TEACHER PREPARATION

TEACHER PREP

MERRILL
PRENTICE HALL

See a demo at
www.prenhall.com/teacherprep/demo

Your Class. Their Careers. Our Future. Will your students be prepared?

We invite you to explore our new, innovative and engaging website and all that it has to offer you, your course, and tomorrow's educators! Preview this site today at www.prenhall.com/teacherprep/demo. Just click on "go" on the login page to begin your exploration.

Organized around the major courses pre-service teachers take, the Teacher Preparation site provides media, student/teacher artifacts, strategies, and tools needed to excel in their courses and prepare them for their first classroom.

This ultimate on-line education resource will provide you and your students access to:

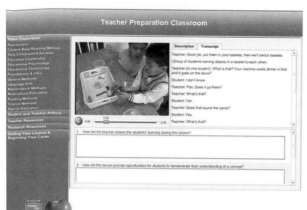

Online Video Library. More than 250 video clips—each tied to a course topic and framed by learning goals and Praxis-type questions—capture real teachers and students working in real classrooms.

Student and Teacher Artifacts. More than 200 student and teacher classroom artifacts—each tied to a course topic and framed by learning goals and application questions—provide a wealth of materials and experiences to help make your students observe children's developmental learning.

Lesson Plan Builder. Offers step-by-step guidelines and lesson plan examples to support students as they learn to build high quality lesson plans.

Research Articles. Over 500 articles from ASCD's renowned journal *Educational Leadership*. The site also includes Research Navigator, a searchable database of additional educational journals.

Teaching Strategies. Over 500 research-supported instructional strategies appropriate for a wide range of grade levels and content areas.

Licensure and Career Tools. Resources devoted to helping your students pass their licensure exam; learn standards, law, and public policies; plan a teaching portfolio; and survive their first year of teaching.

How to ORDER Teacher Prep for you and your students:

For students to receive a Teacher Prep Access Code with this text, instructors must provide a special value pack ISBN number on their textbook order form. To receive this special ISBN, please email: Merrill.marketing@pearsoned.com and provide the following information:

- Name and Affiliation
- Author/Title/Edition of Merrill text

Upon ordering Teacher Prep for their students, instructors will be given a lifetime Teacher Prep Access Code.

Transition Planning for Secondary Students with Disabilities

Third Edition

Robert W. Flexer
Kent State University

Robert M. Baer
Kent State University

Pamela Luft
Kent State University

Thomas J. Simmons
University of Louisville

PEARSON

Merrill
Prentice Hall

Upper Saddle River, New Jersey
Columbus, Ohio

Library of Congress Cataloging-in-Publication Data

Transition planning for secondary students with disabilities / Robert W. Flexer . . . [et al.].
— 3rd ed.
   p. cm.
  Includes bibliographical references and index.
  ISBN 978-0-13-238763-7
  1. Youth with disabilities—Education (Secondary)—United States.   2. Youth with disabilities—Vocational education—United States.   3. Students with disabilities—Services for—United States.   4. School-to-work transition—United States.
I. Flexer, Robert W.
  LC4031.T733 2008
  371.9′0473—dc22

2007003269

Vice President and Executive Publisher: Jeffery W. Johnston
Executive Editor: Ann Castel Davis
Editorial Assistant: Penny Burleson
Production Editor: Sheryl Glicker Langner
Production Coordination: Kelli Jauron, Carlisle Publishing Services
Design Coordinator: Diane C. Lorenzo
Cover Design: Thomas Borah
Cover Image: Super Stock
Production Manager: Laura Messerly
Director of Marketing: David Gesell
Marketing Manager: Autumn Purdy
Marketing Coordinator: Brian Mounts

This book was set in Garamond Book by Carlisle Publishing Services. It was printed and bound by Hamilton Printing Company. The cover was printed by Phoenix Color Corp.

Photo Credits: Center for Innovation in Transition and Employment, p. 3, 21, 29, 39, 54, 82, 88, 103, 112, 129, 134, 136, 154, 161, 173, 179, 187, 203, 205, 220, 230, 233, 239, 277, 290, 303, 317, 321, 327, 340, 351, 367, 376; Gary Harwood/Kent State University, p. 258. All other photos supplied by Robert W. Flexer.

Pearson Prentice Hall™ is a trademark of Pearson Education, Inc.
Pearson® is a registered trademark of Pearson plc
Prentice Hall® is a registered trademark of Pearson Education, Inc.
Merrill® is a registered trademark of Pearson Education, Inc.

Pearson Education Ltd.
Pearson Education Singapore Pte. Ltd.
Pearson Education Canada, Ltd.
Pearson Education—Japan

Pearson Education Australia Pty. Limited
Pearson Education North Asia Ltd.
Pearson Educación de Mexico, S. A. de C. V.
Pearson Education Malaysia Pte. Ltd.

10 9 8 7 6
ISBN-13: 978-0-13-238763-7
ISBN-10: 0-13-238763-8

CONTRIBUTORS

Robert Baer, Ph.D.
Kent State University
Kent, OH

Debra Bauder, Ph.D.
University of Louisville
Louisville, KY

Alfred W. Daviso III, Ph.D.
Kent State University
Kent, OH

Randall L. De Pry, Ph.D.
University of Colorado at Colorado Springs
Colorado Springs, CO

Robert Flexer, Ph.D.
Kent State University
Kent, OH

Pamela Luft, Ph.D.
Kent State University
Kent, OH

Laura Huber Marshall, M.A.
University of Colorado at Colorado Springs
Colorado Springs, CO

James Martin, Ph.D.
University of Oklahoma
Norman, OK

Rachel McMahan Queen, Ph.D.
Kent State University
Kent, OH

Thomas Simmons, Ph.D.
University of Louisville
Louisville, KY

Deborah Durham Webster, Ph.D.
Cleveland State University
Kent, OH

Beyond the meaning of everyday learning and living, all students, on varying timetables and with individual urgency, take on a future orientation during the high school years. Looming in the background is the question, "What am I going to do after high school?" The importance of high school programs and transition activities directly relates to the degree to which they provide learning and experiences that will move students toward or clarify their transition goals. For the student to have an investment in their education, meaningful participation in the "right" programs is essential. For students with disabilities, access is necessary to realize the benefits of participation in regular education, vocational and career and technical education, and school-to-work programs as well as transition and special education programs. *Transition Planning for Secondary Students with Disabilities* (Third Edition) describes the varied transition needs of students with disabilities and the myriad options and career paths potentially available.

The purpose of education and transition is to move students toward selected postschool outcomes. Quality of life is the major benchmark of the Individuals with Disabilities Education Act (IDEA) as assessed through the careers and lifestyles achieved by students. Make no mistake about it. As logical and principled as these assumptions are, there are many competing forces on the national educational agenda. For one, standardized test scores are viewed by some stakeholder groups as the major focus of educational efforts. From a transition perspective, academic achievement is considered very important, but academic achievement alone is insufficient for successful postschool outcomes. Moreover, contextualized and authentic learning in which academics are embedded shows better learner outcomes than academic subjects taught in the abstract.

Since education is a cultural process, new educators need to identify their values and determine which actions are consistent with them. Do we care whether our students enjoy successful careers, meaningful relationships, and community membership? Do we care whether students obtain the best possible foundation to launch them into their young lives? If you answered yes to these two questions, then you will be motivated to learn how transition needs can be met in an academic achievement environment through reading this book.

THE THIRD EDITION

Transition Planning for Secondary Students with Disabilities (Third Edition) provides broad coverage of transition content, ranging from the legislative–policy base to specific transition activities. A framework of four essential elements of transition provides themes to organize each chapter, connecting content across chapters and topics. The resulting integration of policy and practice systematically builds the reader's understanding and provides guidelines for daily transition activities.

This new edition focuses on how to support the in-service and preservice teacher or professional in developing and implementing transition activities that meet a dual criteria. Foremost, the outcomes of special education and achieving a quality of life must remain the broad educational framework from which to judge the merits of transition efforts. Just as important, the process of transition provides the means to these goals. Students achieving quality of life outcomes for themselves is partly dependent on a service system with integrity—basing services on students' needs, interests, and preferences, providing an outcome orientation and planning processes, and effectively coordinating all the services required. When these activities result in movement toward student goals, they are on the right track. The four essential elements (see p. ix) are a quality check on whether things are being done right. As with the second edition, these two broad goals of transition outcomes and process remain embedded in the major reorganization of the content of this edition.

Section 1, "Implementing Transition Systems," still provides the broad background that is required to understand the complex developmental and education process that takes place from early adolescence through young adulthood. A new Chapter 1, "Transition Planning and Promising Practices," provides an evolution of issues of adolescence, a quality-of-life framework, and the four essential elements. The field of transition is traced within a framework of the maturing disability rights movement and government initiatives. The chapter shows that requirements and the need for transition services are no longer debatable. The legislation, models, and exemplary practices that have been developed over the roughly 50 years of the modern era are described in Chapter 2. Chapter 3, "Multicultural and Collaborative Competencies for Working with Families," is now placed in the overall organization so that students get this foundation information early on. A more accessible format is used for the theoretical base of career development presented in Chapter 4, as well. A career development framework remains central to enabling the transition team to view the student as evolving and maturing, and to providing a general approach for fitting the student's transition goals within high school programs and preparation options.

As in the first edition, Section 2, "Creating a Transition Perspective of Education," moves from the foundations of transition addressed in Section 1 to its programmatic implementation at the high school level. The four chapters in this section apply career theory to career and technical education, curriculum options and course of study, and the implementation of these programs through valid assessment and effective instruction. Assessment practices show how to monitor and evaluate programs to ensure success, and instruction and the use of technology guarantee access to these programs as well as a full range of optimizing life and career opportunities.

In order to fill in the practices implied in a broad framework, Section 2 is completely reconceptualized and features three new chapters. As in the prior edition, the section starts with transition assessment, which is important in identifying future environments and the students' needs, interests, and preferences. Transition is unique in that the process always starts with the students' goals and their related postschool outcomes.

The three remaining chapters in succession describe and illustrate: (a) a model for planning a general education curriculum that incorporates transition; (b) instructional planning for transition teaching, and; (c) instructional methods for transition teaching. The information presented will allow transition teams to guide students toward a high school course of study consistent with their transition goals. At times, students with disabilities will be educated and supported in completing high school courses and requirements much like other students but with necessary accommodations and transition services. However, if necessary, the transition team and teachers must make choices that implement career and technical preparation, in conjunction with academic content and life skill areas, that prepare the student for his or her individually chosen transition outcomes. When these choices are integrated and assembled across the student's profile of educational and transition strengths and needs, they become an individualized curriculum.

Integrated throughout all chapters are descriptions of several of the technologies available that allow students to access the full range of curricular and postschool options that lead to a quality adult life. Team members are provided with the processes needed for investigating and making decisions about technology and transition services that will lead to long-term satisfaction with careers and chosen life styles.

Section 3, "Promoting Movement to Postschool Environments," starts with an overview of transition services and collaboration, then makes concrete the issue of employment, postsecondary education, and community living with three updated chapters. These three domains of postschool experience are discussed at length in the prior sections regarding the execution of planning and the formulation of future goals, educational preparation, collaborative enterprises, and joint programmatic efforts. This section is filled with information that will expand understanding of transition issues after students leave school and explore issues that most educators don't think about. The authors believe that these future environments have a very important role, and they often require a special effort by transition teams. Communication and interaction among team members in future environments enhance the goal-setting process and assist students to "keep their eye on the ball."

Section 4, "Developing a Responsive Transition System," moves from a discussion of programs in rehabilitation and special, general, and career and technical education to a discussion of how these programs can be integrated into transition planning and program development for youth with disabilities. These three chapters can be viewed as a technical manual that describes how to weave policy, promising practices, and a myriad of programs and services into transition activities that promote student self-determination, effective transition planning, service coordination, and family involvement.

With the student and family at the center of the process, Chapter 13 moves the reader through the process of developing a transition planning process, preplanning for the IEP meeting, conducting that meeting, and evaluating progress. Still included in Chapter 13 is a question and answer section that can be helpful to parents and professionals in dealing with the jargon of transition. Chapter 14 presents an in-depth look at how students move from passive spectators to involved decision makers, and a step-by-step process for supporting students in this process.

The section concludes with Chapter 15, which talks about transition service coordination from both an individual and a systemic perspective. Overall, Section 4 describes a planning process that places the family and the student in a central position so that exemplary practices can be supportive of the hope for adult life in the community.

The purpose of *Transition Planning for Secondary Students with Disabilities* (Third Edition) is to provide a comprehensive, yet practical, text for advanced students at the undergraduate level and for students at the graduate level from the diverse fields that contribute to the transition process. School-based teachers from regular, vocational, and special education and other professionals, including psychologists, related services professionals, and guidance counselors, will benefit from reading this text, especially if they are in the process of establishing or improving interdisciplinary and collaborative transition services. Families and a variety of postschool service providers (e.g., rehabilitation counseling, case managers, etc.) will also benefit from the broad framework and specific examples that illustrate the varied educational, career, and personal issues that arise in students' transition to postschool life.

In this text, the reader is continuously brought back to the four basic questions raised by the *essential elements*:

1. Is there meaningful student involvement?
2. Are student goals directed toward postschool outcomes shared by the student and his or her family and team?
3. Are all team members working in a coordinated fashion in relation to the student's goals?
4. Are the education and transition services promoting movement toward the student's accomplishing his or her goals?

The application of the essential elements provides a test of transition services both for individual students and across all school and postschool services. Transition is treated in a generalized way by cross-categorical, practical, and real transition examples.

ACKNOWLEDGMENTS

For 22 years, the Center for Innovation in Transition and Employment at Kent State University has had as its mission supporting the efforts of people with disabilities in realizing quality in their lives. In developing programs to prepare transition professionals and in reaching out to schools and communities, innumerable individuals have had an impact on our programs. We hope that they gained insight and useful skills for supporting students. The first author, there from the start, will be indebted forever to his three friends, coauthors, and colleagues for all they have taught him. All the authors thank all of the students with disabilities who contributed so much to us personally and professionally. Likewise, all the Kent State University students and professionals trained in transition at the Center, families of students with disabilities, and Center collaborators who have contributed to our efforts need to be acknowledged for the important lessons they have taught us. All of these individuals with whom we have interacted provided the data and stories upon which this book is based. These relationships brought much joy and will endure into the future. We would especially like to thank John Wachovec, who provided case studies from his transition classes at Kent State. The authors hope that this book will serve you, the reader, in the same way that all our associations have enhanced us as people.

We would like to thank our spouses, Carol, Judy, Drew, and Debbie, whose love and appreciation of us provided much of the "staying power" on this journey. We would like to thank Sherrie Blalock, especially, who kept us organized and provided timely assistance in preparation of the first edition and Valerie Gilbert for the second edition. For this third edition, the first author would especially like to thank Mary Toepfer, Jessica Mackert, Susan Cromwell, Sajid Shaikh, and Tina Bastock. There are no more loyal and hard-working team members. The project teams at the Transition Center were truly remarkable in the giving of their time: George Ackerman, Al Daviso, Stephen Denney, Thomas Hoza, Rachel McMahan Queen, and Gina Metz.

Large projects like a book always involve innumerable individuals who give their time to make the book the best possible product it can be. We are very thankful and indebted to individuals at Merrill and Carlisle Publishers Services who have supported us in a thoughtful, kind way—Ann Davis, Kathy Burk, Penny Burleson, Allyson Sharp, Sheryl Langner, and Kelli Jauron. The individuals who provided reviews of the book provided an invaluable service to us by providing useful suggestions for improvement. We would like to thank these individuals: Mary Ellen Bargerhuff, Wright State University; Everett Pierce, Lock Haven University of Pennsylvania; Patti Whetstone, University of Northern Colorado; and Dalun Zhang, Clemson University.

DISCOVER THE MERRILL RESOURCES FOR SPECIAL EDUCATION WEBSITE

Technology is a constantly growing and changing aspect of our field that is creating a need for new content and resources. To address this emerging need, Merrill Education has developed an online learning environment for students, teachers, and professors alike to complement our products—the *Merrill Resources for Special Education* Website. This content-rich website provides additional resources specific to this book's topic and will help you—professors, classroom teachers, and students—augment your teaching, learning, and professional development.

Our goal is to build on and enhance what our products already offer. For this reason, the content for our user-friendly website is organized by topic and provides teachers, professors, and students with a variety of meaningful resources all in one location. With this website, we bring together the best of what Merrill has to offer: text resources, video clips, web links, tutorials, and a wide variety of information on topics of interest to general and special educators alike. Rich content, applications, and competencies further enhance the learning process. The *Merrill Resources for Special Education* Website includes:

- Video clips specific to each topic, with questions to help you evaluate the content and make crucial theory-to-practice connections.
- Thought-provoking critical analysis questions that students can answer and turn in for evaluation or that can serve as basis for class discussions and lectures.
- Access to a wide variety of resources related to classroom strategies and methods, including lesson planning and classroom management.
- Information on all the most current relevant topics related to special and general education, including CEC and Praxis™ standards, IEPs, portfolios, and professional development.
- Extensive web resources and overviews on each topic addressed on the website.
- A search feature to help access specific information quickly.

To take advantage of these and other resources, please visit the *Merrill Resources for Special Education* Websites at

http://www/prenhall.com/flexer

BRIEF CONTENTS

CONTENTS

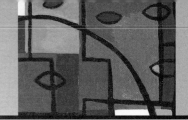

Chapter 15
COORDINATING TRANSITION SERVICES   367

Note: Every effort has been make to provide accurate and current Internet information in this book. However, the Internet and information posted on it are constantly changing, and it is inevitable that some of the Internet addresses listed in this textbook will change.

IMPLEMENTING TRANSITION SYSTEMS

Section 1 of this book examines the "why?" of transition and is designed to provide a background on how the transition initiative came into being, how it has been regulated, its evolving models, and its relation to career development. In Chapter 1, "Transition Planning and Promising Practices," and Chapter 2, "Transition Legislation and Models" the evolution of transition law and policy and practice is traced within a framework of the maturing disability rights movement and other transition initiatives. These chapters are designed to provide the reader with an understanding of the complex interlocking systems of rehabilitation, special education, career education, and developmental disability programs. They also describe major transition models and best practices that have been developed over the last 50 years, delineate the major components of transition as related to IDEA's essential elements, and provide a description of best practices that have emerged from the literature.

Chapter 3, "Multicultural and Collaborative Competencies for Working with Families," describes how the transition process is viewed by various cultural groups and provides strategies for engaging students and families from other cultures in the transition process. This chapter discusses the values underlying various transition models and how these values may conflict with other cultures.

Chapter 4, "Career Development Theories for Transition Planning," is designed to provide a description of career theories and how they relate to the unique needs of students with disabilities and suggests the use of this approach for aligning transition programs with general education programs. This chapter is designed to prepare the reader to develop inclusionary transition practices using mainstream career education programs and models. This chapter also includes a discussion of the problems of using these mainstream approaches for students with disabilities who may lack the life experiences, career maturity, and support systems of their nondisabled peers. A career development framework enables the transition team to view the student as evolving and maturing.

TRANSITION PLANNING AND PROMISING PRACTICES

Robert W. Flexer

Robert M. Baer

LEARNING OBJECTIVES

The objectives of this chapter are:

1. Understand how cultural concepts of disability have influenced special education services.
2. Explain the relationships between typical adolescent development and transition planning.
3. Describe the rationale for transition planning.
4. Describe the various definitions of transition services and their impact on planning.
5. Explain the essential elements of transition and how they are reflected in promising practices.
6. Identify problems in defining promising practices in transition for youth with disabilities.
7. Explain the connections between the nine promising practices in transition and the essential elements of transition.
8. Identify practical implications of promising practices for special educators.

INTRODUCTION

The concept of "disability" has been undergoing a radical change in the modern world. Only three generations ago, it was widely believed that individuals with disabilities were a menace to the health of society, and many were sterilized or even euthanized with the full sanction of the law. This did not simply happen in Germany, but also in the United States. For example, a popular American sex education book stated:

> While everyone will agree there are large sections of our population which are composed of very undesirable individuals, it is hard to get agreement on methods of eliminating them. No one denies the staggering cost to the State of our institutions for the feeble-minded, the insane, and the criminals; if we add to this the costs of courts and legal procedures, of charitable and relief measures, to say nothing of clinic and hospital service which is largely supported by the responsible members of society for the benefit of the irresponsible.... (Richmond, 1934, p. 275)

Following World War II, eugenics fell into disfavor, but the concept of disability as a burden to society remained. A new medical model of disability emerged that promised to wipe out disabilities by providing cures and treatments (Shapiro, 1993). This medical model provided some successes, but persons with disabilities continued to be devalued and excluded from social participation. They were often viewed as "sick" and as "objects of pity" and their participation in society was contingent on them first getting "well" (Shapiro, 1993). Later behavioral-developmental models shifted the focus of disability programs to training rather than medical treatment, but the premise remained the same—persons with disabilities could not fully participate in society until they were cured or rehabilitated.

Despite large investments in medical and behavioral treatment, habilitation, and rehabilitation programs, few persons with disabilities moved into more independent settings and the number of adults in institutional and segregated day programs increased dramatically (Bellamy, Rhodes, Bourbeau, & Mank, 1986). Additionally, advances in medicine sharply reduced mortality rates associated with many disabilities (Shapiro, 1993). By 2000, persons with disabilities made up one of the largest minority groups in the United States, with more than 49.7 million persons (or nearly 20% of Americans) reporting significant disabilities. Of this number, 30.6 million were of working age with 43% of them unemployed (U. S. Census, 2003, May). The number of persons with disabilities in Social Security programs showed a similar trend with more than 10 million persons with disabilities under age 65 receiving Supplemental Security Income (SSI), Social Security (SSDI), or both (Social Security Administration, 2003).

In the 1980s, new community support strategies showed considerable promise in regard to providing integrated employment, residential living, and community participation options for persons with disabilities. The supported employment programs developed in this decade indicated that with individualized supports, virtually any individual with a disability could be employed for pay (Wehman, 2006). Supported living programs showed similar promise by keeping individuals with the most severe disabilities in their own homes with family and community supports (Knoll, 1992). These programs showed long-term benefits not only in the quality of life for persons with disabilities, but also in their ability to become productive and contributing members of society (Storey, Bates, & Hunter, 2002; Baer, Simmons, Flexer, & Smith, 1994).

The transition initiative discussed in this book grew out of this new support paradigm and highlights the need to include and go beyond the general curriculum in promoting quality-of-life outcomes for students with disabilities. In the first part of this chapter, transition activities will be described in the context of typical adolescent development and in the context of the ecological environments experienced by youth in that period. The authors will then explore research on how to promote the successful transition of students with disabilities by fostering their normal development and by supporting them in the typical environments experienced in middle and secondary education.

> **Critical Point**
> There have been dramatic changes in the U.S. approach to disability from models focused on treatment to models based on support.

ADOLESCENCE AND THE TRANSITION TO ADULTHOOD

To understand the problems facing youth with disabilities, it becomes necessary to understand the challenges faced by all youth in this critical period. The transition to adulthood has been a concern of societies from the dawn of humanity when this process was first codified in tribal "rites of passage" (Ferguson, 2001). These rites involved a variety of socially sanctioned activities where youth practiced the roles of adults and participated in important social customs. As societies moved to agrarian economies, adult roles became more specialized and youth were apprenticed to experienced adults who were responsible for seeing that they learned both work skills and appropriate social behavior (Scheerenberger, 1983). This cultural model worked well until the industrial revolution when rapid economic change and growing social complexity meant that youth could no longer expect to enter the occupations of their parents, or even jobs in their community. Increasingly during this period, the transition to adult roles became the responsibility of professional educators and required much longer periods of preparation.

Until recently, youth had the option of moving into occupations without secondary education, with 90% of them exiting school at the middle school level in 1900. Typically these young adults entered occupations (e.g., farm or factory work) where skills were taught on the job (Lichtenstein, 1998). During this period, only students who were expected to enter "elite" positions as managers or professionals continued through high school. However, mechanization and computerization of nearly all economic sectors caused shrinkage in the unskilled occupations from 90% to less than 15% by the end of the century (Levesque, Lauen, Teitelbaum, Martha, & Librera, 2000). For all youth, this meant that the path to adult work roles required relatively long periods of education (Hamburg, 1993). In modern societies, the average age of full transition to adult roles moved from about age 13 in 1900 to the mid-20s in 2000 (Levesque et al., 2000). Additionally, the transition to adulthood now required performance in several spheres, including education, the family, the economy, and the political/ legal system (Pallas, 1993).

> **Critical Point**
> The transition to adulthood has become more complex and extended for all adolescents.

The period of adolescence has become so extended in modern society that it has been defined as three periods—early adolescence, middle adolescence, and late adolescence. Early adolescence has been defined as the period when youth are aged 10 to 14 years and when they begin drawing away from their parents to begin exploring adult roles and to become more oriented to their peers (Lichtenstein, 1998). This period has been conceptualized by Piaget as the period when youth depend heavily on problem solving through trial and error, but begin to think in terms of abstract thought and deductive reasoning (Piaget, 1966). Erikson conceptualized early adolescence as a period

when youth begin the task of reconciling their beliefs, abilities, and desires with adult norms and expectations (Erikson, 1963). During this period, parents usually serve as a secure base from which adolescents can explore new roles and environments and become more focused on peer relations (Erikson, 1963). For all students, transitional objectives for early adolescence must focus on developing self-awareness and knowledge about a range of possible adult roles that are compatible with their unique needs, interests, and preferences. During this period, transition activities related to development of self-determination and career awareness are critical to support the next stage of career development (Palmer & Wehmeyer, 2003).

Middle adolescence has been defined as the period when youth are 15 to 17 years of age and has been characterized as a period when they experience mounting pressure to conform, and engage in risk-taking behaviors. This has been described as the period when the discrepancy between the actual self and the ideal self is most pronounced (Lichtenstein, 1998). Greenberger and Steinberg (1986) argued that too much pressure to conform during this period could result in an "identity foreclosure" where adolescents conform to roles dictated by adults, leading to passivity and an inability to accept responsibility. Some risk-taking behavior characterizes normal middle adolescence as youth experiment with adult roles, but too much risk taking may lead to problems with the legal system (Erikson, 1963). Additionally, the discrepancy between ideal and actual self-perceptions during this period has led many youth, especially students with disabilities, to drop out of school to avoid frustration and embarrassment. Consequently, transition planning for middle adolescence must focus on giving students the chance to take risks in order to experience meaningful work, education, independent living, leisure, and extracurricular activities, and these activities should be designed to develop self-confidence and to reduce the incidence of dropping out. Contextualized learning approaches (e.g., work experiences, community service, and career and technical education) have been used by school programs to increase student retention during this period, and these activities also form the basis for transition to the next stage in adolescence (Barton, 2006).

Late adolescence typically occurs from age 18 to the mid-20s. This period has been characterized as ideally involving closure in resolving problems of personal identity and intimacy. This requires the ability to make sensible decisions, engage in problem solving, and participate in adult roles. For a growing number of students, this period has been extended by participation in postsecondary education where they can continue to explore adult roles and careers. However, for youth entering employment after graduation this period may be much shorter, resulting in problems of identity foreclosure or identity incoherency (Erikson, 1963). Transitional objectives for this period therefore must focus on developing closure related to self-determination, postsecondary education, work, leisure activities, and residential options. For students with disabilities, this transition may require time-limited or ongoing support from adult service programs (Will, 1983).

AN ECOLOGICAL VIEW OF ADOLESCENCE

An ecological view of adolescence has been nicely conceptualized by Lichtenstein (1998) and is included in Figure 1–1. The first ecological domain in Lichtenstein's model is *relationships with peers*. Like all individuals, students with disabilities become increasingly focused on the acceptance of peers as they progress through adolescence. This ecological domain has been identified as important in developing interpersonal skills and in validating self-concepts (Lichtenstein, 1998). Students with disabilities may lack experiences in this domain, if they have significant disabilities and/or are in classes or schools that provide little opportunity for interactions with peers. Research indicated that successful peer relationships ranged from 91% of youth with learning disabilities, to only 56% of students with multiple disability, to 35% of students who were deaf and blind (Wagner, D'Amico, Marder, Newman, & Blackorby, 1992). Additionally, research has indicated that these relationships tended to decline after students with disabilities left high school (Chadsey & Shelden, 1998). Transitional implications of this domain are related to the need to provide students with opportunities to establish social connections and to plan for community participation following high school (Chadsey & Shelden). Approaches such as peer mentoring, peer supports, and peer education may be helpful in this area.

At the 1:00 position on Lichtenstein's model is *mass media*. All youth tend to emulate behaviors of the actors and performers portrayed in the mass media.

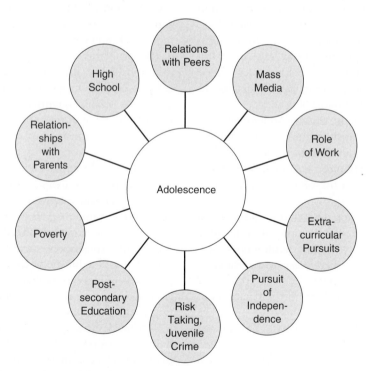

FIGURE 1–1 Ecological influences in adolescence

Source: From Lichtenstein, S. (1998). Characteristics of youth and young adults. In F. R. Rusch and J. G. Chadsey (Eds.), *Beyond high school: Transition from school to work.* Wadsworth Publishing, Boston. Reprinted with permission of Wadsworth, a division of Thompson Learning.

This becomes problematic when they imitate the antisocial behaviors portrayed extensively in movies, computer games, and even professional sports. Additionally, youth with disabilities may be confused by the media's ambiguous and often negative presentations of their disability as something that should be feared, pitied, overcome, or hidden (Shapiro, 1993). The media's use of terminology such as "the disabled" or "the crippled" has continued to create the impression that persons with disabilities are not like other persons, and this terminology has persisted despite more than 20 years of effort by self-advocacy groups to use person-first language such as "persons with disabilities" or "persons with mobility impairments." The transitional implications of the mass media domain include the need to expose students with disabilities to positive role models and to help them develop a realistic and positive understanding of their own disability. Approaches such as mentoring from adults with and without disabilities and exposing youth to positive media regarding persons with disabilities may be helpful in this area.

The next ecological domain going clockwise is the *role of work*. In America, youth work while going to school at a higher rate than any other country in the Western world (Lichtenstein, 1998). The role of work in adolescence has been debated by experts with some arguing that work detracts from schooling and has little value for them as adults (Cole & Cole, 1993; Greenberger & Steinberg, 1986; Stern, McMillion, Hopkins, & Stone, 1990). Another group of experts has argued that work while in high school promotes vocational development and provides "real-life" experiences that students could not obtain in school (Phillips & Sandstrom, 1990; Steele, 1991), and that longitudinal outcome and follow-up studies indicate a strong relationship between high school employment and employment after graduation (Blackorby & Wagner, 1996; Baer et al., 2003). Halpern (1993) found that employment in high school was beneficial to the extent that it related to student career paths. The transition implications of this domain suggest that work experience programs should have clear objectives and be related to students' postsecondary goals. Also, work experiences during high school may be used to help students develop self-esteem, persistence, and confidence.

Extracurricular activities are a fourth ecological domain of adolescence identified by Lichtenstein (1998). These activities have been identified as an important way to promote student attachment to their school and as a way to develop teamwork, loyalty, leisure skills, and peer relationships (U.S. Department of Education, 1995).

For students with disabilities extracurricular activities become particularly important as a means of developing self-esteem, confidence, and peer relationships (Mahoney & Cairns, 1997; Newman, 1991; Sarkees & Scott, 1985). The transition implication of this domain suggests that youth with disabilities need to be encouraged and supported in selecting and obtaining extracurricular activities as part of the Individualized Education Program (IEP) planning process and by systematic intervention to make these extracurricular programs more accepting of persons with disabilities.

The *pursuit of independence* is a fifth ecological domain and has been identified as critical for establishing a sense of responsibility and control (Lichtenstein, 1998). For all students, obtaining a driver's license, getting a job, and spending time with peers is important. Independence also means the opportunity to make important choices. For students with disabilities, the ability to make choices and pursue goals has been called self-determination, which has been positively related to both school performance and postschool outcomes (Wehmeyer & Schwartz, 1997). Transition implications for the ecological domain of independence include the need to help students develop travel, independent living, and self-determination skills and opportunities. Driver's education, self-determination training, life-skill training, and community awareness programs may be helpful for students relative to this ecological domain.

Risk taking is an ecological domain of particular concern for adolescents. Social psychologists have argued that risk taking allows youth to experiment with adult roles and individual choices (Erikson, 1963). However, students with disabilities have often been sheltered from taking risks to the point that they did not participate in experiences that would promote normal development. Perske (1973) identified this concern and developed a concept known as "the dignity of risk," which stated that persons with disabilities should have the opportunity to take reasonable risks in the pursuit of independence and happiness. On the other hand, risk-taking behavior can be a problem when risks are taken needlessly. Students with learning and emotional disabilities may develop risk behaviors of alcohol and drug abuse, unsafe sex, or other dangerous behaviors. Transition implications for the ecological domain of risk taking include activities designed to acquaint students with their rights and responsibilities and the development of activities that are designed to teach them safety precautions, wise choice-making, and emergency procedures.

Postsecondary education has been an ecological domain of growing concern for all students, including students with disabilities. As discussed earlier, education requirements have steadily grown over the past century. This trend accelerated in the 1990s, with 68% of all students and 28% of students with disabilities attending two- and four-year postsecondary education programs. Four-year college enrollment for students with disabilities showed particularly steep increases, rising from 2.6% in 1978 to 9.2% in 1994 (Henderson, 1995) and recent studies indicated that more than 60% of youth with disabilities wanted to go on to attend either two- or four-year colleges (Wagner, Newman, Cameto, & Levine, 2005; Baer, Flexer, & Dennis, in press). The completion of a postsecondary education program is fast becoming as critical as completion of high school was just 40 years ago (Fairweather & Shaver, 1991; Gray, 2002). Additionally, for students with disabilities, postsecondary education provided the opportunity to postpone the transition to adulthood for several years, resulting in considerable advantages in terms of long-term earning ability and career satisfaction. The transition implications for the postsecondary education domain include activities designed to assist students with disabilities in developing study skills, choosing colleges, taking college entrance examinations, applying for financial aid, and using college disability support services.

Poverty has been an ecological concern for adolescents because it exposes them to problems, including lack of opportunity, crime, low expectations, health risks, and high-risk behaviors (Lichtenstein, 1998). Students in poverty often do poorly at school because they may lack parental support, may be required to care for siblings, or may be forced to work to support the family (Kozol, 1996). Poverty is a particular concern for students with disabilities because high proportions of these students come from low-income families (Kozol). Additionally, poverty can worsen the effect of a disability by limiting transportation, employment, social, and educational options. Transition implications for this ecological domain include the need to provide social services, support personal hygiene, and develop financial and community supports. Students may also need considerable counseling and direction in the use of disability benefits and related work incentives.

Parents continue to be one of the most influential ecological domains for adolescents. They serve as role models, provide supports, and serve as important resources in connecting youth with employment, educational, and community resources (Blackorby & Wagner, 1996; Hasazi, Gordon, & Roe, 1985). For students with disabilities, parents typically provide a place to live well into adulthood and can strongly influence decisions about employment, postsecondary education, independent living, and community participation (Blackorby & Wagner; McNair & Rusch, 1991). Additionally, parents of students with disabilities often take over the role of service coordinators when students with disabilities exit secondary education. Transition implications for the parental domain include the need to educate and involve parents in transition planning, to use them as resources in finding and maintaining employment, and to plan for their role in the transition process after school services have been terminated.

The final ecological domain in Lichtenstein's model is that of the *high school*. As students move from elementary to middle and secondary programs they encounter increasingly impersonal relationships with teachers, new challenges in navigating between classes, and greater pressures to compete and perform (Lichtenstein, 1998). During this period students choose or are placed in classes that can have a profound effect on postschool opportunities. For students with disabilities, the transition to secondary education settings often results in less consideration of their unique needs, increased stress, and increasing segregation from nondisabled peers (Lichtenstein). Transition implications for this ecological domain include the need to support students in choosing a course of study, in getting into desired courses, in organizing schedules, and in mastering an increasingly difficult curriculum. As students with disabilities approach graduation, their need for linkages to adult services and postsecondary settings also becomes critical. See Table 1–1 for a summary of transition implications of ecological domains.

In summary, during adolescence numerous developmental tasks and environments present opportunities for growth while at the same time presenting risks and challenges. For each domain, it is important to frame the task from the perspective of typical adolescent while respecting the unique needs of the student with a

> **Critical Point**
> Many environments have an impact on adolescents as they move toward adulthood and each of these environments may present unique challenges to students with disabilities.

TABLE I–1 Summary of transition implications of ecological *domains*

- Relationships need to be fostered with typical peers.
- Students with disabilities need to be exposed to positive adult role models.
- Work experiences should promote students' postsecondary goals and self-confidence.
- Extracurricular activities should be addressed in the IEP and through systemic interventions.
- IEP planning should address mobility, independent living, and self-determination skills.
- Students need to be allowed the dignity of risk and understand emergency procedures.
- Students with disabilities need to consider and be prepared for postsecondary education.
- Students with disabilities may need counseling in regard to disability benefits and work incentives.
- Parents need education and involvement in transition planning.

disability. It is important to remember that the students we work with are youth first and youth with disabilities second.

A RATIONALE FOR TRANSITION PLANNING

For students, whether they have a disability or not, high school is a critical juncture where each year forms a foundation for the next, culminating in the student's graduation and movement to postschool environments. This process of moving from one status to the next is called **transition** and during this period all students must ask the question, "What am I going to do after high school?" High school programs should address this question and provide stepping-stones to the future through a process known as **transition planning.** For students with disabilities transition planning is particularly important because, in addition to the normal upheaval in the transition to adulthood, students with disabilities exchange the security of a single contact point—special education—for the complexity of multiple systems serving adults with disabilities (Baer, McMahan, & Flexer, 2004).

Transition planning helps secondary students with disabilities find meaning in their educational activities. Since the 1950s, high school programs in the United States have become primarily focused on college preparation for four-year programs, leaving many other students wondering whether their high school programs have deserted them in favor of the more "promising" students (Rusch & Chadsey, 1998). This had a particularly hard impact on students with disabilities who responded by dropping out of school at higher rates than their peers (Blackorby & Wagner, 1996; Grayson, 1998). Although school completion rates improved (Wagner, Newman, Cameto, Garga, & Levine, 2005) in recent years, investment and participation in the "right"

programs remains essential—programs tied to students' postschool goals. If they cannot say to themselves, "I'm going somewhere and this is the way or path to my goals," their disengagement is inevitable. Supporting students in setting postschool goals and in choosing educational programs that fit is, therefore, one of the most effective practices in assuring their participation in high school programs.

> **Critical Point**
> Participation in high school requires that students have access to the full range of high school programs and the opportunity to participate in individualized and varied work experiences.

The type of transition services advocated in this chapter draws heavily on postschool outcome research and on the principles of self-determination, person-centered planning, and advocacy on the part of special educators. Educators support students and families in transition planning by conveying positive future expectations and by employing a range of scientifically-supported and individualized transition services (Conley 2002; Pearlman, 2002). This includes helping students with disabilities understand the transition process and requires supporting them in addressing the inevitable obstacles encountered on their road to responsibility and independence. Effective transition planning requires quality learning experiences that have been shown by research to promote movement toward the student's individualized postschool goals (Gray, 2002). The following discussion will address the following questions:

1. What does research say about the postschool outcomes of special education students?
2. Which types of transition services have been supported by outcomes research?
3. Which transition frameworks provide the best means for delivering these services?

Research on the Postschool Outcomes

The **Education of All Handicapped Act (EHA) of 1975** was the forerunner of the Individuals with Disabilities Education Act (IDEA) and established the right to a free and appropriate education for all students with disabilities. The EHA created a combined federal, state, and local system for the delivery of special education and created new and higher expectations for students with disabilities. Several years after implementation of this landmark legislation, researchers began asking how it was impacting postschool outcomes for students with disabilities. They began conducting follow-up studies of the sort that were used in the 1950s and 1960s to evaluate work–study and vocational programs (Cobb, 1972). These early post-EHA follow-up studies were designed simply to provide a snapshot of the status of graduates of special education. Researchers found that, although some students with disabilities benefited from special education, a disproportionate number continued to experience unemployment, low wages, low-level jobs, lack of postsecondary education, and lack of community participation and independent living (Hasazi, Gordon, & Roe, 1985; Wehman, Kregel, & Barcus, 1985).

> **Critical Point**
> Follow-up studies showed that special education graduates continued to experience poor postschool outcomes after the implementation of the EHA of 1975.

In the aftermath of these seminal studies, several outcome studies were implemented at local, state, and national levels to evaluate: (a) the postschool outcomes of special education students, (b) the effectiveness of high school programs and services, (c) the availability and utilization of high school and postschool services, and (d) promising transition practices. In 1983, the National Longitudinal Transition Study (NLTS1) was funded by Congress to assess the first three questions. This study used a random national sample of more than 8,000 special education students from all geographic regions, socioeconomic groups, school settings, and disability categories who were surveyed one, three, and five years after exiting special education (Blackorby & Wagner, 1996). The NLTS1 study began compiling survey results in 1987 and found that ten years after the implementation of EHA, students with disabilities were continuing to experience dismal earnings, employment, postsecondary education, and community participation outcomes. The NLTS1 found that community-based work experiences and vocational education were correlated with significantly better postschool employment outcomes for students with disabilities, but that the availability and utilization of these high school programs varied across schools and across disability groupings.

The IDEA of 1997 funded a second national longitudinal transition study known as NLTS2. It was patterned after the NLTS1 and was designed to evaluate changes in postschool outcomes and in utilization and availability of high school services (Wagner, Newman, Cameto, & Levine, 2005). In the NLTS2 study, the postschool status of two-year-out 2003 special education exiters was compared to students who were two years out in 1987 to evaluate the impact of school, rehabilitation, and special education reforms. This comparison showed both positive and negative changes for students with disabilities. On the positive side, the NLTS2 found the high school completion rates of students with disabilities increased 17%, with 70% completing high school in 2003, a rate comparable to regular education students. It also found that greater numbers of students with disabilities attended postsecondary education in 2003 (32%) approaching half the rate of postsecondary attendance for youth in the general population (Newman, 2005). The NLTS2 also found that 22% more students both worked and went to school in 2003 than in 1987.

The NLTS2 found some negative trends, as well. Full-time employment rates were lower two-years-out for the 2003 cohort (39% vs. 57%) than the 1987 cohort (Cameto & Levine, 2005). No improvement was found in the independent living status of special education exiters, with 90% of them remaining single and 75% living with parents. The NLTS2 also found that over 50% of the 2003 cohort had been subject to disciplinary action at school, fired from a job, or arrested compared to 33% in the 1987 cohort. Utilization of transition services correlated with employment also dropped during this period with vocational education declining 15% (Wagner, 2005).

It should be noted that some of the negative trends reflected in the NLTS2 were probably the result of corresponding positive trends between the 1987 and 2003 cohorts. Lower 2003 postschool employment rates were undoubtedly the result of higher postsecondary education rates, while lower vocational education rates for this cohort may be attributed to higher levels of special education participation in the general education curriculum. The NLTS2 also could be interpreted as indicating positive changes for certain disability groups (such as students with learning disabilities obtaining greater access to the general education curriculum) and negative changes for others (such as students with behavioral disabilities who faced higher levels of suspension and exclusion).

Taken as a whole, the NLTS studies and other outcome research from the 1980s and 1990s have suggested that secondary special education needs to continue to move from a focus on special education process to a focus on postschool outcomes (Kohler, 1998). Otherwise, students whose career paths do not fit the current secondary and special education curriculum focus are bound to suffer. Transition services related to employment (e.g., community-based work and vocational education) continued to remain critical for the 60–70% of students with disabilities entering employment after graduation (Benz, Lindstrom, & Yovanoff, 2000). For these students, simply providing access to a rigorous academic curriculum may not be sufficient (Turnbull, Turnbull, Wehmeyer, & Park, 2003).

For example, Baer, Flexer, and Dennis (in press) found that community-based work predicted postschool employment much more effectively than academic achievement for students with disabilities who were one-year postgraduation. This suggested that at least in the short term, these transition services were a critical bridge to employment.

> **Critical Point**
> National research found both positive and negative special education outcomes between 1987 and 2003 and implied the need for individualized high school programs for students with disabilities.

Quality-of-Life Considerations

The move toward outcome-oriented high school programs for students with disabilities required defining them in a way that they could be measured and evaluated (West, 1991). Consequently, policy makers and advocates began to focus on answering the question, "What quality-of-life perspectives underlie special education's professional philosophy, American cultural values, and the values of the individuals and the families we are serving?" This led to early efforts to define quality of life by asking individuals with disabilities what they valued. Goode (1990) conducted research with focus groups consisting of individuals with disabilities and concluded:

> When an individual, with or without disabilities, is able to meet important needs in major life settings (work, school, home, community) while also satisfying the normative expectations that others hold for him or her in those settings, he or she is more likely to experience a high quality of life. (p. 46)

Quality-of-life research began to be applied to outcome research in the 1990s. Halpern (1993) assessed 41 outcome studies for students with disabilities and found that they did not adequately assess all of the quality-of-life outcomes being identified by persons with disabilities and their advocates. Halpern found that postschool outcome studies typically focused on education and employment with little or no consideration of social networks and relationships, and none on personal fulfillment. His analysis led him to call for an expansion of the focus of postschool outcomes studies to include three quality-of-life domains: (a) physical and material well-being, (b) performance of adult roles, and (c) personal fulfillment. These quality-of-life and related concepts are presented in Table 1–2.

> **Critical Point**
> Quality-of-life studies called for the expansion of the focus of postschool outcome studies to include social networks and relationships and personal fulfillment.

Halpern (1993) suggested that employment outcomes could not be isolated from other facets of a person's life and that problems in one area (e.g., physical

TABLE 1–2 Quality-of-life domains and desired postschool outcomes

Physical and material well-being:
• Physical and mental health
• Food, clothing, and lodging
• Financial security
• Safety from harm

Performance of adult roles:
• Mobility and community access
• Vocation, career, employment
• Leisure and recreation
• Personal relationships and social networks
• Educational attainment
• Spiritual fulfillment
• Citizenship (e.g., voting)
• Social responsibility (e.g., does not break laws)

Personal fulfillment:
• Happiness
• Satisfaction
• Sense of general well-being

Source: From Quality of life as a conceptual framework for evaluating transition outcomes, by A. S. Halpern, *Exceptional Children, 59*(6), 1993, p. 491. Copyright (1993) by The Council for Exceptional Children. Reprinted with permission.

and personal well-being and personal fulfillment) would have a corresponding impact on the others (e.g., performance of adult roles or employment). He argued that transition programs for students with disabilities should address *physical and material well-being* because food, shelter, rehabilitation services, and health care were not an entitlement in the United States, even for persons with disabilities. *Performance of adult roles* was considered prerequisite to achieving physical well-being and personal fulfillment, so Halpern suggested that transition professionals must also develop strategies for students to learn the necessary skills and obtain the necessary supports to participate in these roles. The outcome of *personal fulfillment* was closely connected to Halpern's outcomes of physical well-being and adult competency, but clearly distinguished from them in that personal fulfillment was to be measured subjectively.

Halpern (1993) stated that ultimately, postschool outcome and quality-of-life studies must consider the satisfaction of individuals with disabilities, because only they could assess how well their physical well-being and performance of adult roles met their personal and emotional needs. This, in turn, implied that persons with disabilities had to achieve some degree of self-determination and control over the choices that were made in their lives for this life domain to be fully realized. Halpern noted that although a happy fulfilled life in a caring community was what all persons wanted, the specific desired lifestyle and related personal fulfillment were different for every person.

> **Critical Point**
> Postschool outcomes should be measured according to how well they address personal and material well-being, performance of adult roles, and personal fulfillment.

IDEA-MANDATED TRANSITION SERVICES

IDEA of 1990 and the Essential Elements of Transition

Follow-up studies of special education students generated widespread concern over quality-of-life outcomes and resulted in a legal mandate for transition planning and service provision in the **Individuals with Disabilities Education Act (IDEA) of 1990.** This legislation mandated that public schools develop a "statement of needed transition services" for students with individualized education programs (IEPs) age 16 or older, or younger if appropriate (IDEA Amendments of 1990, P.L. 101-476, 20 U.S.C. § 1401). From that point forward, secondary students with an IEP were required by law to have a transition plan to support postschool activities and goals. The IDEA of 1990 defined transition services as:

> The term "transition services" means a coordinated set of activities for a student, with a disability, that: (A) is designed within an outcome-oriented process, that promotes movement from school to post-school activities, including postsecondary education, vocational training, integrated employment (including supported employment), continuing and adult education, adult services, independent living, or community participation; (B) is based on the student's needs, taking into account the student's preferences and interests; and (C) includes instruction, community experiences, the development of employment and other post-school objectives, and, when appropriate, acquisition of daily living skills and functional vocational evaluation. (Section 602)

According to this definition, transition services can be distilled into four essential elements. They must: (a) be based on student needs, taking into account the students' preferences and interests, (b) be designed within an outcome-oriented process, (c) include a coordinated set of activities, and (d) promote movement from school to postschool activities. All of the transition strategies and programs discussed in this book will be evaluated relative to these four transition criteria, and the degree to which they address them will serve as a basis for discussing their relative merits. Additionally, these four essential elements of transition imply a range of best practices in transition including: (a) student self-determination (i.e., based on students' needs, taking into account students' preferences and interests), (b) person-centered planning (i.e., outcome-oriented process), (c) interagency collaboration (i.e., a coordinated set of activities), and (d) follow-up and follow-along services (i.e., activities that promote movement from school to postschool activities).

> **Critical Point**
> The IDEA of 1990 established four essential elements that define transition services and that implied the need for a number of related practices.

The Division of Career Development and Transition (DCDT) of the Council for Exceptional Children (CEC) (as the primary professional group of transition service providers within special education) provided a "best practice" definition of transition (Halpern, 1994). Under the DCDT definition, consideration of *student needs, interests, and preferences* in relation to transition planning should begin no later than age 14, and students should be encouraged to assume a maximum amount of responsibility for such planning. Their definition specified that the IDEA's *outcome-oriented process* should focus on the change in status from behaving primarily as a student to assuming emergent adult roles in the community, including employment, postsecondary education, independent living, community participation, and satisfactory relationships. The DCDT definition more broadly defined a *coordinated set of activities* as including elementary and middle school programs and services, and it recommended *promoting movement to postschool settings* through career development and education approaches. See Table 1–3.

Critical Point
The DCDT definition of transition expanded on the IDEA definition of transition to extend transition planning to age 14, to focus on attaining adult quality of life, to include transition activities from elementary school on, and to use career development and education practices.

The IDEA of 1997 and 2004

During the 1990s, further transition policy shifts occurred due in part to research that identified a disconnection between transition services and the rest of the curriculum (Stodden & Leake, 1994). This led prominent researchers in the field of transition to call for a "transition perspective of education" (Kohler, 1998). This greater curricular focus was mirrored in the IDEA of 1997, which required both a "statement of needed transition services" focused on postschool outcomes and a "statement of transition service needs" focused on a student's secondary course of study at age 14 (IDEA of 1997). Essentially, the IDEA of 1997 required planning for the transition into high school and planning for the transition into adulthood and elevated coursework into a primary focus of transition planning. The IDEA of 1997 also recognized the need for student self-determination by requiring that families be prepared to transfer control of IEP planning to the student by no later than one year before the student reached age 18 (IDEA of 1997).

The IDEA of 2004 moved transition more significantly toward a coursework focus by defining transition services as a coordinated set of activities that was "results" (rather than outcome) oriented and that was *"focused on improving the academic and functional achievement of the child with a disability to facilitate the child's movement from school to postschool activities"* (rather than a focus on directly promoting movement to postschool activities) [H.R. 1350 § 602 (34)]. The IDEA of 2004 also removed specific language regarding the need to identify linkages with adult services and moved the requirement for transition planning back to age 16. At the same time, the IDEA of 2004 increased outcome (or results) accountability by requiring that the IEP include:

1. Appropriate measurable postsecondary goals based upon age appropriate transition assessments related to training, education, employment, and, where appropriate, independent living skills; and
2. The transition services (including courses of study) needed to assist the child in reaching those goals. ([§300.320(b); Authority: 20 U.S.C. 1414(d)(1)(A) and (d)(6)])

The shift in focus of transition planning in the IDEA of 1997 and 2004 toward academic and functional achievement and away from supports and linkages was, in part, an effort to bring transition planning in line with regular education's focus on achievement of academic standards. The intent of these IDEA changes was to maximize student participation in the general curriculum and to focus transition on outcomes

TABLE 1–3 DCDT transition definition and essential elements

Transition, as defined by DCDT, refers to a change in status from behaving primarily as a student to assuming emergent adult roles in the community. These roles include having employment, participating in postsecondary education, maintaining a home, becoming appropriately involved in the community, and experiencing satisfactory personal and social relationships *[designed within an outcome-oriented process]*. The process of enhancing transition involves the participating and coordination of school programs, adult agency services, and natural supports within the community *[using a set of coordinated activities]*. The foundations for transition should be laid during the elementary and middle school years, guided by the broad concept of career development *[promote movement from school to postschool activities]*. Transition planning should begin no later than age 14, and students should be encouraged, to the full extent of their capabilities, to assume a maximum amount of responsibility for such planning *[based on their needs, taking into account the students' preferences and interests]* (Halpern, 1994, p. 117).

rather than process. This shift in the definition of transition services was portrayed in both a positive and negative light. The removal of transition process requirements contained in earlier versions of the IDEA was mirrored by increases in transition outcome requirements in later versions. Some advocates were alarmed by removal of process requirements noting that the general education curriculum was becoming exclusively academic and that many students with disabilities were being denied transition services that research had shown as critical to quality-of-life outcomes (Turnbull et al., 2003). Others maintained that focusing transition services on improving the academic and functional achievement of students with disabilities would promote higher expectations, improve educational opportunities, encourage better teaching, and increase accountability, and that the consequent improvement of student achievement would lead to better postschool outcomes (deFur, 2002).

> **Critical Point**
> The IDEA of 1997 and 2004 increased the focus on transition results and outcomes and generally reduced requirements and assurances for transition planning and services.

In summary, the focus of transition services was broadened to include academic and functional achievement in an effort to create a better connection between transition and the general education curriculum. At the same time, the IDEA requirements in regard to transition planning have shifted from a focus on process to a focus on results and outcomes. It remains to be seen how these policy changes will be played out in schools and classrooms. It is the authors' position that special educators will need to focus on both process and outcomes to ensure that transition programs are doing *things right* and that they are doing the *right things*. Researchers and advocates for students with severe disabilities are right to be concerned that schools may eliminate many transition services and supports, if they are not specifically required to provide them. The EHA of 1975 was passed because schools were refusing to serve the needs of many students with disabilities (Turnbull et al., 2003). Conversely, concerns about burdensome process requirements that limit the flexibility of educators in dealing with an increasingly diverse

> **Critical Point**
> Ultimately special educators must assure that transition planning does things right and that it does the right things by individualizing services in relation to the four essential elements of transition.

population of students with disabilities hold equal validity. Schools have limited resources and they need to be able to use them in ways that best fit the local context and the needs of individual students. Ultimately, both groups continue to agree that transition planning must address the four essential elements of transition services that were defined in the IDEA of 1990 and restated in the IDEA of 1997 and 2000 and that form a common theme throughout this book. These are that transition services must be:

1. based on student needs, interests, preferences, and strengths.
2. developed through an outcome- and results-oriented process.
3. a coordinated set of activities across student environments.
4. designed to promote student movement to postschool activities.

PROMISING PRACTICES IN TRANSITION

As Paula Kohler noted, "transition planning means different things to different people" (Kohler, 1998, p. 180). Some saw transition narrowly as a process of linking traditional education, rehabilitation, and vocational services to promote postsecondary outcomes, whereas others saw it as fundamentally restructuring the core of education (Kohler, 1998; Stodden & Leake, 1994). Distilling principles of promising practice from transition research can, therefore, be hampered by differing definitions of transition. As Stodden and Leake (1994) noted, the process of importing and adapting the promising practices in transition may be more exportable than the practice itself. This is because unique cultural, community, policy, and individual characteristics often define promising practices in transition. In addition to problems caused by differing transition definitions and local context, the definition of promising practices has been hampered by rapid changes in postschool environments, which have created new economic, independent living, and community involvement demands on individuals with disabilities and their families. For example, the growth in technology jobs created a greater demand for postsecondary education. As more students with disabilities entered postsecondary education, transition practices were needed to address the needs of increasing numbers of students with significant disabilities entering two- and four-year postsecondary education programs.

Policy related to transition also can be seen as both a support and a barrier to student and family access to promising practices in transition (Stowitschek & Kelso, 1989). For example, IDEA's requirement that transition curriculum be aligned with the general education curriculum may have created problems for students needing access to life skills training and functional vocational education. Another policy barrier for some students with disabilities was the requirement for high-stakes graduation tests in many states. These tests have tended to focus exclusively on academics and have often been resistant to accommodations for students with disabilities (Turnbull et al., 2003). This has forced many secondary educators back toward an emphasis on remedial academics and away from providing transition services that have been correlated with positive quality-of-life outcomes.

Any effort to define promising practices in transition must make note that for individual students there may be exceptions. As Kauffman (1999) noted, when selecting rules for any type of practice, professionals must consider: (a) the need for different rules for different purposes, since no single set of rules is a fully satisfactory guide to all aspects of living; (b) all rules are grounded in values and we must specify the values of our rules; (c) the origins and appropriate application of particular rules are often misunderstood; (d) personal experience and popularity of ideas are often unreliable guides to rule making; and (e) all truths are tentative... (p. 266).

> **Critical Point**
> Defining promising practices in transition has been hampered by lack of consensus on the purpose of education, the definition of transition services, and by variations among individuals and localities.

Although the authors are reluctant to endorse any transition practice as being good for all students all of the time, it is possible to establish some general principles that should be considered in the adoption of any transition practice. We have already noted that the four essential elements of transition outlined in the IDEA apply for virtually all students. Other researchers have elaborated and expanded on these essential elements of transition. To thoroughly review all research on promising practices in transition would require more than a chapter. However, recently researchers have begun summarizing and categorizing promising practices to simplify this process. Wehman (2006) identified nine guiding principles for transition implementation, while Kohler (1993) conducted a review of literature to determine what transition promising practices were

well-supported by research. Policy makers have also helped define promising practices in transition by establishing goals for transition grant competitions (Rusch & Millar, 1998). Greene (2003) came up with a taxonomy that divided the transition practices into three categories: (a) agency practices, (b) educational programs, and (c) planning. Agency practices consisted of interagency collaboration and interdisciplinary collaboration. Other researchers have continued to identify transition practices that are highly correlated with specific positive postschool outcomes (Johnson & Rusch, 1993). An overview of promising transition practices that are widely supported by experts is shown in Table 1–4.

A review of transition policy and research support for promising practices shows some areas of disagreement about promising practices in transition for youth with disabilities (Kohler, 1993; Phelps & Hanley-Maxwell, 1997). However, the following list provides some themes and related concepts common to expert opinion and research:

1. Student **self-determination** (social skills training)
2. Ecological approaches (use of formal and informal supports, career education)
3. Individualized backward planning (person-centered planning)
4. Service coordination (interagency and interdisciplinary collaboration)
5. Community experiences (paid work experiences, career education)
6. Access and accommodation technologies (assistive technology)
7. Supports for postsecondary education (postsecondary education)
8. Systems change strategies (secondary curricular reform and inclusion)
9. Family involvement (parent involvement)

Self-Determination

While Nirje (1972) addressed self-determination in the context of normalization, "this seed did not blossom" (Browning, 1997, p. 44) until self-advocacy movements such as "People First," the independent living movement of the 1970s and 1980s, and quality-of-life studies in the 1990s brought it to the attention of policy makers (Goode, 1990; Schalock et al., 1994; Shapiro, 1993). Throughout the 1980s, self-determination was defined from several perspectives, including empowerment,

TABLE 1-4 An overview of promising practices in transition

Wehman, 2006	Kohler, 1993	Rusch & Miller, 1998	Greene, 2003	Johnson & Rusch, 1993
• Self-determination	• Vocational training	• Community-based training	• Interagency collaboration	• Interagency cooperation
• Support focus	• Parent involvement	• Postsecondary education	• Interdisciplinary collaboration	• Job placement
• Family and student attitudes	• Interagency collaboration	• Career placement	• Integrated schools, classrooms, and employment	• Needs assessment
• Person-centered planning	• Service delivery	• Vocational training	• Functional, life-skills curriculum and community-based instruction	• Systems change
• Secondary curriculum reform	• Social skills training	• Job placement	• Social and personal skills development and training	• Outreach
• Inclusion	• Paid work experience	• Cooperative planning	• Career and vocational assessment and education	• Barrier resolution
• Career development	• Individualized transition planning	• Self-determination	• Business and industry linkages with schools	
• Longitudinal curriculum	• Transition and career planning within the IEP	• Follow-up of graduates	• Development of effective IEP planning	
• Business connections and alliances	• Focus on integrated employment	• Use of formal and informal supports	• Student self-determination, advocacy, and input in transition planning	
	• Functional community-referenced curricula	• Student involvement	• Family/parent involvement in transition planning	
		• Assistive technology		

self-advocacy training, and sensitivity to values. Knowlton, Turnbull, Backus, and Turnbull (1988) asserted that "a fundamental aspect of the transition into adulthood involved increasing the exercise of direct consent in making decisions about one's own life within one's inherent capacities and means and consistent with one's values and preferences" (p. 61). Ward (1988) suggested that self-determination needed to address both individual attitudes and abilities. Woolcock,

Stodden, and Bisconer (1992) noted that: "transition is a highly value-driven process in which the values of educational personnel are coordinated with the values of the student's family and, most importantly, the values of the student who is about to enter adulthood" (p. 236).

In special education, self-determination became widely supported after 1992 when the Office of Special Education and Rehabilitation Services (OSERS) funded projects across the country to develop self-determination assessments and curricula for students with disabilities. Some of these efforts focused on promoting the fundamental psychological and emotional development of students. Others focused on the need for "students with disabilities [to] be allowed to assume greater control over and responsibility for educational and transition planning and to be involved in selecting and prioritizing goals and objectives" (Wehmeyer, 1993, p. 144). The self-determination movement was reflected in the IDEA of the 1997's requirement that (at least one year before students reach the age of majority) they and their families be informed and prepared for IDEA rights and control of the IEP to transfer to the student.

The concept of self-determination continued to evolve in the 1990s. Wehmeyer, Agran, and Hughes (1998) provided a synthesized definition of "self-determination" as a combination of skills, knowledge, and beliefs that enabled a person to engage in goal-directed, self-regulated, autonomous behavior. Wehmeyer (1998) suggested that self-determination included individuals being able to take control of their lives and to assume the role of successful adults. He further developed this concept by developing a secondary curriculum that considered student needs in the areas of (a) self-awareness, (b) decision making, (c) self-advocacy, and (d) goal expression and exploration.

> **Critical Point**
> Self-determination has been seen as a critical quality-of-life issue for persons with disabilities since 1992 and students must be prepared to take control of IEP and transition planning well before they reach adulthood.

Practical Implications

Self-determination approaches represent promising practice in addressing two essential elements of transition. First, research has indicated that these approaches are one of the promising ways of identifying students' needs, interests, and preferences because traditional approaches such as career interest inventories are not sufficient alone for students with disabilities (Menchetti & Piland, 1998). Additionally, self-determination approaches involve students in the outcome-oriented process of planning by helping them to become active participants in defining their goals and aspirations. Self-determined students with disabilities understand their strengths and limitations and view themselves as individuals with the ability to take control of their lives and assume adult roles. The purpose of transition planning is to help students get into postschool environments that are "right"

for them and prepare them for success in their chosen endeavors. Preparation in self determination allows students to take control of their lives and the critical planning and preparation processes. Involvement in planning and experience in choosing, expressing, and testing goals is time well spent because students enter life with the tools needed to get the best start possible.

One aspect of self-determination approaches deals with self-knowledge and the student's need for information specific to their disability. When related services providers (e.g., audiologists, physical therapists, psychologists) explain the impact of disability, students are in position to inform others of their accommodation needs. Empowered with technology and strategies that provide both access to their strengths and a compensation for barriers presented by their disability, students become self-advocates able to have an impact on school and community environments. Some students may require psychology services to promote emotional growth and to help them come to terms with a psychiatric disability. Transition specialists therefore need to be sure that students understand their disability and needed accommodations by providing training and opportunities for self-determination and by involving related service providers in helping them understand their disability.

Ecological Approaches

Ecological approaches were designed to provide opportunities to learn about and perform in a *variety* of environments. By assessing and training in settings with varying demands and requirements, students learned about their abilities, talents, and interests in real-life contexts. Ecological approaches placed student goals in relation to specific present and future environments. Szymanski (1994) found that an ecological framework was crucial to: (a) focusing the transition curriculum on the most important student needs, (b) developing a variety of professional (formal) and natural (informal) supports, (c) providing learning experiences in a variety of environments, and (d) generalizing skills across varied environments.

Lou Brown's model of curriculum had a strong ecological focus and was the first to use this approach in IEP planning for students with moderate to severe disabilities (Snell, 1981). In his model, Brown defined four ecological domains: domestic, leisure-recreation, community, and vocational (Brown et al., 1979). He recommended that all four domains be assessed in relation to the actual and anticipated environments of individual students with disabilities. These four domains could then be broken down into specific environments through an ecological inventory that assessed where these students went each day and where they hoped to go in the future. (For example within the community domain, relevant environments might include grocery stores, restaurants, banks, pharmacies, and department stores.) These environments could be further broken down into subenvironments where the student would be spending their time. (For example within the grocery store environment, relevant subenvironments might include the entrance, produce section, and checkout lane.) It was then possible to identify and train students in the specific skills and activities required for each subenvironment (Storey et al., 2002).

Ecological approaches began to be implied in public special education policy as underlying Madeleine Will's initial model of transition that she presented as the director of OSERs in 1983, but her model addressed only the employment domain (Will, 1983). Halpern's 1985 model of transition advocated for a transition model closer to Brown's by including residential (domestic) and social-interpersonal (community and recreation-leisure) domains in addition to Will's employment domain (Halpern, 1985). The IDEA of 1990 adopted much of Halpern's model and added postsecondary and continuing education domains for consideration in transition planning. The IDEA of 1997 further expanded the focus of transition planning to include students' high school academic environments by requiring a statement of transition service needs related to their actual and planned courses of study. Repetto and Correa (1996) went even further to propose application of ecological concepts to early childhood and elementary school programs.

> **Critical Point**
> Ecological approaches to special education were highly successful with students with significant disabilities and were instrumental in the development of transition programs and policy for all students.

Practical Implications

Ecological approaches represent a promising practice in developing a coordinated set of activities that promote movement to postschool environments and have been supported by extensive research and public policy. Ecological approaches will require schools to become more involved in assessing and planning in relation to the current and future environments of students with disabilities. In this process, teachers and students will need to determine: (a) the environments that students plan to enter, (b) the demands of these environments, and (c) the skills and supports students will need to perform in these environments. For many students with disabilities, this will require special educators to become more involved with students' communities and families in order to enlist teachers, parents, adult programs, employers, and friends to provide transition activities. The use of these approaches should make the student's transition experience more relevant and culturally sensitive and will also serve to increase the capacity of stakeholders to support the student in achieving meaningful postschool outcomes.

Inclusion and integrated community employment will be important considerations in the delivery of ecological services under the IDEA of 2004. As noted by Storey (2002) attitude change requires an assumption of equal status in interactions between a labeled individual and a "typical" individual (p. 2). Training in inclusive and integrated environments will help regular education teachers, employers, co-workers, customers, and people in the community see people with disabilities performing competently and promote the perception of students as valued members of society. This is important because a 1991 Louis Harris poll found that 77% of persons in the community still felt pity toward people with disabilities.

> **Critical Point**
> Ecological approaches will require special educators to collaborate more closely with regular education teachers, families, employers, and communities and will be critical in helping them see the student as competent and valued.

Person-Centered and Backward Planning

In transition planning it is important for students to envision a future in which they are living the life they want to live. The development of a positive vision has been hard to achieve for IEP transition teams. Even for students with transition plans as part of their IEP, research showed very little orientation to postsecondary outcomes. Lombard, Hazelkorn, and Neubert (1992) examined IEP transition plans for students with disabilities and found that only 18% of students with learning disabilities, 17% of students with emotional disturbances, and 21% of students with mild mental retardation had any postschool transition goals. This research validated concerns expressed by Stowitschek and Kelso (1989), who warned that transition planners may fall into the same traps as IEP planners. These traps included irrelevant activities, low-quality goals, and infeasible strategies (Gallivan-Fenlon, 1994; Grigal, Test, Beattie, & Wood, 1997). Other studies confirmed the central role of transition goals to high school completion and positive outcomes (Benz et al., 2000).

Person-centered planning has been developed to help students and families develop meaningful adult living goals and the means for achieving those goals through backward planning. It evolved from an approach called 24-hour planning that had students envision an integrated life in the community in terms of day-to-day activities (Holburn & Vietze, 2002). Person-centered planning approaches typically involved a facilitator, a recorder, the student, and various family, friends, classmates, and co-workers who worked together to answer questions regarding the student's: (a) history, (b) dreams, (c) nightmares, (d) relationships, (e) abilities, and (f) plan of action. Person-centered planning has been identified as a promising practice by many researchers, even though its impact on postschool outcomes has been hard to document in research (O'Brien & O'Brien, 2002). However, Miner and Bates (1997) showed that parent participation in IEP meetings increased after person-centered planning activities and that parents perceived enhanced input, qualitatively and quantitatively. Person-centered planning approaches included: (a) Personal Futures Planning (Mount & Zwernick, 1988), (b) McGill Action Planning System (now Making Action Plans or MAPs) (Vandercook, York, & Forest, 1989), (c) COACH (Giangreco et al., 1993), and (d) Life-Style Planning (O'Brien, 1987). These approaches have been recommended as a means of complementing and enhancing transition planning (Wehman, Everson, & Reid, 2001).

The common characteristic of person-centered and other backward planning approaches has been the shift from a focus on short-term developmental and academic goals to a focus on achieving specific quality postschool outcomes. Therefore planning at this level must begin with the end in mind and should systematically plan backwards from those goals to the present time (Steere, Wood, Pancsofar, & Butterworth, 1990). See Figure 1–2. IEP planning has tended to pursue developmental milestones based on progress that has

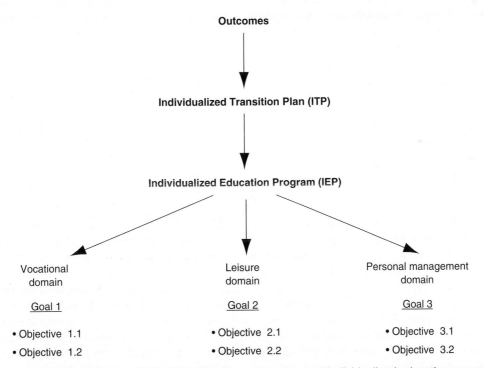

FIGURE I–2 Relationship of outcomes to individualized transition plan and individualized education program

Source: From Outcome-based school-to-work transition planning for students with disabilities, by D. Steere, R. Wood, E. Pancsofar, & J. Butterworth. *Career Development for Exceptional Individuals, 13*(1), 1990, p. 67. Copyright (1990) by The Council for Exceptional Children. Reprinted with permission.

been made in the past and this has led to a focus on remediation of student disabilities. In contrast, backward planning pursued postschool outcomes and developed benchmarks based on progress that would have to be achieved at given points to achieve these goals. Backward planning typically results in higher expectations due to its focus on meaningful outcomes and consequently requires a greater focus on developing student strengths and support systems to achieve these outcomes (Steere et al., 1990).

Practical Implications

Because many students and families may only focus on current issues and stressors, they often ask, "How will we get through the next year?" or "What seems to be the best available program in the high school?" For professionals, besides dealing with current issues, they may have to put extra effort into creating a future orientation and into learning new skills to carry out planning focused on the students' goals. Person-centered and backward planning will undoubtedly create stress for both families and professionals. The use of these approaches must therefore be very open, nonjudgmental, and student focused and use a process of brainstorming to help students describe themselves and their future. Person-centered planning should address not only what outcomes the student desires (going to college or employment) but also why the student desires these outcomes. This helps the student to focus on the future and to delineate his or her strengths, talents, and interests.

In spite of the extra effort required in person-centered and backward planning approaches, they have been shown to provide greater student and family input critical to postschool outcomes (Hasazi, Gordon, & Roe, 1985). Person-centered planning helps students visualize themselves doing something meaningful and fulfilling meaningful roles as adults, and it develops communications and consensus regarding these goals. Team members come to their own understanding of the student's goals and engage in collaboration and sharing as ways to achieve those goals. Because the team plan outlines how the students will pursue their goals, team members must be in communication about how (in what context) they know the students. The transition specialist helps the team develop diverse and varied viewpoints necessary to get a complete picture of individuals and their preferred environments. By creating a brainstorming process that is positive, the coordinator focuses on the students' desired future and capabilities. In subsequent steps and stages in the process, team members support reality testing so that the student and team members gain greater understanding of the postschool goals and environments.

Service Coordination

It is critical that person-centered and backward plans be followed up with effective service coordination. Otherwise, the best person-centered plans quickly fall apart (Holburn & Vietze, 2002). Historically, the problem of integrating services in a transition system (that was really a nonsystem) was discussed by a number of authors. Ward and Halloran (1989) suggested that there was a serious discrepancy between the entitlement philosophy of school programs and the availability of adult services. Szymanski, Hanley-Maxwell, and Asselin (1990) noted that differences between state and local special education programs and state and local vocational rehabilitation programs were rooted in history, definitions of disability, funding differences, and differences in evaluation standards. Kochhar-Bryant and Deschamps (1992) maintained that vocational and special education policies were often at odds in assuring services for learners with special needs, while Kortering and Edgar (1988) emphasized the need for more cooperation between special education and vocational rehabilitation. To address these needs, various individuals have recommended the development of school-interagency transition teams to develop channels of communication and to "iron out" policy differences (Everson, 1990; Heal, Gonzalez, Rusch, Copher, & DeStefano, 1990; Phelps & Maddy-Bernstein, 1992; Wehman, 1990; Wehman, Moon, Everson, Wood, & Barcus, 1988).

Many authors also saw the involvement of employers and other community members as an important function of transition teams. Wehman (1990) stated that a school–business linkage was a critical element of a successful transition program. Rhodes, Sandow, Mank, Buckley, and Albin (1991) indicated that activities involving employers would be the major source of growth for training in a future in which special education and adult service budgets were expected to show little or no growth. Rhodes et al. noted that employer resources were greater than those that were available through special education and rehabilitation. Phelps and Maddy-Bernstein (1992) found that the benefits of business education partnerships included additional resources, employment opportunities, increased personal attention, improved facilities, and better teacher morale.

Practical Implications

Service coordination may involve either transition professionals or transition agencies. At the level of the individual IEP team, service coordination assures that the team members are working toward a common set of goals. This will require the service coordinator to develop a sense of equality among the various team members and some flexibility regarding their respective roles. Training team members in interdisciplinary and transdisciplinary approaches may be required before holding team meetings. Additionally, the team must agree on a single service (or transition) coordinator to assure that the various team members are fulfilling their roles in a timely and coherent manner. The choice of the service coordinator should therefore be a team member who is committed to the student and who is willing to follow up with each member of the IEP team periodically.

Regular and special education staff need to work in concert to help the student achieve his or her programs of choice. The regular education teacher has to be clear about what the student must achieve in the program, whereas the special educator must obtain necessary adaptations and accommodations and work with the regular teacher to use them. Educators must also communicate with representatives of postschool environments and adult service professionals to convey the direction of the students' transition plan and how the high school program connects to the students' desired postschool environments.

At the level of agencies, service coordination creates the opportunity to pool resources toward meeting mutually agreed upon student goals. As with individual IEP team process, each agency will need to come to interagency collaboration meetings as equal partners and appoint representatives that are of equal status to other agency representatives and that are able to make commitments on behalf of their agency. This may require training in interagency collaboration across the agencies before collaboration is undertaken. It is also important at this level for the interagency service coordinator to understand the fundamentals of group development.

Community-Based Learning Experiences

Community-based learning experiences have been found to be critical for youth with disabilities in fostering their transition to postschool activities. Wehman (1990) noted that community work experiences provided students with exposure to social situations and natural contingencies that were unavailable in the school setting. Additionally, research showed a strong correlation between community work experiences and postsecondary employment. The NLTS2 found that students who had work experience as part of a vocational education program experienced significantly better employment outcomes (Cameto & Levine, 2005). Unfortunately in the past, researchers found that many special educators remained committed to training in

Students learn about career interests through community experiences.

classroom settings (Lynch & Beare, 1990; Stowitschek & Kelso, 1989). The IDEA of 1990 actually mandated that community work experiences be part of a student's transition plan unless there was a statement of why these types of experiences were not needed. This requirement was repealed in the IDEA of 1997 as being too restrictive, but was still considered a critical part of transition planning.

Community experiences were also seen as critical to the development of career maturity. Rojewski (1993) found that students with learning disabilities were less able than typical students to identify career options due to limited experiences and opportunities. Additionally, Lombard et al. (1992) found that less than one-fifth of the transition-age students they surveyed had any postsecondary transition goals on the IEP. Having community experiences (e.g., career exploration, job shadowing, and community work experiences) was significantly related to career maturity and postschool outcomes for youth with disabilities (Gill & Edgar, 1990; Halpern et al., 1993; SRI International, 1990; Storey & Mank, 1989; Wehman, Kregel, & Seyfarth, 1985a). Community experiences were also identified as critical to the acquisition of daily living and social skills (Halpern, 1985; Johnson & Rusch, 1993).

Community experiences were seen as a critical component of functional vocational assessment. Research indicated that standardized assessment procedures conducted in artificial settings often lacked validity for students with disabilities because they did not consider the effects of supports, technology, and training on student performance (Menchetti & Piland, 1998). Hagner and Dileo (1993) pointed out that standardized assessment procedures had little or no validity, especially for students with severe disabilities, because they lacked the clues, sights, and sounds of the environments where students would have to perform. They therefore advocated for the use of situational or authentic assessments that were conducted in the environments in which the student was expected to perform.

> **Critical Point**
> Community experiences are important for students with disabilities because exposure to social situations and natural settings enhances the transition to postschool activities and they are critical to the acquisition of work and daily living and social skills.

Practical Implications

It is critical that community experiences be tied to the outcome-oriented process and to the course of study being pursued by secondary students with disabilities (Halpern, 1993). These experiences help them explorie work, living, and community participation opportunities in the community that they would otherwise not be exposed to. A variety of work-based activities can be connected to school activities to both strengthen learning and contextualized academic content, including school-supervised work experiences. The range of experiences should be broad and include not only work, but also postsecondary education, residential, and recreational-leisure settings. For students with significant support needs, these experiences may be supported by job coaches provided through vocational rehabilitation. In some cases, school districts may choose to hire their own job coaches or to use work-study programs to provide these supports. To obtain these supports it may be necessary to make an early referral to vocational rehabilitation to establish eligibility and to involve adult service providers in transition planning.

Community experiences should also consider the student's need for social and interpersonal relationships (Halpern, 1985). Research has indicated that students with disabilities often become more isolated as they grow older due to lack of mobility, income, and social networks. Additionally, students in inclusive educational settings may lose many of their friends after graduation and need help establishing new networks through integrated work and community experiences. Even if they maintain relationships with typical peers, they may have difficulty in making safe choices regarding friends and in meeting people who will direct them toward a good adult quality of life. Membership in religious/cultural affiliations, clubs, and recreational programs and other community activities may provide natural and ongoing support networks that can assist them in developing and maintaining friendships throughout their life.

Access and Accommodation Technologies and Related Services

Access and **accommodation** technologies and related services for youth have been prescribed in the requirements of Section 504 of the Rehabilitation Act of 1973 and the EHA of 1975 and for adults in the Americans with Disabilities Act (ADA) of 1990. They include a particularly broad range of services, strategies, technologies, and professions including reading strategies, rehabilitation technology, assistive technology (AT), audiology, ophthalmology, orientation and mobility training, speech-language pathology, physical therapy, rehabilitation engineering, ergonometrics, and job carving. The application of these strategies has varied in effectiveness based largely on the level of interdisciplinary collaboration and the level of their integration with individual students needs, interests, preferences, and strengths (Cavalier & Brown, 1998). For many students, access and accommodation technologies (including AT) will be a critical determinant of the students' ability to function in community-based environments. Often access and accommodation strategies have been associated with students with severe disabilities. However, students with mild disabilities may depend on access and accommodation technologies or strategies to perform in inclusive academic settings. For example, Behrmann (1994) identified seven areas of support that may be essential in achieving positive academic outcomes. These include:

1. Organizational technologies (e.g., computers and electronic organizers)
2. Note-taking technologies (e.g., optical character recognition, microcassette recorders, videotapes and CDs, and voice synthesizers)
3. Writing assistance (e.g., grammar/spell-checkers, and macros)
4. Productivity (e.g., personal digital assistants, calculators, and software)
5. Access to reference materials (e.g., telecommunication networks and multimedia)
6. Cognitive assistance (e.g., computer tutorials and multimedia)
7. Materials modification (e.g., instructional software)

Access and accommodation technology and related services have also been used to integrate individual assistive technologies with the many technologies used in employment settings. In the year 2000, it was estimated that 75% of jobs would involve the use of computers (Bender, Richmond, & Pinson-Millburn, 1985, cited in Sowers & Powers, 1995). These technologies included telephone technologies, environmental controls, robotics, constructed devices, and other adaptive strategies (Sowers & Powers, 1995). Access and accommodation were an important consideration not only in work, but in the postsecondary education, independent living, and community activities of persons with disabilities.

There have been many types of assistive technology devices that may be used in all or in specific settings. It should be understood in applying assistive technology (AT) that each situation is individualized and that all relevant information must be obtained to effectively decide what accommodation or access strategies will best meet an individual's needs and personal preferences (Esposito & Campbell, 1993; Inge & Shepherd, 1995). Some *common* examples of AT include electric page turners, books on tape, computers, switches, adapted keyboards, orthotics, FM (frequency modulation) systems, prosthetic devices, and augmentative communication devices. Independent living technology (commonly known as daily living aids or DLA) included remote control units, talking alarm clocks, adapted silverware, and gripping cuffs for brooms and mops. Community participation and recreation technology included adapted easels, beeper balls, adapted sport wheelchairs, bowling chutes and audio description services for theatrical events or museum tours (Bauder & Lewis, 2001).

> **Critical Point**
> Access and accommodation technology and related services have been required by legislation and require appropriate assessment and a selection of technologies to enhance the individual's participation in education, employment, and community living environments.

Practical Implications

It is important that technology interventions be tied to students' needs, interests, and preferences so that they are used rather than discarded (Judge, 2002; Lahm & Sizemore, 2002). Many assistive technology devices have been quickly discarded by individuals because they failed to address their individual needs or because they preferred not to use them. Special educators may not be able to keep up with all of the available access and accommodation strategies, but they should be familiar enough with these approaches to be able to make referrals and obtain assessments. Many assistive and accommodation technologies are accessed through related service providers and the special educator must understand the role of these providers and involve them in IEP planning whenever there is even a possibility that a student would benefit from their services.

It is also important for technologies to be developed as part of an outcome-oriented process and maintained as part of a coordinated set of activities. Often assistive technologies stay in the classroom and do not follow the student into adult and community settings. When assistive technologies have been found to be effective and preferred by the student, the special educator will need to assure that these technologies are available to the student and are applied in the full range of applicable environments. This often involves collaboration with adult service providers such as vocational rehabilitation who can purchase or provide these technologies for the student across environments. Additionally, these technologies will need to be periodically updated and may require regular reevaluation.

Determining student accommodations for a particular educational program involves a process that requires communication among team members, who need to understand a student's future goals and the current year's transition activities (O'Brien & Lovett, 1992). Interdisciplinary communication is needed whereby team members have gained knowledge of and respect for the expertise of one another. In the case of access to the general curriculum, the regular education teacher needs to articulate and make clear the curriculum and the classroom philosophy and environment. The special education teacher needs to provide a framework and rationale for individualization and curriculum adaptation within the framework of the regular classroom. The student in question must be able to explain his or her disability and how accommodations are designed to provide an opportunity to participate and complete requirements within the class. Thereby, the student gains an ability to play this role in the process because the process has provided the problem-solving experiences, framework, and practice in being adept at requesting.

> **Critical Point**
> The application of assistive and accommodation technologies requires that the special educator have a basic knowledge of these services and collaborate with related service providers.

Supports for Postsecondary Education

Newman (2005) found that the percentage of students with disabilities that had entered postsecondary education by two years from graduation had more than doubled from 1987 to 2001 from 15% to 37%. Wagner, Newman, Cameto, Garga, and Levine (2005) found that by two years after graduation, 9.6% of special education graduates enrolled in four-year colleges, 5.9% enrolled in vocational schools, and 20.8% enrolled in two-year colleges. In addition to students with disabilities who attended mainstream postsecondary education programs, a growing number of students with severe disabilities such as moderate and severe mental retardation, autism, and other developmental disabilities also entered postsecondary education settings in a variety of programs described by Stodden and Whelley (2004) as including: (a) substantially separate models, (b) mixed-program model with some separate programs for transition skills, and (c) individualized support models with individual services based on preferences and supports consistent with education and career goals. These are described in greater detail in the literature (Hart, Mele-McCarthy, Pasternak, Zimbrich, & Parker, 2004; Neubert, Moon, & Grigal, 2004).

This positive trend was accompanied by some concerns. Murray, Goldstein, Nourse, & Edgar (2000) reported that after five years, 80% of students with learning disabilities had not graduated from college compared to 56% of youth without disabilities. They found that the differences in graduation rates persisted at ten years after graduation with 56% of youth with disabilities not graduating versus 32% of youth without disabilities.

The research on the promising practice in helping youth with disabilities in the transition to postsecondary education has been limited to date. However, Stodden (2001, 2005) laid down several principles for transition programs serving youth who are planning to enter postsecondary education. These included the need to:

> **Critical Point**
> Students with disabilities entered postsecondary education in skyrocketing numbers, but were often not prepared to succeed in these environments, suggesting a need for stronger secondary transition services related to postsecondary education.

1. Provide educational experiences similar to those in postsecondary education.
2. Identify strengths and needs relative to higher education settings.
3. Provide experiences where students with disabilities are outside their familiar support system of family, friends, and teachers.
4. Provide students the opportunity to practice self-advocacy.
5. Familiarize students with the physical environments of postsecondary education.
6. Familiarize students with campus and community supports available to students.
7. Provide instruction related to study skills, time management, test taking, and library use.

8. Provide direct instruction in academic areas such as reading, writing, and mathematics.
9. Provide postsecondary education staff with formal and informal performance data.

Practical Implications

As students with disabilities begin entering postsecondary education in unprecedented numbers, special educators will need to examine how well secondary education is preparing and supporting them. Often these students are overlooked by special educators because they have been mainstreamed and receive few special education services and are often served by tutors who are not part of the regular special education staff. It is important for special educators to recognize that the best providers of transition services may be outside the special education system and include guidance counselors and reading consultants. On the other hand, students with more significant disabilities entering postsecondary education may require the support of special educators who have a strong knowledge of postsecondary education systems and who can develop linkages, services, and supports that allow these students the opportunities to experience these environments through specialized arrangements.

Postsecondary education supports should be developed as part of an outcome-oriented process and should be coordinated with academic activities pursued by the student while in secondary education. Postsecondary options should be explored early in high school to select the proper coursework and to choose a postsecondary program that provides the services and supports that the student will need after graduation. Every postsecondary program has academic requirements that must be met, although state universities and community colleges often have remedial programs for students who have had difficulty in general areas of course work such as mathematics and English. The student should receive training in requesting the necessary accommodations and supports and should visit and/or audit classes from desired schools (Turner, 1996b).

Family Involvement

McNair and Rusch (1991) noted that 63% of the parents they interviewed had a plan for what their child should be doing once school was completed. SRI International (1990) found that parents and guardians had definite expectations about postschool activities of youth with disabilities, with 84% expecting their children to be working in a paying job and 78% expecting them to live independently. Wagner, Newman, Cameto, and Levine (2005) found that 75% of the youth with disabilities they surveyed continued to live with their parents two years after graduation, while Scuccimarra and Speece (1990) and Halpern et al. (1993) found that parents located jobs for 25–30% of the graduating youth they surveyed. Students with disabilities reported that parents and families were their most important supporters (Morningstar, Turnbull, & Turnbull, 1996), and outcome studies showed that after graduation from high school, the family was often the only consistent source of support for these students (Hanley-Maxwell, Pogoloff, & Whitney-Thomas, 1998).

Despite the important role parents played in shaping student career goals and outcomes, they continued to be largely under-involved in transition planning. McNair and Rusch (1991) found in a study involving 200 parents of transition-age students that nearly 70% desired involvement in transition programs, while only 30% experienced involvement. They also found that parents wanted to be involved in finding job placements and community-living arrangements more often than they were afforded the opportunity to do so. Parental lack of information was another concern in regard to student and parent self-determination. McDonnell, Wilcox, Boles, and Bellamy (1985) determined that only 32% of parents they surveyed reported receiving any information about adult services from school personnel. A variety of sources (Turnbull et al., 2006) found that parental ability to make informed decisions related to six factors:

1. Knowledge of the range of options
2. Ability to evaluate options
3. Knowledge of the child's skill
4. Knowledge of the child's preferences
5. Knowledge of how to get services
6. Knowledge of how to advocate for services that are not available

Salembier and Furney (1997) extensively surveyed parents regarding their perceptions of involvement in the IEP process. Several recommendations were provided related to promoting comfort, developing partnerships, and enhancing communication. To foster positive family involvement, Greene (2003) identified the

> **Critical Point**
> Parents continue to be largely underinvolved in transition planning despite their interest and involvement in the student's future.

need for a concerted effort in arranging meetings, sharing information, and coordinating actions to make the school more family friendly and accessible.

Practical Implications

Family involvement represents promising practice in the area of determining student needs, interests, and preferences and in promoting movement to postschool settings, especially when families take over the role of transition coordination after the student exits school. Family involvement should be a major focus of the outcome-oriented process used in transition planning, and family activities should play an important part in developing a coordinated set of activities to support the student's postschool transition. Hanley-Maxwell, Pogoloff, and Whitney-Thomas (1998) outline the four promising practices in family involvement relative to transition planning. These are:

1. Reciprocal family education
2. Cultural sensitivity
3. Personal futures planning
4. Longitudinal involvement in transition planning

Reciprocal family education suggests that professionals will need to be trained both with and by families. This will require some effort by the school to provide training opportunities on evenings and weekends when families are most likely to attend. Cultural sensitivity will require that the school enlist the support of "cultural consultants" who can assist the school in making school programs, meetings, and training more culturally friendly and understandable to families. This will require regular and special educators to examine their values and how they might be different from the families they are serving. Personal futures planning and other person-centered planning strategies will require innovative approaches to finding the time to meet with families in the environments of their choosing and with participants who know and can relate to the student. Finally, longitudinal involvement in transition planning will require that educators communicate information obtained from the family from year to year and assure that families understand the "big picture" in regard to the general purposes and strategies of transition planning across middle and secondary education.

Systems Change Strategies

Researchers, advocates, and policy makers have recognized systems change as an essential strategy for capacity building in transition (Benz et al., 2000; Halpern, Benz, & Lindstrom, 1992). Systems change can occur from "top-down" or "bottom-up" approaches. Top-down systems change efforts in transition were funded by OSERS in the 1990s who awarded grants to states in order to create structural changes in the statewide system of transition services. Two basic objectives had to be met by states in order to receive these grants:

1. To increase the availability, access, and quality of transition assistance through the development and improvement of policies, procedures, systems, and other mechanisms for youth with disabilities and their families as those youth prepare for and enter adult life.
2. To create incentives for the implementation of lasting statewide system changes in the transition of students with disabilities to postsecondary training, education, and employment. (Sec 626([e]) of IDEA)

The results of these projects highlighted what became the central themes of policy debates leading up to IDEA of 1997. These themes included the problem of maintaining individualized transition services while ensuring student participation in the standards-based general education curriculum and found expression in IDEA of 1997.

During the same time period that state system issues were being addressed, bottom-up transition change efforts were also being undertaken. School-level interagency transition teams were developed as a mechanism to address systems issues at the local level based on models developed through Section 626 of the EHA amendments of 1983 (McMahan & Baer, 2001). Members of these school-level interagency transition teams consisted of a full array of people who had a stake in transition outcomes and pooled their efforts in identifying and meeting the needs of students with disabilities at the local level (McMahan & Baer; Wehman et al., 1988).

> **Critical Point**
> Transition systems change occurred largely as a result of OSERs projects at the state and federal level and as a result of school-level interagency transition teams at the local level.

Practical Implications

Often, educational and adult services systems present transition barriers that cannot be addressed at the individual level. To deal with these issues, the transition services coordinator must be aware of exemplary transition practices and be able to mobilize transition stakeholders toward incorporating these practices in the school. The school-level interagency transition team can be an effective way of accomplishing this. Transition system issues that may be addressed by the schoolwide transition team include:

1. Development of accommodations and procedures for proficiency testing of students with disabilities.
2. Adoption of person-centered IEP planning approaches.
3. Definition of graduation requirements for students with severe disabilities.
4. Cross-training for students, parents, and professionals.
5. Strategies to empower youth with disabilities and their families.
6. Development of linkages with providers of career opportunities for students with disabilities.

The membership of the school-level interagency transition team should include all transition stakeholders, including but not limited to: families, adult service providers, administrators, educators, employers, and transition specialists. The makeup of the team may vary from meeting to meeting depending on the issues being discussed.

The implementation of transition systems change will require that special educators have a working knowledge of all of the transition stakeholders and communicate with them regularly. It will also require a knowledge of the team and group processes that can enlist these stakeholders in developing and implementing ideas for improving transition systems and services in the context of the local community and of the students with disabilities they are serving.

CONCLUSION

Transition policy and practice has been a dynamic concept that has evolved along with beliefs about promising practices in education. Its early roots could be traced to work-study and career education programs which evolved into the narrowly focused bridges model and were expanded further to broadly defined transition education models. Defining promising practices for transition remains difficult because of the interaction of local variables, divergent concepts of education, different needs of individuals with disabilities, and the changing environments that youth with disabilities will be entering in the future. The authors discussed how promising transition practices were contingent upon students' postsecondary environments, transition and education policy, and individual student needs, interests, strengths, and preferences. In the remainder of this book, the authors will provide the readers with a more detailed understanding of concepts introduced in this overview chapter.

STUDY QUESTIONS

1. How has the social response to disability changed in the last 60 years and how has that influenced the provision of disability services?
2. What are some of the characteristics of early adolescence and what transition goals should be typically pursued during this period?
3. What are some of the characteristics of middle adolescence and what transition goals should be typically pursued during this period?
4. What are some of the characteristics of late adolescence and what transition goals should be typically pursued during this period?
5. Identify one of the ecological domains in the Lichtenstein model and the transition implications for that domain.
6. What was found in researching postschool outcomes for students with disabilities and what did this imply for secondary education?
7. What quality-of-life concerns were addressed in Halpern's model?
8. When did the IDEA mandate the provision of transition services and how has this mandate evolved in later amendments to this legislation?
9. What are the four essential elements of transition?
10. How are the essential elements of transition in the IDEA reinforced and supported by promising practices developed through research and professional consensus?
11. What national organization developed its own definition of transition services and how did it differ from the IDEA definition?
12. Name two promising practices in transition and discuss how they are related to postsecondary outcomes, transition policy, and individual/family needs.
13. How has alignment of transition curriculum and regular education curriculum helped and hampered the implementation of career education approaches to transition?

WEBSITES

The IDEA and Transition
http://www.ldonline.org/ld_indepth/transition/law_of_transition.html

Quality of Life—Bibliography
http://www.utoronto.ca/qol/biblioqol4.htm

The Real Facts about Disability and "Quality of Life"
Compiled by *Not Dead Yet* in consultation with Carol J. Gill, Ph.D., April 1999.
http://www.independentliving.org/docs3/gill99.html

Quality of Life Indicators
http://www.ont-autism.uoguelph.ca/STRATEGIES4.shtml

Quality of Life for Minorities with Disabilities
http://www.hawaii.edu/hivandaids/Improving%20the%20Quality%20of%20Life%20for%20Minorities%20with%20Disabilities.pdf

Handbook on Quality of Life for Human Service Practitioners
http://www.aamr.org/Bookstore/QUAL/handbook.shtml

Erik Erikson's 8 Stages of Psychosocial Development
http://www.childdevelopmentinfo.com/development/erickson.shtml

Effects of Disability on Psychosocial Development
http://www.ssta.sk.ca/research/students/91-05a.htm#eff

Adolescent Stages of Development
http://www.childdevelopmentinfo.com/development/teens_stages.shtml

Family Ecology Issues
http://www.ncoff.gse.upenn.edu/litrev/fpmlr.htm

National Longitudinal Transition Study–2
http://www.nlts2.org/

National Transition Alliance Model Programs
http://www.dssc.org/

CHAPTER 2

TRANSITION LEGISLATION AND MODELS

Robert W. Flexer

Robert M. Baer

LEARNING OBJECTIVES

The objectives of this chapter are:

1. Explain the disability policy background for each period of legislation.
2. Describe the basic principles and provisions of transition and related legislation for each period.
3. Explain how legislation in different areas is coordinated and what this means.
4. Describe changes in transition focus across the periods of legislation.
5. Know the history of practices to help youth with disabilities in the transition to adulthood.
6. Understand how transition history shaped transition policy.

INTRODUCTION

The provision of transition services became policy for secondary special education with the passage of the Individuals with Disabilities Education Act (IDEA) of 1990. This legislation defined transition services and required incorporation of these services into the individualized education programs (IEPs) of all youth with disabilities. This IDEA transition mandate was designed to address a fundamental purpose of secondary education—preparation for adult life (Turnbull et al., 2003). Moreover, its mandated transition planning process was designed to emphasize student, family, and professional attention to the challenges, uncertainties, and promises of making the transition to adulthood.

Throughout this book, the authors will use the four essential elements of transition as defined in the IDEA to provide a common ground between the legal requirements for transition services and empirically supported transition practices. This chapter will emphasize both the letter and intent of the IDEA transition mandate and emphasize the use of student-determined postschool goals to develop a coordinated set of activities directed toward their accomplishment. Additionally, in this chapter the authors will explore the relationship between transition-related legislation and transition models in special education, general education, career and technical education, and vocational rehabilitation.

In the following discussion, transition legislation and models will be broken into five time periods spanning the five decades from the 1960s to the present time. It will discuss the period up to and including the 1960s in relation to the development of underlying values and beliefs regarding disability issues. It will describe the 1970s as creating a foundation for the delivery of special education and the 1980s as refining this system through the development of new and innovative transition models. The final two decades will be discussed in terms of legislative reforms that translated these innovations into policy and that were designed to reconcile them with parallel reforms in education and vocational rehabilitation.

POLICY, PRACTICE, AND SOCIAL FOUNDATIONS THROUGH THE 1960s

Modern concepts of disability can be traced back to the Elizabethan Poor Laws in seventeenth-century England, which differentiated between the deserving and undeserving poor. The undeserving poor were seen as living in poverty as a result of poor moral character and, therefore, were expected to work and "pull themselves up by the bootstraps." In contrast, the deserving poor, primarily the "crippled" and the blind were responded to with charity and were usually not expected to work (Macklesprang & Salsgiver, 1996). Throughout history, persons with disabilities were seen as both the deserving and undeserving poor, depending on the type of disability and prevailing cultural values. This notion of disability had its drawbacks, both for persons considered as deserving and those who were not. When seen as deserving, persons with disabilities were patronized and not expected to work or contribute. When seen as undeserving, they faced unemployment and servitude, or a life of crime and imprisonment. This Elizabethan disability concept can be viewed as underlying much of Western society's response up to the 1960s. For example in Social Security income programs in the United States, "deserving" persons with blindness received much higher benefits than persons with emotional disturbances who were considered less deserving.

Wolfensberger was among the first to challenge this concept when in 1972 he provided a seminal critique of disability policy in a book titled *Normalization*. In this book, he argued that the value assigned to persons with disabilities was subsequently played out in how they were treated by society and disability programs and noted how, at various times in history, people with disabilities were treated as less than human at worst, or charitable cases at best (Wolfensberger, 1972). Table 2-1 illustrates how perceptions were mirrored in disability service models and professional roles.

These conceptions of persons with disabilities were documented repeatedly in the 1960s and 1970s. Examples of their impact included:

- Institutional exposés like Willowbrook, portrayed in *Christmas in Purgatory* (Blatt, 1966) and reported by Geraldo Rivera, demonstrated that in the 1960s people with severe and profound mental retardation were being abused and living in horrific conditions.
- The exclusion of children with severe disabilities from public school until 1975.
- The segregation of persons with severe disabilities in day activity centers and institutions in the 1970s.

TABLE 2–1 Sociohistorical deviancy role perceptions and resultant service and staffing models

Role Perception	Service Model	Staff Model

Subhuman:
  Animal
  Vegetable
  Insensate object
	Neglect, custody, destruction	Catcher, attendant, caretaker, keeper, gardener, exterminator

Menace, or object of dread	Punitive or detentive segregation, or destruction	Guard, attendant, exterminator
Object of ridicule	Exhibition	Entertainer
Object of pity	Protection from demands	Member of religious bodies, charitable individual
Burden of charity	Industrial habilitation	Trainer, disciplinarian, work master
Holy innocent	Protection from evil	Member of religious bodies, charitable individual
Eternal child	Nurturant shelter	Parent
Sick person	Medical	Physician, nurse, therapist

Source: From Overview of normalization, by W. Wolfensberger in R. J. Flynn & K. E. Nitsch (Eds.), *Normalization, social integration, and community services.* 1980, Table 2, p. 10, Chap. 1. Reprinted with permission.

Early Rehabilitation Influences

Disability reforms also had roots up to and including the 1960s. Early in the 1900s, the concept of disability began to be reformed by the emergence of rehabilitation services. These services were a result of medical and technical progress in World War I and the need to rehabilitate the many veterans injured in that war. In 1917, the Smith-Hughes Act (P.L. 64-347) provided government support for rehabilitation services for veterans with disabilities and was followed by the Smith-Sears Act (P.L. 65-178) in 1918, which provided them with the first government-supported employment services, vocational education, and early forms of disability technology. In 1920, the Smith-Fess Act (P.L. 66-236) extended these services (e.g., guidance counseling, occupational adjustment, and placement) to civilians who had become disabled while engaged in civil employment. This early rehabilitation legislation focused on a small group of "deserving" persons with disabilities and focused on the correction of individual deficits rather than social change. These early twentieth-century concepts of

> **Critical Point**
> Vocational rehabilitation concepts of disability were influenced greatly by World War I, the emergence of rehabilitation technology, and the need to rehabilitate veterans and civil service employees injured in the line of duty.

disability can still be observed in the underlying philosophy and strategies of many current disability professions, including rehabilitation, vocational education, and special education (DeStefano & Snauwaert, 1989).

Legislation from 1917 to 1943 (the period between World War I and World War II) dealt with limited populations and limited disability services. Legislation during this period dealt primarily with the support and training of veterans and civil service employees with disabilities. However, in 1943 the Barden-LaFollete Act (P.L. 77-113) extended these services to civilians who were not government workers. This act also extended rehabilitation services to include medical services such as examinations, surgery, and prosthetic and orthotic devices that were deemed essential to becoming employed. In principle, rehabilitation services were expanded to include people with mental retardation and mental illness, although services were rarely extended to these populations because of their scarcity and the lack of an overall rehabilitation system. While the Vocational Rehabilitation Amendments of 1954 (P.L. 83-565) did not make work-study, sheltered

> **Critical Point**
> Rehabilitation services evolved slowly between the two world wars but began to be viewed as part of an overall system for the promotion of the welfare of U.S. citizens.

workshops, and job placement services generally available to all people with disabilities across states, it did provide "seed" monies for the establishment of pilot programs in these areas and to develop the capacity of states and local programs to make these services part of an overall system.

Development of Advocacy Organizations

Rehabilitation services were gradually extended to more persons as technologies improved; however, persons with severe disabilities continued to be seen as charity cases with nothing to contribute to society. In 1950, a challenge to this concept came from the National Association for Retarded Citizens (now known as the ARC), an organization formed by parents. Initially, the ARC and other parent organizations (such as United Cerebral Palsy) set out to fund and create skill-development programs and activities for children and adults with severe disabilities (e.g., moderate to severe mental retardation, cerebral palsy, autism, and other developmental disabilities). Early childhood programs and special schools were established for children who were excluded from school, and sheltered employment and day activity centers were established for adults. Parent information and support was a cornerstone for these early organizations that supported a rapidly growing number of families who were facing a challenge few professionals understood or had resources to deal with (Turnbull & Turnbull, 1990).

> **Critical Point**
> The first national attention to disability issues stemmed from efforts by family-based advocacy organizations.

These early advocacy organizations were the impetus for community and social awareness regarding the need for special education and rehabilitation services. Consequently, the 1960s was a period characterized by an emerging visibility of disability issues, and it established the first federal commitment to persons with disabilities in regard to helping them fulfill their needs, hopes, and desires. This commitment started with the Kennedy administration, which called for the establishment of public welfare, service, and training programs designed to decrease the prolonged dependence of persons with disabilities. This national commitment was described by the first President's Panel on Mental Retardation (see Table 2–2) and are as relevant today as they were more than 40 years ago. The language was different, but the goals underlying these

TABLE 2–2 President's panel on mental retardation: 1962 recommendations

- The establishment of research centers for the study of retardation, its causes, and especially its prevention
- The improvement of welfare, health, and general social conditions of all the people, particularly those in the greatest need
- Improved educational programs and availability of appropriate education for all: the extension of the definition of education beyond the academics
- The training of professional and service personnel to work in all aspects of retardation, particularly at the leadership level
- The development of comprehensive, community-centered services on a continuum to meet all types of needs

Source: From President's panel on mental retardation (1962). A proposed program for national action to combat mental retardation. Washington, DC: U.S. Government Printing Office.

recommendations have remained central to current efforts to improve the quality of services and outcomes for persons with disabilities.

Legislation of the 1960s

In concert with goals of the President's Panel on Mental Retardation, legislation in the 1960s was directed at meeting the educational and developmental needs of all children with disabilities. In 1965 and 1966, legislation was passed that provided support for the education of children with disabilities in state-operated schools, community hospitals, and local schools. The Vocational Education Act of 1963 (P.L. 88-210) provided for the development of vocational programs for disadvantaged populations and for students with disabilities. In 1968, the Vocational Education Act amendments authorized and set aside 10% of vocational education funding for education and services to students with disabilities. The rehabilitation amendments of 1967 created new programs for recruitment and training of rehabilitation service providers and funded rehabilitation services and research at much higher levels. This act led to the development of work study programs that provided work experiences, functional academics, and life skills training for persons with mild mental retardation.

Developmental disabilities and mental health legislation also expanded during the 1960s by sharpening definitions, eligibility, and scope of services for these two populations. For example, the Mental Retardation and

Facilities and Construction Act of 1963 (P.L. 88-164) established, for the first time, a federal priority to meet the needs of persons with mental retardation on a national level. A framework was set up to define the need and subsequently to develop a national framework for service delivery. Monies became available to states and community agencies to establish community-based services with government support. This legislation was an important start in defining the major life activity needs of persons with disabilities and in establishing a comprehensive system of services and supports to meet these needs.

Early Transition Models

While the transition initiative was yet to be defined in the 1960s and 1970s, many programs emerged prior to and during that period that were later to be called transition programs. Halpern (1992) reviewed the history of the transition initiative and concluded that transition programs were essentially "old wine in new bottles" consisting largely of updated variations of the "tried and true" approaches of the past. He warned transition advocates to avoid the danger of discarding past research in favor of new and untried approaches marketed as a "silver bullet." In fact, he noted that precursors to transition models dated back to the 1930s when educators began to realize that a strictly academic curriculum was not sufficient to meet the needs of students with mild mental retardation. During this period, educators (in urban areas in particular) in some states developed functional curricula that reflected a life-skills and a vocational approach to special education for secondary youth (Clark & Kolstoe, 1995; Neubert, 1997). Similarly, a functionally based job-skills approach was implemented in the early work study programs in the late 1950s (e.g., Frey & Kolstoe, 1965). Studies spanning a 20-year period documented the effectiveness of these approaches for students with mild mental retardation (see Cobb, 1972).

Work-Study Programs

As vocational rehabilitation (VR) became a federal-state partnership (i.e., federal money being matched by state money), various populations of people with disabilities were identified as "in need" of rehabilitation and employment-related services, including high school students with mild mental retardation. Consequently, the **work-study** model emerged in the late 1950s through collaboration between public schools and local offices of state rehabilitation agencies (Halpern, 1992). These programs provided integrated academic, social, and vocational curriculum coupled with community work experiences to prepare youth with mild disabilities for productive community adjustment. Work-study programs were the first examples of formal interagency cooperation between education and rehabilitation agencies. Halpern (1992) observed that work-study programs had many elements in common with transition programs, including:

1. Community employment was legitimized as part of the curriculum and recognized for its educational value, and part-time work experiences were combined with part-time school, with school credits given for work experience.
2. Work-adjustment classes and functional academics supported these work experiences by helping students obtain work-related reading, writing, and mathematics skills.
3. The classroom teacher and the rehabilitation counselor worked as an interdisciplinary team with students being eligible for all services of vocational rehabilitation.
4. Local and state interagency agreements were used to combine school and vocational rehabilitation resources, and local VR offices sometimes had counselors who were assigned exclusively to serving schools.

Through work-study programs, thousands of students with mild mental retardation became clients of the state rehabilitation agency to help them make the transition to successful employment. Although it held great promise, the work-study cooperative with a blended funding arrangement with rehabilitation services lasted little more than a decade. The passage of the Education of All Handicapped Children Act (P.L. 94-142) in 1975 passed the responsibility for work study to schools as part of the requirement that they provide "free appropriate public education" (FAPE).

After 1975, many schools continued to operate work-study programs by hiring specific staff persons to develop programs that were typically designed for students with learning disabilities, behavior disorders, and mild mental retardation. The survival of the work-study model may be attributed to the fact that research continued to find a relationship between work experiences in high school and better employment outcomes (Hasazi, Gordon, & Roe, 1985; Blackorby & Wagner, 1996). Researchers found that work-study pro-

> **Critical Point**
> Although these cooperative agreements no longer exist, most states have work-study programs to serve high school students with learning disabilities, emotional and behavioral disorders, and mild mental retardation.

grams helped students learn the basic skills required in all work settings and to make contacts that led to employment after graduation (Blackorby & Wagner). They also found that these programs provided students with real-life experiences that made their education more relevant and contributed to their staying in school (Blackorby & Wagner). Work-study programs, therefore, strongly addressed the essential elements of promoting movement to postschool settings and creating a coordinated set of activities between rehabilitation and education, but focused less on the other two essential elements of transition.

Summary of Policy through the 1960s

From 1917 to 1945, the primary federal role was rehabilitation for veterans with disabilities and the development of vocational education alternatives in public schools. Beginning in the late 1950s and continuing into the 1960s, legislation was passed for special education, special needs vocational education, statewide

TABLE 2–3 Legislation prior to and during the 1960s

1917–1945
Focus on support and training for disabled veterans Beginnings of a federal government role.
• 1917 Smith-Hughes Act (P.L. 64-347): Provided for vocational rehabilitation and employment for veterans with disabilities and vocational education • 1918 Smith-Sears Act (P.L. 65-178): Provided additional support for veterans with disabilities • 1920 Smith-Fess Act (P.L. 66-236): Provided funding for vocational training for civilians with disabilities who worked in federal civil service jobs • 1943 Barden-LaFollette Act (P.L. 77-113): Provided for vocational rehabilitation for all civilians with physical disabilities and mental retardation
1945–1968
Expansion of training and rehabilitation for the whole population of persons with disabilities Emergence of disability policy and federal government role.
• 1954 Vocational Rehabilitation amendments (P.L. 83-565): Provided funding for research and training of professionals and for expanding and improving rehabilitation • 1963 Vocational Education Act (P.L. 88-210): Provided for expansion of vocational programs and services for person with disabilities • 1966 Elementary and Secondary Education Act amendments (P.L. 89-750): Provided for support of state programs of special education and created federal Bureau of Education of the Handicapped • 1968 Vocational Education amendments (P.L. 90-576): Established set-aside of basic state funding for special populations (10% for students with disabilities and 15% for students with academic and economic disadvantages) • 1967 Vocational Rehabilitation amendments (P.L. 90-99): Provided increased funding for rehabilitation, research, demonstration, and training projects • 1968 Vocational Rehabilitation amendments (P.L. 90-391): Provided increased funding for rehabilitation, research, demonstration, and training projects • 1963 Mental Retardation and Facilities and Construction Act (P.L. 88-164): Provided funding for creation of community-based programs for people with mental retardation

Source: Adapted from School-to-work transition: Overview of disability legislation by R. A. Stodden in F. R. Rusch & J. G. Chadsey (Eds.) *Beyond high school: Transition from school to work,* 1998, Wadsworth Publishing Company.

rehabilitation programs, and a developmental disability and mental health service system. This was the beginning of disability policy and practice and a federal government role in the education and rehabilitation of people with disabilities. Table 2–3 compares and contrasts the federal government role and development of transition services in disability services through the 1960s.

POLICY FOUNDATION, PRACTICES, AND LEGISLATION OF THE 1970s

PARC v. Commonwealth of Pennsylvania, 1972

While continuing to provide community services, the ARC expanded its advocacy role into the political arena in the 1970s. In the early 1970s, students with severe disabilities continued to be excluded from public schools in most states prompting the Pennsylvania ARC (PARC) to file a class action lawsuit. This suit demanded public education for all children regardless of disability under the argument that their rights to education could not be taken away without due process of law (*PARC v. Commonwealth of Pennsylvania*, 1972). The class action suit was won by PARC (the plaintiff) and was instrumental in creating the structure of the Education of All Handicapped Children Act (P.L. 94-142) in 1975. This new act ended the exclusion of children with severe disabilities from public education and established their entitlement to a "free and appropriate public education."

> **Critical Point**
> In the 1970s, political action by advocacy groups established the right to a free and appropriate education for all students with disabilities.

Independent Living Movement

While parents and families were advocating for children and some adults with disabilities, adults with physical and sensory disabilities began advocating for themselves. In Berkeley, California, a small group of young adults challenged the University of California to make all of its programs and education accessible to persons with physical disabilities. This resulted in the "independent living movement," which emphasized that community participation and access to social institutions were the right of all citizens, including persons with disabilities.

With leadership from a variety of self-advocacy groups, the Rehabilitation Act of 1973 (P.L. 93-112) was passed mandating equal access for persons with disabilities to all federally funded programs. However, the implementation of this law was hindered because the government did not write regulations. Five years later, in 1978, advocates and persons with disabilities had to stage a sit-in at the office of the cabinet secretary and in regional offices of the U.S. Department of Health, Education, and Welfare to spur the government into promulgating the needed regulations. This bureaucratic stonewalling was typical of the battles that disability movements faced in affirming the rights of people with disabilities.

> **Critical Point**
> Legislation mandating access to employment, postsecondary education, and the community was achieved by coalitions, including persons with disabilities.

People First

The 1970s was also a period of self-advocacy by other disability groups. The origin of **People First,** the self-advocacy organization of people with mental retardation, was a case in point. Because of cognitive limitations, persons with mental retardation were not being heard, except through their parents. A group of these individuals came together in Oregon to tell professionals what they wanted from their programs. Accounts of the meeting describe a young woman standing up and saying, "We want to be people first!" This sparked a movement in the disability community that persons with disabilities should be referred to and treated as "persons first." The People First movement challenged society and professionals to attach primary attention to "personhood" and to view disability as only a part of a whole person, not the defining characteristic (Perske, 1988).

The People First movement led to a change in thinking and talking about persons with disabilities. Professional and social discourse about persons with disabilities began to discard terms such as "retardate," "cripple," and "the disabled." **Person-first language** and disability etiquette has been characterized as political correctness, but was seen by advocates as being very important in increasing the presence and participation of people with disabilities. Person-first language was designed to convey respect for the person with a disability by:

1. Recognizing a person's right to self-esteem.
2. Recognizing a person's right to be thought of as a person first and foremost in word and in thought (in other words, the person is "first a

TABLE 2–4 Person-first language suggestions

- Refer to people first and disability second.
- Avoid the use of terms which equate a person with his or her disability (i.e., the "quadriplegic" or "epileptic"; instead, use the person with a seizure disorder or the person with quadriplegia).
- Use adjectives that do not have negative connotations (i.e., "stricken," "afflicted," "victim," or "crippled").
- Use the words "typical" and "normal" appropriately (i.e., in comparison to people without disabilities, people with disabilities are "atypical," but the term "abnormal" conveys inaccurate, negative meanings).
- Focus on what a person with disabilities can do rather than what they cannot do.
- Avoid describing persons as having disabilities when it is not pertinent to the conversation.
- Avoid sensationalizing or implying that superhuman qualities are possessed by persons with disabilities (persons with disabilities have the same range of talents and successes as others; to sensationalize their accomplishments implies that they must overcompensate to succeed—most need only a regular effort when they have equal access and reasonable accommodations with which to accomplish their work).
- Avoid using words associated with disability in a manner that has negative connotations (i.e., terms such as "deaf and dumb," "retarded," or "spastic" evoke negative images and are easily replaced by accurate descriptions).
- Avoid the use of terms such as "wheelchair bound" or "confined to a wheelchair" (persons who *use wheelchairs* view them as most people view cars, as tools which enable freedom and independence, not traps! It is inappropriate to associate wheelchairs with helplessness and dependence and to treat wheelchairs as an extension of personal space; to lean or hang on it is like leaning or hanging on the person using the wheelchair).

Source: Adapted from class materials "Disability Policy," developed by Deborah Durhan Webster, Kent State University, 1999.

person" and "second a person with a disability").

3. Accurately describing a person without being judgmental (i.e., just as it is not always necessary to convey the color of a person's hair, it is also not always necessary to mention that a person has a disability).

> **Critical Point**
> People with mental retardation directly experience the rejection and fear resulting from others who define them only through the label of their disability.

Table 2-4 provides both an overview of some issues that are important in interacting with people with disabilities and some useful guidelines to personal and professional behavior. Person-first language should generally be used in talking about persons with disabilities unless they request otherwise. It may also be necessary to educate others (e.g., send guidelines to the media) so that they can support social behaviors that show respect for persons with disabilities.

School-Based Legislation of 1970s

During the 1970s, special education and vocational education were coordinated through cross-references in their governing legislation. The Education for All Handicapped Children Act (EHA) of 1975 (P.L. 95-142) mandated multifactored evaluations (MFE) every three years, parental right to due process, free appropriate public education (FAPE), least restrictive environment (LRE), and the Individualized Education Program (IEP), which were the cornerstones of special education. Under the EHA, the IEP was to include career and vocational objectives for youth with disabilities.

The Education Amendments of 1976 (P.L. 94-482) required coordination of the state plans of special education and vocational education and established priority for access to regular vocational education over specialized vocational education. Assurances that the full range of program options was accessible were an important requirement in state plans for vocational education. The need for vocational teacher participation in the development of IEPs was highlighted in this legislation. The teaming of vocational and special education instructional staff was expected for participation in regular vocational education. Consequently, many states developed a continuum of vocational education services and options for students with disabilities. These continuums were based on least restrictive environment concepts (i.e., regular vocational education, with support, or specialized).

In 1977, the concept of career education was put into legislation and introduced as "the totality of experiences through which one learns about and prepares to engage in work as part of his or her

> **Critical Point**
> The common underpinnings of special education, vocational education, and career education were established through coordinated legislation in the 1970s.

way of living" (Hoyt, 1977). States were to implement programs on:

1. Encompassing the total curriculum of the school and providing a unified approach to education for life.
2. Encouraging all members of the community to share responsibility for learning within classrooms, homes, private and public agencies, and the employment community.
3. Providing for career awareness, exploration, and preparation at all levels and ages.
4. Encouraging all teachers to review their subject matter for its career implications.

Special educators increased their career education emphasis to develop students' functional and life skills, and as a method to link academic and vocational preparation (Clark, 1979). Unfortunately, career education legislation was passed with a sunset provision and expired in 1982 along with funding to states for career education efforts. Nonetheless, the concept and structure of career education continued to be implemented in various ways and some structures still exist in schools today.

Career education's influence can be seen in counseling and guidance, special education, and career and technical education. In fact, the School to Work Opportunity Act of 1994 was in many ways a successor to the Career Education Implementation Incentive Act of 1977.

Rehabilitation Act of 1973

Historically, the Rehabilitation Act of 1973 was of great importance for several reasons. First, the act was completely rewritten as a "new" law and replaced the Barden-LaFollete Act of 1943. Second, it reflected a comprehensive and functional service delivery model. Third, with passage of the Rehabilitation Act of 1973, Congress officially established the notion of disability rights in regard to vocational rehabilitation. Additionally, state rehabilitation programs were to give priority to persons with the most severe disabilities and to provide them the opportunity to receive services in order to become employed. This was the beginning of an ongoing trend in vocational rehabilitation service delivery where extensive services were mandated but insufficiently funded.

A second area addressed by the Rehabilitation Act was the establishment of **independent living centers.** These were included as a Title—a section of the law to cover those kinds of services. Independent living programs emphasized two major points: (a) living in the community and getting help with activities of daily living was as important as working, and (b) independent living made it necessary that the client or consumer of services should have considerable input and control over what services were provided and how they were delivered. The underlying principle of independent living centers was that they should deal with the whole person by addressing all the domains of living in the community.

A third area of the Rehabilitation Act described the rights of persons with disabilities as they pertained to employment and participation in the community. Of particular importance was Section 504, the nondiscrimination requirements pertaining to people with disabilities. Section 504 reads:

> No otherwise qualified person with a disability in the United States ... shall, solely on the basis of disability, be denied access to, or the benefits of, or be subjected to discrimination under any program or activity provided by any institution receiving federal financial assistance or under any program or activity conducted by any Executive Agency or by the U.S. Postal Service (29 U.S.C. § 794).

Developmental Disability and Mental Health Legislation

The field of **developmental disabilities (DD)** was unique because its origins could be traced to congressional legislation. As the mental retardation legislation of the 1960s was expiring, leaders and advocacy groups grasped the opportunity to expand previous laws to benefit not only individuals who were mentally retarded, but also individuals with other types of disabilities (e.g., cerebral palsy) whose impairments were developmental (occurring before adulthood) in nature. Consequently, P.L. 91-517, the Developmental Disabilities Services Facilities Construction

Critical Point
Developmental
disability legislation
extended disability
services for persons
with mental
retardation to other
groups with
developmental
disabilities.

Act of 1970, was enacted for not only persons who were mentally retarded, but also persons who were affected by cerebral palsy, epilepsy, and other neurological conditions found to require comprehensive services similar to those required by individuals with mental retardation.

Since many persons with severe disabilities were not receiving services after the passage of the 1970 DD Act, its 1978 amendments dropped eligibility based on disability categories in favor of eligibility based on substantial impairments in life activity areas. Public Law 95-602, Rehabilitation, Comprehensive Services, and the Developmental Disability (DD) Amendments of 1978, defined developmental disability as a severe, chronic disability of a person which:

a. Is attributable to mental or physical impairment, or combination of mental and physical impairments.
b. Is manifested before the person attains age 22.
c. Is likely to continue indefinitely.
d. Results in substantial functional limitations in three or more of the following areas of major life activity:
   1. self-care
   2. receptive and expressive language
   3. learning
   4. mobility
   5. self-direction
   6. capacity for independent living
   7. economic self-sufficiency
e. Reflects the person's need for a combination and sequence of special, interdisciplinary, or generic care, treatment, or other services that are individually planned and coordinated.

Critical Point
The Developmental
Disabilities Act of
1978 discarded
eligibility based on
developmental
disability categories
in favor of eligibility
based on
developmental
disabilities resulting
in substantial
functional limitations.

The major implications of the definition were that comprehensive, coordinated lifelong management of services would be required to meet the needs of the person with a developmental disability.

Similar legislation to that in the DD amendment was passed in the area of mental health in the 1960s and 1970s. This legislation also focused on community-based services and support over extended periods of time. Individuals had pervasive needs and were referred to as having psychiatric disabilities. These individuals had substantial functional limitations, but due to psychiatric problems, and not mental retardation. In the 1970s hospital work programs laid the groundwork for supported employment programs for persons with serious mental illness, which included transitional work programs and client-employing businesses (Baer, 2003). Transitional work programs stressed the importance of developing work skills and coping strategies in a series of temporary jobs and shared some therapeutic orientation with hospital work programs. Client-employing businesses, like earlier hospital work programs, emphasized the approach of developing supportive environments for persons with serious mental illness and then bringing competitive work to these environments.

Critical Point
In the 1970s, mental
health programs began
looking at the need
to deal with the
employment needs of
adults with psychiatric
disabilities.

Career Education Models

In concert with the comprehensive coordinated legislation of the 1970s, the Career Education Implementation Incentive Act of 1978 introduced a comprehensive model to assist students in their transition to adulthood. Career education models were characterized as: (a) systematic, (b) developmental, (c) focused on self-awareness, and (d) oriented to a wide range of occupations. Halpern (1992) said this initiative could be seen as an extension of the earlier work-study movement, but noted that unlike work-study programs, career education programs spanned elementary, middle, and secondary education and included regular as well as special education students. Career education included a broader curricular focus including students' self-understanding and occupational awareness and a broader ecological focus including interpersonal, domestic, and community domains. Although the Career Education Implementation Incentive Act expired in 1982, career education in special education continued to be an integral approach to transition.

Critical Point
In career education,
added emphasis was
placed on the
elementary and
middle schools as the
foundations for the
development of
career maturity and
life skills.

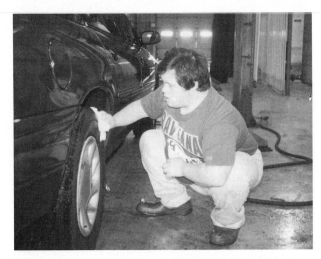

Work experience is vital to career education programs.

Special educators embraced the career education model and developed programs for students with disabilities. The **Life-Centered Career Education (LCCE)** model identified 22 major competencies, which were to be infused into primary, middle, and secondary curricula to address the major life domains of work, home, and academics (Brolin & Lloyd, 2004). Another career education model for students with disabilities was the *School-Based Career Development and Transition Education Model,* which focused on student skill and support needs in the areas of: (a) employment, (b) further education, (c) daily living, (d) leisure activities, (e) community participation, (f) health, (g) self-determination, (h) communication, and (i) interpersonal relationships (Sitlington & Clark, 2006).

Critical Point
The career education programs differed from work-study programs in that they included students of all ages and students with and without disabilities.

For students with severe disabilities, career education approaches emphasized community-based instructional programs. These approaches were developed within the framework of the "criterion of ultimate function" (Brown et al., 1979). Under this approach, education and supports addressed the skills students needed to function as independently as possible in future as well as present environments. Research supported this approach and indicated that students with severe disabilities with training in community environments were much more likely to

function in these environments as adults (Blackorby & Wagner, 1996).

Summary Policy, Legislation, and Practice of the 1970s

Table 2–5 shows the legislative and transition progression through the 1970s. The focus during this period was on appropriate education for special education youth and access and accommodation for all persons with disabilities, including adults. On the special education side, all students were to be provided with a **free appropriate public education (FAPE)** and an education program that met their unique needs (i.e., an IEP). FAPE was to include vocational and career education for secondary-age students, if needed. The focus on career education brought special and regular education closer after years of separation. The career development models of the 1970s were designed to broaden the educational focus from academics to development of skills in all of the life domains. Rehabilitation, developmental disability, and mental health legislation provided guidelines for eligibility and

TABLE 2–5 Legislation during the 1970s

Ensured rights to appropriate education and access for persons with disabilities in general
Established service system supported by federal government

- 1970 Developmental Disabilities and Bill of Rights Act of 1970: Provided support to states' creation of a developmental disabilities service system—emphasized long-term support
- 1973 Rehabilitation Act (sections 503 and 504) (P.L. 93-112): Funded independent living centers, prioritized rehabilitation of persons with the most severe disabilities, provided protection from discrimination
- 1973 Comprehensive Employment and Training Act (P.L. 93-203): Provided manpower services to raise employment levels of unemployed, unskilled youth and adults
- 1975 Education of Handicapped Children Act (P.L. 94-142): Partially funded a free appropriate public education (FAPE) in the least restrictive environment; included vocational education
- 1976 Vocational Education amendments (P.L. 94-482): Emphasized access to regular vocational education and development of new vocational programs; funded vocational assessment and support services for students with special needs

Source: Adapted from School-to-work transition: Overview of disability legislation, by R. A. Stodden in F. R. Rusch and J. G. Chadsey (Eds.), *Beyond high school: Transition from school to work,* 1998, Wadsworth Publishing Company.

established service systems for children and adults with the most severe disabilities who were historically underserved. Integration and participation in the mainstream of schools and communities and society was central to all the disability legislation while, for the first time, rights for people with disabilities were spelled out for both school-age children and youth and adults.

POLICY, PRACTICES, AND LEGISLATION OF THE 1980s

Whereas legislation of the 1970s laid a foundation for special education and a service system for adults with disabilities, the 1980s was a period of consolidation and coordination of disability legislation among vocational education, rehabilitation, and disability benefit programs. The Carl D. Perkins Vocational Education and Technology Act of 1984 (P.L. 98-524) provided clarification of the role of vocational education in regard to providing FAPE for students with disabilities. Within the rehabilitation system, the Rehabilitation Act Amendments of 1986 (P.L. 99-506) provided a specific program and service structure (i.e., supported employment) to serve individuals with the most severe disabilities. The 1980s were especially known for the legislative activity of the 99th Congress, which was particularly active in addressing issues affecting employment opportunities for persons with disabilities (e.g., disincentives to employment such as the loss of Social Security benefits).

Special Education Legislation

As a result of the concern generated by postschool outcome studies, the 1983 amendments to the Education of All Handicapped Children Act (P.L. 98-199) included Section 626, which addressed secondary education and transition and which launched a federal initiative to develop model transition programs. Substantial numbers of discretionary programs were funded for the purpose of researching the transition process and for developing demonstration and capacity-building activities to improve transition services in state and local education agencies. The Office of Special Education and Rehabilitative Services (OSERS) promoted secondary

> **Critical Point**
> In the 1980s, the EHA of 1983 brought national attention to the transition needs of secondary youth with disabilities.

education improvements including projects to develop transition services, community-based education and services, cooperative models, job training, self-determination, and local education agency capacity to deliver transition services. This initiative also funded research and demonstration projects designed to develop follow-up/follow-along systems, address special populations, and provide postsecondary supports and education (Rusch & Millar, 1998). The 1983 EHA amendments also promoted individual transition plans for high school youth and funded model demonstration projects focused on developing interagency teams, teamwork, and interagency collaboration.

Vocational Education Legislation

The strengthening of transition services for youth with disabilities was an important component of the Carl D. Perkins Vocational Education Act of 1984 (P.L. 98-524). The emphasis in this legislation was to assure access to quality vocational education programs and to expand programs that were to be developed from the 10% of funds set aside for students with disabilities. The Carl D. Perkins Vocational and Technical Education Act of 1984 was passed with the intent to:

> ... assure that individuals who are inadequately served under vocational education programs are assured access to quality vocational education programs, especially individuals who are disadvantaged, who are disabled, men and women who are entering non-traditional occupations, adults who are in need of training and retraining, individuals with limited English proficiency, and individuals who are incarcerated in correctional institutions. (P.L. 98-524, 98, Stat. 2435)

This legislation viewed access to vocational education as critical to youth preparing for the transition from secondary education to work environments. Youth who were identified as disabled and disadvantaged were now required to receive vocational assessment, counseling, support, and transition services; and vocational support and goals in their IEPs. Additionally, vocational education was to be provided in the least-restrictive environment and state and local education agencies were to coordinate vocational education programs with special education services. Underlying these legal requirements and assurances was the question of how to encourage students with

> **Critical Point**
> In the 1980s, vocational education expanded services to students with disabilities and focused on enrolling them in mainstream vocational programs.

disabilities to enroll in and complete vocational education. This resulted in a national assessment of vocational education, which found that vocational education was serving students with special needs, except that: (a) students with disabilities were still underserved and (b) access to regular vocational education was still an issue for these students (Boesel & McFarland, 1994).

Employment and Training Programs

Within the U.S. Department of Labor, programs were also developing in a way that required more coordination with education legislation. The Comprehensive Employment and Training Act (CETA) of the 1970s was consolidated under the Job Training and Partnership Act (JTPA) of 1982, which provided significant funding for job training and placement programs directly benefiting youth with disabilities. With CETA and JTPA, the unemployment of both youth and adults was addressed by providing occupational skills to those who were not able to contribute to the nation's economy.

Rehabilitation and Developmental Disability Legislation

The rehabilitation legislation of the 1980s continued to focus on the rehabilitation service needs of persons with the most severe disabilities. The Rehabilitation Act Amendments of 1986 (P.L. 99-506) defined "supported employment" as paid employment in integrated real-work situations at least 20 hours per week. The significance of this legislation was that it made supported employment a regular vocational rehabilitation service, and that it required interagency cooperation between rehabilitation services and other adult service agencies to provide long-term ongoing supports for persons with severe disabilities. There were also corresponding changes in developmental disabilities and mental health legislation to make them supportive of this new rehabilitation focus.

> **Critical Point**
> The 1980s saw the beginnings of rehabilitation legislation that made supported employment a service and that required collaboration between adult service agencies in providing ongoing support.

Social Security: Sections 1619a & b

Supplemental Security Income (SSI) was an income support program administered by the **Social Security Administration** where monthly benefits could be paid to youth or adults with long-term (12 or more months) disabilities, if their individual or family income fell below a certain level. For youth in transition, SSI could supplement their income if they were in postsecondary education or in entry-level work. People who met the eligibility requirements for SSI were typically eligible for Medicaid benefits, which were applied for through the Department of Human Services.

Technology-Related Assistance for Individuals with Disabilities Act

The Technology-Related Assistance for Individuals with Disabilities Act (Tech Act) was passed in 1988 and was designed to establish statewide systems focusing on providing technology supports for individuals with disabilities. Assistive technology (AT) was first defined in this legislation, and this definition was used in other disability legislation for this period. The Tech Act was a state-grants program that provided grants to develop a consumer responsive, comprehensive, statewide program of technology-related assistance for individuals of all ages. The Rehabilitation Engineering Society of North America (RESNA) provided technical assistance to states funded under this act. The Tech Act was important in regard to increasing, maintaining, and improving the functioning of persons with disabilities in natural environments.

Will's Bridges Model

Follow-up studies through the 1970s documented that many students were experiencing poor outcomes after high school (Hasazi et al., 1985). This, coupled with the expiration of the Career Education Act (P.L. 95-207), underscored the need for new legislative initiatives directed toward promoting the movement of youth with disabilities into meaningful adult roles. In 1983, Madeleine Will, a conservative parent advocate and the assistant secretary of OSERS within the U.S. Department of Education, proposed a model for transition from school to work that emphasized "bridges" or linkages between school and postschool environments (Will, 1983). Will's position statement established transition services as a federally recognized school activity. The basic concept behind Will's bridges model was that secondary and postsecondary environments for youth with disabilities needed to be connected by services and supports that overlapped. Will's model addressed the fact that special educators and adult

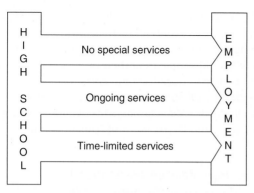

FIGURE 2–1 OSERS transition model, 1984

Source: From OSERS programming for the transition of youth with disabilities: Bridges from school to working life, by M. Will, 1984, U.S. Office of Education.

service providers often labored under differing assumptions about who was to be served, what types of services should be available, and who was responsible (DeStefano & Snauwaert, 1989). Edgar (1987) conducted research on postschool services and supports and found that they were lacking for the majority of students with disabilities after graduation. He argued that school systems would have to change to create the variety of services prescribed in Will's bridges model.

Will's transition model is illustrated in Figure 2-1. It conceptualized transition as three bridges to employment: (a) transition without special services (e.g., postsecondary education), (b) transition with time-limited services (e.g., vocational rehabilitation), and (c) transition with ongoing services (e.g., supported employment). Will's model addressed two of transition's essential elements by prescribing a coordinated secondary-postsecondary set of activities designed to promote movement to postschool settings. However, it was designed to promote movement only to employment settings, providing little guidance in terms of determining student needs, interests, and preferences and in terms of using an outcome-oriented process in planning. This "bridges" concept of transition was therefore narrower in focus than many of the earlier work-study or career education models (Halpern, 1992).

> **Critical Point**
> Will's "bridges" model established transition as a national special education initiative that focused on employment.

Halpern's Community Adjustment Model

Halpern's model challenged Will's total focus on employment. He argued that the residential and interpersonal domains must also be considered in planning for the transition to adulthood (Halpern, 1985). Halpern proposed that community adjustment should be the conceptual framework underlying transition and identified three "pillars" of community adjustment: (a) employment, (b) residential environments, and (c) social and interpersonal networks. According to Halpern, transition programs needed to address each of these three areas in order to affect the overall quality of life and community adjustment of students with disabilities (see Figure 2-2).

> **Critical Point**
> Halpern expanded Will's employment model to include residential environments and social and interpersonal networks.

Like Will, Halpern (1985) addressed the need for "bridges to adulthood" but he relabeled what Will referred to as "no services" as "generic services." Halpern noted that a variety of non–disability-specific social welfare and community programs were also available to young adults with disabilities and were often necessary to help them achieve quality of life after graduation (such as postsecondary education and employment training programs). Halpern's model emphasized that transition was more than a process of the school's "handing off" the student, and his model was very similar to a career education model (Halpern, 1992). Halpern's model was very influential in defining transition services in the IDEA of 1990 (Johnson & Rusch, 1993).

> **Critical Point**
> While Will's "bridges" model focused on linkages alone, Halpern's transition model took more of a career education approach.

Work Preparation Models

Two specific transition approaches emerged during the "bridges" period, including (a) special needs vocational education and (b) community-based vocational training. Special needs vocational education grew out of the legislation that set aside funds to serve special populations (such as students with disabilities) and to serve primarily students with mild to moderate disabilities. **Special needs vocational education** was designed to provide adapted and modified occupational-specific programs with supplemental services to serve students with mental retardation, learning disabilities, behavioral disorders, and sensory and physical impairments (Sitlington & Clark, 2006).

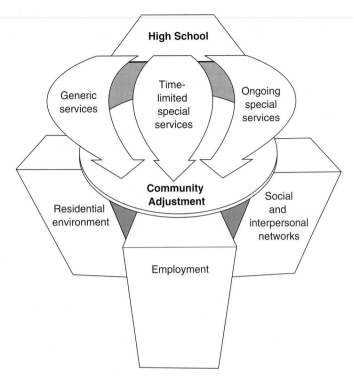

FIGURE 2–2 Halpern's revised transition model, 1985

Source: From Transition: A look at the foundations, by A. S. Halpern, *Exceptional Children, 51*(6), 1985, p. 481. Copyright (1985) by the Council for Exceptional Children. Reprinted with permission.

Community-based vocational training and supported employment programs resulted from rehabilitation and ongoing support legislation to assist students with severe disabilities. Community-based vocational training (e.g., supported employment, on-the-job training services, and community-based instruction) was initiated while students were still in high school. Before graduation, students were placed in a permanent job with the understanding that community agencies would take over support and case management services after the student graduated (Wehman, Kregel, & Barcus, 1985).

> **Critical Point**
> Transition work preparation models included the special needs vocational preparation model and community-based vocational training models.

Summary of Legislation and Models of the 1980s

The 1980s were characterized by legislation and programs that focused on coordinating services across secondary and postsecondary systems affecting transition-age youth. The 99th Congress updated legislation in rehabilitation, developmental disabilities, income maintenance, employment, and health programs with the goal of improving the employment prospects of persons with disabilities. As shown in Table 2–6, legislative adjustments were made across disability-specific and transition-related programs, while interagency collaboration models were being developed to address the needs of various disability groups. The 1980s could be considered the period of policy development, but it should be emphasized that policy development does not equate with implementation of transition programs in every community. Nonetheless, during the 1980s, advocates and policy makers established a general framework that tied together legislation and promising practices and that developed the capacity of state and local programs to implement collaborative transition service delivery.

TRANSITION POLICY, PRACTICES, AND LEGISLATION OF THE 1990s

The 1990s started with the passage of the IDEA of 1990 and the Americans with Disabilities Act (ADA), which established a federal commitment to employing

TABLE 2–6 Legislation during the 1980s

Authorized funds to develop transition models and practices
Provided further clarifications of rights, reinforced coordination of legislation across transition and related areas, and expanded service eligibility

- 1982 Job Training Partnership Act (P.L. 97–300): Provided significant funding for job placement and training programs directly benefiting youth with disabilities
- 1983 Individuals with Disabilities Education Act (P.L. 98–199): Provided funds for grants to demonstrate support and coordination among educators and adult service programs to foster transition to postschool settings
- 1984 Carl D. Perkins Vocational Education Act (P.L. 98–524): Set aside funds to facilitate equal access to full range of vocational education activities through supplemental services; includes vocational education in IEPs
- 1986 Rehabilitation Act amendments of 1986 (P.L. 99–506): Provided definition and funding for supported employment
- 1984 Developmental Disabilities amendments of 1984 (P.L. 98–527): Defined supported employment and emphasized productivity and participation in the community

Source: Adapted from School-to-work transition: Overview of disability policy, by R. A. Stodden in F. R. Rusch, & J. G. Chadsey Eds., *Beyond high school: Transition from school to work,* 1998, Wadsworth Publishing Company.

persons with disabilities. The ADA established the employment rights of people with disabilities in both the public and private sectors by outlawing discrimination in hiring and employment of persons with disabilities who were otherwise qualified to fulfill the "essential requirements" of a job with "reasonable accommodations." The IDEA of 1990 mandated transition services as part of the IEP and established the rights of students with disabilities to be provided assistance and support in attaining meaningful adult roles. Full participation and equal opportunity marked the beginning of the decade and these two pieces of legislation represented a pivotal point in the disability rights and transition movements. The beginning of the 1990s represented a major shift from charity to rights and from separation to integration for persons with disabilities.

The IDEA of 1990 provided the basic definition of transition services used in special education today. Under this legislation, the term "transition services" meant a coordinated set of activities for a student with a disability that were designed within an outcome-oriented process and that would promote movement from school to postschool activities. Included were the following: postsecondary education, vocational training, integrated employment (including supported employment), continuing and adult education, adult services, independent living, or community participation. The IDEA of 1990 emphasized that transition services should be based on the individual student's needs, taking into account the student's preferences and interests. The types of

> **Critical Point**
> The IDEA of 1990 defined the four essential elements of transition that provide the framework for this book.

transition services mentioned in this legislation included instruction, community experiences, the development of employment and other postschool adult living objectives and, when appropriate, acquisition of daily living skills and functional vocational evaluation.

Americans with Disabilities Act

The **Americans with Disabilities Act (ADA)** was comprehensive and provided rights relating to most areas of citizen participation for persons with disabilities. It was an overarching piece of legislation that brought together disability principles from previous laws and that provided a standard for measuring the overall success of disability policies (West, 1991). The ADA dealt more with breadth of disability law than with the introduction of new disability principles. Before the ADA, only federal contractors and recipients of federal funds were barred from discriminating against people with disabilities. The ADA extended this protection to persons with disabilities in most areas of the private sector, as well. The ADA sent three major messages "about what society's attitude should be toward persons with disabilities: respect, inclusion, and support" (West, 1991, p. xviii). The ADA principle of respect suggested that disability was part of the identity and self-concept of individuals, was experienced by most people at some point in their lives, and was a natural way in which persons differed from each other. The principle of inclusion suggested that society should create equal opportunities for persons with disabilities to participate in meaningful adult roles, while

> **Critical Point**
> Respect, inclusion, and support were the underlying principles of the ADA.

the principle of support suggested that society should make a reasonable effort to provide accommodations that allowed people with disabilities to perform to the best of their abilities (West).

The ADA was organized into five sections called "Titles." In the ADA law, the first four titles covered: (a) private employers who did not receive federal money; (b) state and local government agencies; (c) public accommodations (e.g., restaurants, hotels, and theaters); and (d) telephone companies (for "functionally" equivalent relay services: TTY). The fifth title covered miscellaneous areas. These titles of the ADA required nondiscrimination and reasonable accommodations for persons with disabilities in all of these sectors.

Rehabilitation Act Amendments of 1992

Whereas the ADA established a common paradigm for disability services and the rightful place of persons with disabilities in society, the Rehabilitation Act of 1992 specifically addressed respect, inclusion, and support for the customers of vocational rehabilitation (VR). Several parts of the Rehabilitation Act of 1992 illustrated connections to the ADA by noting that:

1. "Disability is a natural part of the human experience and in no way diminishes the right of individuals to live independently; enjoy self-determination; make choices; contribute to society; pursue meaningful careers...."
2. "Individuals with disabilities, including the most severe disabilities, are generally presumed to be capable of engaging in gainful employment."
3. Services to persons with disabilities need to include personal assistance services, transition services, and supported employment services.
4. Families and natural supports can play an important role in the success of a vocational rehabilitation program, if the individual with a disability requests, desires, or needs such supports.

Workforce Investment Act and Rehabilitation Act Amendments of 1998

The Rehabilitation Amendments of 1998 were subsumed under the Work Force Investment Act (WIA) of 1998 (P.L. 105-220). The inclusion of rehabilitation legislation within workforce development reflected an attempt to integrate employment and training programs on a federal, state, and local level. The WIA of 1998 was a comprehensive job-training bill that consolidated over 45 previous federally funded programs. The intent of the bill was to simplify the worker-training system by providing more emphasis on meeting skill shortages in the labor market and on career individualization. Therefore, local business needs and individual employment needs and preferences were two major factors in determining the types of services provided by agencies and the way that they were delivered. WIA provided block grants to states to fund three programs: (a) adult employment and training, (b) disadvantaged youth employment and training, and (c) adult education and family literacy.

Title IV of WIA contained the 1998 amendments to the Rehabilitation Act. These amendments focused on increasing opportunities for persons with disabilities to prepare for, secure, maintain, and regain employment. The Individual Written Rehabilitation Program (IWRP) was now called the Individual Program of Employment or (IPE). Informed choice and a "fair shot" at employment were core principles of these new amendments. Informed choice meant a greater focus on the individual goals of persons with disabilities. The "fair shot" principle was reflected in the presumption of eligibility

for employment services of persons who were historically being determined ineligible for these services because of the severity of their disability. At the other end of the continuum, rehabilitation service clients who appeared less disabled and who were not served because of this new "order of selection" were to be referred for an appropriate service within the WIA system or through other community employment services.

School-to-Work Opportunities Act of 1994 (P.L. 103-239)

Transition was the underlying and defining principle in the School-to-Work Opportunities Act (STWOA) of

1994, which had a sunset provision and expired in 1998. The STWOA called on states to plan and implement transition systems that enabled all youth to make the transition from school to postschool environments. The components and expected outcomes of STWOA **school-to-work programs** included provisions: (a) to enable all youth to acquire the skills and knowledge necessary to make the transition from school to work or further education and training, (b) to impact the preparation of all youth for a job leading to a career and to increase opportunities for further education, (c) to expand ways through which school- and work-based learning could be integrated, and (d) to link occupational and academic learning and to strengthen the linkage between secondary and postsecondary education (Norman & Bourexis, 1995). All these provisions were consistent with special education transition requirements in that they had an emphasis on outcomes, career development, career education, and training beyond high school.

Two of the purposes of STWOA were: (a) "to build on promising school-to-work activities, such as tech-prep education, career academies, school-to-apprenticeship programs, cooperative education, youth apprenticeship, school-sponsored enterprises" and (b) "to improve the knowledge and skills of youths by integrating academic and occupational learning, and building effective linkages

---

Critical Point
Under the School to Work Opportunities Act, transition services were recommended for all students, not just students with disabilities.

---

between secondary and postsecondary education" (p. 5). As with prior education-for-work legislation, STWOA addressed the need for all students to have access to programs, and it specifically mentioned individuals with disabilities, low-achieving youth, school dropouts, and those from disadvantaged or diverse racial, ethnic, or cultural backgrounds (Kochhar-Bryant & West, 1995).

The Carl D. Perkins Acts of 1990 and 1998

The 1990 Carl D. Perkins amendments had two major themes:

a. to improve the quality of vocational education programs, and
b. to provide supplemental services to special populations.

The 1990 amendments moved away from traditional job skills orientation toward integrating vocational and academic skills training. It focused on poor districts, addressed school reform issues, and restructured the state and local administration of vocational education. Perkins emphasized vocational schools getting involved in reform and states developing standards for vocational education. It developed apprenticeships and established "tech-prep" programs. In 1990, Perkins eliminated 10% funding set-asides for special populations. As shown in Table 2–7, the Perkins Act of 1990 had numerous provisions that addressed transition issues for students with disabilities.

TABLE 2–7 Carl D. Perkins vocational and Applied Technology Education Act of 1990

Criteria for services and activities for individuals who are members of special populations—required assurances:

- Equal access to *recruitment, enrollment,* and *placement activities*
- Equal access to the full range of vocational education programs available
- Provision of vocational education in the *least restrictive* environment
- Vocational planning for individuals with disabilities coordinated by representatives of *vocational education, special education,* and *state vocational rehabilitation agencies*
- Vocational education monitored for students with disabilities to ensure consistency with their IEP
- Notification to members of special populations and their parents *at least one year prior to eligibility, including information about specific courses, services, employment opportunities, and job placement*
- Assistance with transitional service requirements for individuals with disabilities
- Provision of supplementary services, including such things as curriculum modification, equipment modification, classroom modification, supportive personnel, and instructional aids and devices
- Provision of guidance, counseling, and career development activities by professionally trained counselors and teachers
- Provision of counseling and instructional services designed to *facilitate the transition from school to postschool employment and career opportunities.*

Source: From Carl D. Perkins Vocational and Applied Technology Education Act. (1990) Pub. L. No. 101–392, 104, Stat. 756.

> **Critical Point**
> In the 1990s, Perkins legislation eliminated set-aside funds for special populations and moved toward a greater focus on meeting academic standards and in setting and meeting vocational standards that were designed to move vocational students into postsecondary education.

The 1998 Carl D. Perkins Act amendments built on the 1990 version but also included provisions that presented challenges to the vocational education system. As Kimberly Green, the executive director of the National Association of State Directors of Vocational Education said: "Legislators want vocational education graduates on the same level as someone who goes through regular academics so that students are just as prepared and have as many options as a person who is college bound."

The 1998 Perkins Act also no longer included set-aside funds for special populations, giving vocational programs more control over how they spent funds, but these amendments also stipulated that vocational educational programs would have to set and meet performance standards. It did not include school-to-work requirements like the STWOA, but it continued to require that school-to-work systems be coordinated with vocational education systems. **Tech-prep** programs (e.g., 2 + 2 programs) were emphasized in Perkins 1998, which established longer reauthorization periods and separate funding streams for these programs.

The IDEA of 1990

The IDEA transition requirements mandated services for the first time and implied the need for several general types of activities in developing and implementing transition IEPs. It suggested activities such as career exploration and job shadowing to help students develop and test their postschool goals and required that the student's postschool goals should be clearly stated in the IEP. The IDEA also recommended that IEPs should include referrals to adult service agencies two or more years before graduation and experiences for students in their desired postschool settings (e.g., colleges, businesses, and other community settings). Student needs, interests, and preferences determined through approaches such as person-

> **Critical Point**
> Transition, as defined by IDEA 1990, established four essential elements of transition and implied the need for coordinated middle, secondary, and postschool activities.

centered planning, student surveys, career inventories, and counseling and community experiences would allow the student to try out or become established in work, education, independent living, and community participation roles. Finally, the IDEA of 1990 suggested that transition activities could also include the acquisition of daily living skills and functional vocational evaluation.

The IDEA of 1997

The IDEA of 1997 incorporated several broad policy shifts reflecting major changes in the way that persons with disabilities would receive an education (Stodden, 1998). One change was that special education must emphasize achievement of educational results rather than adherence to process, steps, and procedures to implement programs. This shift represented an increasing focus on what happened to students when they exited the educational system as evidenced by their quality of life and success in postschool environments. The IDEA of 1997 added "related services" to the list of recommended transition services (e.g., transportation to a work experience; speech language and audiology, physical and occupational therapy, psychological and counseling services). This addition was partly due to the IDEA of 1997's focus on including students with disabilities in the general education curriculum and the important role of related services in providing this access. The primary changes in policy from 1990 were:

1. Access, participation, and progress in the general curriculum so that special education would be in alignment with standards-based curriculum reform.
2. The corresponding requirement of the standards movement of participation in state- and district-wide proficiency tests.
3. Functional behavior analysis, manifest, and behavior management plans for special education student misconduct. If the behavior in question is considered part of the disability, then removal and placement into an alternative program (i.e., in-school suspension) would be considered a change in placement requiring an IEP team decision.
4. The requirement of transition service needs statement at age 14. This would provide identification of high school courses of study (e.g., career and technical education, or advanced academics) leading to postsecondary goals, which adds a middle school transition.

With the IDEA of 1997, special educators were now required to ensure the participation of children with disabilities in statewide performance tests and accountability systems. Within the IEP, annual instructional goals were to be referenced to the general education curriculum and transition planning for students with disabilities was to reflect a course of study. This emphasis on inclusion in mainstream academic programs required participation of general and vocational education teachers in the IEP process.

Kohler's Transition Education Model

During the 1990s, Kohler (1998) offered an infusion-based career education model called a "transition perspective of education." Her model emphasized the importance of a broad view of what education was, or should be, and delineated a taxonomy (or categories) of transition services, namely: (a) student-focused planning, (b) family involvement, (c) program structure and attributes, (d) interagency collaboration, and (e) student development (see Figure 2–3). Kohler saw student-focused planning as inherently important in individualized planning as the main vehicle for determining appropriate goals, objectives, and services. For the second category, student development, Kohler argued

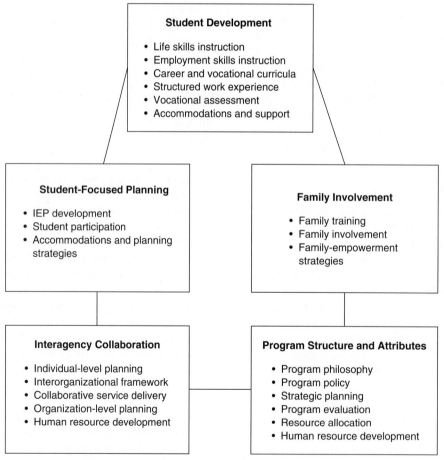

FIGURE 2–3   Emerging model of transition practices

Source: From Implementing a transition perspective, by P. D. Kohler in F. R. Rusch & J. G. Chadsey (Eds.), *Beyond high school: Transition from school to work*, p. 208. Copyright 1998. Reprinted with permission of Wadsworth Publishing, a division of Thomson Learning. FAX 800-730-2215.

that schools must provide activities in which students could learn the skills necessary to become successful participants of society and that these activities should be provided in a number of different settings to enhance the generalization of skill acquisition. Kohler saw interagency and interdisciplinary collaboration as critical to the development of a collaborative framework, and she suggested establishing interagency transition teams where participants could increase their knowledge about other delivery systems, work collaboratively, and share resources. Kohler's fourth category of family involvement emphasized participation, empowerment, and training to deal with the need for greater student and family involvement in transition planning. The final category of Kohler's taxonomy, program structures and attributes, looked at the service system and the need for: (a) systematic community involvement in the development of educational options, (b) community-based learning opportunities, (c) systematic inclusion of students in the social life of the school, and (d) increased expectations related to skills, values, and outcomes for all students.

Career Pathways Models

Siegel (1998) proposed an infusion career pathways model of transition with a heavy emphasis on integrating transition with school-to-work programs. His approach was also designed to address all four of the essential elements of transition. Siegel suggested that the collective educational experiences of students should answer three basic questions:

1. Who am I?
2. What is my community?
3. How do I engage in a meaningful way?

In Siegel's multiple-option school-to-work system, students had the flexibility to adjust their individualized program as their interests and needs changed over time. Career pathways consisted of coursework clustered in five or six career areas (e.g., communication and arts, marketing and business, health occupations, and human services). A career application context for an entire curriculum allowed students to shape their course of study in a way that was meaningful to them. Siegel suggested

that pathways serving all levels of students must be broadly defined (e.g., an introduction to health occupations course may serve future surgeons, students interested in obtaining a nursing license, or students who may be projecting career interests in volunteer or entry-level work in a hospital). Siegel's model of multiple options in a school-to-work system consisted of five levels of transition services. These levels differed by the intensity of student need and were not determined by the student's disability label, but rather by their individualized need to participate with other students and to become independent after graduation. Siegel's levels were not to be used as a tracking system; rather, they were multiple options that students could utilize depending on their individual needs at a given time.

Greene (2003) proposed a career pathways model based on the postschool outcomes being pursued by students. This model included four major pathways: (a) four-year college, (b) community college or technical school, (c) paid competitive employment, and (d) supported employment. For each pathway, Greene suggested that the student's desired postschool environments should help determine the type of assessments used, the type of curriculum employed, the most effective instructional settings, and transition planning and related services concerns. Greene also emphasized that the provision of career pathways should not result in career tracking.

Summary of Transition Legislation and Models of the 1990s

The 1990s was a period when transition became established in the field of special education through legislation. Transition was defined and mandated in special education legislation beginning with the IDEA of 1990. The IDEA of 1990 required a statement of needed transitions no later than age 16, and at age 14 or earlier, if appropriate. The coordinated transition activities required by the IDEA of 1990 necessitated interdisciplinary services reflecting regular, vocational, and special education and closer connections between secondary and postschool education and services. The IDEA of 1997 strengthened the requirements for collaboration between regular and special education, and it required looking at the entire period of education from middle school through postsecondary education and employment. The IDEA was designed to ensure a career path that was based on the student's needs, preferences, and interests. See Table 2–8.

TABLE 2–8 Legislation of the 1990s

Established a policy framework for the rights movement
Refined and extended access, community participation, and quality-of-life perspectives
Established standards-based education and accountability for results for *all* students

- IDEA 1990: Required that a transition plan be incorporated into the IEP by age 16.
- ADA 1990: Provided for equality and integration in all aspects of community life.
- Carl D. Perkins Amendments of 1990: Focused on integrating vocational and academic skills training and eliminated special funding set-asides.
- Rehabilitation Act Amendments of 1992: Increased requirements and provisions for accessibilty to rehabilitation services and self-determination.
- Educate America Act of 1994: Goals 2000: Mandated education based on goals related to achieving student outcomes through reform of education.
- School to Work Opportunity Act of 1994: Provided for state laws for education for transition systems and schoolwide programs for preparation for a career.
- Technology-Related Assistance Act of 1994: Provided for statewide systems of assistive technology.
- IDEA 1997: Required a transition course of study by age 14 and access to general curriculum.
- Rehabilitation Act Amendments of 1998: Increased provision for employment and required coordination with the one-stop employment and training center.
- Workforce Investment Act of 1998: Comprehensive job training that consolidates 45 previous federally funded programs.
- Carl D. Perkins Amendments of 1998: Provided for tech-prep to be centerpiece of career/tech system—2 + 2 programs in technical fields bridging secondary and postsecondary programs.

The IDEA of 2004

The Elementary and Secondary Education Act (ESEA)—the federal law guiding general education and other compensatory programs—was renamed the No Child Left Behind Act (NCLB) in its reauthorization in 2002. Because special education was considered part of general education, changes in the ESEA had a profound effect on the IDEA reauthorization. Prior to the reauthorization of IDEA, President George W. Bush appointed a commission to collect information, hear testimony, and create a report on improving educational achievement for special education students. The commission's final report contained three major recommendations. First, the report recommended a focus on results, not on process. The second recommendation called for a model of prevention before students entered special education. Third, the panel recommended considering children with disabilities as general education children first. The President's Commission on Special Education (2002) made several recommendations within the transition area:

1. There was an emphasis on *full participation* by parents and students and student self-advocacy and the need for a broad array of transition services (e.g., work experience, career exploration, etc).
2. The report called for improving cooperation and collaboration among agencies serving students during the transition period. Several specific recommendations on *interagency collaboration* dealt with more effective implementation of existing legislation for transition services and study and reporting of barriers to transition coordination (i.e., IDEA, Rehabilitation Act, Higher Education Act, Ticket to Work Act, and Workforce Investment Act).
3. The report argued for a uniform age for transition planning (not having different requirements for ages 14 and 16) at a point that makes sense educationally. Graduated diplomas were recommended that "more accurately represented levels of skill and ability."

With both the NCLB Act and IDEA, there continued to be an emphasis on outcomes (Turnbull et al., 2003). Content standards for academic areas and performance standards defining levels of proficiency accompanied this outcomes focus (Thurlow, 2002). Student performance was to be used in determining: (a) the qualifications of the students who got promoted or graduated; (b) the teachers and principals who were promoted, received raises, and kept their jobs; and, (c) the schools and districts that got funding and were accredited under the NCLB Act. Numerous changes were initiated with IDEA of 2004.

- Services changed to emphasize a design "within a results-oriented process" focusing on improving "academic and functional improvement".
- Vocational education was defined as a transition service.
- Strengths as well as needs, interests, and preferences need to be taken into account.
- Purpose of special education included preparation for further education.

- Eliminated reference to transition activities at age 14.
- Included measurable transition goals beyond high school in the IEP.
- At exit from school, students were to be provided with a summary of performance.

See Table 2–9 comparing IDEA 1997 and IDEA 2004.

TABLE 2–9   Comparison of the transition requirements of the IDEA of 1997 and 2004

Transition and the IDEA of 1997	Transition and the IDEA of 2004
Definition of Transition	**Definition of Transition**
The term "transition services" means a coordinated set of activities for a student with a disability that	The term "transition services" means a coordinated set of activities for a **child** with a disability that
(A) is designed within an outcome-oriented process, that promotes movement from school to post-school activities, including postsecondary education, vocational training, integrated employment (including supported employment), continuing and adult education, adult services, independent living, or community participation;	(A) is designed **to be within a results-oriented** process, **that is focused on improving the academic and functional achievement of the child with a disability to facilitate the child's** movement from school to post-school activities, including postsecondary education, vocational **education,** integrated employment (including supported employment), continuing and adult education, adult services, independent living, or community participation;
(B) is based on the individual student's needs, taking into account the student's preferences and interests;	(B) is based on the individual child's needs, taking into account the **child's strengths,** preferences, and interests; and
(C) includes instruction, related services, community experiences, the development of employment and other post-school objectives, and, when appropriate, acquisition of daily living skills and functional vocational evaluation (Section 602).	(C) includes instruction, related services, community experiences, the development of employment and other post-school objectives, and, when appropriate, acquisition of daily living skills and functional vocational evaluation (Section 602).
Transition Statement and the IEP	**Transition Statement and the IEP**
(vii)(I) beginning at age 14, and updated annually, a statement of the transition service needs of the child . . . that focuses on the child's courses of study (such as participation in advanced-placement courses or a vocational education program);	(VIII) beginning not later than the first IEP to be in effect when the child is 16, and updated annually thereafter—
(II) beginning at age 16 (or younger, if determined appropriate by the IEP Team), a statement of needed transition services for the child, including, when appropriate, a statement of the interagency responsibilities or any needed linkages; and	(aa) appropriate measurable postsecondary goals based upon age appropriate transition assessments related to training, education, employment, and, where appropriate, independent living skills; (bb) the transition services (including courses of study) needed to assist the child in reaching those goals; and
(III) beginning at least one year before the child reaches the age of majority under State law, a statement that the child has been informed of his or her rights under this title that will transfer to the child . . . on reaching the age of majority under 615(m) Section 614(d).	(III) beginning at least one year before the child reaches the age of majority under State law, a statement that the child has been informed of his or her rights under this title that will transfer to the child . . . on reaching the age of majority under 615(m) Section 614(d).

CONCLUSION

Modern concepts of disability have been rapidly changing and this has been reflected in the legislation governing disability policy. Social policy toward persons with disabilities could be traced back to Elizabethan Poor Laws that created the concept of deserving and undeserving poor. Overall, disability policy can be seen as moving from a charity model to a rights model, but many vestiges of earlier concepts of disability persist to the present day. The efforts of social policy advocates have continued to focus on promoting quality of life for persons with disabilities, and increasingly this concept has required the promotion of meaningful employment, interpersonal relationships, community participation, and postsecondary education. Ultimately, the measure of the effectiveness of disability policy has been how closely the lives of persons with disabilities mirrored the lives of their typical peers.

The earliest services for persons with disabilities went to groups considered the most deserving of help, including the blind and soldiers who were disabled in World War I. These disability services were extended to include government workers, and after World War II, began to be rapidly extended to other groups of individuals with disabilities. Much of this early post–World-War-II evolution could be attributed to the efforts of parent advocacy organizations that established services for persons with disabilities who were being denied government-funded educational and rehabilitation services. This early advocacy period leading up to and including the 1960s established many of the conceptual foundations of disability policy that was to emerge in later decades.

The 1970s saw two important developments. The first was the start of legal advocacy on the part of parent organizations such as the ARC. A series of class action suits outlawed institutionalization without due process and provision of habilitation services. Another class action suit (*PARC vs. Pennsylvania*) laid the groundwork for the EHA of 1975, which established the right to a free and appropriate education for all children with disabilities and developed due process procedures to protect these rights. In the 1970s, individuals with disabilities also began speaking for themselves and were instrumental in establishing regulations for the Rehabilitation Act of 1973, in creating independent living centers, and developing People First language. The Rehabilitation Act of 1973 barred discrimination against persons with disabilities in all federally funded programs, while the independent living

movement was instrumental in providing access to buildings, transportation, and residential options. The People First movement focused on changing social perceptions of persons with disabilities through language and actions that emphasized their personhood over their disability.

In the 1980s, the concept of transition services was developed by Madeline Will in response to poor postschool outcomes of students with disabilities. Transition services were initially a rebottling of earlier special education and related programs including functional curricula, work study, and career education. Will's model of transition focused on transition to employment and on overlapping services, but this model was quickly replaced by transition models that focused on broader quality-of-life concepts. Though transition services were not mandated in the 1980s, they were encouraged through federal legislation in special education, rehabilitation, and vocational education.

In the 1990s, transition services were mandated in the IDEA of 1990, which established four criteria (or essential elements) of these services by requiring that they be: (a) based on student needs, interests, and preferences, (b) developed through an outcome-oriented process, (c) a coordinated set of activities, and (d) designed to promote movement to postschool settings. The IDEA of 1990 mandated transition planning by no later than age 16, with the student being part of this process. The IDEA of 1997 required transition planning related to students' courses of study by age 14 and required that they all participate in state and district testing to assure their participation in the general education curriculum. Transition services were also supported by vocational education and rehabilitation legislation, and the STWOA of 1994 even extended these types of services to general education students until it expired in 1998. The new millennium ushered in a heavy focus on accountability for academics with the No Child Left Behind Act. In the IDEA of 2004, transition services were redefined to focus on academic and functional "results" to promote movement to postschool settings.

The challenge for the future will be balancing an increasingly rigorous academic curriculum with the need for transition services that have been repeatedly correlated with better postschool outcomes for students with disabilities. On the one hand, these students have been entering postsecondary education at rapidly increasing rates and will need advanced academics to succeed in these environments. On the other hand, an estimated 60–70% of students with disabilities continued to enter employment without completing postsec-ondary education and continued to need help in ob-taining community-based work experiences and vocational education before exiting high school. Future legislation is likely to continue to swing back and forth between the interests of these two disability groups, and the challenge for transition coordinators will be to assure that the right services are getting to the right students.

STUDY QUESTIONS

1. What were the differences between disability services as an entitlement versus based on eligibility?
2. Why is disability considered a rights issue?
3. Why are disability and disability policy generally misunderstood by the general public?
4. Why are access and accommodation important in vocational and regular education and postsecondary education?
5. How would you characterize disability policy and services in the 1960s?
6. How would you characterize disability policy and services in the 1970s and 1980s?
7. How would you characterize disability policy and services in the 1990s?
8. What were the changes in emphasis in legislation among the 1960s and 1970s and 1980s?
9. What were the changes in emphasis in legislation between the 1970s, the 1980s, and the 1990s?
10. Why is general education and disability legislation other than special education (SPED) important to transition and IDEA requirements?
11. What were changes in transition with IDEA of 1990?
12. What were changes in transition from IDEA of 1990 to IDEA of 1997?
13. What were the main models through the 1980s that form today's concept of transition?
14. What are the major differences between Will's and Halpern's models of transition?
15. Why did the work-study movement start and what services were added to improve transition?

WEBSITES

National Information Center for Children and Youth with Disabilities
http://www.nichcy.org

CHAPTER 3

MULTICULTURAL AND COLLABORATIVE COMPETENCIES FOR WORKING WITH FAMILIES

Pamela Luft

LEARNING OBJECTIVES

The objectives for this chapter are:

1. Describe at least two major reasons that transition team members can expect to work with culturally different families and students.

2. Compare the major differences between identified U.S./American beliefs and values and minority group beliefs and values in the areas of worldview, personal identity, disability, and relationships.

3. Describe how cultural differences between team members may impact team processes for identifying and addressing the student's needs, interests, and preferences in the transition process.

4. Describe cultural, class, and socioeconomic differences that impact goal-setting and outcome-oriented processes of transition planning, including movement from school to postschool activities.

5. Describe potential conflicts in developing participatory decision making with families who are not acculturated into the middle-class American interaction style (e.g., represent culturally different or diverse groups) and appropriate approaches to support such decision making.

6. Describe strategies for preparing staff and families in culturally competent and diverse interaction styles and processes.

7. Describe multicultural and collaborative strategies that support participation of all students and families.

INTRODUCTION

It is increasingly likely that residents in the United States will work with and live near those who are culturally different from themselves. Minority populations in the United States are increasing in size (Bose, 1996; Garcia & Yates, 1986; Knopp & Otuya, 1995; Wald, 1996). This has been confirmed by U.S. census data showing that between 1980 and 2000, average, minority populations grew 11 times as rapidly as the white population (U.S. Census Bureau, 2002, November). Within the past 10 years (1990 to 2000) there was a 13.2% increase in overall population; however, minority populations grew even more quickly: 15.6% increase in African Americans, 26.4% increase in American Indians/Alaska Natives, 48.3% increase in Asians, and a 57.9% increase in Hispanic or Latino populations. The 2004 census projections are that Hispanics or Latinos represent 14.2%, African Americans 12.2%, Asians 4.2%, and American Indians and Alaska Natives 0.8% (U.S. Census Bureau, 2004). So, regardless of ethnicity, teachers and students are increasingly likely to have "close encounters" with those who are racially or ethnically different from them.

But how does this impact the work of IEP and transition teams? Well, they are increasingly likely to work with minority students and families, as well as team members. In addition, many of the legal mandates and transition components described in Chapters 1 and 2 are based on American cultural beliefs about disability, optimal outcomes for all people, and how best to achieve these outcomes. These are not shared by all cultures so that, in some ways, by complying with these mandates the team is being set up for cultural conflicts. A pervasive problem is that teachers are most effective in working with those who are culturally similar to themselves (Lareau, 1989). Yet, as professionals they are responsible for providing quality services to *all* students, families, and clients. How then, can the team learn to move beyond cultural habits, as well as some of the legally proscribed education practices, to provide effective services to culturally-different families (and this means anyone who is culturally different from *ourselves*)? This can be approached by looking at what culture means in people's daily lives.

CULTURE AND COUNTRY ISSUES

In the United States people often think of themselves as supporting and accepting cultural diversity—isn't the country populated primarily by generations of immigrants? The Statue of Liberty publicly displays a welcome to the world, and people are proud of the "melting pot" of cultures and ethnicities from around the globe (Bull, Fruehling, & Chattergy, 1992; Cordeiro, Reagan, & Martinez, 1994; DeVillar, 1994; Hanson, 1998a). In truth, our country has not always succeeded—ethnic violence and intolerance erupts periodically, and is not easily resolved. As Bull et al., state (1992, p. 131) "contact between cultures—whether in inner-city New York, between ethnic groups in eastern Europe, among the tribes of Nigeria, or between religious factions in India—has long been the source of profound human suffering as well as mutual enrichment."

It is obvious that, in fact, tolerance for diversity is difficult—and it is because of the nature of people. People have an instinctive preference for cultural homogeneity in their daily lives (Brislin, 1993; Green, 1999). They wish to be with and interact with others who are like them, thus creating comfort, understanding, and the sharing of general lifestyle and beliefs. Often it is a struggle to understand and interact with people who may have significantly different practices and beliefs. Rather than a "melting pot," a better analogy of our country is that of a "salad bowl" consisting of complementary (hopefully!) but different elements, because diverse cultural groups don't often completely "meld" together (Cordeiro et al, 1994; DeVillar, 1994). By reading and examining culture and its omnipresence within thoughts, feelings, behaviors, and interactions, you will better understand how and why conflicts occur and then acquire some strategies for positively negotiating potential differences. This chapter's overall goal is to help you begin the journey toward becoming culturally competent: to start understanding cultural differences, to become more sensitive to their occurrence, and to better mediate between your own beliefs and those that are highly dissimilar.

One fascinating aspect of culture is how its beliefs are translated into practices. The following section examines the four essential elements of transition in terms of cultural practices and reexamines them through a different cultural lens. This gives the reader a sense of some of the conflictual situations into which teams and families are placed when making transition plans.

Cultural Perspectives and Transition Mandates

Legislation and policy are ways in which societal and cultural ideals and values are formalized (Cordeiro et al.,

1994; Nieto, 2000), and the IDEA's four *essential elements* of transition represent a number of these values. The first essential element—*consideration of the student's needs, strengths, interests, and preferences*—mandates that the transition team individually assess the students' preferences for their future career and lifestyle. In the United States, an important cultural value is that of being independent and self-reliant as a means of achieving personal and social success (Althen, 1988; Dunn & Griggs, 1995; Green, 1999; Hammond & Morrison, 1996; Hanson, 1998a; Harry, 1992a; Hobbs, 1975; McPhatter, 1997; Pinderhughes, 1995). However, a number of other cultures place greater value on belonging to a group and do not prefer to be highly independent or self-reliant (Chan, 1998a; Hanson, 1998a; Harry, 1992a; Joe & Malach, 1998; Lynch, 1998b; Pinderhughes, 1995; Zuniga, 1998). These cultures believe that the needs, interests, and preferences of the group (e.g., the extended family, the neighborhood, the community, or the tribe) are more important than those of the individual. Some may not accept the notion of "student choice" but, rather, believe that the group's needs should be addressed before those of an individual (i.e., if the group is functioning effectively, then the individual's needs will be met). Team members need to be cautious in how they implement this "individualized" planning process and do so in a way that may include broader family or "group" needs and preferences in a way that also supports those of the student.

The second essential element of transition planning is to use an *outcome (results)-oriented process*. Results or outcomes which are considered "positive" or "successful" are highly culturally defined (Nieto, 2000). For example, many people who are acculturated into the American value system (are accepting of these values) are likely to have personal goals for earning more money (value financial success), buying a nicer car or home (accumulate material possessions), and having important or successful friends (want social status) as ways to improve their quality of life. Achieving these things leaves a feeling of success and contentment. Team members may very much want the transitioning student to have a well-paying job, to have a nice car and apartment or home, and to make friends with key coworkers and supervisors—these are often considered "high expectations." In contrast, the student's family members may prefer that she or he live and work within the family or community (value on being with the group) and remain loyal to people in the community (personal worth gained through being honorable,

respectful, and loyal) who were helpful in the past. These outcomes are valued much more highly by the family than are high salaries, social status, and so on (Harry, 1992a, 1992b; Turnbull, 1993; Turnbull, Barber, Kerns, & Behr, 1995). Therefore, the family's preferred outcome may be for their child to live at home because of her or his disability and to take a low-paying job with a long-time family friend. Team members must be careful that they do not impose their preferred outcomes or culturally defined "high expectations" on the student or family.

The third essential element of transition planning is a *coordinated set of activities*. School personnel are mandated to invite individuals from adult service agencies and other community service organizations who are or will be assisting the student and family after the student leaves school. However, our families may prefer to work within their extended family and community group. Some cultures have great difficulty in seeking help or in disclosing a need for help, and may not feel comfortable with a large group of individuals ("outsiders") discussing their or their child's "needs." Agency personnel who attend one meeting annually with the parents may be viewed with some suspicion, and families may resist accepting advice or programming support from these individuals who "don't know the family." Teams need to be sensitive to the family's feelings regarding numbers of professionals at these meetings, and the sometimes frequent "turnover" of positions and personnel.

The fourth essential element of transition is *movement from school to postschool activities*. Team members may not have thought of successful transition outcomes as representing cultural values—to live independently (or with a roommate), to have a job, to have friends outside of the family, and so forth. Yet, these expectations may create conflicts with families who view having single, unmarried children living outside the home as indicative of parental dysfunction and failure (Turnbull et al., 1995). Some families expect all income earned by unmarried children to be given to the parents, without question, out of loyalty. Team members need to first ask the students and their families about postschool preferences, and make no assumptions otherwise.

Family involvement remains a critical element in transition success (Salembier & Furney, 1997; Siegel, 1998), and teams who create conflictual situations may be puzzled later to find that transition plans are not succeeding. It is always important to engage the family in identifying mutually agreeable goals *before* moving into the planning phase. Team members need to watch for assumptions they may have about achieving a "high-quality" life, or "high expectations" and what "success" means, or whether self-determination or self-advocacy interventions correspond with the family's vision. For example, cultures that value group harmony and identity (through family, community, tribe, etc.) may not subscribe to American values of independent decision-making or advocacy skills. Such cultures have great faith in the group's ability to respond to the needs of the individual, in contrast with many middle-class Americans who have much more faith in the individual's ability to take care of him- or herself using advocacy and self-determination strategies. The family may even view the team's advocacy strategies as undermining their family and community harmony. Therefore, never presume that specific transition values are necessarily shared by the family (in fact, it's a good idea to ask *all* families first).

Discussed thus far was how cultural differences can lead to tremendous barriers in effective transition planning and some of the cultural "traps" that exist: in the legislation, the essential elements of transition, and in assuming that these values are shared by the family. In these next sections, the reader will learn why analyzing culture can be both difficult and frustrating, and its pervasiveness within societies and organizations.

The Problem of Cultural Awareness

One significant problem with studying and analyzing culture is that it remains largely invisible. Culture consists of the "ideals, values, and assumptions about life that are widely shared among people and that guide specific behaviors" (Brislin, 1993, p. 4). It is also "the complex, changing nexus of values, attitudes, beliefs, practices, traditions, and social institutions ... of a community" that includes religion, language, foods, history, and dress (Cordeiro et al., 1994, p. 20). These fluctuating attitudes, ideals, and assumptions remain largely internalized until called upon to guide behavior. When values are not challenged, there are no visible behaviors that lead people to think about or remember a particular value. For example, cleanliness and personal hygiene habits generally are not an issue in our daily life until challenged by a person who, through physical appearance or smell, does not meet expected cultural standards (Brislin, 1993). When confronted by this difference a typical response is to "protect" the cultural value and to reaffirm how important it is. In this example someone might reaffirm his/her belief in this value by describing how much "better" people are when they practice regular and thorough hygiene (e.g., these people will experience negative consequences at work, socially, to their health, etc.).

Cultural values often remain covert because people are socialized into culture as children, and guided into a particular set of behaviors and beliefs without considering them (Brislin, 1993; Lewis, 1997). These early, formative experiences make it difficult for people to distance themselves enough to analyze them. In addition, people who share the same culture rarely discuss their values and assumptions, reinforcing their hidden nature. For example, only when religious or democratic values are challenged (e.g., through our engagement in the Middle East) do Americans discuss values and assumptions (such as what it means to be a Christian, an American Muslim, or Jew).

With much of culture nicely hidden away, people often respond to cultural conflict by reaffirming their own beliefs and behaviors as being "better." Rarely do they take the time to unearth the underlying core values and analyze them and the contrasting value accordingly. Without training, these cultural conflicts may become intensified with each future encounter. In fact, people often find violations of their culture to be emotionally upsetting and vivid (Brislin, 1993). Such feelings are not likely to be aired or recognized at a team meeting, and, therefore, may never be resolved.

The good news is that learning about cultural differences has been found to decrease negative emotional responses and discomfort when faced with a culturally conflicting situation (Brislin, 1993). Cross-cultural knowledge and skills allow people to feel more relaxed in these situations. Team members may not know much about a particular family's culture but by using more-open and communication-fostering strategies, families will sense that they are working to create a comfortable and positive interaction climate. This is an important first step for establishing open and trusting relationships with culturally different families, and ultimately, to more collaborative and effective interactions among all team members.

Control Issues and American Cultural Forces

By their very nature, societies use cultural values to proscribe and structure interactions (male to female or female to female, adult to child, and so on) and how certain processes or tasks are organized (e.g., making decisions and solving problems) (Brislin, 1993; Lewis, 1997). In these ways, culture acts as a mechanism for social control (Gray, 1997). Societies also organize themselves by assigning power—through status and leadership roles. This same process occurs when two people of differing cultures meet: One culture will dominate, creating a high-status versus lower-status interaction (Althen, 1988; Green, 1999; Hanson; 1998a). It is the dominant culture that receives the higher status: Maintaining equality between diverse cultures is not typical. So another important factor in becoming culturally competent is recognizing the status and leadership role team members often will be accorded when meeting a student or family member. A member's status may be allocated based upon how strongly they represents the dominant culture, or in response to the family's own cultural beliefs about schools, school professionals, and what they believe roles should be in terms of their child's education. So remember that the family will accord you a certain status and expect you to take on certain leadership roles. "Pretending" that they are equals will not lead to honest and open communication; instead, use the role to help ensure that the family feels listened to and respected with regard to their own experiences and beliefs, including cultural values.

DEVELOPING CULTURAL COMPETENCE

The team is likely to work with families who are culturally different from themselves. Because of increasing globalization and fluctuating immigration patterns, it is also likely that the team will meet certain families about whose cultural background they are moderately uninformed (regardless of how much of an expert they become). *Multiculturalism* is a concept used in this chapter that recognizes the diversity of cultures and ethnicities within the people of our schools and public services, and the competencies across these diverse cultures that are important for professionals in these services. Professionals who learn the understandings, concepts, and strategies that support "cultural pluralism" will be better able to develop harmonious coexistence among the different cultures with whom they

work (Green, 1999). *Cultural pluralism* is a belief that represents an acceptance of cultural diversity as a valuable and worthwhile facet of a society. However, it is a belief in *cultural relativism* that advocates that it is neither possible nor desirable to evaluate or judge cultural patterns, practices, or beliefs of a community by using the standards of another community (Cordeiro et al., 1994, p. 20). Developing a resistance to "evaluating" other cultures is one of the first precepts of cultural competence.

Cultural competence then, begins with an understanding of, and respect for, cultures and ethnic backgrounds and their impact on team members (Green, 1999; Lynch, 1998b). It does not consist of a single set of skills or knowledge for working across all cultures because "culture" and "competence" vary with the situation and those people involved (Green; Lynch). Like culture itself, competence evolves and is flexible, to support "the ability of service providers to respond optimally to all children, understanding both the richness and the limitations of the sociocultural contexts in which children and families as well as the service providers themselves, may be operating" (Barrera & Kramer, 1997, p. 217). So there is no one right answer, as there is one correct culture, or set of beliefs, or behaviors (that is *cultural relativism* in practice). The special challenges of trying to maintain a multicultural and cultural relativistic perspective in our schools is discussed next.

> **Critical Point**
> Cultural competence is built upon an understanding of, and respect for, the many different cultures of the world.

Cultural and Racial Inequities in Special Education

For many years, special education programs have enrolled higher numbers of minority children than proportional to their populations within the United States (Donovan & Cross, 2002; Sarason & Doris, 1979; Turnbull, 1993). The first compulsory education laws were passed during the 1880s and early 1900s as attempts to socialize immigrant Catholic children into our traditionally Protestant country (Hobbs, 1975). Special education programs at this time segregated immigrant Irish, Italians, Hungarians, Germans, Russians, and other groups and isolated them from the more established American children (Sarason & Doris, 1979). Intelligence tests were used to "prove" that these children were inferior and needed special classroom placement; we realize now that these tests and their procedures were highly biased.

Students are identified for special education through referral and assessment processes; however several lawsuits have documented that these processes may be biased and unfair (Turnbull, 1993). IDEA's reauthorizations have consistently required that these decisions be based on multiple measures (not just on one test) and that all assessments be done in the child's primary language or mode of communication, administered by trained personnel, with each instrument testing specific areas of educational need (Turnbull, 1993; van Keulen, Weddington, & DeBose, 1998). At least one person on the multidisciplinary team must have knowledge in the area of the suspected disability. The essential problem is that schools refer students to special education who aren't progressing and succeeding as expected. But because definitions of "success" and "typical expectations" are highly culturally-bound, children from culturally-different families are at high risk for inappropriate referral and enrollment in special education programs.

The U.S. Department of Education Office for Civil Rights (OCR) has monitored ethnic proportions in special education classes since P.L. 94-142 was passed in 1975, and results consistently show that minorities are overrepresented in special education programs. Until 1985, twice as many African American students were placed in classes for mild mental retardation, and 1.5 times as many were placed in classes for severe behavior disorders (U.S. Department of Education, 1987). Latino students in Texas were categorized with learning disabilities at a rate of 315%, according to their population (Holtzman, 1986). The U.S. Department of Education data in 1994 and 1997 still showed high placement rates for Native American and Latino students. The Committee on Minority Representation in Special Education recently evaluated OCR and OSEP datasets (1997 and 1999): African American and American Indian/Alaskan Native children remain at increased risk of identification for mental retardation and emotional disturbance; males were more likely to be in all high-incidence disability categories, with significant placement rate variation among states (Donovan & Cross, 2002). Thus, despite IDEA requirements for fair assessment and placement processes, minority students are still enrolled in special education programs at a higher than expected rate (Burnette, 1998; Greenberg, 1986; Harry, 1992a; Markowitz, 1996; Reschly, 1997; Russo & Talbert-Johnson, 1997; Sarason & Doris, 1979; U.S. Department of Education, Office of Civil Rights, 1987, 1994, 1997).

The cultural problem is compounded by the increasing growth of minority groups within the U.S. population. Van Keulen et al. (1998) predicted that by the year 2000, minority children would constitute one-third of all children, and that by 2030 this figure would be 41% of the child population. In fact, in year 2000, 62.5% of the school-age population (or five-eighths, and even less than the two-thirds predicted) was white alone (non-Hispanic) with 14.9% African American, 14.9% Hispanic or Latino, 4.3% Asian, and 1.1% American Indian/Alaskan (U.S. Census Bureau, 2003, August). Increasingly large numbers of students are at risk of being placed in special education (Greenberg, 1986).

What are some of the cultural differences that lead to placement? Differences in behavioral and personal interaction styles and in learning styles (global and holistic versus linear and analytic), as a result of bilingual communication, may be misinterpreted as evidence of a disability (Burnette, 1998; Turnbull, 1993). Few school professionals are trained to provide multicultural special education assessments or classroom interventions (Burnette, 1998; Obiakor & Utley, 1996; Talbert-Johnson, 1998). Consequently, referral teams rarely recognize or examine classrooms or schools for cultural factors that may contribute to a child's difficulties, nor do they identify those culturally specific attributes and skills that the child *is* able to perform successfully (Burnette, 1998; Cummins, 1986; Obiakor & Utley, 1996; Simich-Dudgeon, 1986; Willig, 1986).

These same behavioral, interpersonal, learning, and communication concerns apply to transition team activities. The interest, need, and ability transition assessments a team chooses may not reflect the cultural values or preferences of the student and family with regard to the statements or activities they present, or in the interpretation of results. The plans and interventions identified by the team may not progress as expected, for a number of reasons. At each stage of the transition planning and implementation process, teams should examine and be alert to the potential impact of cultural differences and how to accommodate these.

> **Critical Point**
> Lack of cultural competence in identifying and assessing ethnically diverse children who demonstrate authentic disabilities continues to lead to high rates of referral and placement in special education programs.

Our public schools and agencies are organized to support mainstream American beliefs and values. It is likely that culturally different families and students already have experienced cultural barriers and conflicts during referral and assessment processes; during classroom interactions and activities; and in their previous communications with school or agency personnel. Transition team members who possess awareness, information, and strategies for building trust and negotiating these types of difficulties need to first deal with the frequent lack of cultural training for many professionals.

Setting the Stage for Cultural Conflicts

The high rate of minority group growth and their over-enrollment in special education classes means that transition teams are likely to work with families who are culturally different (Wald, 1996). Unfortunately, the demographics of personnel in education and public services (e.g., counselors, social workers, etc.) show that they are primarily white, middle class, and female (Burnette, 1998; Eubanks, 1996; Moores, 1996). Proportionally fewer members of minority groups become special educators and the number of African American personnel is expected to continue to decline (Sexton, Lobman, Constans, Snyder, & Ernest, 1997). Few students of color, or who are male, can expect to have teachers of similar backgrounds (Knopp & Otuya, 1995; Simpson, 1997).

Individuals who are socially or culturally different usually have much greater difficulty in achieving equal access to societal rewards. This gets back to the issue of comfort and ease of communication. For example, parents who are middle or upper-middle class tend to be more successful in creating genuinely individualized IEPs for their child, with a broader range of options, than are typically made available to minority and lower- or working-class parents (Lareau, 1989; Lynch & Stein, 1987; Mehan, Hertweck, & Meihls, 1986). This is because middle- and upper-middle-class parents interact more easily with school

and agency staff; they feel more comfortable with each other and share the same basic values so that their interactions tend to be much more successful. Sadly, minority parents and their children are unlikely to work with personnel who are ethnically like them, and are also less likely to be successful in their IEP and planning meetings.

Social class differences also impact interactions and family lifestyles and contribute to communication barriers with school personnel (Lareau, 1989). Also, minority groups are more likely to be in lower-income categories, and are among the country's poorest groups (Dennis & Giangreco, 1996; Fujiura & Yamaki, 1997; Harry, 1992a; Janesick, 1995; Miller & Roby, 1970; Rose, 1972). For example, 31% of African Americans, 26% of Hispanics, and 10% of white Americans lived below the poverty level in 1989. In 1999 these figures were 24.9%, 22.6%, and 8.1% respectively, with an overall rate of 12.4%—not much improvement (U.S. Census Bureau, 2003, May).

Immigrants who do not move into an existing and well-established support system can experience lower social status as a result of being a minority, which can result in poorer income potential. Families who struggle with English also are likely to have poor wages and limited employment opportunities. With the addition of the economic, medical, and familial stresses of having a child with a disability, immigrant families often face multiple and substantial barriers. To summarize: minority families are statistically more likely to be poor, their children are more likely to be placed in special education, they will work with educators who are culturally different than themselves, and are less successful in creating individualized IEPs. Not a positive picture!

Given this situation, how effectively can professionals provide high-quality services, regardless of frequent ethnic, economic, educational, and class differences? In fact, it can be difficult to evaluate accurately the quality of services for culturally different families. Perceptions of successful services and family satisfaction often are gauged through culturally based behaviors. For example, family members may smile, greet, and interact with team members pleasantly and appear to have few questions or concerns. Yet, this may not reflect their satisfaction with services. A comparison of African

American and Caucasian early-intervention specialists found that the Caucasian personnel rated their services to African American parents higher than did their African American peers (Sexton et al., 1997), including:

1. openness to input from parents,
2. establishing positive relationships with parents,
3. actively encouraging parents to be involved in their children's program, and
4. services were a positive experience for children and their families.

The families themselves did not concur with the professionals' evaluations and rated the services less highly. Part of the difficulty is the frequent lack of professional training in multicultural competencies (Markowitz, 1996). So team members need to be cautious, get training, and evaluate satisfaction in culturally-neutral or culturally-appropriate ways.

For professionals, good intentions are not sufficient. They need training and awareness of the impacts of communication and behaviors. A few examples of cultural conflicts with transition services have been described, but the team must learn to recognize cultural beliefs—in our schools and agencies, in ourselves, and ultimately, in our families. This requires probing more deeply into some of the common and institutionalized examples of many American values.

EXAMINING AMERICAN CULTURAL VALUES

American Values and Beliefs

Despite the (continuing) history of diverse waves of immigration, the United States has a set of identified American values and norms. These are the typical standards for behaviors and are primarily reflected in the lifestyle of the white, middle and upper-middle class (Althen, 1988; Dunn & Griggs, 1995; Green, 1999; Hanson, 1998a; Harry, 1992a; McPhatter, 1997; Pinderhughes, 1995). This group holds a majority of powerful societal positions and uses its class-based power to influence government, legal, and social processes: Its tax base supports the country; it lobbies for changes in laws; it serves on public school boards, which decide curriculum and teaching practices; and it provides the majority of civil servants, such as police, teachers, and government workers.

Many American cultural values were brought with the Pilgrims and reinforced by pioneer movements into the unknown West. Values include industry, success

and achievement, civic-mindedness, usefulness, individualism and personal choice, self-reliance and independence from others, privacy, equality, informality, future orientation and progress, and a focus on efficient management (Brookhiser, 1991; Hammond & Morrison, 1996; Hobbs, 1975; Stewart, Danielian, & Festes, 1969). These translate into behaviors such as: keeping busy; setting personal goals; reading self-help books (i.e., independent self-improvement); rating importance of an activity and giving time according to immediate "relevance;" expecting meetings to follow an agenda and a time schedule; successfully competing against others (for individual honors, grades, salaries, etc.); addressing problems succinctly and rationally; and using day planners to maintain organization and efficiency (scheduling leisure and family activities as well as professional meetings and appointments, leisure should be goal-oriented to achieve fitness or health).

Table 3-1 describes some typical U.S./American characteristics and contrasting cultural characteristics that impact interactions and, therefore, transition team processes. As the table shows, some expectations about place in the world, ability to control our future, way of viewing time and interpersonal relationships, and family structure are widely variable depending on culture of origin. Knowledge of interaction preferences and styles can greatly enhance professional effectiveness. However, realization of the tremendous impact that behavior can have on those who are culturally different is likely to increase one's anxiety at first and lead to some awkwardness (Brislin, 1993). This will decrease with time and additional cross-cultural opportunities as the information becomes more integrated into one's behavioral repertoire.

Assimilation and Acculturation of Values

Professionals who work with and study immigrant people often view them in terms of steps they have made toward "assimilation" or "acculturation" (Green, 1999; Lynch, 1998a; Joe & Malach, 1998). This becomes a way to categorize individuals in terms of their acceptance of the dominant cultural characteristics of a particular society, in contrast with those who retain their native language and habits (considered to be "traditional"). Green (1999) proposes an alternative view that defines the entire concept of ethnicity and acculturation as "situational" rather than absolute, and is modified to suit the needs of various types of cross-cultural encounters. For example, a family may adhere to ethnic patterns while in their community by

TABLE 3–1   Key cultural differences between U.S. American and other cultural groups

Cultural Characteristic	U.S./American Cultural Value	Culturally Contrasting Value
Cooperation versus competition	Society (and public schools) encourage doing better than others as proof of mastery; games are based on having a winner and loser, winners in a variety of activities are regularly rewarded.	Cooperative societies work together to achieve a mutual goal; children may be taught to wait until everyone has finished so that no one is embarrassed; individual achievement is likely to be less motivating in comparison to roles as family member and group or community pride.
Individual versus family or group orientation	Standard value on small, nuclear family units with little reliance on the extended family. Use of professional assistance and services when issues cannot be resolved within the nuclear family unit.	Importance of extended family or group and blood kinship lineage, with respect for elders and ancestors. Child's achievement (or disability) may reflect upon the entire family. Family and group identity may be of primary importance and contribute to the family's reputation, status, cohesiveness, and sense of collective (group) responsibility.
Time orientation	Time is measured and used efficiently; punctuality is expected and rewarded. People wear watches and professionals use appointment calendars; wasting time or lateness is viewed negatively. Monochronic orientation for doing one thing at a time—for example, "business before pleasure," and students work without talking or distractions.	Time is "given" in many other parts of the world and is generously shared; quality of interpersonal relationships takes priority. Polychronic time orientation handling several interactions and activities simultaneously, encouraging business and pleasurable activities together; appear to have several individuals talking at the same time with intermittent listening, laughing, and commenting.
Gender roles and responsibilities	Traditional nuclear family remains the ideal, with a working father and stay-at-home mother who cares for the family's emotional and physical needs; this is responding to increased single-parent homes and working mothers with greater role and gender flexibility.	Some cultures have strict gender-based roles with pampering of young males and girls caring for younger siblings, with home responsibilities and limited independence. Some discourage conversations between children/adults, or males/females until appropriate times. Some groups have highly adaptable family roles among parents, extended family, and older children.
Interaction style	Tendency to be direct with a topic, factual and impersonal. There is an expectation to identify and address difficulties and conflicts directly, including expression of related concerns and use of a highly verbal style. Laughing and giggling are expressions of enjoyment. Typically, focus on one topic or activity at a time. Americans tend to prefer more interaction space than many Latinos, southern Europeans, and Middle Easterners; less than African Americans and Asians.	May use indirect means to address a topic with requirements to begin serious discussions with initial, interpersonal, and social interactions. May use a more emotive style or an unobtrusive, nonemotive interaction style depending on group. Status, authority, and roles of interaction partners may be very important and dictate specific styles. Southeast Asians may see laughing and giggling as a sign of extreme embarrassment or discomfort. Loud talking or personal contact may be rude or offensive; others see it as natural expression and friendliness. May be comfortable with multiple conversations simultaneously. Interpersonal space preferences vary widely with culture.
Fate versus individual	There is very little that cannot be controlled—cars, services, utilities, or medical interventions. Emphasis is on individual rights and responsibilities, self-determination and autonomy. Is rewarded for taking care of one's own needs independently.	May believe that control lies outside the individual, with external forces largely responsible for what happens to people. Value on harmonious existence with surroundings and circumstances. May feel responsibility toward oneself as is reflected in terms of family and group roles, not through own achievements.

Source: This table is based on Chan (1998a, 1998b), Green (1999), Hanson (1998b), Harry (1992a, 1992b, 1992c), Joe and Malach (1998), Lynch (1998a, 1998b), Sharifzadeh (1998), van Keulen et al. (1998), and Willis (1998).

celebrating festivals, eating traditional foods, and socializing with others; however, they may accept the dominant culture's standards about work, housing, and traumatic health care (Green, 1999; Hanson, 1998a). In addition, degree of acculturation depends on many factors including socioeconomic status, generational status, religion, age at immigration, language ability, education level, gender, cultural attitudes, length of residence in the majority language country, and personality factors (Harry et al., 1995; Lynch & Hanson, 1992). A rigid set of acculturation "stages" does not account for these multiple factors and their degrees of influence.

Instead, an "ecocultural" framework that allows a range of responses according to contextual (situational) variables better reflects a family's or individual's behavior (Harry, 2002). Family members can respond in bicultural ways, according to situational demands. They may retain traditional values that they believe are important, but they also can learn to use IEP meetings in a more "Americanized" way to support their child's development and access to certain societal rewards (social or work status). This view also allows professionals to support families who may wish to learn specific skills that will increase their sense of success at these meetings, without having to address the full range of culturally unique behaviors and values.

A family's affiliation with their cultural group may change over time, often depending upon whether or not they live within a strong minority community, if they have American relatives nearby, if they had previous exposure to American cultural values, if they are recent immigrants, and if they desire to accept American values. The team may need to negotiate changes between generations—grandparents or elders are key decision makers in several cultures, but may not represent the beliefs of either the parents or the student. These perspectives may change as the child develops and has either positive or negative interactions with American cultural values, which will lead to reinterpretations of adult goals (Harry, 1992a). Situational biculturalism may allow the team to negotiate for student trials for specific activities and settings.

Culturally aware professionals need to understand how "success" exemplifies acceptance of standard American cultural values: our advanced degrees, and our socioeconomic status, regardless of our ethnicity. Individuals may display more or less of these typical values depending upon the situation, its context, and those with whom we interact. Educational and professional status often is perceived by others as power, and team members are likely to have a higher social status

than do families (Green, 1999). Teams need to recognize and use this power carefully when interacting and negotiating plans with families. As acculturated Americans, team members may be used to stating opinions and debating options; for these families, those opinions may be interpreted as commands from a social and professional superior.

Transition Values

Table 3-1 lists some of the differences between American and other cultures which may impact transition practices. For example, interaction differences impact how team members establish open, trusting, and collaborative relationships with families. The other ideals, values, and beliefs that are mandated and expected in the transition planning process can lead to cultural conflicts such as were discussed earlier in the chapter. The following sections describe some of the fundamental contrasting values that are embedded in many of our required IDEA services and, therefore, in terms of how we work with families.

Contrasting Values of Identity

Several cultures emphasize group identity rather than individualism, and the child's future roles may be defined as his or her place within the family or group structure. The family also may disagree with, or see as destructive and undermining, transition team goals to develop their child's independence, self-reliance, and abilities to make his or her own decisions and choices. Several cultures have very different values about young adult independence from parents with age expectations that are both younger and older than typical American youths.

> **Critical Point**
> The team should frame the "individualized" nature of the IEP/ITP process in terms of a set of mutually, agreed-upon outcomes that will be achieved through collaboration between the family and the IEP team.

Contrasting Views of Disability

In the United States, people tend to believe in a "medical model" for diagnosing and curing disabilities. The result is an ever-growing list of identified disabilities (Ysseldyke, Algozzine, & Thurlow, 1992). Not all cultures recognize this variety and may focus only on obvious physical or mental disabilities (Harry, 1992a; Zuniga, 1998). Mild disabilities are what other cultures believe are part of a normal range of behaviors. Families may have great difficulty in understanding why their child is being identified as "problematic" and placed in special programs. Or their religious or cultural beliefs may not concur with the school's urgency for intervention planning and remediation—because it is their child's "fate" or a result of God's plan to have this disability.

Families may not view transition planning as important because they do not foresee a future that is problematic. A family may view very positively the vision of allowing their child with a significant disability to remain at home under their protection and love. For a child with a mild disability, the family may believe that the school's elaborate transition plans are unnecessary because their child will be a successful adult within the community and its support system. Other families may believe that the disability reflects poorly upon the family and they are very uncomfortable discussing these issues in the detail that Americans prefer.

> **Critical Point**
> The team should work from the vision of the family focusing on what the child does well.

The team should frame the discussion around improving agreed-upon results and outcomes, and be sure to identify what the child does well (show value and caring for the child) rather than focusing on "disabilities" and needs; additionally, the team could work from the family's vision for their child's future and explore options within that. (Remember: "Fighting" with the family over future visions will only alienate both them and the student—and the family has a lifelong commitment versus the team's very few years. Also, "individualized" transition planning is just that— the team should not try to fit students and families into generic visions of an optimal job or living situation.)

Contrasting Values for Family Relationships

American families use the nuclear family as the center of all primary relationships. Our country's identified "minority cultures" often value wider kinship or community webs and may not view parents as the primary decision makers or caretakers. These parents may consider their signatures on IEP documents as meaningless because they lack the formal approval of their extended family or community group.

Child-rearing practices also are highly culturally based and impact family roles and relationships; some cultures do not focus on independence and self-reliance, or reflect developmental milestones that include the age at walking, talking, and toilet training (i.e., these are often viewed as a *critical* event by both American professionals and parents). In many Asian cultures, young children are not diapered but are expected to relieve themselves freely and are washed as needed. Older children and adults may feed young children for an extended period because caring for a younger child or a child with a disability is not viewed as a burden (Lynch, 1998a). The team should gather information from families (not always by asking) regarding current and expected family roles of their children, and how they perceive relationships as leading to agreed-upon outcomes. Additionally, the team should: be inclusive of extended family and group members and the positive and expanded contributions they can make to the student's adult life; and develop mutually supportive ways to use family expectations in conjunction with school supports and programs to achieve transition outcomes.

The scenario in Table 3–2 demonstrates a possible contrast of time orientation for U.S. cultural values versus other cultures.

TABLE 3–2 Scenario: Cultural contrast for time orientation

Situation:	If you were a parent on your way out the door to an IEP meeting, how would you react when your youngest child arrived from the bus upset and crying about being teased by peers? You need to drop the child off at your neighbor's house within 5 minutes or you will be late—how do you react?
Response (U.S. value):	You might bring the child in the car with you and try to soothe him/her while you are driving, reasoning to yourself that these types of conflicts are typical of children and although upsetting at the time, not overly traumatic—this is part of becoming a self-reliant individual. Or you might take an extra 5 minutes of private time (knowing there is a short "grace period" for most meetings) before heading for the school.
Contrasting Response:	Cultures that value relationships over time would focus on soothing the child's feelings as a priority. Within their cultural group, being 30 or more minutes late would be understood, accepted, and supported as the appropriate response (also showing how the "group" takes care of the individual). The group also would understand if you chose to bring the child to the meeting to be sure that s/he felt protected (rather than abandoned).

The scenario in Table 3-2 illustrates a possible stereotyping that team members may be at risk for if they devalue a flexible concept of time. From this example, perhaps you can think of other ways in which people judge or stereotype the responses of other groups:

She is so "lazy" and won't work hard to be better. [*She doesn't enjoy or value competition, or the task is gender-inappropriate.*]

He has no initiative—he'll never get anywhere or do anything with his life! [*He is not behaviorally or verbally assertive, and lives according to cultural roles.*]

The impacts of many of contrasting values can create fundamental difficulties with transition planning, because a "successful" adulthood is culturally determined. Many of the transition-related competencies are individualized or labeled using "self": self-determina-

tion, self-advocacy, self-reliance, self-sufficiency, and when interpreted literally, these concepts are not a good fit with group-oriented cultures (Leake & Black, 2005). Rigid adherence to a "professionally-based" versus a "culturally-appropriate" definition will exacerbate rather than ameliorate differences. For example, when do people generally define "independence" as occurring for a student: when they (a) graduated, (b) turned 18 or 21, (c) left home? And if it were when they left home, when would that be expected to occur: when they (a) graduated, (b) turned 18 or 21, (c) married? For Latina mothers the answer was (c) in both cases and was when their children could make decisions on their own (Rueda, Monzo, Shapiro, Gomez, & Blacher, 2005).

Table 3-3 summarizes some of the key contrasting values and includes potential negative impacts. Most often these occur when professionals are unaware of the impact of their own values and behaviors, and act

TABLE 3-3 Potential impacts and resolution of cultural differences

	ITP Legislative Mandates and Practices	Contrasting Cultural Values	Results of Unresolved Conflicts	Culturally Competent Responses
Goals of the IEP/ITP planning processes	Identify student's skills, needs, preferences, achievement levels. Identify goals and plan steps to achieve desired outcomes.	Contribute to group and family needs, and listen to others. Build relationships that value communication, harmony, and personal/family honor.	Schools limit the information or choices given to families. Families are offended that key members are excluded from meetings. Families may not voice concerns out of respect or due to status differences.	Be alert to goal and outcome differences; begin with personal interactions (visiting). Establish a trusting relationship with family (regarding cultural preferences for formal/informal, gender, and role-consciousness).
Transition outcomes for students	To develop independence, self-reliance, assertive-ness, and economic success for work, ability to live alone (with minimal support), and satisfying leisure activities.	To develop group interdependence, social harmony, and extended support networks that contribute to the family and community. To develop noncompetitive attributes and skills with a focus on relationships and respect for others.	Schools judge families as unable or unwilling to work toward critical goals. Families withdraw or "ignore" advice from school; may not attend future meetings.	Gradually begin to solicit from family members their description of preferred adult outcomes (in a culturally appropriate manner). Negotiate differences by suggesting a variety of alternatives and explain rationale for professional suggestions in a culturally appropriate way.

within what may be a "professionally accountable" but not "culturally responsible" manner. The table also suggests ways to resolve some of these differences.

Beginning with the typical scheduling of transition meetings, there are several immediate potential conflicts: the one-hour time blocks for meetings promote efficiency and rational decision making; little time is spent in building a relationship with family members because achieving the task is more important; and only key team members are invited because this is more efficient. Instead, families may hope meetings serve as a means of establishing long-term and trusting relationships that will serve them over a number of years—this is *their desired outcome*. The school's focus on the task and time allotment (in preference of relationship-building and connecting with multiple team and family members) can confuse and insult families (who may interpret this as not valuing them as families) (Harry, 2002). Immigrants may also be from countries in which parent participation in education is neither expected nor encouraged (Lai & Ishiyama, 2004; Rogers-Adkinson, Ochoa, & Delgado, 2003).

> **Critical Point**
> When cross-cultural conflicts are not resolved, families and professionals often become increasingly confused and distrustful of each other.

When conflicts are not resolved, initial barriers become more solidified as each responds in culturally appropriate, but cross-culturally different, ways. Minority families may withdraw out of respect, or to allow the school to save face, or may work within their own family or community to address their child's issues in very different ways from school expectations. Families may perceive the minimizing of relationships (with the family, extended family or group members, and their community) as a lack of interest or commitment to developing a genuine understanding of their child. They may interpret meetings based on rapid decision making and problem resolution as rude, overbearing, and controlling (Harry, 1992a; 2002; Rogers-Adkinson et al., 2003).

When parental expectations aren't met, school and agency personnel may conclude that the family is either unable or unwilling to follow through with goals and plans; they may be seen as "bad parents" who lack both caring and commitment to their child (Harry, 1992a, 1992b, 1992c). The result is that personnel often respond by limiting the information and choices presented to parents—because the parents are uncaring or unable to follow through (Lynch & Stein, 1987;

Mehan et al., 1986). Not surprisingly, across 12 studies, Harry found that minority parents were less involved and less informed, and parents felt that the professionals implicitly or explicitly discouraged their participation. The data from those studies was from 15 years ago. Surely, professionals are now more aware of cultural differences, but there is also no evidence that shows that, in general, relationships have improved between professionals and families.

EXAMINING CULTURAL BELIEFS OF OTHER GROUPS

Thus far, this chapter examined some typical American values, how they impact transition services planning, and how initial conflicts can worsen with future encounters and over time. The hope is that you are becoming more aware of your own culturally-influenced behaviors. Without training and intervention, it is likely that neither the professional personnel on the team nor the families will have the skills to resolve these situations. Therefore, this next section describes key information about, and values of, a number of cultural groups within the United States. Information is provided about the range of values that may be encountered in order to increase awareness and sensitivity. It also shows the values that may impede certain strategies—this is because resolutions must be done using culturally-appropriate interaction styles and account for key differences in worldview, family structure, child rearing, and beliefs about disability.

> **Critical Point**
> Acculturation is situational and families and individuals may or may not choose to adhere to more Americanized beliefs or values at any point in time.

The descriptions that follow should be read within a paradigm of diversity: Each family and individual chooses to ascribe to, and to express, each value or belief in potentially unique ways. Culture is continually evolving (Cordeiro et al., 1994; Green, 1999; Hanson, 1998a; Harry, 2002; Harry, Grenot-Scheyer et al., 1995; Lynch & Hanson, 1992). So these descriptions should be used as starting points, to be read with prudence: stereotyping ("expecting" people to behave in certain ways) is helpful to no one. From the examples earlier, "expecting" people to be late, or "off-task" (not following the stated agenda) is divisive and damaging. Understanding a family's focus on relationships (versus task, as establishing trust and understanding with professionals) and time spent with a child as demonstrating ways of caring (by taking time to deal with a child's troubles) helps you reframe these potential conflicts in more appropriately positive ways. Therefore, the information provided is to expand cultural referencing and alertness to cultural conflicts. It should be kept in mind that it is generally through cultural "conflict" that we learn the depth and breadth of our own cultural values. You should approach these descriptions for possible "conflicts" or differences—make this both a self-exploration and cross-cultural learning process.

Native American Values and Beliefs

Native American groups in the United States include 517 separate tribes or nations with over 150 languages. There is tremendous diversity and cultural differences that exist, particularly among the Navajo, Eskimo, and Cherokee peoples (Dunn & Griggs, 1995). General tribal interests and life pathways often are similar, although tribal customs, languages, and life practices frequently are unique (Hanson, 1998b). Their existence has been significantly influenced by life on the reservation, although more than one-half do *not* live there. Native Americans live in most major U.S. cities and although many are part of mainstream society, many also retain their traditional beliefs and values to some degree.

Levels of affiliation with tribal members and traditions may vary greatly; however tribes often continue to provide a strong level of personal and cultural identification. Much of the Native American culture of today has been influenced by adaptive and acculturation strategies from three centuries of contact with a highly dissimilar and somewhat hostile U.S. government, lifestyle philosophy, and social organization. The Bureau of Indian Affairs continues to exert a strong influence and exists as a separate governmental body in the United States (Hanson, 1998b).

Wide cultural belief and value differences exist between Native American people and U.S./American perspectives on relationships with and dominance over nature, paths to harmonious lifestyles, family structure, child rearing, interaction and communication, and causation of disabilities. This can lead to profound differences in goals for transition planning and definitions of an optimal adult lifestyle. Communication styles are much less direct, with times for silence: American values of communication directness and efficiency with meetings, according to a time line and agenda, can very

negatively affect trust, communication, and participatory decision making.

African American Values and Beliefs

This group includes people from West Africa, the Caribbean, and those who have lived in the United States for many generations, resulting in many different cultural patterns, lifestyles, and beliefs. As a whole, they have distinct patterns of thinking, feeling, and acting, some of which have developed as an adaptation to discrimination and their history of slavery. The family, marriage, and kinship bonds are extremely important and the impacts of slavery on relationships can still be seen. African American family members may or may not live together (often misinterpreted by American culture as family instability). Great value is placed on the extended family, blood relatives, and strong kinship networks with multigenerational social networks for relatives, friends, and neighbors.

Family remains the source of their culture, providing socialization and guidance with a great value on communication. The family provides members with a sense of who they are, including their relationship with the dominant white culture. Family structure is significantly impacted by socioeconomic class (lower versus middle or upper class) and rural versus urban location. There is comparatively higher unemployment, which impacts families in terms of health and poverty despite a higher rate of working mothers than found among many white Americans. Family structure is more flexible with collective responsibility and sharing of child care across family and community relationships. The American meeting and communication styles that focus on direct, assertive, and nonemotive recitation of "facts," with expectations of timely decision making can all negatively impact effective collaborative planning with the family. If the team is primarily white, the family may be suspicious and challenge opinions and educational options recommended by the team.

Latino Peoples' Values and Beliefs

Latinos include people from Mexico, Puerto Rico, Cuba, and Central and South America, with specific cultural characteristics that are unique to each geographic area. Puerto Ricans are the second largest Latino group in the United States (Mexicans are the largest), with Central and South Americans the fastest growing group. Cubans tend to have more economic success; Central Americans immigrate for job opportunities but often experience greater levels of poverty. Family commitment is of paramount importance to all, including loyalty to family, a strong family support system, and a view that the child reflects upon the honor of the family. There may be a strongly hierarchical order among siblings with a duty to care for members who have a disability, are ill, or are elderly.

Ethnic networks and supports are very important for teaching families about resources, procedures, and mechanisms of organizations in the United States. This is especially important for Latina women when they no longer have family or community networks from home; the barrio church often provides important sources of help. Many communities offer support groups for parents with some of the more common disabilities (e.g., cerebral palsy or Down's syndrome).

Strong cultural differences with American values may occur in the strong focus on the family and community for a sense of identity and appropriate life roles (gender- and age-specific). Planning processes and outcomes may be influenced by interaction styles that expect greater attention to group issues and familial well-being than to individuals within the group. Relationships are very important and support personal values of trustworthiness, loyalty, and respect.

Asian American Values and Beliefs

An older term, "Asian-Pacific Americans," has been separated to differentiate between the many widely varying beliefs and values (Pacific Island Americans are described separately). Asian Americans include ethnic groups that originate from east Asia—China, Japan, and Korea; Southeast Asia—Burma, Cambodia, Indonesia, Laos, Malaysia, the Philippines, Singapore, Thailand, and Vietnam; and south Asia—India, Pakistan, Sri Lanka, Bangladesh, Bhutan, and Nepal (Chan, 1998a; Dunn & Griggs, 1995). Although several Asian-American groups are known for their industriousness and economic success, other refugees (e.g., from Cambodia, Laos, and Vietnam) tend to have high rates of unemployment and low wages.

These diverse groups represent a variety of religions, beliefs, and lifestyles. Hindus believe in reincarnation, a respect for all living things, and the worship of many gods. Muslims believe in one God and strive to live in accord with the five pillars of their religion, including daily confessions of faith, praying five times daily, charity to those less fortunate, fasting during the ninth month, and a pilgrimage to Mecca at least once during their lifetime. The majority from Southeast Asia practice Buddhism, which believes in peace, harmony, strong family commitment, nonmaterialism, and avoidance of extremes. Those from east Asia practice either Confucianism, Taoism, or Shintoism, which follow a set of ethical standards, including obedience to authority, honesty, kindness, and respect for elders. Refugee groups may retain tribal beliefs such as spiritualist and animist practices.

All these religions share deference to authority, emotional restraint, specified roles defined in paternalism (i.e., men and elders enjoy greater status than women and children); a hierarchical, extended family orientation; interdependence; harmony with nature; and commitment to learning and academic achievement. Although these groups are primarily and strongly patriarchal in their families, there are several strong matriarchal groups.

Wide differences with American culture occur in these religious practices and worldviews, including peace and harmony (nondominance over nature and others), strong family commitments that extend to previous generations, and strong social roles and proscribed relationships. These impact transition outcome goals and self-determination, and also often conflict with American preferences for communication that is flexible in role, informal, assertive, and direct.

Pacific Island American Values and Beliefs

This group includes the Pacific Rim islands (people from the Philippines, Indonesia, and Polynesian islands of Hawaii, Samoa, and native New Zealanders) as a separate cultural group. Indonesia is strongly influenced by Muslim and Asian religions; however, there also is a strong Christian presence. For example, Filipinos are primarily Catholic and Hawaiians are strongly Christian (Chan, 1998b; Mokuau & Tauili'ili, 1998). The Christian religions emphasize brotherly love, justice, and charity as strong values. The influence of Asian religious beliefs encourage obedience to authority, honesty, kindness, and respect for elders with strong links to ancestors. There is a tendency toward paternalism in certain cultures, although Polynesian cultures have strong matriarchal structures. The influence of native folk beliefs and Asian religions provide the most contrasting cultural differences and include diverse social structure and child-rearing practices.

Filipinos tend to be highly educated with professional backgrounds but experience underemployment when their professional training is not recognized in the United States. Native Hawaiian and Samoan families value education but economic and social factors have led to a lower success rate.

BECOMING CULTURALLY COMPETENT

Developing Your Own Cultural Skills

The information provided thus far can alert the team to potential conflicts when teaching students and working with families—examine everyone's assumptions and interactions in order to "understand," and then *modify* the team's responses—building toward mutually caring and respectful interactions. Also, team members need to support each other—beware of using cultural group generalizations to judge, evaluate, or otherwise negatively respond; although this may protect individuals at the moment, it contributes to ongoing historical prejudice and superficial overgeneralizations (Bull, Fruehling, & Chattergy, 1992). Ultimately, this causes long-term harm to both parties, and particularly to the team's role as professionals.

The summaries of cultural groups provided neglect the natural diversity that occurs within these groups: none of us likes being stereotyped due to our gender, appearance, ethnicity, and so on. Within any one group, there is substantial diversity. For example, immigrating groups often are different from each other, depending upon their country and region of origin, and according to the region in which they now live. The cultural responses of Japanese immigrants to Hawaii will be different from those who settled in California as a result of their different experiences (Bull, Fruehling, & Chattergy, 1992). Immigrating Puerto Ricans may identify their ethnicity as "white" on intake forms because they do not have "kinky hair"—their criterion in Puerto Rico (Rogers-Adkinson, et al., 2003).

The journey toward cultural competence starts with a clear understanding of one's own beliefs and values, and an acknowledgment that they will differ from those of others (Dennis & Giangreco, 1996; Fradd & Weismantel, 1989; Hanson & Carta, 1996; Harry, 1992a; Lynch, 1998a). When reading these descriptions, you might find values that you felt were highly similar and compatible to your own, as well as those that were highly dissimilar. This leads to the first step of becoming aware of, examining, and comparing the impact of cultural learning on your personal and professional behaviors and expectations, with values and expectations of other cultures. Any one person will not subscribe to only one set of culturally-prescribed values—and there

are elements that we all will share with other cultures. This is important in helping you and the team to find common ground with family members, an important component for building collaborative partnerships (Friend & Bursuck, 2006).

> **Critical Point**
> Becoming culturally aware involves the impact of cultural learning on personal and professional behavior and expectations.

Wolfe, Boone, and Barrera (1997) recommend a six-step strategy to guide reflection and inquiry to support culturally relevant transition planning:

1. Awareness of culture-related issues that influence collaborative transition planning—knowing one's own attitudes, beliefs, values, and cultural preconceptions;
2. Identification of personal values regarding adult life—including autonomy, independence, interdependence;
3. Perception of family values related to cultural diversity and adulthood—finding out what the family values are;
4. Congruence and incongruence among educator and family values—assessing congruence among all team members;
5. Communication with the family to verify perceptions and obtain additional information—also regarding the family's preference for what role you and they take during the transition process; and
6. Reflection on family meeting and future plans—identifying sources to help resolve disagreements and to promote mutually satisfying outcomes.

The first three steps focus on identifying and understanding values, the base for which has already been presented. The last three steps support communication and using mutual problem solving to resolve important differences: it begins with problem identification (assessment of congruence), then opens up communication between team and family members for problem solving. The last step evaluates the team's success; but culturally different personnel often misinterpret family perceptions regarding satisfaction requiring reconfirming with the family about the process.

While taking courses can help (Bellini, 2002), additional personal introspection and learning often occurs when there is honest and open communication with families; however, they should not be placed in a role of becoming a primary source of cross-cultural teaching.

Green (1999) recommends a three-step plan that includes background readings and research that also uses personal cross-cultural interactions with a chosen cultural guide. This guide explains and interprets frequently scheduled visits to ethnic communities and interactions with minority group members. See Table 3–4. Pinderhughes (1995) also suggests a model for cultural competence and adds important qualifying characteristics of culturally competent individuals, which include being (a) comfortable with difference, (b) willing to change previously held ideas, and (c) flexible with one's own thinking and behavior.

Among the most difficult aspects of cross-cultural learning is dealing with personal discomfort, which often arises when confronting oneself with differences or when realizing that one needs to change. The conflictual situation itself often causes strong emotional pain (Brislin, 1993). As recommended by Green (1999), it is helpful to have a cultural guide to help mediate and debrief (particularly from painful or disturbing experiences). This person should be competent, both as a member of a minority group and one who is articulate and knowledgeable about his or her own culture. Involving the whole team, or at least a few colleagues, can be very helpful in providing support and encouragement through frustrating or troubling situations, which leads us to the next section about school-based cultural activities.

> **Critical Point**
> Cross-cultural skills are learned through guided interactive experiences that involve dealing with difference (comfort, change, and flexibility).

Schoolwide Professional and In-Service Training

The more people on your transition teams, your district, and school who have received training and experience in cross-cultural skills, then the less likely it is that culturally different children and families will be misdiagnosed and poorly treated by the schools or the special education and planning processes. All-inclusive personnel meetings can be effective ways to meet comprehensive needs for information about, and access to, culturally competent practices (Burnette, 1998; Markowitz, 1996; Obiakor & Utley, 1996). Because personal examination and behavioral change can be painful and difficult, it is often helpful and reassuring to be involved in school- and district-wide programs and to work through these issues alongside your colleagues. This broad-based approach also ensures that all school and district personnel share the same information about "acceptable" and "unacceptable" perspectives on cultural pluralism and working with culturally different families.

Bellini's (2002) research shows that courses and workshops are helpful, even if a comprehensive program is not offered through the district or school. Therefore, teams should use courses and workshops as a beginning step, or to continue and expand their

TABLE 3–4 Becoming a culturally competent professional

Steps to develop cultural competence
1. Background preparation: Read descriptions in journals, make a series of visits to the community to learn about the social interactions and characteristics and the resources that are available.
2. Use of cultural guides: These are ordinary people who may or may not be community leaders but who can articulate what is going on around them.
3. Participant observation: This is a long-term commitment to learning in detail about the life of a community with minimal intrusion into the day-to-day activities of the residents by participating in community activities with simultaneous observation of all interactions and details about community life.

Questions to ask in evaluating your cultural competence
1. How much personal and social time do I spend with people who are culturally similar to or different from me?
2. When I am with culturally different people, do I reflect upon my own cultural preferences or do I spend time openly learning about the unique aspects of another person's culture?
3. How comfortable am I in immersion experiences, especially where I am in a numerical minority?
4. How much time do I spend engaged in cross-cultural professional exchanges?
5. How much work have I actually done to increase my knowledge and understanding of culturally and ethnically district groups?
6. What is my commitment to becoming culturally competent? What personal and professional sacrifices am I willing to make?
7. To what extent have I nondefensively extended myself in approaching professional colleagues with the goal of bridging cultural differences?

Source: Adapted from Green, J. N. (1999). *Cultural awareness in human services: A multi-ethnic approach.* Boston: Allyn & Bacon, p. 76.

training. Again, the critical first step is to be committed to the process and become aware of one's own values and cultural beliefs. Rodriguez (1994) also found that (1) involvement with parents and (2) an understanding of the cultural and linguistic background of the family was important to developing competencies. It should be noted that *personal involvement* is the first listed competency: Relationships with families are not typical of American values for problem solving. In addition, the medical model believes that noninvolvement maintains objectivity and, therefore, greater accuracy in diagnosis and treatment. Yet, several cultures consider relationships as essential to receiving satisfactory services from professionals; for them, commitment to forming and maintaining relationships shows commitment to their child's well-being.

One of the benefits of school- or district-wide programming is that it can address personnel who are not equally supportive of multicultural competence. For example, Sue (1996) described four types of resistant beliefs: (1) there is no need to change because current practices are equally appropriate for all populations, regardless of race, culture, ethnicity, gender or otherwise; (2) multicultural competencies are unrealistic for any one individual given the multitude of knowledge and skills that is necessary; (3) we must wait until appropriate standards and guidelines are developed for *all* underrepresented groups including gays and lesbians, and women; and (4) cultural diversity represents reverse racism and quotas, and is biased and unbalanced (Middleton et al., 2000, p. 220). School- or district-wide policies can establish a standard that all are expected to achieve. If your school or district does not have a policy, it is still important to model and utilize culturally competent practices in meetings—competent practices must begin with someone.

School- and agency-based in-services and workshops are excellent ways to implement large-scale training; however, they will never be sufficient unless they are continuous and ongoing, with mechanisms that allow for feedback and evaluation (Green, 1999; Hanson, 1998a). Typically, in-services and workshops are designed to address one or a series of narrow topics through informal or formal training programs. Often they have little or no follow-through and reinforcement

of learnings in order to achieve substantial change. Those who are resistant often take advantage of the short-term nature of such programs. Ongoing involvement of parents with planning teams are important for identifying ongoing needs and topics.

A more complete planning process would involve schoolwide and agencywide planning in restructuring or revising of mission statements and policies (Nieto, 2001; Fradd & Weismantel, 1989). In order to be truly effective, this type of change should address multicultural issues and needs for *all* staff, and not just "key" personnel or faculty. Such a comprehensive approach is the best way to address institutionalized and organizational processes and procedures that create cultural barriers. An organization-wide value is implemented when cultural competence is expected across the range of personnel that interact with families and clients. (Yes, bus drivers and office staff also should have "a cultural clue" when interacting with families.) *Everyone* needs information about cross-cultural interaction styles when making contacts, setting up appointments and meetings, or soliciting information to be used in files. All IEP and transition teams need information about culturally fair assessment and referral/ eligibility processes, identifying and building upon cultural strengths and resources in carrying out IEP plans, and developing appropriate expectations regarding students and families (cf. Markowitz, 1996; Obiakor & Utley, 1996). Each school or agency consists of unique cultural strengths, needs, and challenges that are best utilized and addressed through a school- or agency-focused program that begins with potentially unique cultural groups that reside within the local population. Ongoing feedback ensures that training is continual, addresses new challenges, and revises and sets new goals across subsequent years. Again, a one-shot, one-year, hurry-get-it-over-with approach will not have many long-lasting results (even though it fits so well with U.S. cultural values of efficiency and time management).

Schools and agencies can utilize parents as a potential source of cultural expertise (Brame, 1995; Harry, 1992a), thereby recognizing them for their contributions as well as meeting needs to learn about unique local cultural groups. Parents and community leaders are the best resources in these instances (Harry, 1992a). Parents can serve as members of advisory groups and in assisting with cross-cultural training. Of course, this is best done outside of the IEP meeting and when the parents don't have something personal at stake. Schools and agencies may have minority staff and faculty who are also valuable resources, and who may have excellent strategies for successfully balancing two or more cultures (Harry, 1992a; Obiakor & Utley, 1996). However, they cannot be expected to know about the range of *all* cultures within an area (Luft, 1995).

Parent and Family Training

Families also need basic information and assistance in becoming culturally competent (Brame, 1995; Burnette, 1998). For parents, this includes information about the special education system and transition planning processes, the important documents and rights, as well as how to find support from peers. Peer parent groups are a very important and "user-friendly" resource for providing training, advocacy assistance, and increased participation in educational planning. Such groups have been a highly effective tool because families often feel more comfortable in learning from each other and through the social ties they form (Dybwad, 1989; Harry, 1992a; Gliedman & Roth, 1980). This is especially true if the peer parent groups are of the same cultural group and social/educational status. Transition team members may be included in peer parent groups to provide school-linked assistance and liaison support. Team members also can provide parent-focused transition workshops or programs. Turner (1996a) studied 30 parents and found that an in-service program increased parents' understanding of transition, of their role and its importance, their confidence in participating, and helped them to communicate and advocate during meetings.

Minority families may want to use school resources and support in learning about American culture and services. In this case, combinations of professional and family training could be developed that support cultural competence for both professionals and parents (Correa, 1989). Including family members as part of the organization's training plans demonstrates the school's commitment to collaboration and respect of parents' input. Family members could serve as individual cultural guides, serve on professional development planning groups, and ensure ongoing feedback between parents and professionals of a quality that builds mutual trust and communication. The issues that arise during inclusive planning meetings would also help to develop strategies to be used schoolwide: for example, roles of parents and expectations from professionals, bicultural ways to signal disagreement and to negotiate mutually acceptable goals and practices, and so on could be clarified and addressed. This would establish

an exemplary model in which each member is valued for the skills and experiences they bring to the team and school.

WORKING WITH ALL FAMILIES: COMPETENCE WITH DIVERSITY AND DIFFERENCE

Parental Involvement in Planning Processes

This chapter has focused on issues related to culturally different students and families. However, the sensitivity and willingness to suspend cultural expectations, and the openness to value the contributions of each family member, regardless of how "different," are also the skills needed to be effective with *all* families. In fact, many parents of children in special education have experienced difficulties in IEP and transition processes. Research on family involvement indicates that parents are *not* very involved in IEP or transition planning meetings, or in making decisions, despite legislative mandates to the contrary, even for white, American families. Gilmore (1974) found that parent involvement in decision making was given a low priority rating by educators, and that parent involvement was considered to be desirable but *not very important.* Although there has been some improvement in the past three decades since P.L. 94-142 was enacted, professionals still often do not use suggested parent involvement practices to ensure active participation (Hilton & Henderson, 1993), nor do they consider parents as having equal weight in decision-making processes (Dinnebell & Rule, 1994; Lynch & Stein, 1982; McNair & Rusch, 1987; Pruitt & Wandry, 1998; Repetto, White, & Snauwaert, 1990; Tilson & Neubert, 1988).

Specific roles of parents often lack active or equal contributions. Turnbull & Morningstar (1993) found that parents were likely to participate only passively in IEP and other educational decision-making meetings. Gartner and Lipsky (1987) reviewed several studies and noted that many parents are minimally involved in providing information, making decisions, and advocating for their child's needs (cf. Lusthaus, Lusthaus, & Gibbs, 1981; Vaugh, Bos, Harrell, & Lasky, 1988). Vaughn et al. (1988) studied interactions within meetings, characterizing such conferences as one of decision *telling* rather than decision *making.* Dunst (2002) compared the use of family-centered practices used by professionals and found there was less evidence of these practices at secondary levels, than at early intervention, preschool, or elementary programs. Combined with other studies he concluded that "secondary school practices are generally not at all family-centered" (p. 144).

Minimal IEP participation is even more pronounced for ethnically diverse parents, as we described earlier. School personnel who limit the information and choices presented to parents (because parents are judged as "uncaring" or "incapable" [Lynch & Stein, 1987; Mehan et al., 1986]) are ensuring that parental participation is minimized. Harry's (1992a) review of studies found overall that minority parents were less involved and less informed, and parents felt that the professionals implicitly or explicitly discouraged their participation. The following is an example of transition planning that is unsuccessful. Read the case study and identify what you believe went wrong.

In the case study just presented, much of the difficulty occurred because professionals did not listen and take enough time to probe and examine the issue from a more *understanding perspective*. Teachers and school personnel often frame problems as caused by students and parents. A more caring and sensitive approach would have led to more investigation and thus, more information about the problem with the gloves. Also, the teacher's observation of Maia's interest in gardening could have provided an alternative career path that

CASE STUDY Maia

Transition Planning Gone Wrong

Maia's transition team had not been able to determine a clear career path for her but observed that she was very neat. Based on this, at her 10th grade IEP meeting the team and family agreed to enroll Maia in janitorial coursework that next fall, leading to a part-time community position with additional coursework in the spring. A few weeks into the fall Maia was reported for attendance problems; in fact, the vocational teacher reported that she was absent each of the past Tuesdays. This was the day the class worked as a "crew" to clean rooms and buildings in the community. Maia always brought a note from home stating that she was sick. The teacher called the mother to ask, but the mother also stated that Maia was sick on those days.

On the next Tuesday absence, the teacher arranged for a home visit after the parents returned from work. She was surprised to find Maia working outdoors in the family garden. The mother and father both said that Maia had been sick that day, but felt better and enjoyed working in their garden. The teacher tried to explain the importance of Maia's attendance and asked if Maia was upset about something that was making her "sick." Her mother replied that Maia's hands bothered her and hurt, but the teacher asked how this could be true if she were working in the garden now. The teacher asked Maia about missing class but she also said that her hands hurt. The teacher remembered that Maia disliked wearing gloves when using cleaning chemicals. The teacher said this was very important and that if Maia did this then her hands would not hurt.

Maia continued to miss on Tuesdays. The teacher made several phone calls home but the pattern did not change and the teacher began to give up. Maia was unable to join the community work program in the spring but took another vocational class. At the spring IEP meeting the team became quite adamant about the attendance issue and wrote a specific goal. The parents said little but agreed that attendance was important. Maia repeated the class but continued to miss on community days, and occasionally on other days. Finally, the teacher reported the truancy problem to the principal. The IEP team informally decided that the parents would have to deal with Maia's problem on their own.

Problem Maia was having a bad skin reaction to the gloves she was told to wear. The teacher made some attempts to resolve the problem with the home visit, but assumed it was a compliance issue and didn't assume a more understanding perspective and listen for alternative explanations. In fact, the teacher had seen Maia's cracked and red hands but had assumed it was because she was not wearing the gloves. The parents acted in a protective manner of their daughter; when initial explanations were not listened to, they were not comfortable taking a more confrontational stance. This situation was not resolved and resulted in a negative school response (reporting the parents) and withholding transition assistance.

her family was well aware of (but it hadn't shown up on school-based interest assessments). In fact, Maia's "neatness" and cleanliness did not extend to the use of chemicals so that the janitorial path may not have been appropriate. A few cultural differences further aggravated this situation: parental respect for teachers, suppressing disagreements with teachers/authority figures, solving conflicts with authority within the family or community, and ensuring safety of family members as a priority. Yet not all of these traits are culturally bound: many white Americans will have great respect for authority figures or those who are better educated. Think of a concern you have had with a doctor or dentist and how you responded—we tend to respect their opinion over ours, and we suppress disagreements because we believe we are more likely than they are to be wrong. For many families, team members are well-educated professionals—this shows why the team must be careful with the "power" of words and actions.

Earlier, this chapter described professionals as consisting predominantly of white, middle- and upper-middle class females with advanced degrees. Regardless of individual ethnicities, degrees and income also set team members apart from many families. Economic class has also been found to have its own set of values and beliefs—another set of differences to which we must be sensitive (Banks, 2001). In fact, sensitivity to diversity is quite broad: to local cultural groups, to gender and sexual orientation, and to the many ways that families and children are unique. And these all impact how families envision their children's futures—the core of transition planning. For example, in Ohio and Pennsylvania there are several active communities of Amish and Mennonite people. Their children with special needs often are enrolled in public education; but because they typically leave school before middle school, their futures do not fit into a typical "vision" of what is possible.

Family Contributions to Transition Planning

Research has shown that, in general, parents of students in special education are not well-included in IEP and transition meetings. But how important is their involvement? Kohler (1993) examined the contributions of parents and families to transition outcomes and found that although multiple studies implied that parent involvement was important, there was much less implementation of this involvement. Schalock et al. (1986) found that when families were moderately to highly involved with their children's programs, the

children were more successful on employment-related outcome variables. Hudson et al. (1988) found that of 40 successfully employed young adults between 19 and 25, 94% of the subjects felt that family support (with friends, school program and staff support) was important in completing their education. In addition, 90% felt that family support was an important personal resource for their successful transition. Heal et al. (1990b) studied factors discriminating between successful and unsuccessful employment and found that home support was one of several significant factors. Halpern, Doren, and Benz (1993) reported on a three-year follow-along study showing that most students found jobs either on their own or with the help of family or friends. Informal supports were more important than the program supports for this key employment outcome. Morningstar, Turnbull, and Turnbull (1995) studied transition outcomes and found that the students' families highly influenced and shaped their career goals.

So, in fact, the research shows that parental involvement is very important to successful transition outcomes. Because IDEA 2004 requires documentation of transition results, it is increasingly important to involve parents positively in supporting and contributing to transition outcomes. Also, clearly there is much room for improvement in significantly involving families with disabilities, regardless of their ethnicity. Are there other concerns that make this involvement difficult for families? An important issue is family resources and meeting time. For example, not all families have cars for transportation, or have work schedules that can accommodate meeting times during typical school hours and schedules (Brame, 1995). Lynch and Stein (1987) also found that 54% were unable to attend their last school meeting because of work, time, transportation, or child-care conflicts. Although these were minority families, lower-income and rural families also face many of these same problems. Teams may want to consider holding meetings in the family's home and in the evenings or weekends to show their commitment to the family and supporting their involvement (Brame, 1995; Lynch & Stein, 1987). Such an arrangement would need to be appropriate for the family's values and comfort level.

Combining the research described above with information on cultural practices means that each team member needs to be sure to interact and to communicate appropriately with all families and students. Transition planning is so very critical, and also potentially conflictual, because unique groups and individuals define adult success so differently. The team must begin by carefully listening to and understanding how to work best with the family to provide services to the student, based upon his or her needs, preferences, and interests, and the family's dream.

The use and choice of assessments for transition planning can be confusing or offensive. Terminology or areas of assessment may not be clear to families, or they may not feel the test is a valid or realistic measure of their child's actual performance. It is important for the team to collect multiple assessments across several environments or settings, and to include families by using rating scales, interviews, and survey instruments. Many of the assessments are individual-based, and the rationale and types of results need to be explained in culturally relevant ways. If conflict or disagreements arise over the type or outcome of these instruments, incorporating activities and assessments completed jointly with the family and community members will help ensure balanced data collection as well as important contributions of the family. The team will want to avoid placing the student in a situation where they are engaging in activities that could create difficulties or conflicts, and be sure to give the family's perspectives at least equal deference.

Transition team members typically rely upon a variety of assessment processes to identify transition strengths, needs, interests, and preferences. Design of tests that are culturally neutral has been extremely challenging and difficult, with accurate and culturally fair testing difficulties still unresolved (cf. Markowitz, 1996; Reschly, 1997; Russo & Talbert-Johnson, 1997; U.S. Department of Education, 1987, 1994, 1997). Transition team members must be very cautious about the accuracy and interpretation of these tests when making decisions about appropriate futures for culturally and linguistically different students. Assessment items may need to be modified both when presenting the item (the stimulus) and with the required responses from the student. Culturally appropriate interaction styles can greatly impact on how well children understand directions for each task and their ability to respond to specified testing protocol. Table 3–5 provides suggestions that may be helpful to the transition team in addressing these issues (Keitel, Kopala, & Adamson, 1996; van Keulen et al., 1998).

TABLE 3–5 Suggestions for modifying assessments with culturally different students

Modification of the item stimulus

1. Repeat the instructions using different words, repeat them more often than recommended, or use sign language.
2. Change the pronunciation of words to reflect the child's culture.
3. Use different pictures when getting unexpected responses; use more culturally appropriate pictures as needed.
4. Modify item wording, probe for related responses, and include additional items to give the student every opportunity to respond.
5. Allow the parents or a trusted adult to administer test items.
6. Administer only a portion of the test; complete the testing in several sessions.

Modification of the item response requirements

1. Allow more time than recommended by the test.
2. Accept responses that are different from allowable responses but that are appropriate for the child's language or culture.
3. Allow the student to change responses.
4. Allow the student to clarify responses and ask questions.
5. Allow the student to respond using sign language, a foreign language, or a gesture.

Scoring

1. When altering a standardized test in any way, this must be described in the report and with the results of the testing; be certain to include this.
2. Do not use the modified results to present normed scores, percentiles, or grade equivalents; changes in assessment procedures always impact normed scoring procedures.
3. Use the modified results to explain your findings and results in terms of the student's abilities; this may have helped you to learn that the student possesses certain skills or knowledge that were masked by cultural differences, and explain how these modifications helped you to learn these things.

Source: Adapted from Keitel, M. A., Kopala, M., & Adamson, W. S. (1996). Ethical issues in multicultural assessment. In Suzuki, L. A., Miller, P. J., & Ponterotto, J. G. (Eds.). *Handbook of multicultural assessment* (pp. 29–48) San Francisco: Jossey-Bass; and van Keulen, J. E., Weddington, G. T., & Du Bose, C. E. (1998). *Speech, language, learning and the African–American child.* Boston: Allyn & Bacon, pp. 123–125.

SUPPORTING PARTICIPATION IN TRANSITION

Supporting Student Participation

This chapter has focused so far on family issues and encouraging their participation and collaboration in IEP and transition meetings. But in our culture, students will be expected to be effective self-advocates as they assume adult roles. IDEA requires that transition teams focus their plans on the student's individual needs, strengths, interests, and preferences. In culturally different families, the focus on the student can be seen as undermining and insensitive to their own social and family order. Students may feel highly supported by, and comfortable with, their culture and community resulting in personal interests and preferences that align closely with what their family prefers.

It can be quite difficult if team members strongly disagree with these perceptions, and if only one definition of "individualized" is allowed. For example, Mason, Field, and Sawilowsky (2004) found that school professionals rated the importance of self-determination skills at 100%; however, the article did not address the cultural issues that this creates. Parents are often critical to successful transition outcomes and essentially, the family's involvement is lifelong. Most young adults require some, if not extensive, cooperation from their family and community to complete the process of becoming successful adults, long after the transition team has relinquished its responsibility. Negotiating a mutually acceptable goal that focuses on areas of shared concern remains an important strategy.

An interesting finding regarding student participation in transition meetings was that student participation was rated as improving the clarity of purpose and interactions of parents and professional team members (Martin, Marshall, & Sale, 2004). However, the students themselves rated their own understanding of the meeting's purpose, role, comfort, and other key aspects as the lowest of the key meeting stakeholders. The authors conclude that meaningful student participation is still difficult.

Teams may face conflict when a student expresses preferences that do not align so closely with those of the family, or wishes to take a more active role in meetings than the family desires. Sometimes these differences can be negotiated on a step-by-step approximation process that allows all team and family members (including the student) to feel comfortable with the new preference. Groups with strong community interpersonal networks, cultural or otherwise, may want students to work and live within this community. The team may be able to negotiate for trial work in a similar position inside the community, and then move to a position outside but near the community. Both the family and student can use this to learn about how comfortable they are, or are not, with this situation. It also is typical of adolescents to require a number of trial learning experiences before being able to make realistic decisions about their future; therefore everyone benefits (and the student gains experience and time regarding the "fit" of this decision).

At no point should the team put the student in a position that would increase family conflict, or support the student's acculturation in a way that leads to discord. Again, planning changes through a series of steps that the family, student, and team can agree upon, can be used to evaluate everyone's comfort level with specific paths toward adulthood. The team certainly wants to avoid being in a position of mediating an escalating conflict between a highly "Americanized" student and culturally traditional family members. Although United States culture views some degree of teenager/parent conflict as typical, the team would be wise to use its cultural skills to avoid additional pitfalls resulting from bicultural and acculturation issues.

Supporting Family Participation

Although the student is the identified focus of the IEP and transition plans, it is through parental support that many of these plans become successful. A key role of parents is in acting as the legal protectors of their minor children; thus, P.L. 94-142 provided tremendous rights to children, through their parents. Communication of these rights can be complicated. Many states have developed brochures and packets to ensure families receive standardized and thorough information. Yet clearly, if parents are not fluent in English and there are no translated versions, written materials are of no help. In addition, many of the rights and responsibilities carry embedded middle-class values and processes (including due process, equal opportunity, etc.) that may not be understood if not communicated in culturally appropriate ways. Lower income groups and social classes may not feel these rights are accessible to them because they lack critical financial, legal, and educational resources. Some groups may not subscribe to inherent and assumed beliefs within these rights. For example, the Amish do not recognize the U.S. government; therefore, providing them with meaningful information about their rights is quite complicated.

For many families, sharing critical information about these rights, about school processes, and about perceptions of their child may require personal contact, and a period of time that begins with "visiting" and getting to know each other. Team members should be sensitive to cultural or interpersonal dissonances: When communication appears to break down or expectations are widely discrepant, they should stop the meeting process to begin ascertaining, in culturally appropriate ways, the nature and extent of the possible potential cultural conflicts. This process is much slower and less "efficient" than typical American information sharing, but is the best way to ensure that families understand their rights, the referral-diagnosis-placement process, and program and placement options. The team needs to begin with what the family currently understands about these issues, relative to their values and beliefs.

Participatory Transition Planning

One of the most important aspects of collaborative planning is to begin with shared goals and values (Friend & Cook, 1990; Friend & Bursuck, 2006). A good place to start is with how the family defines their child's ultimate adult outcomes. This may lead to a discussion of related beliefs and values regarding the student. Again, soliciting family input should be done in a culturally- and family-supportive manner rather than the typically "direct" and *efficient* American or "medical model" style. Because team members are successful, degreed (and acculturated) individuals, they will probably feel uneasy departing from typical school and professional (American) practices. The family's response may be difficult to gauge as well. As trust and comfort develops between all members, the communication and negotiation processes will become increasingly easier.

Once the team has obtained a fairly comprehensive description of the family's vision, it can begin to suggest and then establish some mutually agreeable goals. This vision should include, as much as possible, if and where their child will work, live, and participate in leisure and recreational activities, and with whom. Some of these may be very different from the team's vision because of views of disability, gender, or family honor. Negotiations can begin by presenting a potential alternative that leads to a similar outcome, as a trial. The team may need to present a rationale in terms of its benefit to the child and family/community (i.e., from their cultural or

group perspectives) and why this is a good alternative (e.g., when the student goes to his or her job, the boss will typically expect skills that include . . .). Also, identify shared goals by agreeing on some initial steps rather than asking the family to support an entire program. Over time the family may see the benefits to themselves, their community, and their child that they at first had difficulty envisioning or resisted implementing. Developing consensus on aspects of a plan can lead to broader goal agreement later. In terms of equality, the same can be said about the team: they may need to try part of the family's vision and over time, come to understand how it best fits with the child's anticipated future.

When describing a vision of adulthood, the team must guard against a temptation to present only one, optimal "American" set of outcomes as the transition program, or to limit options presented to families, especially if the family is believed to be struggling. This can be particularly challenging with cultures that have difficulty expressing their goals (long-term planning is not an activity valued by all cultures [Lewis, 1997]) or are reticent in discussing these topics. Families may not be comfortable or able to express this directly to team members, but also may be very accepting of this ambiguity (not typical of American values). They may see attempts at decisiveness as being pushy and overbearing (when the team attempts to resolve discomfort with ambiguity), which then further reduces their willingness to participate in decision making.

Another aspect of vision that is impacted by culture and socioeconomic status is the choice and availability of assistive technologies (AT). Although these devices have opened many new opportunities for students with disabilities, families may perceive them very differently (Parette, Huer, & Scherer, 2004). Those of lower socioeconomic status (SES) may have had far fewer experiences with technology in general, and regard these devices much differently than the team. Family is very important to supporting ongoing use and maintenance, so supporting family preferences for device choice, use, and repair/maintenance is extremely important. Teams may not realize that repair can involve time off work, transportation, child care, and other costs to families with often more significant impacts on culturally diverse and low-SES families (who may not have work benefits, or salaried vs. hourly positions). Cultural and class-based values may not be considered in typical, fact-based decision-making processes for determining AT choices (Parette et al., 2004). The recommendation of an AT professional may not be the solution that works for the family (and therefore, the team).

Creating visions, developing transition plans, and implementing these through school and agency programs all involve decision making. Typical IEP meetings assume that this all will be accomplished within an hour or so. However, some cultural and family groups need more time to make decisions, and may prefer to share meeting suggestions with their larger community group or decision makers who are not present. This can present a problem, particularly with some school administrators who prefer not to continue at a later time, or to end a meeting without a parental signature. This type of "American" pressure must be negotiated carefully—just one more reason why involving the entire school or agency can be very helpful.

Throughout interactions and meetings with them, it is important to let the family know how much their efforts with their child are valued. Sometimes their actions may be hidden or they do not feel it is appropriate to share them with "professionals." This is also where our stereotyped "expectations" can serve as barriers—very poor and challenged families can contribute substantially toward their child's literacy and academic achievement (Harry & Klingner, 2006). The team must allow them the opportunity to utilize their abilities and resources to their best advantage. As with special needs children, significant "challenges" that families face can lead to lower expectations instead of seeking the positive and supporting the optimal.

Strategies to Support Cultural and Diverse Competencies

A number of planning and professional practices have been suggested to support effective partnerships with parents. Dunst (2002) identified family-centered practices as consisting of both relational and participatory components (cf. Dunst & Trivette, 1996). Relationship components consist of:

a. clinical skills: active listening, compassion, empathy, respect, nonjudgmental responses; and
b. professional beliefs and attitudes: positive beliefs in capabilities and competencies of families.

Participatory skills include practices that are:

a. individualized, flexible, and responsive to family concerns and priorities; and

b. provide opportunities for families to be actively involved in choices and decisions, and collaboration that achieves desired goals.

Truly effective professionals need to combine both sets of skills. In addition, implementing these components through knowledge of cultural and individual diversity will further eliminate interaction barriers and maximize meaningful family involvement.

Many transition meetings adhere to rigid time and agenda schedules that are not amenable to rich and meaningful interaction. Instead, person-centered planning presents a meeting-based strategy for IEP and transition planning in a way that ensures a person and family focus (Callicott, 2003). It uses a creative process as a way to integrate divergent voices, and includes persons most important to the individual or family (not only professional personnel). These may be used to replace or augment IEP meetings—again, schoolwide acceptance of this practice is very helpful.

Harry (2002, p. 136) identified six principles for providing appropriate services to families who are different because of culture or socioeconomic status. These principles can be applied to transition planning as follows:

1. addressing differences in definitions and interpretations of disability;
2. accepting differences in family coping styles and responses to disability-related stress;
3. accommodating differences in parental interaction styles, and expectations for participation and advocacy;
4. accommodating and equalizing differential access to information and services;
5. preventing and addressing negative professional attitudes to, and perceptions of, families' roles in educational processes; and
6. overcoming dissonances in the fit of educational and transition programs.

These six principles summarize much of the content of this chapter. It is important to focus on the family's understandings and beliefs in order to learn about or verify their perceptions. These understandings can be used to identify shared goals and values. This, then, can form the basis for developing a trusting relationship in which all team members are valued for their contributions—the start for collaborative family-professional planning and partnering.

CONCLUSION

The cultural understandings described in this chapter impact cross-cultural relationships that go far beyond transition and IEP planning meetings. In fact, the need for cultural and diversity competence impacts all aspects of family and student interactions. Every conversation with the child or their parents, every note, telephone call, written report, and meeting convey beliefs and opinions, many of which unintentionally convey culturally- and professionally-based expectations. In fact, many of our assumptions about children's learning also are culturally based. Many classroom instructional tasks and transition activities expect analytical and cause-and-effect thinking. This is quite different from cultures that value global and holistic perspectives and thinking processes (Dunn & Griggs, 1995). The classroom routine and structure, the nature of visual or auditory cues, physical contact, disciplinary procedures and presumed student responsibilities may be quite different from those within their own culture or background (Winzer & Mazurek, 1998).

The steps toward becoming culturally competent are gradual, and require time as well as perseverance. Team members must learn to recognize the power of their own cultural beliefs and values, and to understand the ways in which these differ from the families with whom they work. These differences frequently include race, educational level, economic status, and social class. The process of learning about culture and diversity requires being flexible and having a willingness to abandon previous ways of thinking. Most importantly, it is allowing oneself to have one's beliefs challenged through interacting with those who are different, by visiting their communities, and by reading and studying about these differences. Although most people are likely to feel awkward at first, communicating positive intentions and asking for suggestions can smooth the path toward family trust, and help people to become increasingly comfortable and effective.

Skills in cross-cultural and diverse interactions will become increasingly important with the continuing immigration and changing demographics of the United States. Many families will not have high levels of English or educational skills, nor the cultural competence or training to interact effectively with American institutions. The unique adult-focused and outcome-oriented nature of transition planning, with its requirements for participatory decision making, creates situations that can lead to substantial cultural barriers and conflicts between families and transition team members. The current lack of cross-cultural diversity and family-centered expertise in many schools and agencies makes the skills we acquire even more valuable. It is an ongoing professional challenge to effectively elicit information from those who are culturally, ethnically, socially, and economically different—their customary interaction patterns, or our perceived higher "status" often make open communication difficult. The team must seek ways and understandings that lead to shared goals and outcomes that will focus the full team on positive results, and allow all to work together.

This chapter has provided a starting point in terms of information and insights for improving cross-cultural transition planning and team interactions. This is a time of opportunity and change, with U.S. public services becoming more willing to recognize culture and diversity as areas of professional need. Readers of this book may become one of the few members of their workplace with a background in cultural and family-centered competence. Those who continue to develop their competence can play an important role in seeing that all members of the transition planning team, and the workplace, have the necessary knowledge and skills to provide high-quality and effective services.

STUDY QUESTIONS

1. What are the reasons and processes that lead to overrepresentation of minority students in special education programs? From your experience in schools and agencies, what could you do as an individual that would help to correct these patterns?
2. What are the major differences among white, middle-, and upper-middle-class values and minority group beliefs and values in the areas of identity, disability, and relationships? What are your beliefs and values, and how closely do they align with some of these cultural values?
3. How can team processes accommodate culturally different or diverse families in terms of (a) determining student needs and preferences, (b) setting goals, (c) determining appropriate outcome-oriented processes, and (d) in moving from school to postschool activities? Where would you start and how would you proceed if you began to sense a difference in values in these areas?

Asian Pacific Americans represent one of the largest current groups of immigrant peoples in the United States (Chan, 1998a, 1998b). Examine your cultural competence by planning how you would work with these two students and their families. Use Table 3–4 as a start.

Case Study

Tru Lang is a 15-year-old Vietnamese student who has a visual impairment and mild/moderate developmental delays. He once showed you a scar on his chest that he said was from a camp. You know that as a child he spent some time in a war orphans camp separated from his parents and had moved to the United States to stay with an uncle. He was reunited with his parents and siblings when they were able to leave Vietnam a few years later. He is very outgoing and animated, with strong vocational interests in working outdoors. He seems very interested in being like other American teenagers. You know little about his family at this point but believe that his uncle and aunt lived here for several years before Tru joined them and may be important acculturating factors and bicultural interpreters for the family.

Case Study

Crystal is a 17-year-old Cambodian girl who lives with her family, which includes an older sister. She has developmental disabilities and had little or no language until she entered school here at age 11. You know little about the family and they have not shared much in past interactions or in school records. You have been told that her "parents" are really her aunt and uncle although it is her real sister. She and her sister were able to escape but you believe that her real parents were killed. You do not know whether or not she and her sister witnessed this. Crystal, like her family, expresses little about herself or her activities. Although her name is Americanized, she does not seem to have strong desires to act like other American teenagers. She does not have strong friendships with the other students (girls or boys) and does not talk much about the TV shows she watches. Only occasionally have you seen her express strong anger, which surprised you, perhaps as the result of someone doing something culturally offensive to her. Crystal has done job shadowing and trial work experiences across the major occupational categories, but it has been difficult for you and the other team members to get a strong sense of any of her preferences. She is a very compliant and pleasant student to work with in other ways; however, it is becoming important for her to make a vocational choice soon.

4. A family does not speak during the annual IEP meeting and does not respond (as expected) to direct questions from team members. What are (a) some of the cultural or diversity-related reasons that this family might not do so, and (b) how would you approach the family to support their greater participation in a future meeting?

5. One of the interagency members of your transition team has a very directive approach that you believe is causing the family to withdraw emotionally from the team. This agency member has informed you that the family is poor, a minority, and, from what the agency member perceives, uncaring and uninterested. You disagree with this conclusion. How would you try to keep the communication open with this person and then further engage him or her in considering some less judgmental conclusions?

6. Your principal/supervisor has asked you to help plan a program to increase diverse and culturally-sensitive interactions and planning within your school/agency. How would you begin such a program, whom would you include in the planning process, and what would be your specific outcomes of this training? What would you try to accomplish in the short term versus the long term?

WEBSITES

The Center for Research on Developmental Education and Urban Literacy
  www.gen.umn.edu/research/crdeul
Council for Exceptional Children:
  http://www.cec.sped.org
Division for Culturally and Linguistic Diverse Exceptional Learners

Standing Committee on Ethnic and Multicultural Concerns Council of the Great City Schools
  www.cgcs.org
The Center for Research on Education, Diversity, and Excellence (CREDE)
  www.cal.org/crede
Intercultural Email Classroom Connections: (IECC)
  www.stolaf.edu/network/iecc

CHAPTER 4

CAREER DEVELOPMENT THEORIES FOR TRANSITION PLANNING

Pamela Luft

LEARNING OBJECTIVES

The objectives for this chapter are:

1. Describe how lifelong perspectives of career development contribute to comprehensive transition planning.

2. Describe at least two ways in which a disability can negatively impact career development processes and outcomes.

3. Identify differences between the four major categories of individual-focused and interaction-focused career development theories views of: (a) the worker, and (b) the work environment in contributing to achieving career success.

4. Describe how the four stages of career development can be used to integrate career development and transition planning across existing career theories.

INTRODUCTION

Faced with turning everyday teenagers into successful adults, teachers and other team members take on a rather daunting task. So how does knowing about theories of career development help them accomplish this? In many ways, a good theory is like a map; it helps focus selecting a path to reach a goal (Krumboltz, 1996). But, there are many types of maps. For example, a road map is different from an elevation map or a map of natural resources. Although each type of map is valid for a specific purpose, team members must be sure that their purpose matches that of the map.

Like a map, a theory oversimplifies certain aspects of reality by focusing in on critical aspects—highways, rivers, and so on—with regard to a specific task. Career development is a very complex process; therefore, career development theories also focus on a set of specific beliefs or relationships that they identify as being most important to a person's career success (Krumboltz, 1996; Patton & McMahon, 1999). Each creates a "map" of how to achieve this success. Members of the IEP team need to be sure that the entire team accepts these theoretical beliefs—so no one is looking at natural (or personal) resources when the student and the team are really trying to find the nearest career highway!

Another similarity between theories and maps is that both assume that the characteristics and features they identify are stable and unchanging. In terms of career theory, globalization is leading to rapid changes in work relationships and duties, requiring modern workers to do more of "what needs to be done" rather than following a strict job description (Krumboltz, 1996). The nature of the workforce is changing as well, with portions of jobs that are outsourced or moved between individuals or subcontractors. Modern career theories must account for much more fluid "work" situations if they hope to accurately describe the experiences of today's workers. Many older theories assume a "universal" model of workers' lives and experiences—one set of "factors" or "events" fits all (Holland, 1996). Theories that approach work and the worker with assumptions of "stability" may not be appropriate to new and evolving careers and work conditions, or to the growing diversity of workers and the importance of race/ethnicity or gender in workers' lives (Arbona, 1996; Patton & McMahon, 1999).

Many of these older theories remain very popular and widely used. Knowing how and when they may be useful will help the IEP team make wise planning decisions. This chapter describes a number of these commonly used theories and their related materials, and some of the newer and emerging frameworks, as well. Several of the older theories have developed well-known assessment instruments and curriculum materials, some of which may be widely used within the team's school system. This information will be part of the discussions in Chapters 5 and 6 as the IEP team must choose assessment and curriculum materials. Understanding of the theoretical assumptions (remember, each theory must oversimplify in order to organize the complexity of career development) will help in choosing and using these materials effectively, as the reader continues through the transition planning process in these later chapters.

IN THE BEGINNING: SETTING THE STAGE FOR THEORY CHOICE

Here is a question to think about: If a room full of successful people were asked if they had been fired from their first job (usually as teenagers), often a surprising number of hands are raised. So is this career development gone wrong? Are these people unusual because although they failed, they later become successful? And what about students with disabilities—what if they "fail" at an initial job? If this is a job that the IEP team has identified and developed specific training and experiences to support, what does this "firing" mean in terms of the student's career and transition plan? Thinking of these questions when reading through the chapter, the reader will find some of the key contrasts between theories.

The past several decades of career development research has strengthened the belief that career development is a lifetime process of growth and experiences, both positive and negative, which results in some type of work—and that this specific type of work may change over the person's life (Beveridge, Craddock, Liesener, Stapleton, & Hershenson, 2002; Sitlington, Clark, & Kolstoe, 2000; Super, 1990). This perspective has important implications for the IEP and transition team, for although the team is responsible for school-based career and transition planning, the broader aspects of career development go far beyond school-based learning.

This perspective defines an individual's career development as a lifetime process that encompasses the growth and change process of childhood, the formal career education in school, and the maturational processes that continue throughout a person's working adulthood and into retirement (Brown & Brooks, 1984; Clark & Kolstoe, 1995; Hoyt, 1977; Sitlington, Clark, & Kolstoe, 2000; Super, 1990). This broader perspective includes the many life and transition-related decisions that impact a career, such as marriage, children, community and leisure activities, and so on. The team's view of career development should address choices that respond to changing development and needs, and include influences from other life roles and responsibilities and ultimately, lead to a satisfactory quality of life.

Using this broad theoretical perspective will impact how the team defines quality of life and work in developing transition plans and postschool outcome statements with the student. The team should be cautious with theories that focus narrowly on a single career choice that occurs during young adulthood and also assume that individuals will remain in that career field throughout their work-life (Brown, 1996; Hershenson & zymanski, 1992). Globalization and patterns of multiple job change no longer support one single, career-defining, decision point.

A lifelong career perspective is helpful to students with disabilities because they may need additional time or planned opportunities and experiences in order to fully develop, express, and refine their career and life interests (Clark & Kolstoe, 1995; Hershenson & Szymanski, 1992, Szymanski & Hershenson, 1998). Students may need supplementary information or experiences to help them make choices and to learn about their needs, preferences, and abilities, which can then help them make a more empowered and self-determined career choice. This lifelong perspective allows multiple life experiences and influences that begin in childhood, to continue throughout the student's working years and beyond (Hershenson & Szymanski, 1992; Super, 1990). These experiences can support students and their families in developing more positive perspectives regarding their competence and identifying goals and options that are both realistic and favorable.

> **Critical Point**
> Viewing career development from a life-span perspective allows students with disabilities multiple opportunities and extended time lines to move into fulfilling life and employment roles.

The broad and lifelong process of career development is leading some of the older theories to expand their focus on factors that influence an individual (Chen, 2003; Patton & McMahon, 1999; Vondracek & Porfeli, 2002). For example, the family's, neighborhood's, and the community's beliefs about career and life goals are important factors that impact the student's decisions about career development and adult roles (Garcia, 2002; Hershenson & Szymanski, 1992; Wolffe, 1997). The school also transmits values about working, and evaluates the child's successes and failures in comparison to other children beginning in elementary school (cf. Erikson's Stage IV: Industry vs. Inferiority and Stage V: Identity vs. Role Diffusion; Erikson, 1968). These fundamental experiences with values, attitudes, habits, human relationships, and valuing oneself strongly influence the success of later career education programs and possible career choices (Clark & Kolstoe, 1995). The lifelong and broader theories are more sensitive to addressing these early influences in terms of current team planning.

An important consideration for the team is that only a few theories have been developed to specifically include the experiences of individuals with disabilities (Conte, 1983; Curnow, 1989; Szymanski et al., 1996; Wolffe, 1997). Several older theories have attempted to add ways to incorporate specific needs of diverse ethnic and racial groups and the importance of race in their life experiences (Arbona, 1996). Newer theories often incorporate a wide range of factors that impact individuals from their inception, in order to be inclusive of all experiences and influences, including those due to disability, race and ethnicity, gender, socioeconomic status, and so on. The team should remain sensitive to whether or not the students' and family's experiences are represented within the assumptions of the theories and related materials they choose. Depending upon the needs and preferences of the student, their experiences with disability and as members of diverse groups, their family and social circumstances, a particular theory may not match well and as a result, the related instruments and interventions will not always be successful or helpful (Savickas, 1996).

> **Critical Point**
> Career development theory is an important element in supporting the team's definition of comprehensive transition planning and successful compliance with these requirements.

CAREER EXPERIENCES FOR INDIVIDUALS WITH DISABILITIES

How does disability impact a person's perceptions and experiences of building a career? First of all, work is a highly valued activity in the American society. Not only does it provide economic support, but it also has a major impact on one's social status and self-image (Szymanski & Hershenson, 1998).

Unfortunately, people with disabilities often encounter obstacles to participation in the workforce. Although almost 80% of people with disabilities in the United States report a preference for working, approximately 76% were unemployed according to one report about 10 years ago (LaPlante, Kennedy, Kaye, & Wenger, 1997). More recently, Burkhauser and Stapleton (2003) commented on unprecedented decline in the employment of persons with disabilities, and noted that both men and women had substantially lower income growth than their counterparts without disabilities. From interviews in 2002, the number of workers who reported a disability aged 21 to 64 and held a job for the past year was 56% (U.S. Census Bureau, 2006), although people with severe disabilities had an employment rate of 42%. Employment rates for persons with nonsevere disabilities were 82% and those without a disability, 88%.

Hagner and colleagues (1996) point to several interrelated factors that contribute to the high unemployment rate among people with disabilities:

1. discrimination in employment and other aspects of life,
2. practical difficulties (e.g., transportation, nontraditional means of communication) that make it difficult to seek employment,
3. limited access to the "hidden job market" and those jobs not advertised by formal means, and
4. employer presumptions about the characteristics and abilities of qualified job applicants.

As one can see, the barriers just listed have no relation to demonstrating important job skills and abilities. Other factors create deterrents to continued working: physical and attitudinal barriers within the work site, health insurance issues (rejected coverage due to existing disabilities and possible medical conditions), and work disincentives inherent in the social security system (medical insurance is provided when one is *not* working in addition to basic subsistence support). These function as deterrents to career maintenance (strategies to keep and improve one's position) and the person's motivation to stay in the current job choice, especially when these workers encounter attitudinal or practical barriers at the job site. Transition teams often do not adequately identify these less obvious employment problems, and,

therefore, do not fully address the multiple aspects facing transitioning students in moving successfully into the world of work. Again, this emphasizes the broad perspective needed when planning for career development: work preparation does not end with acquiring job skills.

> **Critical Point**
> The use of a career development theory that helps the team to identify and address important career issues potentially improves employment outcomes.

Teams are likely to face a number of challenges in terms of the students' own school and work outcomes, many of which will be less positive than those of their peers. In a review of research on postschool outcomes, the National Longitudinal Study II (NLTS2) (Wagner et al., 2004) found that students with disabilities have many difficulties. They:

1. are more likely than their nondisabled peers to drop out of school;
2. experience difficulties in other areas of their lives such as independent living and relationship building;
3. are less likely than their nondisabled peers to participate in postsecondary educational programs;
4. receive low wages when they do obtain employment; and
5. experience higher rates of unemployment (for some disabilities) regardless of whether or not they graduate from high school.

The authors attribute these poor outcomes to a variety of factors that include the method of school leaving (lower rates of graduation), type of disability, special education placement, a low percentage of time spent in regular classrooms, limited vocational experiences, and lack of employment during high school. In addition, students with disabilities often have limited exposure to the variety of employment options available and, therefore, have restricted opportunities to develop generalizable work skills that could enhance their performance across a variety of jobs. Many studies, like the NLTS2 (Wagner et al., 2005), also identify the research on postschool outcomes that has "consistently supported the critical connection between high school employment and postschool employment" (Hanley-Maxwell, Szymanski, & Owens-Johnson, 1998, p. 152). Unfortunately, few high school students with disabilities have opportunities to work part-time or during the summers. The poor employment rates and barriers experienced by adult workers with disabilities suggest that finding part-time or summer work, even though a critical developmental experience, will be quite challenging for the IEP team.

The nature of a student's disability can affect the student's self-perceptions and career-related developmental experiences. Students with early onset disabilities may experience developmental barriers that result in potentially limited career experiences (Szymanski & Hershenson, 1998). Functional limitations may restrict the child's ability to participate in important activities that contribute information about life and work capabilities (e.g., play, chores, extracurricular activities, and after-school jobs). These experiences facilitate development of the student's occupational interests, career decision-making skills, work competencies, and a positive occupational self-concept (Conyers, Koch, & Szymanski, 1998). Limited experiences, in addition to low expectations of parents, teachers, service providers, and employers also can severely impede the development of a healthy self-concept and appropriate career aspirations. Ochs and Roessler (2001) tested 95 special education students and compared them with 99 general education students, finding that special education students were less confident about their career decision-making abilities, did not have clear and stable vocational identities, and were somewhat less optimistic about the outcomes of their career activities. These concerns can become major career development barriers for students with disabilities and their teams (Conyers, Szymanski, & Koch, 1998; Luft & Koch, 1998).

One optimistic note is the contribution made by adaptive technologies to increasing access and opportunities of individuals with disabilities. The team's knowledge of reasonable accommodations and newly developed and adaptive technologies can be used to greatly augment and improve what may have been the student's prior limited work-related learning experiences and career opportunities. These new opportunities need to be considered when viewing career theories and their instruments, as well (Szymanski & Hershenson, 1998). However, if the team is using normed and standardized assessment instruments, then changes to any of the procedures (such as allowing more time or providing certain prompts) or to instrument items (such as providing alternative and more familiar choices that are within the student's experience) will, of course, impact their interpretation.

Knowledge about successful and effective adaptive technologies, access to successful role models with disabilities in a career of interest, or contacts with community businesses who successfully employ workers with disabilities often is beyond the expertise of school-based IEP team members. Linkages with other agencies are essential for addressing the complexity of these career issues and in creating the necessary supports to ensure optimal program completion. For example, even though a team may have identified an excellent community-based work site, the student's group home staffing schedule may limit the hours and transportation during which the student can work. A student in an urban setting may begin living independently at age 16 or 17, but be too young to sign a lease, and soon learn that their SSI is insufficient to afford safe housing, thus placing them at risk for dropping out and getting full-time work.

Resolving these types of situations will require all of the resources of the team, as well as the agency and employment linkages they are able to make. Including these individuals, as well as employers, supervisors, co-workers and the family's support networks during school-based transition planning can greatly help the student and his or her family when it is time to leave school: they will still have a network of nonschool supports. These people can help with potential adult-based career development decisions and issues that arise, and can help adult agency personnel to provide continuous, high-quality services. This collaborative network is the key to ensuring maximum success as the student moves to postschool phases of his or her career development (Gajar, Goodman, & McAfee, 1993; Sitlington et al., 1997).

> **Critical Point**
> Adaptive technologies for increased access and networks of nonschool supports can empower the team to take advantage of opportunities and to deal with issues that overlap the school and adult career path.

These potential negative employment and schooling outcomes underscore the team's need to incorporate appropriate career development activities and curricula into the IEPs of students with disabilities. The Individuals with Disabilities Education Act (IDEA) 2004 requires outcome-oriented services including career and technical education and integrated employment. Appropriate career and technical education decisions, leading to sustained and satisfying employment are the culmination of successful career development and transition planning. It is important that these career planning decisions be based on a theory that utilizes the needs, strengths, interests, and preferences of the student, as well as their family's and life situation's realities.

The potential vastness of career development factors has resulted in multiple theories, each of which provides a unique description of the experiences, attitudes, values, and competencies that individuals need in order to choose and maintain a satisfying and optimal career path. The next sections describe important career planning stages and an overview of major theory categories to help the team with understanding these theories and ultimately, choosing appropriate assessments and curriculum to meet the student's transition planning goals.

EXAMINING TYPES OF CAREER THEORY

A variety of career development theories have been generated in the past 70 years and as a result, there is no universal or all-encompassing perspective for teams to use. Career development has alternately been described as the "lifelong process of getting ready to choose, choosing, and typically continuing to make choices from occupations available in our society" (Brown & Brooks, 1984, p. ix) and, more broadly, as "the total constellation of psychological, sociological, educational, physical, economic, and chance factors that combine to shape the career of any given individual over the life span" (Herr & Cramer, 1992, p. 27). As stated earlier, a broad and life-long definition is most supportive and inclusive of potentially unique life paths and diverse experiences of individuals with disabilities.

A broad definition of career development allows the transition team to examine all possible adult roles that a student may wish to undertake, and to include multiple factors and life situations in their transition plan development. The rationale is that life roles intersect and interact: What one does on the job, including time schedule and constraints, physical and mental energies expended, impacts how and when one assumes family roles, engages in recreation and leisure; and how the responses of family members, co-workers, and other key individuals and situational conditions further impact the individual in a reciprocal and interactive manner. This is the true nature of career and transition planning, organizing these multiple roles and settings in ways that support an optimal career plan and minimizes conflict between roles and settings.

Many of the career theories in this chapter have been adopted from career and vocational research done with people *without* disabilities. These theories bring insights about careers in general, but also can lead to difficulties, particularly in their lack of attention to the unique experiences and abilities of people with disabilities (Szymanski & Hershenson, 2005). Conte (1983) and Curnow (1989) found three factors that left existing career theories inapplicable to persons with disabilities: (a) limitations in early career exploration experiences, (b) limited opportunities to develop decision-making abilities, and (c) a negative self-concept resulting from societal attitudes toward persons with disabilities (Sitlington et al., 2000). Patton and McMahon (1999) reviewed a range of theories and stated that "conclusions within the literature generally agree that it remains inadequate and incomplete . . . and lacking in comprehensiveness and coherence . . . particularly in its failure to account for diversity within the population" (p. 5).

One reason for the lack of universality of career theories is a result of the variety of their originating disciplines: counseling, organizational psychology, sociology, and business, to name a few (Szymanski, Fernandez, Koch, & Merz, 1996). Several decades ago, theories were designed according to one of three perspectives: occupational choice, work adjustment, or career development. Szymanski and Hershenson define these three concepts as follows:

1. *occupational choice:* the process of choosing a specific job at one point in time through examination of personal and situational factors that lead to a satisfactory job choice;
2. *work adjustment:* an examination of conditions within both the worker and the work environment that support a good "match" and including adjustment to the work process itself, independent of the occupation in which it is performed; and
3. *career development:* examine lifelong work patterns and change, often examining the impact and interrelationships of multiple life roles with those of just being a worker, and the developmental processes of one's lifelong sequence of occupationally relevant choices and behaviors (Szymanski & Hershenson, 2005, p. 228).

From these definitions one can see that *occupational choice* assumes that a person will make one choice in early adulthood, and remain in that career across their lifetime. *Work adjustment* focuses on the work processes and tasks themselves and is slightly broader in its examination of related variables in a particular work setting, but assumes a match between person and these environmental variables. *Career development* is the broadest in viewing multiple work and life factors.

Career development is a lifelong process.

These three perspectives have evolved with time. For example, until the last two decades or so, career counselors believed that young adults made one occupational choice prior to entering the workforce, which remained intact and unchanged throughout their lifetime. More recent studies of adult work patterns show that workers make multiple job changes during their work career, and this trend continues to grow. The Bureau of Labor Statistics (1992) reported that an employee typically remains with a particular employer for a median of 4.5 years. This has now increased to 10 jobs, held between the ages of 18 to 38 (Bureau of Labor Statistics, 2004). Globalization and changing workforce patterns have only increased the challenges that modern workers face (Herr, 1996).

> **Critical Point**
> The three concepts of career development are about choosing the "right" career, adapting to a specific job, or developing multiple work and life roles.

These three perspectives and their related theories have continued to be used and modified to accommodate differences in lifestyles, work, and social conditions. Theories of *occupational choice* now allow this choice to occur at various times during a person's working life. *Work adjustment* theories also may be applied at multiple points in the person's life when a new career decision is imminent. *Career development* theories have worked to ensure inclusion of diverse populations of workers, including those with disabilities, and have also addressed areas of growth and change that occur throughout adulthood.

Theories can be categorized in a number of ways. One perspective is to examine how each views the individual: Is the *individual* seen as the primary actor and decision maker to study (individual-focused theories) or is the *interaction* between the individual, other persons, events, and environments seen as the primary dynamic for study (interaction-focused theories) (Herr, 1996; Krumboltz, 1996)? Many of the older theories have been used and tested for several decades; they have both data-based results with assessment instruments and intervention activities that practitioners can use for transition planning. Yet, many of these also have an individual-focus, partially because older statistical methods were unable to integrate multiple factors and variables (Vondracek & Porfeli, 2002). Newer theories often have less data on their usage and outcomes, and are less likely to have developed assessment instruments and curricula. Yet, these theories attempt to be more descriptive about a comprehensive array of factors, events, and circumstances that impact career development. As a result, they also are more inclusive of unique experiences based on disability, diversity, gender, family status, and so on. Typically, they present a broad array of these factors for practitioners to work among, rather than a limited set of factors to focus on and "match." The breadth of newer theories, therefore, adds to their complexity for practioners. This next section reviews a sample of both types of theories.

> **Critical Point**
> Individuals with disabilities should have the same opportunities to change jobs and careers that individuals without disabilities have.

> **Critical Point**
> Each career development theory views the individual, the environment, and critical factors differently. "Successful" career development is also defined uniquely.

EXAMINING FOR FIT: A SELECTION OF CAREER DEVELOPMENT THEORIES

What follows is a description of commonly-used individual-focused theories across four different categories (structural, developmental, **work adjustment,** and learning theories) and one interaction-focused theory. The four individual-focused theories were identified as major types originally by Osipow's review in 1990 and they remain as examples of these theories today (Brown, 2002; Szymanski & Hershenson, 2005). The

CASE STUDY   Miguel

Miguel is a physically active, 18-year-old male who enjoys sports. He has a moderate cognitive delay and his teacher suspects he had some ADHD (which has not been diagnosed) because he is highly distractible (noise, bright colors, movement, or activity by others) with a short attention span (5–10 minutes is the usual maximum). He communicates best nonverbally with strangers using appropriate gestures and vocal approximations, although he has approximately 50 spoken words that are understood by family and friends. He has a communication book but frequently forgets to use this. He tends to be easily angered and frustrated when he is not understood. Miguel can be physically aggressive at times, although he is small and thin for his age with a low tolerance for lifting or strength-based activities. He has expressed strong interests in working in an autobody shop and is involved with activities with his family that support this interest (washing cars, observing others doing informal car repair, helping to bring tools).

How would one describe Miguel's career development in terms of the three major perspectives? What might be important relative to ensuring a good choice of career? What might be some issues that he might face in adjusting to specific work environments? What might contribute to his overall growth and maturity in the career domain?

CASE STUDY   Aza

Aza is a 15-year-old-female who has just entered high school. She has a mild to moderate cognitive delay with moderate vision loss and moderate/severe bilateral hearing loss. She wears glasses but needs nonglare lighting and high-contrast work papers. Her hearing aids frequently bother her (she complains of headaches) but when she takes them out, she hears very few environmental sounds and no speech. She has a spoken functional vocabulary that is adequate for simple tasks and does not use sign language. Aza has not had any work exposure, partly because the prior principal believed she would be a safety hazard. Her parents have not asked her to do many chores up to this point although they recognize that she should start fairly soon. Given her disabilities they are not sure how to teach her to do these things.

How would one describe Aza's career development in terms of the three major perspectives? What might be important relative to ensuring a good choice of career? What might be some issues that she might face in adjusting to specific work environments? What might contribute to her overall growth and maturity in the career domain?

chapter will describe each theory and end with a summary of their perspective on the student and work environment, and a list of related instruments. Remember the key questions about how each theory defines career "success" and how each would respond to an individual who was "fired" from a job. This will help team members choose among the theories regarding "fit" with the student, and subsequently will influence the types of information the team gathers in determining intervention strategies to promote successful career development and transition planning.

Individual-Focused Theories

Structural Theories

These theories have been extremely popular at times and are still applied to many work and interpersonal

situations today. Structural theories categorize specific characteristics that lead to correspondence or a "match" between individuals and work environments. From this correspondence, individuals make an appropriate *occupational choice* that is assumed, will lead to a satisfactory career. Structural theories date back to the early 1900s when Parsons introduced the idea of matching client attributes or traits (e.g., aptitudes, abilities, interests, and functional limitations) to workplace demands (Wolffe, 1997). Parson's model became known as the trait-factor approach and is still used extensively in modern career counseling and vocational rehabilitation practice (Szymanski et al., 1996; Wolffe, 1997). His theory examines occupational choice and three variables that are keys to this decision:

a. the individual—aptitudes, abilities, interests, ambitions, resources, and limitations;

b. the occupation—requirements, conditions of success, advantages and disadvantages, compensations, opportunities, and prospects; and

c. the relationship between these two groups of factors (Brown & Brooks, 1996; Crites, 1981; Szymanski et al., 1996).

More recent theories have incorporated constructs of midlife career change as well as multiple and lifelong factors impacting individuals and society, and have given increasing attention to diverse groups (Brown & Brooks, 1990). These theories view the individual and the environment as a set of variables that should be as similar to each other as possible, in order to ensure job success.

One of the most prominent and popular structural theorists today is John Holland. Holland's (1992) theory of career development categorizes *personality* into six general types with six corresponding work environments: realistic, investigative, artistic, social, enterprising, and conventional (abbreviated as RIASEC). People are identified as having a dominant personality pattern, with their personalities typically fitting into two or three general types. Holland developed his career assessment instruments to use combinations of each person's three most dominant personality types to identify congruent occupational matches. These instruments include the *Self-Directed Search* (Holland, Fritzsche, & Powell, 1994) and the *Vocational Preference Inventory* (Holland, 1985).

The transition team would typically use Holland's proposed three-step process: (1) to identify individual traits according to the six personality types, (2) to classify the work environment by type, and (3) to match the two sets of factors as a basis for establishing congruency and a series of success and satisfaction cycles (Brown, 1990; Spokane, 1996). Personalities and environments also vary along the attributes of consistency, differentiation, identification of strength, congruence, and consistency between the person and the environment. These, in combination with each person's six personality factors (RIASEC), should match the work environment type in order to establish congruency and satisfaction. Teams may find this useful based on a study by Mattie (2000) who found that the *Self-Directed Search* was both reliable and valid for middle and high school students with learning disabilities and mild mental retardation, some of whom were unable to read the form. They also may want to use a lower-reading version of the *Self-Directed Search* that is available (cf. Szymanski & Hershenson, 2005). However, the team may want to be sure that students have sufficient prior experiences to answer appropriately. Krumboltz (1996) argues that such inventories and their interpretation force responses of like/indifference/dislike even though most individuals have had little or no direct experience with these things, and they cannot respond that they "don't know," "have not tried," or "would like to learn more" about these occupations first. In addition, such inventories assume a common and stable set of jobs and job expectations, aspects that may no longer exist in certain work settings (Krumboltz, 1996).

Work-Adjustment Theories

The Minnesota Theory of Work Adjustment was borne out of a focus on persons with disabilities through the Department of Vocational Rehabilitation and the University of Minnesota (Dawis & Lofquist, 1984; Hershenson & Szymanski, 1992). The framework

CASE STUDY Questions

Examine the prior experiential and life opportunity histories of the two students. How would these contribute to, or serve as barriers to, using Parson's or Holland's career theory?

For Miguel: How would his distractibility and verbal skills impact his ability to take or respond to data collection or interviews to determine his personality type? What modifications or adaptations might the team need to make when evaluating results? Would this theory be more of a help or a hindrance in evaluating his strengths as well as his needs?

For Aza: How could her vision needs be accommodated in using instruments related to this theory? What modifications or adaptations might the team need to make when evaluating results? Would this theory be more of a help or a hindrance in evaluating her strengths and needs?

consciously focused on work adjustment and work behavior rather than on occupational choice or career development models because of the authors' concerns with adequately addressing the unique life circumstances that disability status and experience often bring (Hershenson & Szymanski, 1992). This and other theories of work adjustment focus on the concept of identifying factors of the worker and the environment that lead to meeting the needs and requirements of each.

The Minnesota Theory of Work Adjustment identifies *work personality* as an important characteristic of each individual that contributes to work satisfaction. *Work personality* consists of needs that the worker expects to have fulfilled on the job and the specific abilities that he or she possesses to perform required duties. The workplace is analyzed in terms of its ability requirements (knowledge and skills needed by the worker), and its potential to meet a worker's needs. *Work adjustment* is defined as the interaction of two sets of indicators, "satisfaction" and "satisfactoriness." *Satisfaction* relates to the overall work conditions and to various aspects of the individual's work environment, as well as to the fulfillment of personal aspirations and expectations held by the worker. *Satisfactoriness* is indicated by the individual's ability to meet the work site's requirements including productivity, efficiency, and his or her evaluation by supervisors, coworkers, and the company (Dawis, 1996; Dawis & Lofquist, 1984; Lofquist & Dawis, 1969; Szymanski et al., 1996). Job tenure is a product of satisfactoriness and satisfaction.

This theory has recently been termed a "person-environment" correspondence (Dawis, 2002). It views the person and the environment as each presenting factors that lead to satisfaction/satisfactoriness when matched. One benefit of using this theory is that it was developed specifically to address the unique needs and coping strategies of individuals with disabilities (Szymanski, Hershenson, Enright, & Ettinger, 1996). For transition teams, this theory may be most useful for supporting a specific work position planned for a student. This theory would assist the team in examining both the student's and the particular work setting's characteristics, and trying to make an optimal match. If a team had several work options, it could help identify the better match (and the team should also recognize that if none of these positions would fit these categories, then they should continue searching for positions). When minor mismatches occurred (major mismatches would tend to disqualify the position as a "match"), the team could explore ways to accommodate both the student and the environment, and achieve better congruence. The team also could use the theory to prepare the student for ongoing changes both to him/herself and in the work setting, resulting in *work adjustment* as a dynamic and lifelong process (Patton & McMahon, 1999). Instruments include the *Minnesota Importance Questionnaire* and the *Minnesota Satisfaction Questionnaire* (Harrington, 2003).

Developmental Theories

These theories tend to divide the life span into stages that impact career development. They view occupational choice as *one* aspect of a person's work and adult life, in contrast to the structural theories that focus primarily on making one career choice. Developmental theories examine *career development* as the result of lifelong work patterns, change, and the positive interrelationships between the elements of a person's life as leading to a fulfilling career and life. Super (1990) provides one of the more comprehensive and well-known theories. He defines occupational choice as the implementation of self-concepts that unfolds across a lifetime (Brown & Brooks, 1996; Super, Savickas, & Super, 1996). His life-span, life-space approach identifies multiple roles (e.g., child, student, leisurite, citizen,

---

CASE STUDY   Questions

How would the Minnesota Work Adjustment theory describe the work personality of each of the two students? What type of work-adjustment factors would be important considerations that could lead to satisfaction and satisfactoriness?

How could this theory be applied to Miguel or Aza? Are they ready for such a "match" to be made—why or why not? What unique insights might this theory provide to the team for each of the students?

worker, and homemaker) with five life stages across time (i.e., growth, exploration, establishment, maintenance, and disengagement). The time dimension uses a developmental perspective to address how people change and make transitions as they prepare for, engage in, and reflect upon their life roles, and particularly, their work role (Super et al., 1996; Super, 1984, 1990). Within each stage are recurring roles and "transitions" as the person changes and develops.

Super (1990) also investigated a number of career patterns in his research to define the concept of "career maturity." This comprises a person's ability to cope with environmental demands, which increases with experience. The complexity of the theory means that specifics regarding personality, life experiences, or the work environment are less well-specified than some other theories. Since the 1970s, this theory increasingly has addressed changing women's roles, ethnicity, and cultural context (Szymanski, Hershenson et al., 1996). Super also has made a determined effort to make his theory applicable to persons with disabilities (Beveridge, Craddock, Liesener, Stapleton, & Hershenson, 2002; Super, 1957, 1990). Related instruments include the *Career Development Inventory* (Super, Thompson, Lindeman, Joordan, & Myers, 1981), *Career Maturity Index* (Super, 1974), *Work Values Inventory, Values Inventory, Work Salience Inventory,* and the *Career Rainbow* (Super, Osborne, Walsh, Brown, & Niles, 1992). However, some of the assessments have been critiqued for their lack of cultural validity for minority groups and the differences in results found with these groups (Leong & Serafica, 2001).

The team's perspective with this theory would view the student as a developing and changing person, who will assume multiple life roles, and move toward increasing career maturity. The description of life stages may be helpful in ensuring that the team considers a range of life roles and career experiences, including the need for coping skills in preparing for lifelong change. This complex and broad theory may serve as a checklist to ensure that the variety of life and career experiences are included in planning the strategies and activities that best prepare the student for his or her preferred roles. Although this theory may resemble interaction-focused theories because of its attempt to be comprehensive, its focus was on the individual and specific events or activities that impacted life-span paths.

Learning Theory

The application of Krumboltz's social learning theory to career decision making has its roots in the learning theories work of Bandura. Krumbolt incorporated elements of reinforcement theory, classical behaviorism, and cognitive information processing to Bandura's original theory (Mitchell & Krumboltz, 1996). The origin of a person's career choice is then explained as a result of learning; and the career counselor uses learning theory during counseling and for developing interventions (Mitchell & Krumboltz, 1996). Krumboltz's theory is less easily classified by major concept (i.e., occupational choice, career development, or work adjustment), but its lifelong growth and learning focus would make it more characteristic of a developmental category.

This theory proposes two major types of learning experiences that result in individually based behavioral and cognitive skills and preferences. *Instrumental learning experiences* occur when an individual is positively reinforced or punished for behaviors. For example, a student does poorly in assigned household chores and is scolded and reprimanded. *Associative learning*

CASE STUDY Questions

What characteristics of each of the two students might be the most important considerations in planning a career path using this theory? What type of experiences or interventions might be suggested using this approach?

For Miguel: How could this theory be sensitive to his special strengths as well as his needs? How could it help the team look at both his strengths as well as his needs? How might results need to be modified or accommodated?

For Aza: How could this theory be sensitive to her special strengths as well as her needs? What unique insights into her career development might it provide? How might results need to be modified or accommodated?

experiences occur when the individual associates some previously affectively neutral event or stimulus with an emotionally laden stimulus. The student is doing the laundry and opens the washer during its cycle and is sprayed with warm water. This recalls an episode when the student spilled boiling water on himself, and, thereafter, he is very afraid of doing the laundry.

These instrumental and associative learning experiences explain why people enter particular programs or occupations, why they express preferences, and why they may change their preferences at selected points in their lives. In addition, four categories of factors influence career decision-making paths, which include (1) genetic endowment and special abilities, (2) environmental conditions and events, (3) learning experiences, and (4) task approach skills. These four factors interact in infinite ways to form a set of beliefs (Mitchell & Krumboltz, 1996). Individuals develop self-observation generalizations that assess their own performances, and worldview generalizations that predict certain expectations about the future. Faulty self-observations, generalizations, or inaccurate interpretations of environmental conditions can lead to a variety of problems in career decision making.

> **Critical Point**
> Learning theories examine the numerous learning experiences which may shape the career path.

This theory views the individual as changing through learning. This change is potentially continuous: counselors work within an appropriate learning environment, using learning strategies to modify and correct faulty perceptions. The *Career Beliefs Inventory* (Krumboltz, 1988) helps to identify beliefs that may block achievement of career goals. Interventions may include expanding an individual's capabilities and interests beyond existing characteristics, preparing for changing work tasks, or empowering the individual to take action. This theory has been expanded: the social learning theory of career decision making (SLTCDM) now describes how the vast number of learning experiences are combined to shape a person's particular

career path (Krumboltz, 1996). Additional work is focusing on its application to career counseling, although many of the theoretical ideas have also been incorporated into the social cognitive career theory (Szymanski & Hershenson, 2005) that will be covered in the next section.

The social learning theory may be useful to the team because it emphasizes lifelong learning opportunities; current barriers or faulty perceptions are addressed through learning; and these interventions ultimately build successful career and transition outcomes. The theory's expansion incorporates multiple variables that can be addressed through learning experiences to develop positive self-observation generalizations.

Interaction-Focused Theory

Although some of the individual-focused theories may appear to be comprehensive and address multiple factors, their focus has been on the individual and his or her decision making. In contrast, interaction-focused theories do not examine the individual without also considering the other situational and interpersonal influences that are impacting behaviors and decisions. Where individual-focused theories tend to look for standard or "normative" patterns, interaction-focused theories examine how situations and factors influence an individual. One is described next.

Social cognitive career theory (SCCT) is based on Bandura's social cognitive theory that identifies self-efficacy expectations as a major influence of behavior and behavioral change (Harringon, 2003). Lent, Brown, and Hackett (1996, 2002) developed this theory to describe how vocational interests developed and related to career choice, and how perceptions of competence shape interests, decisions and actions, and performance. Three central constructs of self-efficacy, outcome expectations, and personal goals influence the individual's construction of their own career outcomes. Three interlocking and interacting mechanisms affect these career outcomes: personal attributes, external environmental factors, and overt behaviors (Lent et al.,

---

CASE STUDY   Questions

How would one describe Miguel's work preference in terms of this learning theory? How would one describe Aza's lack of a preference? Do either one show some potentially faulty beliefs about themselves or the world? What types of interventions and experiences would this theory suggest as the next steps for the students?

2002). These authors have developed a framework or model for testing, and a series of research data are examining these relationships. For example, perceptions of abilities influence expectations for outcomes, and are linked to a sense of importance (goal), that result in performance. This model also accounts for racial/ethnic and disability factors, so that a person's own influence over their career development can be enhanced or constrained by contextual supports and barriers: workplace discrimination, disapproval of career goals by significant persons in one's life, and so on (Lent et al., 2002; Szymanski & Hershenson, 2005).

The team may find this theory useful to identify prior or potential barriers that the student might face across postsecondary, training, employment, independent living, and community environments; and to plan for accommodation or self-advocacy strategies. This theory includes the importance of finding supportive persons and conditions across these environments, and how environments as well as individuals change according to local and global market or social conditions. Some of the instruments that have been used with this theory are the *Strong Interest Inventory* with the companion *Skills Confidence Inventory*, and the *Kuder Occupational Interrest Survey* with the *Kuder Task Self-Efficacy Scale* (Brown, 2002).

To summarize across all of the theories, the various individual and the interaction-focused theories presented in this chapter represent a range of those presently used in transition, vocational rehabilitation, or career counseling services. Each theory views students and their interaction with the work and adult world somewhat uniquely. A challenge for the team is in choosing a theory that best addresses an individual's needs, abilities, and preferences particularly when the individual is still developing, growing, and changing across these dimensions. Another challenge is that although the older theories may seem limited in focus, they currently have developed more of the commonly-used assessments and curriculum materials. The team may choose to use some of these materials, but keep in mind some modifications and adaptations to better fit the experiences of their student.

> **Critical Point**
> Not all career assessments address all issues, so it is important for the team to have a general understanding of the student's career issues first in order to choose the assessments and interventions that are most appropriate.

INTEGRATING THEORY WITH PRACTICE: USING CAREER DEVELOPMENT STAGES ACROSS CAREER THEORIES

Although numerous career development theories have been formulated and tested over the years, many practitioners believe that no single theory, in and of itself, adequately explains the career development of people with (or even without) disabilities (Beveridge et al., 2002; Chen, 2003; Conte, 1983; Curnow, 1989; Szymanski et al., 1996; Vondracek & Porfeli, 2003; Wolffe, 1997). It is also difficult for practitioners to be widely read across multiple theories, and many professionals tend to have "favorites" (Savickas, 1996).

In addition, people with disabilities represent a large and heterogeneous group (Beveridge et al., 2002). The diversity of their abilities and limitations, supportive or limiting life experiences, as well as gender, cultural, and the myriad of other unique factors limit the degree to which any single theory is applicable or nonapplicable to their unique situations (Szymanski et al., 1996; Szymanski & Hershenson, 2005). As experience bears out, the nature of a person's disability cannot reliably predict how that individual will proceed through the career development process: Two individuals with the same disability may have extremely different life experiences and career concerns. This all complicates the choice of a theory, and the essential career planning decisions of the team. The very presence of a disability often adds further risk factors to this complicated career development process and positive transition outcomes.

Suppose that a team can find no one theory that best describes a particular student's career strengths and needs. How should the team proceed? A number of researchers have suggested models and methods (Beveridge et al., 2002; Brown, 2002; Chen, 2003; Savickas, 1996; Szymanski & Hershenson, 2005; Vondracek & Porfeli, 2002); yet, there is no consensus at this time. Herr (1996) describes the problem between theory and practice being that no one theory is sufficiently comprehensive or integrated. In particular, individual-focused theories select and study a limited set of conditions, a particular time (adolescence, adulthood), or event in a person's life (decision making, integrating into the workforce, etc.) in a person's total life experiences (cf. Chen, 2003; Vondracek & Porfeli, 2002). Yet, it is unclear how a single decision can lead to subsequent success across the person's lifespan, adult roles, and environments. The result has been the creation of interaction-focused theories in an effort to link multiple situational and interpersonal influences on events and decisions of individuals, that lead to certain types of career and life outcomes. The SCCT described earlier attempts to combine a broad array of contributing factors but is still relatively new and incomplete.

Proposed Frameworks and Models

Several authors have proposed models to integrate multiple theories and utilize both research and instruments for each. Szymanski and colleagues (Szymanski et al., 1996; Szymanski & Hershenson, 2005) have developed an **ecological model** across a comprehensive array of variables and career development theories. They utilize five groups of factors or *constructs*: individual, contextual, mediating, work environment, and outcome. These constructs interact to enhance or impede the career development process of people with disabilities (Szymanski & Parker, 1996; Szymanski et al., 1996). Szymanski and Hershenson (1998, 2005) expanded their original model to include six interrelated career development processes: congruence, decision making, development, socialization, allocation, and chance. These are mechanisms by which the constructs can be addressed, with related questions and suggested interventions for each construct and process across multiple theories.

A second comprehensive career development framework was developed by Savickas (1996) that is based on six key questions that represent primary concerns faced by practitioners. The framework serves as a problem-solving model to determine which of the theories and interventions best address the individual's issues. Each question is linked with specific career instruments and interventions across several theories. Subsequently, Savickas has used Super's life-span, life-space model as a means to converge multiple theoretical models (Savickas, 2001, 2002). He included four theoretical segments to integrate these theories: individual differences, development (including stages and career maturity), self-concept, and context (including life roles). Work to further specify this integration is continuing.

McMahon and Patton (1999) have proposed a systems-based theoretical approach that examines the interaction of the individual with persons, environments, and social influences as a comprehensive perspective that can accommodate all career theories. Yet, they have not developed an overarching framework which could help

to organize or systemize the work of practitioners (Brown, 2002). Lent et al. (2002) suggest that their social cognitive career theory (SCCT) is a comprehensive theory that can serve as a bridge (Brown, 2002). Yet, it appears that no one convergent model is sufficiently developed, given the rapid changes in the workplace and workforce, to provide a framework for transition teams.

Instead, using career development tasks or issues may be a logical way to organize theoretical choice, assessment, data collection, and transition planning until a more organized framework has been developed. Beveridge et al. (2002) take such an approach in their INCOME framework, utilizing Imagining, iNforming, Choosing, Obtaining, Maintaining, and Exiting tasks to choose appropriate theories, instruments, and curriculum.

Four Stages of Career Development

Another suggestion is to use the four stages of career development and track students' progression through the stages. Although Brolin (1995) suggests grade levels, using the four stages as a nongraded developmental model allows older students who are missing key experiences and information to "catch up" and move through the stages, according to their own, unique career path. The four stages could be used to organize and monitor career development, shown as follows:

1. *Career awareness*—Explore or choose theories, assessments, and activities that support building an awareness of work and how the student will fit into a work-oriented society;
2. *Career exploration*—Choose theories, assessments, and activities that support student's exploration of their interests and abilities in relation to lifestyle and occupations, including hands-on and community experiences;
3. *Career preparation*—Use theories, assessments, and activities that support appropriate career decision making and skill acquisition, based upon specific interests and aptitudes;
4. *Career assimilation*—Use theories, assessments, and activities that support postschool movement into training and community settings in which students participate in satisfying avocational, family, civic, as well as paid employment activities. See Table 4-1.

TABLE 4–1   Stages of career development

Name of Stage	Tasks	Activities
Career awareness	• awareness of work • fit into a work-oriented society	• interest inventories that are linked with related experiences and visits to work sites • activities that explore the social and individual importance of work • identification of strengths and needs that correspond with interests and hobbies
Career exploration	• exploration of their interests and abilities • hands-on and community experiences	• interest inventories that increasingly narrow career path choices • self-evaluations and ratings of work experiences • integrating of aptitudes and interests across vocational and avocational activities • exploration of career as contributing to self-esteem, insight, and development
Career preparation	• appropriate career decision making • skill acquisition, based upon specific interests and aptitudes	• observational and other assessments that validate a single career choice • experiences and opportunities to confirm choice or change • utilization of "failure" or dissatisfaction to identify more satisfying choices
Career assimilation	• movement into training and community settings • participate in satisfying avocational, family, civic, as well as paid employment activities	• assessments and experiences for skill, attitude, and knowledge readiness • certificate or degree-level academic and vocational skill development • career entry, maintenance, retraining, advancement, and exit preparation • stress-management and multiple role coordination and balance strategies

These four stages are specific to employment, but a broad definition of career development incorporates all life areas. These same stages of awareness, exploration, preparation, and assimilation could be applied to other environments as well: education and postsecondary training, independent living, and community participation. Students should first become *aware* of the tasks, expectations, and roles within each; should *explore* their options and responses to the tasks, expectations, and roles (and use these to develop strategies and interventions); should *prepare* and have trial experiences with each, and then *assimilate* into these settings. Thus, the four stages truly support a comprehensive view of career development and transition planning.

CASE STUDY   Questions

Earlier, Miguel's and Aza's primary strengths and primary needs in terms of the three career perspectives were described. Are there any additional interventions that could be suggested as the most important at this point for each student? How would the team use the four stages to track the students' career and transition development as they move into postschool environments?

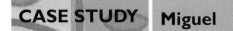

Career Development Needs of Miguel

This last section uses the information across the practices suggested in this chapter and required by IDEA to demonstrate how they can be implemented by the team. It uses Miguel, the case described throughout, as the example for implementing these practices.

The following is an example of how the four stages of career development can be used successfully with Miguel:

1. *Career awareness*—Miguel has a stated preference in autobody and car-related work but could benefit from learning about different types of work that people do, earning wages, benefits, and qualifications needed;
2. *Career exploration*—Miguel has a stated preference but should explore other potential interests and relate these to his skills and abilities; for example, his strength limitations will limit certain tasks and his learning abilities might be more appropriate for noncertificate or licensed positions; wider interest exploration and preparation will help should his preferred positions be downsized or eliminated at a later time; the team should build his informal friend-and-family repair assistance experiences into a series of exploratory hands-on and community experiences that identify specific abilities and needs within specific job descriptions;
3. *Career preparation*—Miguel and his team should use his prior neighborhood and community experiences to choose specific vocational coursework to build on personal abilities and address areas of need in preparation for available jobs in his preferred location for adult living;
4. *Career assimilation*—Miguel and his team should prepare for postschool training for apprenticeship or pre-licensure/licensure or certificate-based positions that will lead to employment in his preferred community setting; the team should incorporate realistic labor market information into decisions that prepare him for ongoing or later job training/retraining; employment decisions should be integrated with community living decisions and supports he may need.

That summarizes his career path: Even though he is currently a tenth grader, Miguel is expanding his career *awareness* and *exploring* possibilities within the automotive path (his teachers also are exposing him to other career areas although he is fairly determined to stick with "cars" at this point). The team expects that Miguel will move into *career preparation* activities near the end of this year.

The team also needs to be sure that the plan meets the IDEA requirements, as well. It is based on *the student's needs, interests, and preferences* with automotive being the strongly indicated preference, according to his family and teachers. The four stages move Miguel toward postsecondary training and a community-based position in his preferred living area, also addressing his living area *preference*, showing an *outcome-oriented process* that *promotes movement to postsecondary environments*. His current awareness and exploration is a *coordinated set of activities* using family-and-friends networks (suggested by the parents and grandparents) with instruction and community sites from the teacher (using community and employer contacts). The vocational education teacher attended last spring's IEP and transition planning meeting and has suggested that Miguel shadow some classes this spring in preparation for next fall.

In terms of a theoretical choice, the team is using the career development stages to ensure that important experiences occur in a supportive sequence. However, because of Miguel's communication needs, physical challenges, and his cultural background they are using the SCCT theory to be sure that key interpersonal and cultural factors are mutually positive to support his success in the workplace. The team will provide additional learning experiences (integrating learning theory) and explore multiple adult roles (community involvement, dating and marriage) as Miguel shows an interest.

A Vision and Transition Goals for Miguel

Vision Statement

Miguel will work full time in a neighborhood autobody repair shop doing detailing work and assisting with (nonphysical) painting preparation and related tasks. He will live with his family (culturally appropriate

(Continued)

preference of student and family) or with siblings and their families as he enters adulthood, and the family is supportive of his dating and possibly marrying, if he chooses.

Postsecondary and Lifelong Education

Miguel will enroll in the district's autobody/automotive vocational classes, as are appropriate for his career goals and abilities, and will have a coach/aide assist him with learning and communication issues. He will need to be prepared for potential job or career change; his vocational rehabilitation counselor will be invited to this spring's IEP to establish this long-term link for training and job-change preparation. Miguel will need to improve his self-monitoring for remembering to use his communication book and problem solving (using appropriate communication strategies) when he becomes frustrated or angry when others do not understand him. The team will ask the speech/communication pathologist to investigate other communication devices to ensure that Miguel's options are user-friendly and appropriate for the automotive "work culture" (job-specific expectations and interaction patterns).

Career and Vocational

Miguel will complete appropriate coursework at the vocational high school in conjunction with hands-on placements in the community. His training will continue at the local community vocational-technical training school after he graduates so that Miguel can attain the highest level of certification or licensure for which he is capable. The availability of continuing coaching/aide support at his classes and in work experiences will be determined through vocational rehabilitation services, and made possible through a **PASS** plan (that uses a portion of his earnings to pay for support services). This will lead to full-time placement at an automotive business in his neighborhood.

Community Living

Miguel will continue to help his father and brothers at home doing appropriate chores; his family and community have fairly defined gender-specific roles so he will not be expected to do cooking or housecleaning, but will be expected to contribute to house and yard maintenance and repair. The team will explore the availability of a community/adult-education course in this topic for Miguel to provide the "teaching" information to support what his family provides in hands-on experiences.

In summary and as can be seen with Miguel, the vision for career development extends far beyond the adolescent and early adulthood age range of transition, and functions as a central focus of transition planning. It contributes to IEP team compliance with IDEA mandates and successful functioning of the four essential elements of exemplary planning practices. The theoretical or organizing framework that a team chooses to guide its career development, through the use of assessments and interventions, will also support the implementation of essential elements of comprehensive transition planning. More of this is scheduled and identified in annual transition meetings and through coursework choices.

CONCLUSION

The career theories described in this chapter offer a variety of perspectives that can be useful to the transition team for supporting educational and career development of students with disabilities. Yet, because individual career theories provide unique perspectives regarding work and the worker, each is not appropriate for every career task or concern, or for every student. Teams may find a particular theory that suits a student very well, or may use key issues across the four stages of career development to integrate assessments and activities from several different theories.

Remember the question asked early in the chapter about people who get fired from early jobs? Often this is a formative experience for people who use this information to: (a) choose a more suitable and satisfying career, or (b) learn an important lesson about work expectations. Although initially perceived as highly negative, this can provide a real-life opportunity with important consequences to think over the differences between school (and teachers/parents who need each team member to attend and comply with truancy laws) versus employers who can replace a team member with someone they might like better. It also can help students learn how to, and how not to express frustration or anger, and how to exit more gracefully from a job they dislike (because references for future jobs are often needed).

So, getting fired isn't the "end" of someone's career, especially in the early stages. However, these same opportunities and experiences have not always been applied to individuals with disabilities. For example, Pumpian, Fisher, Certo, and Smalley (1997) believe that individuals with disabilities should be allowed the same opportunities for job change and should not be "stuck" in a position that they do not enjoy, or find challenging and rewarding. This means that the transition team will need to allow for job movement, and to view job changes and even "negative" work experiences (where the student is "fired" or asked to leave) as important learning opportunities. Ultimately and when used wisely, these experiences will help the student make more realistic choices, will lead to jobs that better fit a student's needs and abilities *and* will teach the student how to make these changes more positively. Across the career theories, this episode would be seen as the result of a possible mismatch, an opportunity for learning, an unsatisfactory adjustment, an episode in a life-span process, or an interaction of multiple factors and influences.

This chapter took a brief look at some of the most popular and comprehensive theories, with a few suggestions regarding their use. Chapter 5 will describe transition assessments more thoroughly, including several of the assessment instruments from these theories. Chapter 6 will describe curriculum issues across career education, life skills, and academic curriculum choices. From the background information in this chapter, the reader may recognize how aspects of these theories are utilized in these chapters and how career development forms a central and guiding function for much of the team's transition planning processes.

In general, the better the team's understanding of theoretical career models and their related assessment instruments and intervention strategies, the more likely the team will choose a theory and assessment instruments that are appropriate to the student's needs. In much transition work, the team will apply their understanding of different theoretical perspectives to gathering appropriate information through assessment, and choosing from an array of curricula, programs, and instruments. This background will allow the team to better choose *compatible* assessment and intervention programs, to link these to complementary coursework and curriculum options, and eliminate possible contradictions and conflicts across transition planning activities. Ultimately, this individualized career and transition foundation will lead to an optimal lifelong plan and a satisfying and fulfilling adulthood.

The career experiences of successful people are not necessarily always "positive." But all such experiences can be used to learn a lot: about oneself, about others, about situations and tolerances, and how and when to end a working relationship. Each event represents one more experience with career development and career stages along their lifelong path, one experience with career type or job satisfaction/satisfactoriness mismatch, and an opportunity for significant learning regarding faulty self-observations, and responding to multiple factors and influences that culminate in a decision-making event. So this is this not career development gone wrong, but one part of a lifelong process. And the same opportunities to experience and to learn (and to occasionally fail as well as succeed) should be afforded to students with disabilities!

STUDY QUESTIONS

1. Compare how one of the narrow definitions (occupational choice or work adjustment) compares with the broader, lifelong perspectives definition of career development when doing comprehensive transition planning.
2. Describe at least two ways in which a disability can negatively impact career development processes and outcomes, across the four stages of career development: career awareness, career exploration, career preparation, and career assimilation.
3. Choose three of the career development theories from this chapter: structural, work adjustment, developmental, learning, or SCCT. Identify the perspective that each theory takes in defining key elements of the individual, the workplace, and the interaction between the two. From each of these, determine and compare how one might use

important interagency linkages differently to accomplish the primary goal of each theory.

4. Compare these same three theories in terms of planning for a student's movement from school to postschool environments. Based on their perspective of the individual, the workplace, and their interaction, how do they differ in prioritizing and organizing potential movement to postschool environments? How would each of these fit with one's own personal career development up to this point?

5. Imagine three different students with disabilities who are (a) entering a work exploration experience (observing a series of work sites spending two weeks at each site), (b) beginning a job try-out/job shadowing experience (spending one month working/following a worker in each of several work sites), and (c) beginning a part-time community work experience in an area of his or her preference. How can you use Brolin's four different stages of career development to help identify specific aspects for the collection of these data, and developing and monitoring a comprehensive transition plan?

WEBSITES

Office of Career-Technical and Adult Education, Career Development/Ohio Career Information System: Career Development and Ohio Academic content Standards: English Language Arts From: Ghilani (2005)
www.ode.state.oh.us/ctae

Self Assessment Websites

Holland's Self-Directed Search:
www.self-directed-search.com.
Costs $9.95.
The Career Key:
www.careerkey.org.
Based on Holland's personality types.
The Career Interests Game:
http://career.missouri.edu.
Based on Holland's personality types.
Workplace Values Assessment:

www.quintcareers.com/workplace_values.html.
Individuals assess what they value in work.

Career Exploration Websites

Learn More Resource Center:
www.learnmoreindiana.org.
Information about careers and work for high school and college students.
Schools in the USA:
www.schoolsintheusa.com.
Search for colleges with a collection of 1,000 career profiles.
Bureau of Labor Statistics for K–12:
http://stats.bls.gov/k12/html/edu_over.htm.
Also access from the BLS homepage by clicking "Kid's Page."
Career Zone:
www.nycareerzone.org.
A free, career exploration and planning system for middle- and high-school students.
Next Step Magazine:
www.nextstepmagazine.com.
Includes career and college information and articles.
Your Vocation:
www.yourvocation.com.
Not-for-profit project to help youths, including e-mail capabilities.

Women and Minorities

Cool Jobs for Girls:
www.work4women.org.
Nontraditional careers.
Women's Work:
www.womenswork.org.
Resource center with professional women discussing their careers.
The Black Collegian:
www.black-collegian.com.
Career resources for students of color.
Saludos Hispanos:
www.saludos.com.
Promotes the careers and education of the Hispanic community.

SECTION 2

CREATING A TRANSITION PERSPECTIVE OF EDUCATION

The four chapters in Section 2 are designed to identify the key players in transition programs and how they can be brought together to develop school transition programs. Chapter 5, "Transition Assessment," describes common assessment practices and how they can be used in determining special education eligibility, in developing a course of study focused on postschool outcomes, and in the monitoring of students' progress. This chapter is designed to provide the reader with a knowledge of the major assessment approaches (e.g., informal, formal, situational, and curriculum-based) and how they can be used to support students' postschool outcomes. It also includes a discussion of common concerns of using assessments for persons with disabilities that have been normed on nondisabled populations.

Chapter 6, "Standards-Based Curriculum and Transition," examines educational approaches and how students' transition needs can be addressed by aligning these educational programs to create a transition perspective of education. As with the legislation chapter, this chapter examines the sometimes contradictory goals of these educational systems and how these contradictions can be resolved by developing broad and inclusive curricula.

Chapters 7 and 8, "Instructional Planning for Transition Teaching" and "Instructional Methods for Transition Teaching," provide strategies for adapting curricula to the needs of students with disabilities using a variety of support, accommodation, and assistive technology approaches. They also provide an overview of strategies that allow students with disabilities access to the general curriculum and to community participation. They also touch on issues of using technology and curricular adaptations across classrooms and environments.

CHAPTER 5

TRANSITION ASSESSMENT

Robert W. Flexer

Pamela Luft

LEARNING OBJECTIVES

The objectives of this chapter are:

1. Describe the characteristics of transition assessment.

2. Describe the types of skills that are tested in each of the four transition domains: current and future education, work, living, and personal-social areas.

3. Explain the purpose and contributions of formal (standardized) and informal (nonstandardized) transition assessments.

4. Describe the kinds of information each can provide to support comprehensive data gathering, and describe their advantages and disadvantages.

5. Describe how functional or ecological assessments can be used in each of the four areas of transition assessment and give examples.

6. Explain the process of assessment planning and decision making for transition teams.

INTRODUCTION

Sitlington, Neubert, Begun, Lombard, and Le Conte (1996) state that transition assessments "should provide the foundation for the transition process" (p. 3), including the information from which the team will identify the student's specific preferences, strengths, and needs. Transition assessments are critical in addressing the IDEA's essential transition element of determining students' strengths, needs, interests, and preferences because they can be used to identify career interests, aptitudes, transition goals, curricular needs, or even to assess the environments that students plan to enter. Transition assessments also support implementation of other essential elements of transition in the IDEA. For example, they can provide data on how students might respond to postschool work, education, independent living, and community situations, thereby supporting an outcome-oriented planning process. In addition, they can help determine whether educational programs and transition activities are actually promoting movement toward students' postschool goals.

Assessment, therefore, provides the informational framework from which all transition planning occurs, and it is critical that the techniques employed are accurate, relevant, and comprehensive in addressing all areas that will be important to the students' adult life. The transition team needs to understand the uses and limits of different types of transition assessments and be able to translate these assessment results into plain English without jargon for students, families, and community members. Results that truly reflect the student's current abilities and future potentials will result in quality transition plans, and, ultimately, in the student's successful movement into adulthood.

This chapter is organized to provide a foundation in transition assessment practices that are critical for transition planning. The authors provide definitions and purposes of assessments to make the reader familiar with the variety of assessment approaches that have been developed from several professional disciplines. This breadth of knowledge is needed because the transition to adulthood is a complex process and no one perspective or professional discipline can meet the need of any single student across all situations. These transition assessments are then described in terms of how well they address the four postschool transition domains (i.e., postsecondary and lifelong education, career and vocational, personal-social, and community living) and their use in transition planning.

IDEA REQUIREMENTS

IDEA 1990 and 1997

Well-done and appropriate assessments are the basis for all successful special education and transition programming. In order to ensure appropriate testing practices, IDEA addressed assessment concerns in 1990, 1997, and 2004 amendments. The IDEA of 1990 required IEP assessments to be unbiased and given in the native language of the student. In addition, placement in special education was based upon a multifactored evaluation that included multiple assessments across more than one environment (Turnbull, H. R., 1993).

The IDEA of 1997 represented a significant shift in assessment processes. It included a greater emphasis on informal assessments that examined the student's performance in specific environments according to each environment's expectations. In contrast, formal assessments tend to be given under strict, neutral conditions; that is, often in a room without distractions, following a standard set of directions, using paper and pencil, or copying or manipulating objects or tools.

Informal assessments allow the team to examine the student's behavior within the variety of environments that are natural to the individual's life, including the anticipated future environments (Bates, 2002; Clark, 1996; Sax & Thoma, 2002; Sitlington et al., 1996). Formal tests can provide important general information but are usually isolated from critical environmental contexts that frequently either support or create barriers for the student. The greater emphasis on informal assessments also allows greater participation from students and parents in the assessment process because these assessments can be more individualized to better fit their current preferences and visions of possible futures.

> **Critical Point**
> The use of both informal and formal assessments provides the transition team with a holistic view of the student.

Two types of functional assessments were required under the IDEA legislation. Under IDEA 1990, a transition option was added in which a team may use a functional vocational evaluation to determine which employment positions are most likely to lead to success within a particular preferred career area for a student. The evaluator may measure functional skills at a work site to determine if the student performs at adequate levels and is able to integrate socially and personally in the work environment. When preparing to seek a specific job, the team may ask for an evaluation at a specific company to ensure that the physical conditions and co-workers/supervisors at that company are compatible with and supportive of the student's needs. Teams will choose to use each assessment to meet their specific needs for information.

Under IDEA 1997, further options were added for students with behavior that may get them expelled. The functional behavioral assessment determines the purpose of a behavior so that an intervention can be developed to address problem behavior before removal from school. A variety of strategies are utilized to identify the purpose of a target behavior and enable the IEP team to identify and individualize an effective intervention. The strategies and techniques most often used to collect data include: questionnaires; interviews with students, teachers, parents; and observations (Quinn, Gable, Rutherford, Nelson, & Howell, 1998). IDEA 1997 also specified that all children who are identified as having special education needs (including transition needs) must be considered for assistive technology.

> **Critical Point**
> Informal assessments test for variability in performance across environments in order to create a realistic picture of the student's abilities.

An additional aspect of IDEA 1997 that the transition team needed to address was the extent to which the student should be integrated into the general education curriculum and classroom as part of the IEP plan. In conjunction with access to the general curriculum, the IDEA required that students with disabilities be part of the accountability systems and that they participate in state and district proficiency testing. The 1997 amendments emphasize placement with peers, and if the team does not feel this is appropriate, then it provides a statement as to why this is so. This issue is very important in terms of the preferences of the student and family. Team members may hold contradictory views in terms of what constitutes "peers." Some may believe that integration into a work and community environment with typical adult co-workers represents the ultimate goal of transition and integration and, thus, complies with IDEA. Others may believe that work and community training is "atypical" for most high school students and, thus, represents a "handicapping" placement that contradicts the IDEA. The preferences of the student and family are probably the best gauge of what is most appropriate.

IDEA 2004

The IDEA of 2004 added significant requirements for the provision of transition services. IEPs now must include measurable postschool goals. In terms of assessment, team members will have to evaluate students in terms of those postschool environments matched to their interests and preferences (Test, Aspel, & Everson, 2006). At the conclusion of their school career, students will create a document (called a Summary of Performance) summarizing achievement and their transition needs. See Table 5-1 for an overview of the numerous legal transition assessment requirements.

CHARACTERISTICS OF TRANSITION ASSESSMENT

Assessment has been defined as the gathering of information for purposes of planning, instruction, or placement to aid in individual decision making (Taylor, 1997).

TABLE 5–1 IDEA requirements for assessment and evaluation

1990 and 1997
• Functional vocational evaluation
• Increased emphasis on functional and developmental information
• Specific requirement for information from parents
• Functional behavior assessment
• Assistive technology assessment
• Information about how the student can best succeed in the general education classroom
• Participation in state and district proficiency testing

IDEA 2004
• Measurable postschool transition goals through appropriate assessment in the IEP
• Summary of performance of academic and functional achievements and of transition needs
• Determination of strengths, needs, interests, and preferences for transition goals
• Requirement for consideration of vocational education

For effective transition planning, assessment strategies must involve the student, the family, and multiple disciplines including educators (i.e., special, general, and vocational), related service providers (e.g., school psychologists, diagnosticians, speech therapists, occupational therapists, and physical therapists), and other individuals involved in the student's transition to adulthood. As the student nears graduation, this list may expand to include personnel from rehabilitation counseling, health or mental health services, colleges or universities, developmental disability services, income maintenance programs, and other assistance or employment services depending on the student's potential future (Halpern, 1994; Sitlington et al., 1996). Transition assessment also needs to include the evaluations of nonprofessionals such as paraprofessionals, concerned business leaders, church representatives, or civic group representatives who can be important sources of information about the student and about the community's resources and support (Luft, P., Rumrill, P., Snyder, J., & Hennessey, M., 2001 Test et al., 2006).

One of the most important aspects of assessment in the transition years is that it should be ongoing and continuous. Adolescent and young adult students are experiencing tremendous developmental changes. These changes, the impact of their peers, and their learning from transition activities and experiences will clarify and perhaps change their values and preferences throughout the transition process (Rogan, Grossi, & Gajewski, 2002). As the student and the team learn more about these abilities and preferences, they may decide to alter and modify strategies to reach the student's desired adult outcomes. Ongoing evaluation is vital to ensuring that final adult plans represent the accumulation of the student's growth, education, and experiences before leaving high school (Sitlington et al., 1996).

> **Critical Point**
> A comprehensive transition assessment synthesizes all assessment results in a comprehensive manner to depict accurately the student's abilities, interests, and needs.

Transition assessment may include some of the same tests as those used by special educators for the development of the Individualized Education Program (IEP) to determine eligibility and to test general areas of achievement, performance, and behavior. However, transition assessment also must address abilities and needs related to specific individualized adult outcomes, including the student's success with specific tasks in actual environments. The team, therefore, needs to assess the student's success in the environments that reflect his or her lifestyle preferences and abilities (Rogan, Grassi, & Gajewski, 2002). This requires clear identification and specification of these environments and of persons who can assess student performance in these settings. Transition assessment involves decisions relative to both school and postschool environments. For students interested in technical careers, for example, decisions may have to be made for career and technical education (school) or technical or community college (postschool). The same current and future framework applies to all the transition domains as well as individual postschool goals. Table 5–2 summarizes transition implications of major purposes of assessment.

> **Critical Point**
> The transition team chooses assessments that provide technically sound data to promote the student's movement toward his or her postsecondary goals.

Transition assessment involves more than administering, scoring, and reporting tests and results. It involves careful analysis of the assessment results that provide functional, relevant, appropriate recommendations and decisions. The integration of assessments into an understandable language for all team members is a difficult task that generally falls to the coordinator of the IEP team in which transition is discussed. This assessment information must be free of professional jargon and specifically address student strengths, needs, interests, and preferences in a way that emphasizes potential and abilities and that promotes an atmosphere of positive expectations for the student with a disability. Transition planning remains most effective when all members understand these results sufficiently to be able to contribute their own analyses and interpretations. It is particularly important that the student and the family recognize how these assessments can contribute to planning for a positive future.

> **Critical Point**
> Transition assessments are ongoing, specific, and individualized according to the students' goals and programs.

DEFINING TRANSITION DOMAINS

In accordance with the three domains of postschool community adjustment established by Halpern (1985), the CEC Division of Career Development and

TABLE 5–2 Purposes for transition assessment

Category	Description
Placement/Eligibility	To determine requirements in education, working, living, and personal/social environments.
	To find out where the student ranks in terms of proficiency, admission standards, or agency eligibility.
	To match an individual's preferences and abilities with appropriate program options.
Planning	To identify abilities, interests, capabilities, strengths, needs, potentials, behaviors, and preferences.
	To "try out" different tasks or activities and to determine how preferences match abilities for program options and postschool outcomes.
	To develop a comprehensive description of transition assessment data to help students, their families, and team members identify concrete ways to assist students in achieving their goals.
Instruction/Intervention	To implement the techniques or strategies that will help a student to explore performance requirements in transition environments.
	To recommend types of adaptive techniques and/or accommodation strategies that will lead to improved performance in transition environments.

Transition (DCDT) has defined the important areas of transition assessment as follows:

> Transition assessment is the on-going process of collecting data on the individual's needs, preferences, and interests as they relate to the demands of current and future *working, living, and personal social environments*. Assessment data serve as the common thread in the transition process and form the basis for defining goals and services, to be included in the individualized education program (IEP). (Sitlington, Neubert, & Le Conte, 1997, pp. 70–71)

This definition categorizes transition assessment into three broad areas of current and future environments for the student. The following discussion expands on the three transition domains of Halpern (i.e., current and future working, living, personal-social). In the last ten years, educational environments are necessary in categorizing the various types of assessments that can be used in transition planning. Postsecondary and lifelong learning environments were added to this list because continuing and lifelong education and postsecondary transition is now a needed and expected domain for most students with disabilities (Stodden & Whelley, 2004). Personal-social knowledge and skills are required in all postschool environments so they are covered within all three domains discussed here: postsecondary and lifelong learning (educational), career and vocational, and community living.

Current and Future Educational Environments

In the last ten years since the passage of IDEA 1997, transition to some type of postsecondary program is the expectation for many students with disabilities. The transition period has been extended for all students (about to age 26 or 27), and postsecondary and other educational programs throughout the life span provide opportunities for further exploration and preparation for adult life and personal and career development. Participation in postsecondary education for students with disabilities grew significantly in all types of settings—there was very rapid growth in community college enrollment in this time period, and in the development of new programs for students with significant disabilities (sometimes referred to as community-based or 18–21 programs) (Wagner et al., 2005). As adults, these youth will continue to seek enrollment in educational programs to enhance personal and career interests—continuing and lifelong education.

> **Critical Point**
> Transition to postsecondary programs increased dramatically for students with all types of disabilities over the last ten years.

For students planning to enroll in four-year colleges and universities, assessment of academic skills and accommodation needs is critical. With the trend toward graduation tests, preparation and success in state- and district-wide assessments is critical. Coupled with admission tests like SATs and ACTs, the team and students need to focus on access and learning content required for these tests and probably, more importantly, performing in the next environment (the college or university). The team needs to support the integration of the performance requirements in the setting of choice with the student's skills and supports available in that environment. Assessments are needed regarding the appropriateness of the choice given the student's career goals, and of the likelihood that the chosen college environment is a good fit for the student.

Similar issues arise for students with community or technical college transition goals. Ecological assessments of the performance and skill requirements and accommodation resources are compared against the student's present level of functioning and accommodation needs. Further assessment is required in terms of the correspondence between the career opportunities for completers of the two-year programs and the individual student's career goals. These kinds of assessments provide the kind of inputs needed for course of study, program selection, and academic and occupational skill goals and activities for the transition plan.

New 18–21 programs for students with severe disabilities combine the opportunity for further educational and career development with a full curriculum of transition goals and objectives and community-based instruction (Neubert et al., 2004). Students enroll at the university or college under a transition status— they may not be enrolled in baccalaureate or associate degree programs. Other models use the campus as a community environment with its various opportunities for learning and participation.

> **Critical Point**
> The increased importance of post–high-school transition led to the evolution of new models and the need for enhanced resources in postsecondary programs.

Current and Future Career and Vocational Environments

Work and career assessments provide information on student needs, interests, and preferences that are designed to lead ultimately to career selection. These assessments may focus on career maturity, development of work behaviors, personality characteristics, cultural factors, or other constructs of career development (see Chapter 4 for a more complete discussion of career

models). Some of the most effective assessments for students with disabilities measure career development and maturity, since many of these students lack experiences to help them make career choices (Rojewski, 2002). These assessments may focus on general abilities and interests in early stages or may examine specific aptitudes and career attitudes needed for employment success in later stages. Assessments are critical to ensuring that the student's career development is leading to a preferred career path.

> **Critical Point**
> Career assessments look at the life span as a series of stages toward career maturity and measure abilities and interests.

Vocational assessment deals with the role of the worker and demands of the workplace for specific vocations or occupations. When the student's employment goal narrows into a specific job type, typically in the later stages of career development, the vocational assessment can provide detailed information critical to success in that occupation. The Interdisciplinary Council on Vocational Evaluation and Assessment describes this type of assessment as comprising:

> Services to measure, observe, and document an individual's interests, values, temperaments, work-related behaviors, aptitudes and skills, physical capacities, learning style, and training needs. (Smith, Lombard, Neubert, Le Conte, Rothenbacher, & Sitlington, 1996, p. 74)

Vocational assessments focus on work-related characteristics and aptitudes of the student within finite vocational and work-oriented approaches (Le Conte, 1986). Areas that vary with the individual include special aptitudes and special needs, work habits and behaviors, personal and social skills needed for work. Other areas such as values and attitudes toward work, work tolerance and work adjustment, physical abilities, and dexterity are also areas that need to be addressed in vocational assessments.

> **Critical Point**
> Vocational assessments focus on the worker and the demands of various workplace environments and measure work-related aptitudes and characteristics of the student.

Current and Future Living Environments

This third category of transition assessment is extremely broad and variable, depending on the student's lifestyle preferences and potential for independence. The transition team should use assessments in this area to ensure that the student has developed a range of necessary self-care and management skills. When independence is limited, students should have skills that allow a maximum sense of independence and choice within a supported living environment. Some skills that the team may need to assess include basic health and hygiene, medical and dental, home care, safety and community survival skills, and self-advocacy. Some students also may need to learn community travel and transportation skills, shopping, cooking, housecleaning, and money management depending on their current and anticipated levels of independence.

The family, the student's residential staff, or personal care providers can be extremely helpful in providing information about current levels of performance in the area of residential living. Additionally, developmental disability agency staff may provide important information on supported living options as well. All of these individuals can help to define realistic future alternatives and the ongoing monitoring and support that may be needed as the student moves into adulthood. This area of transition is less well defined by testing and assessment instruments; therefore, including the individuals who can assist with gathering relevant data is very important.

Importance of Personal-Social Skills and Relationships

This importance of personal-social areas for transition is an area that is highly dependent on the preferences of the student. Most students have desires for friendships, but the number and types of friends they need in order to feel satisfied varies greatly. Consequently, hobbies and community participation, including sports teams or interest groups, should be supported according to the student's preferences. Additionally, some students may plan to marry and have children of their own, so the team may need to address issues relating to dating, sexuality, child care, and possibly, sexual vulnerability in the community. Because friendship, dating, marital, and parenting skills are areas where there are few assessments, teams will need to rely upon gathering information from the student and those individuals who know the student best. Team members who see the student regularly will have valuable perspectives on the student's current abilities in making, maintaining, and, when necessary, ending relationships and

friendships with others. The involvement of all important community members on the team can greatly assist in addressing all important transition areas and in better predicting future needs and potential environments.

A unique aspect of the personal/social domain is its influence on success in all the transition domains, and the team may have to address social skill needs in school and work and in community living environments as well. A number of assessments address behavioral and interaction aspects of personal-social skills that the team may find helpful. The team may need to develop an integrated assessment approach that identifies related strengths and needs across all three domains with an intervention plan that addresses all simultaneously (Sax & Thoma, 2002).

Summary

Transition assessment is broadly inclusive of competencies that are needed for adulthood. These competencies can be categorized into three main areas: current and future education, work, and living. Personal-social permeates all three domains. The team chooses among a range of standardized and informal assessments, including functional and ecological assessments. These provide both general and specific data that are used in planning for desired transition outcomes. The nature of transition implies that assessments be ongoing, have a specific purpose, and be effectively summarized. The next section further describes the types of tests that the team uses in gathering the required information to create a comprehensive transition assessment.

FORMAL TRANSITION ASSESSMENTS

Assessments can be classified into two general categories: standardized (formal) and nonstandardized (or informal). A norm-referenced test (one type of formal assessment) is designed for the purpose of determining a person's relative standing within a group for a general trait or characteristic. Typical examples include intelligence tests (i.e., a number is calculated that compares the student's ability to learn with others of the same age) and achievement tests (i.e., a grade equivalent or stanine score is given that ranks the student's progress compared with others of the same age or grade). In addition to intelligence tests and achievement tests, special education and transition programs often use formal adaptive behavior scales, transition skill and self-determination scales, personality tests, and vocational and career aptitude, interest, worker characteristic, and occupational skill tests for evaluating student potential for a variety of careers.

Some newer transition tests are being developed that are designed to assess knowledge and skills specifically required in community functioning. These tests are criterion referenced. A criterion-referenced standard is used to evaluate mastery of specific tasks required, for example, in career/technical and community and employment environments. For some work-related and community tasks, there may be specific industry, union, or site-based standards of production quality and quantity that the student must meet. These are examples of socially validated or external criteria, which the team will want to follow. Formal assessments, including many statewide proficiency tests, often use criterion-referenced standards to establish categories of attainment.

It has been long recognized that standardized tests give a limited view of the individual (e.g., a focus on deficits) and are not perfectly reliable and valid, particularly for individuals with disabilities. However, there are certain qualities and circumstances that make standardized tests valuable.

Formal, standardized tests go through a development process that strengthens their reliability and validity and allows comparisons between individuals. Reliability refers to stability of scores. For example, a student taking a social skills test should get approximately the same score if he or she takes it again without instruction (of course, we hope that training and practice will raise scores in any areas of need). Validity means that a test accurately measures what it is intended to assess. For example, if the results of a vocational abilities test show an aptitude in a particular career area, the student will also demonstrate those aptitudes successfully in a work situation.

The difficulty for students with disabilities is that few students (or none) are included in the development of most tests or in the norming processes that establish the norms. In addition, students who need specific accommodations or who do poorly on certain types of tests (e.g., those that are timed or require transferring answers onto a standardized "bubble" test form) are not likely to perform in ways that represent their true abilities. While comparisons with other students can provide some useful, general information, the team should combine formal test results with those from informal tests to evaluate the student's potential. When both types of tests identify patterns of behavior or gaps and needs for programs or environments, the team can be fairly certain that these are trustworthy and accurate results. Any one test, whether formal or informal, should never be used as the sole indicator or predictor of success or difficulty potentially experienced by a student.

Current and Future Educational Environments

Transition teams often need academic assessments because of the transition goals of students with disabilities. The extent to which the team addresses academic performance and outcomes will depend on the student's academic potential and career/lifestyle preferences. For some students, education transition goals may include two- or four-year college or postgraduate and professional training. For other students, postsecondary education will involve further development of work and life skills. The team must also realize that not all students are appropriately tested through the standard method, in which case accommodations and alternative performance options will need to be investigated. However, teams will still need to plan for entrance requirement tests for a variety of postsecondary programs ranging from technical training through graduate and professional study.

Although it is usual for all students to be assessed in the realm of academic performance, many of those assessments are more closely allied with classroom curriculum and activities. They may not address the individual student's projected needs in postsecondary environments (Thurlow & Elliott, 1998). Academic assessment for transition purposes must focus specifically on those academic skills that will provide the foundation needed for success in postsecondary education and community and work life. Students who plan to live and work independently in the community also need job-related academic skills as well as functional and survival skills in communication (either written or oral), math, science, social studies, and government/civics. They must be able to budget their income and to balance their checkbook, as well as, for example, to read directions on cleaning products and recipes. Their adult goals will determine the extent and nature of the academic testing that the team needs to pursue (Hart et al., 2004; Stodden, 2005).

Many academic tests use formal and standardized procedures although informal procedures also can provide valuable information. Students who wish to enter academically focused postsecondary programs need to develop abilities to take general achievement tests. In addition, they should consider participating in mandatory statewide testing, which is required of regular education students in many states. IDEA requires that students with disabilities should be part of the system of assessment and accountability that is part of school improvement and reform efforts. The type of high school diploma a student receives may depend on his or her ability to take and score well on achievement and state proficiency tests. An academic diploma is increasingly important for assuring entry into postsecondary programs. The team may need to be creative in devising appropriate accommodations and methods to ensure that this testing reflects the student's actual skills and accomplishments and not an access issue.

Table 5–3 shows general categories of standardized achievement and ability tests and possible accommodations. Accommodations are necessary in many instances to allow the true abilities of the student to be determined. Because of the technical issues of test standardization, the interpretation of the test results is unclear. Tests taken with accommodations are under different conditions so that comparing scores with others (e.g., norm group) may not be valid.

Current and Future Working Environments

The area of work has been fairly well developed for formal assessment through career counseling and vocational rehabilitation programs. Assessment often begins with identification of career interests. The *Becker Reading-Free Interest Survey*, *Career Development Inventory (CDI)*, *Career Maturity Inventory (CMI)*, *Knowledge of the World of Work Scale*, *Kuder Vocational Preference Record*, *Reading-Free Vocational Interest Inventory*, *Self-Directed Search*, and the *Wide-Range Interest and Opinion Test (WRIOT)* all provide for some aspects of interest assessment. Additional information about these and other instruments listed in this chapter can help team members to evaluate which, if any, are appropriate for their student (see Clark & Kolstoe, 1995; Gajar, Goodman, & McAfee, 1993; Kokaska & Brolin, 1985; Linn & DeStefano, 1986; Luft, 1999; Sitlington et al., 1996). The use of visual mediums may assist in assessing the interests of students with communication

TABLE 5–3 Transition-related large-scale standardized tests and accommodations

Types of tests/examinations
Proficiency: Measures of accomplishment of standard curriculum; knowledge and/or performance in academic subjects at different grade levels
High School Graduation: Measures on attainment of certain levels of competence to receive a regular diploma
General education development: Tests on meeting high school requirements in reading, mathematics, writing, social studies, and science in lieu of a diploma
Entrance to College or Professional School: Tests on level of preparation for college course work (e.g., ACT, SAT) or graduate/professional school level work (GRE, LSAT, etc.)
Credential: Tests to determine proficiency preparation to enter a line of work/occupation (e.g., BAR, medical boards, teacher license exams, etc.)

Types of accommodations
• Increased time • Different setting • Different response types (e.g., oral versus written) • Revised formats (e.g., enlarged print)

Source: Adapted from Thurlow, M. & Elliott, J. (1998). Student assessment and evaluation. In Rusch, J. R. & Chadsey, J. G. (Eds.), *Beyond high school: Transition from school to work* (pp. 265–196), New York: Wadsworth.

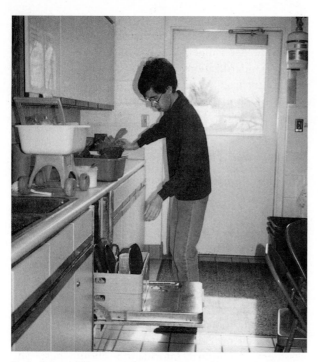

Daily living skills are an important transition curriculum.

difficulties. Besides pictures and drawings, assessments using videos were developed that provide multiple choice-making opportunities coupled with experience (Martin, Marshall, et al., 2004; Morgan & Ellerd, 2005).

Another well-developed area of assessment is work skill and aptitude measurement. Some of these instruments are the *Bennett Hand-Tool Dexterity Test*, *Differential Aptitude Test (DAT)*, *Macquarrie Test for Mechanical Ability*, *Minnesota Spatial Relations Test*, and *Purdue Pegboard Test* (Clark & Kolstoe, 1995; Gajar et al., 1993; Kokaska & Brolin, 1985; Linn & DeStefano, 1986; Luft, 1999; Sitlington et al., 1996). The team may want to consult with a vocational evaluator in order to select specific tests that best assess a student's skills in a particular area.

Use of work samples is another popular format that was developed by rehabilitation and vocational education to examine work tasks and performance variables. A work sample is "a well-defined work activity involving tasks, materials and tools that are identical or similar to those in an actual job or cluster of jobs. Work samples are used to assess a person's vocational aptitudes, work characteristics, and vocational interests" (VEWAA, 1988, p. 16). Because a work sample approximates an actual job, the evaluator can observe actual work behavior in a controlled situation (usually a testing room or classroom). Commonly used examples include *Apticom*, *McCarron-*

Dial Work Evaluation System, *Singer Vocational Evaluation System*, and *Valpar Work Sample* (Clark & Kolstoe, 1995; Gajar et al., 1993; Kokaska & Brolin, 1985; Linn & DeStefano, 1986; Luft, 1999; Sitlington et al., 1996). These typically involve asking the students to perform certain specific tasks that are evaluated for speed, accuracy, quantity, and quality. *Vocational Evaluation and Software:* A *Consumer's Guide* discusses and analyzes 30 work sample systems (Brown, McDaniel, Couch, & McClanahan, 1994) and is a good resource for general and specific issues of work sample batteries. (The work sample method can also be an informal [nonstandardized] method to determine how students respond to specific task and setting characteristics that may be relevant to local employment or program settings.)

These formal and standardized work samples, like other standardized measures (e.g., intelligence tests, adaptive behavior scales, and the others described earlier), do not predict job success perfectly because they are based on performance of job tasks that only resemble actual jobs and do not occur in a real work environment with typical distractions and conditions. They continue to be used as a means of identifying a student's relative areas of strengths and aptitudes for certain kinds of jobs. Although it can change their interpretation and scoring, some experienced evaluators choose to modify these assessments to learn valuable information about a student's rate of learning these tasks, responsiveness to suggestions, and related work behaviors. These modifications can provide helpful information to the team when standardized scores are not necessary.

Rating scales also are a common tool used to assess general work and employability skills. Some scales are appropriate for use with students with any disability (Brady & Rosenberg, 2002) while others were developed for students from a specific disability group (Bullis & Davis, 1996). The *Job Observation Behavior Scale (JOBS)* is a standardized rating scale based upon supported employment practices and expectations. The *Scale of Job-Related Social Skill Knowledge (SSSK)* and *Scale of Job-Related Social Skill Performance (SSSP)* are assessments of social competence with specific situations for students with emotional/behavioral disabilities.

Current and Future Living Environments

An important area to assess for independent living is whether students have sufficient survival skills to live safely and happily. Several instruments that assess general areas of survival skills include the *Independent*

Living Behavior Checklist, the *Street Survival Skills Questionnaire*, and the *Test for Everyday Living*. These typically use an interview or survey format (Clark & Kolstoe, 1995; Gajar et al., 1993; Kokaska & Brolin, 1985; Linn & DeStefano, 1986; Sitlington et al., 1996). A student's satisfaction is the ultimate measure of transition success. Although there are few such instruments as yet, an additional assessment is the *Lifestyle Satisfaction Scale*, which might provide some useful information for the team. Community living skills also are included within subtests of general adaptive behavior or transition skills assessments (discussed later under transition skill assessments).

Survival skill needs may have related effects on personal-social skills and skills needed for work (Menchetti, Rusch, & Owens, 1983; Rusch, 1979). A key feature of survival skill measurement is that the instruments should have social validity and should meet the expectations and beliefs of the community and family regarding environments in which the student will live, work, and play. The team may need to interpret some of these standardized tests cautiously; conditions vary considerably between urban, suburban, and rural settings as well as across ethnicity, social class, and disability. What meets the expectations of one community may violate those in another community.

Formal Tests of Personal-Social Skills

This area has fewer standardized measures although a number of instruments recently have been developed that assess aspects of personal-social functioning. The *ARC's Self-Determination Scale* (Wehmeyer, 1995; Wehmeyer & Kelchner, 1995) is a formal assessment that is a student self-report instrument designed for use with adolescents with cognitive disabilities, including mild mental retardation and learning disabilities. Through this instrument, students can evaluate their own beliefs about themselves and their self-determination skills or needs, and can assess their progress.

Abilities or needs in this domain can greatly impact the other three transition domains. An inability to form satisfactory relationships can lead to unacceptable behaviors in any environment, ranging from social withdrawal to aggression and violence toward others. Not many formal assessments address formation of friendships and dating/marital relationships, but they do address more general social abilities. Some of these assessments include the *Progress Assessment Chart of Social and Personal Development, Social and Prevocational Information Battery, Waksman Social*

Skills Rating Form, and the *Leisure Time Activities Scale* (Clark & Kolstoe, 1995; Gajar et al., 1993; Kokaska & Brolin, 1985; Linn & DeStefano, 1986; Sitlington et al., 1996).

An assessment that combines work with social skills is the *Test of Interpersonal Competency for Employment (TICE)*. This is a 61-item survival skill measure that has been validated in terms of important skills that are specific to job tenure (Foss, Cheney, & Bullis, 1986). The student's competence is evaluated in terms of responding to criticisms/corrections, following instructions, and requesting assistance from supervisors; working cooperatively, responding to teasing/provocation, and coping with personal problems as co-worker issues. The instrument accompanies a comprehensive training curriculum (Foss & Vilhauer, 1986) so that need areas can be efficiently addressed.

Comprehensive Transition Skills Assessments

A number of instruments provide general assessments of transition skills that can help the team to identify broad strength and need areas. Adaptive behavior scales often are used in multifactored assessments and typically request individuals who know the student well (e.g., teachers, parents, etc.) to rate the individual on the skills required for functioning in the community or school. An example is the *American Association on Mental Retardation (AAMR) Adaptive Behavior Scales*. Teachers and parents rate the student's abilities across a number of life-skill areas (e.g., basic academics, self-care, meals, and hygiene). Results provide an age-normed score with 100 as the "average." The *Vineland Adaptive Behavior Scales* is another commonly used instrument with a similar format.

Halpern (1996) developed the *Transition Skills Inventory*, which is completed by the student, parent, and teacher. The skills inventory consists of four broad areas and their respective subdomains, including the following areas:

- Personal life: communication with other people, relating to authorities, relating to peers, responsibility, solving problems, controlling anger, personal safety;
- Jobs: knowing about jobs, finding a job, skills on the job;
- Education and training: reading, writing, math; and
- Living on your own: self-care, nutrition and fitness, money management, home management, community and leisure activities.

Halpern's inventory uses a self-report student form in conjunction with forms for parents and teachers. This helps students to learn about their interests, strengths, and weaknesses and then to use the information obtained to make important decisions that affect their lives. Students can use this to enhance their self-evaluation as a foundation for greater participation with the team in developing their transition plans.

The **Transition Planning Inventory (TPI)** is designed to help its user identify and comprehensively plan for the student's transition needs (Clark & Patton, 1997). The instrument assesses employment, education, daily living, leisure, health, self-determination, communication, and interpersonal relationships. There are three forms completed by the school, home, and students. There are over 600 transition goals that are correlated with transition planning statements. Together, these results can assist the team in integrating perspectives from several people regarding the student's needs, preferences, and interests.

Sample items from the various categories of the TPI are:

- Can take care of physical problems that arise (Health Scale)
- Has the work habits and attitudes for keeping a job (Employment Scale)
- Takes care of his/her own money (Daily Living Scale)
- Knows and accepts own strengths and limitations (Self-Determination Scale)
- Makes friends in different kinds of settings (Interpersonal Relationships Scale)

The individual doing the rating (parent, teacher, self) then indicates whether he/she strongly agrees or disagrees with the statement relative to the student being rated.

Some transition assessments have a more narrow focus. The *Social and Prevocational Information Battery (SPIB)* assesses knowledge of skills and competencies for the vocational and community adjustment of students with mental retardation (Halpern & Irvin, 1986). The nine subtests examine knowledge of job search skills, job-related behavior, banking, budgeting, purchasing, home management, health care, hygiene and grooming, and functional signs. The battery is intended primarily for junior and senior high school levels and consists mostly of true-false, orally administered items. One important note for team members is that students who have difficulty responding to questions asked in this manner may not give reliable answers.

The comprehensive **Life-Centered Career Education (LCCE)** curriculum program includes a related assessment program and employs criterion-referenced measures (Brolin, 1992a, 1992b; Brolin, 1995; Bucher & Brolin, 1987). This comprehensive curriculum is designed to prepare students with disabilities with the important skills needed to function successfully as productive workers in the home and community. The three accompanying curriculum-based measures are the LCCE knowledge battery, LCCE performance battery, and the competency rating scale. There are two versions of the LCCE and the accompanying measures—LCCE Mild and LCCE Moderate (Brolin & Lloyd, 2004). The following discussion is of the measures for the LCCE Mild.

The Competency Rating Scale (CRS) evaluates students on the 22 competencies and 97 subcompetencies comprising the LCCE. The subcompetencies and their objectives become the test while the test manual provides specific behavioral criteria to judge student performance. Teachers who have worked closely with students are in the position to accurately assess their competency levels, given helpful and appropriate guidelines from the manual. A three-point Likert Scale is used to evaluate each of the subcompetencies as: not competent (0), partially competent (1), or competent (2). See Figure 5-1 for listing of competencies and subcompetencies of the LCCE.

CASE STUDY | Helen

Using the LCCE Assessments

Helen is described here in terms of her present level of educational performance, her background, and assessment results from the LCCE (see Figure 5-1). She is currently in the 11th grade at County High School and attends a separate class for students with disabilities, with inclusion in Environmental Biology (with modifications), PE, and women's chorus. She reads at the fourth-grade level, with listening comprehension at the fifth-grade level. Mathematically, she can add, subtract, multiply, and divide, using a calculator and decimal form. Money exchange and figuring change are difficult practices for her.

Although physically able to do most things, she does have significant limitation in fine- and gross-motor activities, and bilateral use of her left leg and arm is limited. She also has had to wear a brace on her lower leg to assist with ambulation and balance. She is, however, physically able to take care of most of her self-care needs. Although she likes her hair to look nice and enjoys makeup and nail polish, her fine-motor skills make it hard for her to apply makeup evenly, and she needs help with thoroughly washing and styling her hair.

She is familiar with cooking and can complete simple meals independently, wash dishes, vacuum, and dust; and she contributes at home by completing these and other chores. When Helen participates in community, recreation, and leisure skills, she requires moderate supervision or support, mostly in the areas of social skills and personal safety. Based upon evaluations using the LCCE criterion measures, the following instructional need areas were identified in the Daily Living Skills domain:

- DL 1   Count money and make correct change
- DL 16 Practice personal safety
- DL 20 Purchase food
- DL 34 Choose and plan activities
- DL 38 Demonstrate knowledge of traffic rules and safety

Helen displays moderate communication deficits due to dysphasia. She has learned strategies that help make her speech more understandable, but Helen can appear withdrawn when around strangers. People unfamiliar with her speech patterns may experience difficulty understanding her at first.

Socially, Helen interacts appropriately with adults but can appear immature, especially around peers. With peers, she often seeks attention in inappropriate ways, such as poking, hitting, yelling, or interrupting conversations. Helen can verbalize that this is an ineffective way to get peer attention, but she becomes frustrated in her inability to replace the behavior with more appropriate responses and resorts to familiar means. Helen does not display the ability to independently select and/or access community recreation, leisure, or other activities. She requires support when selecting and participating in new activities and she may not always recognize unsafe situations. Based upon evaluations with the LCCE criterion measures, the following instructional need areas were identified in the Personal-Social Skills domain:

- PS 42 Identify physical and psychological needs
- PS 56 Demonstrate listening and responding skills
- PS 67 Recognize and respond to emergency situations
- PS 68 Communicate with understanding

Helen participates in community-based vocational training once a week at the Food Bank. She is required to follow food safety and hygiene practices while sorting, weighing, packaging, and labeling food. She is able to complete a learned task with minimal supervision, at about 40–50% of the standard work rate. Needing one to four reminders per session to stay on task, Helen also requires occasional cues to begin and end scheduled breaks. Helen volunteers at a horse stable once per week, where a peer helps her complete the tasks of grooming, feeding, and mucking the stalls. In the summer, she mows her lawn and the neighbor's lawn, with supervision from her parents, to earn money.

In work situations, some social intervention is needed, such as working as a team, understanding the social norms of the work place, and rules of the job. Helen has difficulty with attention at times. However, high-interest activities tend to increase her motivation to learn. Based upon evaluations with the LCCE criterion measures, the following instructional need areas were identified in the Occupational Guidance and Preparation domain:

- OGP 53 Demonstrate appropriate behavior in public places
- OGP 81 Follow directions and observe regulations
- OGP 85 Work with others
- OGP 87 Work at a satisfactory rate
- OGP 94 Demonstrate stamina and endurance

Curriculum area	Competency	Subcompetency: The student will be able to:	
Daily Living Skills	1. Managing personal finances	1. Count money and make correct change	2. Make responsible expenditures
	2. Selecting and managing a household	7. Maintain home exterior/interior	8. Use basic appliances and tools
	3. Caring for personal needs	12. Demonstrate knowledge of physical fitness, nutrition and weight	13. Exhibit proper grooming and hygiene
	4. Raising children and meeting marriage responsibilities	17. Demonstrate physical care for raising children	18. Know psychological aspects of raising children
	5. Buying, preparing, and consuming food	20. Purchase food	21. Clean food and preparation areas
	6. Buying and caring for clothing	26. Wash/clean clothing	27. Purchase clothing
	7. Exhibiting responsible citizenship	29. Demonstrate knowledge of civil rights and responsibilities	30. Know nature of local, state, and federal governments
	8. Utilizing recreational facilities and engaging in leisure	33. Demonstrate knowledge of available community resources	34. Choose and plan activities
	9. Getting around the community	38. Demonstrate knowledge of traffic rules and safety	39. Demonstrate knowledge and use of various means of transportation
Personal-Social Skills	10. Achieving self-awareness	42. Identify physical and psychological needs	43. Identify interests and abilities
	11. Acquiring self-confidence	46. Express feelings of self-worth	47. Describe others' perception of self
	12. Achieving socially responsible behavior—community	51. Develop respect for the rights and properties of others	52. Recognize authority and follow instructions
	13. Maintaining good interpersonal skills	56. Demonstrate listening and responding skills	57. Establish and maintain close relationships
	14. Achieving independence	59. Strive toward self-actualization	60. Demonstrate self-organization
	15. Making adequate decisions	62. Locate and utilize sources of assistance	63. Anticipate consequences
	16. Communicating with others	67. Recognize and respond to emergency situations	68. Communicate with understanding
Occupational Guidance and Preparation	17. Knowing and exploring occupational possibilities	70. Identify remunerative aspects of work	71. Locate sources of occupational and training information
	18. Selecting and planning occupational choices	76. Make realistic occupational choices	77. Identify requirements of appropriate and available jobs
	19. Exhibiting appropriate work habits and behaviors	81. Follow directions and observe regulations	82. Recognize importance of attendance and punctuality
	20. Seeking, securing, and maintaining employment	88. Search for a job	89. Apply for a job
	21. Exhibiting sufficient physical-manual skills	94. Demonstrate stamina and endurance	95. Demonstrate satisfactory balance and coordination
	22. Obtaining specific occupational skills		

FIGURE 5–1 Life-centered career education competenices

Source: From *Life-centered career education: A Competency-based approach* (4th ed., pp. 12–13) by D. E. Brolin, 1993. Reston, VA: The Council for Exceptional Children. Copyright 1993 by The Council for Exceptional Children. Reprinted by permission.

3. Keep basic financial records	4. Calculate and pay taxes	5. Use credit responsibly	6. Use banking services	
9. Select adequate housing	10. Set up household	11. Maintain home grounds		
14. Dress appropriately	15. Demonstrate knowledge of common illness, prevention and treatment	16. Practice personal safety		
19. Demonstrate marriage responsibilities				
22. Store food	23. Prepare meals	24. Demonstrate appropriate eating habits	25. Plan/eat balanced meals	
28. Iron, mend, and store clothing				
31. Demonstrate knowledge of the law and ability to follow the law	32. Demonstrate knowledge of citizen rights and responsibilities			
35. Demonstrate knowledge of the value of recreation	36. Engage in group and individual activities	37. Plan vacation time		
40. Find way around the community	41. Drive a car			
44. Identify emotions	45. Demonstrate knowledge of physical self			
48. Accept and give praise	49. Accept and give criticism	50. Develop confidence in oneself		
53. Demonstrate appropriate behavior in public places	54. Know important character traits	55. Recognize personal roles		
58. Make and maintain friendships				
61. Demonstrate awareness of how one's behavior affects others				
64. Develop and evaluate alternatives	65. Recognize nature of a problem	66. Develop goal-seeking behavior		
69. Know subtleties of communication				
72. Identify personal values met through work	73. Identify societal values met through work	74. Classify jobs into occupational categories	75. Investigate local occupational and training opportunities	
78. Identify occupational aptitudes	79. Identify major occupational interests	80. Identify major occupational needs		
83. Recognize importance of supervision	84. Demonstrate knowledge of occupational safety	85. Work with others	86. Meet demands for quality work	87. Work at a satisfactory rate
90. Interview for a job	91. Know how to maintain post-school occupational adjustment	92. Demonstrate knowledge of competitive standards	93. Know how to adjust to changes in employment	
96. Demonstrate manual dexterity	97. Demonstrate sensory discrimination			
There are no specific subcompetencies as they depend on skill being taught				

FIGURE 5–1   *Continued*

The Knowledge Battery (KB) provides teachers and team members with a more objective instrument for assessing students on their level of competency attainment. The KB is a functional transition criterion-referenced assessment with 200 multiple-choice questions for the three LCCE domains. It is important to remember that the KB, like any other assessment, is just a sample of basic knowledge. No measure should be considered to reveal every student's actual functional competence. Rather, such instruments are useful screening devices to assist special educators in instructional/transitional planning efforts.

The Performance Battery (PB) is a nonstandardized criterion-referenced instrument and provides a functional, real-life measure of the competencies. Evaluation is done with open-ended questions, role-playing scenarios, card sorts, and several hands-on activities that require the student, for example, to prepare a meal, use a telephone directory, and fill out a credit application. Many teachers prefer the PB because it is the most natural and realistic measure of their students. Collectively, these criterion measures make it possible to evaluate the knowledge and skills to determine individually appropriate instructional goals related to daily living skills, personal-social skills, and occupational guidance and preparation skills.

FUNCTIONAL AND INFORMAL TRANSITION ASSESSMENTS

In the early 1980s, contemporary and functional assessment emerged as an alternative approach to supplement limitations of norm referenced tests of student characteristics and abilities (Halpern & Fuhrer, 1984; Pancsofar & Steere, 1997). IDEA 1997 emphasizes the use of functional or informal assessment because of limitations of standardized tests. Bullis, Kosko, Waintrup, Kelley, & Issacson (1994) further noted: "the relevance of traditional intelligence, personality, and neuropsychological instruments and their respective results to the pragmatic educational, work, and community adjustment focus of rehabilitation programs is unclear at best, and may be totally unrelated to the rehabilitation process" (p. 9).

> **Critical Point**
> Informal assessments are emphasized in IDEA 1997 to supplement the use of standardized tests.

Informal assessments are used to determine what the students' strengths, needs, interests, and preferences are and how well they are progressing in reaching their transition and IEP goals. Informal assessments also can be functional to determine performance on some specific task directly relevant to the educational program of the student. The student's performance or behavior is measured in a specific environment, for example, the classroom or community setting. The functional assessment consists of a standard or criterion of performance of what, in fact, is required for success/achievement within that setting, in comparison to the individual's own performance (Hughes & Carter, 2002).

One important concern about informal assessments is their potential lack of validity and reliability; in other words, are they really testing what is desired (and not other irrelevant or obscure factors), and are the results reliable (e.g., if different people observed the student over several weeks, would the results be the same?). Clark (1996) identified some conditions for determination of the validity of nonstandardized assessments. He believed that the team's agreement that an assessment is an accurate reflection of a student provides some face validity for an informal assessment. When these results are supported by what is already known (e.g., other informal assessments or formal assessments), then the results may be considered affirmed and useful for program planning.

Informal assessments are a vital complement to standardized test results in transition planning by providing examples of specific successes, strengths, and needs in relation to transition planning and IEP outcomes. Because informal assessments do not meet the technical standards of formal tests, describing how the information was obtained, providing caveats and limitations in their interpretation, and examining the assessments as a whole and among several sources (e.g., different team members in different situations) become very important. Nonetheless, because informal assessments occur in specific environments, their results provide authentic information about how the student performs in these environments and their needs for training, resources, and accommodations in order to be successful.

Informal assessments include several types of formats that address all four transition domains depending on the setting in which they are used. The key in informal assessments is to accurately identify demands in future environments and to assess the student reflective of those demands. The assessment provides a starting point for instruction and a method to track progress toward goals. Table 5–4 lists various types of items from informal assessments that might take place in the three transition environments. Several are described next.

> **Critical Point**
> Informal assessments provide detailed information on a student's specific successes, strengths, and needs that are directly related to his or her transition and IEP outcomes.

Rating Scales

Rating scales of transition skills can be nonstandardized tools used by an individual team member or by the

TABLE 5–4 Types of informal assessments in various environments

	Education	Work	Community Living
Ecological Assessment	Identifies addition of 3-digit numbers in all environments: home, school, community, and future environments	Examine quality and quantity of work performed in bussing tables/janitorial at fast food restaurant; compare with similar tasks at home	Safely prepares nutritious meal in supported living apartment
Rating Scales	Teacher, parent, and student rate (1–4) addition skills and usage	Employer, site supervisor, co-workers rate (1–4) on job tasks and compare with self-evaluation on quality and quantity of work.	Level of independence (rated 1–4) in preparing a meal
Surveys and Interviews	Ask teacher and parents to identify potential use of addition skills in daily life	Ask employer, site supervisor, co-workers to evaluate their satisfaction with student	Question mother about cooking skills
Situational Assessments	Teacher creates scenarios and observes use of 3-digit addition skills	Observe job tasks and settings for implementing self-monitoring of job quality and quantity evaluations	Knowledge and skills related to planning and preparing a meal
Curriculum-Based Assessment	Demonstrates 3-digit addition skills with regrouping, in isolated and applied situations	Follows safety procedures; uses math skills to self-evaluate quality and quantity of work performed	Appropriate/safe use of appliances in home, etc.
Task Analysis and Behavioral Assessment	Follows steps in task analysis for regrouping to solve 3-digit addition problems	Performs all steps for specific job skills, in correct sequence, and according to site standards for quality and quantity	Perform multiple step tasks for how to follow a recipe; Engages in appropriate interactions

whole team. The number provided from rating scales is a collective judgment based on the rater's observation of the student in a variety of situations over time. The rater indicates his or her perception of the typical performance of the student. For example, the teacher may indicate that the student turns in his or her work on time most of the time, or rarely.

Table 5-5 shows sample items from the **Employability and Life Skills Assessment (ELSA)**, a representative rating scale of general transition skills. The ELSA is a rating scale on important life and work skills designed for teacher or parent assessment. A unique feature of the ELSA is that it can be used from elementary through the secondary level. If used every year, valuable data on student development over time can be accumulated. This type of scale is useful to identify a student's general transition skills and needs and tracking the student's progress from year to year.

Surveys and Interviews

Surveys and interviews are an effective means of gathering information directly from the student and others who are involved with the student in important settings. These individuals include parents, work supervisors and co-workers, group home staff, transportation staff, and a variety of community persons and friends. The team may need to seek out some of these individuals for their help in identifying either factors or conditions that lead to the student's success, or that create barriers.

Interviews are generally conducted face to face or by telephone. Surveys can be either self-administered or completed orally. The value of this method is that the information is obtained directly from the source. Students are the best source for their likes, dislikes, and other transition-related preferences; employers, supervisors, and co-workers are the best sources for what is important in the work environment and how students are performing; parents and families have a unique perspective on the student and their own views on the student's personality and developmental history; and friends and community members have information about interests and participation in other environments.

A number of the instruments listed previously in the formal testing section utilize an interview or survey format. These differ from informal procedures and

TABLE 5–5 Employability and life skills assessment

Self Help Skills

A. Demonstrates personal hygiene and grooming by:
• Meeting teacher expectation for good grooming (hair combed, shirt tucked in, etc.)

B. Dresses appropriately by:
• Identifying when clothes should not be worn (dirty, ill fitting, etc.)

C. Travels independently by:
• Walking or riding to school, following safety rules.

D. Communicates effectively by:
• Expressing self, answering and asking questions.

General Work Habits

A. Attends regularly/arrives on time by:
• Arriving at class, school, or work on time.

B. Stays on task by:
• Returning to work if distracted.

C. Works independently by:
• Beginning work promptly.

Task-Related Skills

A. Cares for tools, materials, and work area by:
• Locating and returning tools to the proper storage area.

B. Practices safety rules by:
• Using tools and materials only for their specified purpose.

Quantity of Work

A. Completes work on time by:
• Completing work on time with teacher prompts.

B. Exhibits stamina by:
• Maintaining an acceptable level of speed without tiring.

C. Adapts to increased demands in workload by:
• Attempting new tasks without demonstrating frustration.

Quality of Work

A. Makes appropriate choices and decisions by:
• Choosing an appropriate solution when given options.

B. Recognizes and corrects mistakes by:
• Using self-check methods to evaluate work.

Relationship to Supervisor/Teacher

A. Accepts constructive criticism from supervisor/teacher by:
• Making specified changes based on constructive criticism.

B. Follows directions from supervisor/teacher by:
• Correctly completing tasks following verbal directions.

C. Seeks help when needed by:
• Asking for assistance when help is needed.

Relationship to Peers

A. Works cooperatively with peers by:
• Seeking help from co-workers.

B. Shows respect for the rights and property of others by:
• Asking permission to use another's property.

C. Uses appropriate language and manners with peers by:
• Using language appropriate for a given situation.

TABLE 5–5 *Continued*

Work Attitudes
A. Develops and seeks personal goals by: • Demonstrating short-term personal goals such as completing daily work.
B. Shows initiative by: • Beginning a task without prompting.
C. Accepts societal values and rewards by: • Recognizing when good work has been done.
D. Takes pride in working by: • Working for positions requiring improvement in skills.

often include scoring procedures that are based on asking the full set of questions, which are asked in the manner described in a manual.

With informal interviews and surveys, the team members may decide that certain types of information that have not been gathered by other methods are needed and so they design questions to solicit this information. It is important that when creating such an instrument the questions should be relevant, clear, and well-designed. Team members may want to have their interview or survey reviewed by several other individuals to ensure it's effectiveness. Also, consideration must be given as to how the respondent will answer; that is, yes-no, multiple-choice, or an open-ended format. Students may have difficulty with certain types of questions and answers, requiring that the linguistic structure and conceptual complexity be controlled. In addition, there are dangers with self-report formats because people, for example, may answer in ways that they believe will please the committee or put the student or themselves in the best light. Answers may be well-intentioned but not entirely factual; therefore, it is best to compare interview and survey responses across several individuals to find a consensus. Figure 5–2 provides a sample of a needs and preferences survey.

Ecological Assessments

The assessments that provide information that is directly related to a student's transition outcomes are sometimes called functional or ecological assessments. The student's performance or behavior is measured in a specific environment. Gaylord-Ross and Browder (1991) contended that although functional assessment has been defined broadly, it has some of the following characteristics: (a) a focus on practical, independent living/work skills that enable the person to survive and succeed in

the real world; (b) an ecological emphasis that looks to the individual functioning in his or her surrounding environment; (c) a process for examining learning and performance; (d) prescriptions for intervention techniques that may be successful; and (e) specification of ongoing monitoring procedures that can evaluate performance progress (p. 45). A functional assessment begins with an ecological or environmental assessment.

Functional assessments require a relationship between data collection and the transition decision-making process (for examples, see Bates, 2002; Miller, Lombard, & Corbey, 2007). They must provide information directly related to current or future environments (e.g., regular or special classes, or community, work, or home settings), tasks (e.g., basic work literacy, home care and personal hygiene, soldering integrated circuits onto the mother board), and behaviors (e.g., adhering to medical restrictions, following safety precautions, and taking the correct bus). For transition planning, functional assessments also should relate directly to the student's transition outcomes.

Ecological assessments are directly related to transition outcomes. They are used to assess all aspects (e.g., people, places, and things) and interrelationships among these elements within a particular environment that impact a student's performance. Important aspects can include environmental conditions (e.g., heat, light, indoors/outdoors, proximity of others, number of co-workers, size and condition of building, etc.), relationships with others (e.g., impact of the student on co-workers and supervisors, quality of mutual interactions, acceptance and mutual regard, abilities to give and take feedback), and performance accommodations/adaptations. A functional ecological assessment examines the interactive and mutual nature of these relationships to evaluate the student's success in meeting both formal and informal expectations within the setting.

This survey is designed to help the school determine what type of experiences and education you will need to prepare for life after graduation from high school. It will be used to develop a long-range plan (or transition plan) that will be discussed at the next IEP meeting.

Please answer the following questions based on what you know about yourself (or the student, if filled out by a parent/guardian).

Student name: Parent/Guardian:

Student age: Today's date:

1. **What kind of work or education do you hope to see yourself in after graduation from high school?**

Full-Time   Part-time

❑	❑	University or College—*academically oriented four-year program*
❑	❑	Community/Technical Colleges—*technical/paraprofessional training*
❑	❑	Adult Vocational Education—*advanced job training (e.g., secretary)*
❑	❑	Military Service—*Army, Navy, Air Force, Coast Guard, Marines, etc.*
❑	❑	Competitive Employment—*a job trained by employer (or job coach)*
❑	❑	Supported Employment—*a job with job coach training and then support*
❑	❑	Sheltered Employment—*low pay work activities and training*
❑	❑	Other_____

2. **What age do you want to exit school?**   18   19   20   21   22

3. **Is there a particular kind of work or education that you are currently interested in or other comments? If so, specify:**

4. **Where do you hope to ultimately live as an adult?**

   ❑ Independently in a home or apartment—*generally requires more than minimum wage*
   ❑ Independently in subsidized housing—*usually requires minimum wage or higher income*
   ❑ Wheelchair accessible housing—*ability to live on own or with personal care attendant*
   ❑ Supported living—*staff assist a few hours per day cooking, shopping, budgeting, etc.*
   ❑ Group home/foster care—*staff provide 24 hour care and help in self-care, health, etc.*
   ❑ With parents or relatives—*sometimes with help of support staff or Medicaid services.*
   ❑ Other _____

5. **Is there a neighborhood, city, or locality you hope to live in?**

6. **What types of community participation do you hope will be available to you as an adult? (check all that apply)**

   ❑ Clubs or groups that meet to talk about a common interest (e.g., computers, astronomy)
   Specify, if possible _____

FIGURE 5–2   Transition needs and preferences survey

Source: From *Transition Planning: A guide for parents and professionals* (p. 9), by R. Baer, R. McMahan, and R. Flexer, 1999, Kent, Ohio: Kent State University. Copyright 1999 by Robert Baer. Reprinted with permission.

- ❏ Community recreational activities (e.g., YMCA, community centers, out with friends)
  Specify, if possible _____
- ❏ Religious and cultural activities (e.g., church, synagogue, temple, study groups)
  Specify, if possible _____
- ❏ Transportation for work and leisure activities (e.g., car, bus, friends, parents, bicycle)
  Specify type(s) and for what purpose _____
- ❏ Continuing education (e.g., computers, cooking, sewing, home repair)
  Specify, if possible _____
- ❏ Political participation (e.g., voting, involvement in political groups)
  Specify type of participation if possible _____
- ❏ Other/ Comments: _____

7. Check any of the following services that you feel would be helpful to you in achieving your goals.

❏ Interest Inventories (e.g., OASYS)	❏ Entrance Exam Training (e.g., SAT)
❏ In-School Job Placement	❏ Job Shadowing (i.e., observing a job)
❏ Work Adjustment Training	❏ Guidance Counseling
❏ Community Work Experience	❏ Vocational Education
❏ Summer Jobs	❏ College Experience
❏ Other/Comments: _____	

_____

❏ Transportation and Driver Education	❏ Training in Handling Emergencies
❏ Consumer Sciences/Home Economics	❏ Training in Cooking and Nutrition
❏ Money Management Training	❏ Home Repair and Maintenance Training
❏ Sewing and Clothing Care Training	❏ First Aid Training
❏ Other/Comments: _____	

_____

❏ Language and Hearing Services	❏ Occupational or Physical Therapy
❏ Accommodations and Technology	❏ Self-Advocacy Training
❏ Relationships and Marriage	❏ Vocational Rehabilitation
❏ Psychology, Social Work, Psychiatry	❏ Community Awareness Activities
❏ Other/Comments: _____	

_____

- ❏ *Evaluation(s) (Specify Type Needed):* _____

- ❏ *Referrals (Specify to Whom):* _____

FIGURE 5–2 *Continued*

See Figure 5-3 for a sample ecological/job analysis format that may be used to assess a variety of work environments. As illustrated in in Figure 5-3, an ecological assessment for a work environment requires obtaining a variety of information that deals with general characteristics (e.g., social atmosphere, transportation, etc.) as well as specific job-related and task skills. Criterion within skills are also specified (e.g., orienting is broken into small areas only, one room, several rooms, building-wide, building and grounds). With an ecological assessment, the evaluator is going to the specific environment and collecting the data for that specific environment. These data are then compared to the skills of the student.

Adapted from Virginia Commonwealth University

Job Title: _____   Job Site: _____

Job Site Supervisor Name: _____   Phone: _____

Transition Coordinator Name: _____   Date: _____

1. Hours Needed	Weekend work	Morning work	Evening work	Part-time work	Full-time work
Comments:					

2. Training Location	On public/ accessible route	Off public/ accessible route			
Comments:					

3. Street Crossing	None	Two-lane with light	Two-lane without light	Four-lane with light	Four-lane without light.
Comments:					

4. Employer Attitude	Supportive of workers with disabilities	Supportive with reservations	Indifferent toward workers with disabilities	Negative toward workers with disabilities	
Comments:					

5. Job Financial Requirements	Paid position	Possible paid position	Nonpaid position		
Comments:					

6. Physical Mobility	Sit or stand in one area	Stairs and/or minor obstacles	Full physical abllities needed		
Comments:					

7. Strength Required	Very light work (4–5 lbs.)	Light work (10–20 lbs.)	Average work (30–40 lbs.)	Heavy work (50 + lbs.)	
Comments:					

8. Endurance	Work < 2 hours with no break	Work 2–3 hours with no break	Work 4–5 hours with no break	work 4 + hours with no break	
Comments:					

9. Orienting	Small area only	One room	Several rooms	Building wide	Building and grounds
Comments:					

10. Appearance Requirements	Appearance of little importance	Cleanliness required	Neat and clean required	Appearance very important	
Comments:					

11. Communication required	None/minimal	Key words and signs needed	Unclear speech accepted	Clear signing required	Clear speech required
Comments:					

12. Social Interactions	Interaction not required	Appropriate responses only	Infrequent instructions	Frequent instructions	
Comments:					

13. Behavior Acceptance Range	Many behaviors accepted	Few behaviors accepted	No unusual behaviors accepted		
Comments:					

FIGURE 5–3   Kent state university cooperative transitional services program job analysis/requirements

Source: From Cooperative Transition Services Program, Center for Innovation in Transition and Employment, Kent State University.

14. Initiative/Motivation	Staff will prompt to next task	Volunteering helpful	Initiation of work required		

Comments:

15. Attention to Task/Perseverance	Frequent prompts available	Intermittent prompts/ high supervision	Intermittent prompts/ low supervision	Infrequent prompts/ low supervision	

Comments:

16. Reinforcement Available	Frequent reinforce-ment available	Reinforcement daily	Reinforcement weekly	Minimal reinforcement	Paycheck only

Comments:

17. Sequencing	One task performed at a time	2–3 task changes	4–6 task changes	7 or more task changes	

Comments:

18. Work Rate	Slow	Average-steady pace	Above average/ sometimes fast	Continual fast pace	

Comments:

19. Discrimination Skills	No need to distinguish between work supplies	Must distinguish between supplies with external cue	Must distinguish between work supplies		

Comments:

20. Time Awareness	Time factors not important	Must identify meals/breaks, etc.	Must tell time with cue	Must tell time to hour	Must tell time to minute

Comments:

21. Functional Reading	None required	Sight words and symbols	Simple reading required	Fluent reading required	

Comments:

22. Alphabetization	None required	To first letter	To second letter	All letters	Letters and numbers

Comments:

23. Functional Math	None required	Simple counting	Simple addition/ subtraction	Complex computations	Cash register use

Comments:

Attach job description if available.

List job duties of position (sequentially if possible):

1. _____
2. _____
3. _____
4. _____
5. _____
6. _____
7. _____
8. _____
9. _____
10. _____
    _____

FIGURE 5–3 *Continued*

TABLE 5–6 Example of a functional assessment

Using a Laundromat

- Compare students' performance with typical customer
- Identify skills that help performance:
    Watching clock
    Measuring soap
- Identify distracters that hinder performance:
    Watching others or television
- Identify reminders that work:
    Using picture cue cards for types of cycles or task sequence
    Going with a supportive neighbor
    Setting a timer
- Identify checkpoints for monitoring:
    Keep checking sorting because colors and whites are still being mixed

Table 5–6 provides the major activities of a hypothetical functional assessment for using a laundromat. Using a typical customer, a general analysis could be done of the major groups of tasks (sorting, operating washer and dryer, folding, and any social etiquette). Then a general assessment is done of the student relative to these functions/tasks. Table 5–6 further illustrates individual student instructional needs that may impact performance: time-telling skills, distractions, helpful instructional cues, and instructional probes.

> **Critical Point**
> Functional assessments focus on practical skills, compare student's performance in different environments, examine the process of learning and performance, and specify evaluation procedures to determine progress.

Situational Assessments

The primary purpose of a situational assessment is to observe, record, and interpret a student's general work behavior and adaptation in a specific work or community setting. The assessment provides a measure of the overall behaviors of the student and also provides the opportunity to observe the student's reaction to specific environments and demands. The student and the team member conducting the assessment can learn information on a wide range of behaviors that are important to the student's transition goals.

The open nature of this type of assessment requires that the team provides the assessor with a specific list of behaviors to observe. The team may want

information on general interaction or performance in global, descriptive forms. If the team wishes the observer to note specific types of behaviors or responses, it will need to provide specific definitions and examples of what to observe in order that this is clear. Some examples of types of observational goals include:

- Getting along with co-workers
- Accepting criticism
- Following directions
- Punctuality and attendance
- Greeting known neighbors in apartment building and stores
- Crossing streets safely
- Waiting for change when paying for items

Situational assessments can be used across a variety of settings. They also can be used in school to create "simulations" of community environments as a type of training assessment. Their usefulness is in being able to identify variables that may be problematic to the student and those that support their success. When done well (accurate observations of specific behaviors and conditions) by a number of persons who have the same conclusions, these are a useful tool in helping to select potentially successful future environments.

Curriculum-Based Assessment

One of the most common alternatives to traditional measurement is curriculum-based assessment. These measures assess a student's progress through a particular curriculum, either academic or vocational. Some better curriculum-based assessments also use a criterion-referenced measure that sets a standard reflecting real-world expectations (e.g., the driver's education curriculum expects the same driving and testing performance as found on the state exams). This is the case for many career and technical programs as well.

These assessments are based on the specific activities and objectives within the curriculum, making it a highly accurate test of the student's progress in the program. This type of test was developed because many standardized tests were far removed from the activities of daily instruction and, therefore, were not an accurate measure of "progress" in that program. Curriculum-based assessment also allows for an analysis of content or skills to be completed so that these can be broken down into smaller curriculum objectives or tasks as needed to promote student success.

These assessments require that the student should be taught from an existing curriculum program. Although IDEA 1997 strongly encourages inclusion of all special education students in the regular curriculum, for some students this may not be practical, or may not meet with some of the transition outcomes that are determined to be important by the team. Students enrolled in career and technical education or vocational training programs can be evaluated using curriculum-based vocational assessment, which documents their progress within the training program and ultimately, toward achieving industry-level skills.

For a student enrolled in a welding program, for example, the vocational and special education teacher could develop curriculum-based measures in order to determine the student's progress and instructional needs in completing the program (Sitlington et al., 1996). The tasks and activities in performing the welding operations are broken down to assess student learning (e.g., a competency checklist). Additional tests or ratings are developed to measure student interest and motivation, the ability to use equipment and tools in the program, and the ability to communicate with the instructor and other students. In the process of assessing and teaching, the two teachers devise any instructional or equipment accommodations/adaptations that are required for

the student to perform welding operations and related or academic tasks. The student and the two teachers are in regular communication while the student progresses through the program.

School programs typically use criteria in an informal way to measure attainment of IEP and instructional objectives. Some of these standards are arbitrary (e.g., is 70 or 80% an appropriate measure of what is "good" for any particular student?) and others are based on common sense and safety. For example, skills in crossing the street should be mastered at 100%; defining mastery at 80% means that in one out of five times the student will be in danger, an unacceptable level of error in this case. The team should ensure that objectives and programs that use criterion-based assessment reflect upon community and real-world standards as much as possible.

Task Analysis

An effective assessment tool is the task analysis subsequent to the environmental analysis. Academic competencies and related learning strategies can be broken down by task analysis into their component skills. Task analysis assessment has also commonly been applied to functional community living task sequences (Test, Spooner, Keul, & Grossi, 1995).

To conduct a task analysis in a work setting, the job trainer should observe a coworker doing the task and record each discrete behavior that occurs. The task analysis assessment delineates the specific behaviors that the student must be able to perform to complete the task successfully and can be quite detailed. For example, Snell (1987) identified 14 steps involved in hand washing, including these separate aspects of rinsing: "put hands under water," "rinse palm of hands (until all visible suds are removed)," and "rinse back of hands (until all visible suds removed)" (p. 75). The needs of the student and the complexity of the task determine the number and detail of steps. For instance, a fairly proficient student may use the task analysis primarily to guide them in the proper sequencing of specific behaviors which they have already mastered or may require only a few number of general steps specified (using the preceding example, simply list "rinse hands" without detailing palm and back of hands). A student with more severe disabilities or less job experience, alternatively, may need each step broken down into its most basic components.

Another example illustrating general versus specific task analysis follows: walk to card holder, select correct card, place card in machine, remove card from machine, return card to original slot in folder, walk to cooler, open and put lunch bag inside, close door securely, walk to office, take off coat, and hang coat on coat rack. The task of preparing for work as shown could be as few as three steps: (1) punch in, (2) store lunch, (3) walk to office and hang up coat, or 11 steps.

Portfolio Assessment

Portfolio assessment with regular and special education students uses student performances (or products) that display accomplishments and improvement over time (Airasian, 1994). Various types of student information or experiences can be included that range from academic to career development to job and community preparation. Through portfolios, a very individual record of the student's growth and development and performance in specific contexts can be recorded, making it somewhat unique (Carey, 1994). Sarkees-Wircenski and Wircenski (1994) recommend portfolio assessment as a good tool for documenting a variety of transition competencies and for directly involving the student in the assessment process. They suggest using videotapes to record students who are successfully performing a variety of tasks. This can be very convincing to a prospective employer or community individual who might not be able to see a student's potential. These types of career or transition portfolios can reflect upon progress over time in critical areas such as: employability skills, work-related social skills, self-help/independent living skills, generalization skills, job-specific skills, home management, independent travel, and safety and survival skills.

The portfolio method also has disadvantages in terms of being subjective, difficult for the student who needs a lot of structure, time-consuming, and difficult for establishing reliability and validity. These issues can be addressed particularly if the team knows of specific performance or behavioral standards that are required in a work or community situation. The portfolio can be used as an alternative way of documenting the student's ability to perform at these levels.

> **Critical Point**
> The portfolio assessment provides an alternative means to evaluate a student's work and improvement over time.

Behavioral Assessment

Behavior assessment (including instructional task analysis) is used to assess functional relationships between training and observed behavior. Many of these processes are based on the use of applied behavioral analysis to identify and thoroughly examine factors that are contributing to the existence of certain behaviors. Although this process is quite detailed and deserving of separate study, a brief summary will be included here.

Observation and documentation of behaviors is the basis for much of our work with students with disabilities, with written goals and objectives that are observable and measurable. Many techniques described here can be applied to the range of student behaviors (e.g., improving quantity or quality of work products and improving quality of hygiene practices) and are not limited to undesirable interpersonal behaviors.

Five major recording procedures are employed in behavior assessment. Anecdotal recording is for the purpose of identifying a behavior and its antecedent events, and reinforcing consequences. The behavior must be specifically defined so that all observers know exactly what to measure. For example, a "tantrum" must be defined as the exact series of behaviors that a student demonstrates so that if they just stamp their feet or engage in one aspect but not the full tantrum episode, this can be accurately noted. (When more is known about the behavior, the staff may choose to watch for "early" signs, which have been shown to indicate that a tantrum will soon begin; however, initial observations must first identify all aspects of a sequence.)

Antecedent events are those incidents that happen right before the behavior. They suggest possible causes or triggers and, thus, they are important. The consequences are events that happen immediately after the behavior, such as "time-out," lots of attention from other students and adults, and so on. The following example is based on a case presented by Browning (1997). Through an analysis of antecedents and consequences, an intervention program can be designed around the behavior under consideration: "When Bill has a tantrum at his work site, what occurs immediately prior to that outburst, and what happens immediately following it?" The analysis may show that the antecedent is that Bill becomes angered by a certain co-worker who won't talk with him (because the co-worker is focusing on his work), and the consequence of the tantrum is that it gives Bill considerable attention from others, which reassures him that he is "likable." Another explanation (depending on which antecedents and consequences are found to be related) is that Bill becomes bored with work (antecedents being that he becomes increasingly agitated, makes increasing attempts to talk with others, or asks to go to the rest room) and the tantrum provides the consequence of removing him from the workstation and also reducing the amount of work he has to do.

Observers can use one or more ways to count how often and at what times the target behaviors occur. Event recording assesses the frequency with which the event occurs: "How often does Bill have tantrums on the job-training site?" Time sampling is for the purpose of determining the time period in which the behavior occurs: "Do Bill's outbursts seem to happen in the early mornings/late afternoons, beginning or end of week, when few or many work peers are around?" Interval recording is an observation period that is divided into a number of equal time intervals in which the presence or absence of the behavior (activities) is recorded, especially when the behavior is relatively frequent. Finally, duration recording refers to the length of time that the behavior (activities) occurs. "How long do Bill's tantrums last?" All of these types of measurements help to identify specific conditions that lead to the behavior, prolong it, and lead to its happening again. The type of recording depends on whether the behavior occurs frequently or infrequently, or if time-related patterns are suspected. Observing periodic tantrums, how often Bill stopped working to try to talk with a co-worker, or how often and long he engaged in "off-task" behaviors would be measured using different techniques.

These observational techniques are used to identify a pattern of behavior and then to document behavioral changes. First, behavioral assessment is used to establish a "baseline" of measurement prior to any training or intervention. This establishes the type, rate, and frequency of the behavior under "typical" conditions. Powell et al. (1991) refer to this baseline assessment as "a process of obtaining information about the worker's current ability to complete (a behavior or) an activity before any instruction" (p. 64). From this baseline pattern, the team can gauge if and how much change, if any, has occurred as a result of instruction or intervention.

The area of behavioral change is extremely complex and the team may need to consult a specialist. Improving behavior does not merely consist of reducing or eliminating problematic behaviors but also must teach appropriate replacement behavior. For example, a team may feel successful in reducing Bill's frequency and duration of tantrums. However, this will be short-lived if they realize a few weeks later that he has now become increasingly physically violent with training staff and co-workers.

When done consistently and conscientiously, behavioral assessment and management is an important informal assessment tool. It can be used across the range of transition settings to meet the requirements of a variety of work, independent living, and personal-social environments.

Transition planning includes multiple outcomes.

INTERDISCIPLINARY ASSESSMENT PROCESS

The assessment process begins with consensus among team members on a student's potential future. They use this to identify the kinds of information that are necessary to assemble a comprehensive transition description of the student. From this, the team shapes future transition potentials by matching interests and talents with potential job requirements and career profiles, lifestyles and living arrangements, and community participation and socialization opportunities.

Sitlington et al. (1997) provided a specific set of guidelines for method selection as shown in Table 5–7. These authors reinforce the need for ongoing evaluation that samples behavior across multiple settings, using several assessors and different methods or instruments. All assessments must be appropriate to the individual and accommodate learning, linguistic, cultural, and technology/assistive device needs. The results must be reported and synthesized into a format that all team members can understand in order to maximize their usefulness in planning.

The process of identifying assessment needs, carrying out the assessments, interpreting the results, and compiling them into a succinct overview is facilitated when the process involves all team members and collaborative relationships (Gajar et al., 1993). A trusting and open relationship will allow the many professional disciplines and community representatives that may be present, including the student, parents, and interested neighbors and friends, to share their perceptions and to participate in providing support and services in planning and achieving transition outcomes.

The amount and variety of information collected across types of instruments and observers/assessors may be difficult to summarize and synthesize (Miller et al., 2007; Neubert & Moon, 2000; Trainor, Patton, & Clark, 2005). Results may be contradictory or raise additional questions. Team members may be unfamiliar with or doubtful about some types of testing. Establishing and maintaining open communication will allow issues and questions to be addressed early and while there is still time to explore alternatives.

As noted earlier, IDEA 1997 specifically indicated that all children receiving special education services must be considered for assistive technology (AT). Each domain area (e.g., physical, communication, cognition) needs to be specifically addressed and considered in terms of potential AT for identified barriers. As with other types of assessment, it is impossible for any single individual to be an expert in all types of AT (Holder-Brown & Parette, 1992). Therefore, the appropriate identification and implementation of AT usually relies upon the knowledge of several disciplines (Holder-Brown & Parette) including occupational therapists, special education teachers, and speech language pathologists. Regardless of what AT assessment model one might use, there are three common characteristics that are embedded within all assessment models: (1) the environmental demands placed on that individual; (2) the individual's needs, abilities, and preferences (Chambers, 1997); and (3) the technology characteristics (Thorkildsen, 1994).

TABLE 5–7 Guidelines for transition assessment processes

- Assessment methods must be tailored to the types of information needed and the decisions to be made regarding transition planning and various postsecondary outcomes.
- Specific methods selected must be appropriate for the learning characteristics of the individual, including cultural and linguistic difference.
- Assessment methods must incorporate assistive technology or accommodations that will allow an individual to demonstrate his or her abilities and potential.
- Assessment methods must occur in environments that resemble actual vocational training, employment, independent living, or community environments.
- Assessment methods must produce outcomes that contribute to ongoing development, planning, and implementation of "next steps" in the individual's transition process.
- Assessment methods must be varied and include a sequence of activities that sample an individual's behavior and skills over time.
- Assessment data must be verified by more than one method and by more than one person.
- Assessment data must be synthesized and interpreted to individuals with disabilities, their families, and transition team members.

Source: From Sitlington, C. L., Neubert, D. A., & LeConte, P. J. (1997). Transition assessment: The position of the division on career development and transition. *CDEI, 19,* 69–79.

Additionally, an AT evaluation should be done in a variety of environments to determine the impact on school activities across curriculum areas, in vocational sites, and in community and home settings (Bauder, Lewis, Gobert, & Bearden, 1997; Blackhurst & Cross, 1993; Craddock & Scherer, 2002; Reed, 1997; Zabala, 1994).

One strategy that may help the team to synthesize assessment data and to prioritize the results into achievable goals is by using a comprehensive planning format. This technique involves collaboration between professional and community individuals who begin with conceptualizing present and/or future life goals for the student. These may best suit transition teams who prefer open-ended and highly individualized approaches. The benefit gained is from the supportive networks that are developed through this process and that can continue well beyond the end of the student's schooling. However, not all agencies and individuals will be equally accepting of a highly student-centered approach (Luft, P., Rumrill, P., Snyder, J., & Hennessey, M., 2001).

Curriculum guides (Kohler, 1996; Brolin & Lloyd, 2004; Clark, 1998) also can provide a comprehensive delineation of elements needed for transition success. Teams who prefer a detailed product focus for planning may wish to use programs which generate transition goals from a comprehensive checklist of transition skills (for example, TPI, LCCE criterion assessments, etc.).

When teams do not choose to use a comprehensive planning tool, they may wish to make checklists of services, providers, and specific transition goals with more specificity across the three broad transition domains. Wehman, Moon, Everson, Wood, and Barcus (1988) recommend a detailed listing for assessing the student's needs in the following areas: (1) employment, (2) vocational education/training, (3) postsecondary education, (4) financial/income needs, (5) independent living, (6) transportation/mobility, (7) social relationships, (8) recreation/leisure, (9) health/safety, and (10) self-advocacy/future planning.

Use of a comprehensive planning guide or a task-focused process with checklists such as described earlier can assist the team in determining and coordinating the assessment, data synthesis, and needs-prioritizing processes. However, for some students, this is likely to necessitate moving beyond current models and requiring ingenuity and creativity from team members (Luft, 1999). Much success of the assessment and transition planning processes depend on the dedication and motivation of the team to meet challenges and to design appropriate solutions.

CONCLUSION

Transition is a process in special education that combines a common frame of reference with transition-specific requirements for assessment and planning for students with disabilities and their families. Interdisciplinary assessment and planning use student and family-generated transition goals to form a framework for consensus-based planning with professional and community individuals. Assessment processes provide the informational foundations upon which these interdisciplinary processes operate in planning and implementing transition goals.

The multiple steps that comprise transition assessment processes result in a comprehensive profile of needs, strengths, and preferences of the student that is updated and evaluated in an ongoing manner. Transition assessments provide information and data that are necessary for the planning, curriculum, and instructional decisions that guide youth with disabilities, their teachers, and other members of their teams. These assessments consist of both standardized (formal) and nonstandardized (informal) assessments, which provide the variety of information that the team will need in completing its tasks. Ongoing assessments are needed to modify goals as a result of growth, training, and experience; and to choose programs and guide program and service delivery so that students are supported for success. Interdisciplinary and team efforts are necessary for effective communication and to ensure consensus throughout the assessment and planning processes. When transition assessments are effectively and conscientiously carried out, team members will have confidence that their resulting transition plans are based on accurate and reliable data and are likely to lead to the student's successful movement into adulthood.

Previously, an appropriate transition assessment was presented for Helen that outlined some transition and instructional needs based on the LCCE curriculum. The next steps in appropriate assessment include determining needs, interests, strengths, and preferences relative to future environments (developing a vision), relating that vision to Present Level of Education Performance (PLEP), and then developing and assessing transition activities in support of transition goals.

1. Developing a Vision

In IEP preplanning sessions, Helen, her family, and the team determine that she enjoys taking care of animals and being around people. She would prefer to work with animals, as a horse trainer or a stable worker, or with young children. Her parents envision her working in retail stocking shelves, or working with animals in some capacity. It is important to Helen to be with people, and she really responds to small children and babies.

2. Present Level of Educational Performance (PLEP)

Helen has had the benefit of a huge variety of opportunities socially, recreationally, and vocationally. She is a good listener and very quick to learn a new task, as long as it does not involve too many steps to learn at once. She enjoys working with animals and is currently involved in working with horses. She volunteers at Horse Heaven Farms to tend the horses, which includes grooming them, bathing them, cooling them down, feeding them, watering them, and mucking stables. She would be comfortable with cleaning up after other animals and is familiar with animal behavior, as she has been working around the barn. She is limited, though, in the amount of heavy lifting she can do and has some limitations through partial use of her left hand to lift and stabilize things.

Helen has participated in community-based and school-based vocational training experiences during which she has demonstrated competence in learning a simple task. She can complete learned tasks independently, with moderate supervision at the start and end of the task. Willing to try new things, Helen enjoys challenges and is hardworking. She enjoys being around both people and animals and can be very polite. She is involved socially in many groups, both at school and in her community.

3. Transition Activity to Support Helen's Vision

The following factors were determined to be important in exploring and assessing potential sites for her community experience. Helen would like to work for a few hours during the school day. She would "shadow" an employee of the pet store, learning the procedure for caring for the various pets available for sale. She also would learn how to stock and straighten shelves and keep the pet store clean by dusting, sweeping, and emptying trash. She could work one to two-and-a half hours per afternoon from 11:30 to 2:00, several days a week. She would be working on a nonpaid basis, as she is mainly interested in exploring the job conditions and expectations.

A community experience to explore job/task preferences and to evaluate response to various work environments and work adjustment was developed. This activity supports movement toward the postschool goal of supported employment in jobs involving animals and has potential to meet her need for challenges and social interaction.

Numerous accommodations and supports are necessary to ensure her success. Helen's speech may be difficult to understand. She is easily distracted and her concept of time is not well developed; therefore, she would need guidance to determine how long to work, when to take a break, and so on. She would probably do better working in the afternoon as she doesn't like to get up early. She has no health restrictions but has difficulty lifting loads heavier than 20 pounds. Helen's behavior might be a challenge; although if the experience provides variety, it may keep her behavior in check. She will need structure, limited supervision, and support, but also would thrive on opportunities to problem solve and be as independent as possible. Helen's tendency to overlook details and rush through a task may reduce the quality of her work. She also will have to keep in check her desire to tell others what to do and to be in charge. A classroom aide would be available to help Helen adjust to the demands of a new environment and to facilitate communication until employees become familiar with her.

Pet Land is located within a few miles of her home. Helen could walk to the nearest safe intersection, cross the street, and walk to the pet store. She would need training to safely cross this very busy intersection. The pet store is on the bus line, so Helen could take a bus home, or her parents could pick her up. Mom works within 0.5 miles of the store and is available if needed.

STUDY QUESTIONS

1. Describe the similarities and differences between special education assessments and transition assessments.
2. What are the three transition domains and the skills tested in each area?
3. Describe the purpose of formal and informal assessments.
4. What kind of information do formal and informal assessments provide?
5. What are the advantages and disadvantages in using formal and informal assessments?
6. What types of information can be gained from the use of functional or ecological assessments?
7. How can academic assessments be used to complement informal assessments?
8. What is the purpose of the comprehensive transition planning approach to informal assessment development?
9. In your opinion, what is the best method of assessment in transition?

WEBSITES

Assessing Students for Workplace Readiness:
   http://vocserve.berkeley.edu/centerFocus/cf15.html
Vocational Evaluation and Work Adjustment Association:
   http://www.fairaccess.org/vewaa_policy.htm

CHAPTER 6

STANDARDS-BASED CURRICULUM AND TRANSITION

Robert M. Baer

Thomas J. Simmons

Debra Bauder

Robert W. Flexer

LEARNING OBJECTIVES

The objectives of this chapter are:

1. Describe legislation tying special education to standards-based and general education.

2. Explain the evolution of the three traditional educational models in American education.

3. Describe how standards-based education changed traditional education systems.

4. Name and define the critical elements of a standards-based general education curriculum.

5. Describe the three curriculum perspectives: intended, taught, and learned curriculum.

6. Explain the role of student self-determination in transition curriculum planning.

7. Give the use and examples of backward planning in regard to curriculum.

8. Describe methods to assist students in developing their courses of study.

9. Explain the links between transition planning and standards-based curriculum.

10. Identify trends in curriculum and how they affect the role of transition specialists.

INTRODUCTION

Curriculum is the foundation of any student's education and ultimately determines how educational programs and opportunities are to be provided. It is a statement about the philosophy of the school and about the purpose of education, and it is a reflection of the values of the community. From the student's point of view, the curriculum is all-important because it lays out what the student will be taught and how such subject matter content and educational experiences will be organized. Given the very subjective character and community-driven nature of schools and curriculum, it is not surprising that there are many opinions and perspectives of what it is. A very narrow view of curriculum is as the content of books and media associated with academic courses, while a very broad view is that it encompasses all content, teaching methods, and incidental experiences (Armstrong, 1990; Berman & Roderick, 1977; Schloss, Smith, & Schloss, 2001). In this chapter, the authors define curriculum as "a master plan for selecting content and organizing learning experiences for the purpose of changing and developing learners' behaviors and insights" (Armstrong, 1990, p. 4). This definition was chosen for the purpose of discussing curriculum in the context of standards-based education and as a way of differentiating it from transition services.

In this chapter, the *general education curriculum* is defined as standards-based education. This standards-based definition of the general education curriculum can be traced back to the 1983 publication, *A Nation at Risk*, which reported that U.S. students were falling behind students in other countries and recommended the application of rigorous *standards* to educational curricula in the United States. The standards-based reforms recommended in *A Nation at Risk* were designed to hold schools and educators accountable for their students' progress in relation to a common set of learning expectations (Hitchcock, Meyer, Rose, & Jackson, 2002; Nolet & McLaughlin, 2005). These learning expectations were sometimes referred to as "curricular aims," "common curricular goals," "standards," and "benchmarks" (Ferguson et al., 2001).

Although the general education curriculum is discussed as standards-based, the authors of this chapter also view curriculum from a career education perspective that focuses on addressing the skills and competencies students need to perform in desired adult roles in the community. The authors describe how *students' needs, preferences, strengths, and interests* must be considered in the development of curriculum and in determining their courses of study. It will describe *an outcome-oriented process* designed to focus the general education curriculum on both postschool and in-school results. Finally, it will show how special educators can develop a *coordinated set of activities* that focus academic, career/technical, and life-skills curricula on *promoting movement toward postschool outcomes*.

CURRICULUM LEGISLATION

Inclusion in the general education curriculum has been a concern of special education policy makers and advocates for some time and was embodied in the Education for All Handicapped Children Act (EHA) of 1975 as the concept of **"least-restrictive environment."** However, the concept of least-restrictive environment was not translated into progress in the general education curriculum for many students with disabilities (Kochhar-Bryant, 2003). With the development of educational standards, special education advocates and policy makers saw an opportunity to hold schools accountable for the progress of all students with disabilities in relation to the general education curriculum. It was anticipated that greater accountability for results would provide students with disabilities greater access to the general education curriculum resulting in better postsecondary education and career outcomes (DeFur, 2002; Kochhar-Bryant, 2003; Metheny, 1997; Pugach & Warger, 2001, Thurlow, 2002).

The IDEA of 1997 and 2004

The IDEA of 1997 was the first piece of special education legislation to require that all students with disabilities be involved in state and district performance tests [20 U.S.C. § 1414 (d) (1) (A)]. Under the IDEA of 1997, all students with disabilities were expected to be included in the general education curriculum to promote improved achievement and results (Hitchcock, Meyer, Rose, & Jackson, 2002; Marzano, 2001; Nolet & McLaughlin, 2000; Wehmeyer, Lattin & Agran, 2001). In the appendix to the IDEA regulations (34 C.F.R. Parts 300 and 301) it was noted that:

> In enacting the IDEA Amendments of 1997, the Congress found that research, demonstration, and practice over the past 20 years in special education and related disciplines have demonstrated that an effective educational system now and in the future must maintain high

academic standards and clear performance goals for children with disabilities, consistent with the standards and expectations for all students in the educational system, and provide for appropriate and effective strategies and methods to ensure that students who are children with disabilities have maximum opportunities to achieve those standards and goals. (34.300 58A)

The IDEA of 2004 strengthened the focus on participation in the general education curriculum and redefined transition services as a *results-oriented* process that was focused on improving the *academic and functional achievement* of the child with a disability to facilitate the child's movement from school to post school activities." It also redefined the purpose of special education to prepare students with disabilities for *further education*, employment, and independent living [Section 601(d)(1)]. Under the IEP [Section 614(d)(1)(A)(i)] the IDEA added the requirement for the statement of measurable annual IEP goals as *including academic and functional goals.* The IDEA of 2004 changed the qualifications of special educators who were teaching content classes (e.g., English) by requiring advanced preparation in that subject matter area. Taken together the IDEA of 1997 and 2004 moved special education firmly into the arena of standards-based education.

> **Critical Point**
> The IDEA of 1997 and 2004 required that all students with disabilities should participate in the general curriculum.

Standards-Based Reform and No Child Left Behind

The No Child Left Behind (NCLB) Act of 2001 moved standards-based education into a "high stakes" policy that reformed or re-organized schools and staff whose students failed to perform adequately on state- and district-wide tests. Title I of this act (formerly the Elementary and Secondary Education Act or ESEA) had been historically concerned with providing educational parity for children from low-income families and under the NCLB, standards-based reforms emerged as the primary strategy for assuring this equity. The No Child Left Behind Act required the states to: (a) develop challenging content and standards, (b) assess school effectiveness in teaching these standards, and (c) provide incentives and penalties for schools based on these assessments.

Standards-based reforms required that schools be held accountable for what students should know and be able to do at various times in their school career

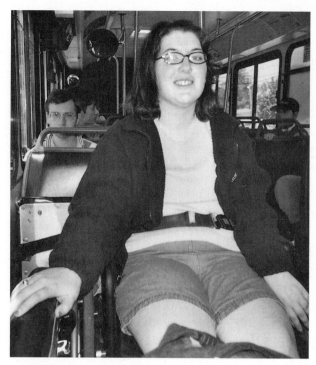

Successful postschool outcomes depend on broad curricular standards.

(Nolet & McLaughlin, 2005). Unfortunately, states and schools passed on much of this accountability to individual students in the form of "high stakes" tests that determined their promotion and graduation. Additionally, as schools tried to meet their targets for student performance, the focus of their curricula became almost exclusively academic (Stodden, Jones, & Chang, 2002; Turnbull et al., 2001). For students with disabilities this move toward an academic focus was evidenced by a 15% drop in career and technical education between 1989 and 2000 (Levine, Marder, & Wagner, 2004). The loss of vocational education and transition-related instruction in the 1990s alarmed many advocates. Turnbull et al. (2003) noted that:

> Despite the four outcomes that IDEA and other federal policy have established, there is gross inattention to all of them, except as they are addressed indirectly through the academic curriculum; indeed, as noted earlier, academic outcomes are unacceptable and too narrow: They do not encompass the global quality of life approach that IDEA implicitly justifies. (Turnbull et al., 2003, p. 73)

> **Critical Point**
> Inclusion in standards-based education held schools accountable for students with disabilities, but it also had the effect of narrowing their curriculum.

GENERAL EDUCATION AND STUDENTS WITH DISABILITIES

While standards-based reform has had the effect of creating a single curriculum, educational services for students with disabilities continued to be delivered through general, career and technical, and special education models developed prior to its advent. Gray (2002) identified three predominate educational models in U.S. education: (a) academic, (b) career education, and (c) general and life skills. Typically, academic models were the focus of high schools, career education models the focus of vocational or technical schools, and life-skills models the focus of self-contained classrooms for students with disabilities. However, some high schools (especially comprehensive high schools) provided career and technical training, while vocational and technical schools also provided academically intensive courses. Following the IDEA of 1997, life-skills programs began to focus on academics, as well. Additionally, students with disabilities increasingly moved in and out of these program models, taking some career/technical courses, some mainstream classes, and some life-skills training.

Within these three educational models, a few researchers have tried to provide general descriptions of curricular pathways to better define the role of each of these models in promoting postschool outcomes for students with disabilities. Greene (2003) identified four major *transition pathways* as including: (a) mainstream academics leading to college, (b) semi-integrated academics and/or career/technical education leading to two-year colleges, (c) semi-integrated academics and/or career/technical education leading to employment, and (d) life-skills training leading to supported employment. Greene identified coursework and transition requirements for each of these transition pathways. See Greene's Career Pathway in Figure 6–1.

Baer, Flexer, and Dennis (in press) conducted a cluster analysis of 705 students exiting special education and identified seven major transition pathways within these three models: (a) advanced academics leading to four-year college; (b) semi-integrated academics leading to two-year college; (c) career/technical training leading to technical school; (d) semi-integrated academics leading to employment;

> **Critical Point**
> The educational system has consisted of three major educational models, but students moved between these models in various career pathways.

(e) career/technical training leading to employment; (f) semi-integrated academics and transition services leading to part-time college and employment; (g) semi-integrated academics or life-skills training leading to entry-level employment, or supported employment. A comparison of the Greene (2003) and Baer et al. (in press), pathway models is included in Table 6–1.

Academic Models

Historically, approximately 70% of all students participated primarily in academic models of education (Gray, 2002). The coursework standards for academic models were first recommended by the National Commission on Excellence in Education (1983) who identified the characteristics of a basic, mid-level, and advanced academic education as including:

> *Core curriculum or below:* 4 years of English, 3 years of mathematics, 3 years of science, and 3 years of social studies.
> *Mid-level curriculum:* exceeds core curriculum by the addition of at least 1 year of a foreign language; also, two of the mathematics courses must have included algebra I and geometry, and the science courses must have included two of the following: biology, chemistry, or physics.
> *Rigorous curriculum:* at least 4 years of English, 3 years of a foreign language, 4 years of mathematics (including precalculus or higher), 3 years of science (including biology, chemistry, and physics), 3 years of social studies, and at least 1 honors or advanced placement (AP) course or, if missing, an AP test score.

In response to demands for more rigorous learning, many states enlarged the number of courses required for graduation. This had the effect of crowding out the other curricula such as career/technical educational programs but also was related to higher numbers of students entering both two- and four-year colleges (Wagner et al., 2005; Baer et al., in press).

Within the academic model, Greene (2003) identified two major career pathways called Pathway 1 and Pathway 2. Greene identified the mainstream academic model leading to a four-year college as *Pathway 1*. He described this pathway as including fully-integrated academics and college-preparatory courses, with a focus on passage of state graduation tests and college entrance examinations. Greene's Pathway 1 students were defined as needing academics that were similar to rigorous or at least mid-level curricula as defined by the National

IDEA 1997 transition services language requirements	Pathway 1	Pathway 2	Pathway 3	Pathway 4	Transition programming components
Instruction	Fully integrated high school college preparatory curriculum leading to passage of district proficiency exams, graduation requirements, and application requirements for entrance into a four-year university.	Semi-integrated high school curriculum leading to passage, with differential standards applied if necessary, of district proficiency exams, graduation requirements, and all requirements for entrance into a community college or professional vocational school.	Semi-integrated high school curriculum leading to passage, with differential standards applied if necessary, of district proficiency exams and graduation requirements or a certification of attendance.	Semi-integrated high school instructional program that focuses primarily on daily living skills, community-based instruction, and obtainment of a certificate of attendance.	Assessments General education curriculum access and school foundation Instructional setting
Community experiences	Function fully independently in the community.	Function fully independently in the community.	Function semi-independently in the community with necessary supports.	Function semi-independently in the community with necessary supports.	Related services and supports
Employment and other postsecondary adult living objectives	Career exploration and paid work experience in high school; full-time competitive career employment with salary and benefits as an adult.	Career exploration and paid work experience in high school; full-time competitive career employment with salary and benefits as an adult.	Career exploration and paid work experience in high school; integrated paid competitive employment with necessary supports as an adult.	Career exploration and paid work experience in high school; integrated paid competitive employment with necessary supports as an adult.	Transition planning considerations
Functional vocational evaluation and daily living skills	Not needed.	Not needed.	Participate in a functional vocational evaluation that identifies competitive employment skills, obtain daily living skills needed for semi-independent living.	Participate in a functional vocational evaluation that identifies competitive employment skills; obtain daily living skills needed for semi-independent living.	Transition culmination considerations

FIGURE 6–1 Pathways to successful transition model

From: Greene, G. (2003). Transition pathways. In Greene, G. & Kochhar-Bryant, C. A. *Pathways to successful transition for youth with disabilities* (pp. 198–229), Upper Saddle River, NJ: Pearson Education, Inc. Copyright 2003 by Pearson Education. Reprinted with Permission.

Cluster and Features	Greene Pathway's Model
Cluster 1—Low academic achieving students planning to enter work and likely to use SSI. Services included semi-integrated academics, more work-study, and supported employment. More IEP focus on residential and community goals.	Pathway 4—Semi-integrated instructional program focused on daily living skills, community-based instruction, career exploration, and paid work experiences. Need daily living skills for independent residential and community living.
Cluster 2—Low academic achieving students primarily with cognitive disabilities planning to enter two and four-year colleges and somewhat more likely to use SSI. Services included semi-integrated academics and some work study. More IEP focus on community goals.	No equivalent career path.
Cluster 3—High academic achieving students generally planning to enter employment after graduation. Services included high levels of fully integrated academic classes, higher levels of career/technical education.	No equivalent career path.
Cluster 4—Low achieving students mainly with learning disabilities planning to enter college and/or employment. Services generally included semi to fully-integrated course work and higher levels of career/technical education.	Pathway 3—Semi-integrated high school curriculum leading to passage with differential standards, if necessary, of district proficiency exams and graduation. Services include career exploration, paid work experiences, and vocational evaluation.
Cluster 5—Fairly high achieving students planning to enter two-year colleges. Services generally included regular academics, some career and technical education, and often work study.	Pathway 2—Semi-integrated high school curriculum, completion of graduation requirements for entrance into a community college or professional school. Services include paid work experiences.
Cluster 6—Very high achieving students who generally plan to enter four-year colleges. Services included regular academics. Less likely to be in work study or career/technical education.	Pathway 1—Fully integrated high school college preparatory curriculum and requirements for a four-year university. Services include career exploration and paid work experiences.
Cluster 7—High achieving students who plan to enter technical school. Services include very high levels of career-technical education.	Pathway 2—Semi-integrated high school curriculum, completion of graduation requirements for entrance into a community college or professional school. Services include paid work experiences.

Commission on Education (1983) standards. In Ohio, Baer et al. (in press) found about 21% of special education graduates in this fully-integrated academics to four-year college pathway that passed the requirements for a regular diploma. They also found that these students received few special education supports or transition services.

Greene (2003) described *Pathway 2* for students planning to enter community colleges or career and technical colleges and schools by participating in fully or semi-integrated academic preparation. These students would need to participate in a mid-level curriculum, but may also be able to enter the two-year colleges with a core curriculum. He described Pathway 2 as focusing on passage of graduation requirements with differential standards, if necessary. Baer et al. (in press) found two groups in this pathway. About 15% of the Ohio sample in the fully-integrated academics to two-year college pathway graduated with regular requirements. Another 10% were in the semi-integrated academics to two-year college pathway who graduated with differential standards. Students in this semi-integrated academics group typically took more work study than their fully-integrated counterparts (Baer et al.).

Career and Technical Education Models

Historically, **vocational education** (now career and technical education) was the focus of secondary education for about 25% of the secondary school population (Gray, 2002). Generally, students received this

> **Critical Point**
> For students with disabilities, the academic model of education was the predominate career pathway leading to four-year and two-year colleges.

type of training in joint vocational schools, career and technical centers, or in comprehensive high schools equipped to provide training in areas including: (a) food service, (b) auto mechanics, (c) computers, (d) construction, (e) industry, (f) marketing, (g) clerical, (h) building maintenance, (i) agriculture, (j) child care, (k) cosmetology, (l) health care, and (m) human services. Cobb and Neubert (1992) developed a broadly defined model for vocational education that is presented in Figure 6-2. In their vocational education model, the middle school years were focused on developing employability skills and awareness of the range of vocational options, and the secondary school years were focused on occupational preparation and work experiences. These experiences then served as the basis for the student's selection of postsecondary options and determined the need for ongoing support (Cobb & Neubert).

Career and technical education programs began to replace vocational programs after career education models emerged in the 1970s with a broader learning focus than that of vocational education (Halpern, 1985). In 1971, Sidney Marland, the U.S. Commissioner of Education, defined career education as a process of "learning about living" as well as "earning a living" (Brolin, 1997; Clark & Kolstoe, 1995). Kokaska and Brolin (1985) later expanded this definition as follows: "Career education is the process of systematically coordinating all school, family, and community components

together to facilitate each individual's potential for economic, social, and personal fulfillment" (p. 43).

In keeping with this trend, in the 1990s, vocational programs were renamed "career and technical education" (CTE) as vocational educators began moving toward approaches more diverse than occupation-specific training programs (Gray, 2002). Increasingly, secondary career/technical programs became focused on higher skills and on students entering postsecondary education. In the Carl D. Perkins Act of 1990 (P.L. 98-524), tech prep programs (sometimes called "2 + 2 programs") were funded to provide specialized training designed to lead into advanced postsecondary technical education. The CTE model was designed to meet regional employers' labor needs and generally identified the need for a more flexible and educated workforce.

The Carl D. Perkins Act of 1990 also required that career and technical education develop standards. One example of this effort was the Secretary's Commission on Achieving Necessary Skills (SCANS) that was organized to identify skills and knowledge that secondary students needed to succeed in the world of work. The overall goal of the SCANS was to focus on a "high-performance economy characterized by high-skill, high-wage employment" (U.S. Department of Labor, 1991). As a result of their work, the SCANS determined that a high performance workplace required workers to have solid literacy, computational, and thinking skills and positive personal

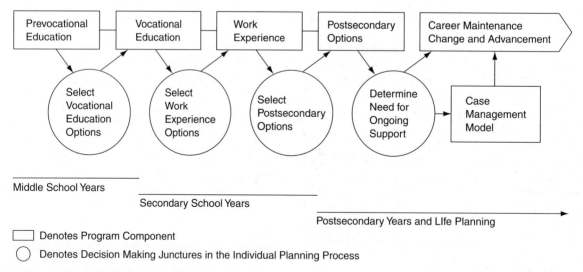

FIGURE 6–2 Model for vocational education

From: Greene, G. (2003). Best practices in transition in Greene, G. S., Kochhar-Bryant, C. A. (Eds.), *Pathways to successful transition for youth with disabilities.* (pp. 154–196), Upper Saddle River, NJ: Pearson Education. Copyright 2003 by Pearson Education. Reprinted with permission.

attributes. In their report, *What Work Requires of Schools: A SCANS Report for America 2000* (U.S. Department of Labor, 1991), the Commission outlined a three-part foundation of what schools needed to accomplish for individuals to be high-performance employees. This foundation is outlined in Table 6–2.

Greene (2003) identified two career pathways that might have a focus on career and technical education

(CTE)—Pathway 2 and Pathway 3. Greene's Pathway 2 students planning to "enter professional vocational education" would be the first group. This career pathway included students who graduated with regular requirements and those who graduated with differential requirements (Greene). Baer et al. (in press) found about 10% of their sample focused on CTE, graduated with regular requirements, and planned to enter technical school.

Greene (2003) identified Pathway 3 as emphasizing semi-integrated academics leading to employment. Baer et al. (in press) found that Pathway 3 students tended to focus more on CTE and transition services.

TABLE 6–2 SCANS foundational skills

Skill	Description of Skill
Basic Skills:	Reads, writes, performs arithmetic and mathematical operations; listens and speaks
A. Reading	Locates, understands, and interprets written information in prose and in documents such as manuals, graphs, and schedules
B. Writing	Communicates thoughts, ideas, information, and messages in writing; and creates documents such as letters, directions, manuals, reports, graphs, and flowcharts
C. Arithmetic/Mathematics	Performs basic computations and approaches practical problems by choosing appropriately from a variety of mathematical techniques
D. Listening	Receives, attends to, interprets, and responds to verbal messages and other cues
E. Speaking	Organizes ideas and communicates orally
Thinking Skills:	Thinks creatively, makes decisions, solves problems, visualizes, knows how to learn, and reasons
A. Creative Thinking	Generates new ideas
B. Decision Making	Specifies goals and constraints, generates alternatives, considers risks, and evaluates and chooses best alternative
C. Problem Solving	Recognizes problems and devises and implements plan of action
D. Seeing Things in the Mind's Eye	Organizes, and processes symbols, pictures, graphs, objects, and other information
E. Knowing How to Learn	Uses efficient learning techniques to acquire and apply new knowledge and skills
F. Reasoning	Discovers a rule or principle underlying the relationship between two or more objects and applies it when solving a problem
Personal Qualities:	Displays responsibility, self-esteem, sociability, self-management, and integrity and honesty
A. Responsibility	Exerts a high level of effort and perseveres toward goal attainment
B. Self-Esteem	Believes in own self-worth and maintains a positive view of self
C. Sociability	Demonstrates understanding, friendliness, adaptability, empathy, and politeness in groups
D. Self-Management	Assesses self accurately, sets personal goals, monitors progress, and exhibits self-control
E. Integrity/Honesty	Chooses ethical courses of action

Source: Adapted from U.S. Department of Labor. (1993) *Learning a living: A blueprint for high performance* (SCANS report). Washington, DC: US Government Printing Office.

They found 13% of their sample had a CTE focus, passed with regular requirements, and planned to enter employment after high school graduation. They also found another 18% in the CTE-to-employment pathway who graduated with differential requirements.

Life-Skills Curricula

Gray (2002) found that life skills curricula were provided to from 1–5% of students (NCES, 2001). This type of education was typically used for students who were not going to college (Edgar & Polloway, 1994; Hanley-Maxwell & Collet-Klingenberg, 1994) and emphasized a comprehensive, life-span approach. In the 1970s and 1980s, life-skills curricula became the primary focus of education for students with the most significant disabilities who (prior to the Education for All Handicapped Children Act of 1975) were considered "uneducable." Life-skills curricula were sometimes provided in separate schools for students with developmental disabilities and more often in self-contained classrooms in the student's home school. At the secondary level, these programs included functional job-related skills, daily-living skills, and social skills (Edgar & Polloway; Hanley-Maxwell & Collet-Klingenberg).

In the field of disabilities, Life Centered Career Education (LCCE) is a common skills curriculum and was specifically recommended by Greene (2003) for *Pathway 4* students entering supported living and employment. The LCCE focused on the elementary to high school levels and covered a wide array of skills and experiences. As a career educational model, the LCCE identified life skill competencies organized across four interrelated stages of career education. As an ecological model, it described critical skills in the three transition environments similar to those described by Halpern in 1985: (a) daily living skills, (b) personal-social skills, and (c) occupational guidance and preparation. Under these three domains it identified 22 competencies and 97 subcompetencies (Brolin, 1966). Table 6–3 lists the competencies and curricular areas addressed by the LCCE.

Students with disabilities that participated in life-skills training typically participated in the core curriculum as identified by the National Commission on Education

(1983) mentioned earlier. Some of these students fitted in Greene's Pathway 3 that focused on semi-independent living, and the remainder fell in Greene's Pathway 4 focused on supported employment and supported living. Baer et al. (in press) found that about 17% of students in their sample were in a curriculum that focused on life skills and transition services with little or no mainstream academics or career and technical education.

THE COMPONENTS OF STANDARDS-BASED EDUCATION

Standards-based education (SBE) required the development of discipline specific standards describing what students should know (e.g., enduring ideas, concepts, issues, dilemmas, and knowledge essential to the discipline) and be able to do (e.g., ways of thinking, working, communicating, reasoning, and investigating). SBE programs developed by states generally included: *(a) content standards, (b) benchmarks,* and *(c) performance standards*. Content standards described generally what the student should be able to do and included a number of indicators. Benchmarks identified specific grade-level steps related to the content standards and often were the basis of lesson plans and textbooks. Performance standards defined how the students would demonstrate their knowledge and skills and often were connected with specific assessments (Nolet & McLaughlin, 2005; Tomlinson & McTighe, 2006).

Content Standards

Standards-based education required schools to connect the material taught in a particular discipline (or content strand) to content standards for that strand (Nolet & McLaughlin, 2005). Content standards were designed to move educators from focusing on coursework credits (e.g., Carnegie units) to a focus on critical knowledge and skills for a given strand of knowledge. For example, in Ohio content standards were divided

TABLE 6–3 Life-centered career education competencies

Curriculum Area	Competency
Daily living skills	1. Managing personal finances 2. Selecting and managing a household 3. Caring for personal needs 4. Raising children and meeting marriage responsibilities 5. Buying, preparing, and consuming food 6. Buying and caring for clothing 7. Exhibiting responsible citizenship 8. Utilizing recreational facilities and engaging in leisure 9. Getting around the community
Personal-social skills	10. Achieving self-awareness 11. Acquiring self-confidence 12. Achieving socially responsible behavior—community 13. Maintaining good interpersonal skills 14. Achieving independence 15. Making adequate decisions 16. Communicating with others
Occupational preparation	17. Knowing and exploring occupational possibilities 18. Selecting and planning occupational choices 19. Exhibiting appropriate work habits and behaviors 20. Seeking, securing, and maintaining employment 21. Exhibiting sufficient physical-manual skills 22. Obtaining specific occupational skills

Sources: From Brolin, 1989, 1996, 1997; Kokaska & Brolin, 1985.

TABLE 6–4 Sample content standard for english language arts—Reading

Content Area: *English Language Arts—Reading*

Standard: 02 *Acquisition of Vocabulary*

Indicators: Students acquire vocabulary through exposure to language-rich situations, such as reading books and other texts and conversing with adults and peers. They use context clues, as well as direct explanations provided by others, to gain new words. They learn to apply word analysis skills to build and extend their own vocabulary. As students progress through the grades, they become more proficient in applying their knowledge of words (origins, parts, relationships, meanings) to acquire specialized vocabulary that aids comprehension. *http://www.ohiorc.org/content_stds/ohio_stds/standards/?type=2&std=35&disc=3*

across twelve content strands (*http://ims.ode.state.oh.us/ODE/IMS/ACS/*):

1. Arts—Dance
2. Arts—Drama/Theatre
3. Arts—Music
4. Arts—Visual Art
5. English Language Arts—Reading
6. English Language Arts—Writing
7. Foreign Language
8. K–12 Science
9. K–12 Social Studies
10. Library
11. Mathematics
12. Technology

In Ohio, each of these content strands contained 5–7 content standards (*http://www.ohiorc.org/content_stds/ohio_stds/standards*). For example, Table 6-4 shows one of five content standards for the English Language Arts—Reading strand. In this case, the content standard is named "Acquisition of Vocabulary."

> **Critical Point**
> Content standards were small numbers of broad descriptions of critical knowledge related to a particular discipline or content strand.

Benchmarks

Benchmarks were defined as "the specific components of the knowledge and skills identified by an academic content standard [that] . . . serve as checkpoints of

TABLE 6–5 Ninth-grade-level benchmarks for content standard "acquisition of vocabulary"

1. Define unknown words through context clues and the author's use of comparison/contrast and cause and effect. *(ORC Resources)*
2. Analyze the relationships of pairs of words in analogical statements (e.g., synonyms and antonyms, connotation and denotation) and infer word meanings from these relationships. *(ORC Resources)*
3. Infer the literal and figurative meaning of words and phrases and discuss the function of figurative language, including metaphors, similes, idioms, and puns. *(ORC Resources)*
4. Examine and discuss ways historical events have influenced the English language. *(ORC Resources)*
5. Use knowledge of Greek, Latin, and Anglo-Saxon roots, prefixes, and suffixes to understand complex words and new subject-area vocabulary (e.g., unknown words in science, mathematics and social studies). *(ORC Resources)*
6. Determine the meanings and pronunciations of unknown words by using dictionaries, thesauruses, glossaries, technology and textual features, such as definitional footnotes or sidebars. *(ORC Resources)* *(http://www.ohiorc.org/content_stds/ohio_ stds/standards)*

cumulative knowledge and skills over a band of grades" (*http://ims.ode.state.oh.us/ODE/IMS/ACS/FAQ/*). Benchmarks provided greater specificity than content standards and were divided according to grade levels (often including kindergarten and pre-kindergarten). For example, in Ohio, the content standard "Acquisition of Vocabulary" was broken down into six ninth-grade level benchmarks described in Table 6–5.

Teachers have traditionally relied on textbooks to help them develop lesson plans, and after the adoption of standards-based curricula, publishers began developing textbooks aligned with the grade-level benchmarks of states. However these textbooks often created curricular overload, because they were designed to address the content standards of multiple states. This meant that teachers were often forced to present their material "a mile wide and an inch deep" (Tomlinson & McTighe, 2006). This problem was illustrated by researchers who analyzed 160 national and state-level content standards and extrapolated 255 standards and 3,968 benchmarks (Marzano & Kendall, 1998). They estimated that addressing all of these standards and benchmarks (at 30 minutes per benchmark) would require approximately nine more years of schooling than was currently available to students in the United States (Marzano & Kendall).

> **Critical Point**
> Benchmarks are more specific than content standards and describe what students should be able to do at each grade level.

Performance Standards

Performance standards were designed to specify *how well* the student should perform relative to the benchmarks and indicators contained in the content standards. Performance standards were closely related to types of questions asked on state and district-level assessments. For example, a primer for taking of the Ohio Graduation Test for English Language Arts—Reading stated:

> In general, each form of a reading test contains one passage of significant length (900–1,200 words), two passages of medium length (500–900 words), and two short passages (under 500 words). About 35% of the points on the reading test are based on fiction and about 65% are based on nonfiction passages. Each form of the reading exam will contain a combination of item types: multiple-choice, short-answer, and extended-response. There will be a total of 31 multiple-choice items per form, 6 short-answer items per form, and 2 extended-response items per form. Total points for multiple-choice items will be 31, 12 for short-answer items, and 8 for extended-response items. The test will include 39 items with a total value of 51 points. (Ohio Graduation Test for Reading—Test Sampler, November 2002 retrieved from *http://www.ode.state.oh.us/ proficiency/PDF/OGT%20Reading%20Test%20Sampler.pdf*).

Increasingly, performance standards have become associated with "high-stakes" testing that governs student promotion and graduation. Efforts were made to make high-stakes testing better at probing in-depth knowledge, but researchers have reported that the expense of grading all of the tests required under the No Child Left Behind Act has led many states to adopt assessments emphasizing short answers and multiple choice questions. Thurlow (2002) noted that:

> Currently, state assessments are primarily structured as multiple-choice tests, with the addition of writing

tasks, sometimes incorporated into other subject areas besides writing. All states focus on language arts and mathematics, but many also add in social studies and science as areas that are covered in their large-scale assessments. These changes in the assessments of standards have been unfortunate, because they result in assessments that are fairly traditional and perhaps less adaptable to use with students with disabilities. (p. 197)

State content standards were also the basis for the performance standards used in *alternate assessments* that were developed for students who could not participate in regular state and district assessments. In a document dated August 24, 2000, the Office of Special Education Programs (OSEP) stated that "alternate assessments need to be aligned with the general curriculum standards set for all students" (2000, Question 10). A study by Thompson and Thurlow (2000) indicated that most states had alternate assessment standards that were the same as the general education standards, although they could be reduced or expanded to allow for demonstration of progress toward the standards in a different way (Thompson & Thurlow, 2000).

> **Critical Point**
> Performance standards describe how students must demonstrate their mastery of content standards and related benchmarks.

CURRICULUM PLANNING AND TRANSITION

Standards-based education was designed to bring academic, career/technical, and life-skills education in line with a common set of rigorous standards. Under SBE, these three educational systems no longer had separate curricula, but continued to use their educational models to help students master content in academic, career and technical, and life-skills contexts. For example, if a state had a core content standard related to addition, an academic approach would entail the learning of the rules and abstract processes involved in adding numbers. A career/technical approach might address this same content standard by having students solve work-related problems using addition. A life-skills approach might address this standard by having students balance a checkbook or count out change. The students would be expected to

> **Critical Point**
> Standards-based education resulted in the merging of the three educational models toward achieving the same standards.

master the same content, but would do so in a way that best addressed their unique needs, interests, preferences, and strengths.

The Three Levels of Curriculum

Deciding on the best curricular approach for a student requires some understanding of curriculum and how it is internalized by students. The three concentric circles in Figure 6–3 show how curriculum can be conceptualized as moving outward from content standards, to what is taught, and then to what is learned by the student. These three dimensions of curriculum have been respectively referred to as: (a) the intended curriculum, (b) the taught curriculum, and (c) the learned curriculum (Cuban, 1993; Nolet & McLaughlin, 2005), The first level—the *intended curriculum* (shown as the middle circle) includes broad descriptions of philosophy, standards, subject matter, content domains, benchmarks, and objectives that students are expected to meet (Nolet & McLaughlin, 2005). Additionally, this dimension of the curriculum includes the course work that students must take to complete their graduation requirements. Under the IDEA and No Child Left Behind Act, this curriculum must be the basis for educating all students, with the IEP used to make it more "immediate and student specific" (Nolet & McLaughlin, p. 17).

The *taught curriculum* (shown as the second concentric circle) emanates from the intended curriculum when content standards, indicators, and benchmarks are translated into teaching activities (Cuban, 1993). The taught curriculum includes the textbooks, worksheets, lesson plans, and electronic media used by the teacher, but also refers to how topics are taught, the cultural context of teaching, how much time is allotted to topics, and the kinds of activities used (Nolet & McLaughlin, 2005). For students with disabilities, the taught curriculum becomes more accessible if it includes universal design, contextual learning, and differentiated teaching approaches. (These methods are discussed in detail in the next chapter on instruction.)

The *learned curriculum* (the third concentric circle) emanates from the taught curriculum and is concerned with how well students can apply the taught curriculum in authentic work, education, life,

> **Critical Point**
> Curriculum can be seen from three perspectives: What is intended by curriculum developers, what is taught to students, and what is learned by students.

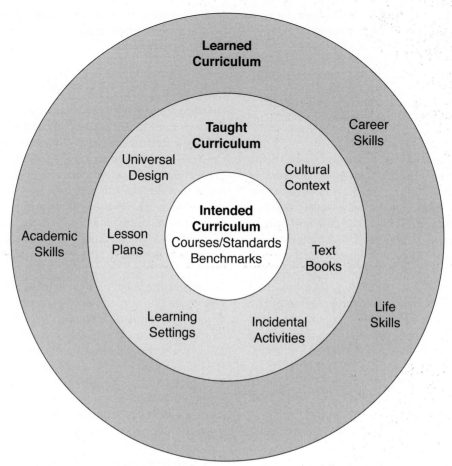

FIGURE 6–3 The three levels of curriculum

and social settings (Cuban, 1993). The learned curriculum may be enhanced by having students solve academic, career/technical, and life-skills problems with the content being taught. This learned curriculum also includes the incidental learning of attitudes and behaviors critical to the postschool success of all students (Nolet & McLaughlin, 2005). For students with disabilities, the learned curriculum can be enhanced by providing them with courses of study related to their postschool goals.

Transition Curriculum Planning

Transition curriculum planning has become an increasingly important part of transition planning. In the IDEA of 1990, instructional activities related to transition were just one of six transition services identified in the legislation. In the IDEA of 1997, instructional activities related to transition were included as a transition service, but identification of a student's

courses of study and related support needs became a focus of transition starting at age 14 or earlier. The IDEA of 2004 focused all transition services on the development of academic and functional skills as a way of promoting movement to postschool settings. This change in transition focus toward academic and functional achievement moved a large portion of transition services under the rubric of standards-based education and raised the question of how to reconcile transition models focused on postschool outcomes (outcome-oriented) and transition models that focus on school achievement and the standards governing this achievement (results-oriented).

The literature on transition planning has not yet addressed the changes resulting from the IDEA of 2004's change in transition focus from an outcome-oriented process to a results-oriented process. In the past, transition literature has typically addressed transition planning and curriculum planning as two separate activities. This may no longer be possible under the IDEA of

2004, which requires that transition services be focused on academic and functional results. On the other hand, if transition services are simply designed to promote student achievement without consideration of postschool outcomes, it is likely that advocates for students with severe disabilities will consider this insufficient (Turnbull et al., 2003). In an effort to address this issue, the authors spent considerable time coming up with a model designed to align transition and curriculum planning. This model drew heavily on the transition pathway model of Greene (2003) and on career education models.

In Figure 6-4, the black boxes superimposed on the three levels of curriculum show how transition curriculum planning can be conceptualized as addressing the four essential elements of transition (used as the framework for this book) *and* the requirements of standards-based education. The steps of transition planning related to curriculum are numbered sequentially and are superimposed on areas of the standards-based curriculum they are most likely to support and impact. Steps 1–4 generally involve special education in a leadership role, while steps 5–7 generaly involve special educators in a consultative role.

Box (or Step) 1 describes the development of a vision of postschool settings that are based on self-determined student choices. This step was inferred from the IDEA requirement that transition planning start with students' *needs, interests, preferences, and strengths* and that the IEP include measurable transition goals. Step 2 focuses on developing students' *courses of study* as

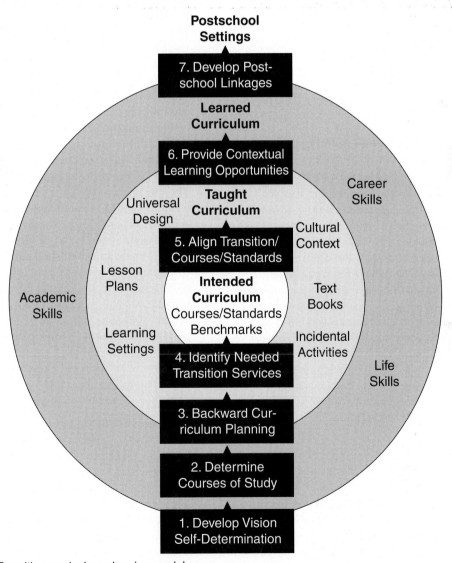

FIGURE 6–4 Transition curriculum planning model

required in the IDEA of 1997 and 2004. Step 3 describes the process of backward planning, which is a critical component of any *outcome or results-oriented process*. Step 4 identifies *transition services* that will be needed to support the student's courses of study (IDEA 1997 and 2004) and additional needed transition activities to *promote movement to postschool settings* (IDEA 1990, 1997, and 2004). Step 5 involves aligning student's courses of study and transition activities with the content standards to ensure *participation in the general education curriculum* as required in the IDEA of 1997 and 2004. Step 6 involves developing contextual learning opportunities within the general education curriculum that are designed to *facilitate the child's academic and functional achievement* as required under the IDEA of 2004. Finally, step 7 describes a process for *developing interagency linkages* as required in the IDEA of 1990 and 1997.

> **Critical Point**
> Transition curriculum planning must align the outcome-oriented focus of the IDEA with the standards-based focus of the general education curriculum.

STEPS FOR CURICULUM PLANNING

Step 1—Developing Student Self-Determination and Vision This first step in transition planning focuses on developing student **self-determination** and a positive productive vision of the future. This requires the development of such a large number of skills that must occur from the beginning of a student's education and that must be a primary objective of the transition planning. However, self-determination goals have been rarely found in the IEPs of students with disabilities (Wehmeyer & Schwartz, 1998; Test et al., 2001). Agran, Snow, and Swaner (1999) found that 75% of middle and high school teachers rated self determination skills as very important and a priority, but 55% either did not include self-determination in students' IEPs or only in some IEPs. Related findings from other studies were:

1. No self-determination goals in a survey of 895 IEP transition goals (Wehmeyer & Schwartz, 1998)
2. Half of teachers surveyed reported self-determination goals only for some students, while one-third of the teachers reported including *no* self-determination goals in IEPs (Wehmeyer, Agran, & Hughes, 2000).

3. Less than 10% of teachers and administrators were satisfied with their approach to self-determination (Mason, Field, & Sawilowsky, 2004).

Despite this lack of self-determination objectives in the IEP, researchers have continued to identify the positive outcomes of these approaches when they have been implemented. Student self-determination has been correlated with increased motivation and decreased likelihood of dropping out (Benz et al., 2000; Karvonen, Test, Wood, Browder, & Algozzine, 2004). Algozzine et al. (2001) conducted a meta analysis of 9 group studies and 13 single subject studies and found that self-determination programs were reported as being used by schools in: (a) teaching choice making to individuals with moderate to severe mental retardation and (b) teaching self-advocacy for students with learning disabilities or mild mental retardation. Test, Fowler, Wood, & Brewer (2005) provided preliminary evidence that individuals of varying ages and disabilities could learn self-advocacy skills, although the majority of participants who were included in self-determination activities were persons with learning disabilities. The curricular content of self-determination training may be varied from student to student. Karvonen et al., (2004) found that self-determination curricula: (a) included both teacher-made and published curricula, (b) typically progressed from information to modeling and from role play to generalization, (c) addressed diverse areas such as requesting accommodations, job search, interviewing, and participation in educational planning, and (d) typically used some form of student-driven educational or personal planning. Wehmeyer (2001) identified the component elements of self-determination as including:

1. choice-making skills
2. decision-making skills
3. problem-solving skills
4. goal-setting and attainment skills
5. self-management skills
6. independence, risk-taking, and safety skills
7. self-advocacy and leadership skills
8. internal locus of control
9. positive attributions of efficacy and outcome expectancy

10. self-awareness
11. self-knowledge

The use of these self-determination skills in transition curriculum planning will require that they be applied to developing a positive vision of the future. Lombard, Hazelkorn, and Neubert (1992) examined IEP transition plans for students with disabilities and found that only 18% of students with learning disabilities, 17% of students with emotional disturbances, and 21% of students with mild mental retardation had any meaningful postschool transition goals. In response to this problem, **person-centered planning** approaches began to be applied to transition planning in the late 1980s. These approaches had been used primarily for individuals who had difficulty developing career goals due to the extent of their disability or due to a difficulty in expressing preferences (Menchetti & Piland, 1998). Person-centered planning approaches typically involved a facilitator, a recorder, the student, and various family, friends, classmates, and co-workers who worked together to answer questions regarding the student's: (a) history, (b) dreams, (c) nightmares, (d) relationships, (e) abilities, and (f) plan of action (Pumpian, Fisher, Certo, & Smalley, 1997).

> **Critical Point**
> Transition curriculum planning starts with the development of student self-determination and the use of person-centered planning to develop a vision of the future.

Step 2—Determining Courses of Study
Often, students have been placed in courses of study based on their disability rather than their postschool goals. For example, a student wanting to go to a four-year college might not be given access to advanced academics because of his or her disability. As a result, the student graduates without the necessary courses to gain entrance to a four-year college. The IDEA of 1997 addressed this issue by requiring that **transition planning** include a statement of the student's courses of study and related transition service needs. The IDEA of 2004 went further to require that this transition planning be directed toward measurable transition goals further cementing the link between students' courses of study and their postschool goals. The following list shows postschool goals and typical course of study focuses that would be appropriate:

- Four-year college = advanced academics and four-year college-level classes
- Two-year college = regular academics and two-year college-level classes
- Technical school = career/technical training and college-level classes
- Employment = regular or career/technical training and community work experiences
- Supported employment = functional academics, life-skill training, and community work experiences

A single course of study may be the focus of a student's transition pathway, but typically students will need multiple courses of study to attain their postschool goals and bring relevance to the general education curriculum. Figure 6–5 shows how the three traditional educational systems (i.e., academic, career/technical, and life skills) can be combined to form courses of study for a student under standards-based education. These three educational systems are depicted as overlapping in the middle because under standards-based reforms all students are expected to demonstrate proficiency relative to the common educational standards (Bauder, Simmons, Baer, 2005). They are depicted as overlapping between one another to suggest that teachers in each educational system need to adopt curricular approaches from the other two to effectively teach material to students with different learning needs and postschool goals. For example, the overlap between academic and career/technical education suggests how academic teachers need to adopt some of the career/technical approaches to bring greater relevance to learning, while career/technical teachers need to adopt rigorous academic approaches, especially for their students who are entering postsecondary education. Likewise, the academic teacher will find that applying academics to life-skills problems (such as checkbook balancing) promotes deeper understanding, while the life-skills teacher must focus on academic content, especially literacy and mathematics, to prepare students for supported employment and supported living. Life-skills and career/technical approaches may be combined when competencies in these two areas are mutually supportive (e.g., social skill development and workplace behaviors).

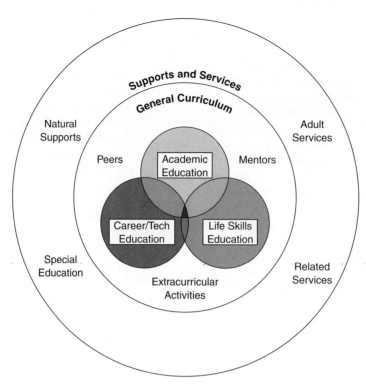

FIGURE 6–5 Standards-based curriculum model

The nonoverlapping areas of the three circles represent areas not covered by state content standards, but that may be critical to a student's development or postschool success. Typically, academic content would be augmented for students seeking a four-year college degree, while the career/technical content would be augmented for students seeking entrance into two-year colleges, technical schools, or competitive employment after graduation. Life-skills content might be augmented for students with the most significant disabilities seeking supported employment and/or supported living after graduation (Greene, 2003).

The initial courses of study statement can be very broad focusing on broad postschool goals such as employment or postsecondary education. As the student gets nearer to graduation, these statements may become more specific. For example a student in career/technical education may need specific courses to obtain certification to practice

> **Critical Point**
> Student courses of study should relate to their postschool goals and may include a mixture of educational approaches.

in a given field. Table 6–6 shows how "tech prep" training might relate to specific job outcomes.

As noted earlier, under standards-based education students must receive appropriate grade-level course work at each point in their schooling to adequately move to the next level. Clarke and Kolstoe (1995) proposed a pathways model that delineated programs and services at the elementary, secondary, *and* post-secondary levels. Their model included instructional methods, materials, and guidance to assist in the implementation as well as a description of needed interagency linkages and is shown in Figure 6–6.

> **Critical Point**
> As students near graduation, their courses of study may become more focused on occupationally specific outcomes or on critical linkages to postschool environments.

Step 3—Backward Planning
Steere, Wood, Panscofar, and Butterworth (1990) described a critical component of transition planning as **"backward planning,"** where students' postschool goals drive the development of the transition plan. This involves planning

TABLE 6–6 Examples of tech prep training and job outcomes

High School	
Earn a high school diploma and take these high school courses	**Train for these entry-level jobs**
Business Communications, Accounting I and II, Advanced Accounting, Mathematics of Finance, Mathematics, and English	Cashier; Night Auditor/Bookkeeper; Brokerage/Statement Clerk; Billing Clerk; Payroll/Timekeeping Clerk
Receive an *A* or *B* in above course and gain college credit in an articulated program at member colleges and universities	
Community College	
Skill Training	**Skilled Jobs**
Earn an associate degree from a member technical and community college and take required courses in: • Computers and Word Processing • Accounting • International Business • Business Law and Economics • Marketing and Management	Accounting Clerk; Tax Preparer; Internal Auditor; Head Bookkeeper; Assistant Controller; Business Manager; Small Business Owner; Hotel Auditor; Computerized Payroll Accountant

backward from the student's postsecondary goals to identify critical steps and then breaking these steps up evenly across the years leading up to the student's graduation. When applied to curriculum planning, backward planning identifies course work and related supports that must be provided each year up to the student's graduation, and it provides a sense of immediacy by showing how each year's activities are critical to activities in the following years (Steere et al., 1990). Overall, using backward planning in developing the curriculum has the effect of: (a) helping students master the intended curriculum, (b) motivating them to learn the curriculum by providing greater relevance, and (c) promoting deeper learning of the curriculum by applying it to social, work, academic, and living environments (Kohler, 1998).

Backward planning also forces educators, parents, and students to make the hard choices about the secondary education curriculum. The fact is, there is only so much that can be fitted into a student's schedule and with the advent of rigorous academic curricula, it may be necessary to trade off some transition services in order to obtain all of the needed course work. For

example, Baer et al. (in press) found very few transition activities in the transition pathways of students with disabilities who were taking rigorous academics leading to a four-year college. Greene (2003) attempted to identify how secondary education transition pathways affected: (a) assessment, (b) course-work needs, (c) instructional settings, (d) related services and supports, (e) transition planning, and (f) transition culmination. The following case examples show how secondary course work might look for students in each of Greene's four pathways in relation to the areas of assessment and coursework needs.

Pathway I

Sarah would like to prepare for further study at a four-year college. She needs assessments and course work related to a rigorous-level curriculum including at least four years of English, three years of a foreign language, four years of mathematics (including precalculus or higher), three years of science (including biology, chemistry, and physics), three years of social studies, and at least one honors or advanced placement (AP) course

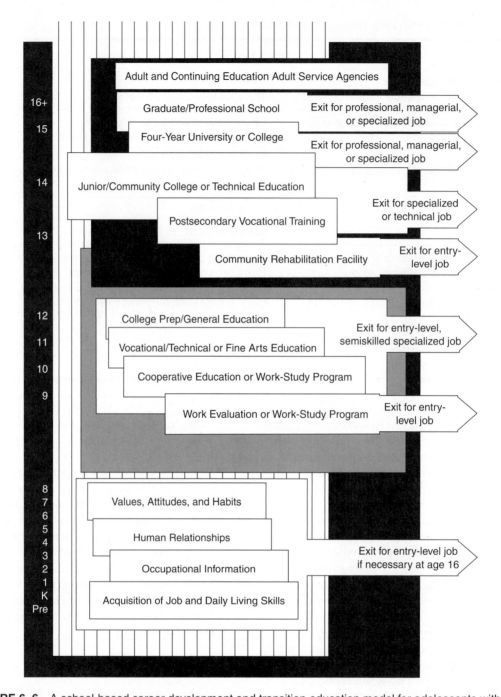

FIGURE 6–6 A school-based career development and transition education model for adolescents with disabilities

Source: From Clark, G. M., & Kolstoe, O. P. (1995). *Career development and transition education.* Copyright (1995) by Allyn & Bacon, Reprinted with permission.

or, if missing, an AP test score. Using backward planning, her coursework and assessments might appear as follows:

1. *Course work (electives will include self-determination training and study skills training).*
   a. English, precalculus, physics, honors course, social studies—12th grade
   b. English, foreign language, algebra, chemistry, social studies—11th grade
   c. English, foreign language, geometry, biology, social studies, health—10th grade
   d. English, foreign language, mathematics, science, consumer science—9th grade
2. *Assessments (may include related service, technology, and assessments of study skills and support needs).*
   a. Development of career portfolio and Summary of Performance—12th grade
   b. Successful completion of SAT, ACT—11th grade
   c. High school graduation test passage, SAT, ACT—10th grade
   d. PSAT and Achievement tests—middle school

Pathway 2

Fred would like to prepare for a community college. He will need to take a midlevel academic curriculum that exceeds the core curriculum by the addition of at least one year of a foreign language; also, two of the mathematics courses must have included algebra and geometry, and the science courses including biology, chemistry, and physics. His curriculum will need an emphasis on transition services and/or career and technical education. Using backward planning, his course work and assessments might look as follows:

1. *Course work needs (electives will include self-determination training, work study or internships, two-year college courses, and study skills training).*
   a. English, CTE coursework, social studies—12th grade
   b. English, CTE coursework, algebra, physics, social studies—11th grade
   c. English, career classes, geometry, chemistry, social studies, health—10th grade
   d. English, foreign language, mathematics, biology, consumer science—9th grade

2. *Assessment needs (may include assessments of related service, technology, and assessments of study skills and support needs).*
   a. Development of career portfolio and Summary of Performance—12th grade
   b. High school graduation test—11th grade
   c. Functional vocational assessments—10th grade
   d. Career interest and aptitude inventories—middle school

Pathway 3

Cindy would like to prepare for employment after graduation and would like to focus on employment skills and a diploma with differential requirements. She will require a core curriculum including four years of English, three years of mathematics, three years of science, and three years of social studies. Using backward planning, her coursework and assessments might look as follows:

1. *Course work needs (electives will include self-determination training, life-skills courses, and community-work experiences). If necessary, Cindy will delay graduation to participate in job club to obtain employment.*
   a. English, CTE coursework, work study, social studies—12th grade
   b. English, CTE coursework, work study, science, social studies—11th grade
   c. English, career classes, mathematics, science, social studies, health—10th grade
   d. English, career classes, applied mathematics, science, consumer science—9th grade
2. *Assessment needs (may include assessments of related service, technology, vocational, and support needs).*
   a. Development of career portfolio and Summary of Performance—12th grade
   b. High school graduation test—11th grade
   c. Functional vocational assessments—10th grade
   d. Career interest and aptitude inventories—middle school

Pathway 4

Jeremy would like to obtain supported employment and supported living, as an alternative to sheltered employment, and graduate with differential requirements. He will require a life skills curriculum that is infused into the core curriculum including four years of English, three years of mathematics, three years of science, and three years of social studies. Using backward planning, his coursework and assessments would look as follows:

1. *Course work needs (electives will include self-determination training, life-skills courses, and community-work experiences). Jeremy plans to delay graduation to obtain additional transition services leading to supported employment and supported living.*
   a. Work study, CTE courses, supported employment, and life skills—age 18-22
   b. English, community work, life skills, science, social studies—12th grade
   c. English, in-school job, mathematics, science, social studies—11th grade
   d. English, career classes, mathematics, science, social studies, health—10th grade
   e. English, career classes, mathematics, science, consumer science—9th grade
2. *Assessment needs (may include assessments of related service, technology, vocational, and support needs).*
   a. Development of career portfolio and Summary of Performance—12th grade
   b. Alternative assessments for graduation—11th grade
   c. Situational work assessments—10th grade
   d. Career interest and aptitude inventories—middle school

Step 4—Determine Transition Services and Supports

After defining the courses and assessments that support the student's postschool goals, it will become necessary to identify transition services to prepare and support students in regard to: (a) participation in their courses of study and (b) attainment of their postschool goals. The types of transition services mentioned by the IDEA of 2004 include: (a) instruction, (b) community experiences, (c) career development, (d) related services, (e) daily living skills training, (f) functional vocational evaluation, and (g) linkages with adult services. For example, students participating in courses of study emphasizing academics might receive extensive *instruction* in learning strategies and study skills, while students participating in courses of study leading to supported employment may need *related services* such as occupational therapy and *community experiences*. The IDEA requires the IEP team to identify how transition services support students' courses of study. Some examples of statements that could be included in the IEP/transition plan to address this requirement might be worded as follows:

> **Critical Point**
> Backward planning should be used to assure that critical courses, transition activities, and assessments fit into the student's schedule year by year.

Participants of a college preparation program at Kent State.

- In order to participate in advanced academics leading to a four-year college, John will need instruction in study skills and the Strategies Intervention Model (SIM).
- In order to participate in a community-based and functional academics leading to supported employment, Susan will need occupational therapy, job coaching, and alternate assessment of skills.

Transition services and supports for students' courses of study should be provided within the general education curriculum, whenever possible. An integrated systems model for all students developed by the U.S. Department of Education suggested that supports be provided within the general education curriculum for about 70% of student needs, through targeted "at-risk" services for about 25–30% of student needs, and through intense individualized services for only about 1–3% of student needs. Additionally, under the IDEA of 2004, students should be allowed to participate in reading and remedial programs for "at-risk" students, and the IDEA of 2004 allows up to 15% of special education monies to be used to offset this cost. These targeted interventions can also serve as a means of addressing the needs of students who tend to be overrepresented in special education, such as African-American students.

In addition to supporting the courses of study, the IEP team needs to identify a coordinated set of transition activities that will promote the student's movement to postschool settings. These generally include transition instruction, community experiences, and career development activities, which were required under the IDEA of 1990 unless the IEP team made a statement that one or more of these activities were not needed and why. This requirement was waived in the IDEA of 1997, but these activities were still recommended for the majority of students with disabilities. Related services may also be considered a transition activity in this area if it promotes movement to postschool settings.

The IDEA also identified three types of transition services that should be considered for students "if appropriate." These were daily living skills training, functional vocational evaluation, and linkages to adult services. Daily living skills training would be important for students who needed skills and supports related to moving into independent living. Functional vocational evaluation should be considered for students needing clarification of postschool goals or the means to achieve them. Linkages to adult services would be required for students who were eligible and who needed adult services to promote movement to, and retention in, postsecondary environments. A number of curriculum accommodations, adaptations, alterations, and augmentations may also be considered in supporting the student's courses of study and these are discussed in detail in the following chapter.

> **Critical Point**
> Transition services will need to support students' participation in their courses of study and their movement toward postschool outcomes.

Step 5—Align Transition Activities and Curriculum Standards

After identifying course work, assessments, and needed transition activities, it becomes important to apply them to achievement of content and performance standards and benchmarks. Depending on career choices made by the student and the IEP team, a variety of course work, program, and experiential options may be appropriate in addressing the student's grade-level content standards. As stated previously, because academic content standards are tied together from grade to grade, teachers must ensure that all grade-level standards are addressed either by the student's transition activities or through the general education curriculum. Students entering employment after graduation generally benefit from transition activities that address content standards by applying them to work settings. Students entering postsecondary education typically benefit from transition activities that address content standards as they are applied to postsecondary academic settings. However, the team must honor student choice, whenever possible, on how grade-level content is to be taught. The following example shows how the content standard "Writing Applications" can be addressed as part of a student's community-based work experience.

Identify what is to be taught and how it will be assessed.

✓ The student can currently use Microsoft Word for typing. The student needs to learn how to write business letters in English class using grade-level vocabulary and grammar for 10 consecutive trials without errors by the end of the year. This skill will be assessed by the English teacher and by the student's work-study employer using grade-level classroom tests and by collecting samples of student work in a career portfolio with employer comments.

Identify how the student will use these skills in relevant and authentic settings.

✓ The student will use these skills in her work-study job as a clerical assistant and in her college applications.

Example—Identify grade-level standards, benchmarks, and indicators to be addressed.

    a. Domain—English and language arts 8-10th grade
    b. Subdomain—Writing applications
    c. Grade level—8-10 grade
    d. Indicator—The student will produce letters that follow the conventional style appropriate to the text.

The type of assessment used may also impact how the student needs to be supported. Currently, the IDEA of 2004 provides four options for assessment (Browder, Courtade-Little, Davis, Fallin, Karvonen, 2005). These are:

1. General assessment/grade level achievement standards
2. Alternate assessments/grade-level achievement standards
3. Alternate assessment/modified achievement standards (limited to 2% of students)
4. Alternate assessments/alternate achievement standards (limited to 1% of students)

As noted previously, assessments based on academic tests may require teaching approaches that closely resemble the solving of academic problems. On the other hand, career portfolio assessments may require teaching approaches that show the student engaging successfully in socially valued work, education, community, and social roles. Best practice researchers suggest that multiple teaching approaches and evaluations should be used to develop deep learning (Wiggins & McTighe, 1998).

> **Critical Point**
> Students' courses of study, transition activities, and other transition services need to address grade-level benchmarks and performance standards.

Step 6—Provide Contextual Learning Opportunities

Transition activities can be effective in helping students understand and apply academic content, especially when classroom training lacks social validity (Kazdin, 1989; Menchetti & Piland, 1998; Patton & Poloway, 1990). A number of approaches have been developed to convert content standards in meaningful and authentic educational activities. Tomlinson and McTighe (2006) have presented a general education model that is highly compatible with transition planning called "Understanding by Design." The planning template in this model uses backward planning that starts with the desired results, determines acceptable evidence of performance, and then plans learning experiences and instruction. In looking at desired results, Tomlinson and McTighe suggest the use of the following "filters" in identifying specific content to be taught:

1. Does the content have enduring value beyond the classroom?
2. Does the content reside at the heart of the discipline?
3. Does the content require uncoverage (i.e., it is not obvious)?
4. Does the content offer potential for engaging students?

Under the Tomlinson and McTighe (2006) model for each content standard, the teacher determines what students need to know and what students must be able to do. These classroom and transition activities are then assessed through a series of performance tasks and other evidence (such as a career portfolio). Because the learned curriculum is concerned with what the student can actually use to solve real-life problems, it is a focus of transition activities at the secondary level. Halpern (1985) identified three general areas that graduates with disabilities must perform—work, residential, and social/interpersonal—to which is added postsecondary education as a skyrocketing expectation of students with disabilities (Baer, et al., in press; Newman, 2005). There are many formal and informal ways to assess the students' preparation in these areas, and assessments should be functional—that is, descriptive of what the student can do in relation to the demands of postsecondary work, residential, social, and education settings.

Some important considerations in developing contextual learning opportunities include: (a) social validity, (b) cultural context, and (c) method of assessment. For some students, the teaching of content must closely approximate the knowledge and skills required in the settings that the student is expected to perform. This level of approximation is frequently referred to as the "social validity" of the teaching. For example, students planning to enter postsecondary education can be taught many of the necessary skills in the classroom but may benefit from taking some college-level courses. Students entering employment after high school may learn occupational-specific skills in career/technical education but may also obtain greater social validity by participating in community work experiences.

<table>
<tr><td>Critical Point
Students' courses of study, transition activities, and transition services need to provide opportunities for students to apply knowledge and skills in authentic contexts.</td></tr>
</table>

Step 7—Transition Culmination and Linkages
Greene (2003) described transition culmination as an important consideration in transition planning. A number of activities may be needed to ensure a successful transition to postschool environments including linkages with adult service programs. These are discussed in greater detail in the chapter on transition planning. In this chapter we will look at some of the final products of the curriculum and their importance in preparing students with disabilities for adult living.

DOCUMENTS FOR THE EXIT TO POSTSCHOOL

The Summary of Performance

The IDEA of 2004 requires that schools provide graduating students with IEPs a *Summary of Performance (SOP)*. It should be viewed first and foremost as a tool for the use of the graduate with a disability and only secondarily as a tool for eligibility. This means that schools must solicit student input and self-determination in the development of this document. This document provides information about the student's progress and accomplishments, postsecondary goals, and recommendations to support the student's postschool goals. It also typically includes professional assessments to document the student's disability and accommodations provided by the school. The Council for Exceptional Children (CEC) Division on Career Development and Transition (DCDT) has developed a format for the SOP (2005). The major components of a summary of performance include: (a) the student's level of functioning with a focus on strengths, (b) the student's postsecondary goals, (c) recommendations for accommodations and supports, (d) supporting documentation, and (e) the student's perspective.

As part of the SOP, the *student's level of functioning* should include a description of how the student's disability affects academic and functional performance. It should also include the results of the student's most recent state and district assessments, the results of any college entrance exams, and the results of the most recent special education evaluation of the student. This section of the SOP should emphasize student strengths and include a description of other honors, special awards, vocational, and extracurricular accomplishments.

In describing students' *postsecondary goals*, the SOP should include measurable transition goals from the student's most current IEP. As previously noted, the IDEA of 2004 requires that these goals be measurable and that they include goals relative to postsecondary employment and education. Measurable goals might include: (a) full- or part-time employment, (b) full- or part-time enrollment at a four-year college, (c) full- or part-time enrollment at a two-year college or technical school, or (d) enrollment in a professional certification program.

The SOP should also include *recommendations for assisting the student.* These recommendations should be tailored to the environments indicated in the student's postsecondary goals. They may include recommendations for accommodating the student's disability in the workplace and recommendations for accommodating the student's disability in postsecondary education. If the student is entering supported living, they may also include recommendations for accommodating the student's disability in residential settings. This section should also include contact information for the teacher completing the summary.

In addition to this narrative information, the SOP may also include *copies of assessments and reports*. These assessments and reports may serve one or two purposes. The first purpose is to assist persons in receiving environments that accommodate and support the student. These reports should be functional rather than normative. The second purpose of attaching reports and assessments to the SOP is to assist the student relative to becoming eligible for services. These reports and assessments may be normative or descriptive of the student's disability. The following list includes the types of reports and assessments that may be included with the student's SOP:

- psychological/cognitive
- response to intervention (RTI)
- neuropsychological
- language proficiency assessments
- medical/physical
- reading assessments
- achievement/academics
- communication
- adaptive behavior
- behavioral analysis
- social/interpersonal skills
- classroom observations (or other setting)
- community-based assessment
- career/vocational/transition assessment
- self-determination
- assistive technology
- informal assessment

Fifth, it is recommended that the SOP include the *student perspective*. The student should be able to put in their own words how their disability affected their school work, school activities, and any jobs that they held while in high school. They should also be able to describe accommodations, technology, and supports that have helped them succeed in school, as well as those that did not help. Finally, they should also be able to describe their strengths and how they can be used to support postsecondary education, employment, and community living. Self-determination training will be required for most students to be able to present their perspective effectively, but they may also be provided key phrases in the SOP development relative to presenting their disability to their employer, postsecondary educators, and adult service programs.

Diplomas and Transcripts

In addition to the SOP, the student will need to understand when and how to use their diploma and transcripts. The diploma is evidence that the student has learned the intended curriculum and met the state standards for graduation. It is also a critical qualification for postsecondary education and for many types of employment. However, not all diplomas are the same, with some states providing qualified diplomas such as "certificates of attendance" for students who do not pass the required high-stakes tests or complete the required coursework.

Student transcripts are also used as evidence of the learned curriculum. These include the grades and grade point averages (GPAs) for coursework taken. Four-year colleges typically have GPA and coursework requirements and these may vary from college to college. Two-year community colleges will often accept students with lower GPAs and provide course work for individuals seeking a G.E.D.

Career Portfolios

A **career portfolio** will be critical for students entering employment and for many students entering postsecondary education. The career portfolio is typically designed to include samples of the student's best work. It often emphasizes areas that are not covered by a diploma or transcripts. It can be used by the graduate as a marketing tool and as a reference tool for filling out job applications and conducting job searches. It is not limited to print presentation and can include videos of the student working, samples of the student's work, and video or audio testimonials from teachers, classmates, and employers.

Career portfolios can also be a way of assessing the learned curriculum. **Career portfolio assessment** typically involves identification of standards to be addressed and then the presentation of triangulated data to

> **Critical Point**
> Students should be provided information that summarizes their achievements and that outlines their needs, interests, preferences, and strengths in relation to the environments they will be entering postschool.

demonstrate the level of mastery of that standard. Under standards-based education, the portfolio assessment was often used for students who could not participate in state- and district-wide achievement testing.

CONCLUSION

The chapter described how the IDEA of 1997 has made the general education curriculum a critical concern for special educators by holding students with disabilities to the same standards as their peers, and it has described some of the positive and unintended consequences of this legislation. In the coming years, special education teachers and transition specialists will need to understand how to infuse scientifically-based transition practices into a general education system that is rapidly evolving under standards-based reform. Students with disabilities have a critical stake in this process, with more than 60% of them planning to continue into some form of postsecondary education. However, it is important to remember that postsecondary education, especially four-year colleges, is only one of several career paths taken by students with disabilities. Career and technical education and life-skills education remain critical and must be infused into the general education curriculum. Transition professionals need to assist in this process by guiding academic, career/technical, and life-skills educators toward a seamless and flexible system that can be easily navigated by students with disabilities.

Special educators must also have a good understanding of the components of standards-based education and the importance of being able to assess education according to common criteria. They must understand the relationship between standards, age-level benchmarks, and performance assessments and the importance of addressing age-level content standards either through transition activities or the general education curriculum. On the other hand, transition educators must also understand how standards can be misapplied to students with disabilities through curricula that are exclusively academic or through testing procedures that fail to consider or accommodate their needs and develop opportunities for deeper understanding and authentic learning.

In this chapter, the authors provided a multilevel perspective of curriculum and how it relates to standards-based education and its critical components—content standards, indicators, benchmarks, and performance standards. It described the purpose of the general education as moving students from the intended curriculum to curriculum that is applied to authentic academic, employment, and life-skills settings. This chapter provided an overview of how transition planning can drive and be supported by the general education curriculum. The authors showed how transition planning drives the curriculum by using students' postschool goals to determine their courses of study. Finally, it described how contextual education can support learning of the general education curriculum by providing opportunities for students to apply their academic knowledge to real-life problems and authentic settings.

STUDY QUESTIONS

1. Compare and contrast traditional course-based curricula and standards-based curriculum.
2. Describe the legislation that has involved students with disabilities in standards-based curriculum.
3. Explain the positive and negative impacts standards-based curriculum has had for students with disabilities.
4. Compare and contrast the three traditional educational models.
5. Explain how career pathways of students with disabilities are related to the three educational models.
6. Describe the three levels of curriculum and how they relate to standards-based education.
7. Describe how transition can drive the standards-based curriculum.
8. Explain how students' postschool goals can be used to determine appropriate courses of study.
9. Describe how backward planning of curriculum helps students make year-to-year choices and test the feasibility of their postschool goals.
10. Explain how transition services might be used to support progress in the general education curriculum.
11. Describe how the general education curriculum can be used to support student learning and postschool goals through contextual learning activities.

12. Describe the five components of the Summary of Performance required by the IDEA of 2004.
13. Describe the basic information that needs to accompany the student after leaving high school and how this information might differ for a student entering different postschool environments.

WEBSITES

CAST
    http://www.cast.org/
Closing the Gap
    http://www.closingthegap.com/
EASI (Equal Access to Software and Information)
    http://www.rit.edu/~easi/
Disability Resources, Inc.
    http://www.disabilityresources.org/

National Council of Teachers of Mathematics
    http://standards.nctm.org/
National Science Teachers Association
    http://www.nsta.org/index.html
State Online Standards Database
    http://www.aligntoachieve.org/AchievePhaseII/basic-search.cfm
Gutenberg Project
    http://www.gutenberg.org/
High Tide Project
    http://www.ccpo.odu.edu/~arnoldo/hightide/hightide.htm
Access Standards
    http://www.ed.gov/G2K/standard.html
Creating Graphic Organizers
    http://www.teach-nology.com/web_tools/graphic_org/

CHAPTER 7

INSTRUCTIONAL PLANNING FOR TRANSITION TEACHING

Pamela Luft

Robert W. Flexer

LEARNING OBJECTIVES

The objectives of this chapter are:

1. Describe the ways through which instructional environments and curriculum are made accessible for students with different disabilities.

2. Define the difference between the art and science of instruction.

3. Describe the four aspects of instructional environments and how to manage their impact on student learning.

4. Describe the four aspects of instructional groupings and how to manage their impact on student learning.

5. Describe the four aspects of instructional materials and how to manage their impact on student learning.

INTRODUCTION

The previous chapter dealt with curriculum—which might be considered the "what" of teaching. It described how the core curriculum standards were incorporated into the three different postschool outcome domains comprising academic, life-skill, and vocational knowledge and skills. Each of these domain areas are associated with a location such as a particular classroom, building or school—the "where" of teaching. All of this teaching should prepare students to be successful across these three programs in the ultimate "where"— the community in which each student plans to live and work. The three outcome areas also include state- or district-identified courses of study—often the "when" of teaching. Certain courses and programs of study are recommended during middle or high school, and sometimes specifically by year.

This chapter will describe the "how" of teaching—the ways in which learning outcomes across the three different programs, including the state's core curriculum standards, are achieved. The instructional methods in the next chapter provide a framework across four major teaching methods that move from teacher-directed through student-directed learning. But, first, this chapter examines the various factors that impact the instructional setting and the teacher's choice of methods: instructional environments, groupings, and materials. Throughout this chapter, the authors also will address several types of "who"—the students, including those with mild-moderate, moderate-severe, sensory, and physical/ health disabilities. Between the curriculum and the instruction chapters, all major instructional factors—the "who," "what," "where," "when," and "how"—are covered.

In this chapter, the essential element of student interests, strengths, needs, and preferences is reinforced by advocating for instruction that has a clear transition focus, heightening motivation and relevance for the student. Further in this chapter, instruction for transition references the postschool goals envisioned by the student and family in the outcome-oriented process. Transition instruction is described as part of the coordinated set of activities through provision for organized, sequential learning of IEP objectives with sufficient repetition and practice in appropriate environments. Transition instruction promotes movement toward postschool activities when it provides the student with knowledge and skills needed to become responsible successful adults and methods are provided to monitor these impacts of instruction.

MAKING CURRICULUM AND INSTRUCTION ACCESSIBLE

In order for effective instruction to take place, students need to have access to both the instructional environment (the classroom, laboratory, work site, and community) and the curriculum (programs and materials). Special education addresses very heterogeneous abilities and needs across students, who at times have posed challenges to access. Fortunately, increased experience, instructional creativity, perseverance, and the development of assistive and other technologies is providing new levels of access for students with physical, health, sensory, cognitive, behavioral, and learning disabilities—to the environment and to the curriculum. In addition to technologies like motorized wheelchairs and elevators, environmental access also can be achieved by low-technology solutions: rearranging the classroom, modifying seating or lighting, repositioning, and so on.

Curriculum access can also be provided through low- or high-tech modifications. Wehmeyer (2002) describes three levels of modification to be considered for students that provide for a continuum of options. See Figure 7–1. If the student is successful in the general curriculum (sometimes because of environmental or other accessibility aides and devices), then no curricular modifications are needed. When students are not successful, the teacher must first consider adding assistive or other technologies, or reconsidering and reevaluating what is currently used. This would include personal care assistants (PCAs) or medical interventions to maintain health and well-being, or educational interpreters for students who use sign language.

> **Critical Point**
> Access to environments and curriculum for students with physical, health, sensory, cognitive, behavior, and learning disabilities is provided through a variety of technologies and modifications both general and specific to disability.

If an individual student remains unsuccessful and these technologies and aides have been thoroughly considered, then the teacher moves into curricular modifications. The first level is to *adapt* the curriculum— to change how the curriculum is presented to the student. Digital technologies (computerized media) greatly expand the ways that students can both receive and respond to the curriculum. Visual presentations can be manipulated and modified, audio can be

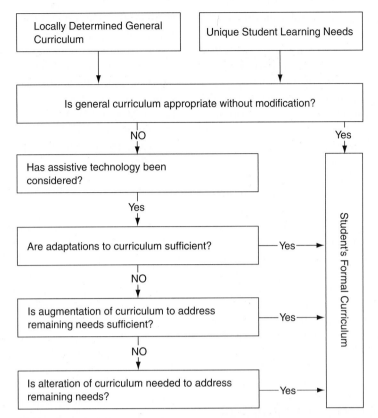

FIGURE 7–I   Access to the general curriculum model

Source: From Wehmeyer, M. L., Agran, M. & Lattin, D. Achieving access to the general curriculum for students with mental retardation: A curriculum decision-making model. *Education and Training in Mental retardation and Developmental Disabilities, 36*(4), p. 335. Copyright 2001 by Council for Exceptional Children. Reprinted with permission.

added or utilized alone, and students can manipulate joy sticks, mice, or keyboards to make their responses, based on their individual needs and preferences.

If change in presentation of information is insufficient, then the second level is curriculum augmentation in which additional learning experiences and activities are provided to support student progress through the curriculum. Students with disabilities often have had to face developmental, health, or communication barriers that have reduced their opportunities for typical childhood experiences and activities. Good teaching builds on prior experiences, moving from what is known or familiar, to what is new and unfamiliar. Special education students may be missing key preliminary experiences or have been unable to develop certain skills to the level of their peers. Curriculum augmentation is a critical means for providing these skills and experiences.

If curriculum augmentation is not successful, then Wehmeyer (2002) suggests examining curriculum alteration to address key student needs and characteristics. At this point, the standard curriculum goals are modified in some way. Students may be placed in an alternative or a functional curriculum that the IEP team believes will ultimately lead to student success.

> **Critical Point**
> Curriculum adaptation, augmentation, and alteration are modifications that address presentation of content, additional learning experiences, or the actual content itself.

The Center for Applied Special Technology (CAST) (1998–1999) had developed the Universal Design for Learning (UDL), a program to design materials that can be successfully used by all students, regardless of needs and abilities. It is based on architectural principles to provide physical access to all people. UDL could be applied in using the first two curricular modifications described by Wehmeyer: curriculum adaptation and augmentation. Adaptation for students struggling with reading text material would allow clicking an embedded link (made possible by digital text) or a button to access an audio or a sign language translation of the same text. Augmentation would provide basic skill review or practice (reading, math, social studies or science principles or processes) or background experiences (relationships between and rotating of geometric figures, multimedia presentations of key historical or scientific events, simulations of developing civil laws or mathematical/scientific principles). Less extensive augmentations would include linking key vocabulary to a picture, text, or multimedia dictionary of the word.

> **Critical Point**
> With the first prerequisite of good instruction, teachers must be sure that students have environmental access to the place of instruction, and curricular access to the content of instruction.

PROVIDING HIGH-QUALITY INSTRUCTION

Now to explore the details of "how" to provide high-quality instruction. Just to review, curriculum describes the "what," the three educational paths identify the "where," and the course of study provides the "when" of instruction. Examples were provided on how varied abilities in the "who"—students—may require different types of accommodations and accessibility. This accessibility must be assured according to the "what," "where," and "when."

The "how" of instruction comprises a complex set of behaviors that are both an art and a science. It is a *science* because good teachers thoroughly study the many variables that impact the teaching process. They often begin with their students' strengths and needs through records, conversations with family members and prior teachers and staff, and observations across different settings. They assess each of their students across the various curriculum options chosen as appropriate by the IEP/transition team. Teachers mentally align each student's learning profile (strengths, needs, interests, age, gender, family and culture, etc.) with the curriculum content and relevant IEP outcomes (annual goals and objectives) to develop an instructional plan. The teacher uses these to evaluate the teaching methods, materials, sequencing, and related factors that will support the student's maximal success with the content. This is a complex task for just one student, and managing this across multiple students within the same group, is even more so. This is why teachers get better with experience. Like with all tasks, aspects of this synthesizing and evaluating process become routine and much easier to manage, with experience.

> **Critical Point**
> Teaching as a science allows teachers to align the student's learning profile with the curriculum and IEP outcomes.

The "art" of teaching is displayed in teachers' interactions with real students—whose own interactions with best friends, girlfriend/boyfriends, or parents affect their behaviors on any given day. Transition-age students are also teenagers and are typically experiencing very rapid and profound developmental changes, both physically and emotionally. Each time teachers deliver instruction, they face all that the students bring and do not bring to the situation—this begins the *art* of teaching. Teachers use their personality, appearance, and intellect to effectively motivate and engage the students into trying out, practicing, and mastering a body of knowledge, or a skill.

> **Critical Point**
> The art of teaching involves less direct aspects, like the use of the teacher's personality, to motivate students.

Skillful teachers modify their moods, energy levels, verbal and nonverbal behaviors, and abilities accordingly to stimulate and perpetuate student learning. The interplay of the interpersonal and environmental characteristics that make up this art includes the effective transmission and implementation of skills in the instructional science aspects. The art skills include being creative and innovative in planning for and implementing these activities; the science skills include critically analyzing and evaluating the results.

Within each science and art aspect of teaching, there also are knowledge, skills, and attitudes. In order to be effective, educators need science-based:

> *knowledge:* about curriculum, instructional strategies, student strengths and weaknesses, developing units;
> *skills:* aligning profiles and curricula, finding and using curriculum and instructional strategies; and
> *attitudes:* our feelings and beliefs that impact our science-based knowledge and skills, etc.

These are combined with aspects of the art of teaching:

> *knowledge:* understanding our own personal strengths and weaknesses as a teacher, using these with those students with whom we seem less effective;
> *skills:* effective implementation, our abilities to monitor effectiveness, and also modify and adapt while teaching, etc; and
> *attitudes:* using our own and our students' attitudes to support effective implementation, or modifying accordingly.

See Table 7-1 to examine the comparison between the art and science of teaching.

Good instruction encompasses a broad as well as thorough knowledge and set of skills effectively implemented across the art and science of teaching, with a positive and professional attitude. Because this is very difficult to achieve, good teachers are always learning and striving to improve. Daily practice helps develop multitasking abilities for managing all of these aspects effectively. Good teaching may seem overwhelming at first, but beginners should be encouraged to remember the first day they climbed in the driver's side of the car. As with driving a car, many aspects of teaching will become routine and automatic over time, allowing good teachers to multitask without undue mental stress.

The material on instruction in the next two chapters uses four categories of instruction and their elements that are based on Friend and Bursuck (2002) and Wood (1998), with some modifications. The four basic categories are: instructional environments, instructional groupings, instructional materials, and instructional methods (see Table 7-2). These first three categories (the contents of this chapter) are listed and then described in the following sections (instructional methods are discussed in the next chapter). An important aspect of these categories is that many elements can be controlled or modified.

TABLE 7-I Art of teaching versus science of teaching

	Science of Teaching	Art of Teaching
Knowledge	• Curriculum • Instructional methods • Student strengths and weaknesses • Instructional unit planning	• Understanding own personal strengths and weaknesses as a teacher • Using our strengths and monitoring our weaknesses to improve student learning
Skills	• Aligning profiles and curricula • Finding/using curriculum • Choosing instructional methods	• Effective implementation of instruction • Abilities to monitor effectiveness • Ability to adapt while teaching
Attitudes	• Feelings and beliefs about instructional contend and skills	• Ability to use own attitudes to facilitate student success • Ability to build upon student attitudes

Teaching Tip: Teaching and Automaticity

With practice comes automaticity, but herein also lies danger—of becoming a nonthinking, mechanical teacher. Back to the driving analogy: Aren't there a lot of careless drivers on the road who have stopped thinking about driving, or are focused on something else? And maybe there are times when even the best drivers drive on "automatic pilot" and wake up to a near miss. Or they're finding that new CD player, or the cell phone rings; or they're groovin' to a new song and daydreaming about life. We've all had teachers like this too—those on automatic pilot, or daydreaming through each day—or counting down the days until retirement. Teachers have *plenty of challenges* left to keep them energized and enthusiastic, so there's no fear of slipping into a rut!

Therefore, if one or more of these are interfering with student learning, the teacher and IEP team are able to make changes to improve the situation. The description begins with variables that impact instruction less-to-more directly, beginning with the instructional environments.

Table 7–3 provides the outline for instructional environments and shows how topics get organized under this category. The outline format used in the table aids the learner to structure new material and promotes better understanding and retention.

MANAGING INSTRUCTIONAL ENVIRONMENTS

Physical Location

Traditionally, instruction has been located within classrooms with students seated in desks: in rows or sometimes half-circles. However, students need to learn and to apply skills not only in academic but also vocational and life-skill settings. Consequently, instructional settings should include a number of locations within the community. Teachers need to be aware of these possibilities and *think outside of the "traditional classroom" box*. Some instruction may occur best in science or computer labs. Daily living practices may be best taught in home-economics classrooms or the school cafeteria. Activity centers, gyms, and auditoriums often can be scheduled when not in use. These all are resources for optimizing instruction. Certainly, moving instruction outdoors can change attitudes and motivation in addition to providing relevant instructional opportunities.

Regardless of curriculum path, all students should know where and how to find information about their adult life: community living (apartments and homes, food and clothing, family relationships, medical, legal, personal, recreational, citizenship); career and vocational (community employers, job-finding sources, human resources and services); and educational

TABLE 7–2   Chart of instructional variables

Instructional Environment	Instructional Groupings	Instructional Materials	Instructional Methods
Physical Location	Whole-Class	Print Materials and Resources	*Teacher Directed*
Physical Structure	Small Group	Non-Print Materials and Resources	*Teacher Guided*
		Manipulatives and Models	
Emotional Structure	Pairs or Triads	Technology Resources	*Student Guided*
Behavioral Structure	Individualized	Human Resources	*Student Directed*

Teaching Tip: Learning from Change

Over the course of 15 years of real-life teaching, I noticed that adolescents' preferences and interests *change*. It happens monthly, weekly, if not daily! And even we, as elementary, middle-school, high-school, and college students changed our friends, our career, and our lifestyle preferences. Student *needs* also vary across environments, by age, across peers/colleagues, and hopefully, as a result of instruction. As team members, we may make transition plans without remembering the prevalence of these changes, and then become frustrated. Instead, this is a wonderful opportunity to help students use change as a learning opportunity—how to adapt to and plan for change—a skill they'll need the rest of their adult life.

TABLE 7–3 Management of instructional environments

- Physical Location
  - School Site
    - Academic—Indoor/Outdoor
    - Classroom
    - Lab
    - Activity-based
    - Nonacademic—Indoor/Outdoor
    - Auditorium
    - Lab
    - Activity-based
  - Community Site—Indoor/Outdoor
    - Daily Living Sites
    - Community Resources
    - Occupational Sites and Resources
- Physical Structure
  - Space: walls, lighting, floor layout, storage
  - Instructional appearance and design: decoration, information
- Emotional Structure
  - Classroom climate
  - Attitudes and acceptance
  - Roles and responsibilities
- Behavioral Structure
  - Rules and resolutions
  - Routines
    - Academic
    - Nonacademic
  - Time and Scheduling
    - Academic
    - Instructional time
    - Transition time
    - Nonacademic
    - Noninstructional time
    - Transition time

opportunities. Students benefit most from on-site activities and experiences and teachers should take advantage of partnerships to teach academic, career/vocational, and life skills in an integrated "classroom + community" approach.

Physical Structure

Across these school and community environments are physical aspects that impact students and teachers. There are pluses and minuses to every environment, whether it is a noisy, inner-city environment or a quiet or noisy, rural setting. Teachers and students will vary in their ability to cope with different conditions. There are teachers and students who do or do not respond well to specific aspects of

each type of environment. Teachers need to watch for nonobvious indicators such as different behaviors across different settings and work to optimize these.

Certain aspects of instructional space teachers may not be able to change. However with some creativity and assistance from a custodian, other desks, dividers, tables, and cabinets, or cubbies, centers, and activity corners can greatly enhance physical as well as emotional accessibility for the students. Through painting (if allowed) and decoration, walls can be optimized and windows emphasized.

Color and classroom appearance, however, is highly personal. As a teacher you may thrive in a colorful, lively, and "busy" classroom—or you may prefer a minimalist, zen-like atmosphere. Regardless, some students will and some will not respond well to the teacher's preferences. The classroom environment may need to be altered if this creates a barrier to a particular students' learning (Friend & Bursuck, 2002; Wood, 2002).

Applying the physical location and structure issues to transition services instruction, suppose the teacher needs to instruct a student who is highly distractible on how to cross an extremely busy four-lane intersection. The instructor may need to begin within a structured, quiet classroom to learn basic procedures. The instructor would then move to increasingly more authentic (community-based) and distracting (busy intersections) environments. Gradually, the student would be helped to develop the knowledge and skills to successfully cross a variety of streets, and develop compensatory strategies for dealing with the nonessential but highly distracting environmental conditions.

> **Critical Point**
> Physical aspects across school and community environments need to be analyzed then utilized to create conditions to further learning.

In terms of an academic outcome, when teaching geometry and angles, initial instruction would be done in the classroom. Then, the class would go outside to examine a dead tree on the school property. Perhaps the tree needs to be professionally removed and the school needs to collect estimates based on approximate height. The students calculate the height of the tree using its shadow and the Pythagorean Theorem and congruency with another shorter and measurable, nearby tree. They present results to the principal.

Emotional Structure

The emotional structure of the classroom is important for ensuring a sense of emotional safety and security. Without a positive and accepting classroom climate, students are unlikely to risk learning new things and making mistakes. A climate that does not support bullying or scapegoating is critical for ensuring authentic integration of students with diverse needs and backgrounds. This begins with teachers who model positive attitudes toward difference, acceptance of genuine learning attempts, and confidence in persevering toward optimal outcomes.

This is another example of the need for balance. Teachers need to assert control in assuring emotional safety and security within their classroom—it is their role and responsibility to do so. Yet, this should not stifle students' needs to engage in serious discussion and criticism of classroom and community issues. Ultimately, teachers must use their role to support students in also assuming roles and responsibilities that build a positive classroom climate as future citizens of their communities. Again, teachers need to be alert to students who may be struggling or uncomfortable due to classroom dynamics. Recent immigrant students may be uncomfortable with typical American interaction styles and emotional engagement. Teachers may need to modify and support these students as they acclimate and perhaps become bicultural, in moving between their family and school environments.

> **Critical Point**
> With a positive and accepting classroom, students will risk learning new things and making mistakes.

Teachers can expect that certain students will challenge classroom expectations and interaction patterns—but how the challenger is addressed also further reinforces the classroom tone. Climate includes how a teacher either supports or discourages acceptance of diversity, an issue that includes ethnicity, but also gender and a variety of personal characteristics. Students who resist and challenge authority also represent authority.

Behavioral Structure

Rules and Resolutions

The teacher's behavioral structures should be used to support the desired emotional structure and used particularly when behaviors warrant consequences. For example, bullying or scapegoating should result in negative consequences and classroom-wide discussion of the issues. Successful resolution of these problems should similarly result in positive consequences. Ultimately, positive behavioral resolutions of any kind should also build students' skills in self-management and choice-making. The situations can be used to develop insights into their own needs and motivations and how these can be fulfilled in more positive ways.

A few, positively stated *classroom rules* that are taught and reinforced consistently throughout the school year, provide the foundation for classroom control (and compliance with instruction). If well conceived, they can be applied equally well to school or community-based settings (e.g., respect others' persons and property, try your best, etc, are universally applicable). Clear and effectively implemented rules will also support a positive classroom climate. The teacher will need to spend extra time and energy establishing these with each new class, but once rules and routines have stabilized, the teacher can focus everyone's energies on learning.

Behavior Programs

A note about behavior systems: It is not within the scope of this chapter to review the many potentially

Teaching Tip: Fair Standards and Individual Students

Every teacher needs to establish "fair" standards across students of varying abilities, background, and motivation, regardless of class size or alleged homogeneity (no two students are identical!). Students are quite aware of the effort versus achievement conflict but can be very accepting of individually defined "fair" standards (the teacher must be consistent with this). For nearly identical behavior, a teacher may lavish praise on a highly distractible student crossing a busy intersection, but reprimand a typically calm and attentive student who suddenly engages in distracting, attention-seeking behavior—and the treatment would be "fair" because the calmer student can achieve at a higher standard regarding attentiveness.

effective systems for encouraging and rewarding positive behaviors. The choice of system depends upon the needs and abilities of the students as well as the needs and preferences of the teacher—a disregard of either can "break" even the best system. And regardless of what is used—behavior management, token economy, contract, or positive behavioral support systems—all can be quickly made ineffective by inconsistency. Rewards and disincentives work only when they are consistently applied (no matter how tired, or irritated, or inconvenienced the teacher may feel).

When designing a behavior system, like other aspects of teaching, teachers need to examine the *science* (analysis) and the *art* (implementation) components. This should begin with a thorough analysis of the behavior such as a functional assessment (cf., Smith et al., 2001) to determine the exact nature of the behaviors, who and what are contributing to this, and as much as possible, *why* they believe the behavior is occurring. The student who behaves marvelously on the job but abysmally in the classroom (or vice versa) is telling the teacher something, and it's their job to identify the conditions supporting the *appropriate* behaviors. This analytical and positive framework (looking for when and where the "good" behavior occurs) is part of the strategy of using "positive behavioral supports."

An effective and positive behavioral program will reinforce other aspects of behavioral structures: positive rules and a positive, accepting classroom climate. Another point: The ultimate goal of behavior systems is to return to more "normalized" contingencies (i.e., primary reliance on verbal praise, warnings, and reprimands). Once behavior is positive and stabilized, teachers should systematically and gradually decrease the frequency and intrusiveness of the system (much of this depends upon the age, needs, abilities, and prior experiences in and out of school, of the students). As students near the end of their schooling, behavior programs need to be adaptable to adult settings. Systems where the student is able to self-monitor and self-check, with periodic oversight (and praise) by a colleague or supervisor can be a relatively nonintrusive and successfully applied in many environments.

Schedules and Routines

Another important behavioral structure is the students' daily schedule and routine. All students benefit from some degree of routine, and also from learning to cope with change (nonroutine events). Some students may work best in the morning, or in the afternoon. This is very evident for students with chronic illness, who are medically fragile, or who take medications several times each day. Teachers who are aware of these issues can greatly support student learning by scheduling the most challenging coursework during the student's optimal learning time.

Students also need to cope with change of routine. This is best done by presenting the schedule change early in the day or when it becomes known. It is important to identify how it will impact scheduling, how the class will prepare and carry out the change, and how/when the class will return to its typical schedule. Providing reasons for the change, when known, also helps students learn cause-effect or problem-solution reasoning, skills which help them later with decision- and choice-making. Students need preparation for coping with change and the unexpected in every sector of their lives!

With a clear set of rules and a daily and weekly routine, teachers will have the structure for optimizing use of instructional time. A number of studies show the importance of time-on-task for achieving learning outcomes. A well-managed classroom leads to effective use of time during instruction and transition times (between classes or activities). When routines and rules are consistently adhered to and implemented, there is a substantial reduction in wasted time. Of course, a teacher can still have all of these aspects well designed, but be unfocused during instruction.

Within the schedule, delineation of both instructional and transition times is important (Friend & Bursuck, 2002). Students need to be taught and prompted to end and begin tasks in a timely manner; and to leave, change, and return to work areas; with increasing amounts of self-monitoring and responsibility in doing so. And don't be fooled into thinking that academically-focused students don't also need to be taught and prompted about this. (Don't we all remember classes where we *manipulated* the teacher into wasting class time, or how we dawdled and delayed some teachers by 5, 10, or 15 minutes between tasks?!) Once learned, these "time management" skills are easily generalized to: work settings (even coffee and lunch breaks), postsecondary settings (self-scheduling of appropriate homework sessions, time for class preparation and arrival, etc.), and across other adult environments.

> **Critical Point**
> Elements of instructional environments can either enhance or impede learning: teachers must be alert to possible barriers to reduce and must build on positive aspects.

Teaching Tip: Staying Positive

It is often very difficult to consistently maintain a positive classroom demeanor and to avoid temptations to become punitive. Like television, people often give much more "air time" to problems than to positive events. But we should ask ourselves—when was the last time *we* were nagged, lectured, or berated into cheerful, enthusiastic compliance? It's important to maintain positive routines, climate, and rules, and to be consistent in carrying these out, despite students who challenge us. Positive classroom climates require regular student praise and attention for behaving well, and also a clear sequence of warnings and consequences for defiance. The most effective tool is the teacher's attention and the "air time" given to positive events!

TABLE 7–4 Management of instructional groupings

- Whole-class
- Small-group
  - Same-skill groupings
  - Mixed-skill groupings
  - Mixed-age groupings
  - Cooperative learning
- Pairs or Triads
  - Peer tutoring
  - Instructional or social "buddies"
- Individualized

To summarize, this section presented four aspects of instructional environments (physical location, physical structure, emotional structure, and behavioral structure) for supporting instruction and described how to positively use classroom and community environments, how physical location and structure can impact learning, and how emotional climate and behavioral structures can be applied to optimize student performance. The next section describes ways of organizing the *students* for learning. See Table 7–4.

PLANNING INSTRUCTIONAL GROUPINGS

Whole-Class or Large-Group Instruction

What works best: "one big happy class," small groups, pairs, or individuals? The answer depends on several things: the teacher and students, the physical classroom arrangements, the lesson content and materials available, and the instructional methods chosen. Grouping arrangements are more variable in general education classes because larger class sizes lead to more possible combinations of students. Self-contained special education or resource rooms often have students on different academic levels and so groupings are less often used.

However, grouping arrangements should be considered in planning *all* lessons. Students both with and without disabilities should have learning and practice opportunities in working by themselves, in pairs or triads, in small and in large groups (Friend & Bursuck, 2002; Wood, 2002). When they move away from their parents, students will probably live with a roommate or two at one point or another.

> **Critical Point**
> In both postsecondary and work settings students will be expected to be able to work alone or with peers or colleagues across all of these grouping arrangements, for special projects, or at meetings.

Students in special education may have much greater experience with individualized instruction and following instructions of teachers. Instructional groupings require communication and interpersonal skills that special education students may not have had opportunities to develop, despite demonstrating appropriate academic skills. *All* students who work with peers will also need some strategies for giving and receiving feedback, for problem solving, and conflict resolution—and how to be appropriately tolerant or assertive, and when to ask for help (cf. Tileston, 2000).

Whole-class grouping arrangement is the *most efficient way* of providing instruction or information. This is best used when the whole class needs basic information, or steps and processes to follow, for a particular lesson or activity. Not all students do well in this arrangement because teacher attention is dispersed across many students. Typically, there are a few who will be "left behind" and possibly confused, even within the general education student body. Students with attention and learning challenges often find it difficult to maintain their focus on the teacher when surrounded by a classroom *full* of potential distractions.

Small Group Instruction

When some type of differentiation is required to meet student needs, and as a way to provide additional support to students who struggle with whole-class arrangements, smaller class groupings often are effective. *Same-skill groupings* are efficient in providing targeted instructional lessons to meet specific needs. However, students consistently placed in "low" groups can be stigmatized, sometimes to the point of reducing their motivation for learning and retention of material. Therefore, teachers need to be creative in varying the groupings across the students and in allowing all students to work with all classmates. Both *mixed-skill, mixed-age groupings* are terrific opportunities for students to learn interaction and communication skills through work with all of their class peers. Innovative teachers will utilize every student's learning profile of strengths and needs to teach others their particular strengths. Mixed-age-groupings have been used very successfully to allow older students to reinforce and display their own academic skills and become role models to younger students (Friend & Bursuck, 2002; Wood, 2002).

Cooperative learning is an effective small-group instructional strategy for inquiry (discovery) learning activities or multiphase research projects. It can effectively accommodate mixed-ability groupings by assigning specific roles according to individual student strengths. However, teachers must be sure to provide students with the skills they will need in group-based learning: they will need the instructional steps and processes for each phase of the project, as well as communication and feedback skills and checkpoints (coupled with behavioral consequences for noncompliance), in order to be successful. Transition-age students are adolescents, and are increasingly peer focused. As a result, they may ridicule or ostracize (especially covertly) those who are "different" or don't fit in (cf. Heaven, 2001). Yet, their increasing peer focus also makes them more amenable to group assignments and projects. Teachers still will need to monitor the groups and make deliberate grouping choices, particularly at first, to help set the tone and promote positive interactions. Some research shows that friends often are more open and honest with each other, leading to improved products and outcomes. Therefore, rather than preventing friends from working together, teachers can use these relationships to support increased learning.

Pairs or Triads

These arrangements often are used for types of tutoring or specific skill practice and mastery. Students may be more used to working in pairs; however, triads can help students practice multiple roles and turn-taking. This is especially helpful as preparation for small and cooperative group work with multiple roles. In triad arrangements, students typically take turns as the tutor, tutee, and observer (who gives feedback to both the tutor and tutee) (Mosston & Ashwurth, 1990). Working in pairs and triads will still require preparation in the specific skills, feedback and communication processes, and potential problem-solving and help-seeking strategies for working together effectively. Some very successful pair-programs teach tutoring "scripts" so that students have a set of effective

> **Critical Point**
> As educational and work sites move toward group-centered and problem-solving interactions, classroom groupings provide important developmental opportunities for learning appropriate strategies that students will need as adults.

parameters within which to work for giving corrective and instructive feedback, decision making, and evaluating their work. The Classwide Peer Tutoring (CWPT) Program is an example of a scripted program (cf. Salend, 2005).

Transition-age students can benefit from complex or multistep projects to evaluate their own and others' learning regarding food purchase and preparation, home repair and maintenance, problem solving, decision making, and so on, as practice for when they will be living independently. A number of "buddy" programs for social interaction and academic support are other examples of successful pairings that can be utilized in the community as well as at school. Work programs that utilize "natural supports" identify a key co-worker to provide work and sometimes social support as well.

Individualized Instruction

This arrangement traditionally is used to remediate or "catch-up" students with knowledge or skill gaps (Friend & Bursuck, 2002). It is best used for students whose skills are quite different from the rest of the group. When combined with self-monitoring, it can help students assume responsibility for their progress, rather than remaining so highly teacher-centered. Self-contained special education and resource room classes have traditionally used this approach for instruction because of the potential variety or intensity of the unique needs presented by each student. Regardless of placement, ultimately the instructional goal is to return the student to a more typical grouping arrangement.

Viewed more broadly as an instructional option, there are times when all students can benefit from some individualized attention and skill training. Within general education classes teachers have implemented this approach through miniconferences to track student progress as well as to provide skill support and instruction. For example, the use of "writers' workshops" allows students to work individually on writing projects while teachers monitor and give individualized feedback. Teachers often use a weekly monitoring grid to take notes on progress as well as needs. At the work site, supervisors may do similar monitoring by moving from worker to worker for quick assessments and making progress notes as well as giving immediate feedback or correction to a worker.

In summary, teachers should view instructional groupings as another variable that can enhance learning outcomes. Both instruction and students' skills will improve by varying groupings appropriately. *All* students should have opportunities to give and to receive tutoring, to lead and to follow in groups, and to work across multiple learning roles. Work settings need workers who can function successfully with others and in groups. Peer tutoring and cooperative learning activities offer opportunities for students to develop learning as well as interaction and problem-solving skills (Tileston, 2000).

> **Critical Point**
> Students should have opportunities to work across all grouping options.

Special and general educators need to prepare students for inclusive classrooms and adult settings by providing a variety of grouping options, a process that helps all persons meet diverse learning and adult needs. IEP team members all need to watch for situations and opportunities in which students can display strengths and skills, across the many instructional environments, within the school and broader community. They can use these opportunities to help all students expand beyond their standard roles: they can help with loading/unloading buses, monitoring and assisting younger students at recess or lunch, assisting or participating in after-school activities and sports, helping to track or monitor locker checks, assisting with crowd control at assemblies, or couriering messages and announcements.

Up to this point, the chapter has described instructional groupings: using variations in grouping students to build upon information about utilizing instructional environments. To review, think of these groupings and how and when they can be used to support student learning: whole-class, small group (same-skill, mixed-skill, and mixed-age), pairs or triads, and individualized instruction. Then combine that with how the physical location and structure can be used with these groupings, and add emotional and behavioral structures to support optimal and positive learning experiences. (The next section will build upon this to include instructional materials, as shown in Table 7–5).

INSTRUCTIONAL MATERIALS

Print Materials and Resources

Instructional materials are the important supports of daily content instruction. Curriculum provides the long-term organization and goals for instruction; yet, curriculum benchmarks and standards are frequently too broad to provide the specifics of daily or weekly planning (Wiggins & McTighe, 1998; Popham, 2001). Many school districts identify textbooks to provide the more specific

TABLE 7–5 Management of instructional materials

- Print Materials and Resources
    - Textbooks and basals
    - Trade books
    - Periodicals
- Non-print Materials and Resources
    - Manipulatives
    - Models
- Technology Resources
    - Audiovisual aids
    - Telecommunications
    - Computers for instruction
    - Assistive technology
- Human Resources
    - Parents and volunteers
    - Business partners
    - Community agencies and local "heroes"

Access to the general curriculum can include a personal computer.

content of the general education curriculum. In the past, special education content has been much less delineated, particularly for those who cannot be accommodated by the standard curriculum. Remembering back to the discussion of curriculum modifications, students who can succeed through *curriculum adaptation* will require minimal modifications to accommodate their learning and behavioral needs, and will typically use general education texts and materials. Students who need *curriculum augmentation* will use the general education texts and materials, plus additional unique materials to supplement their learning and prepare them for use of the general materials. Students who require *curriculum alteration* may not use the general education texts and materials as a result of the intensity and nature of their needs (cf. Wehmeyer et al., 2001).

For students in the special education classroom, teachers must be especially concerned that materials are age-appropriate, regardless of the student's current grade-level skills or developmental age. Teachers searching for materials to augment or alter the standard curriculum need to be particularly concerned. For example, a second grade reading level *does not* mean that juniors in high school should still be practicing on second grade books—dating, and "Dick and Jane" are *not* *compatible*. It is very important that all materials be *authentic* and *relevant* to the students' current lives, and their achievement of adult living objectives. Special educators generally spend a good part of their at-work and off-work time making appropriate materials—be prepared! Vaughn, Bos, and Schumm (2000, p. 474–475) offer some criteria for reviewing textbooks.

Students in the general classroom need abilities to read, comprehend, and study from the textbooks effectively. These classrooms depend far more on textbook-based instruction; Gunning (2003) estimates that 75%–90% of learning in content area classes is from textbooks. Therefore, students with disabilities need strategies to use texts effectively. Generally, schools do a poor job of preparing students for nonfiction and text reading (Gunning, 2003). For example, there are five primary text strategies used to structure nonfiction writing. They are: time order, listing, cause-effect, problem-solution, and comparison (Cooter & Flynt, 1996; Schirmer, 2000). Special education teachers need to provide explicit skill instruction and practice opportunities to build up students' abilities to read, comprehend, and respond to textbooks and other nonfiction materials (research articles, biographies, etc.) using these five text strategies.

Basal textbooks used to be standard for literacy instruction. However, many teachers prefer "authentic" literature and provide reading instruction that is integrated with reading of trade books, library books, and literary periodicals. Basals offer some organizational advantages: they often come with prepackaged workbooks and activities for teachers (Schirmer, 2000). Teachers who use same-skill reading groups can assign workbook or activity pages (with a set of answers for easy correction) to one group while providing oversight and intervention to another group. A desire for authentic stories and chapter books, written by highly talented and engaging authors (thereby increasing student motivation to keep reading), has led some teachers to abandon basal texts. Self-selecting books and managing the range of literacy skills needed across a classroom of students requires organizational skills and confidence. These teachers typically use a variety of grouping arrangements (by interest, same- or mixed-skill) with independent journaling and learning center activities to allow individual progress monitoring and time to provide minilessons to students.

One of the important benefits of using authentic literature is that it allows teachers to pick topics of interest to students: urban settings, runaways, family abuse, and other topics that are frequently very engaging to students and can help them ponder some of their own personal concerns (supporting a key purpose of reading: personal growth). Teachers can easily incorporate transition topics using the same approach (e.g., stories about coping, decision making, and living independently). A note: special education students moving from a highly structured, basal-focused reading class into a more wholistic and trade-book reading experience will need some preparation. Flexible groupings and movement between journaling, independent reading, and skill instruction may result in special education students feeling lost, unsupported, and insecure; if not also tempted to engage in distracting or disruptive behaviors! Teachers need to be sure these students are adequately prepared for these new environments.

Content-area textbooks can be a challenge for special education students to navigate and comprehend. As mentioned earlier, schools typically do a poor job of preparing students to read across the five nonfiction text strategies. For example, think of how familiar you are with the typical "story grammar" or elements of fiction (characters, setting, plot, and theme) versus how well you can describe the five basic nonfiction text patterns (time order,

listing, cause-effect, problem-solution, and comparison). For many special education students, the lack of nonfiction comprehension strategies is compounded by their fundamental difficulties with reading and writing. Students who are still "learning to read" struggle in content classes that depend upon their skills in "reading to learn" and acquire new information. This is where the *adaptation, augmentation,* and *alteration strategies* from curriculum design should be applied to textbook usage and choice. Students requiring adaptation would have basic nonfiction comprehension strategies, but require modification on how much or how (font, color, auditory support) text material is provided. Students requiring *augmentation* may need specific instruction and practice on the five text strategies, gradually increasing the conceptual challenge and new information presented using these five strategies prior to resuming their work in the classroom text. Students needing *alteration* would need different materials; augmentative instruction in the text strategies would not be enough for them to be successful in learning from the classroom text.

Math and science textbooks often are conceptually dense and generally more difficult for students to read (Gunning, 2003). Mastropieri and Scruggs (2002) found that readability of science texts was often higher than the assigned grade level. Therefore, students will need skills in reading nonfiction text strategies as well as practice in the unique ways of *applying* various *reading* strategies to these content areas (Mastropieri & Scruggs, 2002). Content area teachers rarely instruct students on the appropriate reading strategies for their subject; yet it can't be left *only* to reading teachers. Professional periodicals may be used for research or for augmenting other text materials.

> **Critical Point**
> Adaptation, augmentation, and alteration strategies from curriculum design may be used to facilitate effective textbook usage and choice.

Teaching Tip: Books and Reading: Ask a Librarian

When looking for books related to topics of interest, no one can beat a good children's librarian! Within one or two days, they can provide a stack of potential books for the teacher's review. Some librarians are willing to visit classrooms (or arrange regular classroom visits) for read-alouds. Although often ignored by middle- and high-school settings, read-alouds allow students struggling with reading comprehension to participate equally in discussion of sophisticated topics and concepts. Repeated oral exposure to the text structures supports all students when they must later read independently—a win-win situation (cf. Salend, 2005).

Teachers often assume that the organization and nature of these magazines is clear to students, but that may not be so—it is important to verify student skills before making these assignments.

Across all types of reading materials, students need strategies in monitoring their own comprehension, and in independently selecting from a range of strategies to support comprehension (i.e., one's teacher or parent is not always available, sometimes the dictionary definition is more complex than the word itself). For example, teaching students to (a) reread for context clues, (b) look at beginnings and endings of words and make a guess, (c) look at the type of word (syntax and semantics), (d) make a guess based on the topic (context), and (e) read ahead (or reread) to confirm the meaning are five strategies students can use independently that will at least move them closer in approximating the word meaning. Study strategies also can help in establishing the topic and the chapter organization, and in self-monitoring for questions and confusions along the way.

> **Critical Point**
> Student will read more independently when they can select strategies to support comprehension.

Students moving into work-site or postsecondary settings need practice reading and responding to commonly-used materials, books (e.g., texts or handbooks), information sharing (e.g., e-mail, bulletin boards, flyers, etc.) and forms (e.g., absence, insurance, vacation). Transition teams should collect a variety of materials and instructions from potential postschool environments and use these as authentic materials to practice reading and help-seeking strategies. Work settings may be able to provide frequently-used customer- or product-processing forms that students will need to use. Computerization means that many of these forms may be on handheld or portable work stations that workers are expected to navigate through (i.e., read and comprehend).

Nonprint Resources: Manipulatives and Models

The opportunity to physically move and manipulate objects or models can be helpful for the initial learning of abstract principles and concepts (Friend & Bursuck, 2002). Often this is a necessary component of facilitating understanding and internalization of key concepts that may be presented in print materials. Recent state standards and professional academic societies (National Council Teachers of Mathematics) are focusing much more on ensuring that today's students understand "big ideas" and concepts that are central to and that cross curriculum disciplines. A concept is a culturally based classification system that is acquired through exposure and experiences, and that is integrated into each person's unique world schema when fully "attained." Therefore, a concept is much more complex than factual learnings that can be memorized—in fact, concepts must be "acquired." This means that teacher demonstration is not enough, but must include adequate student opportunities and, eventually, fluent student use, including abilities to provide a thorough verbal explanation (Friend & Bursuck, 2002).

In order to be effective, manipulatives and models must match the conceptual and developmental stage of the student. They can be quite effective in providing the student with critical experiences that build to full concept acquisition. For example, learning the Earth's position in the solar system is *not* intuitive: through use of a model (Earth and sun) that is manipulated (showing day and night) and then linked with the students' experiences (sun rising and setting) eventually leads to concept attainment.

As can be seen, manipulatives and models can be very helpful, *if not essential*, in building concepts and "big curriculum ideas". Depending upon the students' learning needs, these may need to be *adapted, augmented,* or *altered*. Certain physical, cognitive, or sensory disabilities will require modified and adapted materials to make them accessible, and some students will need *augmented* models. If a student is unfamiliar or doesn't recognize the appropriate scale model of the Earth and sun (Earth represented by a marble, to a giant sun), the teacher may need to begin with a globe, and sequentially reduce size and physical similarity of Earth-like models until approximating the correct representational size. Students with difficulty in interpreting abstract models (globe represents the Earth) may also need to be taken to *real* places or use an *altered* model (e.g., not to scale).

Many teachers will be required to provide instruction in sex education. For this topic, verbal descriptions or even colored diagrams may not be enough (for example, students have never *seen* their internal organs so they may struggle to interpret their significance). Teachers need to check that students understand these as *their own* current or future bodies. Certainly, it can be embarrassing to be explicit in demonstrating hygiene or other activities on these models, but teachers also need to be clear. A case in point is the classic story (perhaps an urban legend) of students who misunderstand the teacher's demo and think they are having "safe sex" by putting their condom on a banana, or a broomstick. Enough said!

Technology Resources

Developments in technology provide many new ways in which teachers can interact with, and instruct, students. But technology should only be used to enhance or improve the learning of an identified outcome, and should *never* become the goal itself. The initial novelty and attraction of technology is tempting, but poor instruction cannot be improved by adding technology.

Audiovisual aids are pretty old but still can be useful to support learning and retention, and provide images and vicarious experiences that can broaden understandings. Movies and videos (as well as older filmstrips and photos) can vitalize descriptions of countries, peoples, environments, flora, fauna, and so on, and help students visualize the environments and circumstances that led to our concepts and understandings of today's world. Visual (overhead projectors) and auditory media (tape recorders) are still helpful and may guide certain students to better focus on key conceptual factors. Students who become overwhelmed or overstimulated (autistic or with learning, attention, or cognitive challenges) may react poorly to multimedia presentations. Desensitizing them through single-sensory introductions may help them be able to participate in using or creating classwide multimedia products. Kinesthetic and proprioceptive experiences also aid learning (e.g., manipulatives and models, movement and dance, etc.). For students who are moving into adult settings, it is critical that they know their own learning strengths, preferences, and weaknesses across these modalities and can identify these clearly—to future supervisors, or disability office personnel and postsecondary faculty.

Telecommunication capabilities allow teachers, classrooms, and students to engage in greatly expanded learning, exploration, and research activities, and to explore issues that are occurring throughout the world, in real-time or asynchronous fashion (at a time convenient to the students). VTEL links allow students to enroll in specialized classes (for example, American Sign Language as taught to several Ohio public school classes from the Ohio School for the Deaf). Many telecommunications capabilities are linked to the Internet, giving students online access to content area experts, diverse classes around the world, and nearly-overwhelming lists of resources. Transition-age students often will be expected to have skills in finding and using Internet resources and using e-mail for jobs and at postsecondary settings. As community and work information is increasingly posted and accessible on the Web, students will need skills in effectively finding and utilizing this information effectively.

Computers continue to provide new resources for instructional content (Friend & Bursuck, 2002). Drill-and-practice and tutorial software provide endless practice and reinforcement, without human tendencies for frustration and impatience. Simulations are unique ways to present real-life environments to teach knowledge and skills that will be used later. As virtual reality becomes more of a classroom presence, it will be more possible for students to have virtual experiences in a variety of careers or job placements, and to "virtually" practice particular work or independent living skills. Digitizing of textbooks and instructional materials also is the basis for the Universal Design for Learning. Computers allow tremendous range of input or output devices (Braille, enlarged print, voice output, joysticks, head pointers, etc.) that all can be converted from one to another, allowing for equal access across differing abilities (e.g., *adaptation*). Hypertext and hyperlinks allow additional support and extension materials associated with specific concepts or events referred to in texts (e.g., *augmentation*).

High-quality technology still remains merely a tool that supports effective instruction: the primary path to the learning goal. For example, a particular path (instruction to meet a goal) may be quickly and efficiently

Teaching Tip: Materials Management

When passing out instructional manipulatives or "toys" (from a student perspective) remember that students don't care how much they cost, how long you waited for the order, or any of your other entreaties, pleas, or threats to the contrary. Plan ahead, and make sure to give clear guidelines for their use.

Give these guidelines *prior* to passing anything out, and *then* distribute them in an orderly fashion (use routines) with your eyes scanning in all directions. Once your prized tools are flinging across the room, boomeranging against the wall, in the latest version of "Class Olympics," it's too late to impose order.

traversed using a car, but at other times teachers must walk, swim, or take a boat. Similarly, computers are not always appropriate for every path. Thoughtful and well-planned technology use is *critical* to effective teaching outcomes (e.g., what's the point of spending a lot of money on computers if they are only used as behavior reinforcements to play games? Students are happy using earned "free time" in other ways, at much less expense.) (cf. Gillingham & Topper, 1999). Highly effective teachers provide successful instruction, regardless of the particular tools available. Unfortunately it is often the wealthier and suburban schools at which students (and teachers) have access to the latest technology, both at home and at school, leaving the poorer students, who are less likely to have access at home, to have minimal, if any, access at school. Teachers are expected to achieve the same state curriculum outcomes, regardless.

Assistive technology (AT) is a different story because it provides access to the curriculum and educational setting as guaranteed through IDEA and ADA. If teachers don't use purchased technology then they are denying the student this access (Gillingham & Topper, 1999). AT has allowed *tremendous improvements* in supporting inclusion of students with disabilities. Again, if instruction is the path to the learning goal, students who previously couldn't keep up with the class, or who couldn't walk or swim now have special vehicles to allow them to do so—voice synthesized or manual communication boards, voice-recognition systems, enlarged or specialized keyboards or input devices, more flexible manual or electric wheelchairs, large print, Braille translations, and computerized American Sign Language, to name a few. As described earlier, computer-based assistive technology allows the computer-as-instructional-vehicle to be even further adapted. Digital technology allows a variety of input and output choices by simply changing interfaces (cf. PACER Center, 2002). Voice recognition systems have greatly expanded and improved to allow faster training and a much broader vocabulary. Even use of word processing and spelling or grammar checkers allows a broader range of learners to communicate their thoughts in ways more commensurate with their other abilities. Word-prediction software can greatly help those struggling with English or writing.

The presence or availability of AT does not always solve access problems. AT adds a level of complexity to classroom and learning settings that is not thoroughly addressed by many IEP teams (Todis, 1996) and students with mental retardation often underutilize some potentially helpful devices (Wehmeyer, 1999). For example, choosing the appropriate AT is a complicated process. This field is changing quickly (e.g., a new wheelchair that goes up stairs) with far too many options for one section of one chapter. A good decision requires input from specialized software and hardware experts who also are knowledgeable about disabilities. Team and schoolwide education about devices is critical as well because students and teachers can feel stranded when devices break, there are no backups available, and repairs will require several days or weeks—everyone must be prepared.

> **Critical Point** Instructional materials and technologies should be carefully selected to support curriculum and learning objectives, and to meet individual student needs and abilities.

Human Resources

People resources that live in our communities are an often underutilized resource. Yet, they can bring invaluable information and ways for students to form personal connections with key content and ideas. Parents and school volunteers may have had very unique experiences or represent diverse perspectives, and are willing to share these. Alternative points of view can remain flat and lifeless until students can vicariously reexperience these through individuals who have "lived through them." Some schools have very strong business linkages and partners for academy-based school units or through work-study and apprenticeship programs. These relationships provide established resources including speakers and ongoing classroom involvement. However, any local business can be a source of content-area resources and larger organizations often have community relations officers or personnel.

Community agencies often want to establish strong linkages with future consumers and with schools as community services. A portion of their mission may be for local outreach, and education and classroom teachers can integrate these agency goals with students' instructional goals. Children's librarians were mentioned earlier as classroom resources, and some may attend classrooms for book readings or presentations across a variety of topics. Community agencies may know of local "heroes." For example, disability organizations can be very helpful in knowing of individuals with disabilities who can serve as role models and explain strategies they used to overcome barriers or discrimination.

Teachers sometimes overlook local persons who can greatly enhance and add meaning, relevance, and authenticity to curriculum content.

CONCLUSION

This chapter has presented three of the four categories of instruction variables: instructional materials, instrumental groupings, and instructional environments. The remaining category of instructional methods will be described in the next chapter. In review, think again about the benefits as well as concerns in using print materials (differences in use between special and general education, reading issues, and real-life applications), and nonprint materials (manipulative and models) to support conceptually-based and thorough learning. Then add technology to enhance learning and to provide access to materials for students: through AV, computer software and hardware, telecommunications, and AT. Then consider the different instructional groupings and how to support this through effective structuring of instructional environments. This shows why teaching and planning are so complex.

STUDY QUESTIONS

1. Describe the ways through which instructional environments and curriculum are made accessible for students with different disabilities, using assistive technology and curricular modifications.

Describe at least two examples of assistive technologies, and one example each of curricular adaptation, augmentation, and alteration.

2. Choose one of the teaching situations described in this chapter (or create one of your own) and describe the differences between the art and science of instruction as shown in this example.

3. Describe the four aspects of instructional environments and how you would manage their potential impact on student learning across both community and school; and urban, suburban, and rural settings.

4. Describe the four aspects of instructional groupings and how you would utilize and manage these across academic, career-vocational, and life-skill transition-based instruction to enhance student learning. (Refer back to Chapter 6, "Step 2: Courses of Study.")

5. Describe the four types of instructional materials and how you could vary these to optimize student learning, including ways to adapt, augment, and alter their presentation or use.

6. You are a teacher of a group of students (visualize a diverse group in terms of strengths/needs and ethnicity—challenge yourself! Include those with mild-moderate, moderate-severe, sensory, and physical/health disabilities). What are some of the ways that you will want to modify your (a) instructional environment, (b) instructional groupings, and (c) instructional materials, to (1) reduce barriers and (2) to facilitate maximum class learning?.

CHAPTER 8

INSTRUCTIONAL METHODS FOR TRANSITION TEACHING

Pamela Luft

LEARNING OBJECTIVES

The objectives of this chapter are:

1. List, explain, and illustrate (a specific task) the basic elements of direct instruction.

2. List, explain, and illustrate (a specific problem, conflict, or choice) the application of basic steps of problem solving.

3. Describe the difference between direct and nondirect instruction in terms of content, approach, and learning strengths and needs.

4. Illustrate for a learning objective the use of direct and non-direct instruction.

5. Explain the role of student-guided and student-directed learning in transition and community environments.

6. Explain the process of lesson planning.

7. Describe how to develop a transition-focused, interdisciplinary thematic unit.

INTRODUCTION

Instruction is extremely complex—as it should be: It is the heart of the teaching-and-learning process. Chapter 6 described curriculum choice and the three courses of study from which the transition team crafts a transition plan. Chapter 7 described how to arrange instructional structures and materials across a variety of instructional settings and environments. This chapter finishes the "how" of instruction by focusing on the actual teaching—the ways in which learning outcomes across the three career paths are achieved. This integrates all of the instructional variables—different environments and classroom structures, student groupings, and materials and resources—within four major teaching methods that move from teacher-directed through student-guided learning.

Much of the information in Chapter 7 addressed the science aspects of teaching—characteristics of the *instructional environment, instructional groupings,* and *instructional materials.* However, instructional methods often are considered more of the "art" of teaching because it is the process through which instruction is actually "delivered." In reality, it is rarely so neatly divided because the interaction between delivery and the students' utilization of knowledge and skills also influences the effectiveness of: the instructional environment and structure (for example, a hopelessly boring delivery often leads to behavior problems even with a "super" behavior system); the instructional groupings (the lesson can be so engaging that students "forget" to annoy each other); and instructional materials (even "cool" materials can become frustrating if the teacher gives too few directions on their use).

The choice of instructional method is fundamental to how teachers best achieve specific learning objectives and outcomes. Much of the effectiveness of these choices depends upon the teacher's skill in sizing up the students' strengths and needs, and evaluating/analyzing the complexity and organization of the intended content (another *science* aspect of teaching). Each teacher has his or her own personality characteristics that contribute to teaching style and interaction preferences in terms of instructional implementation (more *art* aspects). The volume of information and detail required to fully understand the complex process of teaching can seem overwhelming—but the rewards of learning it are immeasurable.

There are four basic types of instructional methods. These four methods begin with teachers in the most directive role, and move toward a less teacher-directed and increasingly student-directed focus. Ultimately, society needs for all students to become independent and lifelong learners. In fact, rapid changes in the global economy and marketplace increasingly require all workers to learn new skills and, at times, to change and learn new careers. The chapter begins with teachers in the most directive role.

TEACHER-DIRECTED INSTRUCTION

Content and Approaches

This method often is called direct instruction with the teacher in a role of providing a specific sequence of learning steps through which all students proceed. It is most effective in promoting mastery of rote-learning *content:* basic facts (e.g., spelling, grammar, math facts, names of animals and classifications, three houses of government) or fundamental skills (e.g., identifying misspelled words, long division, reducing fractions, measuring and recording observations, recognizing and identifying countries or continents). In terms of transition and life skills, when instructing students how to cross the street or to drive a car, instruction consists of teaching a specific set of skills and sequences and continues until students reach mastery.

There are several approaches within this method for supporting student success: *demonstrate* how to look both ways on the street or how to turn the ignition in the car; *model* (with self-talk or explanation) about criteria for when to walk or when to pull out into traffic (look both ways to see if things are clear and judge the necessary distance or clearance); *explain* or lecture what may or will happen if distances are misjudged.

Teaching Tip: Life Long Learning

Although you will become much more skillful after a few years of teaching, good teachers are always learning and striving to improve—with all students, with all methods, and in all environments. And if the goal for students is to become lifelong learners, isn't it important that teachers model these same attitudes and skills to students?

Teachers may also use some additional strategies to support these approaches and help students remember key aspects: they may develop a mnemonic using first letters of words, a picture-based cue card, or tape-recorded instructions that students will play to themselves at intersections (using an age-appropriate MP3 device). An example of a mnemonic device is as follows:

C ome up to the street edge

R each and push the walk button

O bserve the walk box

S tart walking when "walk" blinks

S top after you cross

Critical Point

Direct instruction strategies (demonstrate, model, explain) may be supported by additional strategies to help students remember the steps of the task.

The number and type of strategies are nearly endless depending upon the students' strengths, needs, and abilities, the situations and age-appropriate materials for each, and, of course, the teacher's creativity.

The student then performs each of these skills, in sequence, and the teacher monitors and gives feedback. Often the teacher presents a portion of the total sequence based upon a *task analysis* that accounts for learner characteristics and needs. A task analysis is a planning strategy that helps teachers divide large or complex activities into smaller portions that can more easily support student success. When developing a task analysis, it is important to accommodate different student needs and experiences: students may need smaller or larger portions or steps in the sequence. For example, students who independently walk to the store for their parents using controlled intersections (with traffic lights) will need fewer steps to learn the ways to monitor an uncontrolled intersection than a student who does neither independently. For a student who already knows how to vacuum and pick up her bedroom, then, a task analysis of how to vacuum and bus a restaurant at closing time would adjust for that. A student who had never used a vacuum would need smaller steps for this same task. A student with visual impairments will need different steps than a student who is deaf or who uses a wheelchair. Teachers examine the students' learning strengths and needs, the size and complexity of the task, develop a system of cues and prompts, and make a

Critical Point

Some students may need smaller portions or more steps for a task analysis while others may learn with larger portions and fewer steps.

decision about whether to use backward or forward chaining—accounting for both the students' characteristics and the nature of the activity to learn.

Teachers identify the starting point and sequence for teaching, sometimes using forward chaining—teaching from the beginning and working forward, one step at a time. At other times, teaching takes place from the end and working backward—backward chaining. Many students learn long division in math with forward chaining and going one step at a time. When teaching a child to zip a jacket, parents may let the child do the last step, zipping up, but they would align, and then insert the one side into the mechanism, allowing the child to do increasingly more steps in this backward chaining process.

As students do these steps, they get feedback on their performance using a hierarchy of prompts and cues. Typically, teachers add prompts or cues on a least-to-most basis, building upon what the student can already do with some ability. Teachers might use verbal cues (reminders, directions, etc.), physical cues (pointing, touching key objects), or hand-over-hand prompts according to what is needed. Then they would fade or withdraw these cues and prompts gradually until the student could perform each step, or all steps together, on an independent basis. Some students may replace cues with self-talk reminders and self-monitoring cues, either verbally or mentally. For some tasks and students, they may continue using a written or pictorial checklist that replaces verbal cues.

Critical Point

Direct instruction is most effective in promoting mastery of basic facts or fundamental skills.

Table 8–1 describes a series of steps that can be used to implement teacher directed instruction, although this is a generic task analysis and not specific to a set of students and their needs and abilities. The table uses an example with teaching laundry skills; however, the outline can be used as a guide across many potential applications. This is the same way in which students learn math procedures and basic facts, phonics and sight words, spelling and dictionary skills, names of states and their capitals, and the names for scientific phyla. Not all teachers provide as much demonstration, explanation, and graduated practice (from teacher-supported to independent mastery)—but then, sometimes students struggle because they need more or one or all of these elements. This method is the most effective means for teaching transition students specific facts and skills, such as the rules of the road or household repair and maintenance. There are tasks and skills they will need to memorize and follow in their adult lives.

TABLE 8–1   Generic task analysis for doing laundry

Element	Explanation	Application
Element 1: Establish the lesson's purpose by explaining its goals and objectives.	Use an anticipatory set: introduce content, include a motivation for learning and the lesson's relevance; provide an overview, a schedule, and relevance.	Tell students they will learn how to use the washing machine; ask who washes their clothes, link to when they are on their own. Explain that they will be going to the home-ec room (schedule), then to the laundromat.
Element 2: Review prerequisite skills.	Review previously learned and relevant skills to ensure readiness to proceed.	Ask them to describe parts of a washer, what is needed to wash clothes.
Element 3: Perform a task analysis and introduce content in discrete steps followed by practice.	Present points in small, incremental, sequential steps (base these on students' abilities).	Task analyze: sorting wash, when to wash, steps in loading, turning on, and unloading machine.
Element 4: Give clear directions, explanations, and relevant examples.	Use clear, explicit statements with terminology that the students understand. Rate of presentation will depend on students' skills and content complexity.	Explain each chunked task explicitly and how it fits in the sequence. Have students copy own set of cue cards as needed.
Element 5: Provide time for active and guided practice.	Allow time for practice after covering small amounts of difficult or new material. Include a variety of activities that require varying levels of difficulty.	Model with self-talk each task chunk; repeat this with students repeating after you; repeat with greater student physical involvement. Put chunks together.
Element 6: Promote active responding and check for comprehension.	Have all students actively respond (active learning), question, and probe.	Each student copies task from instructor, taking turns; other students join in self-talk.
Element 7: Give prompt, specific feedback.	Frequent, prompt, clear, constructive feedback during: lesson, learning checks, and practice; use prompts and praise.	As prompts are withdrawn, give students immediate feedback on performance; praise for success.
Element 8: Offer time for independent activities.	Develop automaticity of skills and knowledge; build on previously learned content; provide examples, divide content into sections, highlight directions and key words.	Assign students to pairs to work independently on washing; have students bring in clothes weekly to wash; demonstrate mistakes. Continue monitoring and feedback.
Element 9: Summarize main points and evaluate mastery.	Summarize main points and follow with 1–5 minute quick probes; maintain skills with weekly/ monthly maintenance probes.	Once mastery is attained, add dryer use. When both are mastered, reduce laundry to once each month in a community laundromat.

Based on Mastropieri & Scruggs (2002) and Salend (1998, 2001).

Monitoring and Evaluation

In teacher-directed methods, monitoring and evaluation are under the control of the teacher. There is usually one right answer for this content (spelling words, basic math facts, animal names or categories, washing-drying sequence, crossing intersections, etc.) so this method provides the specific information (facts or skills) to be memorized and retained. But what if students struggle to learn these basic facts and skills? Despite the teacher's best efforts, sometimes students fail to learn. Following is a series of steps that often can help:

1. Activate background knowledge.
2. Teach and review preskills (prerequisites for lessons).
3. Provide direct instruction, practice, and review for individuals with poorly developed preskills.
4. Select and sequence instructional examples to fit students' interests and needs.
5. Modify rate for introducing new skills—slower at first, faster for review and interest.

This list is not comprehensive and there are a number of books with fairly comprehensive lists of accommodations, by disability (cf., Friend & Bursuck, 2002; Mastropieri & Scruggs, 2000; Smith, Polloway, Patton, & Dowdy, 2001; Vaughn, Bos, & Schumm, 2000; Wood, 1998). If certain students are struggling to learn something, a teacher might check their background experiences (also very important when teachers and students do *not* share the same cultural, linguistic, or socioeconomic background).

1. *Activate background knowledge.* Building a bridge between what students *do* know and what the lesson requires often means a discussion or asking questions—Why do we wash clothes? What do you know about it? What are some things you've seen people do? In some cases, teachers will need to provide additional background experiences (video and movies help, assigning students to watch the next time their family does the washing, sometimes field trips are needed—going to the home ec room to show them a washer and dryer and then asking what they are for). Use what they remember and have experienced to build to the needed skill or knowledge mastery— move from the known to the unknown. And if they look lost or confused at this point, it often means that teachers have moved too quickly. If background seems sufficient, check for evidence of preskills.

2. *Teach and review preskills.* It is helpful to identify these preskills as *prerequisites* for lesson plans because it is so important that they have really mastered prerequisite skills. For example, if students get stuck while remembering basic subtraction facts then this will be a barrier to their giving their full attention to your presentation on subtraction of fractions—because they are struggling to remember, they don't catch key aspects of the process with fractions. If you are teaching students to use the telephone book or an alphabetical Internet resource and they are struggling to remember alphabetization, your lesson is likely to fail. The students' basic skills may simply be weak and they are taking extra time and falling behind. For example, students may have very poor typing skills, spending a lot of time looking for each letter which is impacting their computer and Internet use for the class. Similar to teaching preskills, the way to address weak basic skills is to provide more instruction.

3. *Provide direct instruction, practice, and review for individuals with poorly developed skills.*

4. *Select and sequence instructional examples to fit students' interests and needs.* When selecting practice examples for these skills, try to find personally relevant practice examples that can help students stay motivated. This can be hard with rote tasks (e.g., basic math facts, spelling lists, housecleaning steps), but describing things related to their home and their life, their friends and families as part of the practice exercises can make it more interesting. Another strategy is to develop a self-monitoring chart with an age-appropriate skill resulting from mastery of this task—working with others on a project, balancing a checkbook, and so on. Students may not have serious preskill or basic skill weaknesses that can be found.

5. *Modify rates for introducing new skills.* Students may need additional time in order to fit this skill into their schema (their internal instructional framework). Also, students from other cultures vary in terms of their analytic versus holistic learning (specific skills taught in isolation versus "the whole picture"), and auditory versus visual learning preferences. Teachers may need to alter aspects of their presentations and give students more time and opportunities to develop some of the culturally-based learning preferences (analytical, linear, and visual

> **Critical Point**
> In addressing skill and knowledge gaps in the community, team members need to communicate about basic strategies like activating background knowledge and prerequisites.

tend to be American preferences). Some students may simply need more time for initial skill acquisition, but then are able to move quickly through practice and application. It often is good to plan for variation and also to vary the pacing. Teachers can purposefully mix up their pacing (after basic mastery is achieved) to keep the class lively and interesting.

These five steps can be used for addressing a range of skill or knowledge gaps—at school, in the workplace, or for independent living. Supervisors in all environments will appreciate information on these basic steps to try, to teach job skills, social skills, or home-based living skills. But these are only useful when combined with being an alert, sensitive, and analytical team member or supervisor; a person who observes the conditions that optimize each student's learning, then replicates those across other activities.

> **Critical Point**
> Independent student practice is critical to knowledge and skill retention; however, material must first have been mastered, and practice should be specific and systematic.

Thus far, this chapter identified the basics of teacher directed instruction, but how can this be applied to transition? In fact, many jobs (establishing and maintaining files, data entry, busing tables at a restaurant) and independent living skills (cooking meals, doing simple household repairs, doing laundry), as well as academic skills (outlining a chapter, doing the four basic math operations, using the scientific method) can be taught very effectively using teacher-directed instructional methods. The teacher identifies a task and divides it into smaller skills or components—the task analysis—to use as the basis for instruction, using prompts and cues, practicing to develop mastery, and then generalizing to community and adult-living settings.

Teacher-directed instruction is often used with whole class instruction but fits easily with tutoring and other grouping arrangements. For example, most class instructions for lessons are given through direct instruction—how to complete an activity, how to earn points or rewards for the lesson, or how to work cooperatively in the group and negotiate individual work assignments for the project. Teachers use this when lecturing, describing, identifying, explaining, listing, demonstrating, and so on. They also use it when passing out materials or using new equipment—wanting to give quick, clear directions (and to avoid students "exploring" their way into yet another version of "Classroom Olympics"). Teachers also use direct instruction to give a quick summary (an advanced organizer) prior to discussing a new chapter in a textbook, or to give a student group-specific or modified instructions with feedback.

A well-run classroom will use many examples of teacher-directed instruction. Yet, even with driving or crossing the street, there comes a point when the learner needs to "experiment" with his or her own timing, pacing of procedures, making judgments, and applying the procedures under varying circumstances and environments. A student at this stage may need feedback, but eventually, caring, nurturing, and possibly terrified teachers will need to "turn them loose on their own." So even under strict direct instruction, more inquiry- and discovery-based instructional methods of coaching and facilitating are useful, after a student has acquired basic skill or fact mastery. In fact, many tasks or activities should combine aspects of both teacher-directed and teacher-guided instruction, to be sure the student can actually use the knowledge and skills in the appropriate situations. In contrast to learning specific facts or skills, when the instructional goal is to promote learning and development of higher-order thinking and use of problem-solving abilities, teachers need to use primarily nondirect or inquiry-based teaching methods.

Teaching Tip: Learning From Change

We all have instructional strategies that we do better than others, and some that feel "downright awkward" to us. Once you have experience and establish a style, *any new strategy* feels somewhat awkward—because you haven't practiced it, it's not yet "automatic." You have just answered the question, "Why do some teachers never change, year after year?" The answer is, because (1) it takes work to practice anything new, and (2) it will feel uncomfortable or wrong for a while—and they're not used to that anymore! So the moral of this tip is: To improve is to change, to grow is to change—and this will always feel awkward at first.

TEACHER-GUIDED OR NONDIRECT INSTRUCTION

Content and Approaches

Teacher-directed instruction occurs when the instructor tells or shows how to do something. In contrast, teacher-guided instruction occurs when the instructor scaffolds and supports the students' cognitive manipulation (thinking about and applying) of information that leads to accomplishing a specific goal. The teacher's role or approach in this method can be described as the "guide on the side." With teacher-directed and direct instruction, the teacher's role is more of the "sage on the stage." Teacher-directed instruction is highly efficient (quick!) in communicating ideas. In contrast, teacher-guided methods often take longer to allow a more exploratory and constructivist learning process. Other names associated with this method are "inquiry-based" or "discovery learning" approaches (Salend, 2005; Mosston, 1972; Mosston & Ashworth, 1990). General education classes more often use these teacher-guided approaches; special education classes more often use teacher-directed instruction (for tutoring and remediation, and specific fact or skill instruction). Students who are moving from special education classes or resource rooms and into inclusive settings should have some basic skill instruction and practice in inquiry-based learning activities (through direct instruction for basic information, followed by their own exploration and use). Students need to be prepared for this type of learning and to take a more active role in their learning.

What type of *content* is most effective with teacher-directed versus teacher-guided learning? Teacher-directed methods are efficient and effective, particularly for fact or skill learning. Teacher-guided methods are best for higher-order learnings—applying principles and rules, problem solving and conflict resolution, evaluation and synthesis (Friend & Bursuck, 2002; Mosston, 1972). These higher-order learnings require more than remembering specific facts or the steps in performing a skill. They require synthesis of information and evaluation of circumstances that influence the use of processes or procedures, often based upon knowing a set of basic facts and skills. Often

> **Critical Point**
> With inquiry, discovery, or constructivist activities (teacher guided), the teacher typically assumes a coaching or facilitating role to foster higher-order thinking.

students will need to explore several possible options through their inquiry and exploration. Rarely is there just "one right answer" as there is with teacher-directed methods. During the students' inquiry, discovery, or constructivist activities, the teacher typically assumes a coaching or guiding role, and challenges the students to consider more complex cognitive relationships or "solutions" to their task. This is very much related to Vygotsky's "zones of proximal development."

Teacher-directed and teacher-guided methods often can be used in mutually supportive ways as the student moves from memorizing specific facts or skills, to their application and use across new environments or circumstances (also called "generalization"). For example, in teaching the transition and life skills of crossing streets or driving a car, the teacher should begin with specific skill sequence instruction (using teacher-directed instruction). Using teacher-guided methods at this point is inappropriate: arranging an environment in which students "explore and construct" their own knowledge and skill schema could risk their physical safety. Pointing students toward the nearest crosswalk or merely handing over the car keys as part of students' "discovery learning" would severely call the teacher's judgment into question, risking the student's safety and the teacher's career.

Yet, after students have learned the basic facts and skills, they *should* be given opportunities to try their skills across several settings. It is critical that teachers not only train students to cross one street, or to drive only on a few local streets. Students will need opportunities that require synthesizing relevant situational factors to help them make judgments about when and how to apply their facts and skills: when it is safe to cross intersections without stoplights; when it is safe to pull out from an entrance ramp, or how much stopping distance is needed at different speeds when a stoplight turns yellow. The point of education is not only to provide students with a body of knowledge (facts and skills), but also to give them guided and structured experiences in using and working with this knowledge.

> **Critical Point**
> Teacher-facilitated methods are best used to teach higher-order learnings and often involve the application and use of facts and skills learned through teacher-directed instructional methods.

Table 8-2 (Mosston, 1972; Mosston & Ashworth, 1990) shows a categorization of several types of facilitated and inquiry-based teaching lessons with classroom and transition examples.

TABLE 8–2   Examples of Nondirect/Inquiry Teaching Lessons

Discovery of facts	About a historical period, about a sport, a career, a lifestyle, etc.
Discovery of a relationship among facts	Facts that explain an outcome (cause-effect; relationship between "work" and "play") Similarities between sets of facts (comparison of civil rights and disability rights movements)
Discovery of concepts	Citizenship rights and responsibilities Ethics Self-determination
Discovery of cognitive behavior skills	Application of problem-solving processes (at work, at home, with friends) Synthesis of information (about careers, utility costs, potential work environments) Drawing conclusions (about budgeting, affordable living) Comparisons and contrasts (among apartment options, career options, friendships) Evaluation using a rubric (fitting lifestyle choices to income realities)

An organizational *approach* commonly associated with teacher-guided instruction is cooperative learning. A teacher assigns tasks or projects to the class or small groups of students who work together to achieve a goal (Friend & Bursuck, 2002; Wood, 2002). Individuals may be assigned specific tasks within the group, that are combined into their own group's or the class's project. The group's task might be fairly structured (e.g., solving a math problem in an exploratory way, completing a multicomponent research project or investigation, using the scientific method to compare conditions for plant growth) or less structured and open-ended (e.g., identifying and designing a community project to clean the neighborhood; examining relationships between weather and frog population in a local pond; conducting on-site interviews with local employers or independent living facilities to determine which are most accessible). Chapter 3 discusses multicultural competence and describes how cooperative or collaborative learning is preferred by many non-European cultures; a number of your students may prefer this type of activity. In addition, the SCANS report (1991) identified working with a team as key skills expected in the workplace. Cooperative learning activities also can lead to more acceptance of students with disabilities than using individualized or competitive instructional approaches (Stevens & Slavin, 1995; Reutzel & Cooter, 1999).

On the other hand, teacher-guided activities are not grouping-specific. Some classroom teachers can provide individualized exploration through centers and self-guided instructional activities. This requires time for design and set-up, and organizational systems for students (and the teacher) to monitor progress across the centers or stations. Yet, centers can be especially effective with theme-based instruction across several related topics or categories. For example, a theme of "careers" could allow students to individually explore career areas at focused learning stations, and provide reinforcement of adult-level vocabulary: education, salary, benefits, schedule, and so on.

Whether using a competitive or cooperative organizational approach, teachers utilize teacher-guided methods to help students learn and apply principles or concepts, develop insights about relationships, and solve problems or conflicts (Salend 2005; Schirmer, 2000). Students are asked to apply basic knowledge and skills to a situation, and to synthesize and evaluate the results. Teachers identify and organize a series of discovery or constructivist learning activities that will promote and elicit the specific cognitive processes and skills. These activities and experiences are used to meet a set of requirements or guidelines, which makes evaluation and grading possible, as well.

> **Critical Point**
> Teachers often use conversational approaches such as guided discussion, role play, and scripting as a means to probe for cognitive thinking, or prompt and scaffold to new insights.

Suppose that the teacher wants students to learn about budgeting for independent living. The teacher facilitates guided discussions regarding how much apartments in their area cost per month. Then they guide students' awareness of affordable options in contrast to *their ideas* about preferred lifestyles. Next, the teacher coaches their exploration of salary realities of their preferred careers, beginning with entry-level positions (a postgraduation reality). Guidance is provided for the collection of typical utility and monthly bills, and typical paycheck deductions to help them discover budgeting complexities. The teacher may use role play or drama to help make certain concepts clearer to the students (Schirmer, 2000).

During this exploration, the teacher is likely to use scaffolding procedures by giving hints and clues that support key insights. For example, the teacher may scaffold student learning of concepts that:

gross pay ≠ net pay (no, your boss is *not* stealing from you), and

net pay ≠ liquid cash (as in, much of your net pay is encumbered by *monthly expenses*).

The teacher first determines the students' current understanding of these concepts, then develops small teaching steps (task analysis) that will lead them to these understandings through key questions and discussions to help in establishing the number and type of inquiry-based steps to include in instruction. Hierarchically spiraling through these two concepts (gross pay and net pay) may lead to increasingly higher conceptual levels and applications.

In this example, beginning with costs of apartments may be effective because many students proclaim a desire to live on their own, in the "lap of luxury." This is a motivating (fits their needs, interests, and preferences)

Transition skills are often taught in the community as well as in the classroom.

exploration into defining "luxury." Then the teacher could bring in one level of reality with "typical" entry-level earnings (salary comparison), with a goal of comparing this to typical apartment costs. The discussion could progress to realization that rent is not the only significant cost. Next, salaries—net vs. gross pay—are compared to apartment + utility costs. Fitting these figures into an overall budget, the teacher lets the *students* explore if there are ways they can still live the "lifestyles of the rich and famous."

In contrast, teacher-directed instruction would *tell* students that their apartment and salary dreams are unrealistic, and then *explain* how and why; or give the students a realistic budget to work with, with a brief explanation as to why these teacher figures are more realistic. There are definitely times when exploratory, student-focused learning is preferable. Confronting them with unabashed "reality" often results in denial, and prevents important learning. However, before beginning this teacher-guided lesson, students must have the necessary facts and skills (learned through teacher-directed methods) to complete this activity (e.g., basic addition and subtraction facts at mastery and fluency levels). Otherwise, they may lose the focus on judging and decision making because they are frustrated or unable to do the fundamental calculations. Clearly, teachers using guided learning methods need to carefully design the necessary components and steps to successfully complete these projects.

The following is a series of steps that can be used when presenting a cognitive process for students to use with any number of guided learning activities. The example here identifies problem solving. In teaching problem-solving skills, the teacher would proceed through these steps:

1. Present the new cognitive strategy.
2. Regulate difficulty during guided practice.
3. Provide varying contexts for student practice.
4. Provide feedback.
5. Increase student responsibility.
6. Provide independent practice.

The most effective and efficient way to introduce the steps of problem solving is through teacher-directed instruction. The first step is to *present the new strategy*—the teacher will need to explain each step of the problem-solving process and possibly demonstrate or model specific problems with self-talk. Next will be to *regulate difficulty during guided practice*—use a familiar example and talk/walk the students through the process several times until they show mastery. The next four steps—*varying contexts, providing feedback, increasing responsibility, and providing independent practice*—increase the students' ability to generalize across contexts and move toward independent use and mastery. Again, initial trials and practice will need to occur through teacher-directed learning.

When the students have shown basic mastery, their increased use across contexts will signal that the teacher may begin more of the teacher-guided learning. The teacher will monitor and facilitate through scaffolded conversations and guided discussions with individuals and groups. Ultimately, the teacher may move from group work to individual work (practice) to validate that each student can use problem solving in an independent manner.

Below is an example of a problem-solving model that teachers can use with teacher-guided learning that requires student exploration and inquiry. This problem-solving model can be easily adapted to address conflict resolution or choice making, by changing a few key words. This demonstrates how one model can be taught to students (direct methods) but

then its use can be experienced across a number of different choice-making or conflict situations—generalization of use that occurs through teacher-guided methods.

Steps for the problem-solving model include:

1. Identify the problem.
2. Consider all possible solutions.
3. Identify the pros and cons of each listed solution.
4. Develop a plan of action.
5. Put the plan into effect.
6. Evaluate the success of the plan.
7. Modify the plan as needed and begin again at step #5.

(Based on Downing, 1996; Hobbs & Westling, 1998; Jayanthi & Friend, 1992; Nezu & D'Zurilla, 1981; Salisbury, Evans, & Palombaro, 1997; Wood, 2002)

Students can learn this one basic set of steps to address a number of similar issues. In fact, it is similar to the scientific method, which develops a hypothesis instead of a solution, and the hypothesis is evaluated based upon the data (here, the plan). Table 8–3 shows an example of how to utilize this process across problem solving, conflict resolution, or choice making.

> **Critical Point**
> Problem-solving skills can be taught by direct methods and then applied across different situations.

TABLE 8–3 Example of the problem-solving process

	Problem Solving: Argument with Friend	**Conflict Resolution: Insulted by Co-worker**	**Choice Making: Job Choice**
Step 1	Friend wants to spend summer traveling with family; student anticipated friend would be home.	Co-worker called him/her lazy and laughed with others about it.	Interested in two possibilities.
Step 2	Beg friend to stay home, offer a gift to friend if s/he stays, try to find other activities or friends, look for a summer job, etc.	List out what to do: report to supervisor, talk with co-worker, ignore, etc.	List key or important factors: wages, benefits, promotions in 10 years, and fit with anticipated lifestyle, etc.
Step 3	Compare each option for possible success, impact on friend, and impact on self, long-term and short-term consequences.	Compare each option for possible success, impact on co-workers, impact on self, long-term and short-term consequences at work.	Compare for each job.
Step 4	Develop a plan for the preferred solution that identifies short- and long-term consequences.	Develop a plan for the preferred solution that plans for short- and long-term consequences.	Develop a career plan for the preferred choice, and how factors will change with time (promotions, raises, etc.).
Step 5	Choose the preferred plan and identify how the friend responds.	Choose the preferred plan and identify how the co-worker responds.	Choose the preferred job; begin tracking key factors.
Step 6	Compare the plan with the real-life consequences.	Compare the plan with the real-life consequences.	Evaluate the key factors and how well they fit with the plan.
Step 7	Change the plan, if possible or needed, and try again.	Change the plan, if possible or needed, and try again.	Change the plan if needed, and try these changes.

The application of one plan across potentially difficult life circumstances and transition skills is nearly endless: *problem-solving skills*—waking up on time, finding the best bus route, meeting and making more friends; *choice making*—deciding if I have "positive" or "negative" friends, choosing a good career or workplace, choosing a hobby; *conflict resolution*—settling an argument with my parents, or friends, or partner, or boss, or co-worker.

Monitoring and Evaluation

Monitoring and evaluating teacher-guided activities is more complex than for teacher-directed instruction in several ways. Teacher-directed methods often result in one right answer; teacher-guided methods often have open-ended outcomes with more than one right answer. The use of clearly identified components with a rubric is critical for clear monitoring and evaluation. Although multiple correct outcomes are possible, teachers must have a clearly-identified *type* of outcome they expect, from which to develop the rubric. In addition, a clear outcome means that teachers can successfully monitor progress through the activity in order to determine when to scaffold and intervene. For example, clear outcomes can make it apparent that students are missing key aspects of a component or implications/insights from their application of facts and skills.

> **Critical Point**
> Before beginning teacher-guided learning, it is *vital* to be sure that students have the necessary *basic skills* needed to complete the activity, often provided through a teacher-directed session.

Teacher-guided instruction also depends on ongoing observation and monitoring of individual and group progress, to know when and how to apply probing questions, scaffolded prompts, or guided discussion of issues. Another outcome of this monitoring is with what is called "teachable moments." These occur when the teacher note a unique convergence of student interest and inquiry (a question or statement), with a teaching topic or link. These are opportunities to illuminate new concepts and facilitate higher-order relationships. Teachers take advantage of a particular example, draw parallels and explore relationships (cause/effect, problem/solution, time sequences, etc.), and scaffold student insights to a higher level.

Teacher-directed instruction is used to acquire knowledge (facts and skills); however the application of this knowledge across different conditions and circumstances is best taught through teacher-guided methods of exploration and inquiry. The teacher leads, guides, and facilitates the development of insights into, and interpretations of what occurred both during individual or small-group exploration, and during larger-group discussions. Before students can competently engage in inquiry or discovery, they must: (a) have a deep foundation of factual knowledge, (b) understand facts and ideas in the context of a conceptual framework, and (c) organize knowledge in ways that facilitate retrieval and applications (Donovan, Bransford, & Pellegrino, 1999). This is based on theory and research done with Bloom's Taxonomy—knowledge, comprehension, application, analysis, synthesis, and evaluation. Students cannot explore nor inquire into various career standards without understanding what "work" means and how jobs are different from each other (in terms of conditions, educational requirements, and so on).

> **Critical Point**
> Teacher-directed and teacher-guided methods are intimately linked in ensuring successful student-learning outcomes.

As part of an inquiry- or discovery-based learning experience, the teacher needs to explain to the teams and the class the procedures for the activities, and the components and rubrics on which they will be evaluated. And this is most efficiently done through teacher-directed methods—lecturing, modeling with self-talk for complex procedures that involve decision making

Teaching Tip: Importance of Application

Have you noticed how students may do okay in a math text, but can't seem to balance a checkbook to save their life? We can forget that skills or processes that we teach in isolation are not always generalized to outside or real-life contexts—students need practice with this. That's why incorporating authentic and relevant examples is so important—because if they can't use a skill in the real world, then we haven't really *taught* them.

and judgments, and periodic review of key aspects. Therefore, teacher-directed and teacher-guided methods are mutually supportive: direct methods provide the basic skills and procedures; guided methods allow for the critical experiences in using this knowledge.

STUDENT-GUIDED OR PROJECT-BASED LEARNIING

This next type of learning is becoming increasingly used in schools. In a way, it is another "practice" step in applying higher-order thinking processes to real-life situations, but with some oversight provided by teachers. It is an important intermediary step in moving students from inquiry and discovery learning activities that are under the guidance of teachers, to completely self-directed learning. Schools are increasingly incorporating student-guided projects into their curriculum or graduation requirements. Senior projects often require students to design and implement an activity that contributes to the community in some way. Theses or dissertations can be considered another type of student-guided learning.

Content and Approaches

The teacher role in this method is to provide assistance and guidance, often according to needs or questions identified by the student. The teacher does not design the activity as they do for teacher-guided learning. Instead it is the student who must create the project, its focus, and its components. This is a major role change because the student, rather than the teacher, now assumes primary responsibility for his or her own learning. Because these projects and activities are completed within an educational organization, teachers still provide some degree of oversight to be sure that projects address appropriate topics using acceptable means for their completion.

The *content* of student-facilitated activities is quite varied; however the school or district frequently has guidelines that these projects must meet or address. Essentially, they are an application of a problem-solving model described earlier, and modified in Table 8–4 as a research activity.

This process can help students organize their project to accomplish their goal successfully. It begins with identifying a problem (or topic) to solve (or investigate), identifying possible solutions (or arguments), considering pros and cons, developing a plan; and then implementing, evaluating, and modifying the plan as needed. Teachers may provide more, or less, guidance in assisting each student's choice and method for implementing these steps in accomplishing the project goal. Ultimately, it is the student who must complete the project.

Much of the student-guided *approach* uses conversation and scaffolded discussions. Teachers often negotiate with students regarding the frequency and type of assistance they will provide. However, teachers typically provide general progress monitoring and discuss concerns, barriers, and overall project achievement; a minimum and a maximum level of supervision and guidance often are described within the school's set of expectations.

> **Critical Point**
> The students' greater responsibility is designed to yield greater insights and understandings than are available through teacher-identified learning steps and activities. Assuming primary responsibility leads to greater overall student empowerment through self-direction and self-monitoring skills. Teacher support helps in addressing barriers and issues that can arise in relation to the topic or issue, and in the student's developing skills in self-direction.

TABLE 8–4 Problem-solving model or research model

1. Identify the problem. [research problem or issue]
2. Consider all possible solutions. [identify major arguments, sides, or issues]
3. Identify the pros and cons of each listed solution. [of each argument or side]
4. Develop a plan of action. [research plan with adequate sources and steps]
5. Put the plan into effect.
6. Evaluate the success of the plan.
7. Modify the plan as needed and begin again at step #5.

Source: Based on Downing, 1996; Hobbs & Westling, 1998; Jayanthia & Friend, 1992; Nezu & D'Zurilla; Salisbury, Evans, & Palombaro, 1997; Wood, 2002

Monitoring and Evaluation

Evaluation procedures typically are more authentic and relevant to real-life situations than with teacher-directed or guided learning. Students take more responsibility for monitoring and evaluating their own progress, which is much of what is expected of adults—throughout their work, friendships, and other independent living situations. Yet, teachers also provide support and can intervene if they see that progress is impeded. It often is helpful to set up regular "check-in" points with timelines for when certain portions of the project should be completed.

Students who begin these types of projects must have a range of *basic skills* that will support their success. Experience and practice with using problem-solving processes across several contexts is one important preskill. Students who have had limited experiences with inquiry- or discovery-based learning activities may expect much more involvement from teachers in student-guided projects, and may flounder. Therefore, in order to be successful with student-guided learning methods, each student must have all of the necessary basic skills (learned through teacher-guided methods), and higher-order thinking and problem-solving skills (teacher-facilitated methods).

An example that we might not typically consider as student-guided learning is what occurs in a "job club" for students or adults seeking employment. Such clubs have an assumed or stated goal that each student will continue until she or he has been successfully employed for a period of time. There are regular meetings to discuss issues in which the teacher or leader scaffolds participants to new insights or understandings, and provides some oversight with regards to strategies used. However, each student is ultimately responsible for their own employment success.

Another example is special education programs that have established independent living facilities for students in which minimal supervision is provided. Students have living and work responsibilities that they must successfully complete, with teacher oversight and support provided. Typically, students must achieve certain goals while living there—again, these programs

> **Critical Point**
> If *all* students should be lifelong learners and if much of this learning needs to be self-directed and done to solve adult-living issues or "problems," then student-guided learning is a critical intermediary step in teaching students to be self-directed.

serve as an intermediary step before completely independent and self-directed living. This provides the next level of supported "real-life" experiences. Those who are missing these skills need to review or repeat these prior learning experiences in order to be successful with these methods.

As with other instructional methods, student *practice* leads to fluency and mastery with these controlled "real-life" experiences. Some students may need extended time in supported living situations or job clubs. Having extended practice with teacher-guided learning, across different contexts, provides practice with basic processes and higher-order thinking and monitoring skills upon which student-guided projects are based. Teacher-facilitated activities within the classroom or school program can be modified to give students increasing individual responsibility, and prepare them for student-facilitated projects. For example, teachers can allow students access to laundry facilities that they schedule and use on their own, but provide scaffolded discussions to address how to wash specialty items and remove stains, with students performing self-evaluations (that are compared with teacher observations). Job-related social interactions may be taught first through a teacher-directed curriculum, and then utilized through on-site experiences with teacher-guided problem solving and conflict resolution. Students who need less teacher facilitation could move naturally toward the next step of resolving situations with minimal teacher oversight in student-guided experiences.

Because there is school or institutional monitoring of these student-guided activities, and because they occur within the purview of the school, *evaluation* often is structured within a set of predetermined guidelines. Although it is the students who are responsible for completing these activities, there often is one teacher, or a panel of teachers and professionals who ultimately evaluate the success of the activity or final product. It is very helpful when the program area, panel, or school has developed a rubric within which the project or product must fit. Rather than use letter grades, sometimes products are given pass/fail determinations—the student is allowed to graduate or progress in her or his program rather than receive a grade. This provides a "gate" that schools or programs use to ensure certain skills and abilities: a student whose graded project receives a "D" may still graduate, but a "fail" mark will not allow graduation (or progress in the program) to occur. At times, the project may have additional expectations for results that are not part of the evaluation criteria: community projects are expected to demonstrate positive community participation and involvement. These "real-world" expectations may not be included as part of the evaluation rubric.

STUDENT-DIRECTED LEARNING

This last method is the ultimate goal of education: to produce lifelong, self-directed learners. In today's global job market, workers are now expected to be flexible and amenable to learning new skills or jobs within their career path. Marketplace pressures and technological developments also mean that certain jobs of today may no longer exist in the future. Citizens must educate themselves about how these changes affect our local governments and where or how we live. Global warming, environmental and health impacts of pollution are topics that have emerged in importance as graduating seniors were just being born: today's adults have had to educate themselves on these issues.

Much of adult learning is self-directed; and teachers need to be sure that their students are fully prepared to assume this responsibility. Thus, the task is to ensure that special education students, just like their general education peers, have the skills and experiences that will allow them to do this effectively, including how to ask for help when needed. Students with disabilities often are found eligible to receive adult services but becoming dependent upon these services hinder, rather than help, in becoming fully-functioning and satisfied adult citizens. Describing some of the characteristics of this learning will help teachers provide students with the necessary prerequisite skills in order to be successful and self-determined lifelong learners.

Content and Approaches

The *content* of this instructional method is self-determined. Therefore, students must be able to identify a problem or need area, and have some strategies for addressing these needs. Once again, using a problem-solving format provides a flexible process for identifying the issue and then developing, implementing, and evaluating a plan. Transition provides many potential examples of possible content, because everyone has strength and need areas across the many different life arenas. Self-directed learning is used to figure out: how to install a new appliance, build a child's toy, operate a new DVR or cell phone. Some people read and study the directions thoroughly, some "shoot from the hip," and some immediately ask for help from a knowledgeable

friend. Regardless, people are using problem-solving and learning strategies to figure these out—Do they know enough to read and understand the directions? Do they prefer to let someone else do this? And is there a friend who is knowledgeable? Self-directed and problem-solving strategies are also used to: resolve a mistaken utility bill (it's often not as simple as making a phone call), find a health or service professional that they like and trust, and so on.

The *approaches* for carrying out this type of learning are typically student-determined as well. Therefore, it is extremely important for the student to understand his or her own learning strengths and needs, and to recognize when certain types of resources are and are not available or helpful, and with whom to meet and ask for help. Because this is student-directed, it is also the student's decision as to whether or not to accept the advice or help—very different from the other types of instructional methods. This includes students enrolling for additional coursework or training, but choosing not to complete it if this no longer meets their needs. Teachers may be used as resources when a student asks for help or guidance in planning a learning path, or they may teach a class that contributes one element to an individual's path.

Monitoring and Evaluation

This area also is student-determined; it is the student who must decide whether or not his or her goal has been achieved, and even if this goal continues to be important. The extent and nature of *monitoring and evaluation* is quite flexible. Students may choose to ask for assistance and support, and arrange for co-direction in monitoring their progress, or work primarily independently or with feedback from friends and family members.

This type of learning requires a range of realistic self-knowledge and self-evaluation abilities. Lack of *basic skills* may include these self-determination skills, or may be more specific to abilities needed to achieve goals—in work, social relationships, or independent and community living. Those who do not have basic skills and don't realize this may flounder, or may eventually seek or be referred to teachers or agencies for assistance in determining how to acquire these skills and experiences.

Students and adults all become more skillful with identifying and accomplishing self-directed learning goals and *practice* with the different environments and circumstances. But it definitely can seem rather daunting to have such independence. Schools rarely provide ample practice opportunities to develop mastery and fluency with partially self-directed learning (e.g., teacher-guided and student-guided methods). Many students actually feel fearful about "graduating" from their programs. Teachers don't typically offer completely self-directed learning activities—part of their job is to supervise and assist.

In special education and transition services, tears frequently discuss "self-determination" as an important topic, and identify its various components and specific activities (cf. Field, Hoffman, & Spezia, 1998; Loyd & Wehmeyer, 2004). Yet in terms of the continuum of instructional methods, it is the culmination of teaching across teacher-directed (that provides basic facts and skills), teacher-guided (that introduces supervised student inquiry and application of facts and skills), and student-guided activities (that oversees student-initiated learning). Foundational skills for success in this method are focused on accurate self-appraisal, monitoring, and evaluation. Because student-directed learning encompasses and is built upon all of the previous types of learning, it is the ultimate "test" of success—Can students utilize these learnings in their lives to successfully meet the challenges of living in today's complex society? It is the final goal and outcome that teachers work to meet—one day, one lesson, and one student, at a time—the measure of our "transition" success.

Chapter 6 discussed curriculum paths and options, Chapter 7 discussed instructional environments, groupings, and materials, and this chapter described the four different instructional methods that one would need to organize and utilize to be an effective teacher. The next important step is to synthesize this information, that is, to put this all together in organizing and delivering instruction for students. Although this chapter can't take the reader into the classroom, it will move from the informational and theoretical into some ways to manage it all. This next section describes the process for organizing and synthesizing all of this into a manageable plan.

PREPARING FOR INSTRUCTION

The classroom is arranged; the rules and routines are ready. The teacher has chosen lesson content from the curriculum and identified ways to use various types of students' groupings. They have found and made some terrific materials that support active student learning and higher-level learning, and have identified instructional methods that have a good chance of being effective as well as some accommodations—with plenty of practice opportunities for all. They will be observing and monitoring, and have a rubric for grading and evaluating student work, with specific examples to be added to the students' individual learning portfolios. Laying this groundwork is a tremendous accomplishment.

The challenge to teachers is in keeping the critical pieces in their head as they stand in front of the class (or move from student to student) every day, all day. There is a tool available: daily lesson planning. A lesson plan summarizes this key information (from across the four categories of instructional variables) so that instruction will achieve the intended outcomes. Although all necessary science-based analysis has been conducted and modified as needed across the four categories, the teacher needs to be very clear and focused for each lesson (and not overwhelmed with considerations). When well done, lesson plans provide a built-in rubric for teachers to evaluate whether or not they have been successful, or if certain portions need to be reviewed and retaught (including helping to evaluate if the methods used were effective).

Lesson Planning

Essentially, a lesson plan is a tool to assist teachers in making sure that all critical aspects of an instructional activity will be addressed. With experience, many teachers are able to do much of this mentally, needing only topic listings to remind them of their plans (like a mental macro-command). Sometimes teachers will shortcut these processes until teaching becomes a process of "going through" a list of materials or topics, rather than providing experiences that provide for and reinforce *student learning*. "Going through" material is not teaching.

The lesson plan is very specific and rather lengthy—a format for beginners. With practice (remember that practice should be individualized, specific, and systematic, with high levels of success), much of the lesson planning process will become automatic. Excellent teachers can use their mental "macro-command" topics to call up their objectives, lesson sequence, adaptations, prerequisites, and so on. But when experienced teachers learn new teaching strategies or plan new types of units, then they too must write and plan their instructional activities.

The lesson plan format is as follows:

1. *Relationship of lesson to unit or theme.* It is important to be clear how this lesson links with others. Have you been in classes that seem to be a series of isolated and fragmented activities? This is *not a good thing*—this step helps us prevent this.

- *Students will learn to do their own washing and drying as part of their preparation to live in an apartment.*

2. *Behavioral objective(s).* Special education likes very clear and precise objectives, moreso than many general educators are used to. Practice in writing clear, concise objectives with observable and measurable outcomes is important (the book by Mager, 1962, is self-instructional and will take about an hour). A clear behavioral objective names a clear and observable *terminal behavior* with the *conditions* (what the student can or cannot use—resources, notes, unlimited time, with teacher or peer assistance, in a group, on his/her own, etc.), and the *criteria* (amount of work, accuracy—number or % correct) for this behavior. A mnemonic self-checking formula for writing behavioral objectives uses the ABCD method:

A = audience (usually students)
B = terminal behavior (measurable, observable demonstration of intended outcome)
C = conditions (what is available or not available to the student—time, resources, persons)
D = degree or criterion (amount of work, degree or % correct)

Now let's check to see how the objective in the example meets this formula:

- *Each student* (audience) *will sort the clothes, identify proper settings, add soap, load, turn on the washer, and unload the washer* (terminal behaviors—lists out each one that is important) *with or without using their own written prompts* (conditions), *requiring no teacher prompts* (another condition) *on 4 out of 5 trials* (degree) *in the home ec classroom* (another condition).

The objective meets all of the requirements and in fact, includes several key behaviors and criteria—because these are what will be important when the student is functioning independently.

Another important aspect of writing a behavioral objective is to focus on teaching something new. In fact, if you are just doing a review exercise, don't bother with doing an entire lesson plan. You may

simply be extending your more thorough lesson plan in which you *taught* the skill, by ensuring appropriate levels of mastery and fluency. So always begin with a new concept or skill to teach—identify this *before* you begin writing your objective. Then use the ABCD or other method—and if done well, the objective also is your evaluation step for the lesson. You simply check the students' performance to see if it matches or exceeds your objective.

3. *Materials.* It is important to make sure you are prepared and have everything ready. Especially when you need several items from different resources (reservation of the home ec room, supplies request filled out a week in advance to get needed materials, etc.) you can use this as a checklist. It will prevent you from jumping into a lesson and *then* realizing you've forgotten a key item. Consider it "humiliation prevention." You may also want to list key vocabulary and concepts (with pictures, cue cards, video clips) that are important to the lesson. Many times these function as prerequisites—do the students "have a clue" about these even before you teach them to recognize or read what they mean?

- *Students bring own clothes weekly, classroom purchased detergent, home ec room facilities (already scheduled for Oct.–Nov.), note cards of choice (index or smaller), home ec room blackboard to write list of steps.*

4. *Key teaching methods and conceptual links.* This is where you identify the instructional methods you will use, based on the students' basic skills and the higher-order thinking needed to achieve the lesson's objectives. After you list out what you intend to use here, then review it after you have listed out your procedures in step 6—you may not have used the methods you had anticipated. You may need to review/revise the behavioral objective, your methods, and/or the teaching steps. At this step it is also important to list conceptual links (where relationship to other lessons in Step 1 helps). In this lesson, the students need to move toward self-directed and independent functioning across types of machines and settings. This helps remind the teacher to focus on key characteristics as they continues to use this basic plan in the community to provide generalization activities.

- *Teacher-directed: Explain rationale, steps, outcome, schedule; narrate/use self-talk through demonstration and modeling of decision making—sorting clothes, water temperature and level, amount of soap (small vs. large load); use verbal and physical prompts that are faded—use only as reminders as students demonstrate mastery.*

- *Teacher-guided: After full-class demonstration, provide guided practice that progresses to working in pairs to sort and wash their clothes— monitor and give feedback. Use guided discussion prior to using laundromat about similarities and differences (what they will expect), then monitor their use in the laundromat facilities. Continue experience and bring "special care" clothing for each pair to examine and wash appropriately.*

- *Conceptual links: Students compare and contrast between home and multiple laundry facilities to support generalization and later independence; have students focus on key features—washer and dryer settings, design (front vs. top-loading), types of cycles, cost, etc.*

    5. *Prerequisite skills, knowledge, and experiences.* This is another humiliation and frustration-prevention step. We often assume that students already know and can talk about things they have done or learned about in the past. This is a frequent cause of lesson failure—we have assumed things that they don't have. With experience, you'll get very good at identifying these. It is somewhat similar to the process of task analysis and dissecting where we will begin our lesson, into the many things that we are building upon. The better we get at this, the more we will be able to identify the missing preskills that are causing our lesson to flounder, even while we are teaching. This is the skill often referred to when we talk about "thinking on our feet" to rescue a lesson.

- *Have seen their family wash clothes, know some effects of hot vs. cold water on clothes (will review), can use measuring cup, read/recognize key words in basic detergent and laundry instructions (inside of washer).*

    6. *Procedure.* This is the main teaching activity and consists of two parts—the introduction and the teaching.

    6a. *Teaching step(s) to motivate, engage their thinking, review past learnings* is the way you will get them thinking and linking to their past learnings. Remember, we should always move from known to unknown, and the way to do that is to start with the known, often called a review. It also is good to do this in a motivating way—present an intriguing idea, an authentic/relevant task, or a challenge to students. The example asks students to remember the problem

with their clothing. You could pose this as a situation and make it "funny" as well: ask if they had "stinky" clothes before and how they would solve this problem in the future, for example.

- *Remember our unit on living independently? What was one problem we had with our clothing? Who takes care of your dirty clothing now? How much have you helped? What things were easy … were difficult for you when you helped? (forgot things, got confused, didn't know how to sort or made mistakes with that).*

- *Tomorrow we're going to the home ec room to do our laundry, but right now we're going to sort— who remembered to bring some dirty clothes from home?*

    6b. *Instructional strategies/steps to develop target behaviors/skills* are the series of steps and activities you will use to accomplish the behavioral objective. The steps should start from your introduction and end with the students performing your objective. In between, you will use your instructional methods (listed in Step 4) and steer the students from initial learning, to guided practice, and to eventual mastery and fluency with the knowledge and skills. It is often helpful to do a task analysis of the skill and include this as part of your steps.

- *Why should we sort clothes? What happens if we don't? So how should we sort them? [Build on past experience.] Yes, we don't want everything to look pink or gray. That happens because dark colors spread to light colors when they get wet. So we need to divide the clothes into dark and light colors. Everyone show me one light thing … one dark thing … Now put each in separate piles. Sort the rest of your clothes into these piles. I will check.*

- *Next day: Who brought their light and dark clothes with them today? Which one is the washer and which is the dryer? What do these buttons/this dial mean? [Build on past experience.] Let's read them and see (students stand around the washer and read). The dial (buttons) is for different types of washing. You can see wash, spin, rinse, spin, and off. Look again. What do these words mean for washing clothes?*

- *Find some of those words in another place. Yes, if you look below you can see heavy, normal, and spin-only. We will use normal. You would use spin-only if you needed to rinse something but not wash it with soap—if something got left out in the rain. You would use heavy for blankets or washable coats or things that were very dirty from being in the mud. Now you need to pick the setting (show how to use dial or buttons to select, then continue in this process through steps in getting and adding soap, loading, turning on the washer, and unloading the washer when it's finished).*

7. *Instructional probe/prompts to summarize, bring closure to the activity, and/or put it in long-term context.* This is how you conclude your lesson. You may have students review and reflect on what they've learned, or link and review how this fits with other learning. It's always good to reestablish the relevancy and authenticity of their learning and identify how it is useful or prepares them for something they will need to accomplish. This step also helps avoid the problem of being able to do something in the classroom, but unable to use it in real life. In the example, the students generate self-monitoring and self-cueing cards that also serve as a review of the lesson.

- *Who would like to have some help remembering these steps? I have two different kinds of cards for you to write down the steps, or you can use another type of paper. Let's first write these on the board to make sure we remember them correctly—who remembers one step? (continue to list all steps and ask students to evaluate and correct the full list, have students copy/draw pictures of each step as needed).*
- *Today we washed one load of clothes and tomorrow we will wash the other. Who can remember one important reason to sort clothes? What is important to remember about the dial/buttons? We will spend this month learning how to wash our clothes each week. Next week we will start washing and drying our clothes. After*

next month we will go to the laundromat so we need to practice and remember these things.

8. *Self-evaluation.* This is where you rethink how effectively you both planned and implemented your lesson—the combination of your *science* and *art*-based teaching skills. When using written lesson plan forms, teachers will sometimes make notes to themselves. Experienced teachers may make notes directly in their planning books while at school. Much of your self-evaluation is likely to occur at home when you have time to reflect on both the strengths and needs of your lesson, free from your other teaching responsibilities—looking for materials or resources, lunch or bus duty, and so on.

- *(Write comments about what went well and what was a little rough, which students understood clearly and which need additional practice or prompting, if the steps seem appropriate, or are too big/too small.)*

Until teachers have practiced to achieve mastery, they will need to write and review (even several times) the various aspects of this plan. But the plan is to help when things go wrong. For example, misjudging students' preskills and prior learning experience is a chief source of lesson failure in any classroom, and even if the lesson was well planned and well executed some teachers plow ahead until failure. When students look lost, a good teacher reviews the prerequisites in the lesson plan.

Integrated Thematic Units

Even wonderfully-planned lessons can be chaotic and fragmented without some link to a larger whole. Of course, lessons should be based on the state or local curriculum that leads to the achievement of standards. But jumping from benchmark to benchmark is productive for neither the teacher nor the student. Research shows

Teaching Tip: A Lesson on Planning

We start teaching a lesson on grocery shopping but become very frustrated when the students don't remember seeing store "aisles" before. How can this be? What's wrong with them? Well, maybe they haven't been in stores very often. And although last year Mrs. Rodriguez took her students on grocery-shopping trips, this class didn't have Mrs. Rodriguez. Also, several mothers have said they prefer to shop alone (to save time). So maybe they haven't had these background experiences. Lesson learned: We need to be aware of our assumptions. Identifying preskills or prerequisites gives us an immediate checkpoint for floundering lessons. We also need to provide these missing experiences if they are foundational to later learning: a field trip—with cameras and video to help their recall if things begin to flounder again.

that organizing knowledge and skills into integrated instructional units is an efficient and effective way to teach (Schirmer, 2000; Siu-Runyan & Faircloth, 1995; Tomlinson & McTighe, 2006; Wiggins & McTighe, 1998). Units are organized around central themes, so that repetition of ideas and concepts occurs naturally—providing for repetition and practice. Teaching based on integrated thematic units helps *all* students (including culturally diverse students) (Siu-Runyan & Faircloth, 1995) learn concepts, vocabulary, knowledge, and skills at higher levels of mastery (cf., Mastropieri & Scruggs, 2002). It also is a way to be sure that students learn the "big ideas" that transcend any particular or specific curriculum area, and that help them learn relationships between skills needed in adulthood. The earlier demonstration showed how one problem-solving sequence can be modified to address decision-making, conflict-resolution, and research/project planning. Applying a cognitive skill across different contexts and concepts within a unit gives students this critical practice.

But developing integrated instructional units is not easy—organizing and synthesizing multiple benchmarks and curriculum activities is a very complex set of higher-order thinking tasks. Teaming across content and within grades can greatly help middle and high school teachers who often are assigned subject-specific classes (Siu-Runyan & Faircloth, 1995). Teachers of self-contained classes (across multiple subjects) may find it easier to organize such units because they can pull together what they need according to the students they teach. School support of collaboration among special and general educators allows for more opportunities for cross-disciplinary or integrated thematic unit planning, and a sharing of resources as well. It often is not easy to develop schedules with common planning and development time. However, shared unit teaching is an excellent way to prepare special education students for inclusion; students can attend selected activities in general education classrooms and return to special education classes for additional support regarding new cooperative or group-based learning experiences.

Many transition topics can be easily integrated into thematic teaching units. By including authentic and relevant outcomes into all units (cf. Tomlinson & McTighe, 2006; Wiggins & McTighe 1998), units would theoretically *always* support transition outcomes (which are based on students' needs, interests, and preferences, and therefore are authentic and relevant). Content that integrated outcomes that students truly needed in adulthood was the idea behind Brolin's LCCE—to integrate career education into the regular K-12 curriculum as well. In Figure 8-1 are two integrated thematic unit examples based on transition needs.

The two units identify the key theme and then each of the key content areas that are linked through this theme. These brief diagrams do not specify the possible state standards or benchmarks that could be included. This would vary by state, disability, and strengths/needs of your particular students. Although standards can be difficult to work with, because they can be either overly broad or overly specific (Popham, 2001; Wiggins & McTighe, 2005), skills in task analysis can help parse out key elements in those that are broad, and link several of those that are highly specific, into appropriate outcomes for units. Wiggins and McTighe (1998) have developed a three-step "backward design" process for unit development that begins with identifying outcomes, then ways to assess across six facets (to ensure thorough understanding), and finally to the lessons and activities that support the outcomes and assessments. In addition, of some assistance in identifying how transition outcomes can link to state standards, the website at *http://www.educ.kent.edu/fundedprojects/TSPT/priorities/priorities.htm* provides state-standard links across Brolin's LCCE transition competencies and subcompetencies (look under *Priority 3,* and *standards*—examples are at the 5th grade and 10th grade).

In review, use lesson plans to focus instruction on key strategies and outcomes. Teaching is a complex process so it's all too easy to "overload" on things to consider, manipulate, and address. But using thematic unit planning as a "map" through the current "regions" of the curriculum creates a structured path through the content and curriculum standards to help you navigate across your multiple lesson objectives to achieve your long-term curriculum learning outcomes.

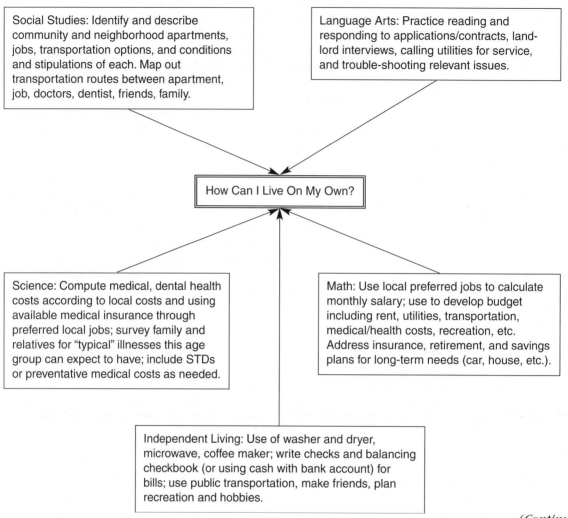

Social Studies: Identify and describe community and neighborhood apartments, jobs, transportation options, and conditions and stipulations of each. Map out transportation routes between apartment, job, doctors, dentist, friends, family.

Language Arts: Practice reading and responding to applications/contracts, landlord interviews, calling utilities for service, and trouble-shooting relevant issues.

How Can I Live On My Own?

Science: Compute medical, dental health costs according to local costs and using available medical insurance through preferred local jobs; survey family and relatives for "typical" illnesses this age group can expect to have; include STDs or preventative medical costs as needed.

Math: Use local preferred jobs to calculate monthly salary; use to develop budget including rent, utilities, transportation, medical/health costs, recreation, etc. Address insurance, retirement, and savings plans for long-term needs (car, house, etc.).

Independent Living: Use of washer and dryer, microwave, coffee maker; write checks and balancing checkbook (or using cash with bank account) for bills; use public transportation, make friends, plan recreation and hobbies.

FIGURE 8–1   Thematic transition units

(*Continued*)

Teaching Tip: Stick to the Plan

At times your students' behaviors may seem quite challenging, but remember the principle of successive approximations—you have a whole year to work on these things. For me, I would focus the first two weeks to one month on establishing rules and routines, rewards and consequences (e.g., compliance and attention). And although they frequently gave me some of the "worst" behaviors, I was amazed at how this plan paid me *untold dividends* of instructional time throughout the year! And I would grin while listening to teachers with "nice, compliant students" shriek in frustration at the frequent misbehaviors they had—while my "special" students were focused and conscientiously applying themselves to the task at hand!

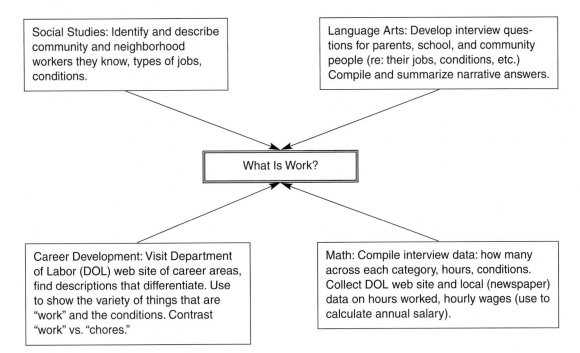

FIGURE 8–1 (*Continued*)

CONCLUSION

The ultimate outcome of good teaching is student mastery of skills and knowledge that they can use in their daily lives, at home, at work, and in the community. Community citizens and politicians are highly aware of the importance of achieving outcomes at this level; therefore, teachers are increasingly accountable. Unfortunately, there are mixed messages regarding how students should demonstrate their mastery: from transition legislation that requires broad and lifelong outcomes, to education legislation that mandates statewide proficiency testing on highly specific knowledge and skills. IEP team members may feel potentially torn in their responsibilities to ensure that students learn important community-based and transition skills (e.g., using the laundromat or automated teller machines) or demonstrating acceptable levels of progress on the curriculum and statewide performance tests.

But what teachers do, and do best, is to provide quality instruction. Teaching is too complex a profession to be done well by those who are not committed professionals. Teachers must understand and be able to skillfully use environments, groupings, materials, and instructional methods, and to articulate the research-based rationale

for each choice. In addition, they must be ready to provide data-based (not just narrative) evidence of students' learning outcomes and achievement (for example, data from the behavior objectives that guide lesson planning and that lead to accomplishment of unit goals and state standards).

The intent of Chapters 7 and 8 was to help present the vast array of variables within what is called "instruction" and to better understand their use; and ultimately, to help with better implementation through practice and guided instruction. The goal is to prepare teachers and transition team members for a range of possible roles. Special educators are increasingly working in co-teaching or collaborative teaching situations. In these cases, they must not only have the skills to identify appropriate learning strategies for particular students, but they must accommodate teaching styles other than their own, and communicate their expertise effectively to partner teachers. Teachers must be prepared to communicate and explain what they do, what choices they make, and why they make those choices. They must be sensitive to how best to modify instructional methods, environments, groupings, and materials; for themselves, and for other professionals, and with strategies for how to integrate them within a curriculum that will often need some adaptation or augmentation. Teachers must also be prepared to modify "instructional language" for roles in work and community settings. They will need to be skillful translators so that the same important instructional methods, materials, groupings, and environmental characteristics are used effectively by co-workers, supervisors, and human resource personnel who will train and supervise students.

Therefore, more than ever teachers must not only be skilled in their teaching, but be able to consult and advise others regarding their choice among instructional variables. They have a very important role on IEP teams in providing information and options regarding appropriate instructional and curricular decisions, their modifications and adaptations, or alterations when needed.

The four instructional methods described in this chapter provide a clear continuum that moves students from learning basic knowledge and skills, to becoming self-directed, lifelong learners. The chapter also provides lesson planning and unit development formats that help synthesize the key instructional variables that impact student success. By integrating well-planned lessons and units with instruction that prepares students for self-directed learning, we have set the stage for successfully attaining transition outcomes.

STUDY QUESTIONS

1. You are a teacher of a group of students (visualize a diverse group in terms of strengths/needs and ethnicity—challenge yourself). What are some of the ways that you will want to modify your (a) instructional environment, (b) instructional groupings, (c) instructional materials, and (d) instructional methods to, first of all, reduce barriers and secondly, to facilitate maximum class learning?

2. You will be utilizing a mix of the four instructional methods in your classroom. What are at least two transition activities you will want to teach your students that are most suitable for each of the instructional methods? For each of these activities, what role will you take as a teacher and prepare your students to take as learners? How will you prepare the students and what types of prerequisite skills will they need for each activity?

3. In your classroom, you now realize that your diverse group includes some learners with (a) high incidence disabilities, (b) low incidence disabilities, and (c) sensory disabilities (define these as you like). How will you plan to accommodate these diverse students when teaching your two transition activities, by varying: (1) instructional approaches (individual, competitive, and cooperative); (2) instructional strategies (options within the direct and nondirect choices); (3) using basic skill accommodations; (4) independent student practice activities; and (5) evaluation activities? Use the lesson planning form to turn these ideas into a full-planned lesson.

4. Brainstorm your ideas and curriculum links (with others if it helps), then refine and create an interdisciplinary thematic unit using one or both of your transition activities (and lesson) from Questions #2 and 3, if possible. Use the lesson planning form to develop another fully-planned lesson.

PROMOTING MOVEMENT TO POSTSCHOOL ENVIRONMENTS

Section 3 of this book examines the demands and supports available in the postsecondary environments of employment, postsecondary education, community participation, and independent living. Chapter 9, "Collaborative Transition Services," examines the roles of educational and adult service professionals and describes several interdisciplinary planning approaches commonly used by these professionals. This chapter is designed to provide the reader with an overview of common transition service providers and describe how these professionals can collectively support the vision of the student with a disability.

Chapter 10, "Transition to Employment," discusses various employment situations available to graduates with disabilities, including competitive employment, individual supported employment, enclaves, mobile work crews, and sheltered work and the general demands and supports of these settings. This chapter is designed to provide the reader with an understanding of the pros and cons of these employment situations, the students who are likely to be eligible for services of this kind, and agencies that typically provide one or more of these services.

Chapter 11, "Transition to Postsecondary Education," discusses various postsecondary education options for students with disabilities, including two- and four-year colleges, technical schools, and other continuing education options, and the general demands and supports characteristic of these settings. It includes a discussion of the role of student disability services and the importance of students understanding their disability needs, of researching supports offered by postsecondary programs, and of advocating for themselves in postsecondary education settings.

Chapter 12, "Independent Living and Community Participation," provides an overview of adult residential options for individuals with disabilities, including independent living, group homes, and supported living. Chapter 12 provides a brief history of residential services and restates the value that people with disabilities should be able to live and recreate in their own homes and communities. Finally, recreation and leisure activities are critical for a complete life in the community. This chapter also describes recreation needs and preferences and how to link the student to the community.

CHAPTER 9

COLLABORATIVE TRANSITION SERVICES

Thomas Simmons

Robert W. Flexer

Debra Bauder

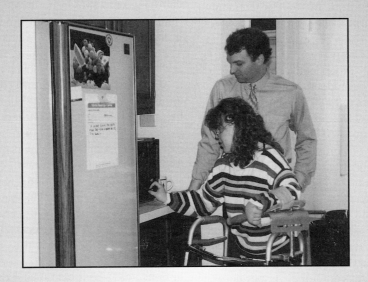

LEARNING OBJECTIVES

The objectives of this chapter are:

1. Describe the importance of collaboration in transition professional and agency services and practices.

2. Describe the different transition disciplines and services.

3. Explain how the interface of transition disciplines may affect the delivery of transition services.

4. Describe transition services and the roles of school professionals on the transition team.

5. Describe transition services and the roles of adult services and postschool professionals on the transition team.

6. Describe the importance of transdisciplinary teams and interagency linkages.

INTRODUCTION

The chapters in Section II set out the components of assessment, curriculum, and instruction for a secondary transition foundation; described the service delivery system of transition in high schools; and delineated some of the "promising practices." This chapter describes the roles of the principal transition disciplines (special education, vocational education, and rehabilitation) and transition services as provided by a variety of other school and adult service professionals. Each professional service within the individual transition plan needs to provide support to the student and family in clarifying and refining postschool goals. The functioning of the transition team has a great bearing on students making progress each year. The team contributions, both individually and collectively, should promote movement toward the students' postschool goals.

The IDEA Amendments (1990, 1997, 2004) require that a variety of transition services be available and that they be provided in a coordinated fashion. The services provided to students are supportive of student-derived transition goals and promote progress toward those goals. Transition services span a broad spectrum of activities. For example, transition services can be instruction— teaching of knowledge and skills from classes or community activities. These instructional activities should clarify and refine student transition goals and result in concrete learning necessary to achieve the goal. Other transition services include: community experiences, development of employment and other postschool living objectives, and related services. Three additional transition services are to be included when needed or appropriate. They include: interagency linkages, daily living skills training, and functional vocational evaluation. This chapter describes each of these service domains and the respective roles of various professionals along with the collaborative and team interactions (contributions) required for a coordinated set of activities.

KEY CONCEPTS IN TRANSITION COLLABORATION

Because transition services require extensive communication among professionals, collaboration and consultation among school and postschool educators and service providers are required under the IDEA. Eber, Nelson, and Miles (1997) further described the broad range of skills required of professionals involved in transition and came to the conclusion that individual personnel alone cannot accomplish the requisite desired transition outcomes. deFur and Taymans (1995) highlighted the need for significant degrees of communication, coordination, and collaboration among vocational rehabilitation, vocational education, and special education programs and staff. As collaborators, team members develop shared values, develop appreciation of unique team member contributions, and derive student- and family-driven transition goals that are consensually developed (Everson & Guillory, 1998). By clarifying who should be involved and their responsibilities, transition teams enable the coordination and utilization of the myriad programs and services available in schools and the community.

The essential element of a *coordinated set of activities* relates directly to the need for interdisciplinary approaches and to the IEP requirement that consensus be obtained from a team. Moreover, transition requirements add services provided by professionals from postschool agencies and environments to the team effort. The uncertainty of the future of the student makes services from these additional team members tenuous and ambiguous at times. For example, although many students may benefit from vocational rehabilitation, few of them will actually receive services, because the need for the service is not the only criterion for eligibility. Similar challenges exist for access to secondary options such as vocational education and school-to-work programs. When transition needs of students are identified, questions of availability and access to an appropriate service usually arise. Often possible options lie in interdisciplinary team functioning. Developing and implementing IEPs based on consensual goal development and interdisciplinary education and services remain both the ideal and the challenge in special education as well as in transition.

The delivery of transition services can be viewed as occurring on three levels. Transition services can be viewed programmatically at a federal, state, and local level. Policies and funds flow from one level to the next within corresponding and mutually supporting structures. Working from the federal structure, statewide and local interagency teams need to be established in order to make transition services accessible and to address barriers.

> **Critical Point**
> Transition services involve the collaboration of many professionals with different philosophies, service delivery approaches, and legal frameworks.

Individual transition teams are another level at which groups of professionals work with students and families in obtaining transition services. Statewide, local interagency, and individual teams all utilize team processes and are what the three groups have in common. Team processes assist in meeting transition needs through establishing joint values and common goals. An understanding of services as delivered by transition teams is facilitated by a foundation in individual and shared expertise of the various professionals involved.

INTERFACE OF TRANSITION COLLABORATION

Integrated services that incorporate the education and expertise of special education, rehabilitation, and vocational education (now also called career and technical education) are necessary to meet the comprehensive needs presented by the diverse populations of students with disabilities. All three transition systems are needed, but how they fit together and meet the needs of students in a unified manner requires a working framework among all three systems. An understanding of the relationships among the three systems is necessary to develop such a working framework, which is sometimes referred to as the "interface."

Szymanski, Hanley-Maxwell, and Asselin (1992) described the interrelationships among special education, vocational rehabilitation, and vocational education as being imperfect and frequently working against one another during these most important stages of the transition process. In general, the history and emphasis of the three delivery systems share similar concerns and emphasis on education and counseling processes. Although complementary, the three systems have distinct features as well. Szymanski et al. described this interface as follows:

> The three service delivery systems share many common concerns. Specifically, special education and vocational education share concerns for education; special education and vocational rehabilitation specialize in serving people with disabilities; and vocational education and vocational rehabilitation share interests in employment preparation. Nonetheless, these service delivery systems are administered by separate federal agencies, which may or may not facilitate coordinated efforts. (p. 165) (See Table 9-1.)

From Table 9-1, each category of difference (e.g., funding, etc.) creates the potential for a conflict or

Teamwork is critical for coordinated services.

barrier in the interactions of two given systems. Because the authorizing legislation for each system is different, there are different policies, rules, and regulations for each—a different purpose and target populations. Because vocational rehabilitation receives major funding from the federal government, they are more affected by those rules, while special and vocational education is funded largely by local and state funds. So, although federal rules need to be followed, individual school districts may have more variability. For every category of difference, there exists a potential for conflict among the systems—who is served, what kinds of services are provided, and the background, training, and professional services of principal staff within the systems. Due to the different systems in which they work and their different backgrounds, team members may experience communication difficulties and struggle with team functioning. Identifying common goals and emphasizing complementary functions need to be the focus of teams in order to serve transition students and help them achieve their goals.

TRANSITION DISCIPLINES

Not only are special education, rehabilitation, and vocational education the three major transition systems, but professionals in those systems also comprise one major interdisciplinary framework for understanding transition services. Taken together, the two education systems, the rehabilitation service system, and their professionals provide the comprehensive support for moving from school

	Vocational Rehabilitation	Special Education	Vocational Education
	Rehab Act	IDEA	Perkins Act
...on	Office of Special Education and Rehabilitative Services, Rehabilitation Services Administration	Office of Special Education and Rehabilitative Services, Office of Special Education Programs	Office of Vocational and Adult Education
...unding	75% federal, 25% state; no local funds	Federal, state, and local; largest share local and state	Federal, state, and local; largest share local and state
Eligibility	Disability, and potential to benefit	Disability, need for special education services	Attendance
Populations served	Adults and adolescents with disabilities	Persons with disabilities from birth through age 21	Adolescents and adults
Scope of services	Range of services for employment and independent living	Range of special education and related services	Vocational assessment, vocational instruction
Service mechanism	District vocational rehabilitation offices/ rehabilitation counselors	Local school districts/ special education teachers and related service personnel	Local school districts, postsecondary programs/teachers, etc.
Evaluation	Numbers rehabilitated; percents with severe disabilities	Compliance with law; service in least restrictive environment	Number of students served
Personnel qualifications	Relevant education in counseling	Usually certified to teach	Usually certified to teach

Source: Adapted from Szymanski, E. M., Hanley-Maxwell, C., Asselin, S. B. Systems interface: Vocational rehabilitation, special education, and vocational education. In *Transition from school to adult life: Models, linkages, and policy* by Rusch, F. R., Destefano, L., Chadsey-Rusch, Phelps, L. A., Szymanski, E. (1992). Sycamore Publishing Company; Sycamore, IL. Reprinted with permission.

to employment and other postschool environments. There are connections between the system and the professional. A given professional identity (e.g., rehabilitation counseling) is frequently tied to a given service system (e.g., a federal-state program of rehabilitation). The association between the sytems and the professionals is also evident in special education and vocational education. Special education and special education teachers are concerned with the delivery of education to students with disabilities within a federal-state-local system of public and private schools. Vocational education and vocational education teachers are concerned with the delivery of specific occupational education to adults and high school students within a federal-state-local system in varied settings. The correspondence of services is the system interface, whereas the interaction of the professionals is an interdisciplinary process. Special education and rehabilitation and vocational education are described as the transition disciplines, with corresponding professional identities, scope of practice, and service delivery systems.

> **Critical Point**
> Three important transition disciplines are typically involved in transition planning for youth with disabilities: vocational education, special education, and rehabilitation.

Scope of Practice of Rehabilitation Counseling

A rehabilitation counselor's preparation and practice is based in counseling with application to issues of instilling or restoring function and performance for persons with disabilities in major life activities. The federal-state vocational rehabilitation (VR) system provides services to eligible persons with disabilities to become employed and to live independently. Qualified rehabilitation counselors are the professionals who are at the direct service level in the VR system; however, rehabilitation counselors can apply their practice in any environment or in programs where persons with disabilities are in the process of treatment, recovery, rehabilitation, integration, or reintegration into work and community roles.

Scope of Practice of Vocational Education

Vocational educators' preparation and practice is based on teaching occupational skill development and academics as they apply to particular vocational programs. Vocational educators also can provide a wealth of information, counseling, and assessments pertaining to careers, in addition to apprenticeships or other community-based work training. Vocational educators are concerned with addressing both social and work-related skills and behaviors, as well as the self-determination skills that are vital to the success of all students.

Scope of Practice of Special Education

Secondary special educators' preparation and practice is based on teaching individual students with disabilities specific skills, such as those involved in self-determination, social skills, learning strategies, and, where appropriate, academic content. They also must have an understanding of all the aspects involved in transition planning, including coordinating assessments, setting and evaluating transition goals and objectives, collaborating with students, their families and communities, and other appropriate service providers, both within and outside the school, to ensure a smooth transition to adulthood.

Transdisciplinary Teams

The characteristics of the three transition systems partly define the professionals' duties. Vocational educators focus on occupational preparation; special educators emphasize transition skill instruction; and rehabilitation counselors use counseling and service coordination as a primary means of promoting employment. Although preparation varies, transition professionals share similarities in their scope of practice. As

an example, rehabilitation counselors and special educators both have expertise in disability, even though special educators focus on instruction and school settings, and rehabilitation counselors focus on counseling and postschool settings. An interdisciplinary transition identity requires that team members understand their complementary roles and contributions in relation to all other team members. To promote movement toward student goals, the broad background and specialized skills appropriate to transition services must be applied in a team context in which all members speak the same language, share the same assumptions and beliefs, and draw from a common culture (Flexer, Simmons, & Tankersly, 1997).

The team coordinator should promote collaboration in a way that minimizes the barriers among the student, family, and professionals; and that also improves collaboration among the professionals themselves (Baer, Goebel, & Flexer, 1993). In this regard, the team leader or coordinator must foster processes that move team members from a multidisciplinary approach (where professional roles are rigid and specialized) to an interdisciplinary or transdisciplinary approach where professional, student, and family roles are less circumscribed. Multidisciplinary models of service delivery are more prevalent in medical programs where professionals typically work in a professional/patient relationship with only limited consultation with other disciplines. Interdisciplinary approaches are more prevalent in nonmedical disability programs where professionals typically work in a professional/consumer relationship as part of a team. Table 9–2 compares and contrasts these models and their implications for assessment, planning, and service delivery.

More than any other approach, personal strengths models of service coordination imply the need for a transdisciplinary approach to service provision. In this approach, professionals work as consultants to individuals with disabilities and to other professionals on the team. Both services and planning are provided collaboratively. *Role release* is an important characteristic of the transdisciplinary model where team members work as part of an integrated program providing services and supports that are organized around individual needs rather than professional services (Baer, Goebel, & Flexer, 1993). In this approach,

> **Critical Point**
> The transition coordinator should develop a team process that equalizes relationships between families and professionals and that minimizes barriers between the disciplines.

TABLE 9–2   Comparison of service models

Multidisciplinary	Interdisciplinary	Transdisciplinary
Participation of the student is limited to a professional-student relationship.	*Participation* of the student is as a member of a team.	*Participation* of the student is as a member of a team.
Assessment is done or interpreted by the professional seeing the individual student	*Assessment* is based on needs and preferences, as seen by the student and each team member, including nonprofessionals.	*Assessment* is based on needs and preferences, as seen by the student and each team member, including nonprofessionals.
Planning is confined to organization of individual treatments provided by the professionals.	*Planning* is based on functional needs within professions, coordinated to obtain outcomes desired by the student and the family.	*Planning* is based on functional needs and preferences, across disciplines, in which activities are shared to obtain outcomes.
Implementation consists of a series of individual treatments.	*Implementation* consists of services and activities coordinated by the transition coordinator.	*Implementation* consists of services and activities collaboratively provided by professionals and team members.
Evaluation is based on progress in regard to year-to-year goals.	*Evaluation* is based on progress toward individual postsecondary goals set by the team and the student.	*Evaluation* is based on progress in achieving the student's total quality of life before and after graduation.

Source: Adapted from R. P. Baer, G. Goebel, & R. W. Flexer (1993). An interdisciplinary approach to rehabilitation. In R. W. Flexer & P. L. Solomon, *Psychiatric rehabilitation in practice.* Boston: Andover Publishers.

students, family members, and other professionals may participate in implementing physical therapy, behavior programming, and training as part of an integrated community program focused upon individual goals.

Integrated services based in role release require that each professional involved make his or her contribution in a way that is supportive of other team members' efforts. For example, consider the roles of the vocational and special education teachers, the guidance counselor (a transition professional from general education), and the rehabilitation counselor in supporting a student's vision to work as a chef. The special education teacher could provide adapted instructional strategies to support performance as required in the culinary arts taught by the vocational teacher. The rehabilitation counselor could assess the student in actual or simulated restaurant environments, which could provide information on accommodated performance in potential employment or jobs where chefs work. The guidance counselor could provide career assessments to determine if interests and abilities match the skill and other requirements that correspond to a career as a chef. The level of sharing is such that the implementation of the culinary arts program is dependent on the expertise of the special education teacher and is required by the

vocational teacher to instruct the student. The expertise of the guidance counselor and the rehabilitation counselor provides a validity check that shows how to accommodate the student's performance in the vocational program and performance in the future available work/job environments.

The transition coordinator is likely to encounter conflict in efforts to promote collaboration. A common myth about any collaborative process is that collaborators will agree, have shared values, and develop consensus without conflict (Koch & Rumrill, 1998b). Strong working relationships with transition team members should assure that conflict and disagreement can occur without destroying the relationship. Koch and Rumrill (1998b) define a four-step process for resolving conflicts: (a) accurately defining the conflict, (b) clarifying misconceptions, (c) generating options, and (d) implementing and evaluating resolutions. It is important to identify conflicts and resolve them as they arise to avoid breakdown in relationships and disruption of decision making and team process. Transition coordinators should deal with conflicts discreetly, preferably outside student or agency meetings. If a conflict threatens to disrupt an IEP/transition team meeting, the coordinator should recess or adjourn the meeting until the conflict is resolved. The coordinator should set up a meeting between the conflicting members, preferably in a relaxed neutral setting, and follow the four-step process for conflict resolution. In conflict resolution, the coordinator should assume the role of mediator and periodically reassure participants that conflict is normal in a good working alliance (Koch & Rumrill, 1998b). If the coordinator is directly involved in the conflict, he or she may bring in an outside person as an arbitrator.

The transition planning process and the coordinated set of activities suggest roles for numerous transition service providers. *Transition coordination* and team process require that program development and monitoring be provided collaboratively across all the components of the **transition plan**. Numerous individual team members and programs may be part of the transition plan. With so many players and programs, teamwork and collaboration are necessary in order to achieve consistency in program implementation. Team process provides a mechanism that fosters the collaboration, coordination, and communication discussed thus far. Team activities are evident in many transition services and functions like work experiences, referral to adult service agencies, interagency coordination, coordinated student assessments, resource development, and training consultation. Because transition collaboration goes well beyond activities in the classroom, the team is required to keep diverse activities on a straight course regarding individualized transition plans and schoolwide transition initiatives.

> **Critical Point**
> The function of transition collaboration transcends the typical role of the special education teacher and includes collaboration and systems change activities.

The role of the transition team shows that major activities are involved in developing a coordinated set of activities for students with disabilities. This role draws upon the strengths and contributions of each system and each professional's expertise for a coordinated effort to effect a meaningful array of transition services. The team provides leadership to guide the family/student in accomplishing appropriate outcomes.

OVERVIEW OF TRANSITION SERVICES

Instruction, community experiences, development of objectives, and related services are the minimal transition services that provide support of students' participation in the various school programs directed toward preparation for life in the community. Interagency linkages, functional vocational evaluation, and daily living skills instruction are provided as appropriate given the student's transition needs and goals. Examples of each transition service requirement include:

1. *Instruction:* tutoring, employability skills training, vocational education, college entrance exam preparation
2. *Community experiences:* job shadowing, community work experiences, tours of postsecondary settings
3. *Development of employment and postschool adult living objectives:* career planning, interest inventories, self-determination training
4. *Related services:* occupational and physical therapy, speech therapy, psychology services
5. *Daily living skills training:* self-care training, home repair, health training, money management
6. *Linkages with adult services:* referral to vocational rehabilitation, summer youth employment programs, developmental disability and mental health boards, independent living centers
7. *Functional vocational evaluation:* situational work assessments, work samples, aptitude tests, job tryouts

A variety of school and postschool collaborators are important for all the services and program options needed to meet diverse student needs and preferences. Involvement ranges from those who directly deliver instruction and services (e.g., teachers, rehabilitation counselors) to those who are responsible for program development regionwide (e.g., administrators). Various staff work together to meet all the transition needs at the high school level.

The many areas of expertise within schools that are relevant to transition are described by deFur and Patton (1999). They indicate that the emphasis on interagency collaboration with adult services may overlook many of the school professionals' transition resources and expertise. High schools deliver many diverse programs and services and have become integral to the successful delivery of transition services to students with disabilities (Wehman, 1992). Today, the school is a place for academics, recreation, athletics, and all sorts of programs that benefit students and society. In order to accomplish the broad goals of schools, school personnel need to demonstrate a diverse array of skills and expertise to enable effective program implementation.

For example, a case in point is the classroom teacher. The roles that teachers play can vary widely depending on the school district and staffing issues within that district (deFur & Taymans, 1995). However, Foley and Mundschenck (1997) reported that secondary education professionals expressed that lack of collaboration with other professionals and knowledge about community-based services seems to detract from successful transition. An understanding of various roles and responsibilities of team members provides a foundation for determining school-based personnel's competencies and their type of involvement in the implementation of transition services for students with disabilities.

Many of the adult and postschool service providers are counterparts to school-based personnel. They may provide support, services, or instruction in a variety of postschool and community settings and contexts. Often, transition goal attainment occurs after high school graduation. By utilizing counseling, education supports, or community services provided by postschool professionals, students continue along a career development path consistent with their goals.

INSTRUCTION

Instruction as a transition service is any instructional activity that promotes access to the school curriculum and movement toward the student's transition goals. Curriculum includes academic subjects, career and technical classes, and life skills, as well as adaptations and accommodations appropriate to unique individual needs. Instructional activities related to transition cover a broad range. They may be tutoring, preparation for college entrance examinations, preparation for proficiency tests, career and technical education, applied academics, employability skills and social skills training, and peer tutoring among others. The transition service concerning the acquisition of daily living skills was not mandated for all students with disabilities but may be incorporated into the instruction of those who need preparation concerning specific life skills (e.g., self-care, money management).

Academic and Career Skill Development

Transition services to support development of both school-based academic and career/vocational competencies are important to students achieving their postschool goals. Attainment of academic skills may be important to the student's preferred transition outcomes and often need to be given consideration in the planning process. For students continuing on to **postsecondary education**, particularly in a two- or four-year-college program, high-level academic skills will be a requirement. The students should be placed and supported in inclusive settings and be able to demonstrate success in an academic-based program. Support to meet academic entrance requirements for college and for possible professional licensure or certification may be the transition services that promote movement toward the student's goals. Some vocational-technical programs require specific documented competency levels. Although these may be primarily skill-based, a certain level of academic skills also may be required in the process of becoming qualified. At some point, information from representatives from postsecondary institutions and professional licensure or certification groups are required to ensure that the team is addressing all key requirements.

Career and technical programs often are a major course of study requiring transition instructional services. Table 9–3 lists representative career/technical education that may be used to fulfill the student's transition goals. All of these areas listed are broad career clusters that provide vocational education/instruction options for students' goals. Each area can be adapted, altered, or modified to suit the student's needs. While many of the vocational fields may have specified fairly high entrance criteria, students, once accepted, can gain critical skills to help them become more independent and able to find a career.

General education teachers working with students with disabilities should be active members of the student's transition team. By playing an active part in a student's transition meeting, content teachers will increase their understanding of transition and provide valuable insight into the student's strengths and abilities. They also bring a network of community resources that may provide linkages necessary for the student's successful transition to adult life.

TABLE 9–3   Programs that represent vocational career and technical education

1. *Agricultural education:* Includes occupations in horticulture, agribusiness, selected food and crop production industries.
2. *Business education:* Focuses on secretarial, administrative, office and business management occupations.
3. *Marketing education:* Includes occupations in retailing, marketing, merchandising, and services, such as real estate, hospitality, and financial.
4. *Family and consumer sciences:* Prepares workers for occupations in the consumer and homemaking occupations, such as day care, lodging, and food service.
5. *Trade and industrial education:* Includes a wide range of occupations in the trades such as graphic arts, metalworking, automotive technology, and manufacturing.
6. *Health occupations:* Focuses on preparation for careers in nursing, medical and dental assisting, nurse's aide, radiology, and other medical occupations.
7. *Technology education:* Prepares students to work in a wide assortment of technical occupations related to manufacturing, construction, transportation, and other industries.

For students who are following a life skills and special education and functionally based academic curriculum, instruction is likely to have a more direct relationship with content of career and vocational courses. For example, in language arts class, students may be practicing vocabulary from their work sites, refining interaction and communication skills used with co-workers and supervisors, and practicing with forms for self-evaluating their work preferences and performance. In math class, they may sum and average their self-evaluation forms and practice fractions when measuring ($\frac{1}{2}$, $\frac{1}{3}$, $\frac{1}{4}$ cup). In science class, they may practice safety rules and procedures for their job, master hygienic procedures used in a restaurant kitchen, or learn how to apply and work with different cleaning chemicals.

> **Critical Point**
> Functional academics have a more direct relationship with the content of career education and vocational courses.

For students at these levels, transition services for the acquisition of foundational interpersonal and daily living skills become more important aspects of their personal repertoire of skills. Instruction in functional competencies may include academic skills, such as reading basic directional words, telling time, and following directions, as well as life skills, such as selecting and buying goods, maintaining a healthy body, following directions, and abiding by designated rules and laws. These competencies strengthen many of life's experiences, and failure to acquire them often cannot be isolated from a person's success or failure in the world of work (Clark & Kolstoe, 1995).

Classroom-Based Career Development

Functional academic and regular academic courses can, and should, include many work-related literacy and mathematics skills that students need for successful work. However, not all important information can be covered through academic courses only. All students will need career classes of some type to complete their preparation. These classes should occur at varying levels in a student's career development to reflect the necessary and relevant information at each stage. During *career awareness* and *exploration* phases, classes should focus on the values, attitudes, and habits that comprise a valued employee. They may include investigations into different career domains and encourage students to indicate initial career preferences. These classes should be integrated with career exploration and job shadowing experiences that the students also are having, and focus on related terminology and important job and daily living skills that contribute to successful work evaluations and performance.

During the *career preparation* stage, classes should focus on aptitude and interest descriptions that match with the student's career preferences. Instruction should address specific terminology and concepts that relate to employment, such as payroll deduction, taxes, Social Security, benefits, and the like, according to the student's academic skill levels. The class should include important interpersonal skills, including interviewing, accepting feedback from coworkers and supervisors, maintaining good relationships with coworkers and supervisors, and terminating employment appropriately.

Classes during the *career assimilation* stage may take on a different format. Students may spend much of their day at the work setting and some may be in a post-secondary environment. Course issues would consist of job tenure and maintenance skills, negotiating and resolving interpersonal issues, and the implementation of self-advocacy and self-determination skills for advancement and ultimate career and life satisfaction. Rather than be scheduled as a typical class, these courses may be organized in the form of a job club that meets at the school site, an adult agency, or at a convenient community facility.

> **Critical Point**
> Individuals with disabilities will frequently need information, strategies, and support to maintain employment, often because they have lacked access to this information and support while growing up.

COMMUNITY EXPERIENCES

Community experiences involve a variety of activities and environments. In the employment, career, and job domains, activities range from *job shadowing* for a few days, to exploring occupations, or to community job experience or cooperative education, which involves learning knowledge and skills to meet requirements of an occupation. The purpose, intensity, and structure of community experiences for postsecondary education show a similar variety. When students are exploring postsecondary education, tours may be arranged to a number of schools. Some

> **Critical Point**
> Community experiences provide schools with many opportunities to teach students the necessary skills for adulthood as well as to provide exploratory activities.

CASE STUDY Durmond

Role of Community Experiences

Durmond is a young man with mild mental retardation just entering high school. He has not had any career awareness or exploration activities to this point in his education. The school teachers and counseling staff decide that Durmond would benefit from some interest inventories; however, those may not be beneficial since Durmond does not really understand potential career/employment possibilities. The school counselor and teacher invite the vocational special needs teacher from the vocational school to attend the IEP meeting. In that meeting a variety of potential jobs are discussed. They also discuss the issues of systematically assessing Durmond's awareness/preferences to deal with his understanding of the work world. The team itemizes a list of potential job skills and places these skills can be attempted. Much effort is placed on a variety of environments and skill performance requirements.

Over the next year or so, Durmond visits local radio stations, metal plating companies, car repair shops, the post office, various clerical and administrative offices, and the local airport. Durmond takes notes and is encouraged to ask about the jobs. A plan is also developed and implemented where Durmond will spend longer periods of time at the sites in which he has expressed an interest. In the subsequent year preferred work environments and skills are identified and the team determines to have Durmond job shadow and attempt to perform jobs within the selected work environments. Systematic data is collected on Durmond's performance along with information collected from his supervisors and co-workers. After the initial two years, Durmond, with the assistance of the IEP team, decides on a career in metal plating.

During his last two years, Durmond is involved in several vocational education classes that deal with foundational course work that enable him to understand the issues around chemical acids, etcher solutions, and cleaning materials. Additionally, he begins exploring several metal plating companies and eventually is placed in Wayne Metal Works. There Durmond shadows in greater depth and is assigned to work in the cadmium plating area. After Durmond's third year, a review is conducted to determine whether this job and work environment are appropriate. Durmond seems to like it and as he progresses in learning skills, management considers him as a candidate for a chrome plating apprentice and potentially working full-time during school breaks and vacations. Upon graduating from high school, Durmond becomes a full-time employee and is promoted to apprentice a chrome plating position.

transition programs provide summer activities and programs in colleges or universities to give students a taste of college life and its demands.

Many skills are taught more effectively in the community, such as: transportation, using community facilities (e.g., stores, laundromats, and public services), learning to care for and maintain personal living space, developing hobbies and recreational and social interaction skills, and using workplace skills related to employment. The community provides an important setting for practicing skills in the environments where students will be when they are living and working in the community.

> **Critical Point**
> Community-based career exploration activities may be the student's first experience away from school.

Community activities often begin in middle school and become increasingly focused on one preferred career domain as the student matures (Brolin, 1995). Early experiences usually involve visiting a variety of job sites. They may include job shadowing experiences in which a student observes and follows a worker as he or she goes about his or her job tasks. At the high school level, community experiences often are more focused at providing specific work-adjustment or vocational skill development. These experiences function best when used as an extension of the classroom educational program and can be supplemented by classroom activities. School-based activities can also include business or work simulations in which the students create a business and assume various roles to "run" this company.

An additional caution for professionals developing community work experiences is that they must structure them in line with the U.S. Department of Labor, Fair Labor Standards Act. This act allows students with disabilities to participate as a "trainee" in unpaid community-based experiences pertaining to school vocational goals. Each of the six criteria presented in Table 9–4 must be met in order for a student to be considered a "trainee."

DEVELOPMENT OF EMPLOYMENT AND ADULT LIVING OBJECTIVES

The transition services that apply to this area deal with *career planning:* the processes whereby students develop, test, and finalize their goals. As implied, career planning transition services are helpful in the process where students gain experience or obtain resources for the purpose of crystallizing their goals—making them more specific and detailed. Again, all transition domains are pertinent—work and school, living, and community participation goals. The activities and resources available in the goal-setting process are numerous and all the transition professionals (special education, vocational education, and rehabilitation) as well as other school and postschool service providers get involved in these transition services.

> **Critical Point**
> Assessment and planning activities are the major types of activities that assist a student in identifying and clarifying transition goals.

The team needs to ensure that students with disabilities are provided career assessments by the eighth grade and again during sophomore and junior years. Career assessment centers may provide evaluations for regular education students and for students who have a "mild disability." Students with more significant cognitive disabilities require assessment through a functional approach that includes vocational, recreation, and community-related environments.

TABLE 9–4   Criteria for "trainee" status under the U.S. Department of Labor fair labor standards

1. The training, even though it includes the actual operation of a business facility, is similar to that which would be given in a vocational school.
2. The training is for the benefit of the trainees or students, not the business.
3. The trainees or students do not displace regular employees, but work under close supervision.
4. The business providing the training derives no immediate advantage from the activities of the trainees or students, and on occasion business operations may actually be impeded.
5. The trainees or students are not necessarily entitled to a job at the conclusion of the training period.
6. The business and the trainees or students understand that the trainees or students are not entitled to wages for the period of time spent in community-based vocational instruction.

Source: Fair Labor Standards Act.

Various team members have the responsibility to explain the results of these assessments to students and parents. The information gained from these assessments should be embedded into the curriculum, helping students to explore all aspects of specific career interests, as well as to expand possible career choices. This can be done in a variety of ways, including (1) providing speakers from different career clusters, (2) taking students to potential job sites for job exploration, and (3) providing mentoring/shadowing experiences. If vocational or technical education is appropriate, the special education teacher has the responsibility to collaborate with the vocational and technical education teachers to develop accommodations and the specially designed instruction needed to help a particular student succeed.

Successful career planning requires both self-awareness and an understanding of the world of work. An important part of this is the transition team's involvement in collecting information that will support the student and team in making appropriate decisions about realistic outcomes. Students also need to be actively involved, according to their abilities, in gathering information about their interests and abilities, in learning about the labor market, in setting short-term and long-term career goals, and in formulating plans for achieving their goals (Szymanski, Hershenson, Enright, & Ettinger, 1996). Teams will need to provide varying levels of support in assisting the students with these tasks.

Monitoring Career Information on Students

Career-related information about the student should be compiled from a variety of sources, including interviews, interest inventories and aptitude tests, work samples, vocational assessment, and portfolio assessment. Inventories provide a range of career options for students to choose from and define a profile of career characteristics that represent the student's pattern of choices. Work samples provide important information about the student's performance under real-life work circumstances using accurate and reliable observation techniques. Curriculum-based vocational assessment provides information collected directly on the students while they are enrolled in vocational-technical education or other training programs, using identified curriculum goals and standards. The portfolio documents the student's career interests, academic accomplishments,

and vocational skills. Guidance counselors, rehabiliation counselors, transition coordinators, and vocational evaluators, among others, are involved in activities of information gathering on the student and potential careers.

Information about potential work environments should examine the tasks involved in occupations of potential interest, the skills and worker characteristics that are required, and the availability of local job opportunities within occupational categories. State and local job classification resources, job analyses, informational interviews, and job shadowing all can provide information about potential jobs to students and team members aiding in goal development and refinement. The *informational interview*, as seen in Table 9–5, is a strategy that students can use to collect a detailed, up-to-date, and personalized perspective on a specific occupation. In this strategy, the student conducts an interview of a potential job site (which also supports self-determination and empowerment strategies). The list of questions that guide the interview should focus on educational or training requirements, employment outlook, description of a typical day, likes and dislikes about the occupation, appropriate training programs, salary ranges, advice for those interested in pursuing the occupation, and related occupations. Transition team members or teachers can assist the student by providing guidelines for conducting such interviews. *Job shadowing* can be considered an expansion of the informational interview. Used in this way, job shadowing is the process of observing an employee at the work site as he or she performs his or her job. This type of career exploration activity enables students with disabilities to acquire firsthand knowledge about what specific tasks and worker skill requirements are involved in any given job.

Interventions such as situational assessments and **trial work experiences** provide opportunities for team members (1) to observe directly how students

TABLE 9–5 Steps the student takes to conduct an informational interview

1. Schedule an appointment with someone working in the occupation of interest.
2. Develop a list of questions to guide the interview.
3. Conduct the interview and record interview information.
4. If possible, get a brief tour of the business.
5. Send a thank-you note to the interviewee.

function in different work situations, (2) to determine the appropriateness of different occupations and living environments, (3) to identify optimal conditions for student success, and (4) to evaluate the effectiveness of different adaptation or accommodation strategies. A *situational assessment* is a means of evaluating student/environment "fit" through direct observation of students in actual or simulated work or living situations. They are particularly useful for transition teams in planning across comprehensive lifestyle choices.

Monitoring Community and Job Placement Information

As transition team members work with the student to explore different employment options, it is especially important to establish community linkages with informal, professional, and employer contacts. Employer linkages are critical to making appropriate job placements that meet the needs of the students. School systems may wish to institute a central clearinghouse for job referrals to support all the transition-age students (Baer,

Martonyi, Simmons, Flexer, & Goebel, 1994). Establishing these linkages can occur through job fairs held at high schools and at postsecondary institutions. They also can be developed through community service agencies, including chambers of commerce, and service organizations such as the Kiwanis. Employer advisory boards can be an important means to gain input from local employers about how to better utilize vocational programs for students with disabilities as a labor resource (Baer et al.).

Job development is an important strategy used by transition professionals to identify employment opportunities and secure employment for students with disabilities. The transition professional works to match an employment opportunity with the interests, needs, and abilities of a specific student. Ideally, the student would be able to perform all of the requirements of the potential job but in some cases, due to their disability, they cannot. In this instance, the professional may negotiate with the employer to create or adapt a position that meets the needs of the student and organization. **Job carving** is similar, in that it creates a position that

---

CASE STUDY Katya Part I

Assessment and Exploration of Future Environments

Katya was diagnosed with cerebral palsy at birth and uses a wheelchair but has good use of her arms. When Katya entered school she was found to have mild mental retardation but has been able to use the regular education curriculum with some modifications. Katya's parents were very concerned that she would have to live at home, but the special education teacher on the team was able to show the parents the impact of ADA on increasing options and accessibility in the environment. Katya's team began integrating basic foundational skills into her classwork and at home. Katya was somewhat shy, so the regular classroom teacher helped to identify two classmates who showed some interest in her. Katya's parents agreed to invite one of these girls to their home once a month. They also began identifying movie theaters and recreation centers that were accessible. Both the teacher and Katya's parents began talking to her about work and work expectations to build her confidence as a future worker. The team developed a list of people who worked in wheelchairs to act as potential role models. Katya's team ensured that she had some career awareness instruction during elementary school. When she entered middle school, the team provided all her teachers with a list of foundational skills on which she was working. Katya was getting mostly Bs and Cs in her academic classes and the IEP team believed this provided a good program for her. During eighth grade, Katya's team enrolled her in a career exploration course that visited workers in the community and included activities about work values and habits, and about occupational clusters. Katya completed her career exploration class with a love of computer work. In high school, her guidance counselor gave her several interest inventories, which confirmed that office work was a preferred option. The transition team placed her in a business course and she did well in learning word processing and data entry. Her parents were not sure she could perform for a full day because she complained of fatigue when using the computer at home.

meets the needs of both the student and the organization. The difference is that the transition professional may accumulate parts of several job descriptions to fit the abilities of a student and simultaneously increase organizational efficiency.

Job and career maintenance clubs offer support to students and adults with disabilities who are looking for a job or currently working. Job clubs can be developed and implemented by guidance counselors, rehabilitation counselors, teachers (regular, vocational, and special education), or teams of these individuals. *Job clubs* utilize a small-group format to provide counselor support, encouragement from other club members, and prospective job leads to people who are actively seeking employment (Azrin & Phillips, 1979). Job seekers meet in groups of 8 to 12 every day for about two and a half hours until employment is secured. The job club method emphasizes group support to club members as they cultivate and follow up on job leads.

Lindstrom, Benz, and Johnson (1996) describe a job club model for special education students between the ages of 16 and 21 who are either actively seeking employment or who are already employed. The emphasis of this model is on preparing students for "the transition from the structure of the school environment to the unpredictable and often confusing adult world" (Lindstrom et al., 1996, p. 19).

Whereas job clubs emphasize ongoing support to students participating in a job search, career maintenance clubs emphasize ongoing support to students who have already secured employment but need additional assistance in order to keep their jobs. Group members meet weekly or biweekly to address career maintenance concerns, such as initial adjustment to a new job, employer expectations, appropriate work habits, problem solving, time management, social skills, co-worker attitudes, transportation issues, and reasonable accommodations.

CASE STUDY | Katya Part II

Planning and Preparation for Future Environments

Katya enrolled in a program for business education taught at the county vocational technical high school. She was very nervous about changing environments and her team scheduled several preliminary visits to show her where the accessible entrances and facilities were located. The team knew that Katya might not be able to develop competitive level skills, and this was the case. After graduation she met the entrance requirements for the local community college and continued to work on her skills there. The vocational rehabilitation counselor attended the last two years of meetings in the high school and continued to work with Katya while she attended community college. Katya was given the options of possibly job sharing with another worker to split business productivity requirements, or having an employment specialist do job development/job carving to identify a position that would take advantage of her typing and data entry skills but would not overtire her. Katya completed her community college and moved into an accessible apartment with a cousin. Her vocational counselor found her a part-time job and continued to look for an arrangement that could be full time. Katya found the daily work environment to be challenging despite her preparation in school. When she became overly tired, she was likely to get sick and have to miss one to two days of work. Katya decided to join a career maintenance club to help her learn to better gauge her health needs. She also learned some assertiveness and was able to talk to others about barriers she encountered in the environment. After one and a half years, Katya was hired full time at her job. The employment specialist realized there were places in the office that became backed up (e.g., mail room and filing end-of-month reports). This gave Katya a break from typing and the office made sure that the mail work and filing were accessible to her. A few years later, Katya asked her boss if she could get training to learn the network systems software packages that she saw the office managers using. The boss was reluctant at first and unsure whether she would be successful. She got some books and showed them to her boss to convince him of her sincere interest. Katya knows that she may not become an office manager but this will allow her to increase her skills and work abilities, and probably qualify for a raise.

Students and/or their advocates must possess accurate information about their legal rights under the ADA and be able to communicate their needs assertively to employers. The transition team plays a central role in assisting students to access information about their legal protections, to develop skills at disclosing disability-related information to employers, to identify their accommodation needs, and to request and implement accommodations (Luft & Koch, 1998). Career classes or job-seeking skills workshops, in which role-playing activities and videotaping are used to facilitate the development of these competencies, provide ideal scenarios for addressing these important topics.

RELATED SERVICES AND ASSISTIVE TECHNOLOGY

In Section 1401 (22) of the IDEA Reauthorization in 1997, related services were defined as: transportation, and such developmental, corrective, and *other supportive services* as may be required to assist a child with a disability to benefit from special education, and includes the early identification and assessment of disabling conditions in children with disabilities. Other supportive services encompass speech-language pathology and audiology services, psychological services, physical and occupational therapy, recreation (including therapeutic recreation), social work services, counseling services, including rehabilitation counseling, orientation and mobility services, and medical services, except that such medical services shall be for diagnostic and evaluation purposes only.

When related services were added to the list of required transition services, policy makers wanted transition teams to consider the supports that students may need to benefit from the available transition services. With this requirement, transition teams and related service providers now needed to assess whether this type of support could provide access to more integrated work, education, and living environments, support demonstration of higher level skills, or support objectives for transition goal attainment. This would be consistent with the underlying legislative philosophy of IDEA providing students access to the general curriculum and to integrated settings.

Related Services

Many related services support the IEP and transition services through either assessment, consultation, or direct services. The National Association of School Psychologists provided an early example for vocational school psychology and transition services, and in fact, incorporated both vocational assessment and intervention practices into its *Standards for the Provision of School Psychological Services* (Thomas & Grimes, 1995). In the case of school **psychologists,** these support services would involve: psychological and psycho-education assessments that focus on career and vocational development, aptitude, and interests (assessment); skill enhancement activities for school personnel, parents, and community members regarding learning, development, and behavior (consultation); and programming designed to enhance cognitive, social, and vocational development (direct service).

The school psychologist, through assessment, consultation, or direct services can provide services supportive of transition instruction, community experiences, and goal development. School psychologists are highly qualified to give and interpret tests and assessments, provide services, and assist others in the use and interpretation of activities directly relevant to vocational and transition goal development and accomplishment. However, Staab (1996) surveyed school psychologists and found that about half felt that their school psychology skills were underutilized in transition activities.

Speech and language therapy (SLP) services also can include assessment, consultation, or direct therapy. To be supportive of transition goals, the related services of SLPs should adhere to the transition services of instruction, community experiences, development of objectives, daily living skills, linkages, and functional vocational evaluation. Table 9-6 provides sample goals and activities conveying how transition services language in curriculum content areas might look in IEPs written by the SLP. From the table's sample goals and activities, it is evident that the expertise of language and language development is applied in an instructional context of transition skills (e.g., vocabulary in job résumés).

In addition to speech and language therapy, occupational and **physical therapists** work with students to ensure access and participation in various environments (e.g., school, home, work, community). Physical therapists evaluate and recommend activities to increase a student's strength, endurance, and ability to maintain postures while participating in his or her chosen environments. Working in conjunction with physical therapists, **occupational therapists** teach techniques and adaptations to allow student access to

TABLE 9–6   IEP transition services language

Transition Service Language (TSL)	Content Area	IEP Goal Example	Sample Activities
Instruction	English/language arts, writing, math	Tommy will identify appropriate vocabulary for completing his résumé (education, work experience, interests).	Select vocabulary from sample résumé or job application; explore interests.
		Johnny will recognize and identify sequence of events on a daily picture schedule.	Choose and act upon activity from a picture schedule.
Community experiences	English/language arts, writing, social science, health	Tommy will identify and access community and employment resources.	Obtain and complete job application.
		Johnny will walk to an off-campus site and follow safety and traffic guidelines.	Use the vocabulary and concepts for travel and safety issues.
Employment/ postschool adult living	English/language arts, social science	Tommy will participate in a prearranged job interview.	Develop language communication scripts appropriate for job interviews; role-play mock interview; discussions.
		Johnny will use public transportation with supervision to a work site.	Practice social greeting, vocabulary of transportation.
Daily living skills and functional evaluation	Family life, health, English/language arts	Tommy will appropriately interpret body language/social cues of peers and adults in his community.	Situational role-playing, mock interviews, school office, and so forth.
		Johnny will maintain personal hygiene.	Referral to daily schedule; develop checklist of daily hygiene responsibilities.

Source: From Harrell, P. *Speech & language services.* In deFur, S. H., & Patton, J. R. (Eds.). *Transition and school-based services: Interdisciplinary perspectives for enhancing the transition process.* (pp. 77–115). Austin: PROED. Reprinted with permission.

daily living activities (e.g., eating, dressing, toileting). Wehman, Wood, Everson, Goodwyn, & Conley (1988) suggested that therapists play a role in the transition process by providing input on student's physical capacities, modifying daily activities, and/or designing, fabricating, or prescribing adaptive equipment to enable performance in community settings. Specifically in work environments, Sowers and Powers (1991) recommended that occupational therapists help conduct job-site and task analyses, develop job-design strategies, and develop supports for job-related activities like eating, drinking, and using the bathroom. Tables 9–7 and 9–8 describe the possible roles in the transition process for occupational and physical therapists.

Fitness, leisure, and recreation are very important for many students served by special education. In not realizing the full benefits of the contributions and interdisciplinary efforts from adapted physical education and therapeutic recreation, students' development as complete human beings and participation in preferred environments are severely compromised. Although instruction in physical education is defined specifically in IDEA as part of special education for students with disabilities, the reality is that appropriate physical education for such students is often missing in public schools nationwide at any level of the curriculum. This is particularly disturbing when noting that a significant number of students with disabilities have marked deficits in physical fitness and motor skills that can adversely affect their life adjustment (Dattilo, 1987; Jansma & French, 1994). Improving physical fitness and motor skills leads to learning lifetime sports skills, with improved health and greater participation in community recreation or sports programs. Professionals trained in adaptive physical education and therapeutic recreation can be major contributors to successful transition

TABLE 9–7 Possible roles for the occupational therapist in the evaluation, service planning, or delivery of transition services

1. Teach functional tasks related to temporal aspects (age, maturation, ability/disability, and life stage).
   a. Activities of daily living
      i. Self-care (e.g., dressing, feeding, hygiene, toileting)
      ii. Communication
      iii. Socialization
      iv. Mobility within home, school, community
   b. Home management (e.g., cooking, cleaning, money management)
   c. Work and health habits
   d. Work skills
   e. Leisure
2. Evaluate environmental supports and barriers and recommend adaptations if needed.
   a. Physical characteristics
      i. Accessibility (e.g., terrain, furniture, objects)
      ii. Sensory stimulation (e.g., tactile, visual or auditory cues or distractions)
      iii. Types of objects, tools, equipment
      iv. Temporal cues (e.g., watches with alarms; toothpaste left out on the countertop)
   b. Social characteristics
      i. Activities (e.g., individual or group)
      ii. People
      iii. Role expectations
   c. Cultural characteristics
      i. Customs, expectations
      ii. Values
      iii. Beliefs
3. Adapt tasks.
   a. Change the physical characteristics of the task (e.g., sit instead of stand)
   b. Change the social characteristics of the task (e.g., increase or decrease the number of people involved)
   c. Change the demands (e.g., do part of task; checklists)
   d. Work simplification (e.g., get all items together before shower; reorganize kitchen so able to find objects)
   e. Use instructional techniques (e.g., task analysis, forward and backward chaining, partial participation, positive supports, systematic instruction, natural cues)
   f. Teach compensatory techniques
4. Adapt materials or recommend assistive technology.
   a. Increase or decrease the size, shape, length, or sensory characteristics of materials and objects being used
   b. Adaptive aids (e.g., button hook, reacher, lap board, talking watch, book holder, memory aids, talking calculators)
   c. Switches, computers, appliances, augmentive communication devices, telephones, wheelchairs, environmental control units, positioning devices, alerting systems
5. Develop interpersonal and social skills to support participation in the school, community, home, or work environment.
   a. Awareness of interests
   b. Stress management

(*Continued*)

TABLE 9–7 (*Continued*)

    c. Time management
    d. Self-management/coping techniques
    e. Leisure activities to promote socialization and develop friendships
    f. Assertiveness training
    g. Decision-making and problem-solving skills
6. Educate others and learn from others in the home, classroom, community, or workplace.
    a. Student training
    b. Family training
    c. Staff training
    d. Peer training
7. Promote self-advocacy, prevention, and health maintenance.
    a. Legal rights and responsibilities
    b. Disability and health awareness
    c. Talk to others about disability and needs
    d. Promote habits to maintain health (e.g., hygiene, medications, pressure reliefs, birth control, equipment maintenance, etc.)

Source: From Shepherd, J., & Inge, K. J. (1999) *Occupational & physical therapy.* In deFur, S. H., & Patton, J. R. (Eds.). Transition and school-based services: Interdisciplinary perspectives for enhancing the transition process. (pp. 117–165) Austin: PROED. Reprinted by permission.

through their focus on lifetime fitness, recreation, and leisure skills.

As just described, these transition services are of critical importance to quality-of-life outcomes for youth with disabilities. Although all possible related services were not discussed, their omission does not mean that they are of less importance. In the past, many of these services have been provided as pull-out programs. As students become actively involved in the transition process, it is essential that the related service personnel work with students within the environments in which they will be living, working, and playing. People involved with a particular student must understand and support this method of instruction. For example, it is obvious that a student receiving speech therapy will benefit from learning how to be understood at his or her job site. A collaborative effort among the speech pathologist, the job trainer or special education teacher, and the employer may make the difference between a successful job placement and a failure.

> **Critical Point**
> Related service providers must become involved in transition planning and assess and provide interventions in a variety of student environments.

Related service providers form an integral part of the transition team, providing information on the student's strengths, essential instruction in areas of need, and critical resources for overcoming the barriers that students with disabilities often encounter. The aforementioned related service providers are

self-explanatory in terms of the types of services provided (e.g., speech therapy: a speech clinician providing interventions that are intended to improve the stu-

Students learn functional academic skills in the community.

TABLE 9–8 Possible roles for the physical therapist in the evaluation, service planning, or delivery of transition services

1. Develop or compensate for skills that support participation in the school, community, or work environment.
   a. Strength
   b. Endurance
   c. Movement patterns
   d. Assume and maintain postures
2. Improve the student's mobility within the home, school, work, and the community setting.
   a. Ambulation
   b. Wheelchair mobility
   c. Climbing stairs
   d. Opening doors
   e. Transfers
   f. Carrying items
   g. Public and private transportation
3. Promote self-advocacy, prevention, and health maintenance.
   a. Exercise
   b. Nutrition
   c. Body mechanics/positioning
   d. Disability knowledge and precautions
   e. Legal rights
4. Adapt tasks and environments so the student can participate.
   a. Accessibility
   b. Position of student and activity
   c. Job-site analysis
5. Recommend or adapt assistive technology.
   a. Mobility aids (e.g., walkers, canes, wheelchairs, standing tables)
   b. Computer access and positioning
   c. Augmentative communication device
   d. Exercise equipment
   e. Accessibility
6. Educate others and consult in the home, classroom, community, or workplace.
   a. Student training
   b. Family training
   c. Staff training
   d. Peer training

Source: From Shepherd, J., & Inge, K. J. (1999) *Occupational & physical therapy.* In deFur, S. H., & Patton, J. R. (Eds.). Transition and school-based services: Interdisciplinary perspectives for enhancing the transition process. (pp. 117–165) Austin: PROED. Reprinted with permission.

dent's speech production). However, increasingly incorporating interventions within school and community environments requires that activities performed are the basis of the intervention. Services may be integrated into the setting in order to reduce the discrepancy of the student's performance with working peers or to allow learning to occur with little if any disruption to the daily work routine. Consequently, related services must be developed so that the intervention is easily implemented and effectively integrated into the teachers' or co-workers' daily routines.

Much of the input provided by related services personnel provided in the transition meeting will be consultative in nature. However, the related services specialists also may (1) provide services during times of the day that the student is away from the workplace; (2) provide technical assistance to the individual providing the one-on-one training to the student; or, in some circumstances, (3) provide services on the job, demonstrating the necessary training techniques to the direct service provider or co-worker. Any of the preceding strategies would have to be implemented based on the needs of the student and the availability or freedom in the workplace.

Assistive Technology

Assistive technology (AT) services and devices along with occupational or physical therapy are other related services considered. The AT services and devices are usually integrated into the IEP and the student's environment by an assistive technology practitioner (ATP). The ATP would provide necessary AT assessments and appropriate technology if the student required it. Occupational and physical therapists tend to provide the positioning, orthotic or mobility services. Both sets of professionals need to be involved in the placement and services provided in the community. An example of this interaction would be Casey, an individual with spina bifida. The occupational or physical therapist would attempt to ensure that Casey would have appropriate gait, positioning, and ambulation throughout the work environment. The ATP would observe Casey's work environment, determine the most appropriate interface between the student and the job, and integrate the selected technology into the student's job. Related personnel perform their duties on the job integrating their expertise with the job placement or vocational experts. Many ATPs are also trained in positioning and other more-therapy-related issues and might be able to deal with the full range of environmental adaptations.

It is important to understand that universal design for learning (UDL) and assistive technology (AT) are not the same; however, both complement one another. For example, UDL is how curriculum is designed and developed with or without technology. AT provides access to the universally designed curriculum. Assistive technology includes a vast number of devices designed to help individuals with disabilities communicate more effectively, control their environment, and achieve greater mobility (Blackhurst & Shuping, 1990; Raskind, 1997/1998).

To a novice or beginning service provider, the thought of AT can, at best, seem overwhelming. To help individuals better understand AT devices, seven major functional areas have been developed: (1) existence; (2) communication; (3) travel and mobility; (4) body support, protection, and positioning; (5) environmental interaction; (6) education and transition; and (7) sports, fitness, and recreation (Blackhurst et al., 1999). Descriptions of the functional categories and possible AT devices and services are displayed in Table 9–9.

AT can be as simple as a pencil grip or as complex as a computer with voice activation capabilities. In addition, it is important to understand the implications of the continuum of AT from low-technology solutions through high-technology solutions. A general principle is that the simplest level of technology that will meet the individual's needs should be considered first. Generally, individuals with disabilities want what will be the most useful for them in providing greater access to their environment (i.e., school, home, and community). The latest, most expensive device is not necessarily the most appropriate or may not meet the needs of an individual. However, the level of sophistication of the device is determined by the needs of the individual.

The process in the selection of AT starts with the assessment process. Several models (e.g., Blackhurst & Cross, 1993; Reed, 1997; Zabala, 1994) have been developed to assist evaluation teams to determine AT devices for individuals. The three important characteristics that are embedded within all assessment models are (1) the environmental demands placed on an individual; (2) the individual's needs, abilities, and preferences (Chambers, 1997); and (3) the technology characteristics (Thorkildsen, 1994). The goal of these models is to address a person's functional responses in light of their environmental demands (Blackhurst, 1997).

A school-based assessment team may be able to assess what is or is not working for a student and determine how AT can be applied to evaluate whether specific AT devices and services are necessary to meet the specific needs of a child (Reed, 1997; Scherer, 1997). However, the IEP team may determine that they do not possess knowledge of resources or do not have knowledge to evaluate AT needs (Chambers, 1997). In these situations, the team would seek additional support from individuals with the level of knowledge or resources necessary to assist the team in evaluating a child's specific educational needs for AT. Additionally, an evaluation to determine appropriate AT should be done in a variety of environments to determine the impact on school activities across curriculum areas, in vocational sites, and in community and home settings (Bauder et al., 1997).

TABLE 9–9   Examples of assistive technology by functional categories

Functional Category	Assistive Technology Example
Existence. Technology that provides assistance in basic function areas needed to sustain life	Respirators, feeding devices, and adapted potty chairs
Communication. Primarily consists of augmentative and alternative communication systems, (AAC). Augmentative/alternative communication refers to any technique to enhance or augment communication	Gestures, sign language, nonelectronic augmentative communication systems (e.g., dial scans, communication boards), voice output communication aids, tactile speech aides, visual doorbells, alert and alarm systems
Body support, protection, and positioning. Devices that provide stabilization, body support, or protection to the body	Braces, crutches, standers, walkers, splints
Travel and Mobility. Devices that help a person move about, either horizontally or vertically	Wheelchair, lifts, and electronic travel aids (ETA) with obstacle detection indicators; adapted buses and vans
Environmental interaction. Devices and accessories designed to assist a person perform daily living skills, both indoors and outdoors	Environmental controls that activate appliances such as telephones, lights, TV, and blenders
Education and transition. Devices that support the educational and vocational needs	Computer-assisted instruction software, work-site adaptations, such as electric staplers, switch-activated filing systems, and adjustable desks
Sports, fitness, and recreation. Assistive technology that promotes participation in individual or group sports, play activities, hobbies, and crafts	Bowling ball chutes, audible baseballs, adapted recreational snow equipment (e.g., adapted ski poles and adapted sleds)

During individual transition planning the team needs to consider all aspects of an individual's life from high school to adulthood, understanding what technology might be required as part of the job and what modifications or adaptations, including determination of the AT, must be part of the planning process (Fisher & Gardner, 1999). One also needs to have a sense of what aspects of postschool environments relate to technology. Teams look at each postschool setting in which the person needs to function and evaluate the needs of the individual for AT that are unique to each of those environments.

> **Critical Point**
> An interagency team sorts out what and how each agency should contribute its resources to assure access by the individual and the proper AT for each desired setting.

INTERAGENCY LINKAGES

Transition Services from Postschool Service Providers

The public sector (governmental agencies and not-for-profit community organizations) can provide a significant amount of assistance regarding the transition needs of students with disabilities. The primary services that should be considered in the transition process are those provided by:

1. The state department of vocational rehabilitation
2. State employment services
3. One-stop employment and training (funded under the Workforce Investment Act)
4. The regional adult mental retardation and developmental disabilities provider
5. The regional mental health provider

Transition services are based on the laws of special education, rehabilitation, vocational education, ongoing lifelong supports, higher education, employment and training, and general education. Special education and transition as defined in IDEA is a basic right and as such is described as an entitlement. If a student has a disability, as defined in IDEA, he or she is entitled to an appropriate education and transition services. For services not prescribed by IDEA and those provided in postschool settings, additional criteria may need to be met—making them eligibility-based.

Eligibilty-based transition-related legislation deals with laws that fall into the rehabilitation and the ongoing supports domains, a major service delivery system for postschool services and supports for students who are in transition. A major shift in the status of students in moving to adulthood is that supports and services go from being an entitlement to being based on **eligibility** criteria. This means that these students may or may not receive services, depending on whether they meet specified criteria. The kind of disability and its severity in some instances constitute the criteria of eligibility.

Rehabilitation services are those that are provided under rehabilitation legislation and deal with supports and services for entry or reentry into the labor market and meet the rehabilitation needs and goals of those found eligible. Generally, a service is viewed as a one-time investment to move an individual into a new or improved role and status (e.g., employment versus unemployment). Thus, rehabilitation services are often referred to as time-limited services.

Other legislation dealing with adults and students who are in transition are adult/postschool services that are assumed to be ongoing. Eligibility in these agencies has specific criteria related to the severity of disability and the need for long-term, ongoing support (in many instances, for the person's lifetime). Still other services and supports are provided primarily only to enable participation and access, not to meet specific disability needs for individuals, such as services that are part of postsecondary education or general community services like employment and training programs.

Regardless, legislation within each legislative area, even those that are not specific to disability, has provisions to protect the rights of persons with disabilities. For example, because employment and training under the **Workforce Investment Act (WIA)** is a delivery system dealing with preparation for and entry into employment, programs and services are important to some students with disabilities in order to attain or maintain transition outcomes. WIA provides assurances that youth with disabilities will have access to the range and variety of program options where appropriate (i.e., if qualified). Moreover, although transition services for students with disabilities are not referenced in WIA, supplemental aids and services can be provided to

> **Critical Point**
> The essential elements of needs and preferences and postschool goals may require programs outside the purview of special education requiring coordination among special education, regular education, and postschool service providers.

support participation and program completion. Understanding the unique provisions of legislation and how they are related to transition requirements is part of what transition teams need to know in their role in providing a coordinated set of activities.

Within various acts and legislation, transition services fall into one of three categories: (1) those provided to students with disabilities in special education who have an entitlement to an education through age 21, (2) those provided to adults who must meet specific criteria and must be found to be eligible in order to receive specialized services, and (3) those provided to any individual with a disability who needs programs and activities that are required to be accessible and not to discriminate against people with disabilities. Transition services in postschool environments are based in the legal and eligibility framework of two or three above.

Federal/State Vocational Rehabilitation Programs

Vocational rehabilitation (VR) agencies, which have different names in different states, utilize funds via a federal and state program. Acceptance for services from the state VR agency, as it is with almost all adult human service agencies, is not guaranteed. VR agencies follow a process in which all applicants must meet specific criteria to be accepted for receiving services. These are (1) having a physical or mental disability that is expected to last longer than 12 months and (2) this disability results in a substantial impediment to becoming employed. In addition, since the state VR money is not able to serve all people with disabilities, the agency is required to develop a set of criteria that focuses on admitting those individuals whose disabilities are the most severe and who meet certain individualized state needs. This individualized differentiated criterion is called the "order of selection."

> **Critical Point**
> Vocational rehabilitation providers may have differing definitions of disability and typically are able to serve only a fraction of the students who are eligible for services.

In general, counselors who oversee the provision of services represent the VR agency. The VR counselor conducts interviews, helps to develop an individual plan of employment, provides oversight of financial expenditures for services, and provides counseling. The VR agency provides a variety of services. Although the VR agency and the VR counselor operate differently in each state, the services that are offered and coordinated by the counselor include vocational assessments, career/rehabilitation counseling, job preparation activities, job development, AT and devices, follow-up services, and post-employment services. Other services that a counselor may coordinate include driver's license training, commercial license instruction or heavy equipment operation, college tuition, and treatment for physical or mental health issues. In coordinating these services, the VR counselor must ensure that the services provided be related to an eventual outcome of improving the likelihood of employment. The primary method for acquiring the services, once accepted for participation, is through the development of the Individualized Plan for Employment (IPE). This is coauthored by a VR counselor and the individual.

To enable the VR system to work effectively with the public school, school personnel should make initial contacts, indicating the need for the VR agency personnel's participation. Generally, VR has indicated that two years prior to graduation is an optimal time for contact and referral. This contact, however, changes based on the severity and the rehabilitation needs of the individual. In some cases, a VR counselor may not be able to participate in every IEP meeting where transition services are discussed. However, the VR counselor should be able to participate via providing written recommendation, verbal communication to the IEP team leader, or in some other manner.

> **Critical Point**
> Due to large case loads carried by vocational rehabilitation counselors, it is important to use their time wisely and to use flexible means for them to provide input.

Federal/State Employment Training

Another agency that should be included in the development of transition programs regarding employment is the particular state's employment and training programs (ETP). Each state's employment and training system is designed to assist all people who are unemployed to become employed. As with the VR agency, an individual can access the ETP agency's services through a counselor. Employment service counselors are generally able to provide résumé development assistance and job leads. The counselors also may provide access to testing services and other training programs, depending on how the services have evolved within the state. The counselor will work with the VR counselor to coordinate employment-related benefits, and other incentives that might facilitate employers hiring individuals with disabilities.

Career one-stop-shop programs through the Workforce Investment Act typically focus on providing services to persons with low socioeconomic status or those who are too disadvantaged to become employed. As with the other agencies, a counselor is the conduit by which services are acquired. The services provided range from skill training to employment readiness training and General Equivalency Diploma (GED) training. In general, the agency functions much like the VR programs in that they fund other agencies or programs that provide those needed services. Table 9-10 describes the types of services available to transition-aged youth.

> **Critical Point**
> Employment training programs typically focus on students and adults from low-income families but may serve students with disabilities under some conditions.

Long-Term Support Agencies

Another group of agencies that are potential collaborators in the transition process include regional mental health and developmental disability (MH/DD) service providers. These two agencies were covered together because in many locations the agencies are one and the same. Additionally, the two agencies are funded and function, in most cases, in the same manner. The state and regional MH/DD agencies generally receive money from both state and federal funds.

In recent years, MH/DD agencies contracted with managed care agencies to provide mental and physical health services to qualifying clients. The types of services that are funded by MH/DD programs include (but are not limited to) employment programs, a range of independent to more closely supervised living programs, case management, counseling and advocacy programs, physical or mental health services, and, potentially, legal assistance. Furthermore, the services that are provided to the eligible participants of the MH/DD agencies can be provided from the moment of eligibility until noneligibility or death. Consequently, a student may have been receiving services since birth.

The MH agency generally deals with people who have significant and persistent mental health problems, such as obsessive-compulsive disorder, schizophrenia, bipolar disorder, and so on. The participants who receive services provided or funded by the MH agency are usually diagnosed with such disorders by a medical doctor or a psychiatrist and are provided services based on their needs. The range of transition services that would be provided by the MH agency would be

TABLE 9–10   Services provided by one-stop delivery centers

Services Available to Youth (ages 14–21) and Adults (age 18 and older)
• Local and national job announcements and resource libraries for career research • Computers, copiers, and fax machines for creating and sending resumes • Telephone and electronic (computer) linkages to employers and web sites • Assessment tools to measure skills, interests, and academic levels • Vocational counseling, job placement assistance, job search, and retention workshops
Services Available to Adults (age 18 and older)
Core Services • Initial assessment of skill levels, aptitudes, abilities, and supportive service needs • Financial aid assistance for training and educational programs *Intensive Services* • Comprehensive assessment of skill levels and service needs, group and individual counseling, career planning, and case management • Short-term prevocational skills, including communication and interviewing skills, punctuality, professional conduct, and other "soft skills" *Training Services* • Job readiness training, on-the-job training, entrepreneurial training, adult education and literacy activities, and cooperative education programs • Customized training conducted with a commitment by an employer or group of employers to employ an individual upon successful completion of the training

case management, housing/independent living, job placement or employment programs, and counseling/drug management services.

The student with mental health issues should have a counselor/**case manager** assigned to him or her. This individual should participate in the planning of his or her transition services. One could expect that the case manager would participate in most if not the entire transition meeting. Additionally, the case manager should provide liaison services with other agencies such as rehabilitation or employment and training. The case manager has broad responsibilities with regard to the student with mental health issues. However, the case manager does not have legal guardianship or any specific ability to cause or force the student to perform certain activities. The services that are provided by the MH agency, and additionally for the DD agency, are generally voluntary. In any case, if the student has potential mental health problems, the local MH agency should be contacted and a request made to include a representative who is involved with the student's mental health services.

> **Critical Point**
> Mental health agencies typically provide services through the counselor or mental health professional who provides mental health services.

The DD agency operates much like the MH agency. Eligibility is determined through a variety of assessments; however, the primary determination of eligibility is whether the student has significant impairments in three or more of the seven major life activities (i.e., communication, independent living, employment, self-direction, mobility, learning, and self-care). These disabilities should be the result of a physical or mental impairment that occurred before age 22 and are expected to continue indefinitely (Beirne-Smith, Ittenbach, & Patton, 1998). The DD agency is responsible for determining eligibility and should be an active participant in determining goals and services. In many cases, the DD agency will have **supported employment** programs and/or will provide ongoing support services to enable access to funding from VR for supported employment. Supported employment is "a job placement and training model designed to prepare people with severe disabilities for competitive employment in regular community settings" (Reed & Rumrill, 1997, p. 238).

Other services that the DD agency may provide or coordinate are independent living, group homes, and so on. Historically, DD agencies ran or, at the very least, funded sheltered employment programs. Thus, for individuals whose families truly want a sheltered employment setting, the DD agency is usually the agency to contact. Both the MH and DD agencies should be contacted as soon as the school is aware or considers that the student should be eligible for either agency's services. Remember that persons who have a behavior disorder do not necessarily qualify for MH services. Additionally, eligibility for both these programs is limited and because of limited funds like VR focuses its resources on persons with more severe disabilities. School representatives can improve the chances of a student's acceptance by providing full documentation of the student's disabilities and behavioral tendencies when a release of information is requested by the MH/DD agency. Additionally, any classroom behavioral notes or intervention data also may be useful.

> **Critical Point**
> Developmental disability (DD) agencies typically serve students with the most severe disabilities although some services (e.g., case management) may be available to students and adults with milder developmental disabilities.

Transition Services of Postschool Education Collaborators

Collaborators from postsecondary programs include people from vocational/technical schools, community colleges, and universities (Gajar, 1998). Training services could include apprentice programs provided by unions or trade associations and job-readiness training programs. Based on the student's interests and preferences, transition teams explore which, if any, of these programs will meet the needs of the student. The next step is to allow the student and his or her parents to explore the opportunities and requirements that appropriate programs can provide. This can be done by building the exploration into the student's curriculum, building self-advocacy skills and having the student and parents begin making contacts with postschool collaborators, and/or by inviting these collaborators to the next transition planning meeting.

> **Critical Point**
> Postsecondary education and training programs should be involved in the development of transition programs at schools and, in some cases, be invited to individual IEP meetings.

All postsecondary institutions receiving federal funds must provide services and accommodations for students with disabilities (Osborne, 1996). Many community colleges and universities have disability centers that provide these services. However, a major difference exists between the services provided at the high school level and those provided in colleges and universities. In most cases, the postsecondary education institution does not provide services unless the service is requested.

Students with disabilities are expected to ask for accommodations and provide proof of their disability. To assure that the student with a disability is capable of maintaining academic performance, the student must demonstrate a significant amount of independence and assertiveness. Thus, after high school the student should be able to (1) contact the postsecondary institution's office of disability services, (2) provide appropriate documentation (usually the latest psychological tests and/or IEP), (3) maintain records that certify the student's disability and his or her needed accommodations, and (4) advocate for oneself. Obviously, in order for students with disabilities to be successful at the college and university level, they must have strong **self-advocacy** strategies and skills. The special education teacher begins to build these skills as early as elementary school. If students with disabilities leave high school without strong self-advocacy skills, the chances of their success in all aspects of adult life are greatly diminished.

> **Critical Point**
> Students with disabilities need to learn to advocate for themselves before they leave high school because after graduation, unless the students ask for services, there is no requirement to provide them.

Services and Agency Delivery Matrix

Table 9–11 provides an overview of services that generally are needed to support postschool outcomes for students with disabilities. The row across the top of the table indicates agencies, with the initial side column showing the potential services that could be provided. A legend is provided to describe the generic or usual categories of disabilities that one would refer to in delivering services. Although these categories do not match the categories delineated by IDEA, the terms generally are used across the country when referring to diagnostic categories.

The purpose of Table 9–11 is to provide the reader with a quick reference to where an individual with a particular disability could acquire certain services. As was described in prior sections of this chapter and book, all the services are available but all potential participants may not be able to qualify for access to the service. For instance, in row two, "Career Planning," one

TABLE 9–11 Transition to employment service providers

SERVICE	Community Employment Agency	Public School	Vocational Education	Work-Study Voc. Sped Coord	Job/WIA/State Employment Agency	Voc. Rehab./VI Agency	Mental Health Agency	MR/DD Agency	Post-secondary Education Agency	Adult Vo-Tech Agency
Functional vocational evaluation		All	All	All		All	PD	MD, OH		
Career planning	All	All	All	All	All	All	PD	MD, OH	All	All
Job shadowing	All	All	All	All		All	PD	MD, OH		All
Job search training	All	All	All	All	All	All	PD	MD, OH		All
Job placement	All	All	All	All	All	All	PD	MD, OH		All
Technology/AT		All		All		All	PD	MD, OH		
Transportation	All	All	All	All		All	PD	MD, OH		
Job training	All	All	All	All	All	All	PD	MD, OH		
Follow-along							PD	MD, OH		
Employer benefits					All	All	PD	MD, OH		
Case management						All	PD	MD, OH		
Independent living skills		All					PD	MD, OH		
Residential-home services							PD	MD, OH		
Financial supports							PD	MD, OH	All	All
Recreational services		All					PD	MD, OH	All	All

Legend: LD = learning disability, BD = behavior disorder, OH = orthopedic impairment, MD = multiple disability, PD = psychiatric disability, SI = sensory impairment.

Source: Adapted by permission: Baer, Simmons, & Flexer, 1996.

can look across and see that all the agencies would provide career services. However, each agency may have differing restrictions as to whom may receive the service. Further, case management, employer benefits (e.g., targeted job tax credits and reduced wage options) are limited to very few agencies. Other access issues include the particular agencies' conditions on providing services. To make the point, the VR agency may be required to offer various training and employment programs and the individual may qualify for receiving these services; however, the individual may not fit within the VR agencies' priority service categories. Consequently, the individual would not be able to access the service. One can use Table 9–11 as a guide for asking for services, but differences do exist in the practical application of those who might be able to receive the service.

CONCLUSION

A variety of professionals and agencies may be involved in transition planning and services. Each member of the transition team has unique expertise and professional skills that can be applied in the transition process. School-based collaborators need to work together so that education and transition services are effective and relate to the student's goals. General, vocational, career, and transition curricula are delivered in a coordinated manner in high school programs by special, related services, vocational, and regular educators with the support of administrators. Postschool collaborators are involved in the transition process for their contributions regarding future environments. When they contribute to the knowledge of future participation and goal development, they are in a position to provide continuity and to take satisfaction when students achieve the transition to postschool activities. Of utmost importance is that resources of team members should be brought out in support of the student-family determined goals. To accomplish this, the team members must apply their energies in a consistent direction and in a coordinated manner. The team process applied to develop the goal consensus is a prerequisite to transition services that promote movement toward student goals. All members of the team must know the roles and responsibilities of each member in order for the team to achieve the best outcomes for the student. Skills of team membership and, in some cases, team leadership, are requisite for team cohesion: the process underlying goal consensus and productive team interactions.

STUDY QUESTIONS

1. Who should be involved in the transition team? Give at least five examples.
2. What is accomplished through interdisciplinary services?
3. What types of services can a person with a disability receive from a vocational rehabilitation counselor?
4. What are the coordination functions of the transitional coordinator?
5. At what point should a student be referred to adult services?
6. How should related services be included in the transition programming for students with disabilities?
7. Is employment the only goal on which the team should focus regarding postsecondary settings?
8. What are the skills that the transition facilitator should exhibit?
9. How can the school or postschool administrators facilitate or hinder transition practices?

WEBSITES

The Federal Resource Center for Special Education
    www.aed.org/special.ed/frc.html
Transition Research Institute
    www.ed.vivc.edu/sped/tri/institute.html
School to Work Outreach Project (Exemplary Model/Practice/Strategy)
    www.ici.coled.umn.edu/schooltowork/profiles.html
The Office of Vocational and Adult Education
    www.ed.gov/about/offices/list/ovae/index.html
National Institute on Disability and Rehabilitation Research
    www.ncddr.org
Administration on Developmental Disabilities
    www.acf.dhhs.gov/programs/add/
Office of Special Education Programs
    www.ed.gov/about/offices/list/OSERS/OSEP/index.html
Rehabilitation Services Commission
    www.ed.gov/about/offices/list/osers/rsa/index.html

CHAPTER 10

TRANSITION TO EMPLOYMENT

Thomas J. Simmons

Robert W. Flexer

LEARNING OBJECTIVES

The objectives of this chapter are:

1. Describe the careers and job experiences of transition students.
2. Explain the role of the labor market in preparing for and obtaining employment.
3. Identify major employment options.
4. Describe the career possibilities for the visions of students and families.
5. Describe the school and postschool services and programs for preparing for employment.
6. Explain the differences in major approaches to mediating supports for employment.
7. Describe model practices for supporting students in obtaining employment.

INTRODUCTION

Most youth enter the working world, find a job, and begin to develop a career path with opportunities for advancement. Recent trends indicate that individuals may in fact change their careers as many as seven times in their lifetime. However, the paths that youth with disabilities take to the workforce vary depending on the individual's interest, support needs, and the extent to which individuals participated in work-based/employment-related experiences while in school. Some students exit public school programs competitively employed, while others pursue postsecondary education and training prior to beginning their careers. For a small number of youth, productive engagement may not entail competing in the open labor market. Individualized volunteer, community, and/or income generating activities may result from a vision developed by the team. Regardless of the specific postschool outcomes, the student's future should include participation in work and productive activities of choice that contribute to the community and/or economy and that provide for social integration.

An outcome-oriented process in this chapter describes how the student, the family, and the team envision a future that includes a satisfying career and transition goals that meet the values of the student and the family. In this chapter, development and refinement of the student employment transition goals are accomplished through career development activities as described through topics of employment preparation programs. Also described are many strategies of planning and support used by team members and agencies. Each year of high school includes a coordinated set of activities that promotes the development of skills and knowledge that moves the student toward self-determined employment goals.

The purpose of this chapter is to describe alternatives for productive engagement, including employment for individuals with disabilities. Also described are the kinds of services and supports available to assist with preparation for the transition to employment as well as job development, placement, and training programs. Though many of the vocational programs and services that were prevalent in the 1960s still exist today, the current focus of employment programs for people with disabilities emphasizes the provision of customized employment services. Customization focuses on the employment relationship between employees and employers and creates ways of supporting the needs of both. In order to facilitate goal attainment,

a description of comprehensive preparation and employment supports for people with disabilities is presented. School and postschool preparation models and agency-mediated, business-mediated, government-mediated, and student- and family-mediated supports are included. The reader will gain knowledge of the various services and supports available to facilitate becoming employed and retaining employment for individuals with disabilities.

EMPLOYMENT OUTCOMES AND OPTIONS

Employment Outcomes

Follow-up studies of youth with disabilities who exited secondary special education programs provide evidence of the importance of transition planning and programming related to employment. Findings from an extensive national longitudinal study of school exiters (the National Longitudinal Transition Study II) with disabilities revealed that employment rates for youth with disabilities lagged behind their peers without disabilities (Cameto & Levine, 2005). In the general population, 55% of 2003 high school graduates were employed by the following fall (Bureau of Labor Statistics, 2004) while NLTS found that 46% of school completers with disabilities were employed one to two years out of school. In earlier studies, similar findings of differences were reported by Fabian, Lent, and Willis (1998) in that three to five years after high school slightly more than half of young people with disabilities were employed, compared with 69% of their peers. Differences in employment by disability reveal that students with learning disabilities and speech impairments were in jobs 46% and 58% of the time, respectively, while students with mental retardation were engaged only 25% of the time (Cameto & Levine, 2005).

One's severity of disability also has been linked to lower rates of employment. For instance, a survey of 398 high school graduates with severe disabilities showed that 48% were not employed or pursuing postsecondary education. Of those employed, slightly more than one-third (34%) held competitive jobs (Johnson, McGrew, Bloomberg, Bruininks, & Lin, 1997). In fact, relatively few individuals with severe disabilities work competitively in the community. The community-based employment rates reported in several studies varied from 0% to 20% across studies (Benz, Lindstrom, & Yovanoff, 2000; Edgar & Levine, 1986; Edgar, Levin, Levine, & Dubey, 1988; Haring, Lovett, & Smith, 1990).

Underemployment, or chronic unemployment, remains a serious problem for many Americans with disabilities. The most recent National Organization on Disability (2004) survey continues to indicate that approximately two out of three persons with disabilities are not working. Employment prospects for youth 18 to 29 are more positive than the general disability population. In recent years, employment rates for youth with disabilities were 57% compared to 72% for youth without disabilities.

Employment Options

Adult Activity and Sheltered Options

Since the emergence of disability services early in this century, employment options for people with disabilities ranged from segregated settings (e.g., adult activity centers and sheltered workshops) to competitive employment in community-based businesses. The typical practice was that professionals determined the "readiness" of persons with disabilities to compete in the workforce. Under this model, consumers had to earn their right to less segregated employment options by demonstrating the skills and abilities needed. Many individuals with disabilities remained in segregated day services because they were viewed as "not ready to leave."

> **Critical Point**
> Few people actually moved, or progressed from the most restrictive, segregated end of the employment continuum to the least restrictive, competitive employment.

In the 1960s, 1970s, and 1980s, the primary employment options for individuals with severe disabilities included adult day programs that offered activities of daily living, training, prevocational training, "make-work" vocational activities, field trips, recreational activities and other types of special education-related curricula (Wehman, 2001). Another option to meet the needs of individuals with severe disabilities was specialized work training in what has been termed "sheltered employment" (Whitehead, 1977). The goal of the sheltered workshop was to provide individualized work environments to "habilitate" (habilitate, meaning to *train* versus the term "rehabilitate," meaning *retrain*) individuals with disabilities, offering the individual a long-term protective environment for learning work skills.

A primary characteristic of sheltered employment was pay that is less than minimum wage, based upon piece rate for products completed. In these programs, there were limited opportunities for daily interaction with nondisabled people except for paid staff who worked at the facility. A final feature of sheltered workshops was limited instruction or training on work skills that transfer to real jobs in community-based businesses. In the vast majority of sheltered workshops, individuals earned less than minimum wage and were paid on a piece-rate basis for contractual work secured from local businesses. However, the work performed in these environments had little relevancy to preparing people for work in today's labor force.

Adult activity centers and sheltered workshops remain an option for persons with severe disabilities. The important point is whether the individual and family were engaged in a planning process by the team and this choice was consistent with the vision of the individual. Research findings that compare employment outcomes of people with disabilities across employment programs (e.g., sheltered workshops, competitive employment) strongly support competitive options. In these studies, individuals with severe disabilities earn more money, experience greater opportunities for interaction with nondisabled co-workers or customers while employed in community-based businesses (Gilmore & Butterworth, 1996; McCaughrin, Ellis, Rusch, & Heal, 1993; Rogan, Grossi, Mank, Haynes, Thomas, & Majad, 2002; Wehman, Revell, & Kregel, 1998).

> **Critical Point**
> The greatest failing of adult day programs and sheltered employment was that very few people move from segregated programs to real employment opportunities.

Through the delivery of employment-related transition services and the development of comprehensive employment supports, most youth with disabilities, including those with intensive support needs, can transition directly into integrated jobs or postsecondary education. Many students with severe disabilities, who have participated in community-based work experiences during their secondary school years, can and should transition into community rather than segregated employment settings when a person-centered process identifies this as the goal. Rarely are individuals with disabilities given choices about the types of work they engage in, the hours they work, the time they have breaks, or the type of supports they need in segregated settings. This is in direct opposition to the principles of student or consumer choice inherent in the reauthorization of the IDEA in 1992 and 1997 as well as the Rehabilitation Act Amendments of 1992.

Supported Employment

Supported employment (SE) is an employment service option that was developed because of the dissatisfaction with segregated options, such as day activity centers and sheltered workshops. Since its inception as a federal program through the 1986 Rehabilitation Act Amendments, the number of people participating in supported employment in the United States has increased from 9,800 to over 140,000 (Wehman, Revell, & Kregel, 1998b). Supported employment has proven to be an effective vocational service delivery option for many individuals with severe disabilities including individuals with mental retardation (Rusch, 1986; Wehman & Hill, 1985; Wehman, Hill, Brooke, Pendleton, & Britt, 1985), traumatic brain injury (Wehman et al., 1993), physical disabilities (Baer, Simmons, Flexer, & Smith, 1994), and psychiatric disabilities (Bond, Dietzen, McGrew, & Miller, 1995; Collignon, Noble, & Toms-Barker, 1987; MacDonald-Wilson, Revell, Nguyen, & Peterson, 1991).

The environment is a powerful teacher.

The 1992 and 1998 Rehabilitation Act Amendments (P.L. 102-569) defines supported employment as:

> (i) competitive work in an integrated work setting, or employment in integrated work settings in which individuals are working toward competitive employment, consistent with the strengths, resources, priorities, concerns, abilities, capabilities, interests, and informed choice of the individuals with ongoing support services for individuals with the most significant disabilities.
>
> (A) for whom competitive employment has not traditionally occurred; or for whom competitive employment has been interrupted or intermittent as a result of a significant disability; and
>
> (B) who, because of the nature and severity of their disability, need intensive supported employment services . . . and extended services . . . to perform such work. (706[18][A & B])

Supported employment uses the services of a job coach or employment specialist who works with a person with a disability to secure employment, to provide on-the-job training to the individual, and to provide long-term follow-along or ongoing support to the worker for the duration of his or her employment. The employment specialist does not provide training and assistance on a daily basis for the duration of the worker's employment but trains the employee to perform the job and then gradually and systematically fades from the work site. The provision of long-term support is one of the distinguishing features of supported employment over other vocational rehabilitation and career and technical education service options. The most widely implemented SE model involves an employment specialist working one-on-one with an individual with a disability. Although, supported employment service delivery also incorporates group placement (e.g., enclaves, mobile work crews, and cluster placements) of individuals with disabilities who receive fairly constant support and monitoring. Today, supported employment is more broadly defined to include not only the intervention of a rehabilitation professional, but also the involvement of (1) family and friends; (2) community organizations and service groups; (3) co-workers and supervisors who serve as mentors, trainers, and providers of ongoing support; (4) existing human resources and employee assistance programs within the hiring company; and (5) training and support through internal, corporate-driven models of supported employment.

In addition to increased opportunities for integration, wages, and choice, other important differences between supported employment and segregated vocational options revolve around the ideas of "work readiness" and long-term or ongoing support. Supported employment service delivery is based on a "place and train" approach in which employment is secured for an individual with a disability based on an individual's unique abilities, needs, and preferences and then the individual is trained to do that job in the business where the actual job is located. The employee begins receiving compensation for his or her work from day one of his employment, the same time that he is being trained to perform the job. As was discussed previously, the segregated vocational options operate on a "train and place" approach and individuals are required to demonstrate certain skill competencies before they are referred for community employment placements. The positive employment outcomes of supported employment participants have been well-documented in a number of important areas including: employee satisfaction (Test, Hinson, Solow, & Keul, 1993), job placements (Mank et al., 1997), wages and benefits (Kregel, Wehman, & Banks, 1989), favorable employer perceptions (Kregel & Unger, 1993), and effective support strategies (Parent, Unger, Gibson, & Clements, 1994).

> **Critical Point**
> Supported employment participants perform real, meaningful work in integrated settings with ongoing supports.

Though people with disabilities have not traditionally been viewed as candidates for self-employment or small business ownership, *supported self-employment* for individuals with disabilities is gaining increasing popularity across the country as a vocational option for individuals with disabilities (Doyel, 2000; Griffin & Hammis, 2001). An outgrowth of supported employment, supported self-employment has adopted many of the same tools used in supported employment while enlisting the assistance of new community partners such as state Developmental Disability Planning Councils, the Small Business Administration, and financial institutions.

Competitive Employment with Supports

Significant numbers of students are exiting special education and secondary education classrooms unable to fully participate in our society. People with disabilities represent an overlooked and untapped employment resource. Many students lack basic skills necessary to find a job, or know what resources and incentives are available to assist in the job search. The students who do find work and are employed in the competitive market are underemployed.

Competitive employment with supports, while not being a truly recognized category or designation, fits within the new efforts distinguished as *customized employment.* In many cases students with disabilities who are more capable of independent work still don't have the skills to find work. Lack of these critical transition skills often limits their career development. In most cases, unless otherwise trained or assisted, students don't have the job-seeking skills, interview skills, or the ability to represent their skills in a way that

fosters truly competitive employment. This additionally results in limited career advancement and perpetual low-paying positions. The venues that have historically been developed for individuals with career goals requiring more advanced training have been traditional employment structures such as Office of Employment Services and One-Stop-Shops (Simmons & Whaley, 2001). It is also important to note that, if students are provided with appropriate career guidance and planning along with a future plan for postsecondary training, students are better prepared to move on to more challenging careers. In addition to traditional structures for securing employment, students who may need time-limited support to obtain and retain employment could benefit from other categories of individualized or group support mechanisms.

Summary

There are several reasons why it is necessary for special educators and transition specialists to be able to communicate to transition-age youth and parents the differences among employment options for people with disabilities. These include: limited awareness of and experiences with adult service agencies by students and parents; the difference between the entitlement-based special education service delivery system and the eligibility-based adult service programs; and the high unemployment rate of individuals with disabilities. Though many students with disabilities may further their education before beginning their careers, it is also important for them to realize the supports and employment services available to them, not only in completing their postsecondary education, but also in beginning their careers upon successful completion of their college degree program, or changing their educational and career goals after leaving high school.

DEVELOPING OPPORTUNITY FOR EMPLOYMENT

A New Labor Market Landscape

Labor markets in recent years have changed drastically. Generally speaking the labor markets were good with approximately 75,000 to over 200,000 jobs being created monthly (U.S. Department of Labor, 2005). As of May 2006 the national unemployment rate was at 4.6%, the lowest rate since 1974. Trends in the labor market included increases in education and health services, wholesale trade, professional and business services, and mining. Employment in health care continued to be a major contributor in the professional sector with approximately 250,000 new jobs annually. Employment in retail and manufacturing continued to decline.

Types of jobs that are or will be in demand were changing also. The U.S. Department of Labor reported that during the period of 2004 to 2014, of the 30 largest growth occupations (increase in actual number of jobs added), 22 will require some form of either short-term or long-term training or on-the-job training. The remainder will require an associate's degree, bachelor's or advanced degrees. However, of the 30 fastest growing occupations (increase in rate of growth) during that same 2004 to 2014 time period only four occupations will require on-the-job training with the remainder needing at least an associate's degree (eight), a bachelor's degree (10) or a master's or doctoral degree (eight). Within this last category of fastest growing, 16 of those occupations are in the medical or medical-related sector.

> **Critical Point**
> In the future, there will be an increase in available jobs requiring on-the-job training and growth in jobs requiring postsecondary education.

A highly competitive marketplace has been influenced by the use of technology such as telecommuting, Internet usage, computer developments, and automated equipment. Self-employment and temporary work agencies have increased in the market share of outsourcing. Smaller, more lean businesses are increasing in their influence and impact. Small businesses have generated 60 to 80 percent of net new jobs annually over the last decade. They employ half of all private sector employees with 53% of them being home based. They create more than 50 percent of non-farm private gross domestic product (GDP) and pay more than 45 percent of total U.S. private payroll. These influences have all increased the need for new and more innovative methods for becoming and staying employed.

Employment Today: Getting a Foot in the Door

With this new and entrepreneurial environment certain strategies and methods are still effective in attempting to gain employment for all working persons including persons with disabilities. Methods that were tried and true still do work with some modifications. Critical to this process is developing and maintaining contacts or connections with employers. Finding a good employment situation, in the final analysis, is finding the best fit between the employer and employee and how that can be accomplished through a variety of mechanisms. Mechanisms for finding the best fit include but are not limited to marketing and direct contacts, business advisory councils, and mentoring assistance.

Marketing and direct contacts for finding jobs for youth with disabilities has, in some cases, become easier in recent years. The development of new and improved methods of training and job acquisition effort have improved job finding. Legislative and financial incentives for both the employer and the person with a disability have altered some aspects of the landscape. One issue with significant impact is that of the wider acceptance and indication of interest in hiring persons with disabilities (Louis Harris and Associates, 2000).

Blanck (1999) pointed out that employers are more likely to employ persons with disabilities because of workplace culture, attitudes, and business strategies rather than compliance with the ADA. Further, Blanck indicates that the cost of replacement of qualified workers is 40 times the direct cost of the workplace accommodation. For Sears, Roebuck and Company, he indicated that the replacement costs of $1,800 to $2,400 were much more expensive than the average $40 to $60 cost of an accommodation. Finally, Blanck (1999) found that significant economic benefit can occur as a result of accommodations. Blanck points out that accommodations involving universally designed technology (UDT) enable employees with and without disabilities to perform jobs productively, cost-effectively, and safely (for example, reducing the potential for workplace injury). Further, changes have a "corporate ripple effect" in that these UDTs enable the employer to reduce cost of production and effectively increase productivity of employees without disabilities.

PREPARATION AND PLANNING FOR EMPLOYMENT

Developing a Vision for Employment

Being employed and productive is a highly valued accomplishment of adulthood. Moreover, engagement in a satisfying career represents a very important quality-of-life outcome for many individuals in our society. The ideal scenario from the viewpoints of the individual and society is a satisfied worker in a successful business. The transition to employment concerns the processes and outcomes of career development for the individual and meeting the labor needs for the business.

Key to this mutually satisfactory relationship is the outcome-oriented process and the determination of strengths, needs, interests, and preferences. The outcome process first requires an envisioning of a future in which the student is employed in a job that meets individualized needs and preferences and a desired quality of life. Defining the quality job is a highly individualized process. The vision provides the starting point in a search for the kind of work environment that meets the dreams of the individual. A thorough knowledge of the individual requires sufficient time and a process that begins and focuses on the dreams. Through an ecological process, a test of goals in real work environments provides additional information about the individual and potential environments.

A process of planning and experiences follows envisioning in order to shape and refine desired employment outcomes and to identify transition needs. Potential employment environments need to be analyzed and experiences provided to students to learn how jobs can impact their quality of life and meet career aspirations. To help the student make connections, there needs to be a solid knowledge base of what options and opportunities are available or can be developed in the local community. School and postschool agencies and programs provide a coordinated effort to insure that preparation reflects the student's goals.

In the next section, the authors describe the variety of in-school and community options of school to work programs available to make visions a reality.

CASE STUDY   Tim

Background

Tim is a 19-year-old senior at Halibut High School, which is located in a suburban school district on the outskirts of a large city. There are a substantial number of big and small employers within 10 miles of Tim's house, including manufacturing, retail, two hospitals, a large college, and a large military installation. Tim has been diagnosed with a moderate cognitive disability that affects all academic areas as well as fine-motor skills. Tim continues to make some progress in academics though that progress is usually linked to "hands-on" life and job experiences. Tim presents as a soft-spoken young man with a somewhat labored conversational style that includes hesitations and some difficulty with word-finding skills. He will become flustered when trying to speak quickly. Tim has several close friends at school and enjoys video games, playing basketball, and going to movies. Tim has learned to drive and has purchased a car with money from his job washing dishes at a local restaurant. Tim has chores at home but he has not learned to cook or do laundry.

Current School Year

Tim has spent the last two years at the career center in the Construction and Remodeling Program. He has mastered a number of related skills and competencies. His school day consists of needed academics, such as related math, English, and a life-skills class in the morning. Tim receives academics in a small-group setting and he has access to tutoring. He maintains a C average in academics and career-related courses. Tim's schedule for the afternoon is as follows: first semester, he will be in construction and remodeling classes; second semester, he will have an internship or job in his career area. Tim's transition team has agreed to ask the work study coordinator to assist with placement and transition coordination. The work study coordinator has agreed to refer Tim to the Bureau of Vocational Rehabilitation for job coaching and the County Board of MR/DD for employment follow-along. Tim currently works on speech fluency with a speech and language therapist. He also receives occupational therapy for improvement of fine motor skills.

Assessments

Academic testing reveals that Tim's reading comprehension and vocabulary are at the sixth-grade level. Tim shows a relative strength in math where he functions at an eighth-grade level. Tim can read a tape measure to 32nds of an inch. He can perform mathematical operations using whole numbers, decimals, and fractions using a calculator. Tim's verbal comprehension is a relative weakness. Tim has difficulty processing facts or instructions with more than two steps or components. He shows strengths in learning by demonstration and hands-on learning. A career assessment performed in the tenth-grade revealed Tim's desire to work either indoors or outdoors. Tim showed a preference for working with his hands. He also displayed the desire and ability to work well with people. Tim displayed an interest in customer service occupations but no interest in using a cash register or a computer at work.

Vision

Tim has stated that his ideal job would be working as a stocker at Lowe's or Home Depot and living in the same town as his parents in an apartment, possibly with a roommate. He would like to have his own car to participate in community activities. Meetings with Tim and his family revealed numerous values pertinent to his vision.

Tim: "I liked helping my uncle remodel his house and build a garage. I don't really like my dishwashing job but it pays for insurance right now. I worked with the custodian when I was a sophomore. I like video games and the Cleveland Indians."

Dad: "Tim does know a lot about the construction business. When Tim helps on a remodel job, he's real careful because he doesn't want to make a mistake. This causes him to be rather slow on a job site. Tim might do great in a hardware store, maybe even apartment maintenance. He knows about the products and is helpful and good with people."

Tim's parents: "We think that Tim could live in an apartment or house by himself or with a roommate. He may take some support or regular check-ins at first."

Tim has also commented on the activities in which he envisions participating in his community:

* Community recreational activities: "YMCA rec center for working out."
* Religious and cultural activities: "I want to keep going to church."
* Transportation for work and leisure activities: "My car for going to work, shopping, dates, and just fun."
* Continuing education: "I'd like to learn how to cook better."
* Political participation: "I want to keep voting."
* Employment: "I would like to try working in a big hardware store or home improvement store like Lowe's or Home Depot."

The vision for Tim illustrates a forward-looking strategy developed from a positive viewpoint of a future derived from the realities (strengths, needs, and preferences) of today and the stated values in the words of the student and family. Each student served by the transition coordinator and team deserves an individualized and positive approach like Tim's illustration.

Summary of Performance

Figure 10–1 contains a Summary of Performance for Tim. For his employment goal of competitive employment, the present level of performance is described for cognitive and functional areas along with essential accommodations.

School-to-Work Programs

School-to-work program is the generic term often used to describe a variety of school and community-based approaches to employment preparation. In school-to-work programs, workplace approaches are brought to educational settings while educational approaches are brought to work settings. Career and technical educators are required to have occupational competence, for example, and a workplace mentor may provide career guidance.

Benz, Yovanoff, and Doren (1997) pointed to the importance of special educators working with their

Employment and postsecondary goal/outcome: competitive employment

Assessments: Community-based assessments; classroom observations; career assessment; needs and preferences survey

COGNITIVE AREAS	Present Level of Performance (Grade level, standard scores, strengths, needs)	*Essential* accommodations, modifications and/or assistive technology utilized in high school and why needed.
Attention and Executive Functioning (energy level, sustained attention, memory functions, processing speed, impulse control, activity level)	Tim may experience some difficulty controlling his emotions and attending to conversations when he has difficulty with his word finding skills. He has appropriate impulse control, but occasionally needs a verbal prompt for his response.	Tim benefits when given scenarios and a review of social stories prior to social events and when he is going to encounter new people (i.e., work supervisor).
FUNCTIONAL AREAS	**Present Level of Performance** (strengths and needs)	*Essential* **accommodations/modifications and/or assistive technology utilized in high school and why needed.**
Career-Vocational/ Transition/Employment (Career interests, career exploration, job training, employment experiences and supports)	Tim's currently has a desire to work in a stocking/customer service position. He has expressed and interest in working at Lowe's or Home Depot. He is working on gaining employment.	Tim will need services from the Bureau of Vocational Rehabilitation and/or The County Board of Mental Retardation and Development Disabilities. They can assist Tim by offering work incentives and job coaching support.
Additional important considerations that can assist in making decisions about disability determination and needed accommodations (e.g., medical problems, family concerns, sleep disturbance)	Tim's family is concerned with his ability to effectively manage his money and leisure time. Tim has the tendency to become overly fixated on video games and other media-focused entertainment. These fixations may negatively affect Tim's motivation for employment.	Tim's family will work with him to find alternative activities of his choice. Tim will also benefit from participation in a local job club for employed students with disabilities.

FIGURE 10–1 Summary of performance—Tim (Case Study)

Source: This template was developed by the National Transition Documentation Summit © 2005 including representation from the Association on Higher Education and Disability (AHEAD), the Council for Exceptional Children's Division on Career Development and Transition (DCDT), and Division on Learning Disabilities (DLD), the National Joint Committee on Learning Disabilities (NJCLD), the Learning Disability Association (LDA) and the National Center on Learning Disabilities (NCLD). It was based on the initial work of Stan Shaw, Carol Kochhar-Bryant, Margo Izzo, Ken Benedict, and David Parker. It reflects the contributions and suggestions of numerous stakeholders in professional organizations, school districts, and universities, particularly the Connecticut Interagency Transition Task Force. It is available to be freely copied or adapted for educational purposes.

Critical Point

The major types of school-to-work programs in which youth with disabilities participate are career and technical education programs (regular and special needs) and community-based vocational training.

counterparts in the school-to-work movement. In collaborating with other players, special educators and transition specialists could ensure options for multiple pathways and time frames within career and technical programs, reasonable accommodations and support services, relevant performance indicators, and ade-

quate training and technical assistance for all personnel in local programs.

Career and Technical Education

Career and technical education provides a variety of programs and options—some occurring in the school setting and others taking place in the community. The National Assessment of Vocational Education (NAVE) (U.S. Department of Education, 2004a) identified three types of courses offered by career and technical education: (1) specific labor market preparation (occupational

Employer input is key to socially valid curriculum.

education), which teaches skills and knowledge required in a particular occupation or set of related occupations; (2) general labor market preparation, which provides general employment skills that are not specific to any particular occupational area, such as courses in keyboarding; and (3) family and consumer sciences education, intended to prepare students for family and consumer roles outside the paid labor market, including consumer and home economics.

Often, the occupational-oriented programs require two years of specific preparation at either vocational centers or comprehensive high schools. Programs can be linked to specific places of business as in cooperative education which combines academic study with paid work for school credits, or programs can be tied to specific postsecondary programs. A key component of tech prep is a formal articulation agreement between high schools and postsecondary institutions that provides for a pathway from one to the other. The original tech prep design included a "2+2" approach, encompassing grades 11 and 12, plus two years of postsecondary education.

Career and technical programs provide other school-to-work–based approaches like internships, apprenticeships, and school-based enterprises. The School-to-Work Glossary of Terms (National School-to-Work Office, 1996) defines *student internships* as "situations where students work for an employer for a specific period of time to learn about a particular industry or occupation. Students' workplace activities may include special projects, a sample of tasks from different jobs, or tasks from a single occupation. These may or may not include financial compensation"

(p. 31). The National School-to-Work Office (1996) defined *registered apprenticeship* as:

> those programs that meet specific federally approved standards designed to safeguard the welfare of apprentices. The programs are registered with the Bureau of Apprenticeship and Training (BAT), U.S. Department of Labor, or one of 27 State Apprenticeship Agencies or Councils approved by BAT. Apprenticeships are relationships between an employer and employee during which the worker, or apprentice, learns an occupation in a structured program sponsored jointly by employers and labor unions or operated by employers and employee associations. (p. 3)

A *school-based enterprise* is a school-sponsored, work-based learning opportunity in which a group of students (1) produce goods or services for sale or use by other people, (2) participate in multiple aspects of the enterprise, and (3) relate service and production activities to classroom learning.

The National Assessment of Vocational Education (U.S. Department of Education, 2004a) found that career and technical education had important short- and medium-term earning benefits for most students. In addition, NAVE found that over the last decade of academic reforms, secondary students who participated in CTE programs increased their academic course-taking and achievement, making them better prepared for both college and careers than their counterparts were in the past.

Special Needs Career and Technical Education

Students with disabilities are often placed in specially designed programs for one of two reasons: (1) no similar programs are available in general education or (2) even with supports, the student cannot succeed in the general education program. Evers and Elksnin (1998) observed that over the last several years, a number of "specially designed" vocational programs evolved:

1. Career exploration
2. Cooperative work training (work study)
3. Student or school-based businesses
4. Job shadowing
5. Volunteer service learning experiences in the community
6. Classroom and school as the workplace

In other instances, components of regular programs, like automotive, are redesigned so that components of jobs could be learned (e.g., oil change or tire changing).

Figure 10–2 shows one model for providing access to vocational and career education developed by the Ohio Department of Vocational Education. The first level of vocational access applies to students who need no

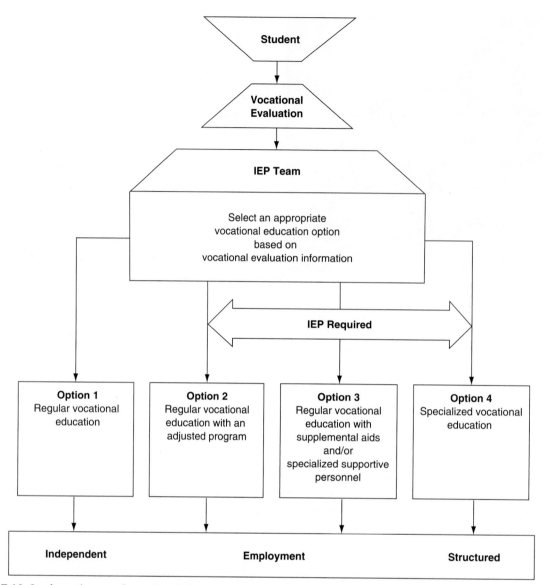

FIGURE 10–2 A continuum of vocational placement options for students with disabilities

Source: From *Vocational education for Ohio's handicapped children,* by Ohio Division of Career and Vocational Education, N.D.

special accommodations. At the second level, students could be served in any regular vocational program with a standard curriculum with supports or tutoring. The first two options apply to all the CTE programs already described. On the third level, access is obtained through a combination of supports and curriculum adaptation. Finally, the fourth level recognizes that some students need not only supports and curriculum adaptations, but also training in alternative or community-based sites, such as supported employment. In Ohio, two positions were created to support this continuum of vocational services. The vocational special needs coordinators

were special educators who focused on curriculum adaptations and supports in Career and Technical Education Programs. The job training coordinators were special and vocational educators who developed and conducted training in community sites.

Community-Based Employment Preparation

Wehman's community-based vocational training model (Wehman et al., 1985) focused on students that typically would have been served in Ohio under job training. Wehman's model was an example of a work preparation model where special education,

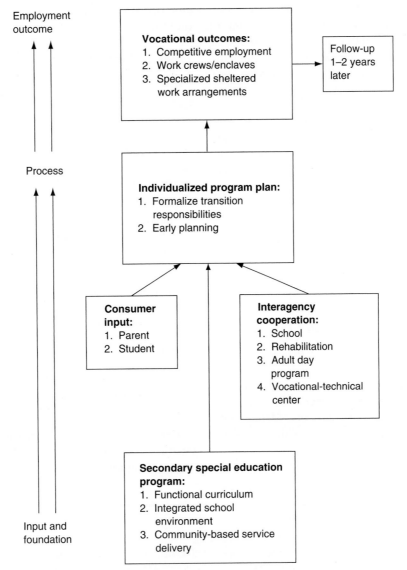

Employment outcome

Process

Input and foundation

Vocational outcomes:
1. Competitive employment
2. Work crews/enclaves
3. Specialized sheltered work arrangements

Follow-up 1–2 years later

Individualized program plan:
1. Formalize transition responsibilities
2. Early planning

Consumer input:
1. Parent
2. Student

Interagency cooperation:
1. School
2. Rehabilitation
3. Adult day program
4. Vocational-technical center

Secondary special education program:
1. Functional curriculum
2. Integrated school environment
3. Community-based service delivery

FIGURE 10–3   Three-stage vocational transition model for youth with disabilities

Source: From School to work: A vocational transition model, by P. Wehman, J. Kregal, & J. M. Barcus, *Exceptional Children, 52* (1), 1985, 28. Copyright (1985) by the Council for Exceptional Children. Reprinted with permission.

vocational education, and rehabilitation were linked to support transition for students with severe disabilities (see Figure 10-3). The principles of Wehman's model were:

1. Members of the multiple disciplines and service delivery systems must participate.
2. Parent involvement is essential.
3. Vocational transition planning must occur well before 21 years of age.
4. The process must be planned and systematic.

5. The vocational service provided must be [of] a quality nature. (p. 26)

Wehman's model required movement through the three stages: (a) school instruction, (b) planning for the transition process, and (c) placement into meaningful employment. The first stage was important because instruction in the public school should support the postschool goals of students with disabilities by including functional curriculum, integrated school environments, and community-based training. The second stage of Wehman's model focused on the planning process, where he argued that students and their families must be core members because they often take over the role of transition coordinators after graduation. Wehman also recognized that adult service providers must also be involved in the planning process to establish linkages and ensure that no interruption in critical services occurs. The final stage of Wehman's model was the vocational outcome of competitive employment, supported employment, or specialized sheltered work.

RESOURCES FOR CUSTOMIZING EMPLOYMENT

Job Development, Placement, and Training

Components of employment service delivery are included in Table 10-1. The team, agencies, individual with a disability and his or her support people work collaboratively during all aspects of service delivery. For instance, the individual with a disability may identify job leads in the local newspaper or network with family and friends to identify potential employment opportunities. Support may be provided by co-workers or other employment supports instituted at the work place.

Types of Employment Supports

One avenue for preparing transition youth for today's labor market involves delivering "customized employment services." Customized employment means:

individualizing the employment relationship between employees and employers in ways that meet the needs of both. It is based on an individualized determination of the strengths, needs, and interests of the person with a disability, designed to meet the specific needs of the employer. It may include employment developed through job carving, self-employment, or entrepreneurial initiatives, or restructuring strategies that result in job responsibilities being customized and individually negotiated to fit the needs of individuals with a disability. Customized employment assumes the provision of reasonable accommodations and support necessary for the individual to perform the function of a job that is individually negotiated and developed. (Federal Register, June 26, 2002, Vol. 67, No. 123, pp. 43154-43190)

Certainly, employment transition services have emerged as a proven approach to delivering customized employment services. Many special educators

TABLE 10–1   Components of employment service delivery

Component	Description
Developing a Customer Profile	A planning tool that provides a "snapshot" of the individual that includes his or her strengths, interests, needs, and expected outcomes. Information is gathered from a variety of sources and across multiple environments including: home, school, and recreational settings, and formal assessment records.
Job Development	Involves working collaboratively with the individual with a disability and key people in his or her life, such as family members, teachers, and friends to network and identify employment opportunities based on student's likes, preferences, and abilities.
Job Placement	Identifies supports to address pre-employment questions and concerns such as securing uniforms, employer tax credits, addressing SSI/SSDI concerns, and facilitating the completion of pre-employment paperwork (e.g., 1-9 form, job application, etc.).
Job Site Training and Support Development	Involves working collaboratively with the employer in developing and implementing employee training. Accommodations are identified, including providing systematic instructional procedures to train the employee with a disability if needed. Assists in determining employee support needs and arranging accommodations. Facilitates the social integration of the employee with a disability.
Follow-up	Identifies and facilitates the use of post-employment supports for the worker with a disability. Assists in the development of a post-employment support plan. Assesses employer satisfaction.

and transition specialists are familiar with employment services and are quite comfortable in communicating information regarding services to students and their families. Furthermore, through their experiences in developing community-based work experiences, many special educators have modified existing jobs or taken tasks from several jobs within one business to create positions that meet the unique knowledge, skills, and abilities of their students while simultaneously addressing a business need. However, they are less familiar with other forms of employment options that emerged from the customized employment approach that can assist students with disabilities in pursuing careers of their choice, such as self-employment and entrepreneurial initiatives. A brief description follows of various employment support structures.

In providing school-to-work transition services for youth with disabilities, special educators and transition providers have a tendency to rely almost exclusively on their own school or program resources to develop community-based training and employment sites and provide support to young adults who may require assistance in securing or maintaining employment. Similarly, human service agencies have relied on a paid job coach or perhaps natural supports to provide assistance or support to individuals seeking competitive employment. In some instances, special educators and human service professionals may be unaware or unable to access these supports and in other instances programmatic or administrative barriers (e.g., lack of interagency collaboration) may prohibit effective implementation of workplace supports. Comprehensive employment supports for individuals with disabilities are typically classified into four categories: agency mediated, business mediated, government mediated, and consumer and family mediated supports (see Table 10–2) (Wehman & Bricout, 2001).

It is beyond the scope of this chapter to include a detailed description of the variety of employment supports in each of these categories. For a more detailed analysis of comprehensive employment supports the reader is referred to the work of Wehman and Bricout (2001). It is important for special educators and transition specialists to be aware of the variety of employment supports available to assist in facilitating competitive employment. The following section will identify the most commonly utilized and accessed employment supports.

Business Mediated Supports

Plan of action, as reported by Griffin and Targett (2001), involves developing a systematic structure for meeting and seeking out employers and employer contacts. This strategy deals with building up employers as a resource. It involves developing a "tickler file" in which one follows up on existing contacts and places new contacts in the file. The file enables one to track and remind one when and where made contacts were made and what issues were raised by employers. This method allows for a consistent means for developing and maintaining a database (a bank of employers and jobs) so that regular communication is possible. This also allows for the individual to develop a plan or strategy of job seeking rather than utilizing a haphazard approach.

The advocate referral approach makes use of an individual who supports the idea of employing people with disabilities and has influence in the business community

> **Critical Point**
> Educators and human service professionals have not utilized the variety of vocational options and work supports that exist to facilitate community employment for young adults with disabilities.

TABLE 10–2 Comprehensive employment supports for people with disabilities

Employment Supports	Description and Examples
Business-Mediated Supports	Job restructuring, workplace accommodations (including environmental modifications, assistive technology, task modification, schedule modification), co-worker mentoring, job creation, employee assistance programs
Consumer/Family/ Community-Mediated Supports	Personal care attendant, peer mentors, family members as job developers, friends, and neighbors used for transportation
Government-Mediated Supports	Social security work incentives, employer tax credits, Medicaid waiver, Ticket to Work, and Work Incentive Improvement Act
Agency-Mediated Supports	Job coach assistance, specialized assistance, compensatory strategies, assistive technology, counseling, substance abuse services, VR counselor

(Griffin & Targett, 2001). This person may be a president of the local Better Business Bureau (BBB) or a philanthropic community organization. This individual could make general or even specific contacts for a person or persons with disabilities. The leader could provide either advocacy or direct input into employment or could just be "cheerleader" for the cause. In any event the advocate could have serious impact on employment for persons with disabilities.

Following up on advertising is another important aspect of acquiring a job. Advertisements are found in the newspaper, on the Web, and in many bulletin boards. Particular attention should be placed on the specifics of the positions being advertised and determining if the job characteristics in part or in full meet capabilities of the individual. Researching the company for its needs and general characteristics of the jobs that are available there is also informative to the likelihood of placement. Reviewing particular job titles and determining turnover rates is also a pragmatic avenue for devising an "in" with respect to employment.

Finally, contacting nonadvertising employers is an important avenue. This involves setting up appointments with the head of personnel or business owner. This could involve developing a rapport and providing them with specific information about yourself or individual(s) with disabilities. This is sometimes called doing "cold calls." The process is not a unique or unusual occurrence. What it entails, though, is a targeted approach. One needs to thoroughly seek out specific information regarding the business and its needs, find the specific jobs that exist within the business, and shape and design your approach to the specific capabilities of the individual and to the needs of the employer. Primary methods of making contacts are through mailing résumés, making unannounced visits, contacting employers via telephone, and so on. Nietupski Vertegen, Reilly, Hutson, and Hamre-Neitupski (1997) studied these procedures and found that all were effective; however, using the referral method leads to more employment than the cold-call method. There are numerous ways that employers become involved in the mediation of the employment process—both directly and indirectly.

Business advisory councils (BACs) have been in use for over 20 years (Rusch, 1990) to engage employers as supports in the employing process. In fact, BACs have been mandated by programs funded through the Projects with Industry (PWI) program of the Rehabilitation Services Administration since the early 1980s (P.L. 93-112). BACs are placement and employment programs that intricately involve employers in their development and oversight. Business advisory councils afford a close relationship with employers by engaging them in the actual implementation aspects of programs and services. While BACs have been required within the PWI programs for numerous years, the degree of involvement of the BACs has varied quite significantly (Hagner & Vander-Sande, 1998).

> **Critical Point**
> Numerous marketing and networking methods for working with businesses (BACs) may be utilized to increase employment opportunities for persons with disabilities.

Baer, Martonyi, Simmons, Flexer, & Goebel (1994), for example, implemented a BAC that was focused on a specific program but utilized the employer participants to market and provide services to individuals with disabilities. Baer, Martonyi, et al. (1994) focused on a systemic approach by enabling the employers to choose the amount of involvement in addressing the community's needs regarding employment of persons with disabilities and utilized a traditional team process approach that focused on stages of team development. The stages included forming, storming, norming, performing, and adjourning phases. These stages were used to both understand the processes and facilitate ongoing development. Baer, Martonyi, et al. (1994) found that their BAC was able to develop marketing and business connections that had a significant impact on the employment of persons with disabilities. Further, they found that the marketing activities cost the disability-related employment agencies far less to develop. In addition, the BAC became so involved that employers developed services that were not in existence before the BACs inception. However, it was found that the BAC did devolve and eventually ceased to exist after several years of operation.

> **Critical Point**
> BACs, as with all committees or groups, follow certain developmental stages of forming, storming, norming, performing, and adjourning.

Consumer/Family Mediated Supports

Very important in the employment process is the job seeker and their personal network. Surveying of personal networks is first accomplished by determining the individual's and family's support structure and connection to the community. Personal and family contacts can be of great use when seeking out employers. Finding leads is the most important means of finding and getting a job. Numerous studies and articles support the often-cited importance of family connections. It still appears that high percentages of the people who found employment, found it via a friend, family member, or acquaintance.

A job club is a program that uses group dynamics and mutual support to enhance employment prospects (Malone, 1996). Azrin and Besalel (1979) developed a job club approach that focused on training in job-seeking skills with the expectation that participants in the club would also be strongly involved in seeking and soliciting job leads. In fact, the job club approach requires the participant to utilize these job-seeking efforts on a daily basis. Primary to this focus is the intensive nature of the job club approach (Azrin & Philip, 1980). Baer, Martonyi, et al. (1994) developed two job club programs meeting the needs of persons with both mental illness and physical disabilities. These respective programs fostered job-seeking skills, making contacts with friends, family members, and potential employers on a daily basis. Further, the job clubs were continued beyond the point of individual placement to facilitate ongoing supports. Baer, Martonyi, et al. (1994) found that a higher percentage of placements and maintenance of employment was attained as compared to other local community employment programs.

> **Critical Point**
> Job club programs have been found useful in developing and maintaining employment through employability skills training and ongoing group supports.

Mentoring also has become a significant programmatic effort in recent years (Siegel, 1998). Mentoring is a process that involves matching the person with a disability with an individual knowledgeable and skilled in work and job-getting strategies (Hagner & Vander-Sande, 1998). In fact, one can implement the mentoring role through several methods. One can be a mentor who discusses and counsels the individual, much like the Big Brother and Big Sister programs. Further, one can be a mentor in the workplace (Hagner & Dileo, 1993; Smith & Rojewski, 1993). The co-worker-mentoring role has been most extensively utilized with persons with disabilities (Mank, Oorthuys, Rhodes, Sandow, & Weyer, 1992). Hagner and Dileo (1993) suggest that selection of the mentor be someone who has worked at the place of employment for at least several months, is well liked by his co-workers, is scheduled to work at the same time as the individual with a disability, and is a willing mentor.

> **Critical Point**
> Utilizing a mentor allows for a more typical approach to job training and ongoing support for people with disabilities.

Government-Mediated Supports

Social Welfare, Social Entitlements, and Work Incentives

Most people with significant disabilities rely on programs administered by the Social Security Administration to provide supplemental income and entitlement income. Most importantly, these programs include Medicaid and Medicare benefits. Most people who attain employment through supported employment work part time. Parent (1996) found that 67% of supported employees received no employer sponsored health benefit. Johnson et al. (1997) reported that nearly 75% of students exiting public school special education programs received Supplemental Security income (SSI) and consequently, Medicaid. Sixteen percent received **Social Security Disability Income (SSDI)** and Medicare coverage.

Social Security/Disability Insurance

The SSDI program strictly limits income for disabled participants to $700.00 per month (effective July 1, 1999). Wages over this amount are considered trial work months. Social Security allows for a nine-month trial work limit and an extended period of eligibility. At the end of this time the Social Security Administration makes a determination of **Substantial Gainful Activity.** This implies that the person with a disability is earning a wage for providing something of economic benefit to an employer. If it is determined that the individual can work in spite of their disability then SSDI benefits are terminated.

Supplemental Security Insurance

The SSI program is a federal welfare subsidy and provides for work incentives to allow people to work. Under Public Law 99-643, SSI cash benefits to recipients are determined on a flexible scale based on countable income. As wages increase, cash benefits decrease. Under Section 1619b, when the cash benefit reaches zero, recipients continue on the Social Security rolls, allowing them to continue working. Medicaid benefits also continue under Section 1619b (extended Medicaid coverage). Medicaid benefits continue so long as wages fall below the federal threshold amounts for earnings. These incentives have allowed thousands of people to go to work. Unfortunately, there is a great deal of confusion as to how to use these benefits. Many people who can go to work do not, due to ignorance of these work incentives or misinformation provided by service providers.

Additional Work Incentives

Two additional work incentives are emerging as effective: *Plans for Achieving Self Support* (PASS) and *Impairment Related Work Incentives* (IRWE). These programs are designed to set aside earned income in order to reduce "countable income" and maintain Social Security eligibility. These programs enable people to purchase equipment or services necessary for individuals to work. West, Wehman, and Revell (1996) determined that 57% of supported employment programs use PASS or IRWE to assist participants. The most frequently purchased services include transportation to work, job coach services, and work site modifications.

Small-Business Incentives

The three core disability employment programs—the federal/state vocational rehabilitation system, the Social Security Administration, and the Workforce Investment Act agencies—represent avenues for financial resources for financing a small-business start-up or entrepreneurial initiatives. They have the capacity to fund a small-business start-up for someone with a disability with free, individual grant-type funds and services as well as pay a small amount to a business consultant to assist in developing a business plan for a prospective business owner with a disability (Griffin & Hammis, 2001). It is important to note that these funds are grants and not loans that the person has to repay. Examples of self-employment and entrepreneurial initiatives that people with disabilities have pursued include: the operation of a cleaning business vending machines, in which the individuals purchase and then place vending machines in businesses, schools, organizations, which they are responsible for restocking and keeping operational; a Kettle Korn™ franchise; and a window washing service. It is important that individuals involved in transition planning and programming recognize that supported self-employment may be a viable employment option for students with disabilities.

Workforce Recruitment Program

The Workforce Recruitment Program for College Students with Disabilities (WRP) is a resource for businesses nationwide to identify qualified temporary and permanent employees from a variety of fields. Applicants are highly motivated postsecondary students and recent graduates eager to prove their abilities in the workforce. To get names, background, and contact information on candidates whose skills match their needs, businesses call the Job Accommodation Network (JAN).

Project EMPLOY

The President's Committee on Employment of People with Disabilities is seeking to expand employment opportunities for persons with mental retardation through Project EMPLOY. Project EMPLOY was initiated as a result of research on best practices. The findings indicated that employment barriers inherent in negative stereotyping can be eliminated through a program of demonstration, outreach, and education when coupled with technical assistance.

Agency-Mediated Supports

Agency-mediated supports are typically originated through a human service agency such as the federal/state vocational rehabilitation program. As you can see from the examples presented in Table 10–2, agency-mediated supports can be in the form of direct assistance from a paid professional such as a job coach or may be in the form of a service authorized or implemented by a human service agency, such as securing assistive technology or developing compensatory strategies that are implemented at the job site. Since agency-mediated supports are widely utilized, a brief discussion of the most frequently utilized adult service agencies that are involved in facilitating employment for individuals with disabilities is warranted.

To facilitate the development of postschool employment outcomes, school personnel should be aware of the general structure and function of adult service agencies involved in facilitating employment outcomes. The agencies that are there to help in the process generally consist of approximately seven different, but in some cases more, related agencies. Examples of the adult service agencies are vocational rehabilitation (VR) programs, developmental disabilities (DD) agencies, mental health (MH) programs, employment and training programs, and community and human service programs.

In general, no state offers or requires a postschool employment agency to provide services to all people who apply for services. In general, the agencies that help persons with disabilities to gain employment provide services through a selection or priority basis. In contrast to special education services, adult service programs are eligibility-based.

> **Critical Point**
> One must either meet the agencies' criteria for providing services or the individual receives services once others who are higher on the agencies' priority list are served.

It is important to note that no individual is guaranteed access to adult services. Programs such as the VR, DD, and MH are primary programs in that they fund or provide the basic resources to accomplish employment. Secondary programs, such as employment and training programs and community and human service programs, usually receive funding from the primary programs, so that the secondary programs can provide their services. In any case, all of these agencies or programs should be involved in the development of employment services for the student who meets the respective agencies' criteria for providing services. Referral to these agencies should be discussed in the initial team meeting as early as possible in the student's educational programming, and a team representative should be given the responsibility to make the initial contact and referral.

Vocational Rehabilitation Agency

As described in Chapters 1 and 2 of this book, VR is a federally designed program. Vocational rehabilitation programs are authorized through the federal legislative process, specifically the Rehabilitation Act amendments of 1998 (now embodied within Title IV of the Workforce Investment Act). The primary emphasis of VR programs is employment. Consequently, any individuals who are accepted for service must have a disability related to performing work. To apply for services, one must either be referred or self-referred. Once referred, a potential client (a person with a disability) meets with the VR counselor and an application is taken and processed. The counselor must determine the potential client's needs and probable acceptance for receiving services. In order to qualify for services, the client must be of legal employable age and have the following characteristics: a physical or mental impairment that results in a substantial impediment to employment. If an individual meets this criteria, he or she will be determined eligible unless there is clear and convincing evidence that the individual cannot benefit from or does not require **vocational rehabilitation services** (Wehman, 1997). Additionally, most VR programs suggest that the potential client should be referred to them only two years before the student is projected to leave public schools. This, however, could change based on the individual needs of the student and the severity of the disability to employment (Wehman, 1997). There have been increasing concerns voiced by parents and transition and rehabilitation professionals regarding the need to have rehabilitation

counselors more actively involved with transition-age youth prior to the student exiting school.

To determine eligibility and to fulfill his or her part of the cooperative relationship, the client must provide evidence of disability, agree to be tested to ascertain employment support needs, participate in a rehabilitation planning process, and be actively involved in training/job seeking. Generally, the initial component of assessment and determination of acceptance should take no longer than 30 days. Once accepted, the client and the VR counselor jointly author and agree to an Individual Plan of Employment (IPE). This plan should spell out exactly what the client's targeted employment goal is and what the counselor and client will do to help the client attain that goal.

The types of services that a VR agency offers are vocational and career counseling, employment training, job skill training, job coaching, money for employment-related expenses, and other employment-related services. All services are provided or purchased by the counselor based on the agreement formulated in the individual plan. Whereas services are provided based on the individual plan, the cumulative success and rehabilitation of the client is based on the client's movement through the VR system and gaining employment. Counselors are evaluated based on the number of their clients that move through the system.

To achieve these outcomes, the counselor usually has a single pool of money to be spent for the caseload of their clients. The determination of the dollar amount that each counselor has is based on the number and severity of the clients in the caseload and the basic amount of dollars coming into the state. The counselor must use his or her best clinical judgment to determine what services will be procured and at what cost for each client.

> **Critical Point**
> It is important for special educators and rehabilitation providers to convey the idea that services offered through the VR program are based on program eligibility requirements, and just because a student is determined eligible for services does not guarantee that the student will receive those services at no cost to the individual.

Visual Impairment Rehabilitation Program

Another agency that may or may not be part of the state VR system is a program that serves persons with *visual impairment* (VI). In some states, the VI agency is separate from the primary VR agency, and the agency uses a differentiated term such as the Department for the Blind or Rehabilitation Services for Visual Impairments. These VI agencies or services are authorized under the same VR Rehabilitation Act amendments, but the services are exclusively offered to persons with visual impairments. These services may begin as early as elementary or middle school. In addition to having an employment focus, the VI agency also focuses upon providing services related to independent living and mobility. Otherwise, the services that are provided by the VI agency are essentially the same as those provided by the VR agency.

Developmental Disabilities Agencies

States also have a developmental disabilities (DD) program that exists in different organizational structures depending on the state. These DD programs, like other programs (e.g., Medicaid, Social Security, etc.), are legislatively authorized and provided the impetus for developing programs and services across the country for persons with more significant or developmental disabilities (Scheerenberger, 1983). The services and funding are generally proportional to each state based on the population size and the number of individuals with developmental disabilities. Each state develops differing methods for delivering these resources. In some states, there are separate entities that are sometimes called Mental Retardation and Developmental Disabilities (MR/DD) programs. Other states combine the DD agency with their mental health services. However, each state and territory has some mechanism for delivering services and providing supports to individuals with DD.

In general, supports for students can be received by getting in touch with either the state or local offices that are contact points for acquiring services. Supports are designed to address the complete needs of the individual with DD. The local agencies' case managers, direct service staff, and/or counselors, are available to provide or assist in the development of appropriate supports to persons with DD (Braddock, 1987). As with the educational services provided in the schools, there is a "plan" Individual Habilitation Plans (IHP) developed that lays out the types of supports that the individual with DD requires to meet their needs. Each IHP is developed in a similar manner as an IEP (individualized education program), IPE (individual plan of employment), or an ITP (individual transition plan). The supports that are needed for the individual with DD

will be acquired through a team approach and be linked to individuals' needs in areas such as living, recreation, relationships, communication, and personal skills. To qualify for services under the DD act, the individual must have a disability that occurred before age 22 and significantly impairs three of seven major life activities. These life activities are language, capacity for independent living, economic self-sufficiency, self-direction, self-care, learning, and mobility (Wehman, 1997).

> **Critical Point**
> Regarding the diagnosis, it is important to note that the DD agency serves individuals based on their capability as opposed to diagnostic labels.

Support services vary according to the local and regional governing board that oversees the programs. Each agency is either a not-for-profit self-administered program (with oversight provided by the state) or a state office directly representing the state. Support services range from providing staff and independent living arrangements, highly structured residences (institutions), resources for supported living, supports for various types of employment programs, a range of recreation and community experiences, counseling, along with other community and institutional support services. Schools can request that the staff of these agencies attend the IEP meeting. The DD programs can offer a great deal of supports in areas listed and may be better able to facilitate some of the outcomes that the school has for the individual with DD. Supports such as **job coaches** or mentoring may be available along with supported employment programs and house supervisors for independent living.

Mental Health Agency

Employment supports can also be obtained from the mental health agency for people that have mental health problems. The mental health organizations operate much like the DD agency/services that was explained earlier. There are state and local agencies: The local agencies can either be a private not-for-profit entity with an oversight board or the state may represent itself through offices and staff employed by the state. Mental health agencies are funded through a combination of funding options. Medicaid, Social Security, health insurance, and a variety of state and federal mental health funding mechanisms are used to support state MH services (Baer, Goebel, & Flexer, 1993; Cook & Hoffschmidt, 1993; Stroul, 1993).

Qualifying for MH support services requires that an individual be diagnosed with a *severe and persistent mental illness* by a qualified clinician. Generally, the phrase "*serious and persistent mental illness*" (SPMI) is the term that is used to describe the disability. A diagnosis of SPMI is defined as:

> Certain mental or emotional disorders (organic brain syndrome, schizophrenia, recurrent depressive and manic depressive disorders, and paranoid and psychoses, plus other disorders that may become chronic) that erode or prevent the development of their functional capacities in relation to three of their primary aspects of daily life personal hygiene and self-care, self-direction, interpersonal relationships, social transactions, learning and recreation. (Goldman & Manderscheid, 1987, p. 13)

Other more specific criteria can be found in the American Psychiatric Association's DSM-IV codes for psychiatric diagnoses. However, key to diagnosis and differentiation from developmental disability is the fact that the delay in three major life activities should be due to a psychiatric cause (Lawn & Meyerson, 1993).

Employment supports can be acquired for individuals with SPMI through contacting the local MH agency. The key mechanism that guides the delivery of services is what Stroul (1995) calls a *community support system* (CSS). The CSS is designed to help maintain the individual with SPMI in the community. Consequently, services are determined based on the need of the individual to live successfully and independently in the community. The individual is able to receive the following services: mental health treatment, client identification and outreach, protection and advocacy, rehabilitation services, family and community supports, peer support, income support and entitlements, housing, health and dental care, and crisis response services (Stroul, 1993, p. 49). These supports can be very useful in planning for transition.

> **Critical Point**
> Involving the caseworkers and support staff in planning will be of great use when developing initial jobs along with long-term supports.

In general, services from an MH program are offered at any time that a diagnosis is made. However, most mental health diagnoses are not made until later in the student's life, so it is uncertain when would be the most appropriate time to make a referral. However, if the individual is exhibiting significant problems and has an initial diagnosis, the student should be referred.

Contract Agencies

The availability of employment supports from private agencies can vary in different localities. As described earlier, the training and employment programs might be part of one of the primary supports network or program providers (VR, DD, or MH). Independent programs may receive funding from those agencies to provide the placement and employment service. Employment and training programs are generally private not-for-profit agencies that have an executive director and an advisory board for administrative oversight. Some programs may be "faith based" that offer additional support services. The programs are funded in part or wholly with fee-for-service contracts with the primary providers. The private employment and training programs are generally small organizations with small-specialized staffs. The staff usually has special training in either community placement/employment or an expertise in a specific skill area. The private employment service providers will perform the tasks of assisting the person with a disability in either gaining the skills to find a job or training the individual with a disability in a particular job. The employment and training staff also may perform a combination of the two components. These private agencies might well be useful in planning for supports in the future because they may either receive funding or develop a funding mechanism that will help long-term job finding and supports.

Another hybrid of the traditional employment and training agency is that of a business, such as a coffee shop or some other service or manufacturing business, that operates primarily to benefit the individual with a disability. Bond and Boyer (1988) have termed these employment agencies *client-employing programs.* These operate as a service or manufacturing business and employ only persons with disabilities. Other similar organizations also may operate a business that employs a mixture of persons with and without disabilities. Additionally, still other employment and training programs will use the client-employing business as a training site for initial skill training. The site is used to facilitate future permanent placements in other similar settings. Although the client-employing business does perform a service and benefits to persons with disabilities, Bond (1991) and others (Simmons, Selleck, Steele, & Sepetauc, 1993) have criticized the model due to business and inclusionary factors.

Other community programs and human service agencies provide employment services that help persons with disabilities to gain access to employment;

however, these programs are not targeted only to meet their unique needs. These programs include the state's agencies of employment services and job training programs through WIA. Each of these programs offers employment and skill-related training to address the needs of individuals who are either not employed or in need of being reemployed.

State Bureau of Employment Services

The state's bureau or office of employment service is a workforce development program that has been in existence since the early 1900s (Droege, 1987). This program is funded through federal and state tax money. The primary focus of this agency is to meet the needs of each state's economic development and to match employers that are looking for employees with individuals looking for work. As with the VR, DD, and MH agencies, there are state and local offices. Local offices of employment services can be found in nearly every state and municipality. The services provided by the state employment agencies include computerized tracking of available jobs, centralized advertising, and referral of those jobs. Additionally, large special-training programs are provided that meet individual employer needs, authorizing tax incentives to motivate employers to hire special classes of people and training programs that enable individuals to gain their high school equivalency diploma (GED, a general education diploma) and job-seeking skills classes. Although they are not the primary targets of the state offices of employment, persons with disabilities are one of the targeted populations that the agencies have a priority to serve. Consequently, state employment services will provide resources for special programs to meet the needs of the individual with disabilities. These special programs, however, differ in various localities.

Accessing services also is similar to the other primary service providers. In each locality, there are counselors, program specialists, employer liaisons, and training specialists. To gain access to the services, one must apply for services and go through some testing to determine the best job-skill match. A referral will be provided if there is a match between the individual's skills and available jobs in the community. The tests that are provided have been developed by the U.S. employment services (USES) and are quite beneficial for individuals who assimilate well into the mainstream of individuals without disabilities. Some problems have been noted about the USES tests for persons with disabilities (Droege, 1987).

One-Stop Career Centers

One of the primary elements of the Workforce Investment Act of 1998 was the expansion of one-stop centers (OSCs). The centers are intended to unify education, vocational training, and employment programs into a single system in each community. There are several principles that guide the development and implementation of the OSC, including: universal access, consumer empowerment, streamlining services, increased accountability, business involvement, state and local flexibility, and improved youth programs. One-stop centers are based on the idea that there should be a single point of entry to various employment services and training programs for all job seekers. Thus, an individual could go to one location and have access to various employment and training programs or services that had traditionally been offered at different locations (e.g., vocational rehabilitation services, State Bureau of Employment Services, etc.). Three levels of services are available through the OSC:

> **Critical Point** Employment supports may come from a wide variety of entities any where from a major state-funded agency to a private "faith-based" support service.

- *Core services*—job-search skills training, interviewing techniques workshops, résumé development preparation, work exploration and referral to employers with job openings
- *Intensive services*—may target specific groups, such as youth, people with disabilities and those with limited income, and include the development of an individual career plan, career counseling, and case management
- *Training services*—targeted for individuals who are not able to become employed through the use of core and intensive services; training may include occupational skills training, adult education, on-the-job training, and customized training for the employer

MODEL EMPLOYMENT PRACTICES

While supported employment has been a primary focus in the employment field for persons with moderate to severe disabilities for many years, the authors feel that the four features of supported employment are a pragmatic means for envisioning all employment practices for young adults with disabilities. Consequently, the four features are described in terms of method and involvement practices that relate to all people, including persons with disabilities.

The four features of supported employment services include: individualized assessment, job development, on-the-job training, and ongoing support. Individualized assessment is a process by which the supported employment provider learns about the unique skills and abilities of the person for whom a job search is being done. There is a similarity between this process and the process described by Richard Nelson Bolles' *What Color Is Your Parachute* (2005). Bolles discussed five effective job-hunting methods. Among these was the "creative job hunting approach." This method urged the job seeker to figure out what his/her best skills and favorite "knowledges" are. This notion of learning what the job seeker has to offer is parallel to the idea of developing an individualized assessment or a person-centered approach to job selection. A person-centered approach begins with the premise that we all have unique skills and interests that define what a good job would be for us. For people with disabilities, the disability can prevent us from getting to know who someone is and what their interests are. Knowing what someone is good at is the first step in creating a job match rather than placing someone at a job site that is available.

Person-Centered Job Selection

Person-centered job selection relies on the use of non-traditional assessment exercises for determining an appropriate job match. As opposed to standardized, norm-referenced testing that is designed to assign a diagnostic category, employment based on needs, interests, and preferences takes a personalized approach to learning about the individual. Where standardized tests can describe what someone cannot do, person-centered activities allow the employment professional to learn the work preferences of the individual. By investing time in getting to know the individual's dreams, interests, and unique skills, the evaluator or team can look beyond the person's disability and develop the "right job" for the individual. By investing the time to get to know a person's dreams, interests, and skills, the evaluator can perform an assessment in a balanced, trusting, and reciprocal way. By spending time in getting to know the person in typical environments, the evaluator can make an assessment of what considerations need to be made in order for the person to be successful at his or her job. This type of assessment is different than finding

a job and hoping the person will be successful. Too often jobs for people with disabilities have centered on entry-level jobs with little regard for matching skills and preferences with the requirements of a job with career possibilities. In fact, the emerging criticism of employment programs is the overreliance on entry-level positions like food service and janitorial jobs. These types of work are characterized by high turnover and low wages. Jobs of this type are an easy job placement for staff trainers who have not taken the time to assess what a "good job" would look like for the participant (Mank, Cioffi, & Yovanoff, 1997). When a person-centered approach is utilized, the job match is individualized and the job more fulfilling for the participant.

> **Critical Point**
> Person-centered assessment and placement can be defined as the opposite of norm-referenced assessment and placement.

The most important consideration in a person-centered approach to job selection is to ensure that the activities used for evaluation are meaningful and occur in everyday life. If the evaluation relies on artificial tasks or environments then the individual will quickly realize the message that the task is not real or relevant. If there is no sense of purpose to the task then what a sad message this must send to someone who, for their entire life, has always faced a life of lowered expectations. What message does this send to family members, employers, and the general public? Tasks used in evaluation should have a suitable level of challenge, should offer the appropriate amount of decision making, and should be appropriate for the age of the individual.

A person-centered approach to job selection leads to a job development approach that places faith in the power of friends and family of the job seeker. A group of friends and family have a personal stake and want to see good things happen for the person seeking work. As opposed to a formal group of therapists and paid professionals, the individuals who participate in a person-centered group are there voluntarily. Paid professionals will be involved in the planning but a balance of nonpaid people can be beneficial. This type of planning group places emphasis on the knowledge and resources of a job-seeker's personal network. This is similar to Bolles (1999), who lists friends and family as the third and fourth most-effective job-hunting method. Very few jobs in our culture are found by looking in the want ads or making phone calls to employers. Bolles (1999) lists classified ads as a least-effective method of job seeking. According to Bolles, answering blind ads in newspapers leads to employment for only 5% to 24% of job seekers. Utilizing our network of friends, family, and acquaintances fills most jobs. In many circumstances the axiom is true that "it's whom you know, not what you know." For too long human service professionals have discounted the power and efficacy of the job seekers' personal network in their job development efforts. See Case Study (Mark) for an example of social network job finding.

> **Critical Point**
> The most important consideration in a person-centered approach to job selection is to ensure that the activities used for evaluation are meaningful and occur in everyday life.

Once a job outcome has been targeted for the individual, the work of job development begins. As with any job seeker, an organized plan will be established for getting a job. As a means of preparation, a decision needs to be made early regarding how much the job seeker will do and how much representation will be required by the service provider. The key is to develop a job-seeking strategy where the individual is empowered in the process and is taking an active role consistent within his or her ability. If too much assistance is provided, the job seeker may be stigmatized by the presence of the service provider. If too little support is provided, then the job search may not be successful. For instance:

- How much assistance will the job seeker need in contacting employers?
- Does the person represent him- or herself well enough that the service provider should not sit in on the interview?
- Should the job seeker, due to the complexity of his or her disability, not attend the initial employer contacts?

- Can the job seeker develop or participate in developing a résumé as part of the job search?
- Has the job seeker been adequately prepared for what to do and say in a job interview? Does the job seeker need more skill training?
- Do the jobs that have been selected allow for career growth?

For some job searches, the paid professional will take the lead in making job contacts and meeting with potential employers. For people who are more capable, the role of the staff person may be to organize the search and provide advice and counseling to the job seeker. For others all that might be needed are supports such as a job club or informal mentor. Regardless of the amount of representation needed to get someone employed, it is essential that the staff person and the job seeker be aware of the accepted protocol for contacting an employer. The first question to consider is "how would anyone contact this employer?" Is it best to send a letter with a résumé before a contact is made? Is it customary to walk in on an employer and make an unannounced "cold call"? Should a formal appointment be made and with whom? Generally, the more typical the contact is to that of any job seeker, the greater likelihood of success.

Job Design

Creativity is essential in job design. One size does not fit all. Targeted job development requires a great deal more flexibility and creativity than typical job acquisition activities. *Targeted job development* means that marketing activities are designed to benefit one person and not designed to sell the services offered by an agency. When an individual interviews for a job, the individual's skills and abilities are being sold. The same should be true for people who require a little extra attention in order to go to work. Service professionals

CASE STUDY   Mark

Social Networks in Job Finding

Within the most recent year, Mark, a man with a disability, was looking for work at a plastic factory. The staff of a local community employment agency made several contacts but after two months the man had no firm job offer. One Sunday night at a church service the congregation was encouraged to stand up and say whatever was on their minds. As Mark, the man with the disability, looked around the church he noticed the owner of the plastics molding company. Mark took this opportunity to stand up and tell the congregation that he had been unemployed for some time and needed a job. He stated "he always thought he'd like to work at a plastic formulating plant." Mark went to work the next week.

should be acutely aware of this fact when they are representing someone at risk of being seen in a devalued role by an employer or the community. The ultimate goal is, of course, to match the skills, preferences, and conditions for work with the setting, task, and decision-making complexity of a particular job. Everyone has individual requirements in regard to where we work, how we work, and when we work. Creativity in job design cannot be undersold when someone goes to work. Flexibility may include job carving or job sharing.

Job carving involves negotiating with an employer to construct a new job description from two or more standardized job descriptions at the business. An example of this process is provided in the Case Study on Dan. Within the job carving process Dan's skills and interests were reviewed. Once the analysis was completed, employment was sought that allowed for Dan to perform either a majority or separate components of presently available jobs. Employers are generally heavily involved in the development of job-carving practices. It is the employer that knows his or her jobs and with the assistance of a community employment specialist, a variety of carved jobs could be developed.

> **Critical Point**
> Creativity is essential in job design.

Job sharing arrangements are effective when individuals with disabilities are primarily interested in working part time (Granger, 1996). Job-sharing arrangements, as the name implies, allow for two people to share a single part-time job. Two people with disabilities or a person with a disability and a nondisabled person may share a job. This arrangement is most effective when the amount of earning is restricted or when personal issues or responsibilities prevent someone from working full time.

Shared jobs or carved jobs can be effective for any job seeker. Job flexibility has found its place in our business culture. People work for a variety of reasons and have different requirements for what defines a good job for them. Salary alone is not the only factor people consider in accepting a job. Issues like child care, proximity to home, flexibility in scheduling, geographic area, and job satisfaction all are issues job seekers consider. This same flexibility is the key to a quality job match and positively correlates with job satisfaction and job longevity (Dentzer, 1992).

In some instances, job seekers do fill an existing job description. Many people with disabilities, at an early age, have indicated that their expectations were high for having a career path. The role of the service provider in these situations is to work with the individual to develop a "road map" on what vocational steps should be taken to get the person to their ultimate job target. A career path involves competency building by working at a series of jobs that lead to the ultimate job target. See Case Studies on Jean and Trevor for two examples of how this can be accomplished.

Natural Supports

The most significant development in the field of employment services is the way people are trained and

CASE STUDY Dan

Construction of a New Job Description

Dan works at a laboratory run by the U.S. Geological Survey (USGS). His job is to sanitize sample bottles used by field workers taking water samples, from Maine to the Mississippi River. The bottle sanitizing job is a time-consuming, complex operation and involves dangerous chemicals. Prior to Dan's employment, this job was part of the chemist's job description. With Dan fulfilling these functions, the chemists have more time to devote to testing samples, preventing the typical spring and summer backlog of work. Dan is employed in a challenging job where he can demonstrate his competency. Additionally, Dan has taken on more complex tasks since he went to work at the lab. The staff of the community employment agency went to USGS with the purpose of designing a job that is specific to Dan's skills rather than trying to have Dan "fit" an existing job description. In developing a carved job, the community employment staff had to spend time in getting to know Dan and what his unique skills were. The community employment staff also had to get to know the employer and the business to learn what tasks would fit Dan's abilities. Close attention was paid to the environment, coworkers, tasks, and culture of the business.

Pursuing a Career Path

Jean is a good example of someone who has succeeded at her career path. Jean graduated from high school in 1969. For the next 11 years, she found herself working at a segregated sheltered workshop. In all those years, she never gave up her dream of working in an office setting. Jean began her career track volunteering at a local university library. At this job, she learned how to organize tasks, how to file, and how to conform to the culture of a business. After a short time, she went to work part time at a steel factory as a file clerk for the sales staff. Jean learned to organize and manage a complex filing system. She also was responsible for taking phone orders and making appointments for the sales staff. After several years, she left the factory to work for the local county clerk's office. This was a full-time position with comparable benefits and wages to her nondisabled coworkers. Jean is responsible for a variety of duties, including processing vehicle registrations, license plate renewals, and vehicle liens. Her present job is challenging and fits the requirements of her dream job of 15 years ago. She works in an office setting performing complex tasks. She works in a downtown office setting where she has contact with professional people. She has the opportunity to develop friendships with her co-workers and to attain respect for her job competency. After going to work at the clerk's office, Jean was able to move from the family home into her own apartment. She has an active social life and is making plans for her retirement.

Pursuing a Career Path

Another example of a career track is the experiences of Trevor. Trevor experienced a brain injury while in college. After several years of rehabilitation services, Trevor was eager to enter the workforce. He worked for an industrial lighting company as a data entry operator. He later worked as an inventory control specialist for a major retail distribution warehouse. These clerical skills allowed Trevor to develop competencies that led to his ideal job, working as a runner for a large downtown law firm. Trevor has returned to school, pursuing an associate's degree as a paralegal.

supported to perform their job. In the early years of employment programs, the accepted method of job training was to develop a job that required no extra planning to teach the new hire to do his or her job. The job developer would analyze requirements at the job site several days before the new employee would begin. This would allow the job developer to develop a training strategy in preparation for the employee to go to work. As employment programs evolved, we have learned that there are distinct liabilities in viewing job sites in a narrow fashion.

With supported employment, a job coach is employed by a supported employment program, but this is ultimately artificial to the job environment. The presence of a job coach on site too often draws attention to the worker with a disability and can stigmatize the individual. Other employees notice the presence of the job coach and look upon the supported employee differently than if the person was trained in a more typical fashion. The presence of a job coach sends a faulty message to other employees at the business that special skills and knowledge are required to work with and relate to the employee with a disability.

The focus of job training has shifted from external job training to the reliance of generic supports that naturally occur at the workplace (*natural supports* in the workplace). Many businesses have training programs in place for their employees (Nisbet & Hagner, 1988). All businesses have a unique culture that enables a new employee to learn their job and to become assimilated into the workplace. The strength of generic supports is to work within the accepted framework of the business to allow the person with a disability to be accepted into the workplace culture, as any other employee would be. The role of the employment staff, in these instances, is to act as a consultant or advisor to the business during the training period. Employment staff will act as advisors to the training staff providing information on teaching strategies, task organization, and other issues that may arise during job training. This role can be more difficult than the traditional job-training role because the **job trainer** is not always present at the business. The results of this type of training are of tremendous benefit to the individual with a disability at work.

Critical Point
The most significant development in the field of supported employment services is the development and utilization of natural supports.

In a landmark study of supported employment, Mank, Cioffi, and Yovanoff (1997) investigated the relationship of employment features and outcomes for supported participants and the use of natural supports in the workplace. The analysis applied to the data in this research studied the relationship between the level of job-site integration and five variables: type of work, level of disability, monthly wages, hourly wages, and the "typicalness" of the employee's circumstances in relation to that of nondisabled coworkers. Mank et al. (1997) found that work-site interaction with nondisabled co-workers was positively correlated with higher wages and longer job retention. Most strikingly, it was found that the correlation holds regardless of the severity of disability of the employee. Conversely, the study concluded that the more atypical someone's conditions are at the start of

employment, the more atypical conditions continue regardless of time on the job or complexity of the task (Mank et al., 1997).

Employment with supports makes a commitment to each person served that they will receive a level of support that is consistent with their needs. Supports are personally designed in order to enable the person to work with maximum independence. Too much support may further stigmatize the individual with a disability. Too little support may jeopardize the person's job. This balance is not stagnant but fluid, allowing for support to change based on circumstances. The provision of support on the job site is essential for both the employer and employee, and includes the following:

1. Addressing management and co-worker changes at the business
2. Retraining, consultation, and new task introduction
3. Advocating for raises, benefits, and job advancement
4. Facilitating job changes as the result of termination, advancement, layoff, or business closure
5. Modeling appropriate work behavior
6. Developing appropriate social interaction skills

Without this valuable service it would be unlikely that many people served in community-based vocational services would be successful. This is especially true for people with long-term mental illness, brain injury, mental retardation, and autism.

CASE STUDY Terry

The Importance of Typicalness

An example of natural supports can be found in a central Kentucky employment agency through which a man named Terry gained a job. Terry has significant disabilities that prevented him from entering the work force. His disabilities included total blindness, midrange deafness, and selective mutism and presumed mental retardation. The central Kentucky agency's staff found that Terry had a tremendous interest in radio and music. His hobby was a music collection composed of thousands of recordings. When initially encountered, Terry worked four days per week at a day activity center putting toys in gumball machine eggs. Terry's ambition was to work in radio. It would have been impossible for the agency staff to learn to operate a radio station and provide the training Terry needed. A radio station was located that employed a disc jockey, Edmund, who was also blind. He agreed to work with Terry in the role of a mentor. By utilizing Edmund's expertise, Terry went to work in an occupation that would have been impossible if traditional job training techniques were utilized.

CONCLUSION

In order to facilitate competitive employment for the youth with disabilities who desire it, transition team members must be more effective in disseminating information and linking students and parents and other participants in the transition process to workplace supports. By becoming more familiar with the numerous employment supports, they can more effectively identify and implement resources or accommodations that will assist more students with disabilities in participating in community-based work experiences and ultimately competitive employment, via further postsecondary education and training or immediate entry into the labor force. There are many supports that students transitioning from secondary education or college and universities can access and utilize to help them achieve their career goals. By identifying the appropriate mix of supports for a student with a disability, the team is better able to inform students, parents, and potential employers of the appropriate resources available. It is important that team members know the resources that are available in the local community so that they can more effectively tap into the array of employment supports. By discussing and distributing information during IEP meetings, students working with their parents or advocates can make informed choices about the type and degree of supports they wish to access. Students and their parents may be more inclined to access services and supports if they are provided with specific contact information, including agency name, contact person, phone number, and eligibility requirements for specific vocational-related postsecondary programs. Representatives from many of these programs should be present at the IEP transition planning meetings. However, the sad reality is that in many localities the seamless transition from school programs to adult service programs or postsecondary education does not occur.

STUDY QUESTIONS

1. Make a list of the various service providers that could assist an individual with a disability in getting a job. Then list the services that the individual might need. How might you as a school transition–related teacher or specialist work with those respective agencies and services?
2. Describe the history of employment for persons with disabilities. What kinds of things were right or wrong with respect to the various aspects of employment services?
3. What is a career path and how can students with disabilities successfully navigate through such a process?
4. What social service programs exist and to what degree can people with disabilities make use of such programs?
5. How can one use the relative plethora of employment supports to facilitate competitive employment for persons with disabilities?
6. What is community-based vocational training and how does it differ from traditional vocational training?
7. Describe supported employment and how it differs from the more traditional methods. Are there advantages to either? Which model appears to be better for students that you have encountered? Why?

WEBSITES

Job Accommodations Network:
   http://www.jan.wvu.edu/
West Virginia Research and Training Center:
   http://www.icdi.wvu.edu/homepage.htm
The Association for Persons in Supported Employment (APSE):
   http://www.apse.org/index.html
The U.S. Department of Labor, Office of Disability Employment Policy:
   http://www.dol.gov/odep/welcome.html
Career One-Stop:
   http://www.careeronestop.org/
U.S. Department of Labor:
   http://www.dol.gov/index.htm
Rehabilitation Research & Training Center on Workplace Supports:
   http://www.vcu.edu/rrtcweb/
Worksupports.com
   http://www.worksupport.com/
Rehabilitation Research and Training Center (RRTC) on Workforce Investment and Employment Policy for Persons with Disabilities:
   http://www.comop.org/rrtc.htm
Training Resource Network, Inc.:
   http://www.trninc.com/
The Center on Education and Work:
   http://www.cew.wisc.edu/

Heath Resource Center—The National Clearinghouse on Postsecondary Education for Individuals with Disabilities:
  http://www.heath.gwu.edu/

Employment Support for People with Disabilities:
  http://www.ssa.gov/work/

Ticket to Work:
  http://www.socialsecurity.gov/work/Ticket/ticket_info.html

Mainstream Inc.:
  http://www.mainstreaminc.org/

National Federation of the Blind:
  http://www.nfb.org/

Closing the Gap:
  http://www.closingthegap.com/

America's Job Bank:
  http://www.ajb.dni.us/

Job Openings *EdHIRES*

  http://www.ed.gov/about/jobs/open/edjobs.html?src=gu

Office of Special Education and Rehabilitative Services (OSERS):
  http://www.ed.gov/about/offices/list/osers/index.html

Job Web:
  http://www.jobweb.com/

The ARC:
  http://www.thearc.org/

YAI/National Institute for People with Disabilities Network:
  http://www.yai.org/

Occupational Outlook Handbook and Career Guide to Industries:
  http://www.bls.gov/news.release/ooh.toc.htm

The Information Network (O*NET®):
  http://www.doleta.gov/programs/onet/

CHAPTER 11

TRANSITION TO POSTSECONDARY EDUCATION

Deborah Durham Webster

Rachel McMahan Queen

LEARNING OBJECTIVES

The objectives of this chapter are:

1. Describe the function of preparation and backward planning in meeting postsecondary transition goals.

2. Describe the importance that academics and independent living skills play in achieving postschool goals.

3. Identify various postsecondary education options and their differences in demands and characteristics.

4. Develop skills on methods to connect to postsecondary options.

5. Explain legislation that applies to the postsecondary sector and how it differs from IDEA.

6. Develop skills to empower students by increasing the understanding of their disability, their ability to self-advocate, and knowledge of their legal rights and responsibilities in postsecondary settings.

7. Be sensitive to the impact of cultural values, attitudes, and beliefs on the students and their families when promoting postsecondary educational goals.

8. Describe how postsecondary education and training goals relate to IDEA's four principles inherent in transition planning and services.

INTRODUCTION

The last chapter addressed issues related to the transitioning process to employment settings. For many students, postsecondary education and training which often takes place right after high school is an important step in reaching employment and career goals. Therefore, this chapter provides an overview of the information needed to guide students and their transition team members in preparing for and succeeding in postsecondary educational environments. The transition from high school to adulthood tends to be a difficult time for all adolescents, but especially for many students with disabilities (Halpern, 1992; Rusch, DeStefano, Chadsey-Rusch, Phelps, & Szymanski, 1992). This process may require greater planning for students with disabilities because they may not have had the supports and experiences necessary to develop confidence, self-determination, social judgment, or self-management skills (Loewen & Iaquinto, 1990), all of which are needed to succeed in postsecondary learning environments (Webster, 2004). Actually, succeeding in postsecondary education can be hard work for anyone. For a student with a disability, it means that many things have had to fall into place. Most sources of information say that planning must begin "early," defined as late middle school or ninth grade, when high school course selection occurs (Cowen, 1993; Turner & Simmons, 1996).

Continuing education after high school is only one option that a student might choose in the developmental process toward adulthood. However, this further step along the road to lifelong learning is a positive choice for obvious academic reasons and because completion of postsecondary education and training enhances job prospects. In addition, continuing education can provide social opportunities that expand upon a student's interests and knowledge of various recreational and community activities. It also provides students with a potential postponement of adult obligations, such as complete financial independence, marriage and family, and job performance. Obtaining postsecondary education is correlated with higher income, lower rates of unemployment, and better overall quality of life (Dohm & Wyatt, 2002; Francese, 2002; Stodden, 2005). Education and a satisfying career are key means to quality of life and a desired lifestyle.

In this chapter, various postsecondary options are described with a focus on matching these settings to student strengths, needs, interests, and preferences, in addition to specific methods used to explore career options based on cultural values and beliefs. For example, a four-year college or university is just one alternative among many types of further education and training available after high school. Vocational and career/technical schools, in addition to community and junior colleges, can all lead to enhanced quality of life and a variety of rewarding employment opportunities. Postsecondary and lifelong education is broader than any specific degree or training program, and contributes to quality of life throughout adulthood in a variety of environments.

The importance of identifying goals and preparing students for postsecondary outcomes through *backward* transition planning is also examined along with coordination and with the process of bringing necessary stakeholders to the team process. Academic as well as nonacademic preparation is viewed as vital for students' success in postsecondary education and for promoting movement toward goals. Throughout the chapter, case study and student voice representations illustrate the planning involved to successfully transition to postsecondary education settings.

Student Voices

"Specifically for most of us with disabilities living independently is like taking a leap off of a cliff without a parachute because this [college] is the first time practicing true independence without the help of parents or a full time aid in the classroom. . . . Unlike our able-bodied peers who get forced to set their own alarm clock, get dressed, prepare meals, and slowly work into independence two or three years before they leave home at the start of their high school career. This is due to the inherent thought processes of our parents that their daughter or son with a disability will never leave their care."

CHARACTERISTICS OF POSTSECONDARY EDUCATION

Postsecondary Options and Career Opportunities

Students with disabilities and their transition teams should be aware of the different types of postsecondary programs that exist, as well as the differences among the types of colleges, universities, and vocational, technical, and proprietary schools. For example, four-year colleges and universities offer programs of study that lead to a bachelor's, master's, or doctoral degree, whereas junior and **community colleges** offer courses that can lead to a certificate, license, or associate's degree, for some programs taking at least two years to complete the prescribed program of study. Community colleges, which are publicly funded, offer a variety of classes, including vocational and occupational courses and have either no or low-cost tuition; whereas junior colleges are usually privately supported, more expensive, and offer a liberal arts program of study. Technical or proprietary schools can also offer certificates, licenses, and associate's degrees and focus on a particular trade or technical career. Community and technical/proprietary schools exist in or near most communities and generally require only a high school diploma or equivalent as an entrance requirement. Local colleges, both community and colleges of continuing education within universities and four-year colleges, have an additional advantage of offering opportunities for lifelong learners to explore all kinds of subject matter, thus enriching the learner's quality of life. Further information on differences among traditional postsecondary programs is shown in Table 11-1.

The purposes, programs of study, entrance criteria, and requirements for completion all vary (HEATH Resource Center, 1995, 2003) between and among the different types of settings. In addition, the individual strengths, needs, and interests of the student also will vary and educational goals may change over time. Therefore, an important step toward a successful outcome is matching the individual's overall needs and goals to the appropriate learning environment.

> **Critical Point**
> Self-determination skills are essential in order for students to clarify their preferred postschool transition outcomes.

Consider the following. Although more students continue to enroll in our nation's postsecondary institutions, roughly half will fail to graduate (Cohen & Besharov, 2002), and 43% of those who do leave with a bachelor's degree report being underemployed two years after graduation (Gray, 2002). In a survey reported in the *Chronicle of Higher Education* (Sanoff,

TABLE 11-1 Postsecondary educational options

Four-Year Colleges and Universities
Colleges provide general academic programs leading to a bachelor's degree in the arts (BA) and sciences (BS). *Universities* offer the bachelor's degree in addition to professional and graduate programs leading to advanced degrees such as a master's degree or a doctorate. Tuition, room and board, and books are generally more expensive per year than at other types of postsecondary programs (HEATH Resource Center, 1995). Some have open admissions (i.e., anyone over the age of 18 and/or with a high school diploma or GED), but most have selective admissions based on high school GPA, class rank, SAT/ACT scores, letters of recommendation, personal interviews, and other evidence of achievement (HEATH Resource Center, 1995). Ninety-five percent of public and private colleges and universities offer "remedial" courses, taken by 40 to 70% of entering freshmen (Gray, 1996), which assist students in developing compensatory skills and strategies for learning, help them to identify necessary accommodations, and to gain confidence.

Community, Junior, Vocational, and Technical Colleges
Community colleges are nonresidential institutions which offer programs less than 4 years in length, generally 2 years or less. Programs can lead to a license, a certificate, an Associate of Arts (AA), Associate of Science (AS), or an Associate of Applied Science (AAS). The cost is generally thousands of dollars less than a 4-year college and allows students to take a few selected courses in an area of interest. Most of them are open admission, but they may require students to take a placement exam (i.e., ASSET). Students who are not academically prepared may be required to take some "developmental" course work. Usually this course work prepares students for the fastest growing jobs identified by the U.S. Bureau of Labor Statistics, such as computer engineers and technicians, dental hygienists, medical technicians, and paralegals (Kent, 1997).
Technical colleges have a special emphasis on training for specific careers in technical fields such as data processing or mechanical trades. Some offer programs leading to an AA or AS degree. They often operate in conjunction with local industry, business, and public and other service organizations (Mitchell, 1997). Some programs are formally linked to programs that students begin during their last 2 years of high school. Such partnerships are frequently referred to as tech-prep, school-to-career, or two-plus-two programs.
Proprietary schools are run-for-profit institutions that offer courses in such areas as secretarial, bookkeeping, or culinary training. Credits from these programs may or may not transfer to 2- or 4-year institutions.

2006), the majority of faculty consider incoming freshmen ill-prepared in written and oral communication, and mathematics. In addition, according to data based on grades, class rank, and SAT/ACT scores, students with disabilities were "much less likely to be even minimally qualified" when compared to students without disabilities (Stodden, 2005). This is not surprising given that it has been estimated that 50% of high school students who enrolled in college did not complete an academic, nor a vocational curriculum integrated with academics (Plank, 2001). Therefore, unless a student is academically and socially prepared, as well as highly motivated to succeed, a four-year college or university may not be the appropriate choice after high school.

Critical Point
Though advanced math courses are often required for college entrance, very few high school students with disabilities are enrolled in these classes.

Another important step toward successful outcomes for students with disabilities is finding the right career—one that is both acquireable and needed by society's workforce. Labor market projections are calculated every two years and can be useful in guiding the transition team through career exploration and identifying an appropriate course of study for students. According to the projections for 2014, overall employment is expected to increase by 18.9 million jobs or 13%. This increase is similar to the previous decade's (1994–2004) increase of 16.4 million. The two fastest growing occupational groups, health care support and computer and mathematical science, are predicted to increase by 33 and 31 percent, respectively (Bureau of Labor Statistics, 2005). In addition, it is projected that an associates or bachelor's degree will be the most significant source of postsecondary education or training for 6 of the 10 *fastest growing* occupations (rate of increase) (see Table 11-2). On the other hand, short-term on-the-job training will be the most significant source of postsecondary education or training for 5 of the 10 occupations with the *largest job growth* (increase in number of jobs) (Bureau of Labor Statistics) (see Table 11-3). The fastest growing occupations and largest growth in occupations differ in that the numbers of jobs that presently exist become an important factor. For example, home health aides, considered the fasted growing occupation for 2014 is projected to create only 350,000 more jobs, whereas retail salespersons, expected to have the largest job growth, is anticipated to increase by 736,000 jobs over the next 10 years. In other words, the *fastest growing occupations* do not produce the most job opportunities in those areas. The amount of opportunity depends on the number of jobs needed to replace workers who move up, move on, or retire than by sheer growth; and, the actual number of positions that will be needed in the field.

TABLE 11-2 The 10 fastest growing occupations, 2004–2014   (Numbers in thousands)

Occupation	Employment		Change		Most significant source of postsecondary education or training
	2004	2014	Number	%	
Home health aides	624	974	350	56	Short-term on-the-job training
Network systems/data communications analysts	231	357	126	55	Bachelor's degree
Medical assistants	387	589	202	52	Moderate-term on-the-job training
Physician assistants	62	93	31	50	Bachelor's degree
Computer software engineers, applications	460	682	222	48	Bachelor's degree
Physical therapist assistants	59	85	26	44	Associate's degree
Dental hygienists	158	226	68	43	Associate's degree
Computer software engineers, systems software	340	486	146	43	Bachelor's degree
Dental assistants	267	382	114	43	Moderate-term on-the-job training
Personal and home health care aides	701	988	287	41	Short-term on-the-job training

TABLE 11-3 The 10 occupations with the largest job growth, 2004–2014 (Numbers in thousands)

Occupation	Employment		Change		Most significant source of postsecondary education or training
	2004	2014	Number	%	
Retail salespersons	4,256	4,992	736	17	Short-term on-the-job training
Registered nurses	2,394	3,096	703	29	Associate's degree
Postsecondary teachers	1,628	2,153	524	32	Doctoral degree
Customer service representatives	2,063	2,534	471	23	Moderate-term on-the-job training
Janitors and cleaners, except maids and housekeeping cleaners	2,374	2,813	440	19	Short-term on-the-job training
Waiters and waitresses	2,252	2,627	376	17	Short-term on-the-job training
Combined food preparation/serving workers, incl. fast food	2,150	2,516	367	17	Short-term on-the-job training
Home health aides	624	974	350	56	Short-term on-the-job training
Nursing aides, orderlies, and attendants	1,455	1,781	325	22	Postsecondary vocational award
General and operations managers	1,807	2,115	308	17	Bachelor's or higher degree, plus work experience

Even though many of the occupations with the *largest job growth* will not require postsecondary education, the reality of wage differentials still exists. For example, the median earnings for male workers aged 25 to 34 with a high school diploma or equivalent was $26,842, compared to over $31,000 for those with some college and over $42,000 for those with a bachelor's degree or higher. For women, the median earnings of those with a high school degree or equivalent were lower at $16,770, compared to $21,008 for some college, and $32,145 for a bachelor's or higher (Cohen & Besharov, 2002).

Postsecondary Participation and Outcomes of Students with Disabilities

Participation in postsecondary education has continued to increase over the past few decades. Based on data from 2000, it is estimated that of all undergraduate and graduate students, 9% and 6%, respectively, report having some kind of disability (National Center on Education Statistics, 2004). In addition, when comparing 15 years of the National Longitudinal Transition Study (NLTS) 1 and 2 data, the rate of postsecondary participation of students with disabilities has more than doubled—from 15% in 1987 to 32% in 2003 (see Table 11-4). The greatest growth in enrollment was at two-year or community

TABLE 11-4 Changes in postsecondary education participation since high school of youth with disabilities by type of institution

Institution type	1987	2003	% Change
Any Postsecondary Education	14.6	31.9	+17.3
2-Year College	3.6	20.8	+17.2
4-Year College	1.3	9.6	+8.3
Postsecondary Vocational/ Technical or Business School	11.7	5.9	−5.8

colleges (17% increase). In addition, youth with disabilities were also more likely to enroll in four-year institutions as shown by an increase of 8%. Unlike the enrollment reported in other types of schools, vocational, technical, and business schools decreased in their attendance of students with disabilities by nearly 6% (Newman, 2005).

Critical Point
The majority of students with disabilities going on to a postsecondary education enroll in two-year (or less) programs whereas students without disabilities are more likely to enroll in four-year programs.

As shown in Table 11–5, the kinds of disabilities reported by freshmen also has changed over the years, with learning disabilities now accounting for approximately 35% of all college students with disabilities, as opposed to 15% in 1987 (Newman, 2005). According to the NLTS2, the percentage increases from 1987 to 2003, across disability categories ranges from 3.2% (students with mental retardation) to 33% (students with visual impairments). Approximately one-third to two-thirds of each disability category were enrolled in some kind of postsecondary education in 2003, with the exception of individuals with intellectual disabilities and emotional disturbance (Newman, 2005).

In spite of the obstacles numerous students with disabilities face in attending postsecondary programs, one study showed that in some instances, students demonstrated a resiliency that enabled them to succeed on their own (Webster, 2004). Colleges and universities have made significant progress over the last 20 years to promote educational access and opportunities for students with disabilities (Rumrill, 1994); yet, availability does not guarantee access to or success in a chosen program of study (Getzel & Kregel, 1996). The increase in the number of students with disabilities who graduate from college with a bachelor's degree or higher has been less dramatic than the increase in enrollment (American Youth Policy Forum/Center on Education Policy, 2002). In addition, young adults with disabilities are less likely to persevere and complete a degree or

certificate program than their peers, and when doing so, take nearly twice as long on average than their peers (Stodden, 2005). In the past to the present day, far too many students with disabilities enter postsecondary programs with little or no preparation and a significant number of qualified students do not attend at all (*Chronicle of Higher Education*, 2006; National Center for Education Statistics, 1999a; Newman & Cameto, 1993). For example, students and their families, teachers, and agency personnel may assume that because a high school student is academically prepared for a postsecondary education, little else is needed in terms of preparation for success in a postsecondary institution (deFur et al., 1996). Furthermore, the discrepancies that exist across secondary and postsecondary environments often leave students unprepared for the higher standards imposed by postsecondary institutions (Stodden, 2006), meaning that effective transition planning must involve more than just focusing on academics.

> **Critical Point**
> The majority of students with disabilities are less likely to be even minimally qualified for admission to a four-year college, compared with their peers in the general population.

Student Voices

"When I went to camp for a week in my younger years, I got a feel of being independent without the safety net of my mother. When I was nine I took a shower only once that week because I didn't ask for one. The next year I had one every day that I was there, because even with the constant push from the greatest mother in the world, I realize that nobody is going to take care of me but me. . . . If I had been pampered and nurtured all the time while at home I wouldn't have lasted the first semester in college."

DEVELOPING A VISION FOR POSTSECONDARY EDUCATION

The process of helping a student to reach her or his postsecondary goal is grounded in the four principles of IDEA: Transition services *must (1) be based on students' strengths and needs, taking into account their preferences and interests; (2) be designed within an outcome-oriented process; (3) be a coordinated set of activities; and (4) promote movement from school to postschool activities.* These principles form the basis of assessment, curriculum, instructional methodology, experiential activities, and formative/summative evaluation

TABLE 11–5 Percentage of postsecondary enrollment by disability type, 1987 to 2003

Disability type	1987	2003	% Change
Learning Disability	15.0	34.7	+19.7
Speech/Language Impairment	24.9	42.7	+17.8
Mental Retardation	10.1	13.3	+3.2
Emotional Disturbance	13.4	21.8	+8.4
Hearing Impairment	32.4	53.1	+20.7
Visual Impairment	32.8	66.1	+33.3
Orthopedic Impairment	20.2	39.7	+19.5
Other Health Impairment	26.1	36.2	+10.1
Multiple Disabilities/ Deaf Blind	—	40.1	NA

Sources: NLTS Wave I parent interview and NLTS2 parent/youth interviews.

of the transition student's secondary education. This planning process, ideally guided by the strengths, interests, needs and preferences of students, must meaningfully include their families. Family participation in this process is crucial as families not only influence career aspirations (Super, 1990; Szymanski, 1994), but they also play a powerful role in developing future visions, which are related to career and lifestyle options (Morningstar, Turnbull, & Turnbull, 1996). Educators also must be aware of attitudes, values, and beliefs from the students' and families' cultural perspective in order to develop strategies to promote success in postsecondary educational settings (Association of Higher Education and Disability [AHEAD], 1998). For example, some cultures may value collectivism or the group more strongly than individualism (Greenfield, 1994; Kim & Choi, 1994; Luft, 2005). Therefore, focusing upon how postsecondary education could increase the status and standard of living for the extended family or group may increase the students' and families' motivation more than emphasizing the benefits to the individual.

Determining Student Strengths, Needs, Interests, and Preferences

Determining the student's strengths, needs, interests, and preferences should begin early and continue throughout the student's school career. Teachers who effectively identify students' expectations, choices, and preferences through observations, conducting interviews and assessments with the students and significant others, are more successful in facilitating a positive transition to adulthood (Wehmeyer, Agran, & Hughes, 1998). Furthermore, students must be involved in the process of choosing and researching their own career interests. The research aspects involving career choice include understanding several factors: (a) the training and education needed, (b) projected earnings, (c) expected job prospects, (d) what workers do on the job, and (e) working conditions. Information concerning these aspects can be found in books and on the Internet (e.g., The *Occupational Outlook Handbook—http://www.bls.gov/oco/home.htm*) and includes additional careers related to student's interests. This can also be helpful when expectations for future careers are either too high or too low when compared to

> **Critical Point**
> Career choices are influenced in part by exposure to a range of opportunities so students from at-risk groups may well have a narrow range of interests merely due to lack of exposure.

abilities. For example, a student interested in the medical or legal fields may only be familiar with popularized careers like "doctor" or "lawyer," not realizing that many related occupations (e.g., physician assistants, paralegals) require fewer years of education.

Although career development should begin as early as elementary school (Benz & Kochhar, 1996; Clark, Carlson, Fisher, Cook, & D'Alonzo, 1991), students should begin formally exploring the world of work no later than middle school, as they begin to discover their own talents and abilities, as well as career areas of interests or career majors. By exploring career options, reflecting upon career interests, and engaging in a gradual process of eliminating choices that are not a good fit (Lindstrom & Benz, 2002), students will be in a better position to understand what kinds of postsecondary programs can best meet their individual needs. In order for career planning to be effective, the transition team must develop partnerships among the student, educators (including career guidance services/school counselors), and community-based service providers, such as vocational rehabilitation personnel (deFur, Getzel, & Trossi, 1996). Activities that can support the career development and exploration of students include, but are not limited to: (a) career speakers, (b) job shadowing and volunteer experiences, (c) informational interviews, (d) developing career portfolios, and (e) participation in job or career fairs.

Student Voices

"My advice to perspective students is to examine and really think about what their 10-year plan is going to be for themselves, because the less time figuring out their career path the more likely they will get funding, especially if they want the government to help. So they [really need] to do research on what they want for themselves by themselves. If people tell the student what they should do, the less likely their heart will be in it to follow through. Therefore, this is a totally independent decision for the student, and once decided they should be ready to give up their whole life for their plan, which may or may not include college. Being happy in life should be the goal no matter how they get to that point."

Identifying Postsecondary Goals and Backward Planning

Since Will (1983) first defined transition as a bridge to adulthood, the main goal of the transition process has been achieving positive postschool outcomes (DeStefano & Wermuth, 1992; Halpern, 1992). In order to accomplish this successfully, goals must first be identified, along with the necessary instructional activities, supports, and services that will facilitate making those goals a reality. To identify appropriate activities, the student and his or her transition team must begin to ask questions, such as (a) what knowledge and skills are needed to make a successful transition to a postsecondary academic or technical/vocational program? (b) what knowledge and skills does the student have at present (and how will they be assessed)? and (c) what knowledge and skills does the student need to acquire? (NICHCY, 1993). As postsecondary programs build upon the skills and knowledge acquired in earlier years, planning the necessary strategies to achieve the student's ultimate goal must start early. For example, a student who does not plan ahead for a college education may have difficulty in completing all the required or recommended courses that are necessary to qualify for a four-year college or university. In addition, students may need to work on acquiring more effective independent study skills or arranging accommodations that are needed for college board or SAT testing. The key lies in the student and transition team first determining the kind of postsecondary program that best fits the student's needs and then planning backward to incorporate activities that will facilitate the achievement of that goal.

> **Critical Point**
> Counseling and access to a variety of opportunities have little impact on postsecondary outcomes unless they lead to a student-directed decision-making process.

The Case Study about Andrew illustrates how his vision of attending college became a reality as his transition team did their best to base his services on his strengths and needs, as well as his interests. As Asperger syndrome

CASE STUDY Andrew

Background. After numerous disability labels through elementary school, a move during middle school would prove to be fortuitous as his new school psychologist suspected Andrew had Asperger Syndrome. She referred him to a clinic where a diagnosis of the syndrome was made. At the start of ninth grade he was put on the medication Paxil, and began to do better in school. Though he had trouble with writing and struggled with abstract concepts, academically he became a "B" student. Social skills remained a challenge and though he made a few friends at school, his parents described them as "fellow outcasts." However, he was very comfortable with himself and seemed to enjoy spending time alone. He liked to play video games, spend time on the computer, and read about weather. These pastimes also became obsessions to the point where he would spend all his money buying computer software and books related to weather.

His transition statement at age 14 included support from special education staff for his writing difficulties, a math tutor, extended time on tests, and seeing a counselor who would try to help him talk through "social autopsies" on situations that he found challenging. For example, he had one experience in high school where he liked a girl, and she totally rebuked him. He was devastated but with the help of his counselor he began to see the part his actions played in her reaction to him. His parents felt that one of the things that helped him most in his transition to high school was being in the marching band because he had to go to the high school every day for a month before school started so he became familiar with the environment and a few friendly faces.

During high school Andrew was very involved in his transition planning. Though he did not have a specific career goal, he clearly expressed his desire to go to college and to follow a course of study that would help achieve that goal. Though he did not know what his ideal job would be, he had stated that he might want to be a paleontologist because he was always interested in rocks and digging for dinosaurs. Career exploration and testing during high school had revealed a potential strength in careers involving art, and Andrew liked to draw.

As he followed a "college prep" track in high school he did not have access to work study programs, but his transition team encouraged him to find summer and/or after-school employment. During the summer after his sophomore year, his family helped him to get a job bagging groceries at a local store. Though he got fired after only two weeks due to inappropriate social skills, it was a positive learning experience for Andrew as his parents worked with him on understanding the role his behaviors played in his dismissal. Role playing paid off as the following year he held down a job at another grocery store for the entire summer.

During his junior and senior year his transition team worked with Andrew on exploring college options. While the team encouraged him to look at community colleges, Andrew was adamant that he attend a four-year

(Continued)

institution and his parents supported his choice. He visited local four-year colleges and decided a small, private school, 30 miles from his home, was the best fit for him. Andrew knew what accommodations he needed in order to succeed in college (e.g., extended time on tests and writing papers) and that the college would accept his latest IEP as documentation of his disability. He was also aware that the accommodations would not be automatically granted to him unless he informed his professors. Therefore his teachers gave him opportunities to practice his self-advocacy skills when asking for accommodations in his high school classes.

Vision. Andrew is interested in following a course of study that will lead him to a four-year college. He is not sure what kind of career he would work toward but his interests lie with paleontology, due to his interests in rocks and dinosaurs. In addition, Andrew seems to show aptitude toward a career in art and he does enjoy drawing. His parents support his vision for college and wish for him to work toward being in social situations in order to prepare for college. They would like for him to get a summer job and perhaps join a club. He is interested in video games, computers, and the weather. He has learned how to play the clarinet and has joined the marching band. His learning needs include: extended time on tests and tutors for math and writing, and his teachers plan to allow the opportunity for Andrew to practice requesting accommodations from his high school teachers.

Summary of Performance. Before Andrew graduated from high school, his transition team developed a Summary of Performance for his postsecondary goal concerning college. They identified his present level of performance and essential accommodations needed for this goal. As seen in Figure 11–1, Andrew's team identified his accommodation needs for transitioning to postsecondary education.

Transition to College. After visiting local college campuses, Andrew chose to attend a small private school close to his home. Once on the campus, Andrew felt he could succeed without the accommodations or any help, though the office of disability services provided extra tutoring. His reluctance to self-advocate and the fact that he finally asked for tutoring too late in the semester resulted in poor grades the first semester and failing grades the second semester. Andrew's first year at college might on the surface appear to have been a failure. However, he achieved a lot through the process of transitioning to the skills involved in succeeding in college life, such as living in a dorm with a roommate, doing his own laundry, budgeting his own money, managing his time, and so on. Not only did he realize he had the ability to live independently, the experience also helped him to recognize his areas of need such as self-advocating and asking for help in a timely manner. At present Andrew is taking a course at a private learning center for adults on study strategies and organizational skills. He is also back working at the local grocery store and his parents engage him in role playing situations where he has to self-advocate. He will be starting at a local community college this coming fall, and plans to transfer to a four-year institution by his junior year.

Case Study Questions

1. List the ways in which Andrew's transition planning was based on his *strengths, needs, preferences, and interests.*
2. What aspects of his transition planning could be described as being *designed within an outcome-oriented process*?
3. With hindsight, what do you think could have been done differently by his team in terms of backward planning and activities to *promote movement from school to postschool* settings?
4. What other activities could Andrew have done to help him explore career possibilities?
5. Do you think Andrew's transition planning was a good example of how *a coordinated set of activities* can *promote movement from school to postschool activities*? Give reasons to back up your answer.

Employment and Postsecondary Goal/Outcome: Four-year college

Assessments: Achievement/Academic assessment; curriculum-based assessments; classroom` observations

Academic Content Area	Present Level of Performance (grade level, standard scores, strengths, needs)	*Essential* accommodations, assistive technology, or modifications utilized in high school, and why needed.
Reading (basic reading/decoding; reading comprehension; reading speed)	Andrew currently reads at the ninth-grade level. He has difficulty with comprehension when the material is of interest to him.	Andrew will need extended time for class examinations to improve comprehension.
Math (calculation skills, algebraic problem solving; quantitative reasoning)	Andrew currently uses a calculator to solve mathematical problems. He can apply these skills in real-life situations such as keeping a checkbook and purchasing groceries and personal items.	Andrew uses a calculator to aid in computation skills.
Written Language (written expression, spelling)	Andrew's written language assessment scores all fall within the average range.	Andrew uses spell-check when using the computer. He will also need assistance in proof-reading skills and will need additional time to complete larger projects.
Learning Skills (class participation, note taking, keyboarding, organization, homework management, time management, study skills, test-taking skills)	Andrew experiences some difficulty in organization and time management skills. He has a tendency to rush through class examinations.	Andrew would benefit from the use of a planner to keep all of his schedules, assignments, and events organized. He should also take a class focused on note-taking and test-taking skills to improve performance on examinations.

FIGURE 11–1 Summary of performance—Andrew (Case Study)

Source: This template was developed by the National Transition Documentation Summit © 2005 including representation from the Association on Higher Education and Disability (AHEAD), the Council for Exceptional Children's Division on Career Development and Transition (DCDT), and Division on Learning Disabilities (DLD), the National Joint Committee on Learning Disabilities (NJCLD), the Learning Disability Association (LDA) and the National Center on Learning Disabilities (NCLD). It was based on the initial work of Stan Shaw, Carol Kochhar-Bryant, Margo Izzo, Ken Benedict, and David Parker. It reflects the contributions and suggestions of numerous stakeholders in professional organizations, school districts, and universities, particularly the Connecticut Interagency Transition Task Force. It is available to be freely copied or adapted for educational purposes.

was not recognized as a disability in the United States until 1994, Andrew, like many other students with the syndrome, was initially misdiagnosed. However, he received the correct diagnosis by middle school and the backward planning done by his transition team, which involved outcome-oriented activities, increased the likelihood that Andrew would achieve his goals.

Students and their transition teams need to become aware of factors that will hinder or enhance a student's postsecondary choices so that they can prepare accordingly. The topics presented in the following sections of this chapter provide the reader with information and skills that have been found to assist students in being successful. Transition teams need to access curriculum resources and to develop individualized intervention plans to focus preparations upon:

1. Choosing from the many postsecondary alternatives that are available,

2. Dealing with a different legal status as a student with a disability, and
3. Spending time in activities that will be required later in college.

PREPARATION AND PLANNING FOR POSTSECONDARY EDUCATION

As the most important part of the transition team, the student must understand their role in identifying and refining their postsecondary outcomes. Students need to be pushed to *educate themselves* in order to understand the demands of their chosen goals. Numerous programs and curricula have been developed to promote such student-directed learning. One in particular is the Career and Self-Advocacy Program (CASAP), which was developed through the Center for

Innovation in Transition and Employment at Kent State University as a model demonstration project to give students, teachers, and parents the necessary resources to prepare for postsecondary education environments through a variety of activities and teaching techniques.

In this program, content enhancement strategies were utilized to create a program that would be accessible to diverse groups of students in which: (a) both group and individual needs would be met, (b) the integrity of the content would be maintained; (c) the critical features of the content would be selected and transformed in a manner that promotes student learning; and (d) instruction would be carried out in a partnership with students (Bulgren, Schumaker, & Deshler, 1994). More specifically, concept maps were used as the technique to visually depict the relationships between and within the three program units: (a) self-awareness and advocacy, (b) postsecondary options, and (c) goal setting and IEPs. Concept diagrams visualize the relationships through labeled arrows to articulate the connections. Each unit builds on the knowledge that is previously acquired through activities specifically designed to engage students in self-discovery. Because, at the heart of a successful transition to postsecondary education lies students' awareness of their strengths, rights, and responsibilities, the impact of their disability, and the ability to self-advocate. (See *http://www.ehhs.kent.edu/centers/cite/CASAP/hom.html*)

Self-Awareness and Advocacy

Self-awareness and advocacy includes: the student's awareness of strengths and needs, disability, and civil rights laws, communication skills, and personal responsibilities concerning advocacy. In all, this segment of the program has students focus on (a) how awareness of their disability translates into accommodation needs, (b) their rights as a person with a disability, and (c) how to effectively communicate their needs through self-advocacy. Following are general approaches for lessons addressing these major concepts (See Figure 11-2 for a concept map on the first unit of CASAP).

Disability Knowledge

Self-awareness begins with understanding the general definition of a disability, the range and kinds of disabilities, and their occurrence in society. However, many students remain unaware of their specific disability and how it impacts their education—usually because the subject matter is uncomfortable for parents, teachers,

and students alike. Approaching the subject of disability is a process that can include: (1) identifying notable people with disabilities, (2) defining each disability category and its occurrence, (3) discussing each student's specific disability, and (4) reframing their disability label into strengths, learning needs and accommodations.

There are many notable and famous people with disabilities, many of whom are recognized by name— including:

- Actors (Tom Cruise, James Earl Jones, Chris Burke),
- Actresses (Whoopie Goldberg, Cher, Patty Duke),
- Musicians (Ray Charles, John Lennon, Carly Simon),
- Composers (Beethoven, Handel, Tchaikovsky),
- Writers (Ernest Hemingway, Truman Capote, Emily Dickinson),
- Artists (Leonardo da Vinci, Norman Rockwell, Claude Monet),
- Athletes (Bruce Jenner, Magic Johnson, Nolan Ryan),
- Scientists (Albert Einstein, Alexander Graham Bell, Thomas Edison), and
- Politicians (Franklin Delano Roosevelt, Sir Winston Churchill, John F. Kennedy)

Students can access additional information on the Internet for more specifics on their disabilities and stories. (e.g., *http://ericec.org/fact/famous.html* and *http://www.disabilityresources.org/FAMOUS.html*).

After learning about people with disabilities they have heard of through history books, news stories, or celebrity magazines, students can learn about what each disability means and how many students are served in schools all over the United States. For example, there are 6,606,702 students aged 3–21 identified as receiving special education services. More specifically, there are 2,892,694 students with learning disabilities, 1,428,568 students with speech and language disabilities, 487,037 students with emotional disturbances, and 83,701 students with orthopedic disabilities (Twenty-Sixth Annual Report to Congress on the Implementation of the IDEA, 2004). Once students understand the basic definition of disability and their prevalence, they can focus on themselves and realize how their disability label relates to their educational programming. For example, a student whose accommodations include books on tape and tests read-aloud will better understand their needs if they recognize that they have a specific learning disability in visual processing and comprehension. The disability label

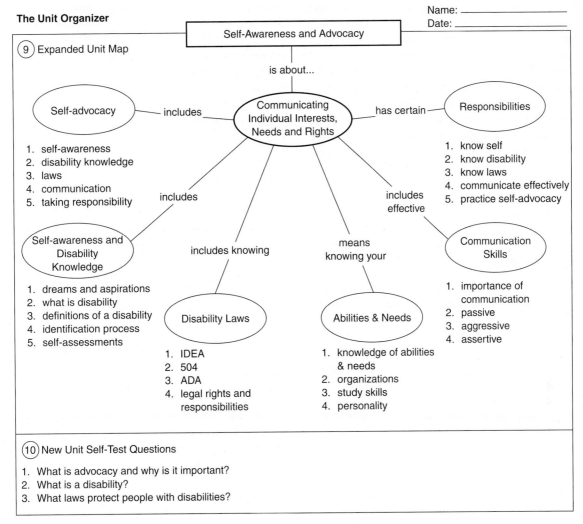

The Unit Organizer

Name: _____
Date: _____

Self-Awareness and Advocacy

(9) Expanded Unit Map

is about...

Self-advocacy —— includes —— Communicating Individual Interests, Needs and Rights —— has certain —— Responsibilities

Self-advocacy
1. self-awareness
2. disability knowledge
3. laws
4. communication
5. taking responsibility

Responsibilities
1. know self
2. know disability
3. know laws
4. communicate effectively
5. practice self-advocacy

includes

Self-awareness and Disability Knowledge
1. dreams and aspirations
2. what is disability
3. definitions of a disability
4. identification process
5. self-assessments

includes knowing

includes effective

means knowing your

Communication Skills
1. importance of communication
2. passive
3. aggressive
4. assertive

Disability Laws
1. IDEA
2. 504
3. ADA
4. legal rights and responsibilities

Abilities & Needs
1. knowledge of abilities & needs
2. organizations
3. study skills
4. personality

(10) New Unit Self-Test Questions
1. What is advocacy and why is it important?
2. What is a disability?
3. What laws protect people with disabilities?

Adapted from *The Unit Organizer Routine.* Copyrights for the template are held by the authors of The Unit Organizer Routine.

FIGURE 11–2   The unit organizer for self-awareness and advocacy

Source: From *The course organizer* by B. K. Lenz, J. B. Schumaker, D. D. Deshler, & J. A. Bulgren, 1998, Laurence, KS.: Edge Enterprises. Reprinted with permission.

then becomes the basis for understanding how they learn best and what they need to be successful in various environments.

Disability Legislation

In addition to understanding their disability, students need to be aware of the antidiscrimination laws in place to protect their rights. To be a good advocate, students, at the very least, need to know their rights and the laws that protect them. If there is not an understanding of this, students will not know if their rights have been violated, and furthermore, that there is a need to advocate for themselves. For example, if a student requests an accommodation from a professor and is refused, they need to know which law protects their accommodation needs in postsecondary environments to successfully advocate for their requests.

The three laws that students need to know include: the IDEA, Section 504 of the Rehabilitation Act, and the Americans with Disabilities Act (ADA). Under the

Individuals with Disabilities Education Act, their secondary school is responsible for identifying and assessing students with disabilities, and for providing appropriate education instruction and related services. However, IDEA does not cover students in postsecondary education—only while they are in secondary school. The students themselves become responsible for some of the services provided by their schools. The two pieces of legislation that impact postsecondary education for students with disabilities are the Rehabilitation Act of 1973 (especially section 504), and the Americans with Disabilities Act (ADA) of 1990 (See Comparison Chart at the end of the chapter). Information in comparing the legal requirements provides the necessary base for students to be knowledgeable of their rights.

Student Voices

"Advocacy to me means speaking up for oneself, knowing the rights granted to you, and making sure you get those rights. To be a good advocator for oneself you need to know about your disability and know your needs. One can't be afraid to speak for oneself if a problem comes about. If one feels they are not getting the rights they deserve they need to speak up. Knowing one's rights is important as well. If you don't know your rights how can you stand up for yourself? A self-advocator must be knowledgeable about their rights as a person with a disability."

Section 504 of the Rehabilitation Act of 1973 was the first piece of civil rights legislation for people with disabilities (Jarrow, 1992). Section 504 states that no *otherwise qualified* individual with a disability be excluded from participation in, or denied the benefits of, or subjected to discrimination under any program receiving federally funded assistance. Although colleges and universities do not have to offer special education courses, subpart E, which focuses specifically upon higher education, further requires that both public and private institutions make appropriate academic adjustments and reasonable modifications to the colleges' procedures and policies (See Table 11-6). This is to ensure that students with disabilities can fully participate in the same programs and activities that are available to students without disabilities (Flexer, 2005).

> **Critical Point**
> While disclosing a disability is a personal choice, students who choose not to disclose to their college office of disability services may not receive the accommodations and modifications to which they are entitled.

TABLE 11–6 Subpart E of Section 504

104.41 Applies to recipients of federal funds

104.42 Admissions and recruitment

- May not limit the number of persons admitted
- Nondiscriminatory criteria and test
- May not make preadmission inquiry

104.43 Treatment of students; general

- Covers overall and general discrimination
- Operaters programs in most integrated settings

104.44 Academic adjustment

- Modification to requirements to include qualified persons
- Does not apply to essential requirements
- Course examinations should reflect achievement, not disability
- Auxiliary aids must be provided to ensure access (i.e., for students with impaired sensory, manual, or speak skills)

104.45, .46, .47

- Also covered are housing, financial and employment assistance, and nonacademic services

Source: Adapted from Section 504 of Rehabilitation Act of 1973, 29 U.S.C. § 794 *et seq.*, subpart E.

Students must know the definitions of specific terms to be able to self-advocate. For example, the term *otherwise qualified* means that the person meets the requisite academic and/or technical standards required for admission to the postsecondary institution's programs and activities (Heyward, 1996). Section 504 also led to the development of disability resource programs in postsecondary institutions—which were to provide appropriate academic adjustments such as the extension of time permitted to complete a degree (Flexer, 2005). Reasonable modifications ensure that students with disabilities are not excluded or segregated from the general student population and apply to areas such as housing, financial and employment assistance, physical education and athletics, counseling, placement services, and social organizations (Flexer). The ADA upholds and extends the Rehabilitation Act's civil rights protection to all public and private colleges and universities, regardless of whether they receive federal funds (Flexer; Frank & Wade, 1993).

Student Voices

"It is my responsibility, being the person with particular needs, to make my needs known to others. It is not their responsibility to assume what I may or may not

Succeeding in College Requires More Than Mere Academics, Michelle's Story. Due to my situation, which is a so-called disability known as cerebral palsy, my schedule and life have always been very structured. Therefore, I have been forced to develop time management skills. I need assistance with daily personal hygiene and eating. I am not able to take early classes or late night classes, unless I am enrolled in the same class as my attendant. To make it easier on both of us, the attendant either works the shift before or after that class.

I have 11 personal attendants who assist me in my everyday life. It is very difficult to find people to work the early and late hour shifts, due to the fact that everyone needs sleep. We all have our own lives and I don't want to impede on other people's lives because the people who work for me most of the time are also my friends. I care about their lives as a friend and not only as an employer. Those special bonds that I form with assistants (because I need so much help with personal things) don't grow unless you are forced to work with them a lot or to take the time to spend quality time with one another. If that kind of friendship does not exist, I feel that it takes a toll on the working relationship, which leads me to my next point. I had to terminate someone's position today.

Lucky for me, I did not really consider her a close friend as of yet. It is very hard to reprimand my friends or to terminate their employment. I terminated her employment because this is the first semester she had worked for me, and she had already asked for approximately six days off, only giving me four days' notice. They were all out-of-town trips, so she knew about them ahead of time. Normally, what we do when a person wants to take off is post a note in my room and then whoever chooses can sign up to take the shift. But for some reason, this person did not understand this concept. At the beginning of every semester, I give each attendant a phone list of all the other attendants' numbers. When they want to take off, they either post a sign or call each other.

The situation today affected my time management plan for the day. That is, because I had to take time out of my schedule to e-mail several attendants to explain the situation and to find someone to fill the shifts. The person whose employment was terminated works both Saturday and Sunday mornings. That shift is really important because I need to get out of bed. For the time being, I am going on a week-to-week basis with that shift. It may get a little harder to manage my time as I get further into my college career, due to class times. However, I made it this far, so I feel that with the help of all my friends and family, I can do pretty much anything.

I do most of my homework on my computers. I am able to type myself, but only six words per minute. In order to utilize my time in a better fashion, I normally dictate to my personal attendants, while they type for me. I also have all my textbooks on audiotapes through the Library for the Blind and Dyslexic. I have a visual perception problem, which means I cannot follow one line of text. It is caused by the cerebral palsy. The muscles in my eyes are weak, so they tend to stray off the line. Sometimes bigger print helps, but not always. It depends how close the lines are to each other.

As for my books on tape, my nightly attendant shift is from 7 to 11 P.M. During that shift I have to eat dinner, dictate any typing, and take a shower. So, usually, when I have a chapter to listen to, I listen to it after my attendant leaves. I leave a little light on and over the 3 years I have been at Kent, I have programmed myself to stay awake. That is just another challenge that comes with cerebral palsy and having to manage my time. During the day, I'm able to spend up to 4 hours alone in my room, although there are always people in the hall. Those times when I'm alone in my room is another chance I get to listen to my books on tape.

During the day, I either take the vans from class to class or have my attendants walk with me. I don't like to walk by myself because of my visual perception problems. I also have trouble seeing curb cutouts and different elevations of land. Also, because I have been in an electric wheelchair since I was seven years old and drive it so much, I have developed tendonitis [sic]. Therefore, when I have an attendant with me, I normally train her to drive for me. My tendonitis [sic] has gotten worse this semester, so having someone drive for me now is basically a requirement. We all have those instructions from my physical therapist at the health center. That is another thing that I am required to fit into my schedule. I go to therapy twice a week, for an hour each session. It helps me to

(Continued)

assist my attendants when they are doing a transfer or helping to move me from one place to another. It also helps me with my stress level. A big part of cerebral palsy is something called "spasticity." It is the contraction and loosening of muscles. How tight my muscles are depends greatly on my mood or how much stress I'm under. My muscles also contract when I get excited or scared. They even contract when I just talk in general because my stomach diaphragm muscles don't work. So, it takes lots of effort to get air out. To get words out, I have to put every muscle into the effort of talking. Cerebral palsy is caused by a lack of oxygen to the brain, which occurred sometime during the birthing process. There are several different variations of it, but in my case, of course, I am not affected cognitively.

There are a lot of people on campus affected with cerebral palsy and I just happen to be one of those who are the most affected physically. To go out with friends also is hard, if I don't go out with someone who works for me, during the normal time that person is scheduled to work, or with someone who's just a friend and doesn't work for me. I have to schedule people around times when I want to have fun. This is very maddening sometimes, but it's an everyday part of life! It's also part of life that some of my friends and I can't drive. All of these things I feel and know because I live my life, and it greatly affects the way I manage my time!

Another part of managing my time in my social life is something I do with a group of friends who are known as the GPC. It stands for Gimp Power Coalition. A "gimp" is slang for someone with a physical challenge, to put it simply. I rely on this coalition throughout my everyday life at Kent to support me in any good times and bad that come along with the challenges that we have. Once a month, our GPC has a movie night; sometimes we end up watching the movies we rent and sometimes we don't because that is the one time in the month when we all get together and just talk or vent if we need to. I feel that I'm a very lucky person because I'm one of the few people whom I know is a part of two coalitions. I have a very strong GPC at home for all through school I was integrated with other people with physical challenges. Some of my friends who are part of the Kent GPC come from different backgrounds and don't have a very strong GPC at home. That is why I feel very fortunate; otherwise, I would not be able to go through my everyday life anywhere at this time in my life without being a part of either one of my GPCs. As a result, being a part of these groups is so important in my life, which is just one more thing that affects my time management in everyday life.

Case Study Question

1. Michelle graduated from Kent State so she obviously had the academic skills needed to succeed in college. Give examples of other skills, abilities, and dispositions Michelle exhibited that helped her to flourish in a postsecondary environment?

(Michelle Marcellus, Kent State University graduate/B.S Degree in Human Development and Family Studies)

need, this can lead to problems. I prefer to do as much as I possibly can for myself even if it would be easier for me to let someone else do it. I have found that the more I do for myself the better I feel about myself, and the more difficult the task, the greater the sense of accomplishment I feel. I thrive off of my challenges and my struggles and when a person attempts to help me when I haven't asked for their help I take offense to it. I know they're only trying to be helpful but in my opinion they are actually hindering me in many ways."

Self-Advocacy

Self-advocacy refers to "an individual's ability to effectively communicate, convey, negotiate or assert his or her own interests, desires, needs and rights. It involves making informed choices and taking responsibility for those decisions" (Van Reusen et al., 1994, p. 1). A vital component of advocacy then becomes the student's ability to "effectively communicate." Students must learn and understand that effective communication involves understanding their rights and responsibilities; and furthermore, communicating those rights and needs in an assertive manner. When the skills involved in self-advocacy are systematically taught and the students are given immediate and specific feedback, along with the opportunity to practice these skills in both training and natural environments, students with disabilities can acquire, maintain, and generalize these skills (Aune, 1991; Durlak, Rose, & Bursuck, 1994). For example, if the student and his or her transition team decide that the student needs extended time to complete tests, then he or she should request the required accommodation with the appropriate mainstream teacher. Roessler, Brown, and Rumrill (1998) developed a self-advocacy model students can use when requesting accommodations at both the high school and college level (see Table 11-7).

> **Critical Point**
> Self-determination in adult life is based on skills related to self-knowledge, self-acceptance, and self-advocacy.

Student Voices

"Self advocacy is something that comes with knowing yourself and taking risk to stand up for yourself. It is a process and takes time. I think self-advocacy is something that someone grows and gets better in over time.

TABLE 11–7 Preparing students with disabilities to request classroom accommodations

Step
1. Establish a good relationship; identify yourself and your relationship to the instructor.
2. Identify your disability and explain your disability in functional terms (i.e., how it affects you in the classroom).
3. Cite an accommodation(s) you've identified as effective, how it benefits you, then state that you would like to use this (these) accommodation(s) in the instructor's class.
4. Describe the resources available to assist in implementing the accommodation and what your role will be (i.e., what action you will take).
5. Ask for agreement from the instructor (i.e., I would like to use this accommodation in your class, how do you feel about that?), then confirm the agreement with an affirming statement (i.e., thanks, ok, good).
6. Restate the accommodation(s), what you will do to implement them and what the instructor's involvement and responsibility will be.
7. Finally, close with a positive statement about the class or the arrangements you've just made and express your appreciation for the instructor's time.

Sometimes it is helpful to have others as role models in self-advocating. Sometimes one is just getting taken advantage of so much and it is the last straw that there is no choice than to advocate for oneself. Besides, who knows me better than I do? Self-advocacy is sort of a neat thing, you can feel the empowerment."

Postsecondary Options

Another indicator of postsecondary success is the ability of the student and transition team to seek out the available postsecondary options, know how to access those options, and eventually select the environment that best matches their strengths and needs (See Figure 11-3). Questions to guide student thinking in this area include: (a) what are my options after high school and how to I do I research them? (b) how are college and other postsecondary education settings different from high school? and, (c) what are my career interests and how do I research them?

Postschool Options and Requirements

Before choosing a postsecondary program, students need to learn how to research their options and, more specifically, what they are looking for in a postsecondary education. Colleges vary widely in terms of their missions, admission requirements, costs, accessibility, faculty and staff, student body, courses and programs offered, community and financial resources (including opportunities for financial aid), size, location, athletics, and social activities (HEATH Resource Center, 1995; Kezar, 1997a; Scott, 1996). For example, research has suggested that a student's cognitive and academic gains are enhanced in an institution where there is greater interaction between faculty and peers and where teaching, as opposed to research, is a priority (Astin, 1993). Traditionally, faculty with a research orientation tend to be in larger public universities, which often place less emphasis on student development and undergraduate education in general (Kezar, 1997b). However, according to Kezar (1997b), many of these institutions have recently begun to focus more upon undergraduate education and student development. More important than the actual size of the university or college is the degree to

> **Critical Point**
> Students need to match their personal preferences and needs to the characteristics of the institution, for example, students with physical disabilities may benefit from a campus that does not have environmental barriers.

The Unit Organizer

Name: _____
Date: _____

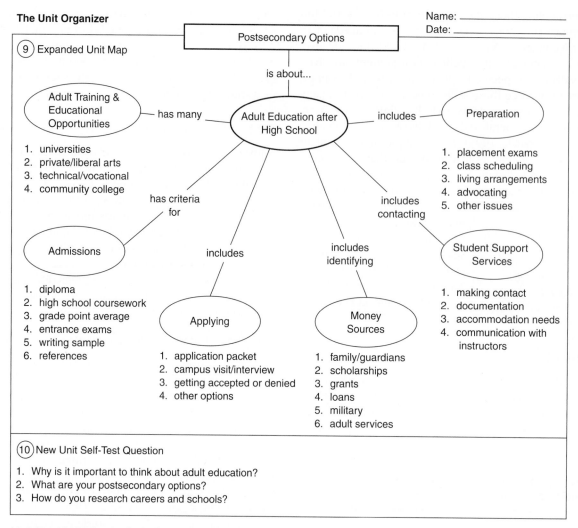

⑨ Expanded Unit Map

Postsecondary Options

is about...

Adult Education after High School

— has many — Adult Training & Educational Opportunities

1. universities
2. private/liberal arts
3. technical/vocational
4. community college

— includes — Preparation

1. placement exams
2. class scheduling
3. living arrangements
4. advocating
5. other issues

has criteria for — Admissions

1. diploma
2. high school coursework
3. grade point average
4. entrance exams
5. writing sample
6. references

includes — Applying

1. application packet
2. campus visit/interview
3. getting accepted or denied
4. other options

includes identifying — Money Sources

1. family/guardians
2. scholarships
3. grants
4. loans
5. military
6. adult services

includes contacting — Student Support Services

1. making contact
2. documentation
3. accommodation needs
4. communication with instructors

⑩ New Unit Self-Test Question

1. Why is it important to think about adult education?
2. What are your postsecondary options?
3. How do you research careers and schools?

Adapted from *The Unit Organizer Routine*. Copyrights for the template are held by the authors of The Unit Organizer Routine.

FIGURE 11–3   The unit organizer for post secondary options

Source: From *The course organizer* by B. K. Lenz, J. B. Schumaker, D. D. Deshler, & J. A. Bulgren, 1998, Laurence, KS.: Edge Enterprises. Reprinted with permission.

which a student participates in clubs, organizations, and activities and the ties they develop with a specific department (Pascarella & Terenzini, 1991). Research has also shown that one of the strongest predictors of a student's satisfaction with his or her postsecondary experience is leaving home to attend college (Astin), as students living away from home tend to be more involved in their campus activities.

Postsecondary programs and institutions vary in their specific entry requirements, which is why it is important for students to establish links early with the prospective institution's postsecondary personnel. Additionally, it is important to start planning for high school classes toward the end of middle school or junior high so that the student will have a greater opportunity to complete all the necessary courses needed to qualify for the postsecondary program of their choice. Therefore, the transition team should work with the school guidance counselor to ensure that the student takes the appropriate required and elective courses that are needed to meet the student's postschool goals. A typical college preparatory curriculum required for admission to most four-year institutions includes: four years of English/literature, three years each of mathematics, science, and social sciences, two years of a foreign language, one or two years of the arts, and one to three years of appropriate electives (e.g., economics, psychology, statistics, computer science) (HEATH Resource Center, 1997).

Differences between High School and College

As students study their various postsecondary options, they need to become aware of the ways in which the various postsecondary environments differ from one another and from the high school environment. Understanding the performance expectations of the individual in postsecondary environments forms the basis for additional transition goals. An example of differences between high school and college demands is shown in Table 11–8.

Support services are available, but students will have to know what each school offers and how to access the various resources. The students need to understand that they will no longer have a team guiding them; will probably not have an IEP (Individualized Education Program, although some colleges do provide these); may have to pay for extra help, such as tutoring services; and will need to understand all the other differences between their current environment and the various postsecondary settings available.

Many school systems destroy records of special testing once a student graduates from high school. Therefore, in order to provide documentation of their disability to colleges and adult service providers, students need to not only request those records, including a Summary of Performance as outlined in IDEA, but also need to make sure they complete an assessment battery shortly before leaving high school. If the testing is relevant and current, colleges may accept the documentation, hence saving the cost of a private evaluation.

> **Critical point**
> It is best to check with the postsecondary institution(s) the student plans to attend to see what types of documentation they require.

Although legally all colleges and universities must provide access and reasonable accommodations, students must understand that the ways in which the services are provided can vary greatly among institutions (HEATH, 1997; Scott, 1996). These services range along a continuum from those where services are practically nonexistent to campuses that offer extensive, comprehensive services (Brinckerhoff, McGuire, & Shaw, 2002; Scott, 1996). Some colleges offer "college experience" summer programs for high school students with disabilities (HEATH Resource Center, 2003; Serebreni, Rumrill, Mullins, & Gordon, 1993) in addition to summer orientations for incoming freshmen (Scott, 1996). As postsecondary institutions and programs can differ in a variety of ways, as can the individual student's strengths, interests, and needs, the key lies in finding a good match between the two.

> **Critical Point**
> Public two- and four-year colleges are more likely to provide a service or accommodation for students with disabilities than their counterparts in the private sector, as are medium- and larger-sized institutions compared to smaller ones.

Students must be knowledgeable about their legal rights and aware of the mandated services available for them in order to have a more realistic expectation about what kinds of help they may expect in college. For transition planning purposes, it is important for students to contact the office for students with disabilities at each school that they may be considering in order to determine the best fit. The Council for the Advancement of Standards in Higher Education (Miller, 1997) described the mission of disability support service programs as being twofold:

1. Assurance that qualified students with disabilities have equal access to all institutional programs and services.
2. Advocate responsibly the needs of students with disabilities to the campus community.

The array of services to students, staffing patterns, and the degree of administrative support varies widely among programs in higher education. One issue common to all colleges is that their requirement to provide disability-related services begins when students request services. Types of services and accommodations specifically for students with disabilities can include: (a) summer or presemester specialized orientation programs; (b) individualized counseling and advising; (c) priority registration and/or reduced course loads; (d) course substitutions, course waivers, and modified materials, program, or degree requirements; (e) taped textbooks, lectures, and the allowance of

TABLE 11–8 Differences between high school and college

	High School	College
Responsibility	Teachers, counselors, and principals are responsible for providing students with support services.	The student is responsible for requesting assistance and advice when needed.
Class time	Students sit in class for 6 hours per day for 180 days, which totals 1,080 hours per year.	Students sit in class 12 to 15 hours per week, 15 weeks per semester. This totals about 450 hours per school year.
Tests	Tests are given weekly or at the end of a chapter, and quizzes are given frequently.	There will be fewer tests, 2 to 3 each semester per class and they will cover more material, perhaps 4 to 6 chapters.
Study time	Homework ranges between 1 to 3 hours per day.	A general rule of thumb is at least 2 hours of homework for every hour spent in class; 3 to 5 hours of homework daily.
Knowledge acquisition	Information is provided mostly through in-class resources, assigned reading, and classroom discussion. Out-of-class research is minimal.	Course work requires more library work and writing; longer papers are required as well as research.
Assignments	Assignments are broken down into step-by-step tasks.	Instructions may be less specific and some may only be given on the syllabus at the beginning of the semester. Students decide how they will complete the task.
Grades	Classroom attendance and participation contributes to grades with numerous quizzes, tests, and homework assignments. Class may be changed for some students with IEPs.	Grades are based on fewer tests and assignments. Attendance is not always a requirement. Students may need a certain GPA to move ahead. All students meet same class standards.
Teachers	Teachers often take attendance, check notebooks, put information on the chalkboard. They monitor progress and will offer assistance when needed. They directly impart knowledge and facts.	Instructors often lecture nonstop and do not always teach from the text. Students are expected to learn from outside readings and research. Students monitor their own progress and need for help.
Parent role	Parents are often advocates and work with teachers and counselors to assure the student is being supported academically.	Parent is a mentor and works with the student to offer support and guidance.
Freedom	Much of the student's time is structured by parents, teachers, and other adults.	Students structure their own time among academics, work, and extracurricular activities. They make their own decisions about schedules, class attendance, and studying.

Source: Adapted from: Mackillop, J. (1996). *Ladders to success: A student's guide to school after high school.* Puget Sound, WA: Puget Sound Educational Service District.

tape recorders in the classroom; (f) services of adjunct personnel such as notetakers, proofreaders, typists, readers, interpreters, mobility guides; (g) alternative testing accommodations such as untimed, individualized, or oral examinations; (h) assistance with study skills, self- and time management; (i) adaptive and regular technological assistance (e.g., calculators, Braille devices, reading machines, computer keyboard modifications, augmentative communication devices, modified word processors, modified telephones); and (j) accessibility adjustments, such as the removal of architectural barriers, designed parking areas, transportation assistance, and barrier guide sheets (Gajar, 1998, p. 391).

Students with disabilities should know that institutional resources that are available to all students also may be of benefit to them. For example, offices of career services can assist students in defining and accomplishing personal and academic goals through career counseling, occupational information, including internships and part-time jobs, job placement and referral, assistance with résumés and on-campus interviews, information on graduate schools and programs, and services specifically designed for students with disabilities. In addition, many other resources are available on most campuses that can provide valuable resources such as academic advising, counseling services, learning assistance centers, office of student activities, office of financial aid, and student orientation programs.

> **Critical Point**
> While almost all postsecondary programs enrolling students with disabilities provide supports to help them succeed, the range of services differs among various postsecondary settings on a continuum from minimal to extensive.

Many life skills are developed at college.

Finding the Right Fit

High schools are called upon to provide instructional programs and career guidance and planning that will result in assisting students in determining a career major that integrates academic and occupational content, with a view to enhancing the students' chances of succeeding in postsecondary programs and future employment (Benz & Kochhar, 1996). Students need to have the opportunity to combine academics with career exploration activities such as:

- Service learning programs that provide community service in nonpaid voluntary positions.
- Job shadowing where the student can get a more realistic view of the essential functions of occupational areas of interest.
- Work experience opportunities where the student works at a particular job for a set period of time, generally two to six weeks.
- A part-time or summer job, which also can teach the student responsibility, reliability, and interpersonal skills, as well as provide a way to save and learn how to manage money for college.

Student Voices

"I am puzzled as to why information related to disabilities is not included in the freshman orientation class. This would be a great way to integrate both those with and without disabilities and increase awareness of the barriers that both groups face, as nondisabled people are crippled by their ignorance as well as their prejudice. Those of us with disabilities struggle with self-esteem and self-confidence issues that can easily be made worse by the negative attitudes of others."

- Informational interviews where the student meets with people working in careers in which the student has expressed an interest.
- Establishing mentors and networks in the local business community as well as encouraging the student to discuss career options with family and friends.
- Working with school guidance or career counselors who should have access to a variety of career interest inventories and vocational assessments.
- Using the Internet and school and public libraries as a resource that can provide information on a variety of careers and the latest trends in the labor market, as well as describe different types of college programs.
- Developing a career portfolio.
- Linking student's hobbies or leisure activities to potential careers.
- Exploring postsecondary programs that offer internships that provide limited intensive learning experience outside the traditional classroom and/or cooperative education programs that work with students, faculty, and employers to help students clarify career and academic goals and expand classroom studies by participating in paid, practical work experiences.

In addition to the various career interest inventories and strategies for career exploration, a vocational assessment also can aid students in deciding upon an appropriate postsecondary program to facilitate their future employment goals.

Choosing a college is similar to the process of choosing a career. The student studies the options and alternatives in terms of their transition goals and other individual considerations. A student's motivation, interactions with faculty and other students, and involvement in campus activities have a greater impact upon educational outcomes than the type of program one chooses (Kezar, 1997a; Tinto, 1993). Although selecting a school depends on the student's interests, strengths, and needs, some may better provide the types of environments in which an individual will thrive and succeed. Many high schools have college counselors who may assist the student and his or her team in choosing a postsecondary school. The key is

finding a good match between the setting and the individual.

Awareness of the types of postsecondary options available and the demands of college life are important to provide an outcome-based transition program for students with disabilities. Additional activities that can facilitate the understanding of this information can include visiting Internet sites dedicated to preparing all students for postsecondary education. For example, the Kuder Career Planning System (*http://www.kuder.com*), utilizes online assessments for career exploration and links to colleges and universities nationwide; FastWeb (*http://www.fastweb.com*), which links its users to over 1.3 million scholarships; and E-Campus Tours (*http://www.ecampustours.com*), where students can view actual college campuses and surrounding areas on the internet. With this background knowledge in place, the transition team, including the student, can begin the process of devising a secondary curriculum that fits the chosen goal. Initially, selected goals may change or be modified along the way, but team members continue to have in mind what choices are available.

> **Critical Point**
> As many postsecondary professors and instructors are unfamiliar with various types of accommodations, students who have the knowledge and ability to self-advocate will be more likely to get their needs met.

Student Voices

"Any student with a disability (or disabilities) should meet up with a student with similar disabilities at that college. I feel it is important to talk to a mentor as much as possible so that the high school student would get the understanding and impression of what it is like to go to college there. In order to make a successful transition, he/she might want to stay at the college for a weekend and 'shadow' the individual around for like maybe one or two days' worth of classes and see what it's like. Then, the student would be able to have a better understanding of what the college will provide in terms of their disability. The student should also meet with the director of SDS and talk about what kind of accommodations would be provided. Be sure to have on hand documentation or any medical records and notes from the doctors."

Participation in Goal Setting and IEPs

A students' active participation in the team process is central to transition planning and decision making (see Figure 11–4), especially if students' needs and interests are to be taken into account. Students should be able to answer questions concerning, (a) their IEP, and (b) their goals, and (c) how they plan to reach their goals.

Far too often students become the passive recipient of instructions and services and have no role in determining their learning needs and goals, or in evaluating their progress (Van Reusen & Bos, 1994). The disservice this does to students who will soon find themselves in a postsecondary program cannot be overstated. At the postsecondary level, the students themselves bear a significant responsibility for the impact of their own college experience (Pascarella & Terenzini, 1991) and, therefore, students who have taken a more active role in their high school education will be in a better position to succeed in a postsecondary program. The different social, academic, and independent living expectations demanded in most postsecondary settings (Shaw et al., 1991) means that students who are college-bound, for

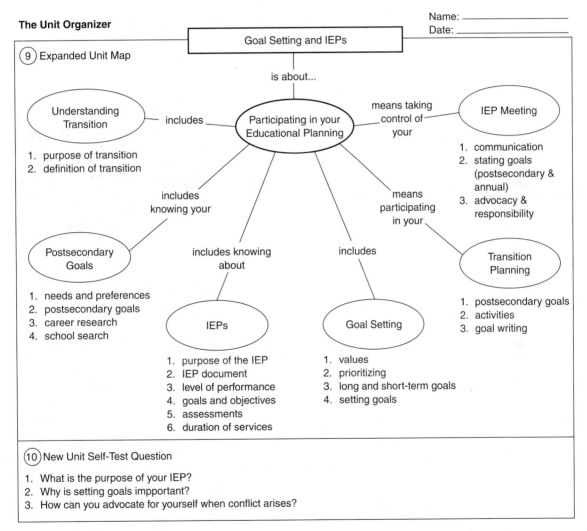

Adapted from *The Unit Organizer Routine.* Copyrights for the template are held by the authors of The Unit Organizer Routine.

FIGURE 11–4 The unit organizer for goal setting and IEPs

Source: From *The course organizer* by B. K. Lenz, J. B. Schumaker, D. D. Deshler, & J. A. Bulgren, 1998, Laurence, KS.: Edge Enterprises. Reprinted with permission.

example, will require more than just academic preparation to meet the challenges that lie ahead. Becoming actively involved in the transition process provides an ideal venue for students to become knowledgeable about the functional limitations of their disability; to develop a sense of independence and perseverance; and to engage in problem solving, which is essential in developing the crucial skills of self-determination and self-advocacy (deFur et al., 1996); as well as greater self-discipline and self-management (Shaw et al., 1991). If students are to succeed in postsecondary programs, they must be provided with the appropriate training that will enhance their skills in self-determination, identifying postschool goals, and choosing appropriate educational experiences (Aune, 1991; Halpern, 1994; Sitlington & Frank, 1990).

Participation in meaningful transition planning and student satisfaction with school instruction is a strong predictor of participation in postsecondary education (Halpern et al., 1995). The challenge is then to get students participating in a meaningful way by giving them the opportunity to state their interests and preferences concerning their postsecondary goals. In order to do this, students need to understand the IEP and transition planning process, goal setting, and their IEP meeting. First, students must have guidance in reading through and understanding their IEP and its various parts (i.e, vision, present levels of performance, transition outcomes, and annual goals and objectives). They are then in a better position to find out what the team presently considers their strengths, areas of need, goals, and accommodations.

Once students have this opportunity to understand the IEP process, or at the very least, what their document says, they can begin to offer their input into their IEP, including postsecondary goals. This next step should include students writing their own goals based on their transition interests. They know what outcomes interest them and must choose and prioritize the necessary educational activities to gain the knowledge and experiences needed. For example, a student with a transition outcome of *going to a university*, might choose activities related to *taking college entrance exams* or *getting a job to save money* for college. At this point, the student has the opportunity to create their own long- and short-term goals, which should be included in their IEP and transition document. A long-term goal for taking college entrance exams could be *to study and do well on the ACT or SAT*. Examples of short-term goals could then include: *to find out when and where to take the exam* or *how to request needed accommodations*.

If they choose the activity to get a summer job to start saving money, the long-term goal could be to *get a job to save money*, with short-term goals of *filling out applications* or *opening a savings account*. By having students write their own goals, they will have more of an understanding of their education and the IEP process. Furthermore, they can then learn how to develop timelines for their goals, how to evaluate their progress, and how to adjust their goals as needed. The skills will serve them well in postsecondary settings.

> **Critical Point**
> As of October 2003, scores from the SAT test no longer indicate whether or not a student used accommodations on the exam.

By providing opportunities for students to make meaningful choices and to demonstrate preferences in what, how, and why they learn, students can acquire the skills of self-determination (Aune, 1991; Halpern, 1994; Sitlington & Frank, 1990) that are crucial for success in postsecondary education. For example, research suggests that when learners are provided a rationale for why they are learning, student motivation and participation in activities increases (Deci & Chandler, 1986). Participation in meaningful transition planning and student satisfaction with school instruction is a strong predictor of participation in postsecondary education (Halpern, Yovanoff, Doren, & Benz, 1995). Although the mere physical presence of students at their IEP meetings may meet the statutory requirements of IDEA on its own, it fails to meet either the spirit or the intent of IDEA (Wehmeyer & Ward, 1995), which calls for student participation to the greatest extent possible.

In summation, active participation in and responsibility for developing transition goals will increase the opportunity for students (1) to become knowledgeable about the functional limitations of their disability; (2) to develop a sense of independence and perseverance; (3) to engage in problem solving and conflict resolution; (4) to develop self-advocacy and self-determination skills (deFur et al., 1996); and (5) to develop greater self-discipline and self-management skills (Shaw, Brinkerhoff, Kistler, & McGuire, 1991).

> **Critical Point**
> Persistence is an essential component of self-determination.

Another way to involve students in their IEP meetings includes the use of transition powerpoint presentations. The TPP offers various levels of participation for the student at their IEP meeting. They can present the TPP, hand it out to the team to read on their own, or show it to their parents and teachers prior to the meeting. The essential aspects needed on the TPP include:

- Career interests (amount of education needed, salary, job outlook, and skills needed);
- Training/education interests (school name, admissions requirements, disability services information, and tuition);
- Transition outcomes (for employment and postsecondary, independent living, and community participation domains);
- Long- and short-term goals related to transition outcomes (for each of the transition domains); and
- Accommodation needs.

Student Voices

In her PowerPoint, one student described what she had learned to conclude her experience in CASAP: "I've learned a lot during these three weeks, about the many options I have after high school, they are called postsecondary options, I learned a lot about my IEP which helped me better understand my settings in school, why things are the way they are in school, I learned about my rights, and how they protect me in many ways, I learned a lot about what types of careers I want to proceed in, and how, and what I have to do to achieve a good status in them, I've learned that there are lot more people with "disabilities" than I thought there were so now, I don't have to feel alone, and that there are A LOT of people willing to help me in a situation if I need it. I learned a lot about self advocacy, and how to better use it to my power to get the help that I need. I learned about the three most important rights that protect me as a person with a disability. Now mind you this is most definitely not all I've learned but, these are the main things that will stick out to me for a very long time." Examples of PowerPoints can be seen at the CASAP website.

Student participation is essential to successful planning for postsecondary outcomes. *A Student's Guide to the IEP* provides a workbook that walks students through the process of understanding the IEP, their disability, and how to participate in their planning meetings (National Information Center for Children and Youth with Disabilities, 2002; *http://www.nichcy.org*). Students cannot be expected to take over their IEP meetings without years of preparation. They can, however, be expected to participate by initially attending; and then, increasing

their level of participation as they mature and become better aware of their strengths, interests, needs, and preferences. In order to fully prepare students for their postsecondary goals, transition planning in the areas of disability awareness, advocacy, goal setting, and career exploration must begin during the middle school years, if not earlier.

Student Voices

"Self-advocacy is something that needs to be taught to us long before we reach college. It should begin at around 14 years of age when we are *supposed* to become an active participant in our IEP meetings. Unfortunately, most school administrations and other involved professionals . . . and parents . . . pay mostly lip service to this 'ideal' situation. Most people with disabilities sit in those meetings while everyone else decides our fate. This encourages and perpetuates 'learned helplessness.' Then, we reach college . . . or the workforce . . . and have no idea what to do, let alone how to do it!"

> **Critical Point**
> Students who are more self-determined in high school are more likely to be employed (and at a higher rate of pay) after high school than students who were less self-determined.

ENHANCING SUPPORTS AND SERVICES FOR DIVERSE STUDENTS

Specialized Programs in Postsecondary Education

Traditional routes to postsecondary education tend to only include two- and four-year programs and technical/vocational programs, when opportunities also exist out of the typical academic college path (Payne, 2001). The NLTS2 found that 13% were students classified as having intellectual disabilities and 40% as having multiple disabilities and/or deaf-blindness went on to a postsecondary education after leaving high school (Newman, 2005), showing in a dramatic increase from earlier data. In one study of students with intellectual disabilities who attended a community college, Page and Chadsey-Rusch (1995) found that although the students had not made significant academic gains, they had achieved interpersonal and social benefits, such as enhanced self-esteem.

An increasing number of community and technical colleges are creating high schools on their campuses that support and accelerate the transition to college through a blend of secondary and postsecondary coursework. Many of these "middle colleges" focus on helping at-risk students, including those with disabilties make successful transitions to postsecondary education (Kazis & Liebowitz, 2003). One such program is the Washtenaw Technical Middle College (WTMC) in Ann Arbor, Michigan. The WTMC is a Michigan Public School Academy chartered by and located on the campus of Washtenaw Community College. The program is a skill-based educational program, in which students acquire academic and life management skills, rather than accumulating high school credits. Students who graduate from WTMC receive their diploma and a certificate or associate's degree from Washtenaw Community College.

Examples of specialized programs are Taft College and Monterey Peninsula College, both part of the California Community College system, offer a range of courses for students with developmental disabilities (Mertz, 1997). Taft's "Transition to Independent Living Program" offers a residential 22-month independent living skills curriculum (i.e., managing money, self-advocacy, and building and maintaining relationships) in conjunction with working on campus and participating in campus activities. Students are eligible for graduation when they complete the required course work and independently demonstrate their acquired skills. In addition, upon graduation, program staff assists the students in transitioning into independent living in their home community.

Landmark College, a private coeducational institution in Putney, Vermont, specializes in serving students with dyslexia, attention deficit hyperactivity disorder (ADHD), and other specific learning disabilities (SLD). It is one of the only accredited schools in the United States designed exclusively for students with disabilities. It offers noncredit foundational courses along with an associate of arts (AA) degree in General Studies and Business Studies; and has articulation agreements with a variety of four-year colleges. Nearly half of Landmark's incoming students start with noncredit skills development courses (i.e, writing, reading, communication, study skills), with most moving into credit courses after one to two semesters.

Some four-year colleges also offer specialized programs for students with disabilities, such as Lesley College's Threshold Program (a residential program in Cambridge, Massachusetts, for students with severe learning and cognitive disabilities). The nondegree program aims to develop the skills that are necessary for independent living through practical courses and field placements in the areas of early childhood and human and business services. Others, such as Beacon College in Leesburg, Florida, offer students with learning disabilities the opportunity to earn AA and BA (bachelor of arts) degrees in Human Services and Liberal Studies (Mertz, 1997).

Although not commonplace, many four-year colleges and universities have comprehensive programs designed for students with disabilities, such as Ohio State University; Southern Illinois University at Carbondale; Wright State University, Ohio; the University of Minnesota; and Ball State University, Indiana (HEATH Resource Center, 1995; Scott, 1996). These programs include services such as independent tutoring in content areas or study and organizational and time management skills, which are beyond those the institution is required to provide under Section 504 or ADA. In addition, there are a growing number of non-degree college-based transition programs for students with cognitive disabilities, such as the College Campus Based Transition Program at Buffalo State College. This program is a collaborative effort between Buffalo Public School, the college, and parent groups, and serves students who have completed their high school education but are still eligible for public school services until the age of 21. Students receive their education in inclusive college settings with their nondisabled peers. Similar programs can be found at many community colleges throughout the country as well.

> **Critical Point**
> Specialized programs in community, vocational and technical schools, and colleges are also available as postsecondary options for students with disabilities.

College guidebooks such as *Peterson's Colleges and Programs for Students with Learning Disabilities* (Mangrum & Strichart, 1997) and the *K & W Guide to Colleges for the Learning Disabled* (Kravets & Wax, 1999) can assist the transition team in finding specialized postsecondary programs.

Student Voices

"... understanding by the teacher not only helps the student academically by having the extra time and use of special services, but it also helps the student integrate socially within the class time. An example of this is my 10th grade English class when I first received my Liberator, and the beginning of my continuing 'motor mouth' habit. So I was typing out every answer in the discussion of the classic epic *Beowulf,* and the first few classes it was hard to get time to fully answer the questions partly because of me getting use to presetting my answers before raising my hand. Also, in part, for everyone, including myself, getting used to me having a voice. Because, before that I had a bliss board which is just a monopoly board covered with 500 words where I had to point and have the person follow building the sentences as they went along. Using the bliss board was very frustrating during class discussions because someone had to come over to see what I was saying, and if [they] got it the first time and kept up with my hand speed it was a miracle. So after two weeks of having the Liberator in school, I learned how to type my answers in before raising my hand and all my [teachers] adapted to calling on me to give answers. My teacher Ms. Barr especially integrated me and my new-found voice into the flow of the discussions by lingering on the subjects a little longer when she sees me frantically typing. She asked me questions more than two times unlike most of my other teachers did or still do. When I [was] going to say her name I always used one 'r' to pronounce it right, but one day of class I wasn't thinking and I put the extra 'r' in the name, and when I spoke I said 'Hey, Ms. Bear,' and the whole class burst out laughing at how I said her name using my Liberator. Everybody started calling her 'Ms. Bear,' and it made me feel so good to hear the whole class, including the teacher, incorporate me into the personality of the class."

> **Critical Point**
> Students with disabilities may need access to instruction in social/interpersonal relationships in an inclusive environment.

First Generation and Rural College Students

First-generation college students (i.e., the first person in the family to attend college) are growing in number (Mitchell, 1997) as the need for an education beyond high school is reflected in the current labor market. Many of these students come from ethnic minority and working-class families (Fox et al., 1993). For all students, making it through the first year is critical to college success and eventual graduation. For students with disabilities who are the first-generation college students, the challenges are greater, as many are less academically and psychologically prepared for college than their peers from college-educated families (Mitchell, 1997). According to Mitchell, some challenges facing the first-generation college students include effectively balancing their time between school and work (as many come from low-income families and must work out of necessity); lack of skills in time management, budgeting, and dealing with education bureaucracies; and the tension created between the student and his or her family and friends who may have difficulty in understanding the demands and rewards of college. In order to aid the transition of these students, parents need to become familiar with the academic, financial, and social demands of higher education. In addition, the transition team should investigate bridge programs (which involve partnerships among high schools, community colleges, and universities) and other services such as special tutoring, counseling, mentoring, and peer support programs that are designed to facilitate the success of first-generation college students. School guidance counselors, as well as colleges, will have information on programs offered to this population of students.

Student Voices

"A mentoring program would help a number of incoming students with disabilities. I keep looking back and telling myself that if I had a mentor of any kind when I first came to college I would not have had such a dramatic first year. I could have used a mentor to help me to better understand college life. I am the first one in my family to come to college and I had no idea what to expect. To make a long story short I had a long and terrifying year at college. But I survived and I am still here. If I can help in any way to prevent this kind of experience for another student I will help in any way possible."

While students from rural communities also may face similar types of challenges to those of first generation students, researchers have primarily focused on employment and service provision issues rather than transition into postsecondary education (Clary, 2001).

Fitcher (1991) proposed several reasons for this limited attention given to rural issues, including (a) urban problems seem so much bigger, with greater support to a much larger segment of the population; (b) the problems of rural America as portrayed by the media seem vague and of little relevance to most Americans, who themselves have only a rudimentary knowledge of rural America; (c) rural problems often are characterized by the unique factors of a particular locale, thus the similarities and interconnectedness of rural problems often go unnoticed.

While definitions of rural vary somewhat, all are characterized by fewer people living in a particular geographic area. It is important to realize that there is a wide array of rural subcultures and rural geographic traits that, in turn, impacts the educational systems of their respective communities (Helge, 1984a; Khattri, Riley, & Kane, 1997). Helge (1984b) noted that designing educational services depends on the consideration of such factors as geographic and climatic barriers, language, population scarcity, cultural diversity, economic lifestyles, and the relationship of the school district to external sources of funding.

The majority of jobs in rural areas are changing; as in most other jobs, they now require skills beyond those acquired by high school graduates (HEATH Resource Center, 1996). Too often rural high school students face limited access to information on postsecondary options. In addition, research has shown that students with disabilities in rural areas frequently must deal with fear, low aspirations, attitudinal barriers such as low expectations from parents, teachers, and the community; lack of counseling and information; lack of family support (and at times family opposition); rural ecology issues such as geographic location, transportation needs, proximity to postsecondary institutions; and need for financial assistance (Clary, 2001; HEATH Resource Center, 1996). To overcome these barriers, the transition team should address the same principles of good transition planning previously discussed in this chapter, in addition to educating students and families about and encouraging them to pursue postsecondary options. For example, many community and technical colleges are taking advantage of distance learning technologies to give students in geographically isolated communities the opportunity to participate in technical courses where they can receive both high school and college credits. Additional recommendations include: developing a parent network; holding parent/ student transition planning events with appropriate guest speakers; providing opportunities for students to acquire experience with adaptive/assistive technology; sponsoring field trips to postsecondary institutions for students with disabilities; and creating mentor programs that pair rural students with college students or college graduates (either in person, as pen pals, or through e-mail connections) (Clary, 2001; HEATH Resource Center, 1996).

> **Critical Point**
> The majority of school districts are located in rural areas of the country.

CONCLUSION

Transition planning for college is really a subset of planning for adult life because postsecondary education is not an end in itself; it is one choice that a student might make in preparing her- or himself for adulthood. If students and their families are to make informed choices, they must be aware of the options and the pros and cons of the various options, and be given opportunities for making meaningful choices based on a self-knowledge of their strengths, interests, and needs. With appropriate preparation and continuing supports, postsecondary education provides an extended educational opportunity for developing social, interpersonal, and cognitive problem-solving skills, as well as academic and career skills that are becoming increasingly necessary in today's society for *all* our citizens.

Student Voices

"We should learn to examine our disability and accept its limitations within our particular culture and society . . . learning to celebrate what we do have . . . our differences . . . without humiliation . . . without trying to fit into the mainstream . . . to celebrate our piece of the mosaic is what empowerment is all about. I would never accept an operation to be 'normal' . . . to have a slight chance of thinking and processing information like the nondisabled . . . I like the kaleidoscope in my head . . . differences are essential to beauty."

This final case study illustrates Michelle's transition planning as it led her to college. She discusses the various activities and people that were helpful as she prepared for postsecondary education.

Transitioning to College

From kindergarten to my freshman year in high school, I was bussed to a school system away from my home district as it was part of a local consortium of districts. However, even though I had the opportunity to move back to my home school in the seventh grade I chose to stay where I was because I had such a great support system in Parma. Then at the end of ninth grade Parma decided they weren't going to service any of us who lived out of district anymore. The explanation was that we cost too much money, which was nonsense because each school district paid into the consortium at Parma. In spite of this uprooting, the move to North Olmsted went relatively smoothly. Also, I had a few friends that were in the same predicament I was and we all transferred schools together. I had the same special ed teacher, all four years of high school, Mrs. Roberts. She moved with us and that made the transition easier. She has been quite an influential person in my life.

In my junior year I was fully included in general ed classes, except for math and that was mostly because I needed someone to be my hands. My senior year was spent in general ed classes and I was one of a selected group of students to be involved in the nationally recognized Student Involvement through Educational Service (S.I.T.E.S) program. It is something like a work study program but instead of working for money, students volunteer at different places throughout the community like schools, hospitals, nursing homes, and even NASA. I fully credit Mrs. Roberts in talking me into joining S.I.T.E.S. The educational basis of the S.I.T.E.S. program was supported by a U.S. Government class and an English class taught by the advisors of the program.

Through S.I.T.E.S., I was lucky enough to work with my 4th grade teacher from the Parma schools, Mrs. Murphy. She also made the transition with the consortium to North Olmsted, but with elementary students. I loved becoming a role model for her students! It was also pretty cool for me to get to know Mrs. Murphy again, this time with the point of view of a young adult working side by side with her, as a help in her classroom. I was a member of Mrs. Murphy's first class out of college. Through all my years of school Mrs. Murphy was always my favorite teacher. When I had the opportunity to spend time with her and her students, I truly saw what a great teacher she was/is! They liked me so much [they] asked me to come back for the second semester so I spent three afternoons a week for a whole year in her classroom.

In the middle of spring semester the highlight of the S.I.T.E.S. program was that all seniors involved got to travel to the Appalachian Mountains in southern Ohio and do service at different places there. It was a life changing week for me and something I will never forget. One of my sites there was a daycare and some of the kids in the daycare had never seen someone in a wheelchair, not even at the mall and by the end of the day I had them on my lap reading stories.

From seventh grade on I was at every IEP meeting I had, and I had a very active voice in them. Along with attending my IEPs, I feel that Mrs. Roberts and the S.I.T.E.S. program gave me great preparation for college, both educationally and personally. I can't tell you how many people made me aware of IDEA and Sec. 504. Also, I can't count how many of my fellow students would come to me with questions about them especially in my S.I.T.E.S. government class.

My IEP team made contact with a counselor for VR Services and I have worked with the BVR counselor for going on ten years now, maybe longer. He was very influential in helping me explore several career opportunities before I chose to attend Kent State and I also had a very extensive tour of Wright State University in Dayton. Since I entered high school I knew I was going to college. I am very determined so that was that! I graduated from Kent in May 2005 and I just got my first job at Easter Seals in Sandusky, Ohio.

My parents also played an important role in helping me succeed. I definitely feel that I learned by example which reinforced my self determination skills. Both of my parents lost their parents at a young age and had built, bought, and sold a business by the age of 24 and were purchasing another one while in the process of

(Continued)

building a house. By the age of 26 they kept a seven day a week business, with fifteen to twenty employees, running for the next 26 years. I don't mean to gloat about my parents, but we have all overcome a lot in our lives. This is what I mean when I say I have learned by example as they have always taught me to keep pushing ahead no matter what life throws at you. To me that is the definition of self determination and the most important thing for an individual with at disability is to always remember to push ahead and if you are determined enough to speak up and stand up with your abilities and say your needs concisely you will be content and happy in the end.

Case Study Questions

1. List all the factors that helped make Michelle's transtition to college successful.
2. Which of her many strengths do you feel was the most important in helping her transtion to college? Give a reason for your answer.
3. What can you do in your role as a special education teacher to ensure that your students experience a similar success and understanding of what it takes to succeed as illustrated by Michelle?

(Michelle Marcellus, Kent State University graduate/B.S Degree in Human Development and Family Studies)

STUDY QUESTIONS

1. Explain the reasons why it is important to incorporate postsecondary goals and objectives into the transition plans of students with disabilities.
2. Why should effective planning for a postsecondary education include more than just academic goals?
3. Discuss why each of the following is crucial to the student succeeding in a postsecondary environment:
    a. Self-awareness of one's interests, needs, and preferences, including understanding the functional limitations of one's disability
    b. Knowledge of the rights and responsibilities of students in a postsecondary environment and how they differ from IDEA
    c. The ability to self-advocate
4. How can teachers assist students and their families in finding the right fit between the student's interests, preferences, and needs and potential postsecondary institutions?
5. Discuss why it is important for students to have meaningful opportunities to take an active role in their transition planning, including leading IEP/ITP meetings.

6. Discuss how issues, such as cultural values of the students and their families, first-generation college students, and students from rural backgrounds can impact the transition planning process.
7. Why are community-based experiences and appropriate linkages to other service providers (including adult services) necessary for a smooth transition to postsecondary education settings?
8. What should teachers be doing to ensure that the postsecondary education and training goals of their students meet the criteria of best transition planning and services, as defined by the four principles in IDEA?
9. Make a list of the things that need to be in place before a student can successfully transition to college.

WEBSITES

College Is Possible:
    http://www.CollegeIsPossible.org
Getting Ready for College Early: A Handbook for Parents of Students in the Middle and Junior High School Years:
    http://www.ed.gov/pubs/GettingReadyCollege Early/index.html

Preparing Your Child for College:
http://www.ed.gov/pubs/Prepare/index.html

The Student Guide: Financial Aid from the U.S. Department of Education:
http://studentaid.ed.gov/students/publications/student_guide/index.html

College Board Online:
http://www.collegeboard.org/

The Education Testing Service Network:
http://www.ets.org/

African American Global Network: Historically Black Colleges & Universities:
http://edonline.com/cq/hbcu/

NICHCY (National Information Center for Children with Disabilities):
http://www.nichcy.org/

The National Center for Learning Disabilities (NCLD):
http://www.ncld.org/

Gallaudet University:
http://www.gallaudet.edu/

AHEAD (Association on Higher Education and Disability):
http://ahead.org/

National Clearinghouse on Postsecondary Education for Individuals with Disabilities [HEATH Resource Center]:
http://www.heath.gwu.edu/

Education Resources Information Center Clearinghouse on Disability and Gifted Education:
http://ericec.org

Disability Access Information and Support (DAIS):
http://www.janejarrow.com

The Council for Opportunity in Education:
http://www.trioprograms.org/

PEPNet (Postsecondary Education Programs Network for Individuals who are Deaf/Hard of Hearing
http://www.pepnet.org/

Closing the Gap: Computer Technology in Special Education and Rehabilitation
http://www.closingthegap.com/

DO-IT (Disabilities, Opportunities, Internetworking, and Technology):
http://www.washington.edu/doit/

Alliance for Technology/Assistive Technology Advocates:
http://www.ataccess.org

Information on Assistive Technology:
http://abledata.com

Division on Career Development and Transition (DCDT):
http://www.dcdt.org

Job Accommodation Network (JAN):
http://www.jan.wvu.edu

National Center for the Dissemination of Disability Research:
http://www.ncddr.org

Independent Living, USA:
http://www.ilusa.com/

Occupational Outlook Handbook:
http://www.bls.gov/oco/home.htm

The Career and Self-Advocacy Program:
http://www.ehhs.kent.edu/centers/cite/CASAP/hom.html

Information on famous people with disabilities:
http://ericec.org/fact/famous.html
http://www.disabilityresources.org/FAMOUS.html

The Kudor Career Planning System:
http://www.kuder.com

FastWeb information on scholarships:
http://www.fastweb.com

E-Campus Tours:
http://www.ecampustours.com

Comparison of federal legislation guiding services for persons with disabilities

	The IDEA	Section 504	The ADA
Purpose of law	To provide a free, appropriate, public education (FAPE) in the least restrictive environment through federal funding to states, with substantive requirements attached to funding	A civil rights law that protects persons with disabilities from discrimination and requires reasonable accommodations to ensure nondiscrimination with no authorization for funding	A civil rights law that provides all persons with disabilities broader coverage than section 504 in all aspects of discrimination, with no authorization for funding
Scope and coverage	Applies to public schools and covers students ages 3 to 21 who have a disability that impacts their education	Applies to any program or activity that is receiving federal financial assistance and covers all qualified persons with disabilities regardless of whether special education services are required in elementary, secondary, or postsecondary settings	Applies to public or private employment, transportation, accommodations, and telecommunications regardless of whether federal funding is received and covers all qualified persons with disabilities, and qualified nondisabled persons related to or associated with a person with a disability
Disability defined	A listing of 13 disability categories is provided in the act, and all must adversely affect education performance	No listing of disabilities, but inclusionary criteria of any physical or mental impairment that substantially limits one or more major life activities, having a record of such an impairment, or being regarded as having an impairment	No listing of disabilities provided. Same criteria as found in section 504. HIV status and contagious and noncontagious diseases recently included
Identification process	Responsibility of school district to identify through "child find" and evaluate at no expense to parent of individual	Responsibility of individual with disability to self-identify and provide documentation. Cost of evaluation must be assumed by the individual, not the institution	Same as section 504
Service delivery	Special education services and auxiliary aids mandated by child study team and stipulated in the IEP	Services, auxiliary aids, and academic adjustments may be provided in the regular education setting, arranged for by special education coordinator or student disability services	Services, auxiliary aids, and accommodations arranged for by the designated ADA coordinator. Requires that accommodations do not pose an "undue hardship" to employers

Comparison of federal legislation guiding services for persons with disabilities   (*Continued*)

	The IDEA	Section 504	The ADA
Enforcement agency	Office of Special Education and Rehabilitative Services in U.S. Department of Education	The Office for Civil Rights (OCR) in the U.S. Department of Education	Primarily the U.S. Department of Justice, in conjunction with the Equal Employment Opportunity Commission and Federal Communications Commission. May overlap with OCR
Remedies	Reimbursement by district of school-related expenses is available to parents of children with disabilities to ensure FAPE	A private individual may sue a recipient of federal financial assistance to ensure compliance with section 504	Same as section 504 with monetary damages up to $50,000 for the first violation; attorney fees and litigation expenses are also recoverable

Source: Adapted from: *Handicapped requirements handbook* (January) 1993. Washington, DC: Thompson Publishing Group.

INDEPENDENT LIVING AND COMMUNITY PARTICIPATION

Robert M. Baer

Alfred W. Daviso III

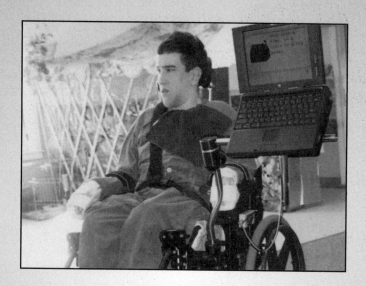

LEARNING OBJECTIVES

The objectives of this chapter:

1. Identify the social factors that contributed to deinstitutionalization and institutional reforms.

2. Identify how normalization contributed to deinstitutionalization and institutional reform and why this concept was revised to include social role valorization.

3. Identify how the independent living movement contributed to the development of supported living options and Medicaid waiver programs.

4. Learn how the history of residential services can be observed in today's residential system.

5. Describe the limitations inherent in older models of residential services such as institutions, ICF/MR programs, and group homes.

6. Describe the factors that should be considered in developing a vision of adult residential options for a student with disabilities.

7. Describe the requirements, skills, and supports that need to be considered in developing a transition plan for residential services.

8. Identify the key agencies for collaboration in developing linkages to adult residential services.

9. Describe the factors that should be considered in developing a vision of adult community participation and leisure options for students with disabilities.

10. Describe the skills and supports critical to developing casual and intimate interpersonal relationships.

11. Describe some of the key agencies and community programs that provide community participation and leisure opportunities for students with disabilities.

INTRODUCTION

Much of the literature on transition has focused on employment and postsecondary education because the primary determinant of a good life in the United States is a good education and a secure job that pays a decent salary. However, this does not mean that transition planning should be limited to these areas. For many people with disabilities, particularly individuals with severe disabilities, issues of employment and postsecondary education must be linked to other aspects of adult life. The place of residence, access to transportation, a range of recreation opportunities, a network of relationships, and needed specialized supports and services are all connected to an acceptable quality of life for adults with disabilities. Career educators have argued for some time that preparation for "independent living" is a critical function of education. Unfortunately, preparation for independent living and community participation is typically overlooked in transition planning, leaving families and adults with disabilities unprepared for the challenges they will confront once they are no longer eligible for a free appropriate public education (FAPE). As Knoll and Wheeler (2005) noted:

> Most parents of young adults with a disability see employment as an important consideration as they look to the future. However, for many parents, particularly those of students with moderate to severe disabilities, a job is a secondary consideration. Knowing their son or daughter as they do, parents are confronted with the question, "Who will look out for them when I am gone?" (p. 425)

This chapter starts with a brief history of residential and community living models and describes how these historical roots have resulted in the current system (or nonsystem) of residential and community services and supports available to individuals with disabilities. It addresses the essential transition element of creating an *outcome-oriented process* by describing how person-centered planning approaches can be used in "building a more compassionate, cooperative community in which persons with disabilities can take their rightful place as respected citizens" (Mount, 2002, p. xxi). It describes how to determine *student needs, interests, preferences, and strengths* through assessments of independent living skills and by helping students explore residential and community options prior to graduation. The authors describe how a *coordinated set of activities* can be developed through resource mapping and development of interagency collaboration. Finally, this chapter discusses how schools can *promote movement to postschool environments* by linking students to community resources and adult service programs.

A HISTORY OF COMMUNITY RESIDENTIAL PROGRAMS

It is important to understand the history of residential services for persons with disabilities to understand how the system works today and to articulate the fundamental shift that needs to occur for persons with disabilities to be afforded the opportunity to live in the home of their choice. This was well stated by persons with disabilities who have advocated for themselves. As ADAPT (Americans Disabled for Attendant Programs Today) pointed out:

> The 20th century began with eugenics taking a primary place in U.S. and world history (it could be called the "Century of Eugenics"). But, it will end with a "qualified" victory for the integration of people with disabilities in all communities ... [in] the 1920's and 30's when states not only sterilized and legally terminated the lives of people with disabilities, their creation of institutions for people with disabilities became widespread; and as the century grew so did these institutions from nursing homes, to institutions for people with psychiatric or developmental disabilities.... Yesterday the question was should people with disabilities live in the community? Today it is how are we to provide services for people with disabilities in the community? (ADAPT, 1999b, p. 1)

Deinstitutionalization and Active Treatment

In the two decades prior to the 1970s, disability services were characterized by "benign neglect," where persons with disabilities were left at home with families or were housed in large state and charitable institutions (Robertson, 2006). Community services for these persons were negligible and families paid most or all expenses of care. Often, the only alternative for families who could no longer care for their relatives was to place them in large state institutions. These institutions provided minimal custodial care and were set up to run as cheaply as possible, typically using unpaid "patient labor" in providing custodial care, food service, laundry, groundskeeping, cleaning, and even farming and construction services (Noll & Trent, 2004).

In the 1970s, this benign neglect period began to come to an end for a number of reasons. First, the use of unpaid patient (or resident) labor in institutions was outlawed in the early 1970s, causing institutional staffing costs to skyrocket. Second, lack of services at the large institutions meant few persons with disabilities ever returned to the community, meaning an ever-growing population in these programs. Third, the impact of the civil rights movement began to be felt in the field of disabilities as families and advocacy agencies began bringing lawsuits to outlaw the institutionalization of individuals with disabilities in programs that provided only custodial care. These social forces collectively resulted in a call for "active treatment" designed to move individuals with disabilities from institutional programs back to the community. This period was characterized as a period of institutional reform (Robertson, 2006).

> **Critical Point**
> The institutional reform movement was brought about by lawsuits that required "active treatment" for persons in institutions.

The reform of large institutions was very costly because the physical isolation of these programs meant that all services had to be provided in-house. Additionally, the advent of Medicaid and Supplementary Security Income (SSI) programs began to provide funding for disability services provided in the community. This led to the development of transitional residential programs known as Intermediate Care Facilities for Mental Retardation otherwise known as ICF/MR. Initially, these programs were similar to nursing homes (otherwise known as Intermediate Care Facilities), and they typically served individuals who were leaving state institutions or who were imminently at risk of being institutionalized. ICF/MR programs were supported with funding from the newly established Medicaid and SSI programs for persons with disabilities. In these early ICF/MR programs, individuals with disabilities received residential and nursing care in-house but were now able to use local physicians, dentists, therapists, and social services, including day activity and sheltered workshop programs (Noll & Trent, 2004).

Concurrent with the development of ICF/MR programs, many states began developing *group homes,* which were less medically-oriented and also less expensive. During this period, group homes were often run by families or charitable organizations and were typically funded through a combination of resident SSI benefits and state and local funding. Some of these group homes operated like foster-care programs where individuals with disabilities were taken into a family home, with the family operator receiving a daily rate for care. Others functioned more like ICF/MR programs but were typically staffed by live-in or minimum-wage workers with little or no training. Though these early group homes generally lacked professional services, they typically had more of a family-style atmosphere and were less restrictive than their Medicaid-funded ICF/MR counterparts. This family-style atmosphere gave group home residents a greater sense of belonging, but it had the drawback of placing them in the position of perpetual childhood (Mackelsprang & Salsgiver, 1996).

> **Critical Point**
> In an effort to control costs and improve services, states began reforming large state-run institutions and replacing them with smaller ICF/MR and group home programs funded by Medicaid and SSI.

Normalization and Integration

The concept of quality of life shifted in the 1970s from a social to an individual perspective. Disability advocates began articulating this shift by defining quality of life for persons with disabilities in terms of how closely their lives mirrored the lives of persons without disabilities (Wolfensberger, 1972). This concept of disability services was called *normalization.* Normalization led disability advocates to question the focus on large congregate settings for persons with disabilities. By the late 1970s, the normalization philosophy began having an affect on how ICF/MR programs were structured, and they now began to physically resemble family homes rather than nursing homes. At about the same time, state-funded group homes began to adopt Medicaid models of service and began to provide active treatment (Robertson, 2006).

Institutions, ICF/MR programs, and group homes began to be woven into a constellation of residential services that were organized according to concepts of **least-restrictive environments** and *continuum of services.* In these organizational systems, individuals with disabilities were "placed" in facilities that were considered appropriate to their functioning level and were expected to progress through the continuum toward greater independence. Residential providers enthusiastically embraced this model and began developing a range of facilities from large ICF/MR down to smaller, family-style group homes. They even began developing clusters of apartment-based programs with two to three persons with disabilities sharing services from staff typically housed in another apartment in the same complex. Unfortunately, research indicated that there was little movement through this continuum, with individuals typically staying in these "transitional" programs for their entire lives (Knoll & Wheeler, 2005).

The reform of residential programs brought about by the normalization principle brought considerable improvements in residential quality of life for persons with disabilities, but it still left them largely disempowered. To address this issue, ICF/MR and group home providers were required to inform individuals of their rights and to establish committees designed to give them greater control of home routines and house rules. However, these changes were largely cosmetic, with the control of major decisions still in the hands of the residential service providers (Knoll & Wheeler, 2005). Additionally, as states began substituting Medicaid funding for state funding of group homes the entire system began to take on more of a medical flavor. This was because Medicaid regulations applied to these programs were derived from nursing home regulations. As Knoll and Wheeler noted:

> Essentially, the federal regulations took the guidance provided for the management of a facility [from programs that were] designed for hundreds, if not thousands, of inmates and "simplified" them for facilities serving 16 or less and located in community settings. The underlying model that shaped these regulations was medical in focus and sought to provide quality care and treatment for "patients" who were defined by regulation as being dependent and "incompetent" to care for themselves. (p. 429)

Additionally, residential providers had to keep these facilities fully occupied to meet their costs and this meant that individuals moved in and out of these programs largely at the discretion of the owners. This often led to groupings of individuals with vastly different needs and functioning levels. No disability group felt this more acutely than persons with severe physical disabilities (such as cerebral palsy and spina bifida) who were often grouped with individuals with cognitive and behavioral disabilities. This often left them isolated and open to abuse from peers (Knoll & Wheeler).

Increasingly, it became apparent that regulations and structures that were designed for the efficient management of large-scale congregate care facilities had little to do with assisting people to achieve their legitimate aspirations as citizens. On a daily basis, service providers, advocates, and family members found themselves struggling to reconcile the dreams of individuals with the medically-oriented requirements of state and federal regulations just so people with disabilities could live a "normal life" (Knoll & Wheeler, 2005).

> **Critical Point**
> The principle of *normalization* began to challenge the medical focus of early institutional reforms and community programs such as the ICF/MR.

Person-Centered Planning

Individuals trained in the normalization principle in the 1970s began to develop a constellation of planning approaches known as person-centered planning (Holburn & Vietze, 2002). Two early influential person-centered planning approaches included **Personal Futures Planning** (Mount, 1984) and **MAPS, Making Action Plans**, formerly known as McGill Action Planning (Forest & Lusthaus, 1989). In the 1980s and 1990s, these approaches began to have an impact on how residential and community services were being conceptualized. Knoll and Wheeler (2005) outlined the common characteristics of person-centered as including:

1. *Real Life, Not "Programming."* Learning should occur in the course of the normal daily routine, not in programs. Support personnel must consider the demands of each individual's environments and daily routines in determining the needs for skill development or supports.
2. *Commitment.* People with disabilities and their families need to know that there are individuals who are committed to supporting them. These individuals and organizations must be willing to work through problems and stay with them through periods of problem behavior.
3. *Personal Advocacy.* People with the most significant disabilities are likely to be the ones with the greatest number of agencies involved in their lives, and shared responsibility has often meant no responsibility (Baer, 1996). A single agency or person must accept a long-term responsibility to bring about change in other agencies including advocating for new and innovative services.
4. *Empowerment and Choices.* People with disabilities often have few choices in their lives. Support personnel must know how to assist them in making real choices in areas of daily life and to be comfortable with the risks involved.
5. *Flexibility and Creativity.* Supports need to build on the strengths and match the needs of individuals, to engage their community supports as partners, and be ready to adapt to changes and uncertainty. Person-centered programs recognize that life is a changing and growing process that requires supports that change along with the individual's changing life situation.
6. *Relationships.* Being in the community means that people have relationships with people other than paid staff. Individuals under the care

of paid professionals tend to lose their natural supports, and it is important for professionals to provide opportunities to develop relationships.

7. *Gaining Access to Typical Community Resources.* Person-centered planning is less focused on developing new programs and services and more on gaining access to community resources. This is because agency-funded programs tend to provide minimal levels of support that often lack the power or flexibility to enable persons with disabilities to reach their goals (Holburn & Vietze, 2002). See Table 12–1.

> **Critical Point**
> Person-centered planning approaches put normalization principles into action by emphasizing community supports over active treatment.

TABLE 12–1   The common characteristics of person-centered programs

Characteristic	Need	Support
Real Life, Not "Programming"	Development and learning should occur in the course of the normal daily routine, not in contrived and artificial programs.	Support personnel must consider the demands of each individual's daily routine in determining the needs for skill development or supports.
Commitment	People with disabilities and their families need reassurance that there are individuals who have made a long-term commitment to support them.	The individuals and organizations that work with them must be willing to stick with them in good and bad times, and during periods of erratic behavior.
Personal Advocacy	People with the most complex needs are likely to be the ones with the greatest number of agencies involved in their lives, and shared responsibility has often meant no responsibility.	A single agency or person must accept a long-term responsibility to work both formally and informally to bring about change in other agencies including advocating for new and innovative services.
Empowerment and Choices	People with disabilities often have had few opportunities to experience making decisions, even small ones, throughout their lives.	Support personnel must know how to assist them in making real choices in areas of daily life and to be comfortable with the risks involved.
Flexibility and Creativity	Person-centered programs recognize that people change over time and the supports they need must adapt to match their changing life situation.	Supports must be developed to match the strengths and needs of the person, to build on natural community resources and be ready to make changes in chaotic times.
Relationships	Being part of a community means that people have enduring relationships with people other than those paid to be with them	With real friendships come natural systems of support that often are able to prevent relatively minor problems. People surrounded by paid professionals tend to lose natural supports. Often the most that the "formal" service system can do is to provide opportunities for people to develop relationships.
Gaining Access to Typical Community Resources	Person-centered planning is less focused on developing new programs and services and more on gaining access to community resources.	This is because agency-funded programs tend to provide minimal levels of support that often lack the power or flexibility to enable persons with disabilities to reach their goals.

The Independent Living Movement

The independent living movement was started by persons with physical disabilities who wanted greater control over the services they were receiving on the campus of the University of California at Berkeley. This consumer-control movement quickly spread to residential settings outside of postsecondary education as advocates for independent living used the Rehabilitation Act of 1973 (which barred discrimination in federally-funded programs) to obtain access to subsidized housing, health services, recreation, and transportation services. Historians of independent living point to its linkage to five social movements: (1) deinstitutionalization, (2) the African-American civil rights movement, (3) the "self-help" movement as seen in organizations such as Alcoholics Anonymous, (4) the movement toward more holistic approaches to health care, and (5) the consumerism movement toward greater responsiveness on the part of providers and manufacturers movement (Knoll & Wheeler, 2005).

The concept of independent living was articulated in the late 1970s by DeJong (1979) as an alternative to the predominate medical and remedial models of the day. In DeJong's model, disability was not seen as an abnormality, but rather as a natural part of the human experience that most persons experienced at some time in their lives. Under the independent living model, the problems arising from disability were seen as residing in the society and in the social and attitudinal barriers that prevent persons with disabilities from becoming participating citizens living in the community. A critical feature of the independent living model was that control over services was exercised by the individual and not by the professional.

The Rehabilitation Act of 1973 also led to the establishment of consumer-controlled Centers for Independent Living that began providing home and transportation supports for individuals with disabilities living on their own. By law, these **Independent Living Centers** had to be under the control of persons with disabilities and be designed to provide supports in the chosen settings of persons with disabilities. The independent living movement coincided with Wolfensberger's elaboration on the concept of normalization to include *social role valorization*, which argued for the attainment of socially valued roles for persons with disabilities that included choices, greater control, and avoidance of services that stigmatized persons with disabilities (Wolfensberger, 1996).

> **Critical Point**
> The independent living movement was started by persons with physical disabilities who wanted better access to the community and more control over their lives.

Supported Living

By 1986, the majority of individuals were receiving residential services in community facilities and residences (Lakin, Hill, White, & Write, 1988). However, although they were now living in communities, this did not mean that they were actively participating in community life (Kregel, Wehman, Seyfarth, & Marshall, 1986). Research indicated that residences could be physically located in the community without being socially integrated (Biklen & Knoll, 1987a). Medicaid regulations focused on preparing staff to provide active treatment but failed to make community membership a clear priority. This led many residential providers to adopt practices that actually erected barriers between residents and their neighbors (Biklen & Knoll, 1987b; Knoll & Ford, 1987).

In the late 1980s, the "People First" movement began articulating how independent living models and social role valorization models could be extended to persons with cognitive and behavioral disabilities needing residential services. "Nothing about me without me," was a rallying call of the People First Movement (Shapiro, 1993) and provided additional impetus for a growing "supported living" movement which maintained that disability services should be provided in residences chosen by individuals with disabilities (Ferguson & Olson, 1989; Taylor, 1988; Taylor, Racino, Knoll, & Lutifyya, 1987). Under the supported living model, recipients of services could lease or own homes or apartments in their own name or contract with a residential provider to find a home on their behalf. They could then use Medicaid and local funds to contract with other disability service providers to support them in these homes. This greatly empowered persons with disabilities who no longer had to change their residence to receive or change services.

As with independent living models, supported living programs rejected the continuum of services as a way of organizing services for people with disabilities. The continuum of services concept required the individual with a disability to achieve certain levels of competency before moving to the next level of independence, but a growing body of evidence showed that the independence of adults with disabilities was largely dictated by their level of community support rather than their functioning level (Hasazi, Gordon, & Roe, 1985). Because continuum of service models did little to address supports, they showed little success in moving persons back into the community. Additionally, their practice of moving individuals with disabilities through "least-restrictive programs" tended to sever the individuals' delicate network of community supports thereby sabotaging future efforts to move them into independent living (Knoll & Wheeler, 2005). In contrast, supported living models conserved these supports by keeping individuals in their homes and communities and by supplementing rather than replacing natural supports.

Medicaid Waiver Programs

Initially, supported living was limited to individuals with milder disabilities whose care could be covered by the individual's SSI in combination with public housing, food stamps, social services, and public transportation. However, in the late 1980s and 1990s, many states began providing Medicaid waiver options that allowed individuals with severe disabilities and their families to "waive" the right to institutional services in return for levels of funding support that allowed them to live in their own homes. Medicaid waiver funding was a voluntary federal program that varied from state to state and was not adopted by all states. Some states provided different levels of Medicaid waiver funding with lower levels of support and flat rates (e.g., $5,000 per year) for individuals remaining at home with their families and at much higher funded individual options waivers (e.g., $40,000/year) for individuals living outside of the family home (Braddock, 2004). Generally, Medicaid waiver programs were "capped" at or below the cost of funding an individual with a disability in an ICF/MR program. In most states, there were **waiting lists** for Medicaid waiver slots and these waiting lists prioritized individuals returning from institutions or in imminent danger of institutionalization. Additionally, some states used Medicaid waiver funds to "convert" traditional ICF/MR and group home programs as these programs began to fall out of favor. The net effect of these prioritized waiting lists for Medicaid funds was to make them very difficult to obtain for persons living in the community who were not in danger of imminent institutionalization.

Medicaid waiver programs did not necessarily allow the individual to live on their own if they needed 24-hour care. Because they were capped at ICF/MR funding levels, and ICF/MR programs tended to share staff among four or more residents, individuals using Medicaid waivers often had to find "roommates" to make ends meet. Individuals and families could address this problem by establishing consortiums or by using earned income to supplement Medicaid funding. Consortium models involved two or more individuals (or their families) creating a nonprofit organization to purchase or lease a home and with 24-hour home care shared by the consortium residents. Another approach was to supplement Medicaid waiver funding with the resident's income from supported employment as part of a "Plan to Achieve Self-Sufficiency" (or PASS) approved by Social Security. Under this arrangement, residents could pay some of the costs of living independently from their earned income, thereby maintaining Medicaid and SSI eligibility for participation in the Medicaid waiver program.

The Residential Service System Today

Due to the incremental evolution of residential services for persons with disabilities, today's service system has become a "crazy quilt" of programs and philosophies. While philosophies have changed, facilities developed under earlier models of service delivery (i.e., institutions, group homes, and ICF/MR programs) have tended to be highly resistant to all but cosmetic changes. The continuum of service model has continued to drive a large part of the disability residential system, with large institutions remaining open in many states to serve individuals considered too "injurious to self or others" to be served in their community. Large ICF/MR programs have also been maintained to serve persons lacking community supports whose health or behavioral needs might otherwise result in their institutionalization. Family-style ICF/MR and group homes have continued to provide services to persons with disabilities who are thought by their families or professionals to need the highly structured activities provided by these programs. Provider-run supervised apartment programs continue to be operated for persons with milder disabilities who are not eligible for Medicaid waiver services. These programs continued to operate because of the costly investment in their facilities and because of the well-organized political efforts of service providers, unions representing employees at state institutions, and family advocates who were instrumental in bringing about the reform of institutions that are now considered obsolete. In many states continuum of service models exist side by side with supported living models of service delivery.

The availability of residential options also continued to vary dramatically from locality to locality and state to state. In some states and localities, a full range of options have been available, while some localities offered only older, more traditional programs. Even when residential options have existed in a community, there have typically been long waiting lists for funding and services. Waiting lists for Medicaid waiver programs often exceeded 10 years, and most states and localities prioritized services to individuals at-risk of institutionalization, meaning that supported living services were not becoming available to families until they were in crisis.

Eligibility for services was another consideration in planning for residential services. Only about 10% of students with disabilities (e.g., moderate to profound mental retardation, or cognitive disability severe orthopedic disabilities, and multiple disabilities) went on to be eligible for residential programs such as group homes, ICF/MR, and Medicaid waiver programs. Students with milder disabilities (who met income eligibility requirements) were eligible for subsidized housing programs (such as Section 8) and could be additionally supported by a combination of social service and transportation programs; however, the majority of students eligible for special education services were not eligible for government-funded residential support as adults. This underscored the importance of person-centered planning approaches focused on developing supports from nongovernment sources such as families and community networks.

RESIDENTIAL TRANSITION PLANNING

Residential transition planning requires an understanding of family and cultural beliefs about residential services and the person with a disability. McNair and Rusch (1991) found that professionals may have different values and priorities when it comes to adult living for persons with disabilities. They found that parents value stability and security more heavily than professionals, who tend to be more focused on independent living and the dignity of risk. Parents may not trust an independent living approach to residential services where there is no established facility and where services are dispersed across disability service providers. This may stem from their lack of knowledge about the community service system or their lack of belief in the student's capability (Carney & Orelove, 1988). Additionally, families may become overwhelmed by the extreme complexity of obtaining residential services when they encounter eligibility determinations, referrals to multiple agencies, waiting lists, and paperwork. The role of siblings may be an important consideration for residential planning. In some families, siblings may be implicitly expected to provide support after the parents, but this may not have been discussed with the siblings in question.

Cultural issues may also affect how parents view residential living alternatives. In some cultures, persons with disabilities have been expected to stay at home under the care of (and often caring for) relatives (Schalock, Jenaro, Wang, Jiancheng, Lachapelle, 2005). Residential options that are planned with these families need to address how the individual can be supported in the context of the family network. Conversely, some families may expect the child to become largely independent of the family as an adult. These families need support in developing individualized residential options for their child through approaches using Section 8 housing and Medicaid waiver options. Some families may be attracted to the security and structure of group home and ICF/MR programs, especially if supported living programs are seen as unobtainable or unreliable.

It is important to realize that a vision of residential services cannot be made in a single transition meeting. Parents may harbor misconceptions and equate planning for residential services to institutionalization of their child. Parents may say that they plan to keep the child at home for the rest of their life and fail to consider the impact this will have on the child with a disability when they can no longer provide for them. They may believe that siblings will provide care when they are no longer able, but have never discussed this with the siblings in question. Some families may be unable to envision their child living independently or in supported living. Some families also may keep the individual with disability as a caretaker who provides both disability income and care of the home or aging adults.

To counter misconceptions about residential services and independent living, families will need the opportunity to explore residential options and to see their child performing in the community. Additionally, families may be preoccupied with the problems of the day and succumb to a natural tendency to postpone decisions that do not require immediate action. They must be made to understand that many residential options will require years or even decades to become available and that early planning is the only way that these services will be ready when they are needed by the individual.

<aside>
Critical Point
Cultural and family values will affect decisions about the person with a disability moving out on their own.
</aside>

Developing a Vision

Addressing cultural and family concerns about residential outcomes requires the identification of student needs, interests, preferences, and strengths. Davis and Faw (2002) suggested that the first step in developing a vision of residential outcomes involved developing a list of residential preferences.

They developed a list of 30 contrasting choices that are presented in Table 12–2. They noted that these choices can be presented pictorially.

After students have identified the characteristics of a residential outcome through contrasting choices, it is important to prioritize the choices systematically. For individuals with cognitive disabilities, Davis and Faw (2002) suggest selecting a desired item chosen from Table 12–2 and then having the individual choose between that item and every other item on the "desired" list of residential options. This process is repeated until all items have been paired. This process yields some items that are chosen consistently over most other items in the list. Davis and Faw suggest then creating a "Top 10" list of items that were most frequently chosen.

<aside>
Critical Point
Students need to identify life-style choices to develop a vision of the type of residential program that will best suit their needs.
</aside>

CASE STUDY Jennifer Part 1

Jennifer was a student with a moderate cognitive disability who was considering moving into a home of her own. After conducting paired choices and prioritizing them, Jennifer's Top 10 list indicated that she wanted:

1. To have a pet
2. Her own room
3. To live with friends
4. Help with her money
5. Help with shopping
6. To use public transportation
7. To have meals on her own
8. To do her own laundry
9. Help with doctor appointments and health care
10. A quiet home

Jennifer then was given a list of these items as questions such as, "Can I have a pet?" Jennifer and her family visited a number of homes and apartment-living situations and asked the providers and residents about each of the 10 areas of high priority to her. After some consideration, Jennifer and her family decided that a supported apartment living program best suited her needs and preferences. This type of home would allow Jennifer to have a pet, live with her friends, and have her own room. To help cover costs she could share an apartment with a friend.

TABLE 12–2 Lifestyle Items and contrasting options

Lifestyle Item	Contrasting Options
Bedroom	You have your own bedroom. You share a bedroom.
Bathroom	You have your own bathroom. You share a bathroom.
Pets	Pets are allowed. Pets are not allowed.
Neighbors	Neighbors live near the home. Neighbors live far away from the home.
Work	You have a job. You do not have a job.
Pay	You receive real money as payment for your job. You do not receive real money as payment for your job.
Handling money	You handle your own money. Staff handle your money for you.
Classes	You take training classes. You do not take training classes.
Visitors	Family and friends can visit whenever they want. Family and friends can only visit during visiting hours on certain days.
Smoking	Cigarette smoking is allowed inside the home. Cigarette smoking is not allowed inside the home.
Number of residents	Many other people live in the home. Only a few other people live in the home.
Curfew	The home has a curfew. The home does not have a curfew.
Getting up in the morning	Staff wake you up in the morning. You wake up in the morning on your own.
Sleeping late	You get up at the same time every day. You can sleep late some days.
Meals with staff	Staff eat meals with you. Staff do not eat meals with you.
Permission to leave the home	You can come and go as you please. You must have staff permission to leave the home.
Counselor	A counselor is available. A counselor is not available.
Keys	You have a key to your bedroom and/or locker. Only staff members have keys.
Telephone	You can talk on the telephone whenever you want. You must have permission to talk on the telephone.
Public transportation	Public transportation is available. Public transportation is not available.
Staff gender	The majority of staff are male. The majority of staff are female. Approximately the same number of male and female staff work at the home.

(*Continued*)

TABLE 12–2 (*Continued*)

Lifestyle Item	Contrasting Options
Staff turnover rate	There is a low staff turnover rate. There is a high staff turnover rate.
Grocery shopping	You shop for your own groceries. Staff shop for your groceries.
Cleaning	Staff clean the home. You and the other residents clean the home.
Laundry	You do your own laundry. Staff members do your laundry for you.
Serving meals	Staff fill your plate and serve your meals. You and the other residents eat family style and fill your own plates.
Fast-food restaurants	The home is near fast-food restaurants. The home is far away from fast-food restaurants.
Doctor appointments	Staff make doctor appointments for you. You make your own doctor appointments.
Familiar residents	You knew some of the residents before moving into the home. You did not know any of the residents before moving into the home.
Noise level	The home is usually noisy. The home is usually quiet.

Source: From Davis, P. and Faw, G. (2002). Residential preferences in person-centered planning. In Holburn, S., and Vietze, P. M. *Person-centered planning: Research, practice, and future directions* (p. 205), Baltimore: Paul A. Brookes. Reprinted with permission.

Addressing Residential Needs Related to the Vision

Once a vision has been developed of how the individual plans to live in the community, transition planning needs to focus on assessing and addressing the individual's independent living skills in the context of the independent living settings he or she is planning to enter. Generally, independent living will require functional skills and supports in the following areas:

1. Health and safety
2. Self-care
3. Home management
4. Transportation
5. Budgeting and finances

Assessing these issues in an ecological context requires the concurrent assessment of: (a) the requirements of the student's desired environments, (b) the strengths, needs, interests, and preferences of the individual, and (c) the availability of individualized supports. The prerequisite requirements of residential programs can often be gleaned from the policies and procedures of agencies or programs. Assessment of student independent living skills may be accomplished through the use of comprehensive assessments such as Life Centered Career Education (LCCE) (Brolin & Llody, 2004). Assessment of supports can best be accomplished through person-centered planning approaches. The following section is designed to discuss these three areas in general terms.

It should be noted that residential services have been rapidly evolving and programs such as ICF/MR may become funded by Medicaid waiver by the time this book is published. However, it is the authors' belief that even with Medicaid waiver funding, these programs will continue to operate in much the same way as they did with funding from older models.

Health and Safety

Health and safety issues are generally the first consideration of whether a student with a disability will be able to live in a particular environment. ICF/MR and group home programs generally packaged health and safety services along with residential services. Most ICF/MR programs have provided 24-hour supervision and many have had nurses on staff or on call to provide daily monitoring of resident medications, therapies, and preventative health care. Group homes generally have staff with some training in basic health care, but their staff are less likely to be supervised by medically-trained staff. Supervised apartment programs may have residential staff on call, but require residents to be able to request help by phone. Supported living programs funded by Medicaid waiver can provide medical services and 24-hour supervision, but families may be required to budget these services to avoid exceeding available funding. Individuals living on their own or in subsidized Section 8 housing may receive health care services with their Medicaid health care card but generally need to travel to health care facilities to receive these services.

> **Critical Point**
> Students with ongoing health and safety concerns often were served in ICF/MR, group home, or Medicaid waiver programs where staff could be shared.

Student residential options are greatly enhanced by developing their health and safety skills as part of their secondary education experience. These skills can be developed through school health education programs or through training from related service providers such as nurses or therapists. They may also be trained in conjunction with the family. Generally health and safety skills should be addressed in the following areas based on individual needs:

1. Avoidance of self-injurious behaviors
2. Avoidance of behaviors injurious to others
3. Recognition of illness and individual medical needs
4. Ability to call for help in an emergency
5. Self-management of routine medical visits and care
6. Self-management of medications and medical treatments
7. Self-management of prosthetic devices and assistive technology
8. Management of personal assistant services

Student support networks can be used to supplement their health and safety skills. Individuals with extensive behavioral concerns may need limited or full guardianship, while individuals with cognitive disabilities and health concerns may need medical guardianship or a durable power of attorney. However, guardianship should be used only after students have had training in self-managing their health and safety needs and to the extent that an individual cannot make informed consent about these areas.

> **Critical Point**
> Teaching students to manage their own health and safety and involving natural supporters in residential planning can greatly enhance residential choices.

Self-Care

Residential programs may vary considerably in how well they provide for self-care needs. ICF/MR programs have traditionally provided a full-range of self-care services, including services to individuals needing help with transfers, bathing, toileting, and eating. Group home programs may not be well equipped to help individuals needing help with transfers and bathing and may screen out individuals who are incontinent. Medicaid waiver programs can provide the full range of self-care services, but cost-saving approaches (such as family consortium homes or dispersed apartments) may need to be employed to afford services that are needed on a 24-hour basis. Generally, individuals living on their own or in subsidized housing will need to be able to call for help in an emergency, get to medical appointments, and to provide routine self-care.

> **Critical Point**
> Students needing extensive self-care supports were often served in ICF/MR, group homes, or in Medicaid waiver programs where staff could be shared.

CASE STUDY Jennifer Part 2

In order to live in a supported apartment program, Jennifer's IEP team determined that she needed to be able to call for help in an emergency and to recognize the common signs of illness. They recommended an LCCE evaluation of Jennifer's health and safety skills and training related to her being able to recognize her medical needs, call for help, and administer routine medications. Through person-centered planning it was determined that her family would be able to assist her in setting doctor's appointments and routine medical care. It was also determined that Jennifer should carry a cell phone for emergencies.

Student residential options will be greatly enhanced by developing skills and supports relative to self-care. Often these areas would be addressed at the secondary level in collaboration with the family, school nurses, and related service providers. Some general areas of self-care that need to be addressed in order of importance are:

1. Transfers
2. Toileting
3. Eating
4. Bathing
5. Dressing
6. Oral hygiene
7. Grooming
8. Good diet and exercise

As before, the individual's support networks can be used where skills cannot be developed. Family members may assist individuals in routine daily care. Sometimes a resident's roommate or spouse can assist in the individual's care, but these individuals should be trained to safely perform these functions.

> **Critical Point**
> Developing self-care skills and involving natural supports in residential planning can greatly enhance residential options.

Home Management

Home management skills have not been a prerequisite for ICF/MR programs, group homes, or Medicaid waiver programs. Some apartment living programs require individuals to be able to prepare meals, do laundry, and do routine cleaning. Generally, individuals living in subsidized housing need to additionally be able to do routine shopping and get around the community using individual or public transportation. Individuals living in their own home may also need to perform some home repair.

Students with strong home management skills will greatly enhance their residential options. At the secondary level, these skills may be developed in conjunction with the family by giving the individual chores to do at home. They may also be developed by having the student take consumer science and vocational courses. Home management skills in general order of importance include:

1. Cleaning
2. Meal preparation
3. Laundering
4. Menu planning
5. Shopping
6. Routine home maintenance

Home management needs can often be met by the use of community and family supports. In some cases, a family or community member may volunteer to assist an individual with menu planning, shopping, or routine home maintenance.

> **Critical Point**
> Home management services can be obtained in a wide range of residential programs, but students with milder disabilities may not be eligible for these services and should receive training.

Transportation

Transportation services have been generally provided in-house by ICF/MR and group home programs and may be included in the services offered in Medicaid waiver programs. Supervised apartment and subsidized housing programs have typically been located on public transit routes and some supervised apartment living programs have offered supplemental transportation services for medical visits and shopping. Student transportation skills and supports can be critical to integration in the community. These skills can be developed in conjunction with the family or as part of a community-based training program such as work study. Students planning to live independently will benefit from transportation skills in the areas of:

1. Identifying local landmarks
2. Asking directions
3. Providing personal identification, if lost

CASE STUDY Jennifer Part 3

In order to live in a supported apartment program, Jennifer's IEP team determined that she would need to be relatively independent in her self-care. Because Jennifer was already independent in most self-care areas, her team recommended a course of study that emphasized proper diet and exercise through physical education and health-related classes. The IEP team felt the pragmatics of grooming and dress should be a focus for Jennifer (e.g., proper work attire, proper hairstyle for work, etc.). Through person-centered planning with her parents, it was determined that they would monitor her grooming and help her make appointments for hair styling and pedicure.

Jennifer Part 4

In order to live in a supported apartment setting, Jennifer's IEP team determined that she would need to be able to prepare meals on her own and do routine cleaning. They recommended that she work on these skills at home by preparing one meal each week with the family and do routine cleaning around the house. Through person-centered planning it was determined that her family would assist her with laundry, menu planning, shopping, and routine home maintenance.

4. Reading maps
5. Reading bus schedules
6. Using disability transportation services
7. Using taxis
8. Using public transportation
9. Driver's education

Individuals may also use community supports to assist in transportation. Some communities offer door-to-door public transportation for persons with disabilities, but this has typically been limited to medical and nonroutine transportation. Even when the individual cannot drive, some individuals with disabilities or their families have purchased cars to make it possible to get around insurance concerns of hiring drivers or using volunteers to meet the individual's transportation needs. If the individual has income through supported employment, the purchase of a car can be made as part of a PASS plan, thereby allowing the individual to accumulate savings without jeopardizing SSI or Medicaid benefits.

> **Critical Point**
> The availability of public transportation is an important consideration in the choice of a residential setting unless the individual has a car.

Transition skills are often taught in the community as well as in the classroom.

Budgeting and Finances

ICF/MR and group home programs generally required that the individual's SSI benefits be used for the cost of residential services with only about $35 per month given to the resident as an allowance. This was a considerable drawback of these programs because residents could not make individual purchases or manage their funds. Medicaid waiver programs can be individualized by giving the individual control of funds and responsibility for purchases or by contracting with an individual or service provider to manage a portion of the individual's funds. Subsidized housing programs generally charge a percentage of the individual's SSI and other income for housing (typically 30%) with the individual being responsible for purchasing groceries, toiletries, and clothing.

Students with disabilities will significantly enhance their opportunities to live in a supervised apartment,

Jennifer Part 5

In order to live in a supported apartment program, Jennifer's IEP team determined that she would need instruction in the use of public transportation. The IEP team agreed that having Jennifer pursue a driver's license was an unrealistic goal. Jennifer will receive instruction in public transportation options, asking for directions, and familiarizing herself with the local area. In person-centered planning meetings it was determined that her sister would be able to help Jennifer in getting to places not reached by public transportation.

Medicaid waiver, or in the home of their choice when they develop skills and supports in the areas of budgeting and finance. These skills may be developed in conjunction with the family, as part of mathematics classes, as part of vocational training, or as part of a community-based program such as work study. Some critical skills include:

1. Keeping money in a purse or wallet
2. Making routine purchases
3. Comparative shopping
4. Managing daily, weekly, and monthly allowances
5. Managing a checkbook
6. Developing weekly, monthly, and yearly budgets
7. Depositing and drawing money from bank accounts
8. Managing a credit card
9. Making major purchases

Individuals living independently may manage their own finances or receive support from a family or community member. For persons who can give consent, a power of attorney may allow a community member to manage finances with their approval. Individuals with significant behavioral or cognitive disabilities may need to have a guardian appointed; however, this decision should not be made until it has been clearly established that the individual cannot give informed consent. See Table 12–3

> **Critical Point**
> Persons with disabilities typically need some support in managing their finances and can appoint a person with power of attorney or receive guardianship for this purpose.

Identifying Resources and Developing Supports

After developing a residential vision and a strategy for assessing and addressing students' training and support needs, it will probably fall to the transition coordinator to identify programs and services that best fit the student's residential vision. This requires a thorough knowledge of the student and the use of residential consultants who maintain up-to-date information about residential services in the community. The transition coordinator should have a contact list that includes the following agencies.

1. Mental retardation and developmental disability (MR/DD) services
2. Alcohol, drug abuse, and mental health (ADAMH) boards
3. Rehabilitation services and independent living centers
4. U.S. Department of Housing and Urban Development
5. Local and state housing authorities
6. Local community affairs, development, or finance agencies
7. The Department of Job and Family Services
8. The Social Security Administration
9. The Federal National Mortgage Association

MR/DD state and local agencies typically provide ongoing support to only 10% of students with disabilities (or about 1% of the total student population). MR/DD residential options include ICF/MR programs, group homes for persons with developmental disabilities, supervised apartments, supported living programs, and Medicaid waiver programs. MR/DD agencies may also provide assistance to individuals or families in the purchase of a home. Typically, families initiate referrals to these programs, though they may need assistance in documenting the level of disability required to access their services. Waiting lists for Medicaid funded programs may exceed 10 years if the individual is not in crisis or in danger of imminent institutionalization. However, Medicaid waiver programs that provide low levels of funding to support individuals living with their families may be more readily available.

CASE STUDY | Jennifer Part 6

In order to live in a supported apartment program, Jennifer's IEP team determined that she would need instruction in budgeting and making routine purchases. She is able to enter money in a bank account and has participated in some lessons about choosing needs over wants in budgeting. In person-centered planning meetings, it was determined that Jennifer's sister will be able to help her in managing her budget, paying bills, and making major purchases. Jennifer was willing to give her power of attorney to do this.

TABLE 12–3 Skills to address across independent living areas

Independent Living Areas	Skills to be Addressed Based on Individual Needs
Health and Safety	Avoidance of self-injurious behaviors Avoidance of behaviors injurious to others Recognition of illness and individual medical needs Ability to call for help in an emergency Self-management of routine medical visits and care Self-management of medications and medical treatments Self-management of prosthetic devices and assistive technology Management of personal assistant services
Self-Care	Transfers Toileting Eating Bathing Dressing Oral hygiene Grooming Good diet and exercise
Home Management	Cleaning Meal preparation Laundering Menu planning Shopping Routine home maintenance
Transportation	Identifying local landmarks Asking directions Providing personal identification, if lost Reading maps Reading bus schedules Using disability transportation services Using taxis Using public transportation Driver's education
Budgeting and Finances	Keeping money in a purse or wallet Making routine purchases Comparative shopping Managing daily, weekly, and monthly allowances Managing a checkbook Developing weekly, monthly, and yearly budgets Depositing and drawing money from bank accounts Managing a credit card Making major purchases

State and local mental health boards may have some residential options for individuals with severe psychiatric disabilities such as schizophrenia or bipolar disorder. However, referral to these programs is usually the result of a crisis situation. Additionally, mental health programs for children do not necessarily interface with mental health programs for adults, so referrals at the secondary level may not be possible until the student reaches age 18.

State rehabilitation service programs and their Independent Living Centers typically have information about accessible housing for persons with physical disabilities and can provide financing to make a home, apartment, or mode of transportation more accessible. Generally, Independent Living Center services are accessed through the state vocational rehabilitation agency, which determines whether an individual is eligible for support. Independent Living Centers may also provide other community support services such as access to personal assistant services and accessible recreational opportunities.

The U.S. Department of Housing and Urban Development (HUD) and local and state housing authorities can provide **Section 8 housing** vouchers and rental subsidies. These typically provide services to individuals with low incomes and often limit rental or mortgage expenses to no more than 30% of an individual's income. HUD also may provide Section 811 funding that is specifically targeted to persons with disabilities.

Local community affairs, development, or finance agencies may provide investment partnerships that assist the individual in buying or renting a home. The Department of Jobs and Family Services may be able to help with covering living expenses by providing subsidies for food, heat, or emergency expenses. The Social Security administration may assist in the purchase of a home by allowing the individual to establish a PASS account to save for a down payment without jeopardizing SSI or Medicaid benefits. Individuals who are not eligible for public housing due to income may benefit from mortgage assistance through the Federal National Mortgage Association (Fannie Mae) Home Choice mortgage program for persons with disabilities.

> **Critical Point**
> There are many sources of financing for residential services and many of these require the individual to have a significant disability and be in financial need.

Implementing the Residential Transition Plan

Under standards-based education, it becomes important to align training in independent living skills with core content standards. Health and safety and self-care training can often be incorporated into health and physical education classes, while transportation training can be infused into driver's education or work study programs. Home management skills can be incorporated into consumer science classes, while budgeting and financial management can be infused into mathematics classes. Students may further develop these skills through career technical education programs such as cooking, home repair, and auto maintenance.

Often the exploration of residential options will need to be done in conjunction with the family. The transition coordinator may start this process by providing families with a list of locally available housing options and by having guest speakers from agencies providing residential supports or services. Students can then explore the advantages and disadvantages of various residential options and of renting versus home ownership. They may also explore the real estate listings in the newspaper to see where affordable rentals and housing are available. In addition to the individual issues identified in the development of the residential vision, families may want to visit residential settings and rate them according to the criteria of:

1. How safe is the residential option?
2. How physically accessible is it?
3. What eligibility, skills, and supports are prerequisite to entrance?
4. Are staff available on-site or on-call?
5. Are staff trained to work with persons with disabilities?
6. Is the facility licensed or regulated?
7. Are facility inspection reports available?
8. How are medical treatments and emergencies handled?
9. Is it in a neighborhood and setting desirable to the individual?
10. Is public transportation available?
11. What community resources are nearby?
12. Is the neighborhood friendly to pedestrians or wheelchairs?
13. What community resources can be accessed through available transportation?
14. What job opportunities are accessible to the place of residence?
15. How conducive is it for visits from family, friends, and community supporters?
16. Does the residence allow for roommates, spouses, children, or pets?
17. Is the residence affordable?
18. Does the residence qualify for rental assistance or purchase by public agencies?

Following the exploration of residential options, the individual will need to consider whether one or more

CASE STUDY | Jennifer Part 7

In order to live in a supported apartment program, Jennifer's IEP team determined that she would be eligible for Section 8 housing and receive additional supports through MR/DD programs. In person-centered planning it was determined that her family would help her make purchases related to furnishing the home.

roommates will be needed to cover expenses. Students may need to explore questions such as, "How many roommates, if any, would be acceptable?" and "With whom would I be interested in sharing a residence?" or "Where might I find a person to share a residence?" In some cases families may need to come together to form a family consortium to purchase or lease a home.

Once a particular residential setting has been decided upon, students and their families may need assistance in navigating the extremely complex system of residential services and supports. Often the transition coordinator will do this in collaboration with one of the residential service or funding agencies that have been previously described. This is important because residential planning and implementation is very likely to extend well into the student's adult years.

PLANNING FOR COMMUNITY PARTICIPATION AND LEISURE

As Strand and Kreiner (2005) noted, if you ask your friends and acquaintances in your community, "What do you do in your spare time?" you would probably have a variety of responses. They may report participation in activities such as baseball, bowling, movies, civic meetings, dates, being with spouses, playing with their kids, watching TV, working in the garden, biking, and so on. If you asked individuals with disabilities the same question, their responses would probably be quite different. They may report going home from work, fixing dinners with or without assistance from paid staff or family members, and then listening to the radio or watching TV. If the individual's residence is a group home, dinner may be made

without their assistance or input, and then the "group" may have a planned activity in the community. If the individual lives at home with parents, he or she might report going straight to his or her room and watching TV.

Community participation and leisure skills are a critical component of the transition process because they provide many connections and relationships essential to quality of life. In his book, *Interdependence: The Route to Community* (1995), Condeluci refers to four basic themes that are vital to every person: (1) a safe place to live, (2) meaningful things to do, (3) intimacy, and (4) rejuvenation. Yet community planning rarely goes beyond residential services and provides few opportunities for intimacy or growth. Additionally, community leisure programs for persons with disabilities have continued to emphasize segregated activities such as Special Olympics to the exclusion of leisure activities with nondisabled peers. That is not to say that special leisure programs are not helpful, but rather to say that persons with disabilities should be given a choice (Strand & Kreiner, 2005).

Community and leisure participation opportunities for persons with disabilities have closely paralleled the development of residential services. During the benign neglect period, individuals with disabilities were warehoused in large state institutions, often remaining tied to benches or confined to rooms with nothing but a television for entertainment. During the institutional reform period, activity therapists provided recreational therapy as part of active treatment with recreation and leisure activities seen as a way of habilitating the individual. Following normalization, individuals with disabilities began participating in activities similar to their age-appropriate peers (e.g., Special Olympics) but generally in segregated programs and settings. Finally, in keeping with the independent living movement, individuals with disabilities increasingly began demanding access to integrated community recreation and leisure programs with the help of supports (Condeluci, 1995).

It should be noted that society's view of community participation and leisure activities has changed considerably

---

CASE STUDY **Jennifer Part 8**

In her visits to supported apartment living programs, Jennifer was able to identify several that met her individual residential vision. After reviewing choices, the family determined to go with a supported apartment program that took Section 8 vouchers and was served by trained MR/DD staff who were available to assist individuals in the mornings and evenings. This program had a good record of health and safety, was in a safe neighborhood, and had access to public transportation. It was determined that Jennifer would need to share expenses with at least one other roommate to cover her expenses.

over time, as well. In the 1950s, the family was the predominate focus of community and leisure activities. Today, peer groups predominate. In the 1950s, religious affiliations were the predominant way of meeting other persons. Today, the World Wide Web has created a network of easily accessible groups of persons organized around specific interests. Bowling nights and trips to the zoo may seem terribly old-fashioned by newer generations of persons with disabilities who may be more interested in computer games, surfing the Web, sidewalk surfing, or going to "raves" (Strand & Kreiner, 2005).

> **Critical Point**
> Community leisure options tend to be closely tied to residential settings and have evolved in a similar manner over the past 30 years.

Developing a Vision of Community and Leisure Options

Often it is difficult to plan for community participation and leisure activities until the student has identified desired work, education, and residential outcomes. This is because community participation and leisure options are heavily influenced by the individual's income and residential setting. Person-centered planning approaches may be particularly helpful in developing a total picture of the individual that includes community participation and leisure options because they are particularly good at eliciting information that can be used to develop ideas about things the individual would like to do as well as things that they do now (Holburn & Vietze 2002).

Another important consideration in the development of community participation and leisure activities is the student's level of self-determination and his or her ability to make choices that: (a) are based on experience and knowledge, (b) have a reasonable probability of outcome, and (c) are free from coercion. Students with disabilities often have limited experience with community participation and leisure activities. For them to make informed and self-determined decisions they will need exposure to a range of different activities including indoor and outdoor activities, individual and team activities, and vicarious, and participatory activities.

Family and cultural preferences will play an important role in planning for community participation and leisure activities. Families may want to play a major role in community and leisure activities, particularly for persons with the most significant disabilities. Other families may prefer more independence in this

area. Though increasingly rare, some families may equate disability with shame and resist efforts to involve the individual in activities that are integrated into the community and highly visible. The element of risk of some activities may be a concern for some families who fear that the individual will be taken advantage of in integrated community and leisure settings.

Cultural issues are another important factor in developing a vision for a person with a disability. Cultural activities related to religious or ethnic affiliation can be a powerful resource in developing ideas for community participation and leisure activities. Religious organizations have a wealth of things to do both in the areas of community participation (e.g., volunteering) and leisure (e.g., socials). Additionally, these religious communities typically provide levels of support for the individual that could not be found anywhere outside of a social service agency.

The community vision does not need to identify specific community participation and leisure activities. It can start by addressing the basic questions of:

1. Who does the individual like to be with?
2. What types of activities do they prefer?
3. Where do they prefer to go for activities?
4. How will they pay for activities?

For individuals with significant cognitive disabilities these questions may need to be answered through observation, interviews with the family, and person-centered planning approaches. For individuals who can make their preferences known verbally, these questions can be elicited through interviews and interest surveys. For individuals who are nonverbal, pictures can be used to explore interests (Strand & Kreiner, 2005). Some individuals may have a very clear idea of what they want to do and only want help in linking to resources. Others may require considerable help in identifying interests.

> **Critical Point**
> Person-centered planning approaches and the use of interest inventories can considerably expand the number of community and leisure options.

Addressing Needs Related to Interpersonal Relationships

The first step in addressing the community vision is to look at who the individual would like to be engaged with as an adult. A student who is peer-group focused will need skills and supports related to functioning in groups and teams. A student who prefers individual activities will need skills and supports related to pursuing individual interests such as conducting research on the Web, consulting interest groups, and going to the library. Students may also need help in pursuing intimate relationships.

Addressing Needs Related to Casual Relationships

Students with disabilities will greatly enhance their community participation and leisure skills by learning how to interact in the environments they wish to enter. Generally, these skills would be taught in partnership with the family or in the context of school activities and extracurricular programs. Some critical skills would include:

1. Greeting others
2. Introducing self to others
3. Conducting small talk
4. Appropriate touching and talking to the opposite sex
5. Dressing appropriately for activities
6. Asking how to join an activity
7. Listening and responding to verbal cues from others
8. Sharing and taking turns in activities
9. Learning to win and lose gracefully
10. Thanking hosts and following up activities

A number of supports can be developed to assist individuals who have trouble learning these skills (e.g., students with Asperger syndrome). Peer mentoring approaches can be particularly helpful in guiding the individual through social situations that they are ill-equipped to handle. It may also be helpful to provide disability awareness training to groups of interest to the individual. The individual may also be trained to describe their disability and to request patience from other participants.

> **Critical Point**
> Students with disabilities may need social skills training and peer supports and mentoring to give them access to integrated community leisure activities.

Addressing Needs Related to Intimate Relationships

Some individuals may need help in regard to developing and maintaining intimate relationships. This must be done with careful consideration of family and cultural mores. Some families and cultures may believe that individuals with a disability should not have intimate relationships and many more believe that they should not have children. Some families may be opposed to the use of birth control and only want abstinence training. Consequently, training and skill development in regard to intimate relationships must be done in partnership with the family and/or counselors who specialize in this area. Additionally, it is very important to assess what the individual knows and is currently doing prior to discussing intimate relationships and to provide information as it is needed rather than all at once. Intimacy generally requires grounding in many of the social skills previously noted. Some additional skills related to developing intimate relationships include information about:

1. Personal space and appropriate touching
2. How to introduce yourself to a person you care for
3. Appropriate ways of showing affection
4. Asking for a first date
5. Proper dress and manners
6. Understanding and managing sexuality
7. Avoiding exploitation
8. Abstinence and birth control
9. Avoiding sexually transmitted diseases
10. Love and lovemaking
11. Considerations in raising children

Supports become very important in guiding a student toward responsible intimate relationships with others. Families and responsible adults should be involved at every step to supervise the individual and prevent injurious situations. It is also important to assess the sexual information that the individual is picking up from other sources (e.g., peers and the media) and address misconceptions as they arise.

> **Critical Point**
> Special educators and transition coordinators need to work closely with the family and respect their cultural values in dealing with student needs related to intimacy.

Addressing Needs Related to Specific Community Activities

The types of possible community and leisure activities are too numerous to list. One of the drawbacks of checklists of activities is that they may not include all possible activities available to the individual and may include activities unfamiliar to the individual. Additionally, many activities have prerequisite requirements that make participation difficult for the individual due to health, safety, or skill level concerns. Generally, activities

Jennifer has a small group of friends that join her in social activities, but she has difficulty making new friends. She has had male friends, but has not dated anyone formally. She is interested in dating; however, she is shy and withdrawn when meeting new people. She has improved her social skills through the use of role-playing activities. Through person-centered planning, it was determined that a nondisabled friend would accompany her to high school dances and help her in social situations.

can be broken into categories that describe features of the activity in terms of:

1. Do you like quiet or noisy activities?
2. Do you like team or individual activities?
3. Do you like indoor or outdoor activities?
4. Do you like to participate, help, or watch?
5. What do you like to do now and why do you like it?
6. What would you like to learn to do?

This initial assessment of activity preferences can serve as a cross-check when lists of possible activities are presented. When developing a checklist of activities the transition coordinator should identify extracurricular activities offered by the school, community activities, and activities that could be offered through the individual's family, religious, and ethnic affiliations. Person-centered planning approaches are particularly effective in eliciting ideas for activities that are unique to the individual. For students who are nonverbal, activities should be assessed by using pictures. To simplify this process, students may be asked to make choices between two pictures of different types of activities. Chosen activities would go into one pile and activities that are not chosen would go in another. This process could be repeated for each pile until the desired number or types of activities are chosen. Kreiner (2005) developed the *Preferences for Leisure Attributes* (PLA)—a forced choice picture inventory that is administered on a lap top.

Activity checklists and assessments will go only so far in determining students' activity preferences. They should be allowed to explore activities by observing and/or participating. After observing or participating in the activity they should assess both what they liked and didn't like about the activity. At this point the activity or picture checklists could be readministered to create a more informed picture of student interests.

Developing skills related to a given form of community participation or leisure activity would be the next step in the student's development. Generally, students need skills and information related to the activity's:

- terminology
- rules
- culture and rituals
- dress
- required skills

These skills and information can be cultivated by having the student research a given activity on the Web or at the library and to view the activity at both the professional and local level. The student may then be assigned to interview individuals who know the activity.

The student may be supported in learning the activity by finding a peer or family member willing to teach basic skills. Rehabilitation professionals may provide supports in the form of activity-related prosthetic devices and assistive technology. In some cases, students may be able to afford the services of a trainer when they have gone beyond the need for basic skills.

> **Critical Point**
> Students with disabilities need to become familiar with the culture of the groups they are planning to join.

Addressing Needs Related to the Location of Activities (Where)

Community participation and leisure activities are often as much a function of where the activity is provided as the activities themselves. Individuals from suburban or rural backgrounds may be uncomfortable participating in an activity at a downtown YMCA. Others may seek activities from familiar places such as their church or neighborhood. After a final list of activity goals has been developed through this process, the transition coordinator will need to research the activity. For commonly chosen and school activities, the coordinator should maintain a file that includes:

1. The name of the activity
2. The contact name, address, and phone number for the activity

Jennifer enjoys activities in small groups or by herself. She likes to spend time at the local mall with her friends. She dresses appropriately for a variety of social situations. She likes quiet indoor activities and will often observe any activity rather than actively participate. Jennifer is also interested in swimming, biking, and playing games on the computer. Through person-centered planning it was determined that a nondisabled peer mentor will be identified for each of her desired activities to help her fit in.

3. Eligibility and prerequisite skill requirements for the activity
4. Availability of supports and accommodations
5. Timelines for referral and participation in the activity

Supports and accommodations for activities vary widely and are generally subject to the requirements of the Americans with Disabilities Act (ADA), the Rehabilitation Act of 1973, and (for school activities) the Individuals with Disabilities Education Act (IDEA). It may become necessary for the transition coordinator to inform the person running the activity of how disability regulations apply, especially if persons with disabilities have not commonly been involved in that particular activity. However, a cooperative problem-solving approach will generally work better than a confrontational one, because the activity coordinator is in a better position to identify how a person with a disability might participate if special accommodations are needed. Training may also help the person coordinating the activity understand concepts such as partial participation where an individual participates in part of an activity or with supports.

> **Critical Point**
> Special educators may need to work with community leisure providers to promote integrated activities for persons with disabilities through transdisciplinary approaches.

Addressing Needs Related to Paying for Activities

The costs of activities will be a barrier for many students, especially when they become adults living outside of the home. If they have no work income, individuals living in ICF/MR and group homes will have only about $35 per month to spend, which virtually rules out all activities involving cost. Often MRDD and charitable agencies will sponsor individual participation in events such as Special Olympics, bowling, and swimming, but these activities tend to be segregated and highly stigmatizing. Families may set up trusts to cover funding for recreational activities for individuals living in Medicaid-funded programs, but these trusts should be set up carefully to avoid jeopardizing SSI and Medicaid eligibility. Another possible source of funding for these individuals are community "friends" who volunteer to take the individual to activities and pay the costs.

Another good choice for individuals with limited funding is public recreational programs. Federal and state parks and recreation agencies often have programs available to the community that charge minimal fees or fees that can be waived for persons with financial needs. The public library often has cost-free alternatives where students can access books, computer games, and library-organized group activities. Local YMCA and YWCA programs may provide access to swimming, organized sports, and exercise activities at little or no cost to persons with limited finances. Religious organizations often offer intramural and other sports activities for members. Neighborhood and senior citizen centers may also provide recreational programs.

Individuals with disabilities should also consider nonrecreational forms of community participation such as volunteering and membership in civic-minded clubs and organizations. Individuals should be encouraged to participate in some form of public service, not only for the good of the community, but also to open the door to recreational activities related with public service. Political activities may provide rewarding experiences and open the door to new relationships. Religious communities typically have missions that can provide interesting activities and sometimes the opportunity to travel. Interest groups such as computer clubs may help the individual link up with like-minded individuals. See Figures 12-1 and 12-2 for Jennifer's Summary of Performance.

> **Critical Point**
> It is important to factor in the costs of community leisure activities and to identify community providers who provide low-cost activities, assistance in paying fees, or volunteer activities.

Residential living goal/outcome: supported apartment
Assessments: Community-based assessments; classroom observations; LCCE assessment

COGNITIVE AREAS	Present Level of Performance (grade level, standard scores, strengths, needs)	*Essential* accommodations, modifications and/or assistive technology utilized in high school and why needed
General Ability and Problem Solving (reasoning/processing)	Jennifer is able to solve simple problems but is easily frustrated. She often needs additional time and prompts (verbal) to process information.	Jennifer uses visual cues to assist her in completing tasks and for problem solving. Jennifer will need a crisis/emergency card with names and phone numbers of those that may assist her. This card will include pictures for ease of use.
FUNCTIONAL AREAS	**Present Level of Performance** (strengths and needs)	*Essential* accommodations/modifications and/or assistive technology utilized in high school and why needed
Independent Living Skills (self-care, leisure skills, personal safety, transportation, banking, budgeting)	Jennifer is currently working on learning personal banking and budgeting skills. She is able to enter money in a checking account and has participated in some lessons about choosing needs over wants in budgeting. She is able to complete a basic grocery list and shop for those items.	Jennifer will need assistance in bill payment and banking procedures. An individual (to be determined) will provide Jennifer with a budget and weekly allowance. This process will be monitored by Jennifer's parents.
Environmental Access/Mobility (assistive technology, mobility, transportation)	Jennifer lives with her mom and sister. She is very mobile, but she is unable to drive. Jennifer will need to learn different forms of transportation so that she is able to use this in case of an emergency.	Jennifer will take part in a life skills class. She will learn how to use different modes of transportation as well as a cell phone in case of an emergency. Jennifer will also receive additional instruction on how to use a map of the city and read bus schedules.

FIGURE 12–1   Summary of performance—Jennifer (Case Study)

Source: This template was developed by the National Transition Documentation Summit © 2005 including representation from the Association on Higher Education and Disability (AHEAD), the Council for Exceptional Children's Division on Career Development and Transition (DCDT), and Division on Learning Disabilities (DLD), the National Joint Committee on Learning Disabilities (NJCLD), the Learning Disability Association (LDA) and the National Center on Learning Disabilities (NCLD). It was based on the initial work of Stan Shaw, Carol Kochhar-Bryant, Margo Izzo, Ken Benedict, and David Parker. It reflects the contributions and suggestions of numerous stakeholders in professional organizations, school districts, and universities, particularly the Connecticut Interagency Transition Task Force. It is available to be freely copied or adapted for educational purposes.

Community Participation Goal/Outcome: Independent participation
Assessments: Community-based assessments; classroom observations; self-determination scale; adaptive behavior; social/interpersonal skills assessments

COGNITIVE AREAS	Present Level of Performance (grade level, standard scores, strengths, needs)	*Essential* accommodations, modifications and/or assistive technology utilized in high school and why needed
Communication (speech/language, assisted communication)	Jennifer is a verbal teenager who expresses her needs, wants, and opinions without the use of prompts.	No accommodations are necessary for Jennifer.
FUNCTIONAL AREAS	Present Level of Performance (strengths and needs)	*Essential* accommodations/ modifications and/or assistive technology utilized in high school and why needed
Social Skills and Behavior (interactions with teachers/ peers, level of initiation in asking for assistance)	Currently, social interactions present a challenge for Jennifer. She has difficulty following directions given by adults and authority figures that are new to her. Jennifer completes most of her assignments independently and is reluctant to work in groups.	Jennifer performs well, when she answers to a single supervisor with whom she has had time to develop a relationship. She is more productive in tasks and situations that do not require her to interact socially with her peers. Feedback should be specific and given in small chunks, focusing on one aspect of her performance at a time. Jennifer also responds well to private positive praise as opposed to being praised publicly.
Self-Determination/ Self-Advocacy Skills (ability to identify and articulate postsecondary goals, learning strengths, and needs; independence and ability to ask for assistance with learning)	Jennifer is able to express a desire for a high school diploma and a job in the local mall. She realizes that her learning is delayed and that she's had many social difficulties. She is not able to articulate her specific strengths and weaknesses. She is able to ask for assistance with academic and functional tasks but often chooses not to.	Jennifer advocates for herself better with specific verbal prompting from an adult she trusts and has improved her skills through the use of role-playing activities with her instructors.

FIGURE 12–2 Summary of performance—Jennifer (Case Study)

Source: This template was developed by the National Transition Documentation Summit © 2005 including representation from the Association on Higher Education and Disability (AHEAD), the Council for Exceptional Children's Division on Career Development and Transition (DCDT), and Division on Learning Disabilities (DLD), the National Joint Committee on Learning Disabilities (NJCLD), the Learning Disability Association (LDA) and the National Center on Learning Disabilities (NCLD). It was based on the initial work of Stan Shaw, Carol Kochhar-Bryant, Margo Izzo, Ken Benedict, and David Parker. It reflects the contributions and suggestions of numerous stakeholders in professional organizations, school districts, and universities, particularly the Connecticut Interagency Transition Task Force. It is available to be freely copied or adapted for educational purposes.

CONCLUSION

This chapter provided an overview of residential, community participation, and leisure opportunities and discussed them in the context of societal views about the roles of persons with disabilities. It described how an evolving concept of these roles has resulted in a nonsystem of services and supports that can vary considerably from place to place. This chapter described how planning for residential services, community participation, and leisure activities starts with the development of a vision of possibilities that is built through person-centered planning approaches and the provision of experiences that allow the individual to actually see and assess the activities. Once the vision has been developed, the chapter presented how to develop congruence between the demands of prospective environments, the skills of the individual, and available community supports. It then described some of the critical gatekeeper agencies for residential and community services and how to use these agencies as consultants in identifying opportunities for the individual. It is the authors' hope that this chapter has provided the essential knowledge that a transition coordinator will need to guide the individual and the family toward obtaining quality outcomes in residential, community, and leisure aspects of the individual's life.

STUDY QUESTIONS

1. Identify the social factors that contributed to deinstitutionalization and institutional reforms.
2. Identify how normalization contributed to deinstitutionalization and institutional reform and why this concept was revised to include social role valorization.
3. Identify how the independent living movement contributed to the development of supported living options and Medicaid waiver programs.
4. Describe the limitations inherent in older models of residential services such as institutions, ICF/MR programs, and group homes.
5. Describe how to evaluate individual preferences in regard to adult residential options for a student with a disabilities.
6. Describe the requirements, skills, and supports that need to be considered in developing a transition plan for residential services.
7. Identify the key agencies for collaboration in developing linkages to adult residential services.
8. Describe the factors that should be considered in developing a vision of adult community participation and leisure options for a student with a disability.
9. Describe the skills and supports critical to developing casual and intimate interpersonal relationships.
10. Describe some of the key agencies and community programs that provide community participation and leisure opportunities for students with disabilities.
11. Describe three methods for developing integrated community activities.

SECTION 4

DEVELOPING A RESPONSIVE TRANSITION SYSTEM

Section 4 moves from a discussion of "why?" and "who?" of transition to "how?" transition planning occurs at the individual and program levels. These three chapters can be viewed as a technical manual that describes how to weave policy, best practices, and a myriad of programs and services into transition activities that promote student self-determination, effective transition planning, service coordination, and family involvement. Chapter 13 "Transition Planning," describes various individual planning strategies and how to prepare for, conduct, and evaluate progress for the IEP meeting in which transition is discussed. This chapter discusses the importance of eliciting student and family input through the use of person-centered, self-determination, and/or career planning models as a base for the IEP and provides practical examples of meeting agendas, transition plans, and IEPs.

Chapter 14 "Participatory Decision Making: Innovative Practices for Student Self-Determination," provides an overview of how students can be involved in developing their own education goals through self-determination curriculum and discusses one self-determination program in detail. This chapter discusses the importance of choice and participation by students with disabilities and their families and provides some practical examples of how individuals with disabilities can take greater control of their lives.

Chapter 15, "Coordinating Transition Services," discusses transition service coordination from a combined individual and systemic perspective and examines state-of-the-art case management and service coordination models and barriers in applying these models in a highly bureaucratic and fragmented transition system. This chapter discusses the important role that the transition coordinator plays in developing interagency collaboration and provides examples of interagency agreements.

CHAPTER 13

TRANSITION PLANNING

Robert Baer

LEARNING OBJECTIVES

The objectives of this chapter are:

1. Develop a general concept of transition planning as it relates to youth with disabilities and the Individuals with Disabilities Education Act (IDEA).

2. Identify some common myths about transition planning that have emerged since it has become IDEA policy.

3. Understand the process of preparing for the transition meeting and the many models,

assessments, and considerations that must be addressed before the actual meeting occurs.

4. Understand the process of implementing the transition plan from the development of the plan to the assessment of progress.

5. Develop a general understanding of common questions that may be asked by families in the development and implementation of the transition plan.

INTRODUCTION

Overall, the transition planning requirements of the IDEA have evolved from accountability for services to accountability for postschool outcomes. However, transition services must continue to address the four essential elements of transition planning for students with disabilities to obtain high-quality outcomes. This chapter illustrates how students' *needs, preferences, interests,* and *strengths* should be considered in the choice of transition assessments, planning approaches, courses of study, transition activities, and linkages with adult service providers. It shows how to design an *outcome-oriented* transition planning process that addresses both academic and functional results and the linkages that students with disabilities need to move into postschool environments. This chapter also describes how a *coordinated set of activities* must involve the full range of educational, adult, and community services. Finally, it explains how the transition specialist can use backward planning approaches to *promote movement from school to postschool activities*.

TRANSITION PLANNING AND THE IDEA 1990–2004

In response to studies that showed poor postsecondary outcomes for students graduating from special education (Hasazi, Gordon, & Roe, 1985) the Individuals with Disabilities Education Act of 1990 mandated that **Individualized Education Programs (IEPs)** include a *statement of needed transition services* developed through an *outcome-oriented process*. The statement of needed transition services (also known as the individual transition plan or ITP) was designed to ensure that students' IEPs included activities that *promoted movement* toward their desired postschool settings. The IDEA of 1990 was the first piece of legislation to mandate transition planning, which it stated should start no later than age 16. This plan was to be reviewed annually and include a *coordinated set of activities* that were *based on students' needs, taking into account their interests and preferences*. The types of transition services identified in the IDEA of 1990 included instruction, community experiences, career development, daily living skills training, functional vocational evaluation, and linkages with adult services.

The IDEA of 1997 (P.L. 105-17) extended the notion of transition to include, by age 14 or earlier, *a statement of transition service needs* related to supporting students' high school courses of study. This transition requirement was added to deal with the concern that students with disabilities were having difficulty accessing the mainstream educational programs critical to achieving their postschool transition goals. The IDEA of 1997 also required that students with disabilities participate in all state- and district-wide testing so that schools could be held accountable for their progress in the general education curriculum. In promulgating regulations for the IDEA of 1997, the committee noted, "the IEP provisions added by P.L. 105-17 are intended to provide greater access by children with disabilities to the general curriculum and to educational reforms [such as school-to-work programs] ... " (p. 55091). The transition requirements of the IDEA of 1997 elevated instruction and participation in the general curriculum to preeminent roles in promoting movement to postschool settings.

> **Critical Point**
> The IDEA of 1990 and 1997 mandated transition planning for all students with IEPs, at first aged 16 or younger, and then aged 14 years or younger.

The IDEA of 2004 redefined transition in a way that weakened its process requirements and strengthened its accountability for results. It no longer required a statement of transition service needs related to students' courses of study by age 14, or earlier if appropriate. It defined transition planning as a "results-oriented" rather than an "outcome-oriented" process and moved its focus from *promoting postschool outcomes* to a focus on *improving the academic and functional achievement of the child* to promote postschool outcomes [20 U.S.C. 1401(34)(A)]. This change in definition suggested that the purpose of transition services was to promote in-school results as a way of promoting postschool outcomes. Additionally, the IDEA of 2004 deleted the requirement that the transition plan in the IEP identify needed linkages with adult services, and it moved the required identification of students' courses of study back to when transition planning was required (i.e., by no later than age 16).

Though the IDEA of 2004 weakened the requirements for schools to provide early transition planning and identify transition linkages, it strengthened accountability for postschool outcomes by requiring that the transition plan include *appropriate measurable postsecondary goals*, including goals related to employment and/or postsecondary education [Section

614(d)(1)(A)(VIII)(aa)]. Additionally, the IDEA of 2004 required that schools develop a "summary of the child's academic achievement and functional performance, which shall include recommendations on how to assist the child in meeting the child's postsecondary goals"[Section 614(c)(5)(B)(ii)].

Determining Student Needs, Strengths, Interests, and Preferences

The IDEA has consistently stated that the school should invite the student to the IEP meeting if the purpose of the meeting is the consideration of transition services for a student. It has also required that the student's preferences and interests be considered if they do not attend the transition meeting. The IDEA has consistently specified that the notice of the transition meeting must inform parents that the student will be invited to the meeting, and since 1997 it has required that the IEP include a statement that students and their parents have been notified in writing of the transfer of IDEA rights to students at least one year prior to them reaching the age of majority [Section 614(c)(5)(B)(i)]. Since 2004, the IDEA has further specified that the determination of student needs, strengths, interests, and preferences be assessed using age-appropriate transition assessments.

Outcome-Oriented and Results-Oriented Transition Planning

Until 2004, the IDEA consistently referred to transition as arising from an outcome-oriented process that focused on adult living objectives including postsecondary education, vocational education, integrated employment (including supported employment), continuing and adult education, adult services, independent living, or community participation. The IDEA of 2004 changed this definition from "outcome-oriented" to "results-oriented" and changed the focus of transition planning to promoting functional and academic achievement to facilitate the child's movement from school to postschool activities. This shift in focus represented a continuation of the evolution of transition from the supports-focused model proposed by Madeline Will in 1983 to a "transition perspective of education" proposed by Kohler (1998). However, the IDEA of 2004 strengthened accountability for postsecondary outcomes by mandating the development of measurable postsecondary goals related to employment and/or postsecondary education.

Coordinated Set of Activities

Until 2004, the IDEA mandated that each student's transition plan include, "if appropriate, a statement of each public agency's and each participating agency's responsibilities or linkages, or both, before the student leaves the school setting." The IDEA of 2004 removed this requirement but continued to require that each transition meeting include "the child's teacher, a regular education teacher (if the student is or might be in regular education) and ... a representative of the public agency other than the child's teacher who is qualified to provide, or supervise the provision of, special education ...". The IDEA of 2004 also continued to require that "the public agency shall invite ... a representative of any other agency that is likely to be responsible for providing or paying for transition services." The IDEA placed the responsibility for coordination of transition plans with schools and required that:

> If a participating agency, other than the local educational agency, fails to provide the transition services described in the IEP in accordance with paragraph (1)(A)(i)(VIII), the local educational agency shall reconvene the IEP Team to identify alternative strategies to meet the transition objectives for the child set out in the IEP. (Section 300.348)

Promoting Student Movement to Postschool Activities

The IDEA required that transition services be designed to move students toward their desired postschool activities and suggested that they should be initiated early enough to achieve those outcomes. The IDEA of 1997 required that, "beginning at age 14, and updated annually, a statement of the transition service needs of the child ... that focuses on the child's courses of study (such as participation in advanced-placement courses or a vocational education program)" be included in the IEP (Section 300.347). The IDEA of 2004 moved this course of study requirement into the regular transition planning process that started at age 16. Both the IDEA of 1997 and 2004 continued to require a statement of needed transition services in the IEP that addresses the need for services including "instruction, related services, community experiences, the development of employment and other postschool objectives, and, when appropriate, acquisition of daily living skills and functional vocational evaluation" (Section 300.29). The IDEA of 2004 added a finding that "as graduation rates for children with disabilities continue to climb, providing effective transition services to promote successful post-school employment or education is an important measure of accountability for children with disabilities" [Section 601(c)].

COMMON MYTHS IN REGARD TO TRANSITION POLICY IMPLEMENTATION

Stowitschek and Kelso (1989) warned that making transition plans part of the IEP would cause them to take on many negative characteristics of the IEP, including lack of year-to-year continuity and low-quality objectives. Research indicated that transition plans often lacked vision, linkages, and methods for coordinating services (Gallivan-Fenlon, 1994; Grigal, Test, Beattie, & Wood, 1997; Krom & Prater, 1993; Lombard, Hazelkorn, & Neubert, 1992; Story, Bates, & Hunter, 2002). Four common myths have become prevalent in schools where educators have focused upon transition "paper compliance" (Baer, Simmons, & Flexer, 1996).

Myth One: There Is One Transition Planning Process for All Students

Transition planning as a career planning process must be individualized and suited to the cognitive and career needs of individual students with disabilities. Some students may choose to participate in regular education career planning processes as part of transition planning (Clark & Kolstoe, 1995; Menchetti & Piland, 1998; Sitlington & Clark, 2006), whereas others may prefer person-centered planning approaches such as Personal Futures Planning (Mount, 1994; O'Brien, 1987; Story, 2002). The principles of self-determination and appropriateness must be concurrently applied in the selection of transition planning approaches. Students with disabilities should be able to take an active role in transition planning, but they also must be provided with planning that is sophisticated enough to address the complexity of school and adult service systems. Consequently, no one transition planning process fits all students. In fact, some students may need multiple planning approaches (e.g., person-centered planning and career planning).

Myth Two: Planning Occurs Only in the Transition Meeting

Transition planning involves much more than a short meeting at the beginning or end of an IEP meeting. In a comfortable environment, students and families should be given time to discuss their needs and desired post-secondary outcomes, and to plan activities for several years at a time. This generally requires a discussion of these issues prior to the transition meeting because students with disabilities and their families have been shown to participate much less in larger meetings with many professionals in attendance (Pumpian, Campbell, & Hesche, 1992; Whitney-Thomas, Shaw, Honey, & Butterworth, 1998). The planning process, Choosing Options and Accommodations for Children (COACH), has suggested that the initial interview limit participation to the teacher/facilitator, family members, and the student to assure meaningful student and family input (Giangreco, Cloninger, & Iverson, 1993).

Myth Three: Transition Plans Cover One Year

Transition plans are by definition long-term plans since they are focused upon postschool outcomes. The IDEA requires that these plans be reviewed annually, but that they should not be discarded each year and started anew. Unfortunately, this presents a logistical problem when the transition plan is part of the IEP. As part of the IEP, transition services are subject to the same requirement as other IEP services, and it has been argued that multiyear transition plans obligate the school to provide services too far in the future to assure that they will be available when the time comes. Yet, without multiyear planning, the transition statement in the IEP becomes nothing more than a list of short-term functional activities. Many schools have addressed this dilemma by developing a long-term transition plan that is passed along from year to year and is used to provide continuity in IEP planning.

Myth Four: Transition Teams Meet Only Annually

The IDEA of 2004 no longer requires that the transition team be reconvened as soon as possible if a school's transition service cannot be provided as planned, if the parent and school agree on an amendment to the IEP. However, the school must still reconvene the IEP if a participating agency other than the school cannot provide services as planned. The general principles of good planning require monitoring, evaluation, and revision of plans whenever major changes occur, including: (a) change in student goals, (b) problems in student performance, (c) failure to obtain services as planned, or (d) new opportunities or programs that may benefit the

Computer-assisted assessments support the determination of career assessments.

approaches may also benefit students with milder disabilities who have no postsecondary goals (Harrington, 2003; Rojewski, 1993). Person-centered planning approaches usually involve a facilitator, a recorder, the student, and various family, friends, classmates, and co-workers who work together to answer questions regarding the student's (a) history, (b) dreams, (c) nightmares, (d) relationships, (e) abilities, and (f) plan of action (Holburn & Vietze, 2002). Person-centered planning approaches include:

1. *Personal Profiling* (O'Brien, 1987; O'Brien & O'Brien, 2002). A planning approach that uses graphics to determine in relation to the individual: (a) important people, (b) important places, (c) critical events, (d) health issues, (e) daily life choices, (f) ways to gain or lose respect, (g) support strategies, (h) hopes and fears, and (i) barriers and opportunities.
2. *Personal Futures Planning* (Mount & Zwernick, 1988). A type of person-centered planning that addresses issues in the areas of: (a) home, (b) work or school, (c) community, (d) choices and preferences, and (e) relationships.
3. *Essential Lifestyle Planning* (Smull & Burke-Harrison, 1992). A person-centered planning approach that focuses upon seven areas: (a) nonnegotiables, (b) strong preferences, (c) highly desirables, (d) personal characteristics, (e) personal concerns, (f) needed supports, and (g) action steps.
4. *COACH* (Giangreco et al., 1993). A form of person-centered planning that stands for choosing options and accommodations for children. This approach includes the family's values and dreams in IEP planning.
5. *Making Action Plans* (formerly McGill Action Planning System (MAPs) (Vandercook, York, & Forest, 1989). A form of person-centered planning that develops "road maps" by defining personal history, identity, dreams, nightmares, strengths, and gifts.

student. Yet, research indicated that less than 25% of secondary schools had a mechanism for reconvening the transition team if services could not be provided as planned (Baer et al., 1996; McMahan, 2005; McMahan & Baer, 2001). Some schools have addressed this problem by developing computer-linked planning, interagency teams, or conference calls to assure regular communication (McMahan & Baer, 2001).

> **Critical Point**
> Implementation of IDEA's transition mandates should go beyond minimum or "paper compliance" requirements.

PREPARING FOR THE TRANSITION MEETING

Choosing Transition Planning Processes

Transition planning must address the unique planning capabilities and needs of students with disabilities and their families. To some degree, all transition planning approaches should be: (a) person-centered, (b) self-determined, and (c) career-oriented. Planning approaches emphasizing person-centered planning have been used primarily for individuals who have difficulty developing career goals due to both the extent of their disability or a difficulty in expressing preferences (Menchetti & Piland, 1998). Although typically used with students with severe disabilities, these planning

Self-determination is an important focus of transition planning. Good person-centered and career-oriented planning processes address the need for students to make their own decisions, but self-determination models may enhance student participation by developing self-awareness and leadership skills. Self-determination approaches typically focus upon improving the student's ability (a) to self-advocate, (b) to make decisions,

(c) to develop goals, (d) to demonstrate leadership, and (e) to take an active role in transition meetings. Self-determination approaches include:

1. *Choice Maker* (Martin, Huber Marshall, Maxson, & Jerman, 1996). A self-determination approach that focuses upon (a) choosing goals, (b) expressing goals, and (c) taking action.
2. *Group Action Planning* (Turnbull & Turnbull, 1993). A self-determination approach that helps students to take charge of personal futures planning.
3. *Whose Future Is It Anyway?* (Wehmeyer & Kelchner, 1995). A self-determination curriculum that is designed for persons with cognitive disabilities consisting of 36 lessons that address (a) having self-awareness, (b) making decisions, (c) obtaining supports and transition services, (d) writing and evaluating transition objectives, and (e) learning leadership skills.
4. *Next S.T.E.P.* (Halpern et al., 1997). A student-directed transition approach consisting of 16 lessons that address: (a) getting started, (b) self-exploring and evaluating, (c) developing goals and activities, and (d) putting a plan into place.
5. *IPLAN* (Van Reusen & Bos, 1990; Van Reusen & Bos, 1994). A form of person-centered planning focused on students with learning disabilities that stands for Inventory, Plan, Listen, Ask, and Name your goals.
6. *TAKE CHARGE* (Powers et al., 1996). A student-directed collaborative approach focused on students with physical disabilities that pairs youth with adults of the same gender with similar challenges, and uses four primary strategies: (a) skill facilitation, (b) mentoring, (c) peer support, and (d) parent support to develop student skills in achievement, partnership, and coping.

Career planning approaches can be effective for many students, especially students who plan to enter postsecondary education and technical careers. Career development approaches tend to be: (a) systematic, (b) developmental, (c) focused on self-awareness, and (d) oriented to a wide range of occupations. Career planning approaches include:

1. *What Color Is Your Parachute* (Bolles, 1995; Bolles & Bolles, 2006). This publication provides an overview of career development and some useful exercises and examples related to identifying interests, researching jobs, developing résumés, and conducting interviews.
2. *Life-Centered Career Education (LCCE)* (Brolin & Schatzman, 1989; Brolin, 1997; Brolin & Lloyd, 2004). This career development approach delineates 22 major competencies that can be infused into primary, middle, and secondary curricula to address the major life domains of work, home, and academics.
3. *Career Maturity Inventory* (Crites, 1978). This assessment, along with the Career Development Inventory (1990), can direct counseling (or the use of a computerized DISCOVER program) to address competencies related to the roles of student, leisurite, citizen, worker, and homemaker.
4. *Myers-Briggs* (Myers & McCauley, 1985). This assessment identifies four personality temperaments that can be used to develop self- and career-awareness (e.g., extroverted, intuitive, feeling, perceptive, or EIFP).
5. *Employability Life Skills Assessment* (Weaver & DeLuca, 1987). This criterion-referenced checklist may be used yearly to assess a student's level of performance in 24 critical employability skills areas in the domains of personal, social, and daily living habits.
6. *Self-Directed Search®* (Holland, 1985b; Holland, 1996). This instrument identifies six personality types and matches them with six matching categories of jobs to help students make a career choice related to their needs and preferences.

The *Self-Directed Search* is particularly effective for transition planning because it provides information on student personality types and matches it with occupations that have a high probability of being a good career choice (Simmons & Baer, 1996). The LCCE is a particularly good assessment and planning approach for students entering supported employment and supported living because it is particularly focused on life-skills needs (Greene, 2003).

> **Critical Point**
> Transition planning approaches should be selected with the student and the family and should emphasize self-determination, person-centeredness, and career orientation.

Time Lines for Transition Planning

Like all people, persons with disabilities go through many transitions in their life (Brolin & Schatzman, 1989; Repetto & Correa, 1996; Savickas, 2002). The IDEA of 2004 has indicated that IEP and transition planning may eventually focus on a number of *transition points* in the educational life span, including the transition to school (currently addressed in Part C of the IDEA), transition to middle school, transition to high school, and the transition to postsecondary environments. In the context of this book, transition planning is focused upon the transition from school to postsecondary environments. However, it is important to view transition in the context of the student's total learning experience since transition planning at the secondary level must build upon the student's developmental experiences up to that time. Table 13-1 shows how transition choices should be developed and formed from primary school on.

Forming the Transition Planning Team

The composition of the transition planning team is a primary consideration in the development of a transition plan. Selection of team members should be a collaborative effort with the student and the family integrally involved (O'Brien, 1987). This is important because research indicates that self-friend-family networks account for more than 80% of the jobs obtained by students after graduation (Hasazi, Gordon, & Roe, 1985; SRI International, 1992). The selection of the transition team also should include representatives from high school and postsecondary environments desired by students so that they can establish contacts and become familiar with the requirements of the programs they want to enter.

> **Critical Point**
> The transition team should be developed with the student and the family and should include core members, natural supporters, adult service providers, and representatives of postsecondary environments.

Core transition team members are persons who should always be involved in the development of the transition plan. According to the IDEA, core members include:

1. The student with a disability
2. Parents and guardians
3. The special education teacher
4. A representative of the local education agency who is knowledgeable about the general education curriculum
5. An individual who can interpret evaluation
6. A regular education teacher (if the student is or might be in regular or vocational education classes).

In addition to these core members, individual students may have specific needs or preferences that require the involvement of other transition stakeholders. These include but are not limited to: (a) work-study coordinators and transition specialists, (b) related service providers, (c) vocational rehabilitation counselors, (d) adult service providers, (e) employers, (f) representatives of postsecondary education programs, and (g) community supporters and advocates. These and other team members should be identified in the process of assessing the student's desired environments related to work, education, community participation, and residential living. The respective roles of transition team members are outlined in Table 13-2.

Transition Assessments

The transition coordinator should assure that students and their families have all the information they need to make informed choices regarding student postschool goals, course of study, and necessary transition services. Prior to the meeting, the educator should collect and obtain the assessments needed for the transition meeting. These may include a range of vocational and life-skills assessments that can help students to identify their strengths, needs, interests, and preferences. It also can include student and family surveys that assess the student's career maturity and family-student agreement on postschool goals. The following list includes some types of assessments that may be useful for specific students (Clark & Patton, 1997; Miller, Lombard, & Corbey, 2007; Trainor, Patton, & Clark, 2005):

* Interest inventories (computer and written)
* Transition surveys
* Employability skills inventories
* Personal futures planning
* Structured situational (i.e., home, community, and work) assessments
* Assessments of postschool environments desired by the student
* Curriculum-based assessment
* Structured interviews
* Social histories
* Adaptive behavior inventories
* Life-skills inventories

TABLE 13–1   Timelines for transition planning

Primary Level: Grades 1–4

Goals: Employability and independent living skills and attitudes

Objectives:
1. To develop positive work habits
2. To appreciate all types of work
3. To develop an understanding of how to cope with disability

Possible Activity Areas:
- Inclusion activities
- Responsibility activities
- Work sample activities
- Career field trips
- Discussions about work
- Discussions of interests and aptitudes
- Exploration of technology
- Decision-making and problem-solving activities

Middle School: Grades 5–8

Goals: Career exploration and transition planning relative to course of study

Objectives:
1. To understand the relationship of school to work
2. To understand interest, aptitudes, and preferences
3. To understand work, education, independent living, and community options
4. To determine a general secondary course of study
5. To identify needed accommodations and supports for secondary education
6. To specify transition services needed to participate in a desired course of study by no later than age 14

Possible Activity Areas:
- Visits to vocational and technical schools
- Visits to high school
- Complete interest inventories
- Functional vocational assessment
- Career fairs
- Survey transition needs and preferences
- Employability assessment
- Daily living skills classes
- Money and budgeting classes
- Community awareness classes
- Political awareness classes
- Job shadowing
- Career guidance
- Self-determination and advocacy training
- Training in use of disability technology and related services
- Computer training
- Mobility training
- Counseling
- Employability skills training
- Decision-making and problem-solving activities

High School: Grades 9–10

Goals: Career exploration and transition planning

Objectives:
1. To develop meaningful and realistic postsecondary goals
2. To develop work, education, residential, and community participation skills and supports relevant to goals
3. To learn to manage disability technology and request accommodations

Possible Activity Areas:
- Technology assessment
- Make agency referrals
- Update transition goals
- Self-determination training
- Develop transition plan
- Vocational education
- Placement in advanced classes
- Work experiences
- Job shadowing
- Job placement
- Job clubs
- Linkages with adult services

High School: Grades 11 and up

Goals: Transition and overlap into postsecondary environments desired by the student

Objectives:
1. To test goals through experiences and activities
2. To secure options for postsecondary education and/or employment
3. To develop residential and community participation supports and contacts
4. To develop linkages with adult services
5. To empower students and families to function in adult environments

Possible Activity Areas:
- Review and revise transition plans
- Involve adult services
- Self-determination training
- Apply for adult services
- Apply for postsecondary education
- Financial planning
- Visit relevant postsecondary environments
- Develop job seeking skills
- Job placements
- Community memberships
- Transfer transition coordination
- Develop follow up supports
- Transfer transition plan to family or adult services

Source: From R. Baer, R. McMahan, & R. Flexer, 1999. *Transition planning: A guide for parents and professionals* (p. 9), Kent, OH: Kent State University. Copyright 1999 by Robert Baer. Reprinted with permission.

TABLE 13–2   Responsibilities of transition team members

Team Members	Responsibilities
Student*	Identifies needs, strengths, preferences, and interests Takes a leadership role in planning with supports Participates in all planning activities Identifies friends, family, and community members who can be part of the transition team Assumes IDEA rights at the age of majority

Parent/Guardian*
Also:
  Siblings
  Friends
  Advocates
	Provides information regarding student needs, strengths, preferences, and interests
	Participates in referrals to transition programs and adult services
	Assists in procuring social security numbers, identification cards, and transportation passes
	Plans for long-term financial support, social security, trust funds, or other supports
	Asks for assistance in obtaining community and residential services as needed
	Provides opportunities for the student to try out adult roles and responsibilities
	Identifies the person who will coordinate the transition plan
	Identifies friends, family, and community members who can be part of the transition team

Special education teacher*
  Collaborating with:
    Vocational education
    Work study
    Related services
    Guidance counselor
	Helps students to identify postsecondary goals and to obtain needed transition services
	Identifies school or community agency personnel to be included in transition planning
	Prepares the student and the family for participation in the transition team
	Writes the statement of needed transition services in the transition plan
	Coordinates transition services and activities in the transition plan (may delegate)
	Provides information and assists families in developing referrals for adult services
	Links the IEP to the student's course of study and required testing
	Collects and monitors information about student progress
	Provides or obtains accommodations and supports for all education services

Regular education teacher*	Connects the IEP to the general education curriculum Helps students to identify postsecondary goals and needed transition services Provides classroom instruction to support the student transition to adult environments Collects and monitors information about student progress Adapts curriculum and provides or obtains accommodation for regular education Obtains or provides accommodations for state and regional proficiency tests
An individual who can interpret evaluations*	Provides assessment information regarding student needs, interests, and preferences Provides assessment information regarding student strengths and aptitudes Interprets assessments and evaluations for the student and the family Identifies limitations of assessments and additional assessment needs Works with the student and family to identify assessment options
Representative of the local education agency familiar with the curriculum*	Provides information about programs offered throughout the school Identifies how the student with a disability can be included in general education programs Assists in obtaining technology, accommodations, and supports for inclusion and transition Helps to identify how to address general education curriculum and competencies Assists the transition team in obtaining accommodations and supports for student graduation, and for participation in state and regional proficiency tests

(Continued)

TABLE 13–2 Responsibilities of transition team members (*Continued*)

Team Members	Responsibilities
Adult service providers,	May provide job training and placement before and after graduation
Including:	May provide case management and service coordination services
VR services	Determine eligibility for Supplemental Security Income and Medicaid (generally VR and Social Security)
MR/DD services	May provide independent living services
Mental health	May provide functional vocational assessments and job counseling
Bureau of employment	May provide health services and supports
Social security	May provide technology and accommodations
Independent living center	May help to fund postsecondary education or vocational training
Employers	May provide recreational and leisure opportunities
Postsecondary educators	May provide counseling and behavioral supports
Human services	May assist in developing peer and coworker supports
	May provide opportunities to try out postsecondary environments
	May provide child support

*Core member
Source: From R. Baer, R. McMahan, & R. Flexer, 1999. *Transition planning: A guide for parents and professionals* (p. 11), Kent, OH: Kent State University. Copyright 1999 by Robert Baer. Reprinted with permission.

- Assessment of prerequisite skills for vocational education
- Aptitude tests
- Personality scales
- Social skills inventories
- Vocational skills assessments
- Professional assessments (e.g., psychology, medical, vision, speech, and mobility)
- College entrance examinations
- Assessment of technology needs
- Career portfolios

The IDEA of 2004 requires the use of appropriate age-level transition assessments. Care must be used in selection of standardized assessment instruments and in presentation of their findings. Assessment information should be: (a) valid for the type of student being tested, (b) related to actual and desired student environments, (c) understood by all members of the transition team, and (d) focused upon student strengths. Research indicates that standardized assessment procedures often lack validity for students with disabilities because they do not consider the effects of supports, technology, and training on student performance (Craddock & Scherer, 2002; Menchetti & Piland, 1998). Hagner and Dileo (1993) point out that standardized assessment procedures may have little use for students

> **Critical Point**
> Transition assessments should be valid for the type of student tested, individualized, strength-focused, functional, and socially referenced.

with severe disabilities since they lack the pressures, cues, sights, and sounds of the environments in which students will have to perform. These researchers advocate strongly for the use of situational assessments, or assessments that are conducted in the actual environments in which the student is expected to perform.

Backward Planning

The transition coordinator should employ a technique known as "backward planning" in developing transition services and the IEP (O'Brien & O'Brien, 2002; Steere, Wood, Panscofar, & Butterworth, 1990). Figure 13–1 shows how backward planning would work for a student desiring supported employment in a clerical situation after graduation. Starting with the final year prior to graduation, the student is established in the environment of choice—in this case, supported employment—to assure that the necessary services and supports are in place prior to graduation so that he or she could be simply transferred to the adult service system. Two years before graduation, the student is moved toward transition into supported employment through job placement, job club, and follow-along services. Three years prior to graduation, transition services are focused upon community experiences and vocational education that lead to supported employment. Four years prior to graduation, the focus of activities is career exploration with a focus upon job shadowing, guidance counseling, and employability skills training. This backward planning approach should be used for

Postsecondary Goal: Supported Employment in a Clerical Setting
Current Age: 18
Age to Graduate: 22

Needed transition service	Age 19	Age 20	Age 21	Age 22
1. Supported employment in a clerical setting			X	X
2. Follow-along support			X	X
3. Job placement services and job club		X	X	
4. Transportation training	X	X		
5. Develop Social Security work incentive plan		X		
6. Vocational education in clerical skills	X	X		
7. Community work experiences during the school year		X		
8. Summer jobs	X	X		
9. Job shadowing	X	X		
10. Guidance counseling	X			
11. Employability skills training	X	X		
12. Apply for social security benefits—done at age 18				
13. Referral to vocational rehabilitation—done at age 16				
14. Referral for MR/DD services—done at age 16				

FIGURE 13-1   Backward planning worksheet

Source: From R. Baer, R. McMahan, and R. Flexer, 1999. *Transition planning: A guide for parents and professionals* (p. 17), Kent, OH: Kent State University. Copyright 1999 by Robert Baer. Reprinted with permission.

each student's postsecondary goals, including postsecondary education, independent living, and community participation. A general rule of thumb for backward planning is, the more severe the disability, the more overlap that will be needed between school and postschool environments. Figure 13-1 shows a sample backward planning worksheet for a transition employment goal.

> **Critical Point**
> The development and implementation of postsecondary goals should drive the student's educational experience each year until graduation.

Preparing for Student and Family Led Transition Meetings

Prior to the transition meeting, the transition coordinator should go over the summary of assessment-identified transition service needs with the student and the family in order to develop consensus on: (a) general postsecondary goals, (b) the student's course of study, (c) the types of transition services needed, and (d) the

Varied transition services are required to meet mandates.

Cindy—Age 16		
Agenda Item	**Time—Presenter**	**Outcome**
I. Introductions	5 minutes—Teacher	Team sharing of names, relationship to student
II. Overview of agenda and meeting rules	5 minutes—Teacher	Team understanding of meeting purpose and process
III. Presentation of student/family postsecondary goals and course of study	10 minutes—Student and Family	Team understanding of student postsecondary goals and preferred course of study
IV. Presentation of student transition service and activity preferences	10 minutes—Student and Family	Understanding of student transition service and activity preferences
V. Discussion of transition service needs/preferences	15 minutes—Team	Consensus on needed transition services
VI. Assignment of responsibilities and timelines	20 minutes—Team	Completed transition plan
VII. IEP development	60 minutes—Team	Completed IEP

FIGURE 13–2 Sample transition meeting agenda

Source: Adapted from R. Baer, R. McMahan, and R. Flexer, 1999. *Transition planning: A guide for parents and professionals* (p. 19), Kent, OH: Kent State University. Copyright 1999 by Robert Baer. Reprinted with permission.

student's self-determination needs. Backward planning can be done with the student and the family to test the feasibility of postsecondary goals and to help them understand the amount of effort that will be necessary to achieve those goals. The results of this discussion should be summarized so that they can be used by the student and the family to drive the transition meeting. The student and the family also should be acquainted with the terms that may be used in the IEP meeting, and the use of Choice Maker or other student-led IEP curricula may aid in this process. A sample glossary is included in Appendix A.

An transition meeting agenda should be developed with time allotted for the student and the family to lead the discussion. The meeting agenda should specify meeting activities, the time allotted for each activity, and the desired outcomes. At the start of the transition meeting, there should be time for all transition team members to introduce themselves, to identify their role, and to state how they know the student. The following is a sample two-hour transition team meeting agenda. Times and agenda items may vary depending on the number of meeting participants, the student transition service needs, and the level of consensus among team members prior to the meeting. The team may want to appoint a timekeeper at the start of the meeting to notify members when the discussion is exceeding the allotted time. Figure 13–2 shows a sample agenda for an transition meeting.

> **Critical Point**
> Educators must plan ahead to ensure student and family participation in the IEP meeting in which transition is discussed.

CASE STUDY JOHN

Writing the IEP with a Transition Plan

The way the statement of needed transition services is written into the IEP may vary according to both the organization of the IEP and the needs of individual students. Typically, an **IEP transition plan** should include: (a) a vision statement, (b) the student's current level of functioning, (c) the student's course of study and related transition needs, (d) the student's postsecondary goals in regard to work, postsecondary education, residential living, and community participation, and (e) needed transition services and the persons who are responsible for each.

1. *The Vision Statement* The vision statement is the opportunity for the student and the family to put their goals and aspirations in their own words. In thinking of a vision, it may be helpful to ask the student and the family to think of a typical day, week, month, and year that would describe the desired goals. For example, a typical day might include work activities, time for rest and leisure, transportation concerns, and communication with friends and family. A typical week might include weekend outings, church, shopping, housework, and visits with friends and family. A typical month might include shopping for clothes, personal items, recreational items and such. Finally, a typical year may include holidays, vacations, time with family, and educational pursuits. The following is an example of a vision statement:

> John would like to work as an auto mechanic after graduation. He would like to live in an apartment and spend his days working and his evenings with friends or a spouse. During the week, John would like to go to movies, shop for groceries, take walks, exercise at the YMCA, and attend church. Periodically, he would like to shop at the local mall and travel to his aunt's house about 30 miles away. During the year, John would like to take driving vacations, attend holidays with family, and spend two weeks camping in the summer.

2. *Present Levels of Performance* According to the IDEA, present levels of performance should be based on a range of formal and informal assessments. This part of the IEP should be written in a functional manner that describes strengths and refers to needs in terms of what the student must do to succeed in a given area. For example, an IQ test is nonfunctional because it gives no direction to the team regarding planning of the student's course of study. Additionally, the current level of performance needs to specify what the student needs in order to progress in the general curriculum. The following is a sample level of performance statement:

> According to a 9/2006 reevaluation, teacher reports, work samples, and parent input, John has strengths in the areas of mathematics skills of addition, subtraction, multiplication, and division using a calculator. He still needs help in converting metrics. John needs to learn to work more quickly and efficiently related to his goal of being an auto mechanic. John also needs to learn to ask for help when frustrated. Grade level expectations of John's peers consist of basic math calculations as well as the application of math calculations in word problems. In order to participate in the general curriculum John will need the help of a tutor, use of a calculator and spell-checker, and curriculum modifications to focus math and English on applied mathematics and reading of technical manuals.

3. *Statement of Transition Service Needs (or Course of Study Statement)* After completing the vision statement and identifying the student's current level of functioning it should be possible to determine what **course of study** would best move a student from his or her current level of function to the desired postsecondary goals. The course of study statement needs to have two components: (a) the desired course of study and (b) the transition services needed to support the student in that course of study. In determining the course of study some general guidelines are that:

1. Four-year college = advanced college-level classes
2. Two-year college = regular and advanced classes, college courses, and vocational training
3. Technical school = advanced vocational training and related academics
4. Employment = applied academics, vocational training, and school-supervised work experiences
5. Supported employment = functional academics, vocational training, and school supervised supported employment

As noted in Chapter 6 and Chapter 7, students may need assistance in accessing these classes including: (a) assistive technology, (b) curriculum adaptations, (c) curriculum augmentation, or (d) curriculum alteration. These accommodations or "transition service needs" should be included in the statement of transition service needs (or course of study statement). An example of the course of study statement would be as follows:

> John will need tutoring, curriculum adaptations, a calculator, and a spell-checker to participate in vocational education leading to employment after graduation.

4. *Statement of Needed Transition Services (or Individual Transition Plan)* The statement of needed transition services was first required in the IDEA of 1990. This statement has also been known as

the Individual Transition Plan (ITP). The transition plan should include: (a) general postsecondary goals and (b) a list of transition services to reach those goals. Postsecondary goals could include goals in the areas of work, education, residential living, and community participation. When the student is younger, these goals may be broad (e.g., competitive employment, postsecondary education, etc). As the student nears graduation these goals may become more specific (e.g., working with autos, four-year college, etc.). If the student has not formed postsecondary goals, the transition goal may be the identification of these goals.

The second part of the transition plan includes activities that will promote movement to the student's desired postsecondary goals. According to the IDEA of 2004, transition services include: (a) instruction, (b) community experiences, (c) development of employment and other postschool adult living objectives, and (d) related services. If appropriate, the transition plan also should include transition services in the areas of: (a) daily living skills, (b) functional vocational evaluation, and (c) interagency linkages. The seven major categories of transition services outlined in the IDEA of 1997 can be described as follows:

1. *Instruction.* Includes tutoring, employability skills training, vocational education, social skills training, college entrance exam preparation, preparation for taking state and regional proficiency tests, and placement in advanced classes.
2. *Community experiences.* Includes job shadowing, community work experiences, tours of postsecondary education settings, and residential and community tours.
3. *Development of employment and other postschool adult living objectives.* Includes career planning, guidance counseling, interest inventories, person-centered planning, futures planning, self-determination training, job placement, and job tryouts.
4. *Related services.* Includes occupational and physical therapy, speech therapy, social services, psychology services, medical services, rehabilitation technology, and other professional supports to move the student toward postschool outcomes. Related services also include special education services to help the student participate in the general curriculum.
5. *Daily living skills training.* Includes self-care training, home repair, health training, home economics, independent living training, and money management.
6. *Linkages with adult services.* Includes referrals or assignment of responsibility for services to vocational rehabilitation (VR), summer youth employment programs, mental retardation and developmental disability (MR/DD) services, mental health services, social security, independent living centers, and agency fairs involving a range of adult services.
7. *Functional vocational evaluation.* Includes situational work assessments, work samples, aptitude tests, and job tryouts.

Many IEP formats include a transition page where postsecondary goals can be identified and then related activities listed below them. For example a transition plan for the goal of working with automobiles might appear as follows in the IEP:

Postsecondary Goal: Working with Automobiles

Transition Activities	Person Responsible	Due Dates	IEP Goal
• Auto mechanics classes	VOED teacher	9/1/07 – 5/1/08	1.1
• Automotive work experience	Work study	1/1/08 – 5/1/08	2.2
• Referral to VR for job coach	Work study	9/1/07	n/a

5. *Annual Goals* Now that the course of study statement and the transition plan has been completed, it is important to tie transition activities into the goals, objectives, and activities in the IEP. The first step

in this process is the development of measurable annual goals. For example, the automotive activity from the above transition plan refers to IEP goal 2.2. This annual goal could be written as follows:

> 2.2. Work experience—John will successfully complete a work experience in auto mechanics.

6. *Objectives* The IEP objectives should be specific components of the IEP annual goal that can be measured. For the above annual goal, the following objectives would help the team determine whether the IEP goal 2.2 has been reached:

1. John will independently complete the 10 duties of his job.
2. John will have no behavior outbursts on his job.
3. John's work will be of a quality acceptable to the employer.
4. John will convert fractions to decimals while using socket wrenches.

Under standards-based education, it is also important to show how transition activities contribute to mastery of state content standards. For example, the conversion of fractions to decimals could be related to age-level mathematics standards.

7. *Assessment of Student Progress* The assessment of student progress should be specified in regard to the procedures being used, who will do it, the target levels, and the schedule of assessments. Assessments must occur at least as frequently as assessments for students without disabilities. For the four objectives just described, the assessment of student progress may be written as follows:

- Procedure—task analysis (#1), behavior reports (#2), employer interviews (#3), and class work (#4)
- Who—work-study coordinator (#1–3) and classroom teacher (#4)
- Criteria
  1. John successfully completes 10 steps in task analysis for five consecutive days.
  2. John requires no behavioral intervention from employer for two consecutive weeks.
  3. Employer rates work quality as acceptable for a regular employee for four consecutive weeks.
  4. John successfully converts decimals to fractions and vice-versa at 95% accuracy.
- Schedule
  1. John will be assessed on completion of his task analysis weekly.
  2. John's behavior will be discussed weekly with his employer.
  3. John's work quality will be discussed weekly with his employer.
  4. John's math teacher will assess decimal/fractions skills weekly.

8. *Needed Services* Once the objectives and assessment procedures have been identified, the IEP team should identify services that will be needed to achieve each of the objectives under the annual goal. For the previously listed objectives needed services may be delineated as follows:

1. Employer/employee training 12/1–12/30/07 by work study
2. Job coaching 1/1–1/30/08 by vocational rehabilitation
3. Evaluation and follow-along by work study 2/1–5/1/08
4. Training and assessment by math teacher 9/1/07–12/1/08

9. *Least Restrictive Environment(s)* Discussion of the least restrictive environment to provide the proposed education and services should commence only after the student's education and support needs have been identified. The least restrictive environment should never be discussed at the beginning of the IEP meeting, because this may result in the student being slotted into a program before consideration of the student's educational needs. An example of the least restrictive environment statement for John would be:

> The least restrictive setting for John's automotive work experience is an integrated school supervised community work experience site. The least restrictive setting for John's classroom training in applied mathematics is a regular education class.

This completes the process of writing John's work experiences into his IEP. This process should be repeated for major transition activities (e.g., auto mechanics class) but may not be necessary for one-time transition services (e.g., referral to VR).

The Backward Transition Planning Process

Cindy was a student who had autism with pervasive support needs relative to self-care, learning, self-direction, communication, and independent living. Her autism was often exhibited in the form of irrational fears, aggression, stereotypical behavior, and rituals. In middle and early high school, it was determined that Cindy was not responding to traditional educational approaches as evidenced by her distractiveness and aggression toward teachers and peers in this environment. At age 14, her parents determined that Cindy should pursue a course of study leading to employment after graduation with transition services in the areas of behavioral supports, direct instruction, and psychiatric consultation. This was written into Cindy's IEP at age 14.

Jill, Cindy's special education teacher, was charged with developing a new transition plan for her since Cindy was turning 16 this year of school. After consultation with Cindy's parents and observation of her interests and preferences, it was determined that Cindy would benefit from personal futures planning, a psychology assessment, and a variety of situational assessments to determine her needs, interests, and preferences. These assessments were arranged with the help of the guidance counselor, the work-study coordinator, and a futures planning consultant from a local university.

> **Critical Point**
> Assessment approaches are to be developed in conjunction with the student and his or her family.

As a result of Personal Futures Planning (Mount & Zwernick, 1988), it was determined that Cindy and her parents wanted her to work in competitive employment and to live in a supported-living situation after graduation. Jill had some concerns that these postsecondary goals may be rather ambitious because Cindy had such extensive behavioral concerns. However, Cindy's parents pointed out that most of these behaviors were exhibited in the classroom and, therefore, could be controlled by the selection of a calm and nondistracting environment for employment after graduation. After some discussion, Jill agreed to support Cindy and her mother in presenting these postsecondary goals to the transition team.

Psychology assessments showed Cindy having considerable difficulty with changes in routine and a history of developing rituals that interfered with daily routines. A variety of situational assessments showed that Cindy preferred quiet and nondistracting environments and was quite interested in matching and organizing things. She did very well in the hospital records room filing records, although she had one outburst when maintenance workers had to work on the lights. She also did very well in delivering magazines and mail to patients. Transitional service needs were identified as follows:

1. *Instruction.* Cindy needed social skills training, behavioral supports, job-skills training, and direct instruction approaches.
2. *Community experiences.* Cindy needed community work experiences related to working in nondistracting clerical settings, experiences in getting to and from the bus, and experiences in living away from her parents.
3. *Development of employment and other postschool adult living objectives.* Cindy needed extensive job placement services and a plan for ongoing behavioral supports in both supported employment and supported living.
4. *Related services.* Assessment showed that Cindy needed related services in the areas of psychology services and augmented communication technology.
5. *Daily living skills training.* As reported by her parents, Cindy needed help to use public transportation.
6. *Linkages with adult services.* Assessment showed that Cindy would benefit from supported employment through VR and DD services, and a Social Security PASS (plans for achieving self-support).
7. *Functional vocational evaluation.* Evaluations emphasized the need to do situational assessments in a variety of environments.

> **Critical Point**
> Assessments must be summarized in a manner that is understandable and focused upon student support needs and strengths rather than upon student deficits.

Jill worked with Cindy and her parents to develop a list of who should be invited to the transition team meeting. Cindy had shown preferences for Jeff Plant, an older friend who had taken her to many community activities and who was the facilitator of Cindy's futures planning meeting. Jill reported that Jeff Ringles, the work-study coordinator, had suggested involving VR services, Social Security, and MR/DD since these agencies would be needed to provide support for community work experiences and supported employment. Cindy's mother recommended Jackie Speaker, an occupational therapist who evaluated Cindy for augmented communication technology, and Leonard James, a behavioral specialist who had worked with Cindy. As required by IDEA, Jill also invited a district representative who was knowledgeable about the general education curriculum, Cindy's regular education teacher, and a vocational-education teacher who was able to interpret evaluations.

> **Critical Point**
> Prepare the student and the family to participate in the IEP meeting and to lead parts of the discussion.

It was determined that, because Cindy was nonverbal, Cindy's mother would start the meeting with a review of Cindy's preferences in regard to employment, residential living, and community environments. She would also discuss transition services that would address Cindy's needs and environmental preferences, including community work experiences, supported employment (before graduation), and vocational education. A meeting agenda was developed and a meeting was set for a time that was convenient for Cindy, her mother, and Jeff Plant, Cindy's friend.

At the meeting, Jill asked team members to address themselves to Cindy and her mother and to identify themselves, their role, and how they knew Cindy. Jill emphasized that the purpose of the first part of this IEP meeting was to generate a plan that would lead to the types of postsecondary outcomes desired by Cindy. The rules for discussion were that the team must start with Cindy's environmental preferences and then brainstorm needed transition services to establish her in those postschool environments. These transition services, then, would be allocated the year prior to graduation.

Jill appointed a recorder and led the transition team in brainstorming the types of transition services that Cindy would need to move into her preferred environments of a quiet nondistractive work setting, a small family-type residence, and leisure activities with her friends and family. To develop supported employment and independent living options, the adult service representatives suggested (1) the development of a PASS plan with Social Security, (2) job placement and training through VR, and (3) ongoing employment and residential supports from MR/DD. Fred Fryman, the MR/DD representative, suggested that their case managers could help to coordinate these services and to obtain residential services for Cindy.

The school representatives identified the need to involve Cindy in applied mathematics, English, and vocational education since Cindy showed interests and aptitudes in these areas. The regular education teacher agreed to give Cindy assignments that would help her to identify words and numbers that were critical to working in the clerical and library settings she seemed to prefer when she job shadowed at a number of locations. The vocational educator agreed to see about getting Cindy into the school's secretarial training program with supports and accommodations provided by her behavioral support specialist and occupational therapist. The work-study coordinator agreed to develop community work experiences and supported employment prior to graduation. The district representative agreed to obtain a waiver on some entry requirements for vocational education so that Cindy could attend.

The team suggested, and Cindy's mother concurred, that Cindy should stay in school as long as possible to assure that she had the needed training, technology, and supports to achieve her postschool goals. It was determined that she would remain in school until age 22. Using backward planning, transition services were planned as follows:

1. Last year in school (age 21). It was determined that Cindy would need to be established in supported employment with supports from both the school and adult service providers. Due to Cindy's concerns about changes in routine, it was decided that this placement should carry on into adulthood.

(Continued)

2. Two years from graduation (age 19). It was planned that this year should focus upon the development of the postschool objectives with needed transition services provided in the areas of job placement, development of ongoing supports including a PASS plan, and continued community and career exploration.

3. Three years from graduation (age 18). It was determined that this year should focus upon the development of community work experiences, situational assessments, and the use of technology and accommodations related to Cindy's desired postschool settings.

4. Four years from graduation (age 17). This year was focused upon completion of vocational education and academics with continued assessment of Cindy's performance and preferences in regard to work and residential and community settings. Intake for all critical adult service program services also should have been completed.

5. Five years from graduation (age 16). It was decided that Cindy's transition service needs for the coming year would be mainly in the areas of academics, vocational education, development of employability skills, social skills training, daily living skills training, and mobility training. It also was determined that Cindy must be trained as soon as possible in order to identify technologies and accommodations that she would need for work.

As a result of this discussion, the following transition plan was developed. Each member was given a list of names, phone numbers, and addresses (including e-mail) to facilitate networking. Jill, then, took the time to address Cindy and her mother in order to explain the plan and to ask if they had any questions. The following transition plan (Table 13–3) was developed as a result of this planning.

Upon completion of the meeting, Cindy and her parents were given a copy of the transition plan and the major points were explained to them. They were informed that the transition team would be reconvened if any problems emerged, and they were encouraged to communicate any questions or concerns to Jill as their transition coordinator.

In the following year, Jill monitored provision of transition services and reconvened the team as needed. She also called each transition service provider and Cindy's parents every three months to determine how Cindy was progressing. At the end of the year, Jill forwarded the transition plan to Joe Lyon, who was to take over as Cindy's special education teacher the following year.

As Cindy moved through high school, there were a number of changes in the transition plan. Cindy was in a variety of work experiences in a library setting, delivering mail, and photocopying for a bank. Despite her success in a couple of her work experiences, she continued to need a great deal of supervision. Collectively, the transition team had to advocate for provision of supported employment because Cindy's MR/DD caseworker felt that she would be safer in a sheltered workshop. After considerable work and support from her family, Cindy was able to obtain a supported employment placement at a government agency delivering mail in-house with ongoing supervision. Her ongoing need for a job coach was partially funded and deducted from her earnings as an **impairment-related work expense (IRWE),** thereby maintaining her eligibility for Social Security and Medicaid. Cindy's parents set up a PASS plan to help her purchase a car so she could be driven to work by her job coach. Cindy also was able to obtain a supported living situation and to participate in community activities with the help of Medicaid funding.

QUESTIONS FAMILIES FREQUENTLY ASK

The educator who is responsible for coordinating the transition team meeting should be prepared to answer frequently asked questions of parents and students. Although it is impossible to know about all the agencies and services, the coordinator should have a basic working knowledge to assist the student and the family in determining who should be invited and involved in transition planning. The following are questions that are frequently asked by parents in regard to transition meetings.

TABLE 13–3   Sample transition plan

Statement of Needed Transition Services			
Name: Cindy Doe Age: 16 Person Responsible for Coordinating Transition: Jill Smith, Teacher	Date: 5/1/06 Age to Graduate: 22		

Postsecondary goals: Supported employment in clerical setting; supported living in hometown; Involvement in integrated clubs and religious organizations; more friends

Course of study and needed transition services: Vocational education (clerical) with direct instruction and behavioral supports. Also classes in consumer sciences, applied academics

Transition Area and Related Activities	Responsible Person	IEP Goal	Start: End:
1. Instruction:			
1. Applied math and English	Pat Claire–math teacher	1.1, 1.2	9/06–6/07
2. Clerical vocational education	Joe Gonzalez–VOED teacher	3.3	9/06–6/07
3. Employability skills	Jill Smith–SPED teacher	3.2	9/06–6/07
4. Social skills training	Joe Lyon–teacher	4.1	9/06–6/07
2. Community Experiences:			
1. Job shadowing in clerical settings	Jeff Ringles–work study	3.4	9/06–6/07
2. Visits to clubs and church groups	Julie Doe–parent		9/06–6/07
3. Community work experiences	Jeff Ringles–work study	3.5	9/07–6/09
4. Supported employment	Jack Point–VR counselor		9/09–6/10
5. Summer camp	Julie Doe–parent		8/06–9/00
3. Development of Employment and Adult Living Objectives:			
1. Job placement and training	Jack Point–VR counselor	5/09–9/09	
2. Development of a PASS plan	Sally Fort–social security	5/09–9/09	
3. Development of residential plan	Fred Fryman–MR/DD	9/08–5/09	
4. Development of ongoing supports	Fred Fryman–MR/DD	5/09–9/09	
4. Related Services:			
1. Behavioral plan	Leonard James–Beh Spec.	4.2	By 9/06
2. Augmentative communication training	Jackie Speaker–O.T.		9/06–5/07
5. Daily Living Skills:			
1. Provide mobility training	Jeff Plant–Friend		4/07–5/07
2. Provide training in home safety	Jill Smith–SPED teacher	4.4	1/07–5/07
6. Linkages with Adult Services:			
1. Vocational rehabilitation services	Jack Point–VR counselor		Age 16
2. Developmental disability services	Fred Fryman–MR/DD		Age 16
3. Social Security	Sally Fort–Social Security		Age 16
4. Residential services	Fred Fryman–MR/DD		Age 18
5. Case management services	Fred Fryman–MR/DD		Age 16
7. Functional Vocational Evaluation:			
1. Situational assessments in a variety of class, home, work, and leisure environments	Jeff Ringles–work study coordinator		9/06–5/07
2. Career portfolio	Sam Smith–guidance counselor		

Comments: Cindy will need a calm and nondistracting environment and ongoing supports.

Source: From R. Baer, R. McMahan, & R. Flexer, 1999. *Transition planning: A guide for parents and professionals* (p. 30), Kent, OH: Kent State University. Copyright 1999 by Robert Baer. Reprinted with permission.

1. *What employment services are available in the community?* There are agencies in each community that provide youth and adults assistance in finding and maintaining employment. These include:

- Vocational rehabilitation (VR) services: Provide or pay for vocational assessment, job placement, job training, postsecondary education, technology, and other time-limited services.
- Mental retardation and developmental disabilities (MR/DD) programs: Provide ongoing supports for students with the most severe disabilities in the areas of sheltered employment, supported employment, residential services, and case management.
- Workforce Investment Act (WIA) programs: Provide time-limited youth employment programs and a variety of job programs, generally for economically disadvantaged students.
- Mental health programs: Provide case management and occasionally supported employment for students with psychiatric disabilities.
- Nonprofit agencies such as United Cerebral Palsy, the ARC, and Goodwill Industries: Provide sheltered employment, supported employment, and other services for youth and adults with disabilities, often through contract with VR.
- Youth services programs: Generally provided to youth who have been in trouble with the law, often through contract with VR.
- Employment agencies: Provide job placement, generally on a fee-for-service basis. Sometimes this service can be paid for by VR.
- Postsecondary education programs: Often provide job placement and career services for their students. Vocational rehabilitation may pay part or all of the cost of these programs for eligible students.

2. *What employment services do school districts provide students with disabilities?* School districts may provide a number of services that are available to students with disabilities. These are provided through general, special, and vocational education. Some examples of programs designed to provide work experience or vocational training are (a) work-study or transition coordinators, (b) occupational work-adjustment staff, (c) vocational educators, (d) school-to-work program staff, and (e) guidance counselors.

3. *What should my child do to get into postsecondary education after high school?* There are four major types of postsecondary education: (a) vocational/technical schools, (b) community colleges (two-year), (c) liberal arts colleges, and (d) state universities. Every postsecondary program has academic requirements that must be met. However, community colleges often have remedial programs for students who have had difficulty in general areas of course work such as mathematics and English. Postsecondary options should be explored early in high school to select the proper course work and to choose a postsecondary program that provides the services and supports that will be needed by the student after graduation. The student also should receive training in asking for needed accommodations, supports, visits, and/or audit classes from desired schools (Turner, 1996). College and other entrance exams should be taken early and applications sent out in the final year of high school.

4. *What can I do to help my son or daughter get a job?* Parents have a very important role to play in their child's getting and keeping a job. The expectation that their son or daughter will work is important to convey to their children as they grow. Supporting the school district's efforts to provide job preparation also is essential. Parents can assure that meaningful vocational goals are written into their child's IEP and transition plans and provide opportunities for their child to develop important work skills, habits, and attitudes by giving them chores and responsibilities. Parents also can assist job placement professionals by providing them with leads and introducing them to employers they may know.

5. *How do I apply for adult services?* Generally, a student with an IEP will be eligible for vocational rehabilitation (VR) services, and the school can initiate a referral at the parent's or student's request, but typically only students with the more severe disabilities obtain VR services. MR/DD programs often serve only students with the most severe developmental disabilities and the family generally initiates referral. Summer youth employment programs often serve students with milder disabilities who are economically disadvantaged, with referrals typically coming from the school. Mental health job programs are commonly accessed through the mental health counselor and generally reserved for students with the most severe psychiatric disabilities.

6. *Is there an alternative to sheltered employment for students with severe disabilities?*

Supported employment is designed to serve students who have traditionally gone into sheltered workshops and day activity centers. This is competitive paid work that is performed in an actual job site by individuals who, because of their disability, need ongoing support services to perform that work. Supported employment has four characteristics: (a) paid employment, (b) integration with nondisabled co-workers, (c) ongoing support after job training, and (d) driven by student career goals. Supported employment models include:

- *Individual placement approaches* that include structured assistance in job placement and job training. A job developer develops a job of interest to the student and a job coach trains job skills and provides other training to maintain employment (e.g., social and travel skills). Once the job coach phases out, a professional, co-worker, or family member provides follow-along services at the job site.
- *Mobile work crews* of three to eight persons are transported to perform contracted work such as janitorial and landscaping services at area businesses. These crews operate under the supervision of one or more employment specialists.
- *Cluster placements* or enclaves of three to eight persons are supervised by employment specialists and work in a business or industry doing the same job as other nondisabled workers.

7. *Can a student have a job coach while still in high school?* VR or the school can provide job coaches for students with intense support needs while they are still in high school. School districts may choose to hire their own job coaches or to use VR services for eligible students. It is important to establish eligibility and to involve adult service providers in transition planning, if they are providing or paying for job coaches.

8. *What are ongoing support services and follow-along services?* Ongoing support services or follow-along services are provided throughout the term of employment after the job coach is phased out. The purpose of these services is to enable the individual to continue to perform the work required by the employer. They may include services that occur at or away from the work site, such as transportation, personal care services, counseling, and behavioral supports. Typically, ongoing support services are provided through MR/DD programs or long-term mental health programs, but employers, family members, or other agencies also may provide them.

9. *What is Supplemental Security Income (SSI)?* Supplemental Security Income (SSI) is an income support program run by the Social Security Administration. Monthly benefits can be paid to youth or adults with disabilities if their individual or family income falls below a certain level, and if their disability is severe and expected to last at least 12 months. SSI can be helpful in supplementing student income while in postsecondary education or entry-level work. Generally, SSI is applied for at age 18 when family income is no longer considered.

10. *What is the difference between SSI and Social Security benefits?* Social Security Disability Insurance (SSDI) is a government insurance fund that is typically paid to a young person with a disability who has a retired, deceased, or disabled parent who paid into Social Security. Social Security benefits are applied for in the same way as SSI; they may amount to more than SSI, or they may be supplemented by SSI if they are less than the SSI amount.

11. *What information is needed to apply for SSI and SSDI?* Application should be made in person at the local Social Security office. The Social Security representative will need to see the following items:

- Social Security number
- Birth certificate
- Information on income and resources: payroll slips, bank books, insurance policies, car registration, burial fund records, and other information about assets
- Mortgage papers and lease arrangements
- Impairment-related information: name, address, and phone numbers of all doctors, hospital or medical facilities where the student has been treated or tested, and any medical reports in your possession
- Work history (SSDI only)

12. *When can SSI benefits be applied for?* SSI benefits may be applied for at any age if the child has a significant disability and if the income of the child and that of the family are very low. After age 18, students may be considered a family of one and receive SSI benefits if their income falls below SSI

guidelines and if the total resources of the student amount to less than $2,000.

13. *How can my son or daughter get Medicaid benefits?* People who meet the eligibility requirements for SSI benefits are usually eligible for Medicaid benefits as well. Medicaid benefits are applied for at the local office of the U.S. Department of Health and Human Services. An individual may be eligible for Medicaid and not receiving SSI if he or she is working and needs Medicaid to maintain health benefits.

14. *If students work, does this cause them to lose SSI?* SSI programs encourage recipients to work through a number of allowances and work incentives. For students, several thousand dollars of earnings can be allowed without affecting benefits by using the **Student Earned Income Exclusion.** Students may also set up a Plan to Achieve Self-Sufficiency (PASS) where (through an agreement with Social Security) earnings may be placed in a bank account to save up for an item that makes the individual more independent (e.g., college, car down payment, etc.). These savings and this income are not counted against benefits.

Generally, SSI recipients lose only $1 for every $2 they earn and are allowed to exclude $85 of earned and unearned income and any impairment-related work expenses (IRWEs) before these SSI deductions are figured. For example, a person who earns $385 dollars a month will lose only $150 of SSI benefits ([385–85]/2). SSI has other work incentives, including deductions for (a) impairment-related work expenses (IRWEs), (b) student earned income exclusion, (c) blind work expenses, (d) plans for achieving self-support (PASS), (e) property essential to self-support, and (f) continued payment under a VR program. These should be discussed with a Social Security representative.

15. *What about Medicaid and work?* Unless recipients earn more than double their SSI check plus $85, Medicaid benefits will be continued automatically. Even if a recipient is no longer receiving an SSI payment, he or she can continue to receive Medicaid if:

- The disabling condition continues.
- There is a need for Medicaid to work.
- A person cannot afford medical coverage.

16. *Why do I need to plan for residential living options?* Whether the student plans to remain at home or to move out, parents should assure that necessary residential supports are provided to ensure that the individual with a disability is cared for after the parents retire or become ill. Depending on eligibility, the student can maintain independence through family supports, Medicaid waivers, low-income housing, personal care attendants, supported living services, or other residential programs. It should be emphasized that residential services often involve long waiting periods and, therefore, should be applied for many years before they are needed.

17. *Why do I need to plan for community participation?* Research indicates that students with disabilities can become more isolated as they grow older. Due to lack of mobility, income, and social networks, they may have difficulty making the right friends and meeting the right people to assure a good adult quality of life. Membership in religious/cultural affiliations (e.g., church or synagogue), clubs, and recreational programs provide natural and ongoing support networks that can assist persons with disabilities to maintain friendships throughout their life.

18. *Can I have a transition plan without an IEP?* If a student has a substantial mental or physical impairment but does not qualify for special education, a transition plan can be developed under Section 504 of the Rehabilitation Act, which requires access to appropriate education for all students with disabilities. Section 504 does not require an IEP, but it does require a plan for any area needed by the student to gain an appropriate education. This can include a transition plan.

CONCLUSION

Transition planning was developed in response to studies that showed poor postsecondary outcomes for graduates of special education programs. The IDEA of 1990, 1997, and 2004 developed a legal definition of transition planning that included four major criteria: (a) based on student needs, taking into account interests and preferences; (b) developed as part of an outcome-oriented process; (c) a coordinated set of activities; and (d) designed to promote movement into employment and other postschool environments. Common myths about transition plans have emerged as they have become part of the IEP, including the need to standardize the process for all students, to limit planning to a small part of the IEP meeting, to plan year to year, and to meet annually as part of the IEP meeting. At most schools, much of the transition planning process must occur outside the IEP meeting in order for the transition coordinator to individualize planning approaches, to conduct planning in a relaxed and creative atmosphere, to conduct multi-year planning, and to meet regularly.

The process of transition planning, therefore, extends far beyond the process of developing a transition statement as part of the IEP transition meeting. Preparation involves consideration of the method of planning and assessment, forming the transition planning team, exploring service options, and planning for student and family involvement. The implementation of the transition service plan starts with the transition meeting and continues through implementation of the IEP, assessment of progress, and coordination of transition services. There are many questions and problems that will arise as part of this process that will require the transition coordinator to continuously update knowledge about adult service options, supported employment, financial support, and postsecondary education.

STUDY QUESTIONS

1. There are four major criteria for transition planning. Discuss one in detail, outlining IDEA's legal requirements and how schools should address this area.
2. Compare and contrast the transition requirements of the IDEA of 1990, 1997, and 2004.
3. Discuss how the transition plan has become part of the IEP, and how this has had unintended consequences for transition planning.
4. Discuss how a school can help students and families become involved in the IEP transition planning process.
5. Discuss what a teacher should do to prepare for the transition meeting, and how this process might differ for students with mild and severe cognitive disabilities.
6. Describe a transition goal and write it into the IEP.
7. Discuss how transition progress can be assessed using standardized approaches.

WEBSITES

National Center on Secondary Education and Transition: http://www.ncset.org/
Transition Planning—NICHCY: http://www.ldonline.org/ld_indepth/transition/nichcy_TS10.html
What Is Person-Centered Planning? http://www.reachoflouisville.com/person-centered/whatisperson.htm
In-Depth Discussion of Person-Centered Planning: http://soeweb.syr.edu/thechp/everyday.pdf
ERIC: Self-Determination and the Education of Students with Disabilities: http://ericec.org/digests/e632.html
National Coalition on Self-Determination: http://www.oaksgroup.org/nconsd/
Self-Determination: Position Statement of CEC: http://www.dcdt.org/pdf/self_deter.pdf
Self-Determination: Selected Bibliography: http://www.isdd.indiana.edu/cedir/selfadvobib.html
ChoiceMaker: http://www.coe.unco.edu/TRAC/choicemaker.pdf
Self-Directed Search: Web-based: http://www.self-directed-search.com/browser.html
Self-Directed Search: Overview: http://www.learning4liferesources.com/special_orders.html
Meyers-Briggs: Overview: http://www.discoveryourpersonality.com/MBTI.html?source=looksmart
ERIC Digest: SCANS Competencies: http://www.ericfacility.net/ericdigests/ed339749.html

PARTICIPATORY DECISION MAKING: INNOVATIVE PRACTICES FOR STUDENT SELF-DETERMINATION

James E. Martin

Laura Huber Marshall

Randall L. De Pry

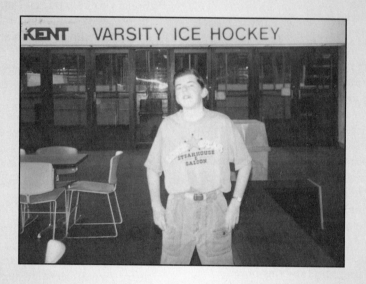

Your life is the sum result of all the choices you make, both consciously and unconsciously. If you can control the process of choosing, you can take control of all aspects of your life. You can find the freedom that comes from being in charge of yourself.

Robert F. Bennett

LEARNING OBJECTIVES

The objectives of this chapter are:

1. Describe the importance of students learning self-determination skills.
2. Define self-determination and describe the major components.
3. Describe how federal laws and regulations support self-determination-oriented instructional practices.
4. Describe how to infuse self-determination into secondary IEP practices.
5. Show how to establish self-determination as an IEP need area.
6. Explain self-determination assessment.
7. Explain how self-determination fits into a standards-referenced IEP format.
8. Describe the *ChoiceMaker* and other research-based self-determination curriculum.
9. Explain how to implement a student-directed summary of performance.

INTRODUCTION

This chapter addresses the issue of how to engage students in their education and planning process. The authors describe self-determination as both a means and an outcome of the transition process. It is described as a means of addressing the essential transition elements of (1) determining the student's strengths, needs, interests, and preferences; (2) coordinating activities; and (3) promoting movement from school to postschool environments. Self-determination also is described as both a means of addressing the essential element of developing an outcome-oriented process and a critical outcome of the transition process itself (Halloran, 1993; Mithaug, Mithaug, Agran, Martin, & Wehmeyer in press, Wehmeyer, 1996).

Educators increase students' self-determination by teaching skills and by providing participatory decision-making opportunities where students practice what they have learned (Martin, Peterson, & Goff, in press). Many typical school functions do not allow student participatory decision making. However, by looking at these typical functions with a self-determination outcome in mind, what are mundane become innovative teaching opportunities: ones that enable students to become participatory decision makers. As students become participatory decision makers, they put into practice their learned self-determination skills.

Four scenarios shown in Table 14–1 depict how typical school functions convert into innovative opportunities to learn self-determination skills. These examples and nonexamples provide a glimpse into what is possible. Our field is just now beginning to realize the numerous opportunities that exist to teach self-determination every day by converting typical teacher-directed school functions into participatory decision-making opportunities.

FEDERAL LAWS, REGULATIONS, AND STATE PRACTICE

Federal special education legislation and regulations include five explicit self-determination statements designed to teach crucial self-determination skills and to provide student participatory decision-making opportunities. First, the Individuals with Disabilities Education Act (IDEA) requires secondary transition-aged students to be invited to attend their IEP meeting. Second, IEP transition goals and activities must be based on *student* strengths needs, interests, and preferences. The spirit of IDEA implies that students of transition age, with support from the IEP team, should determine and implement their own goals, objectives, and activities based on *self-perceived* strengths needs, preferences, and interests—not simply those expressed by parents and educators. Third, the U.S. Congress declared with the Rehabilitation Act amendments of 1992 (P.L. 102-569) that the presence of a disability does not diminish the rights of individuals to enjoy self-determination. Fourth, the Rehabilitation Act mandates that all programs and activities funded by the federal and state offices of vocational rehabilitation must promote the principles of self-determination. Fifth, No Child Left Behind legislation requires that a portion of state funds must be used to facilitate: (a) the successful transition into adult life of students who are Native American, (b) the transition of female youth into technologically-related workplace, (c) the transition of neglected, delinquent, or at-risk youth into further education or employment.

In addition to federal regulations, each state must minimally implement its special education practices to match the expectations established in the federal laws and regulations. States, however, may exceed the federal minimum requirements. The transition vision of the Ohio Department of Education, Office of Exceptional Children, for example, implements the spirit of the law. Special education practice in Ohio could satisfy the minimum requirements by only *inviting* students to their IEP meetings, but instead, students are *expected* to be present at their IEP meeting and to participate actively in the planning and implementation of their transition to adult life educational program (Ohio Department of

TABLE 14–1 Case scenarios

Scenario	Typical Functions	Innovative Opportunities
Scenario 1: The IEP Meeting	The special education teacher invites a student to his IEP meeting, but he is not provided with any instruction about the IEP or what to do at the meeting. The student does not want to attend and does not come to school the day of his meeting. Teachers, support staff, and parents talk about the student's interests, skills, needs, and last year's IEP goal performance. They make plans for this year without any direct student input.	Prior to the IEP meeting, Sean learns about the IEP, the meeting, and prepares a script of what to do and say. During the meeting, Sean actively participates and even directs part of *his* IEP meeting. He begins by stating the purpose, introduces everyone, talks about his interests, skills, and how he did on accomplishing last year's IEP goals. He asks for teacher and parent support to accomplish his goals.
Scenario 2: IEP Goal Attainment	The special education teacher assumes responsibility for attaining the IEP goals. The teacher builds supports, implements strategies, and collects data. The student does not know her IEP goals or how she is progressing toward accomplishing them.	Bekah shares the responsibility for attaining her IEP goals. The teacher educates Bekah on how to accomplish her goals. Each week Bekah completes a plan to accomplish a portion of her goals and then evaluates the success of her plan at the end of the week.
Scenario 3: Course Scheduling	The special education team determines what classes students take for the next semester. The team considers their perception of student skills, limits, and interests in building the student schedule.	Students build their own schedule in consultation with their teachers. Students learn what classroom characteristics they like and learn their school skills and limits. The students next consider their needs and goals, then match their interests, skills, and limits to required and optional courses.
Scenario 4: Functional Assessment	The special education team conducts a functional assessment in reaction to a persistent behavior problem, then develops a behavior support plan.	Sean actively participates in the functional assessment process, helps to analyze and interpret data, and develops a support plan in collaboration with the team. Sean shares responsibility in accomplishing the goals of his behavior support plan.

Education, Division of Special Education, 1999). To this end, special education transition practice in Ohio:

- Expects students to lead their own IEP meetings
- Expects students to describe and discuss their postsecondary transition goals
- Teaches students about their transition process
- Expects students to develop postsecondary goals based on their interests and preferences

To document this transition vision, Ohio school districts must report the number of student-led IEP meetings, documentation of efforts to develop postsecondary goals based on student interest and preferences, the number of students who discuss their postsecondary goals, and a listing of the programs or strategies used to educate students about transition.

In New Mexico, the Albuquerque Public Schools expect students to become actively engaged in their IEP meetings, and to build a student-directed Summary of Performance that they present to the IEP team prior to exiting high school (Martin, Van Dycke, D'Ottavio, & Nickerson, in press). Starting in ninth grade students prepare their Summary of Performance worksheet to share disability and transition information at their IEP meetings. Students use their own words to describe their disability and explain how it impacts their school and work performance. Students describe supports and accommodations that have worked, and they identify where they want to work, go to school, and live after leaving high school. Each year they learn the information on their Summary of Performance form so that they can present the information to their IEP team when they exit high school.

EVOLUTION OF THE SELF-DETERMINATION CONCEPT

Since the late 1960s, special educators have discussed self-determination. One way to understand self-determination is to view it as two strands that have evolved over time: (1) the choice strand and (2) the goal-setting and attainment strand. The self-determined learning model of instruction (Wehmeyer, Palmer, Agran, Mithaug, & Martin, 2000), and the self-determined learning theory (Mithaug, Mithaug, Agran, Martin, & Wehmeyer, 2003) exemplify how our field's understanding of the concept has matured and merged from two strands into one.

The Choice Strand

The earliest, and a few modern self-determination definitions, cluster into the choice definitional strand. Within these conceptualizations, choice becomes a right that people with disabilities exercise (Ippoliti, Peppey, & Depoy, 1994). Self-determination begins with choice and motivates action (Mithaug, 2005). A few of these definitions include:

- Nirje (1972): Self-determination is a critical component of the normalization principle. Choices, wishes, and aspirations of people with disabilities must be considered when actions affect them.
- Deci and Ryan (1985): Self-determination is the capacity of individuals to choose and then have these choices be the driving force behind their action.
- Deci and Ryan (1994): Individuals are self-determined to the extent that they freely choose their behaviors.
- Wehmeyer (1992, 1994): Self-determination refers to the attitudes and abilities required to act as the primary causal agent in one's own life and to make choices regarding one's actions free from undue external influence.

The trend in special education is toward greater involvement of students in their own education by providing them opportunities to make their own choices (Wood, Fowler, Uphold, & Test, 2005). Opportunities to engage first in simple, then increasingly complex choice making must be infused throughout students' education (Post & Storey, 2006). When educators provide individuals choice-making opportunities, students express their individuality, and teachers show that they value and respect their students (Test, Fowler, Wood, Brewer, & Eddy, 2005). Belief in choice making impacts practice, as the following three examples demonstrate. First, when teachers provide students task choice opportunities, disruptive behavior significantly decreases and learning increases (Munk & Repp, 1994). Second, when students are given a choice of vocational tasks, their productivity increases (Martin, Mithaug, Oliphint, Husch, & Frazier, 2002). Third, when students read text materials that interest them, the students comprehend and enjoy the

> **Critical Point**
> Self-determination practices improve learning and productivity because students are engaged in tasks they have chosen and that are meaningful to them.

task better than with material they do not enjoy (Ryan, Connell, & Plant, 1990).

Special educators said in a statewide survey that they consider choice as the primary self-determination strategy. When asked what strategies constitute self-determination, 91% of the special education teachers identified choice making (Agran, Snow, & Swaner, 1999). They identified goal setting as the second ranked strategy.

The Goal-Setting and Attainment Strand

This second self-determination strand includes choice but emphasizes goal setting and the goal attainment process. Ward (1994), who champions this view, wrote that the optimal outcome of the self-determination process is setting a goal and achieving it. A few of the goal attainment definitions include:

- Ward (1988): Self-determined individuals define goals for themselves and take the initiative in achieving those goals.
- Martin, Marshall, and Maxson (1993): Self-determined individuals know what they want and how to get it. From an awareness of personal needs, self-determined individuals set goals, and then they doggedly pursue their goals. This involves asserting their presence, making their needs known, evaluating progress toward meeting their goals, adjusting their performance as needed, and creating unique approaches to solve problems.
- Wolman, Campeau, DuBois, Mithaug, and Stolarski (1994): Self-determined individuals know and can express their own needs, interests, and abilities. They set appropriate goals, make choices and plans in pursuit of their goals, and make adjustments as needed to achieve their goals.
- Field and Hoffman (1994, 1995): A self-determined person defines and achieves their goals from a base of knowing and valuing themselves.

Critical Point
Goal attainment strategies are critical in ensuring that students with disabilities are truly self-determined.

When goal attainment defines self-determination, certain practices result. Martin and Marshall (1995) suggest that students should identify their needs and interests across different transition domains; establish goals that match their interests, skills, and limits; develop a plan to accomplish their goals; evaluate their progress toward meeting their goals; and make adjustments in their support, strategies, or goals. An opportunity for this to occur, for example, exists within the IEP process: getting ready for the meeting, the meeting itself, and the subsequent goal attainment process. When typical school functions change to become participatory decision-making opportunities, students actively participate as an equal team member to help establish goals.

The Strands Merge

Just having the opportunity to make choices and decisions does not ensure that a person will be self-determined (Wehmeyer, 1997, p. 36). Self-determined individuals *choose* goals that match their interests, skills, and limits (Martin & Marshall, 1995). The goal attainment strand includes choice but goes much further. Goal attainment strategies empower individuals to achieve their choices (Wehmeyer, Agran, & Hughes, 1998).

The self-determined learning model of instruction (Wehmeyer et al., 2000) or the self-determined career development model (Benitez, Lattimore, & Wehmeyer, 2005) brings the two strands together with the premise that once a goal is chosen, learning to adjust to attain the desired goals is necessary for a successful transition. The self-determined learning theory (Mithaug et al., 2003) extends the model and postulates that learning is adjustment and that people learn when their attempts to attain goals are blocked. To attain goals, choices, actions, and beliefs may need to be adjusted. Students learn by adjusting, and adjust to learn. When students learn to align their choices, actions, evaluations, and adjustments with their self-identified needs and interests, the likelihood of attaining desired goals increases (Martin, Mithaug, Cox, Peterson, Van Dycke, & Cash, 2003).

Self-Determination Components

Martin and Marshall (1996a) interviewed adults with disabilities, parents of children with disabilities, conducted a multidiscipline literature review, and undertook a national survey to determine a set of self-determination skills. This resulted in seven self-determination constructs (see Table 14–2). These include (1) self-awareness, (2) self-advocacy, (3) self-efficacy, (4) decision making, (5) independent performance, (6) self-evaluation, and (7) adjustment. These seven constructs break down into 37 additional components.

TABLE 14–2 *ChoiceMaker* self-determination constructs

1. *Self-awareness:*	Identify needs; identify interests; identify and understand strengths
	Identify and understand limitations; identify own values
2. *Self-advocacy:*	Assertively state wants and needs; assertively state rights; determine
	needed supports
	Pursue needed support; obtain and evaluate needed support;
	conduct own affairs
3. *Self-efficacy:*	Expects to obtain goals
4. *Decision making:*	Assess situation demands; set goals; set standards
	Identify information to make decisions; consider past solutions for
	new situation; generate new creative solutions
	Consider options; choose best option; develop plan
5. *Independent performance:*	Initiate tasks on time; complete tasks on time;
	use self-management strategies
	Perform tasks to standards; follow through on own plan
6. *Self-evaluation:*	Monitor task performance; compare performance to standards;
	evaluate effectiveness of self-management strategies
	Determine if plan completed and goal met
7. *Adjustment:*	Change goals; change standards; change plan
	Change strategies; change support; persistently adjust
	Use environmental feedback to aid adjustment

Source: Adapted from a table originally published in: Martin, J. E., & Marshall, L. H. (1996a). ChoiceMaker: Infusing self-determination instruction into the IEP and transition process. In Sands, D. J. & Wehmeyer, M. L. (Eds.), *Self-determination across the life span* (pp. 215–236). Baltimore: Paul H. Brookes. Used with permission from University Technology Corp.

Other goal attainment definitions of self-determination include similar conceptualizations. These definitions consider goal setting, planning, evaluation, and adjustment as central components. Field and Hoffman (1994) developed a self-determination model consisting of five areas: (1) know yourself, (2) value yourself, (3) plan, (4) act, and (5) experience outcomes and learn. Mithaug, Wehmeyer, Agran, Martin, and Palmer's (1998) self-determination learning model poses questions that students ask, then answer across three phases: (1) setting learning goals, (2) constructing a learning plan, and (3) adjusting behaviors. The Mithaug et al. (1998) model also provides teacher objectives to facilitate answering the questions. These questions and selected teacher objectives are presented in Table 14–3.

THE IMPORTANCE OF SELF-DETERMINATION

A growing number of studies indicate the positive impact of self-determination skills upon postschool outcomes. Wehmeyer and Schwartz (1997) collected self-determination measures on students with learning disabilities and mental retardation prior to their exiting from high school. After leaving high school, the former students who had higher levels of self-determination while in high school had higher employment rates than those who had lower self-determination scores. Wehmeyer and Palmer (2003) replicated their 1997 study and found that once again students with learning disabilities and mental retardation who had higher levels of self-determination in high school had more positive postschool outcomes than students with lower self-determination scores. Their data also showed that from the first to third year following graduation, students with higher levels of self-determination experienced additional positive outcomes compared to those who had lower self-determination scores.

> **Critical Point**
> Self-determination has been linked to better postschool outcomes for persons with disabilities.

Martin, Mithaug, Oliphint, Husch, and Frazier (2002) determined that job choice options and adjustments support increased vocational success. These researchers compared the employment outcomes of almost 600 individuals with disabilities who completed a systematic "choose and adjust" process to 200 workers who did not. Those who completed the self-directed employment choice process retained their jobs significantly longer than those who did not.

TABLE 14–3 Self-determination learning model

Phase 1: Setting a Learning Goal

Student Questions
- What do I want to learn?
- What do I know about it now?
- What must change to learn what I do not know?
- What can I do to produce that change?

Selected Teacher Objectives
- Enable student to identify specific strengths and instructional needs in a specific area.
- Enable student to evaluate and communicate preferences, interests, beliefs, and values that relate to this area.
- Assist student to gather information about opportunities and barriers in physical and social environment.
- Teach student to prioritize need.
- Teach student to state a goal and identify criteria for achieving that goal.

Phase 2: Constructing a Learning Plan

Student Questions
- What can I do now to change what I do not know?
- What will prevent me from taking action now to produce that change?
- What can I do to remove these obstacles?
- When will I take action and remove these obstacles?

Selected Teacher Objectives
- Enable student to self-evaluate progress toward goal achievement.
- Enable student to determine plan of action to bridge gap between self-evaluated current status and self-identified goal status.
- Enable student to identify most appropriate instructional strategies.
- Enable student to identify and implement strategies to overcome barriers and obstacles.
- Support student to implement student-directed learning strategies.
- Enable student to determine schedule for action plan.
- Enable student to self-monitor progress on implementing action plan.

Phase 3: Adjusting Behaviors

Student Questions
- What actions have I taken?
- What obstacles have been removed?
- What has changed about what I do not know?
- Do I know what I want to know?

Selected Teacher Objectives
- Enable student to self-evaluate progress toward goal.
- Collaborate with student to identify if action plan is adequate or inadequate given revised goal.
- Assist student in deciding if goal remains the same or changes.
- Assist student to change action plan if necessary.

Source: Excerpts taken from Mithaug, D. E., Wehmeyer, M. L., Agran, M., Martin, J. E., & Palmer, S. (1998). The self-determined learning model of instruction. In Wehmeyer, M. L. & Sands, D. J. (Eds.), *Making it happen: Student involvement in education planning, decision making, and instruction* (pp. 299–328). Baltimore: Paul H. Brookes.

Gerber, Ginsberg, and Reiff (1992) interviewed a group of adults who were identified as learning disabled during their school years, to determine why some were successful and others were not. They found that successful individuals with learning disabilities had:

- Control of their lives and surroundings
- A desire to succeed
- Well-thought-out goals
- Persistence

- Adapted to their environment
- Built a social support network that facilitated their success

After conducting the interviews, Gerber et al. (1992) realized that successful individuals decided, long before they became successful, that they would be successful. The authors concluded that successful adults with severe learning disabilities wanted to succeed, set achievable goals, and confronted their learning disability so that appropriate measures could be taken to increase the likelihood of success. One highly successful young man explained it like this: "Successful people have a plan. You have to have a plan, goals, strategy, otherwise you are flying through the clouds and then you hit the mountain" (Gerber et al., 1992, p. 480). These findings, when combined with what we know from other disciplines, strongly suggest the beneficial outcome of increased self-determination skills.

Raskind, Goldberg, Higgins, and Herman (1999) and Goldberg, Higgins, Raskind, and Herman (2003) in a 20-year follow-up study found that successful adults with learning disabilities used self-determination skills. A research review by Konrad, Fowler, Walker, Test, and Wood (2005) found that increased self-determination skills yield increased academic productivity.

INFUSION OF SELF-DETERMINATION INTO THE IEP

Self-determination skills make a difference in the postschool outcomes of people with disabilities. Unfortunately, students with disabilities possess far fewer self-determination skills than do secondary students who do not have an IEP (Wolman et al., 1994). Only a few IEPs include self-determination goals, even though teachers value self-determination skills. For students to learn and use self-determination behaviors in their everyday lives, self-determination skills must be taught and opportunities provided for students to practice self-determined behaviors.

> **Critical Point**
> States and local education agencies need to go beyond the minimum requirements for self-determination established by federal legislation.

Educational practice appears to reflect this view. Agran et al.'s (1999) survey of special education teachers found that 77% considered self-determination as an important curricular area, with only 3% of the teachers rating self-determination as a low priority. However, a discrepancy exists between the teachers' expressed importance and their inclusion of self-determination into most of the IEPs they write. The Utah teachers said that:

- 14% include self-determination skills on most IEPs
- 61% include self-determination skills on some IEPs
- 25% include self-determination on few or no IEPs

What can be done to create more of a match between the perceived importance and the inclusion of self-determination goals into students' IEPs? One answer to this question begins with considering self-determination as a need to be discussed at the IEP meeting.

ESTABLISHING SELF-DETERMINATION AS AN IEP NEED AREA

Educators and parents must consider self-determination as an educational necessity, one to be pursued as seriously and systematically as any other skill area valued (Agran et al., 1999, p. 301). The route to making self-determination an educational necessity begins with establishing it's need in the IEPs present level of performance section (Sale & Martin, 2004). Assessments, either formal or informal, typically document the present level of performance and establish the need. Self-determination assessment tools may assist with this process.

Four available self-determination assessments may help to determine students' self-determination strengths and needs. These include: The *ARC's Self-Determination Scale* (Wehmeyer & Kelchner, 1995); the *Self-Determination Knowledge Scale* (Hoffman, Field, & Sawilowsky, 1996); the *ChoiceMaker Self-Determination Assessment* (Martin & Marshall, 1996b); and the *AIR Self-Determination Assessment* (Wolman, Campeau, DuBois, Mithaug, & Stolarski, 1994). (NOTE: The *AIR Self-Determination Assessment* may be downloaded free of charge at *www.ou.edu/zarrow.* Click on the self-determination button.)

Each tool provides a unique perspective and reports the results in different ways (see Field, Martin, Miller, Ward, & Wehmeyer, 1998; Sale & Martin, 2004, for detailed descriptions of the four assessments). The *ChoiceMaker Self-Determination Assessment* singularly produces suggested IEP goals and objectives.

The *ChoiceMaker Assessment*, as a curriculum-referenced assessment, matches the *ChoiceMaker* curriculum (see Table 14–4 for sample questions). It consists of 54 items that evaluate student self-determination skills and the opportunities at school to exercise these skills. The *ChoiceMaker Assessment* contains three sections: choosing goals, expressing goals, and taking action. The "choosing goals" section assesses goal setting based on students' knowledge of their interests, skills, and limits across school, employment, and post-high-school education domains. The "expressing goals" section assesses students' participation and

TABLE 14–4 Sample choicemaker assessment's expressing goals questions

	Student Skills			Opportunity at School		
Section 2: Expressing Goals	(Does the student do this?)			(Does school provide structured time?)		
E. *Student Leading Meeting—Does the student:*	(not at all)		(100%)	(not at all)		(100%)
E1. Begin meeting and introduce participants?	0 1 2	3	4	0 1 2	3	4
E2. Review past goals and performance?	0 1 2	3	4	0 1 2	3	4
E3. Ask questions if student does not understand something?	0 1 2	3	4	0 1 2	3	4
E4. Ask for feedback from group members?	0 1 2	3	4	0 1 2	3	4
E5. Deal with differences in opinion?	0 1 2	3	4	0 1 2	3	4
E6. Close meeting by summarizing decisions?	0 1 2	3	4	0 1 2	3	4
	Subtotal _____			Subtotal _____		
F. *Student Reporting—Does the student:*						
F1. Express interests.	0 1 2	3	4	0 1 2	3	4
F2. Express skills and limits.	0 1 2	3	4	0 1 2	3	4
F3. Express options and goals.	0 1 2	3	4	0 1 2	3	4
	Subtotal _____			Subtotal _____		
	TOTAL (E + F) _____			TOTAL (E + F) _____		

Source: Excerpt taken from: Martin, J. E. & Marshall, L. H. (1996b). ChoiceMaker *self-determination assessment.* Longmont, CO: Sopris West. © 1997 University of Colorado. Used with permission from University Technology Corp.

leadership in IEP meetings. The "take action" section measures students' goal attainment skills.

Teachers evaluate each of the 54 items using a five-point scale across both the Student Skills and Opportunity at School columns. The raw scores for each of the three sections are summed, graphed, and compared to the total points available to find the percent of available self-determination skills and opportunities. Items assessed as zero, one, or two become possible IEP goals and objectives.

CASE STUDY   Zeke

Assessment of Self-Determination for the IEP

Zeke, a 14-year-old high school student, receives special education services due to the impact his learning disability and emotional problems have upon his educational performance. The special education team at Zeke's high school believes in teaching self-determination skills and in providing many opportunities to practice learned self-determination skills. In preparation for Zeke's first high school IEP meeting, Mrs. Gomez and Zeke jointly complete the *AIR Self-Determination Assessment* and the *ChoiceMaker Assessment* to document his present level of educational performance.

Zeke's *ChoiceMaker Assessment* profile (see Figure 14–1) shows that Zeke's high school provides 33% of the choosing goal opportunities, 100% of the expressing goals opportunities, and 99% of the taking action opportunities. Zeke's skill profile depicts low and variable self-determination levels: a 30% choosing goals skills level, a 10% expressing goals skill level, and a 38% taking action skills level. The skill levels differ significantly from the opportunities provided by his high school program. On the *AIR Self-Determination Assessment* (student version), Zeke obtained an overall rating of 47%.

> **Critical Point**
> Self-determination should be measured in terms of choosing goals, expressing goals, and taking action.

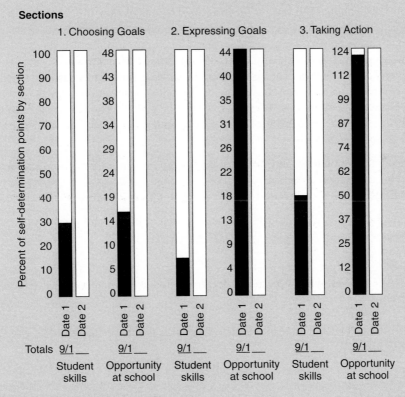

FIGURE 14–1   ChoiceMaker assessment profile

(Continued)

TABLE 14–5   ChoiceMaker lesson matrix

Section	Goals	Lessons	Students
Choosing Goals	A. Student understanding B. Student interests C. Student skills and limits D. Student goals	• Choosing employment goals • Choosing personal matters goals • Choosing education goals	• Middle and high school general education students • Middle and high school students with an IEP and mild to moderate learning and behavior problems
Expressing Goals	E. Student leading meeting F. Student reporting	• Self-directed IEP	• Middle and high school students with an IEP and mild to moderate learning and behavior problems
Taking Action	G. Student plan H. Student action I. Student evaluation J. Student adjustment	• Take action	• Middle and high school general education students • Middle and high school students with an IEP and mild to moderate learning and behavior problems

Source: Adapted from a table originally published in: Martin, J. E., Marshall, L. H., Maxson, L, & Jerman, P. (1996c). *Self-directed IEP.* Longmont, CO: Sopris West. Used with permission from University Technology Corp.

In preparing for Zeke's annual IEP review meeting, Mrs. Gomez writes the results of her assessment into the IEP form's transition present level of educational performance and needs section (see Table 14-5). She then sends a copy of her self-determination assessment and a draft of present level of performance section home for Zeke and his parents to review and discuss prior to the IEP meeting.

At the IEP meeting, Zeke (with coaching by Mrs. Gomez) showed the team his self-determination assessment profiles, and then described his strengths and a few of the self-determination skills he has not yet mastered. Mrs. Gomez then reviewed the school's self-determination expectations. The team realized a large discrepancy existed between Zeke's current performance and the expectations to engage in self-determination activities. Zeke and the team decided he needs to:

• Choose education, employment, and personal goals based on an understanding of his skills and limits
• Learn to lead his educational meetings
• Learn the goal attainment skills needed to take action on his IEP goals

Mrs. Gomez wrote these into Zeke's "transition need" section of his IEP, and then wrote a self-determination IEP goal and related objectives:

Goal

Within the next 20 weeks, Zeke will increase self-determination skills to an average of 83%.

Objectives

Within the next 10 weeks, Zeke will increase taking action skills to 90% as measured by the *ChoiceMaker* self-determination assessment.

In the next 15 weeks, Zeke will increase choosing goals to 70% as measured by the *ChoiceMaker* self-determination assessment.

Within the next 20 weeks, Zeke will increase expressing goals skills to 90% as measured by the *ChoiceMaker* self-determination assessment.

TEACHING SELF-DETERMINATION AND CREATING PARTICIPATORY DECISION-MAKING OPPORTUNITIES

Once self-determination goals are written into the IEP, special education teachers need to make teaching self-determination skills a priority. Teachers may develop their own lessons, or choose to use or modify already-developed lesson packages in order to teach self-determination skills to their students. (Go to *http://www. uncc.edu/sdsp/sd_curricula.as* to look at numerous self-determination lesson packages.) Teachers across the country use the *ChoiceMaker* self-determination instructional packages to teach basic self-determination skills and to practice learned self-determination behaviors.

The *ChoiceMaker* series consists of the *ChoiceMaker Self-Determination Assessment* and six instructional packages. The instructional packages include:

- *Choosing employment goals* (Huber Marshall, Martin, Maxson, & Jerman, 1997)
- *Choose and take action: Finding the right job for you* (Martin et al., 2004)
- *Choosing education goals* (Martin, Hughes, Huber Marshall, Jerman, & Maxson, 1999)
- *Choosing personal goals* (Marshall, Martin, Hughes, Jerman, & Maxson, 1999)
- *Self-directed IEP* (Martin, Huber Marshall, Maxson, & Jerman, 1996).
- *Take action: Making goals happen* (Huber Marshall, Martin, Maxson, Hughes, Miller, McGill, & Jerman, 1999).

Each instructional package teaches specific goals and objectives of the *ChoiceMaker* curriculum (see Table 14–5). The *ChoiceMaker* curriculum, which operationalizes the self-determination constructs identified in Table 14–2, contains three strands, nine broad teaching goals, and 54 objectives (see Table 14–6).

Development of the *ChoiceMaker* Lesson Packages

The development of each lesson package followed the same process. A team comprised of university faculty, public school special educators and administrators, parents, students with an IEP, and adults with disabilities jointly worked on conceptualizing, writing, and field-testing the materials. The development teams wrote the lessons to attain specific *ChoiceMaker* goals and objectives. The teams repeatedly took the draft lessons into middle and high school programs to field-test. Feedback from the teachers and students resulted in numerous revisions. Researchers then conducted rigorous studies to demonstrate the programs' effectiveness. Results of these, studies are described when we explain each lesson package.

> **Critical Point**
> *ChoiceMaker* was developed and field-tested in collaboration with educators, students, adults with disabilities, and parents.

Use of the *ChoiceMaker* Lesson Packages

Each *ChoiceMaker* lesson package may be infused into existing educational programs. Because the *choosing goals* and *taking action* materials are compatible with middle and high school content area courses, they may be used for general education students *and* with students who have an IEP. The *self-directed IEP* materials, which teach the *expressing goals* section of the curriculum, are designed for students with an IEP. The *Choose and Take Action* multimedia software package uses a repeated-measures design within a situational assessment to teach and assess entry level vocational choices of students and adults who cannot read, have more moderate to severe cognitive disabilities, and have limited to no previous work experience. All other *ChoiceMaker* lesson packages teach students who have at least minimal reading and writing skills.

Self-determined choices enhance postschool outcomes.

TABLE 14–6 ChoiceMaker self-determination curriculum matrix

Sections	Teaching Goals	Teaching Objectives							
1: Choosing Goals (through school and community experience)	A. Student interests	A1. Express *education* interests	A2. Express *employment* interests	A3. Express *personal* interests	A4. Express *daily living, housing, and community* interests				
	B. Student skills and limits	B1. Express *education* skills and limits	B2. Express *employment* skills and limits	B3. Express *personal* skills and limits	B4. Express *daily living, housing and community* skills and limits				
	C. Student goals	C1. Indicate options and choose *education* goals	C2. Indicate options and choose *employment* goals	C3. Indicate options and choose *personal* goals	C4. Indicate options and choose *daily living, housing, and community goals*				
2: Expressing Goals	D. Student leading meeting	D1. Begin meeting by stating purpose	D2. Introduce participants	D3. Review past goals and performance	D4. Ask for feedback	D5. Ask questions if don't understand	D6. Deal with differences in opinion	D7. State needed support	D8. Close meeting by summarizing decision
	E. Student reporting	E1. Express interests (from A1–A4)	E2. Express skills and limits (from B1–B4)	E3. Express options and goals (from C1–C4)					
3: Taking Action	F. Student plan	F1. Break general goals into specific goals that can be completed now	F2. Establish *standard* for specific goals	F3. Determine how to get *feedback* from environment	F4. Determine *motivation* to complete specific goals	F5. Determine *strategies* for completing specific goals	F6. Determine *support* needed to complete specific goals	F7. Prioritize and *schedule* to complete specific goals	F8. Express *belief* that goals can be obtained
	G. Student action	G1. Record or report performance	G2. Perform specific goals to *standard*	G3. Obtain *feedback* on performance	G4. *Motivate* self to complete specific goals	G5. Use *strategies* to perform specific goals	G6. Obtain *support* needed	G7. Follow *schedule*	
	H. Student evaluation	H1. Determine if goals are achieved	H2. Compare performance to *standards*	H3. Evaluate *feedback*	H4. Evaluate *motivation*	H5. Evaluate effectiveness of *strategies*	H6. Evaluate *support* used	H7. Evaluate *schedule*	H8. Evaluate *belief*
	I. Student adjustment	I1. Adjust goals if necessary	I2. Adjust or repeat goal *standards*	I3. Adjust or repeat method for *feedback*	I4. Adjust or repeat *motivation*	I5. Adjust or repeat *strategies*	I6. Adjust or repeat	I7. Adjust or repeat *schedule*	I8. Adjust or repeat *belief* that goals can be obtained

Source: Adapted from a table originally published in: Martin, J. E., Marshall, L. H., Maxson, L., & Jerman, P. (1996c). *Self-directed IEP.* Longmont, CO: Sopris West. © 1996 University of Colorado. Used with permission from University Technology Corp.

TEACHING AND CREATING OPPORTUNITIES FOR CHOOSING GOALS

The choosing goals section of the *ChoiceMaker* curriculum provides students the skills and knowledge needed to express their interests, skills, limits, and goals across different transition areas. The choosing goals lesson packages include *choosing employment goals, choosing education goals*, and *choosing personal goals*. As exemplars of the choosing goals lesson packages, in this section, the general choosing goals process and samples from the *choosing employment goals* lesson package are reviewed. Then the *choosing education goals* and *choosing personal goals* instructional packages are briefly described.

Choosing Goals Process

Each of the choosing goals lesson packages includes methodology for students to determine quickly their goals across transition areas. A student video included in each of the three lesson packages, entitled *Choosing Goals to Plan Your Life*, introduces the choosing goals process by showing actual high school students learning and using the choosing goals process.

After watching the video and completing the choosing goals lessons, students complete a choosing general goals worksheet. Figure 14–2 presents a sample section of a choosing general goals worksheet from the *choosing employment goals* lesson package for a high school student who wants to work as an autobody repairman. After the student knows how to complete the form, he simply reads each question and writes in his

answer. If he does not know the answer, then that becomes his goal. In this example, Cal does not know the requirements to become an autobody repairman. So, learning the requirements to be an autobody repairman becomes his goal. Once completed, students may use the form for discussions in their transition class, with their parents, or in their IEP meeting. If students do not know their goals, the lesson packages teach students to identify their goals based on an understanding of their interests, skills, and limits. Cross, Cooke, Wood, and Test (1999) found that the choosing goals process enabled students to provide information on vocational and other transition domains so that they could actively participate in their IEP meeting. When compared to the *McGill Action Planning System*, the results favored the use of the *ChoiceMaker* choosing-goals process.

Choosing Employment Goals

The *ChoiceMaker* curriculum objectives (see Table 14–6) addressed by *choosing employment goals* are:

> Objective A2: Express employment interests.
> Objective B2: Express employment skills and limits.
> Objective C2: Indicate options and choose employment goals.

The *choosing employment goals* lesson sequence is flexible and designed to be mixed and matched with the content and opportunities of existing school curriculum, classes, and schedules.

The lesson activities, which take place at community job sites and in the classroom, teach students to reflect upon their experiences, draw conclusions about

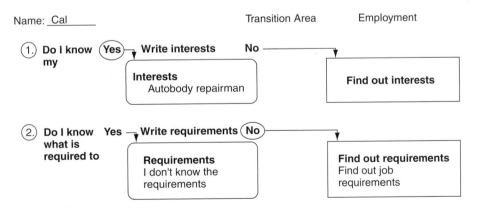

FIGURE 14–2 Choosing general goals

Source: Excerpt taken from: Marshall, L.H., Martin, J., Maxson, L., & Jerman, P. (1997). *Choosing employment goals.* Longmont, CO: Sopris West. © 1997 University of Colorado. Used with permission from University Technology Corp.

themselves, and learn about community opportunities. Students collect and assimilate this information over time so that they can make informed career decisions. The *choosing employment goals* lesson package consists of three parts: (1) choosing general goals lessons (discussed earlier), (2) experience-based lessons, and (3) dream job lessons.

Experience-Based Lessons

Teachers use these lessons and materials with students who are involved in on-the-job activities through work study, on-the-job training, volunteering, or in an after-school job. These lessons teach students to draw meaningful conclusions about their interests, skills, and limits based on their own work experience.

Students learn the job characteristics and job duties they like by completing the *Job Characteristics I Like Worksheet* (see Figure 14–3) and *Job Duties I Like Student Worksheet* process. To examine their on-the-job skills and limits they complete a *Work, Social, and Personal Skills* (see Figure 14–4), and a *Job Duties—How I Did* process. When done repeatedly across time, the results yield a self-directed vocational profile that may be shared with others (see Figure 14–5). Students save their results to develop a self-directed vocational portfolio, which they can show at their IEP meeting and add to the IEP's present level of performance section.

Dream Job Lessons

With the dream job lessons, students in a general education academic or a transition class gather information about a variety of jobs, then research those they think they would like. Students determine how their interests, skills, and limits match those jobs. The lessons may be used sequentially or separately. There are four lessons in the dream job section: (1) job clusters, (2) dream job research, (3) dream job interviews, and (4) dream job shadowing.

Choosing Education Goals

The *choosing education goals* lesson package teaches students to choose high school and postsecondary education goals that match their interests, skills, limits, and available opportunities. The *ChoiceMaker* self-determination transition curriculum objectives addressed by the *choosing education goals* lessons include:

> Objective A1: Express education interests.
> Objective B1: Express education skills and limits.
> Objective C1: Indicate options and choose education goals.

The *choosing education goals* lesson activities all take place in the classroom. The lessons teach students to reflect upon their experiences, draw

---

Name: _____	Job Site: _____	Date: _____

Directions: WHAT I LIKE column: Circle the job characteristic that you like best in each box.

WHAT IS HERE column: Circle the job characteristic in each box that best describes what is at this job.

MATCHES column: Circle YES if the first two columns are the same. Circle NO if they are not.

	What I Like	What Is Here	Matches	
1.	Work alone Lots of people around	Work alone Lots of people around	Yes	No
2.	Quiet workplace Noisy workplace	Quiet workplace Noisy workplace	Yes	No
3.	Work close to home Distance to job doesn't matter	Work close to home Distance to job doesn't matter	Yes	No
4.	Weekdays only Weekends too	Weekdays only Weekends too	Yes	No
5.	Easy job Challenging job	Easy job Challenging job	Yes	No

FIGURE 14–3 Job characteristics I like worksheet

Source: Excerpt taken from: Marshall, L. H., Martin, J. E., Maxson, L., & Jerman, P. (1997). *Choosing employment goals.* Longmont, CO: Sopris West Publishers. © 1997 University of Colorado. Used with permission from University Technology Corp.

How I Did column: Circle 3, 2, or 1, whichever best describes your performance.

Supervisor Thinks column: From the *Work, Social, and Personal Skills Supervisor Worksheet*, copy the numbers that your supervisor chose to describe your performance.

Matches column: Circle Yes if yours and your supervisor's evaluations are the same. If they are not the same, circle No.

Skills	How I Did		Supervisor Thinks		Comments	Matches	
						Yes	No
1. Follows company rules	Very good OK Needs improvement	3 2 1	Very good OK Needs improvement	3 2 1			
2. Comes to work on time or calls if late or absent	Very good OK Needs improvement	3 2 1	Very good OK Needs improvement	3 2 1		Yes	No
Social							
8. Talks the right amount	Very good OK Needs improvement	3 2 1	Very good OK Needs improvement	3 2 1		Yes	No
9. Behaves appropriately	Very good OK Needs improvement	3 2 1	Very good OK Needs improvement	3 2 1		Yes	No
Personal							
12. Works independently	Very good OK Needs improvement	3 2 1	Very good OK Needs improvement	3 2 1		Yes	No
13. Good grooming	Very good OK Needs improvement	3 2 1	Very good OK Needs improvement	3 2 1		Yes	No

FIGURE 14–4 Work, social, and personal skills student's worksheet

Source: Excerpt taken from: Marshall, L. H., Martin, J. E., Maxson, L., & Jerman, P. (1997). *Choosing employment goals.* Longmont, CO: Sopris West Publishers. © 1997 University of Colorado. Used with permission from University Technology Corp.

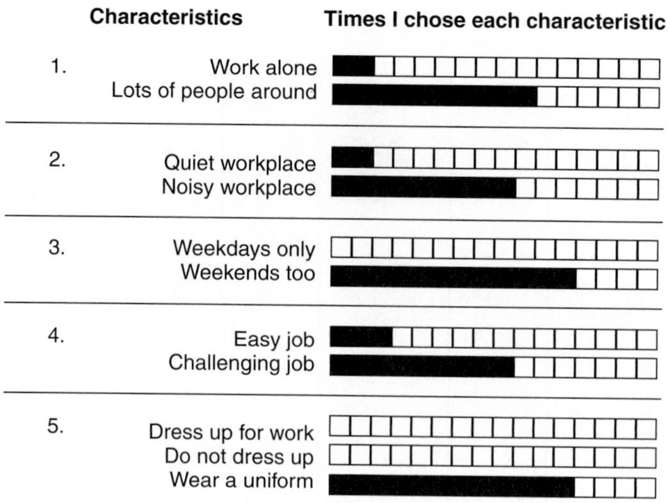

FIGURE 14–5 Job characteristics I like graph

Source: Excerpt taken from: Marshall, L. H., Martin, J. E., Maxson, L., & Jerman, P. (1997). *Choosing employment goals.* Longmont, CO: Sopris West Publishers. © 1997 University of Colorado. Used with permission from University Technology Corp.

conclusions about themselves, and learn about education opportunities. Students will collect and assimilate this information over time to make informed decisions about their secondary and postsecondary education plans.

While using the *choosing education goals* lessons, students complete a variety of activities that are designed to help:

- Determine what students hope to do at different stages of their lives.
- Identify the school subjects that students like.
- Complete a personalized graduation checklist.
- Develop an individualized education performance summary.
- Learn postsecondary education terminology.
- Complete study habits, work habits, and academic skills self-assessment.
- Maintain a study habits log.
- Develop an individualized postsecondary education options information table.
- Choose secondary and postsecondary education goals.

Choosing Personal Goals

The *choosing personal goals* lesson package teaches students how to develop satisfying personal lives and how to spend their free time in safe, legal, and healthy ways. The *ChoiceMaker* self-determination transition curriculum objectives (see Table 14-6) addressed in the lessons include:

Objective A3: Express personal interests.
Objective B4: Express personal skills and limits.
Objective C5: Express options and choose personal goals.

While using the *choosing personal goals* lessons, students complete a variety of activities designed to help them:

- Consider how they interact with other people.
- Evaluate the interactions of the groups in which they are involved.
- Identify the activities they do in their free time to further their relationships, hobbies, talents, recreation; or health and wellness.
- Decide if they would like to make changes in the way they interact with people or in the activities they do and identify ways to make those changes.
- Investigate activities, events, and services that are available in the community or school that can help them to make those changes (e.g., classes,

> **Critical Point**
> Once students identify their goals based on an understanding of their interests, skills, and limits, they then need the skills to express their goals at their IEP meeting.

- clubs, teams, art groups or activities, sports, counseling, and community events).
- Consider their interests, skills, and limits in relation to the opportunities and choose personal goals of activities they want to try.
- Try their chosen activity and evaluate the results.

TEACHING AND CREATING OPPORTUNITIES FOR STUDENTS TO LEAD THEIR IEP MEETING

More than two decades after the passage of the first federal special education laws, students, parents, and general education teachers finally must meet to develop students' IEPs. IDEA mandates that students 14 years old and older must be invited to attend their IEP meetings, and that the IEP discussions and decisions must reflect student interests and preferences (Storms, O'Leary, & Williams, 2000). Implementation of these reforms has been slow, with most states failing to achieve even minimal levels of compliance (Grigal, Test, Beattie, & Wood, 1997; Hasazi, Furney, & DeStefano, 1999). The National Council on Disability (2000) reported that "88% or 44 states failed to ensure compliance with transition requirements" (p. 89). Williams and O'Leary (2001) found that many schools do not invite students to their own IEP meetings. Johnson et al. (2001) indicated that secondary education must improve student attendance at IEP meetings, and prepare students to actively participate in their meetings so they can lead discussions about their plans and goals. The U.S. Department of Education's Office of Special Education Program Expert Strategy Panel Report indicated that today's secondary schools provide too few opportunities for students to learn and practice IEP leadership skills prior to their IEP meeting (U.S. Department of Education, 2001). Even so, a growing number of students do attend their IEP meetings. Many of the statewide transition system change grants sponsored by the U.S. Department of Education encouraged student involvement in their IEP meetings (Williams & O'Leary, 2001).

Research suggests that when students attend their IEP meetings without specific IEP meeting instruction, they do not know what to do, lack understanding of the meeting's purpose or language, feel like no one listens to them when they do talk, do not know their goals or other outcomes of the meeting, and think that attending the IEP meeting would be a meaningless activity (Lehmann, Bassett, & Sands, 1999; Lovitt, Cushing, & Stump, 1994; Morningstar, Turnbull, & Turnbull, 1995). Powers (1997) discovered that if students attended their IEP meetings with no prior instruction in what to do, they did not enjoy their IEP meetings and they did not understand the language or the meeting's purpose. She also found that students (and parents) believed that IEP team members did not talk to the student or ask for student input.

Martin, Marshall, and Sale (2004) conducted a survey of almost 1,770 IEP team members who attended middle and high school meetings over a three-year period. They found that when students attend their meetings, the students talked less and understood less about the reason for the meeting than did all other participants. To verify survey findings, Martin, Van Dycke, Greene, et al. (in press) observed 109 secondary teacher-directed IEP transition meetings using 10-second momentary time sampling. The results indicated that special education teachers talked 51% of the time, family members 15%, general educators and administrators 9%, support staff 6%, and students 3%. They concluded that "it seems naïve to presume that students attending their transition IEP meetings will learn how to actively participate and lead this process through serendipity—yet this is precisely what current practice tends to expect" (p. 4). It does not need to be this way.

> **Critical Point**
> Students' presence at the IEP meeting is not enough because they must learn their role and how to participate meaningfully.

Presence at the IEP meeting without knowledge of the process and skills in what to do achieves very little. Clearly, to make student-directed IEPs a meaningful educational experience, students should learn their role in the IEP process and what they can do to become a meaningful part of that process.

The expressing goals section of the *ChoiceMaker* curriculum provides students the skills and knowledge needed to become actively involved in and to direct their own IEP meeting. While at the meeting, the students learn how to discuss their interests, skills, limits, and goals across different transition areas.

Five available lesson packages help educators to teach students the skills required to participate in and direct their own IEP meetings. These include the *Self-Advocacy Strategy for Education and Transition Planning* (Van Reusen, Bos, Schumaker, & Deshler, 1994); *Whose Future Is It Anyway?* (Wehmeyer & Kelchner, 1995b); *A Student's Guide to the IEP*

(McGahee-Kovac, 1995); *Next Steps* (Halpern, Herr, Wolf, Lawson, Doren, & Johnson, 1997); and the *Self-Directed IEP* (Martin, Huber Marshall, Maxson, & Jerman, 1996c). The *Self-Directed IEP* specifically teaches students to attain the expressing goals section of the *ChoiceMaker* curriculum.

The Self-Directed IEP

The *Self-Directed IEP* teaches students to become active participants in their IEP meetings and to chair the meetings to the best extent of their ability. It teaches students the two goals and 11 objectives that are crucial for student involvement in their own education planning process (see 2. Expressing Goals in Table 14-6). Through the use of the self-directed IEP materials, role-play practice prior to the meeting, and participation in their actual meeting, students learn the leadership skills that they need to manage their IEP meeting. The *Self-Directed IEP* contains several different instructional materials. These include:

- *Self-Directed IEP in Action Video* (7 minutes). This video shows students with different disabilities using the self-directed IEP lessons in their classes and talking about their experiences. This video is used to introduce the self-directed IEP to students, parents, teachers, and administrators.
- *Self-Directed IEP Video* (17 minutes). This video shows a student named Zeke, using each of the 11 steps to lead his IEP meeting while describing the process to a younger, reluctant friend. Zeke's meeting provides a model for each of the 11 steps needed to lead an IEP meeting (see Table 14-7). The meeting

depicted in the video shows an ideal meeting, in which the student viewers focus upon the steps that are necessary to lead an IEP meeting.

- *Teacher's Manual.* This book provides background information, detailed lesson plans, and a teacher answer key to the quizzes and activities. Lessons include a variety of activities to teach each step, including a mnemonic learning strategy, vocabulary-building exercises, role playing, discussion, and brief reading and writing activities. The lessons are all presented in a model, lead, test approach.
- *Student Workbook.* This consumable workbook provides students an opportunity to apply each step to their own IEP. A script, summarizing all the steps, is completed at the end of the lessons for students to use at their IEP meeting.

Instructional Considerations

The IEP is the one unique aspect that defines special education. If educators and families are serious about involving students in their IEP process, then students must be taught their role. This means that even in fully included schools, students who have an IEP must receive instruction about the IEP process and their role in it.

The *Self-Directed IEP* contains 11 sequential lessons that can be taught in six to ten 45-minute sessions. The lessons may be taught in a resource room, study skills class, or other settings. To teach students who are fully included in general education classes may involve meeting with individuals or with a group during study hall or other convenient times. The lessons also may be taught in an elective class.

TABLE 14-7 Eleven steps to the *self-directed IEP*

1. Begin the meeting by stating the purpose.
2. Introduce everyone.
3. Review past goals and performance.
4. Ask for others' feedback.
5. State your school and transition goals.
6. Ask questions if you do not understand.
7. Deal with differences in opinion.
8. State what support you will need.
9. Summarize your goals.
10. Close the meeting by thanking everyone.
11. Work on IEP goals all year.

Source: Excerpt taken from: Martin, J. E., Marshall, L. H., Maxson, L., & Jerman, P. (1996c). *Self-directed IEP.* Longmont, CO: Sopris West Publishers. © 1997 University of Colorado. Used with permission from University Technology Corp.

Impact of the Self-Directed IEP

Sweeney (1996) undertook a pre-post control group study to measure the impact of the *Self-Directed IEP* upon Florida high school students with learning disabilities and mental retardation. In comparison to the students in the control group who did not receive instruction, Sweeney (1996) found that the students who completed the *Self-Directed IEP* lessons:

- Attended more of the IEP staffings
- Had more parents attend IEP staffings
- Talked more about their interests
- Shared more of their dreams for the future

- Talked more about the job they wanted
- Felt like they were the boss of their IEP meeting
- Felt more confident in reaching their IEP goals

Snyder and Shapiro (1997) and Snyder (2002) found that the *Self-Directed IEP* taught adolescent students with emotional and behavior problems the skills needed to direct their own IEP meeting. Allen, Smith, Test, Flowers, and Wood (2001) showed the functional relationship between the *Self-Directed IEP* and increases in participation by students with mental retardation and learning disabilities in their IEP meetings. Arndt, Konrad, and Test (2006) demonstrated across secondary students with various disabilities that the *Self-Directed IEP* increased student participation in their IEP meetings. Martin et al. (2006) used an experimental design and compared the *Self-Directed IEP* to traditional teacher-directed IEP meetings. They found that students who received *Self-Directed IEP* instruction started and led significantly more IEP meetings and significantly increased talking during their meetings. Students also reported significantly improved perceptions of their IEP meetings, and both students and adults both gave the transition discussions higher ratings.

The goals and objectives are the most important instructional outcome of the IEP meeting. In a *Self-Directed IEP* meeting students play a major role in determining the goals. But after the meeting, how are the goals attained? Typically, goal attainment becomes an educator's duty. However, do educators need to be the only people responsible for goal attainment? What about the student?

TEACHING AND CREATING OPPORTUNITIES FOR ATTAINING GOALS

Currently, special education teachers feel it is their responsibility to attain students' IEP goals. However, is this really the best education practice? To the authors, something is wrong with a practice in which the student is absolved of any goal attainment responsibility. After all, whose education is it, and whose goals are on the IEP? If goal attainment is the most important part of being self-determined, then why are students not more responsible for their own goals? Are educators really acting in the student's best interest if teachers carry the entire burden of responsibility for goal attainment?

The authors do not think so. Students should have at least equal, if not greater, responsibility for achieving

their own IEP goals. The authors' dream is that once the IEP meeting is concluded, the goal attainment process begins that students meet weekly with their teachers in order to develop plans to achieve their own IEP goals, after evaluating the progress they made the previous week in achieving the past week's plans. The authors cannot think of a better way to make the IEP process a student-centered, living document. *Take Action: Making Goals Happen* is the *ChoiceMaker* instructional program that teaches goal attainment.

> **Critical Point**
> It is believed that students should take as much responsibility as possible for their own IEP goals.

Take Action Overview

The *Take Action* lesson package teaches students a simple, yet effective goal attainment process. As with the other *ChoiceMaker* lesson packages, this lesson package is introduced with a student-oriented video demonstrating the take action concepts. *Take Action* lessons teach students to plan how they will attain their goal by deciding (1) a standard for goal performance, (2) a means to get performance feedback, (3) what motivates them to do it, (4) the strategies they will use, (5) needed supports, and (6) schedules. This leads to student action, evaluation, and adjustment. These lessons can be applied to any goal or project and, thus, are excellent for use in content classes.

Take Action Lessons

By using a model-lead-test approach, the *Take Action* lessons systematically teach students an easy and effective goal attainment process. Here we discuss four lessons:

- *Lesson 1.* Introduces the *Take Action* process for accomplishing goals. Students watch the 10-minute *Take Action* video, which shows students developing plans and working on attaining their own goals. The students in the video assisted in writing and creating the video. The goals you see them working on in the video use goals from their own lives. Introduced in this lesson are the four major parts of the take action process: plan, act, evaluate, and adjust.
- *Lesson 2.* This lesson begins the process of teaching students how to break long-term

Name _____ Date _____

Find the question that explains each part of a plan. Write it under the correct part of the plan.

Questions

How will I get information on my performance?	What help do I need?	When will I do it?	What will I be satisfied with?	What methods should I use?	Why do I want to do this?

Parts of a Plan

Standard	Motivation	Strategy	Schedule	Support	Feedback

FIGURE 14–6   Take action review

Source: Excerpt from: Marshall, L. H., Martin, J. E., Maxson, L. M., Miller, T. L., McGill, T., Hughes, W. M., & Jerman, P. A. (1997). *Taking action.* Longmont, CO: Sopris West, Inc. © 1997 University of Colorado. Used with permission from University Technology Corp.

goals into short-term objectives. To do this, students participate in an example process showing what a student must do to get her driver's license.

- *Lesson 3.*   Students are introduced to plan making. Here they learn the parts of a plan that is needed to attain their goal. Hands-on activities are used to demonstrate each plan part. One of the concluding activities is for students to match the question being asked to the correct part of the plan (see Figure 14–6).

- *Lesson 6.*   Students learn the importance of evaluation and adjustment to goal attainment. They examine the evaluation and adjustments of earlier plans.

- *Remaining lessons.*   The remaining lessons teach students how to develop their own plans for sample goals, then for their own goals. The last lesson teaches students how to use the take action goal attainment process in other settings, and with a wide range of goals.

Impact of *Take Action* Lessons

German, Martin, Huber Marshall, and Sale (2000) undertook a study to determine the effectiveness of *Take Action* in teaching goal attainment to six students with mild to moderate mental retardation. After completing the *Take Action* lessons, all the students had significant increases in the attainment of specific daily goals. The students went from achieving 0 to 25% of their daily goals during baseline to 80 to 100% after instruction in the *Take Action* lessons. Walden (2002) demonstrated that university students with learning disabilities could learn the *Take Action* goal attainment process and that the strategy generalized.

TEACHING AND CREATING OPPORTUNITIES FOR STUDENTS WITH SEVERE COGNITIVE NEEDS

Most available lesson packages teach self-determination skills to students with mild learning and emotional challenges. Only a few materials exist to help educators teach self-determination skills to students with more severe cognitive needs (Field et al., 1998). Martin, Mithaug, Oliphint, Husch, and Frazier (2002) use illustrations to develop a self-directed vocational assessment and to establish self-directed goal attainment (see Figure 14–7). In their *Self-Directed Employment Program* students complete a repeated-measures situational assessment process to determine preferred job characteristics, tasks, and locations. Second, students learn an on-the-job problem-solving system that utilizes written or illustrated contracts

Name				Date	Job Site		Page 1 of 2
	What I Like before work				What Is Here after work		
Circle what you like. *Star top 10 √4 most preferred		*	√		Circle what is here		Matches
Work alone	Work with lots of people	⊀	√	Work alone	Work with lots of people		Y (N)
Quiet workplace	Loud workplace			Quiet workplace	Loud workplace		Y (N)
Part time	Full time	⊀		Part time	Full time		Y (N)
Weekdays only	Weekends too			Weekdays only	Weekends too		Y (N)
Hard job	Easy job			Hard job	Easy job		(Y) N
Inside	Outside	⊀		Inside	Outside		Y (N)
Few rules	Lots of rules	⊀	√	Few rules	Lots of rules		Y (N)
Standing up	Sitting down	⊀		Standing up	Sitting down		Y (N)
Work mornings	Work afternoons			Work mornings	Work afternoons		(Y) N

FIGURE 14–7 Characteristics I like versus what is here form B

Source: Excerpt from: Martin, J. E., Mithaug, D. E., Oliphint, J. V. & Husch, J. (2002). *ChoiceMaker employment: A self-determination transition and supported employment handbook.* Baltimore: Paul H. Brookes.

to improve social, personal, and work performance. Third, students engage in job adjustment and career advancement decisions. The procedures capitalize upon discrepancy problems that workers must solve. During assessment the students need to resolve the discrepancy between what they like and what may or may not exist at a job site. In placement, this discrepancy exists when the workers' self-evaluations do not match their supervisors' evaluation. The *Self-Directed Employment Program* provides opportunities for students to resolve these discrepancies.

The *Choose and Take Action* program combines interactive software, classroom lessons, and community experiences to enable individuals with developmental disabilities to make practical career choices. Students watch video segments, select a job that matches their interests, try the selected job at a community site, evaluate the experience, and then make new choices based on what they learned. The *Choose and Take Action* instructional activities are designed to teach students numerous self-determination skills, including:

- Choosing from a variety of work options
- Planning whether they want to watch or do the activity
- Completing the plan in the community setting
- Evaluating what they liked and did not like about the setting, activity, and work-site characteristics, and how the students did while they were at the setting
- Using the information gained in the experience to make the next choice

The *Choose and Take Action* software also introduces students to a variety of job and career possibilities and teaches them to identify what is most important to them about a job, the setting, the activity, or the characteristics.

Target Population

Choose and Take Action is designed for students and adults with developmental disabilities, brain injury, and autism who are unable to read and write. The characteristics of students for whom this program will work the best include:

- Students with moderate to significant cognitive needs
- Students who have difficulty getting information from print
- Students who can attend to a computer screen

- Students who can follow simple verbal instructions
- Students in middle and high school
- Students with limited work experience

How *Choose and Take Action* Was Developed

The development of the *Choose and Take Action* software program involved numerous steps. First, a group of teachers, adult-service-supported employment personnel, former students with a disability, parents, advocates for students with disabilities, and university faculty met to brainstorm. The group identified critical self-determination skills. Next, a project advisory panel (made up of transition specialists, teachers, former students, parents, agency and university personnel, and school administrators) voted on the relative importance of each skill area. Third, the development team along with representatives from three states spent several days creating a rough draft of the software specifications and functions. Fourth, the advisory panel reviewed and finalized the software plan. Fifth, the software plan underwent a nationwide social validation process. Experts in transition, self-determination, employment for individuals with disabilities, individuals with disabilities, and parents reviewed the plan. Then, the comments and suggestions were incorporated into the software and lessons. Sixth, the software and lessons underwent extensive field testing in four states, with their findings incorporated into the final product.

Daviso, Ackerman, and Flexer (2003) found that the choices students make using the *Choose and Take Action* program correlates highly with the results of the *Becker Reading Free Interest Inventory*. Students chose the same types of jobs from both picture assessments. Student with severe disabilities demonstrated stable choices supporting the value of preference assessments with these students. Martin, Woods, Sylvester, and Gardner (2005) compared the choices made by individuals with cognitive disabilities to their caregivers. The choices made by individuals with disabilities seldom matched those made by their caregivers.

The *Choose and Take Action* Cycle

The *Choose and Take Action* cycle includes four steps. Students complete the first two cycle steps, choice making and plan development, in one session.

Step 1: *Choice Making.* During choice making, students view pairs of randomly presented videos showing different employment settings, activities, and job characteristics. From each pair, students select the one they like the best. After they have viewed all the videos once, the ones they chose the first time are paired and the students choose again. This continues until students choose one final video option to try. Then, students develop a plan.

Step 2: *Plan.* During the plan part of the program, students determine if they want to *watch* someone do the activity at their selected setting or if they want actually to *do* the activity. Printed plans are produced and shown with pictures that students chose: the setting, activity, two characteristics, and whether they want to watch or do the activities. The evaluation questions regarding these choices are also printed on the plan.

Step 3: *Try It.* Based on the plan, the student goes into the community to "try it" at the chosen setting. Students will interact with the workers at the site as much as possible as they watch or do the activity.

Step 4: *Evaluate.* Students, with the instructor's guidance, evaluate the experience, then enter that information into the computer.

With each step, the teacher provides only instruction that the students require to complete the step independently. Of course, an educator will need to arrange the detail involved in visiting a "try-it" site. The *Choose and Take Action* software is designed for students with limited work experience; therefore, it is critical for students to complete the process a number of times in order to try many different things.

Video Clips

The software contains 31, 20-second video clips, across 14 employment settings, and 15 activities. Twelve characteristics, each shown at least four times, are also included in the 31 video clips. Each video clip shows an employment setting, an entry-level activity, and two characteristics of the job. For each setting, there are two or three video clips showing a different activity, and each activity is shown in at least two settings.

The teacher may limit the number of video clips that a student will see in one session. The settings and activities shown in the video clips represent entry-level jobs and cover most job categories in the Department of Labor's *Occupational Outlook Handbook*. The jobs represent opportunities that are available in most communities. See Table 14–8 for a listing of video settings, activities, and characteristics.

Importance of *Try-It*

Students in the target population may have difficulty generalizing from what is depicted in the video to a real setting. The videos give more information than a text or pictured version of an employment interest inventory, but they still do not exactly replicate the community settings students will visit. Students must go to the settings and *try it* to make their choices meaningful.

TABLE 14–8 List of settings, activities, and characteristics included in the video clips

Settings	Activities	Characteristics
Auto dealer/mechanic	Assemble and disassemble	Spacious
Construction site	Bag items and bring in carts	Cozy space
Factory	Bus tables	Noisy
Florist/Greenhouse/Nursery	Care for animals	Quiet
Grocery store	Care for people	Inside
Hospital/Nursing home	Care for plants	Outside
Hotel	Heavy cleaning	Wear own clothes
Janitorial service	Laundry	Wear a uniform
Landscape/Outdoor maintenance	Light cleaning	Many people
Office	Move materials	Few people
Restaurant	Filing	Messy
Retail	Paperwork	Clean
School/child care	Stock shelves	
Vet office/Kennel/Grooming	Wash dishes	
	Yard work	

Reports

The software records students' choices throughout the program and creates reports indicating the students' choices in the choose, plan, and evaluate sections. There is also a place for instructors to record their observations and notes about the students' experiences and their discussions. Students will be able to graph their results on simple bar graphs. The reports and graphs will help students and the IEP teams to see the students' emerging interests and skill trends. These reports, including the instructor's evaluations and observations, may be included in a student portfolio. This provides information about students' preferences for IEP meetings and vocational assessments. This will give students a starting place for employment decision making.

The *Choose and Take Action* lesson package infuses the best of what is known about teaching self-determination with available technology. The use of interactive video software provides an additional means for students with severe needs to show teachers what they want.

CREATING OPPORTUNITIES TO PRACTICE SELF-DETERMINATION SKILLS

Students with emotional and behavioral disorders (EBD) present a unique challenge to the transition process. Students with EBD have the lowest graduation rate of all students with disabilities, the highest dropout rate, and a high rate of contact with the criminal justice system (Blackorby & Wagner, 1996). Innovative practice for students with behavioral challenges provides the opportunity to combine self-determination instruction *and* effective behavioral support planning. The following case study shows what we mean.

CASE STUDY William

Student Directed Behavior Assessment and Planning

William, a 12th-grade student at a local high school, acts out chronically at his community-based vocational placement. The teaching team decides that a functional assessment is needed, and they spend several hours collecting data and observing William across settings, using both indirect and direct functional assessment methodologies. Upon completion of the functional assessment, the team convenes and develops a behavior support plan outlining a replacement response and teaching strategies to establish new and more appropriate behavior. After three weeks of implementing the support plan, the team becomes frustrated—William's acting-out has actually increased.

William's teaching team is more concerned than ever about William's increased chronic acting-out at his community-based vocational placement. This time, rather than using a traditional teacher-directed functional assessment, they involve William. The team meets with William over a morning snack to determine his beliefs regarding the problem behavior. William talks about his behavior at the vocational setting. With this new information, the team—with William as an equal member—conducts indirect and direct functional assessments. The collected data identify the perceived function or purpose of William's problem behavior. Following the functional assessment, William leads his behavior support planning meeting and shares with the teaching team what he learned. During the meeting, he identifies his interests, skills, and goals. The teaching team (with William as an equal member) writes a behavior support plan with instructional and support strategies, and environmental modifications to help William learn a new replacement response to his acting-out behavior. The behavior support plan is also incorporated into William's IEP.

Data are collected for several weeks by the teaching team *and* William. After three weeks the data clearly show that the problem behavior has decreased and William's replacement behavior is being demonstrated consistently at his vocational placement and across other environments.

Student-Directed Summary of Performance

IDEA 2004 now requires that schools provide students with an IEP a Summary of Performance when they exit (Johnson, 2005). The student-directed Summary of Performance provides another opportunity for students to become engaged in their own transition planning process (Martin, Van Dycke, D'Ottavio, & Nickerson, in press). Rather than educators completing the Summary of Performance and simply handing it to the student at the exit IEP meeting, special educators can instead use the student-directed Summary of Performance.

The student-directed Summary of Performance, when built across the high school years, will increase Students' awareness of their disability, increase their knowledge of useful supports, provide a means for students to understand the results of transition assessment data, and enable students to fully understand the school's recommendation on what must be done to attain post–high-school goals. Sections of the student-directed Summary of Performance will be written in first-person language (my goal for employment is, my primary disability is, and my disability impacts school activities like this). Students, with teacher and parent assistance, complete the Summary of Performance starting in ninth grade to aid with their IEP transition discussions. Prior to exiting school, students will present to their IEP team their Summary of Performance.

Functional Behavioral Assessment

O'Neill et al. (1997) writes that a functional behavioral assessment is the result of an information gathering process that includes an analysis of the person's schedule, activity patterns, curricula, staff support, and physical environment, as well as the observation of the person's behavior in targeted settings where the problem behavior occurs and does not occur. When collected, this data is used to develop alternatives to the problem behavior that are functionally equivalent to the behavior of concern, while at the same time being more appropriate in targeted settings. O'Neill argues that functional behavioral assessments create a context for understanding problem behavior and are best used as a method to "maximize the effectiveness and efficiency of behavioral support" (p. 3).

> **Critical Point**
> Students can participate in functionally assessing their own behaviors and in developing intervention strategies.

In most cases, educators and support staff complete the functional assessment and implement the behavior support plan without direct student input. But, there is an alternative that includes the student as a key person in this process. Students with emotional or behavioral disabilities who have learned to choose and attain goals have the skills that are necessary to set goals about their behavior, make plans to adjust their behavior, take action on their plan, self-monitor and self-record targeted behavior, and adjust goals and plans as the situation dictates. As students learn these important self-determination skills, they can become an increasingly effective member of their behavior support team.

Students with emotional or behavioral disabilities, or other students who exhibit chronic or persistent problem behavior that prevents them or their peers from receiving a reasonable educational benefit from the general curriculum, can and should participate in their own behavior support planning process. Important outcomes result when students participate in their behavior support planning, implementation, and evaluation processes. For example, students will: (a) *choose goals*—identify needs and interest based on the functional assessment data; (b) *express goals*—lead the behavior support planning meeting, which results in the development of a behavior support plan; and (c) *take action*—implement their behavior support plan, evaluate progress toward goal attainment, and make adjustments to their plan as needed.

CONCLUSION

Self-determination skills contribute to a successful transition. Since most students with an IEP lack well-developed self-determination skills, teaching these skills must become a priority in the transition process. For this to occur, self-determination must be considered as a transition need. Once the need becomes established, self-determination teaching goals detail what must be taught. Educators, then, must teach students self-determination skills and provide opportunities for students to practice and generalize their learned skills.

STUDY QUESTIONS

1. You are a member of a high school IEP team and believe that self-determination skills need to be taught to your students. How will you include self-determination in the IEP process?
2. From your knowledge of what takes place in secondary programs, identify at least three

different ways that each self-determination concept depicted in Table 14–2 can be taught and practiced by students with high-incidence disabilities.

3. Write a letter to your Congressional representative detailing how IDEA needs to be modified when the act is again authorized to make its self-determination emphasis even stronger than it is today.

4. Your team has a budget of $1,800 to purchase new materials. Go to the websites of different educational publishing houses and build a purchase request document to submit to your principal. Include a description of the material, its use, how it will help to meet your students' IEP goals, and purchasing information. (See the list of websites at the end of the chapter.)

5. Using your state's academic standards, write a standards-referenced IEP goal and objectives to teach a self-determination construct from Table 14–2.

WEBSITES

Selected list of publishers that distribute self-determination materials:

Sopris West for *ChoiceMaker* materials:
  www.sopriswest.com
Brookes Publishing Company:
  www.pbrookes.com
Pro-Ed:
  www.proedinc.com
Council for Exceptional Children:
  www.cec.sped.org/
Self-Determination Synthesis Project Homepage:
  www.uncc.edu/sdsp
AIR Self-Determination Assessment is available at no charge at:
  www.ou.edu/zarrow
Click on the self-determination button.

CHAPTER 15

COORDINATING TRANSITION SERVICES

Robert Baer

Robert Flexer

LEARNING OBJECTIVES

The objectives of this chapter are:

1. Identify four major approaches to service coordination and their underlying philosophies.
2. Understand how student and family expectations define service coordination.
3. Define the five major responsibilities of the transition services coordinator.
4. Identify the 11 major job duties of the transition services coordinator.
5. Identify competencies needed by the transition services coordinator.

INTRODUCTION

Special education's involvement in providing transition services under the requirements of the IDEA has required educators to work with a staggeringly complex adult service system (Baer, 1996; Paulson, 1993), with differing legislative foundations, eligibility requirements, intake procedures, service definitions, and philosophies (DeStefano & Snauwaert, 1989; Szymanski, Hanley-Maxwell, & Asselin, 1992). Ward and Halloran (1989) suggested that this system represented a serious disconnect between the entitlement philosophy of school programs and the availability-driven philosophy of adult services. Szymanski et al. noted that these differences were rooted in history, definitions of disability, funding differences, and differences in evaluation standards. Kochhar and Deschamps (1992) maintained that adult service and special education policies were often at odds in assuring services for learners with special needs, and Kortering and Edgar (1988) emphasized the need for more cooperation between special education and vocational rehabilitation.

The complex array of school and adult services has pointed to the need for transition services coordinators who can address both the individual and the systems level transition needs of students with disabilities (Kohler, 1998). At the individual level, transition coordinators need to assure the development of a coordinated set of activities designed to promote student movement to postschool environments. At the systems level, they need to address barriers related to intake and referral, information gathering, planning, service delivery, and evaluation (Baer, 1996). This chapter has been designed to discuss these issues by starting with a review of a range of service coordination strategies. It then applies these strategies to the categories of transition activities developed by Kohler (1998), and the job duties of transition coordinators as defined by job audits (Asselin, Todd-Allen, & deFur, 1998; Baer, 1998). The chapter closes with an extended case study to show how these transition activities and job duties were applied in a single case.

THE RANGE OF SERVICE COORDINATION STRATEGIES

Much of what has been published about service coordination (or case management) has emanated from the fields of rehabilitation and mental health, which have had a long history of dealing with fragmented service delivery systems. Service coordination models have ranged from *broker* models on one end of the continuum to *full support* models on the other (Hagen, 1994; Hodge & Draine, 1993). Broker models of service coordination have often been used by service coordinators (or case managers) with large caseloads (Hodge & Draine). Typically these models consisted of an expert case manager who linked the individual to needed services and then intervened only as new services were needed or when a crisis situation arose (Hodge & Draine). Because of the broker model's focus on stabilization in the community and on appropriate use of services (Hodge & Draine), transition coordinators using this model tended to focus their services on assertive individuals and on individuals in crisis (Intaglia & Baker, 1983).

At the other end of the continuum, full support models used ecological approaches to service coordination. These models required much lower caseloads because the service coordinator functioned as part of the interdisciplinary team and provided proactive services that included assertive outreach, development of environmental supports, and promotion of self-determination (Hodge & Draine, 1993). Services and supports were assessed in these models through what Brown, Nietupski, and Hamre-Nietupski (1976) called the *criterion of ultimate function* and Vincent et al. (1980) described as the *criteria of the next environment.* Full support approaches to service coordination have been identified as best practice in both education and rehabilitation programs (Asselin, Todd-Allen, & deFur, 1998; Baer, 1996) but have remained difficult to implement due to their labor intensiveness.

In between these two extremes, two other service coordination models have been identified in the literature: (a) rehabilitation models and (b) personal strengths models (Hodge & Draine, 1993). A unique feature of the rehabilitation model was the use of functional assessments to determine strengths, deficits, skills, and abilities and then the application of this information to help individuals succeed in specific environments (Robinson, 1991). Typically, this included strengthening individual skills and making adjustments in the living and working environments to facilitate independence. The service coordinator in this model served as a buffer between the individual and the service system and success was measured based on individual satisfaction in the environment of choice (Robinson). This model was less time-intensive than full support models because it targeted specific environments (usually work or education) and focused interventions more on the individual than the environment.

Under the personal strengths models, the service coordinator served as a mentor who assisted individuals in identifying personal strengths that could be used to achieve desired goals. This model has been typically used with individuals with greater career maturity and the ability to identify and develop their personal potential. The advantage of this model was that the focus on strengths and individual resources provided new perspectives about the person with a disability. Evaluation of success under the personal strengths model was based on the individual's

Critical Point
Four models of service coordination are the:
(a) full support,
(b) personal strengths,
(c) rehabilitation, and
(d) broker models.

ability to identify and obtain personal goals (Hodge & Draine, 1993). It had the advantage of being most closely aligned with the philosophies of the independent living and student self-determination movements.

Family expectations also played a role in the choice of service coordination strategies. Research has found that family expectations of professionals typically fall into one of four general categories: (a) expectations for support and emotional guidance, (b) expectations for cognitive guidance and evaluation, (c) expectations for assuming personal initiative with professional feedback, and (d) expectations for collaboration (Koch & Rumrill, 1998b). It is important that transition coordinators negotiate rather than impose coordination strategies, since congruence among youth, family, and professional expectations has been shown to be positively related to ratings of the working alliance (Al-Darmaki & Kivlighan, 1993). Additionally, families may have many other concerns and stressors that limit their ability to assume service coordination responsibilities (Hayden & Goldman, 1996).

A number of factors influence the expectations that students with disabilities and their families have regarding the transition process, including the individual's career maturity, availability of resources and natural supports, and the preferences of the individual. The "helping" and formalized culture of the disability service system may not fit well with individuals or families who view disability from the perspective of the emerging consumer culture of the independent living movement, which has defined lack of civil rights, societal responses to disability, and dependence on professionals as the primary concerns in disability service provision

(Shapiro, 1993; Tower, 1994). The independent living movement has stressed self-management of services by persons with disabilities through collective advocacy, self-help groups, generic support services, and access to the community (DeJong, 1984; Tower).

In some cases students with disabilities and their families may expect greater involvement of professionals in service provision. Hayden and Goldman (1996) suggest that the caregiver's marital status, the youth's level of cognitive disability, frequency of maladaptive behaviors, and the health status of the adult family members are important considerations in determining support strategies. Care should be taken in using service-oriented models such as the broker model because an over-reliance on services may create problems for students with disabilities who move from a service-rich environment in high school to little or no services after graduation (DeStefano & Snauwaert, 1989; Ward & Halloran, 1989).

Critical Point
The type and level of service coordination should be based on the needs and expectations of families and students with disabilities

THE RESPONSIBILITIES OF TRANSITION COORDINATORS

The role of transition coordinator may reside in one or more transition specialists at a school, may be assumed by the special education supervisor, or may fall to the individuals responsible for IEP/transition planning. This role may be dispersed across several individuals at a school with some handling transition planning, others directing community-based transition services, and others handling administrative-level interagency collaboration. Regardless of how transition responsibilities are allocated, it is important to coordinate these responsibilities so that all components of transition systems are working together.

Kohler (1998) surveyed transition service providers and administrators across the United States and found that their transition activities generally fell into five categories: (a) student-focused planning, (b) student development, (c) family involvement, (d) collaboration, and (e) development of program structures and attributes. Her transition "taxonomy" showed how the four essential elements of transition in IDEA were being implemented across various contexts and environments. Kohler's categories of *student-focused planning* and *family involvement* identified activities related to determining student needs, interests, strengths, and preferences in the family context. Her categories of *collaboration* and *development of program structures and attributes* were related to developing a coordinated set of activities, but extended this concept to include systems-level interagency collaboration. Finally, her category of *student development* was highly related to promoting movement to postschool activities, but it included a range of activities to promote in-school results as well as postschool outcomes.

> **Critical Point**
> Kohler identified five general categories of transition services: (a) student-focused planning, (b) student development, (c) family involvement, (d) collaboration, and (e) development of program structures and attributes.

Within Kohler's (1998) overall framework, transition coordinators performed a number of specific duties. Asselin, Todd-Allen, and deFur (1998) and Baer (1996) used a job audit process known as Developing a Curriculum (DACUM) to identify the major job duties of a transition coordinator. These were identified by practicing coordinators as:

1. Linking services and instruction
2. Identifying postsecondary opportunities and competency requirements
3. Developing community worksites and work experience programs
4. Coordinating referrals
5. Scheduling and facilitating transition meetings
6. Promoting student self-determination
7. Monitoring fulfillment of transition team member responsibilities
8. Chairing the interagency coordinating body
9. Developing communication strategies, methods to release and share information
10. Developing methods to identify future service needs of families and students
11. Coordinating student follow-up studies

In 2000, the transition competencies from Kohler's (1998) work were organized according to the major categories in the Council for Exceptional Children's (CEC, 2000) standards for a qualified special educator by the CEC Subcommittee on Knowledge and Skills, the University of Illinois' Transition-Related Competencies Project, and the Division on Career Development and Transition (DCDT, 2000). The Subcommittee on Knowledge and Skills and the CEC Division on Career Development and Transition (DCDT) identified the "transition coordinator" as:

> . . . an individual who plans, coordinates, delivers, and evaluates transition education and services at the school or system level, in conjunction with other educators, families, students, and representatives of community organizations. (Division of Career Development and Transition, 2000, p. 1)

When compared with traditional special educator roles, these new competency areas suggested that in addition to special educator skills, transition specialists should have additional competencies in the areas of: (a) knowledge of other transition disciplines (such as vocational education and rehabilitation), (b) ability to develop work and community-based training, and (c) competency to evaluate the effectiveness of transition services in producing desired outcomes (Flexer & Baer, 2005). The following discussion explores each of Kohler's categories of transition services, related job duties, and critical transition specialist competencies.

> **Critical Point**
> Practitioners have identified many job duties and competencies for transition coordinators within the five categories described by Kohler (1998).

Student-Focused Planning

Each member of any working alliance enters the process with unique expectations (Koch & Rumrill, 1998b). These expectations need to be identified at the outset so that any discrepancies among the expectations of the transition coordinator, the individual, and the family can be resolved and a mutually acceptable set of expectations can be established (Koch & Rumrill). These expectations may evolve over the working alliance and include expectations about outcomes and expectations about roles. Koch & Rumrill described a five-step process in developing a working alliance:

1. Address individual expectations routinely as part of the intake process.
2. Clarify expectations about professional roles, goals, and services of the rehabilitation process.
3. Identify discrepancies between what individuals hope will occur and what they expect to occur.
4. Determine if there are differential expectations among members of the working alliance.
5. Reassess expectations at various stages of the process.

Before the IEP/transition meeting, the transition coordinator should develop some degree of consensus among meeting participants about the student and family vision. This is because these meetings typically do not allow time for extensive debate or disagreement, and these time constraints can result in students and families being coerced to accept decisions. If any key IEP/transition meeting participant is likely to disagree with the student and family vision, the transition coordinator should try to resolve these issues prior to the meeting or allocate additional meeting time for discussion.

In some cases, students may disagree with their families or guardians regarding career choices, services, or supports. In this situation, the transition coordinator should mediate by providing students and their families with additional information or career exploration experiences. This could include involving the student and family in informational meetings with guidance counselors, employers, postsecondary educators, community members, or service providers. In the few instances where students and their families cannot reach consensus, the transition coordinator generally should follow the wishes of the family while supporting the student before the age of majority, and vice versa, after the age of majority.

Prior to the IEP/transition meeting, the transition coordinator should define the role that students and their families will play in the meeting. For students and families with self-determination and advocacy skills, the transition coordinator should encourage them to assume the role of directing the IEP/transition meeting. Their leadership role can be supported by developing an agenda and a PowerPoint presentation prior to the meeting. The student and/or the family can use these aids to present their transition goals with the transition coordinator serving as the timekeeper, note taker, and prompter.

As noted earlier, many students and families will expect the coordinator of the IEP/transition meeting to take the leadership role, especially if they have not had extensive preparation and self-determination training. In these cases, the IEP/transition coordinator must act as an advocate by meeting with students and families prior to the meeting to identify their vision and service preferences. The coordinator should then start the meeting by presenting their vision and

> **Critical Point**
> Transition coordinators should clarify and update student and family expectations in regard to their roles in transition planning.

help the student and family defend their choices throughout the meeting. In this advocacy role, it is particularly important that the transition coordinator work out disagreements with the student and family prior to the meeting.

Scheduling and Facilitating Transition Meetings

The transition coordinator should work with special and general educators to schedule meetings in a way that maximizes student and family participation. Approaches include the use of personal invitations to students and family members, offering alternative times for meetings, holding meetings in alternative locations, and helping to arrange transportation for families. The transition coordinator should also develop strategies for maximizing participation of adult service providers using strategies that include grouping IEP meetings to be attended by an adult service provider and by arranging alternative ways for adult service providers to provide input.

The transition coordinator also needs to accommodate the schedules of families, while at the same time assuring maximum participation of key educators and adult service providers. This may be difficult because adult service providers and educators may be reluctant to meet outside their regular work schedules, while families may find day meetings difficult to attend. This issue can be partially addressed by identifying those times that families are free during the day or times that educators and adult service providers are available on the weekends and in the evenings. These key times can be reserved for families that have difficulty meeting during regularly scheduled hours.

The invitation to the **transition meeting** should consist of a written invitation with an enclosed meeting agenda and a simple way to RSVP (e.g., phone call or self-addressed stamped envelope). This invitation should inform the family of who will be at the meeting and provide opportunities for students and families to invite other members. The transition coordinator may need to make follow-up phone contacts to encourage students, key adult service providers, community members, and families to attend. Families, and even adult service providers, may avoid participation in IEP/transition planning as a result of previous experience where their input was not valued, or where the IEPs were essentially developed prior to the meeting. The transition coordinator needs to assure families and adult service providers that their role in the meeting will be critical. One method of doing this is to develop a meeting agenda that includes time allotted for the student, family, and adult service providers to present issues of concern to them.

The transition meeting should be conducted in a way that presents the youth with disabilities and their family in the best light. Starting with seating and introductions, students and their families should be given priority in their IEP meetings. The meeting should always start with the student and family vision of the future. It should not start with a discussion of the student's weaknesses or disabilities because this will limit the possibilities envisioned for the student by the team. If any student background is provided at the start of the meeting, it should focus upon positive experiences and strengths.

> **Critical Point**
> The transition coordinator should organize meetings to assure student and family participation and respect.

Once the vision has been presented, the team should identify students' current level of function and brainstorm services and supports they will need to achieve their postschool goals. This is a critical phase of the planning process because team members may challenge the feasibility of the student's goals in relation to their current level of functioning. At this point, the coordinator may need to redirect the team from a focus on problems to a focus on solutions (Koch & Rumrill, 1998b). This may require persistence because it is safer to discuss problems than to generate solutions. At this stage, the coordinator should assure team members that all ideas will be welcome and that

criticism of ideas in the brainstorming phase will not be allowed.

Generation of ideas may be supported through backward planning where problems are solved one year at a time starting with the final year prior to graduation. The coordinator may aid this process by providing a list of commonly used transition services and supports and then having the team allocate these services and supports year by year. A simple way to illustrate this process to the team is to develop the following grid for each of the students' postschool goals. This grid can be created on the wall using sticky notes by listing the student's postschool goal and the years leading to graduation across the top and the seven types of transition services mentioned by the IDEA down the side. This would create a grid similar to one shown in Table 15-1.

Once this grid has been established, the coordinator can then distribute sticky notes to team members and ask them to write transition ideas related to the goal posted across the top. As transition ideas are generated, the transition coordinator can ask questions such as, "When will this service be provided?" and "Who will provide this service or activity?" (Koch & Rumrill, 1998a). The advantage of using sticky notes for this process is that it allows team members to move transition services around as new ideas are generated.

After generating and scheduling ideas for transition activities, the transition coordinator should ask the question of how these activities will be connected to the general education curriculum by asking "How will

TABLE 15-1 Planning grid for brainstorming transition services

	Postschool Goal:				
Transition Activities	Age 14	Age 15	Age 16	Age 17	Age 18+
Instruction and Courses					
Community Experiences					
Career Development					
Related Services					
Daily Living Skills					
Vocational Evaluation					
Linkages to Adult Services					

this transition activity be supported by class work?" or "How will the student learn the math or spelling needed to participate in this program or activity?" These ideas can also be written on sticky notes and be attached to the relevant transition activity. Once this process has been concluded, the coordinator should be able to generate an IEP/transition plan that includes: (a) a list of needed transition services and activities, (b) time lines for their completion, (c) contact persons, and (d) how transition activities will support and be supported by the general education curriculum.

> **Critical Point**
> The transition coordinator should focus team efforts on generating and prioritizing ideas rather than discussing problems.

Coordinating Referrals

Student-focused planning may also require the development of linkages to planning conducted by adult service agencies. The transition coordinator needs to develop linkages with adult services and the range of educational programs. The Social Security Administration and the Rehabilitation Services Administration are the two most common referrals for funding and services for youth with disabilities. Transition coordinators need to become familiar with Social Security and its work incentives programs, such as plans to achieve self-sufficiency (PASS), impairment-related work expenses (IRWEs), and student income exclusions. They must become familiar with the programs of the vocational rehabilitation (VR) services and with the services it funds, including postsecondary education, vocational school, assistive technology, computers, and job placement and training. Coordinators also should be aware of when students may apply for and begin receiving services since many adult service programs also serve youth and even children. The coordinator should know that adult services vary widely for different disability groups, from location to location, and from year to year.

The transition coordinator may want to sponsor an agency fair where students, teachers, and families can sign up for adult services at the school. As part of an agency fair, each agency representative and representatives of postsecondary environments can fill out a questionnaire. Figure 15–1 presents an example of such a questionnaire. These can be typed, alphabetized, and put together to make a directory that the school can give to students, community members, and families for easy reference. Additionally, the adult service providers can be invited to present to parents, students, and teachers as part of a panel presentation, which is followed by the opportunity for participants to meet with agency representatives and fill out **referrals.**

The transition coordinator should be aware that student and family preferences need to be respected in making referrals for adult services and that some referrals may need to be initiated by the student or the family. Referrals for mental health and developmental disability (or mental retardation) services may be resisted by some students for fear of being stigmatized as "retarded" or "crazy." Additionally, families may have misinformation about adult service programs that need to be addressed. For example, many students and families believe that developmental disability programs provide only sheltered workshop services, when these programs can actually provide supported employment and supported living services in the community.

> **Critical Point**
> The transition coordinator needs to maintain and update lists of agencies and contact persons.

Student Development

Siegel (1998) suggested that because there was no single transition program that served all students with disabilities, all programs should maximize accessibility. According to Siegel (1998), youth with profound disabilities and extremely challenging behaviors should have access to supported employment services, day treatment, residential, and immersion programs and should have follow-along services that extend for up to five years. Youth with mild learning or emotional disabilities should be involved in job shadowing and have access to work experiences during the last two years of school. They also may need to have access to team teaching, vocational special education, community work experiences, participation in career/technical and vocational clubs and organizations, linkages with adult services, and support in accessing a community college program.

Students with disabilities also need access to appropriate course work. As noted in previous chapters, Greene (2003) identified four major *transition pathways* as including: (a) mainstream academics leading to college, (b) semi-integrated academics

> **Critical Point**
> Students with disabilities need access to courses of study and transition services that lead to their desired postschool goals.

1. **Your name:** _____ **Title:** _____
2. **Your agency:** _____ **Phone:** _____
3. Please provide a brief overview of the purpose of your agency:

_____

_____

_____

_____

_____

4. Briefly, what transition services are available to students with disabilities before age 18?

_____

_____

_____

_____

_____

5. Briefly, what transition services are available to students with disabilities after age 18?

_____

_____

_____

_____

_____

_____

_____

6. Generally, what types of students are eligible for your services and how should they be referred?

_____

_____

_____

_____

_____

FIGURE 15–1   Outline for panel presentation

and/or career/technical education leading to two-year colleges, (c) semi-integrated academics and/or career/technical education leading to employment, and (d) life skills training leading to supported employment. Transition coordinators need to be able to identify these pathways within their school and assure that students with disabilities have access to pathways that are appropriate to their postschool goals.

Linking Services and Instruction

Transition coordinators can link services and instruction by assuring that students' courses of study relate to their postschool goals. Though no longer required under the IDEA of 2004, the author recommends that by age 14, student IEPs should include a "statement of transition services needs" related to students' desired courses of study. This statement should: (a) identify the

students' courses of study and (b) identify transition services related to those courses of study. Courses of study could include specific classes or training related to student postschool goals, but the author recommends identifying general courses of study such as career and technical education, advanced academics, or life skills education because coherent and focused courses of study have been shown to promote positive postschool outcomes for students with disabilities (Blackorby & Wagner, 1996).

Access to the general curriculum may be resisted by general education teachers who feel unprepared to teach students with disabilities, so the coordinator may need to advocate for inclusive practices such as team teaching. Additionally, students with disabilities may experience difficulties in accessing career/technical and advanced academic education programs that require them to complete prerequisite coursework.

Transition coordinators must therefore become familiar with these prerequisites (Greene, 2001; Wehmeyer, 2002). This would include planning for student participation in tests required for graduation and promotion. Additionally, transition coordinators should assure that students with postsecondary education goals complete the course work required for entry into the postsecondary education programs of their choice and take college entrance examinations.

> **Critical Point**
> Transition coordinators need to work with general educators to determine how transition services can support and be supported by course work.

Identifying Postsecondary Opportunities and Competency Requirements

A primary role of the transition coordinator is providing linkages to services and supports needed for the development of employment and other adult living objectives for youth with disabilities and their families. Prior to the IEP/transition meeting, the coordinator needs to develop linkages with postsecondary educators and adult service providers who can aid in the development of the transition plan; and with natural supporters, employers, secondary educators, and service providers who can assist in its implementation. The transition coordinator should assist students and their families in identifying and inviting potential postsecondary meeting participants. This requires out-of-school activities such as touring area businesses and educational programs, meeting with employer groups, having students conduct informational interviews with employers and schools, and meeting with career and technical educators. The coordinator can also invite employers to consult as part of individual IEP teams or as part of a school-wide interagency transition team.

It is important to establish the right contact person for each postschool program. It may be much more effective to use a representative of student disability services or learning centers from a two- or four-year college than an admissions officer who is unfamiliar with disability issues. For employers, it may be more effective to establish contact with employee assistance personnel than with personnel managers who are more inclined to screen than to welcome applicants with disabilities. The general rule for selecting contacts is that they should: (a) be able to represent the **postsecondary program,** (b) be as knowledgeable of disability issues as possible, and (c) be supportive of persons with disabilities.

It is critical that the transition coordinator establish linkages with two- and four-year colleges, career and **technical schools,** employers, continuing education programs, residential programs, transportation, parks and recreation, YMCAs, independent living centers, neighborhood organizations, cultural centers, and a myriad of other community programs. Key contacts from each of these programs should be on file and easily accessible, and the coordinator should establish new contacts as needed by individual students. Each contact should be cultivated and rewarded for participating in meetings or providing consults. Rewards can include thank you letters, invitations to school events, recognition dinners, or providing useful information of interest to the contact. It is important to understand that many of these contacts provide consultation on their own time, so their input should be used efficiently and effectively. The coordinator can use career fairs, group together IEP/transition meetings that postschool providers are to attend, and use conference calls to maximize participation of postsecondary contacts while minimizing time demands.

> **Critical Point**
> Transition coordinators need to foster relationships with key adult service and community contacts.

Developing Community Work Sites and Work Experience Programs

Wehman (1990) stated that an employer advisory board was a critical element of a successful transition program. Halloran (1992) asserted that education-industry collaboration was an important strategy for ensuring that students with disabilities had access to employment training opportunities. Rhodes, Sandow, Mank, Buckley, and Albin (1991) noted that involving employers would be the major source of training in a future in which special education and adult service budgets were expected to show little or no growth, and they noted that employer resources already dwarfed those available through special education and rehabilitation. Phelps and Maddy-Bernstein (1992) found that the benefits of business-education partnerships included additional resources, employment opportunities, increased personal attention, improved facilities, and better teacher morale. Other researchers pointed to the importance of employer support for students with mild disabilities who were not eligible for adult services (Scuccimarra & Speece, 1990).

In addition to advisory boards, several researchers have developed mechanisms for forging individual partnerships with employers. Rhodes et al. (1991) noted that employee assistance programs were a potential support mechanism for the worker with a disability, and suggested that legislation such as the Americans with Disabilities Act would enhance transition as employers expanded existing employee support programs to meet the needs of persons with disabilities. Hagner, Rogan, and Murphy (1992) identified strategies for facilitating natural supports in the workplace by using a consultant approach with employers. They found that it was important to get employers to take ownership of services for employees with disabilities, rather than having service providers offer to do it all.

The development of community work sites and work experience programs for youth with disabilities requires the ability to use both the individual's and the school's network of contacts. Some common practices might include hosting an agency or business advisory committee, becoming a member of a business-oriented community group, maintaining a "job bank" with other agencies, or hosting a career fair (Baer, Martonyi, Simmons, Flexer, & Goebel, 1994). It is also important to survey staff, board members, former and current employers, and consumer supporters to develop job leads. The most efficient way to develop job leads is through personal referrals from a person known to the prospective employer.

In developing community work experiences, the transition coordinator needs to be aware of child labor laws and the Fair Labor Standards Act. Some key provisions of these laws include:

> **Critical Point**
> Transition coordinators should be aware of the employer system and laws governing community work experiences.

1. The purpose of the community work experience must be clearly defined in the student's IEPs.
2. They must be voluntary with no expectation of remuneration.
3. They must not result in immediate advantage to business or displace workers.
4. Students should not work before age 15.
5. Students should be supervised by the school.
6. Experiences for the purpose of career exploration should not exceed five hours per job.

7. Experiences for the purpose of assessment should not exceed 90 hours per job.
8. Experiences for the purpose of training should not exceed 120 hours per job.
9. Students should not be considered a trainee for a job with expectation of employment at the end of training.
10. Students under age 18 should not operate dangerous power equipment (Petric, 2002).

Promoting Student Self-Determination

Transition coordinators need to encourage and provide opportunities for self-determination and decision making in the transition process. Many students with disabilities and their families will have had previous experiences with IEP planning that led them to define their role as passive, uninvolved, or dependent. To promote self-determination, the transition coordinator should assess factors affecting the student's ability to make informed choices. Informed choice assumes that the youth with a disability is: (a) free from coercion, (b) has the necessary information and experience, and (c) is able to make choices that have a reasonable expectation of positive outcome (Dinerstein, Herr, & O'Sullivan, 1999).

Assuring that students are free from coercion in setting goals and choosing services is an important role of

Support needs may vary over time.

the transition coordinator. Coercion, unlike persuasion, is based on force rather than information and may be both covert and overt. Overt coercion may come from professionals or family members (Dinerstein et al., 1999). It may come from professionals in the form of threats to discontinue support services, if youth with disabilities choose to participate in settings that make provision of these services inconvenient to providers. It may also come from family members who pressure the student into accepting services that are more convenient for the family (e.g., the convenience of regular day activity programs versus supported employment).

A more difficult concern for the transition coordinator is covert coercion. Covert coercion may include questions such as, "You want to work in a restaurant, yes?" Apart from leading questions such as this, research indicates that even yes and no questions can be coercive since many individuals with disabilities have learned to answer yes to questions posed by persons in authority (Wehmeyer & Kelchner, 1995b). Transition coordinators need to avoid yes and no questions in interviews, whenever possible. Open-ended questions are preferable, with comprehensive lists of well-defined choices provided as support. Covert coercion can also be avoided by developing a script or PowerPoint presentation with the student prior to the meeting. This assures that the student's goals and service preferences are clearly stated and less subject to distortion.

A second consideration in assuring informed consent is that students need the necessary information and experience to make informed choices about their education program and the IEP planning process. Martin, Huber-Marshall, Maxson, and Jerman (1996); Wehmeyer and Kelchner (1995), Van Reusen and Bos (1990); Powers et al. (1996); Halpern et al. (1997), and others have developed self-determination curricula that may be useful in this regard. Transition coordinators should be aware of these self-determination curricula and encourage their use with students. Additionally, students should be aware of service, curriculum, and support options available in their school system.

Determining the reasonableness of the outcome of student decisions regarding the education program is perhaps the most difficult aspect of assuring informed consent. A student who makes choices that do not have a reasonable chance of outcome may be considered unable to provide informed consent (Dinerstein, et al., 1999). However, a student who is not allowed to make some "unreasonable" decisions and experience consequences may never develop the maturity to give

informed consent. The transition coordinator, therefore, must support the right of students and families to make low feasibility choices early in transition planning, while at the same time assuring that these choices do not result in substantial harm. For example, a failing student who chooses a college preparatory career path could meet with teachers of college preparatory high school courses, college admissions officers, and college disability services to discuss the reasonableness of his or her choice. If the student chooses to proceed with a well-informed but possibly unwise decision, the transition coordinator should support this decision while minimizing the harm of failure. For, example the transition coordinator could enroll the student in advanced academics but provide frequent follow-up to assure that progress is being made. If the student succeeds, expectations should be reshaped accordingly, but if the student fails after all supports have been tried, the IEP team should be reconvened promptly to discuss alternative strategies. In some cases, students may succeed against all odds. In other cases, students or families may need to revise transition goals or services.

> **Critical Point**
> The transition coordinator needs to assess student decisions relative to voluntariness, knowledge, and reasonableness of outcome and to provide self-determination training and opportunities to make choices.

Promoting student self-determination becomes a critical issue as the student approaches the age of majority under state law. The IDEA of 2004 requires transfer of IDEA rights and control of the IEP team at that age unless the student has been determined incompetent or unable to give informed consent about the education program (IEP). If the student has become increasingly self-determined and has had opportunities to demonstrate informed consent in the early years of transition planning, she or he is much more likely to be ready to be given IDEA rights at the age of majority. On the other hand, if this issue is not addressed, it is likely that the student will never have the opportunity to assume this role.

In keeping with the concept of self-determination, the transition coordinator should provide opportunities for students to practice advocacy skills in supported situations. Students should know about their disability, the accommodations they need, and how to communicate these needs with educators, employers, and community members. They should request accommodations and services on their own with the support of the transition coordinator. Self-advocacy is a critical skill that may make the difference between a student succeeding or failing in postsecondary education, employment, or social interactions. These self-advocacy skills can be developed through a number of approaches including self-determination training, mentoring from successful individuals with disabilities, or development of advocacy groups.

The advocacy role of the transition coordinator should not be confused with the advocacy role of the student and the family. *Webster's* dictionary defines advocacy as "speaking for or on behalf of a person." Advocacy in this sense can be empowering and disempowering. If the coordinator speaks on behalf of students and families who could speak for themselves, it is disempowering. On the other hand, the transition coordinator may be able to assist individuals and families in communicating with service providers whose culture and technical jargon may be foreign to them. In this sense, advocacy by the transition coordinator may be seen as empowering.

Family Involvement

Families can provide critical insight into student interests, abilities, history, and preferences and may act as surrogate decision makers for students who are unable to give informed consent (Dinerstein et al., 1999). They also play a critical role in improving student performance and attendance in school and in supporting the individual's transition after leaving school. Family involvement in transition planning and programs also can help the parents form realistic expectations for the students as they observe them performing competently in classroom and community environments with supports.

Carney and Orelove (1988) noted that parental influence toward community integration depended on parent beliefs about their children's needs and capabilities, and their beliefs about the availability and appropriateness of community services. They developed a grid that showed how parental perceptions were formed. This grid appears in Table 15–2.

Carney and Orelove (1988) suggested that parent involvement promoted student independence only when their beliefs and knowledge fell in cell 1. They found that parental ability to make informed decisions related to six factors: (a) knowledge of the range of options, (b) ability to evaluate options, (c) knowledge of child's skill, (d) knowledge of child's preferences, (e) knowledge of how to get services, and (f) knowledge of how to advocate for services not available (Carney & Orelove, 1988).

The transition coordinator should be aware of the difficulties that families have in participating in the transition process. They may find transition planning ambiguous and confusing; be reluctant to discuss their child's disabilities in front of a group; and may lack clear, relevant, and timely information about transition services. The transition coordinator needs to address these issues by making families more knowledgeable, connected, and supported. The coordinator can support them in this regard through development of joint family-professional transition training, resource fairs, a single point of contact for all services, support groups, information materials, and networking activities (Kohler, 1998).

The transition coordinator also needs to be aware of how cultural issues affect transition planning. These issues can result in discord and conflict when the culture of a service delivery system differs greatly from the culture of the student and the family (Hanley-Maxwell, Pogoloff, & Whitney-Thomas, 1998). Some cultures depend more heavily on support from extended families, neighborhoods, and churches, while others may reject the idea of social services altogether. For example, a transition services coordinator in

> **Critical Point**
> The transition coordinator should develop a variety of options for families to participate in transition planning and the development of transition programs.

TABLE 15–2 Family perceptions affecting transition planning

	Know Available Services	Don't Know Available Services
Believe in child's capability	1. Parents know community options and believe they are appropriate.	2. Parents don't know community options but believe they are appropriate.
Don't believe in child's capability	3. Parents know community options but do not believe they are appropriate.	4. Parents don't know community options and don't believe they are appropriate.

rural Ohio or Pennsylvania should know that many Amish communities will not accept social services, but may use them if they are termed "educational services." Service coordinators in urban settings must be sensitive to extreme dissonance between social service agencies and minority cultures, while at the same time recognizing the great potential of neighborhood and religious affiliations (Hornstein, 1997). Service coordinators need to understand the youth's culture, explore alternative service and support approaches, discuss individual needs and preferences, and provide choices regarding service providers and supporters.

Collaboration

The transition coordinator should promote collaboration in a way that minimizes the barriers among the student, family, and professionals; and that also improves collaboration among the professionals themselves (Baer, Goebel, & Flexer, 1993). In this regard, the transition coordinator must foster transition team processes that move team members from a multidisciplinary approach (where professional roles are rigid and specialized) to an interdisciplinary or transdisciplinary approach where professional, student, and family roles are less circumscribed. *Multidisciplinary* models of service delivery are more prevalent in medical programs where professionals typically work in a professional/patient relationship. *Interdisciplinary* approaches are more prevalent in nonmedical disability programs where professionals typically work in a professional/consumer relationship. *Transdisciplinary* approaches are more prevalent in independent living models of service provision where services are deprofessionalized and shared among the individual's community supporters.

Independent living models and personal strengths models of service coordination imply the need for a *transdisciplinary* approach to service provision. In this approach, professionals work as consultants to individuals with disabilities who determine how services are to be provided and by whom. Because independent living models of service provision emphasize deprofessionalization, *role release* is an important characteristic of the transdisciplinary model. This allows the individual with the disability to choose how

> **Critical Point**
> The transition coordinator should develop a team process that equalizes relationships between families and professionals and that minimizes barriers between the disciplines.

services are provided. In this approach, students, family members, or community supporters may be substituted for professionals in implementing many aspects of physical therapy, behavior programming, and training.

In directing collaboration, the transition coordinator should be familiar with laws pertaining to youth with disabilities. These include the IDEA, Section 504 of the Rehabilitation Act, the Americans with Disabilities Act (ADA), and other civil rights legislation. Transition legislation and regulations can be difficult to read and interpret, so the coordinator should attend in-service programs and obtain publications by the National Association of State Directors of Special Education (NASDE) and other publications of professional and parent organizations.

The transition coordinator is likely to encounter conflict in efforts to promote collaboration. A common myth about any collaborative process is that collaborators will agree, have shared values, and develop consensus without conflict (Koch & Rumrill, 1998b). The transition coordinator needs to cultivate mutual respect and celebrate the successes of team efforts to assure that conflict and disagreement can occur without destroying working relationships. Koch and Rumrill (1998b) define a four-step process for resolving conflicts: (a) accurately defining the conflict, (b) clarifying misconceptions, (c) generating options, and (d) implementing and evaluating resolutions. It is important for the transition coordinator to anticipate conflicts and have plans to resolve them before meetings to avoid breakdown in relationships and disruption of decision making and team process.

Generally, transition coordinators should deal with conflicts discreetly, preferably outside student or agency meetings. If a conflict threatens to disrupt an IEP/transition team meeting, the coordinator should recess or adjourn the meeting until the conflict is resolved. The coordinator should set up a meeting between the conflicting members, preferably in a relaxed neutral setting, and follow the four-step process for conflict resolution. In conflict resolution, the coordinator should assume the role of mediator and periodically reassure participants that conflict is normal in a good working alliance (Koch & Rumrill, 1998b). If the coordinator is directly involved in the conflict, he or she may bring in an outside person as an arbitrator.

> **Critical Point**
> Transition coordinators should be familiar with conflict management techniques and resolve conflicts outside of meetings whenever possible.

Developing Communication Strategies and Methods to Release and Share Information

In the 1980s the Office of Special Education and Rehabilitation Services (OSERS) began to focus on interagency agreements as a way of bringing the transition disciplines together. Heal, Copher, and Rusch (1990) studied the characteristics and perceived value of these agreements in 29 demonstration projects. They found that while several agencies were involved (average 3.93 per agreement) less than half (11) involved vocational education. Heal et al. (1990) also found that interagency agreements did little to address the problem of fragmented transition services. Generally, the respective agencies invested minimal time and resources in interagency collaboration and collaborative efforts tended to focus on information and referral, rather than developing a truly coordinated set of activities (Heal et al., 1990).

To address this need, authors of best practice have recommended the development of school-interagency transition teams to develop channels of communication and to iron out policy differences (Everson, 1990; Halloran, 1992; Halpern, 1992b; Heal, Copher et al., 1990; Phelps & Maddy-Bernstein, 1992; Wehman, 1990; Wehman, Moon, Everson, Wood, & Barcus, 1988). These teams may focus on a number of issues. Heal et al. (1990) suggested that transition teams focus on service overlaps and gaps, while Wehman et al. (1988) recommended that they be formed to address the need to: (a) share referrals, (b) do local needs assessment, and (c) share funding. Everson (1990) suggested that transition teams address local obstacles (such as funding and lack of parent participation) through collaborative efforts designed to empower parents and students.

Communication among the many programs serving youth with disabilities can be challenging for transition coordinators who spend much of the time out of the office. Ohio's systems change project for transition explored this issue by funding a number of pilot sites to address shared intake, referral, and transition planning. Approaches varied among the sites and included:

- Sharing the transition plan with all agencies serving a given youth, with the agencies then using it as the base of all plans concerning the youth.
- The development of a password-protected computer site where general information on students could be stored and released to agencies.
- The development of common intake and referral sheet used for all agency services (Baer, 1996).

Release of information restrictions can be a major impediment to communication. The transition coordinator may need to look into how information can be shared among transition providers without violating the privacy of youth with disabilities and their families. Collaborating agencies may fall under the jurisdiction of privacy laws pertaining to medical information (HIPPA) or educational information (FERPA). A blanket release of information that allows the sharing of information among all transition agencies for a limited time can facilitate information sharing. This can help students and families who often have to answer the same questions repeatedly to different transition services providers. Some considerations in the development of a blanket release of information form include the option for students and families to control:

1. What information is to be released: identifying information, case information, financial information, sensitive medical information (e.g., HIV and AIDS).
2. How long the release of information is in effect (e.g., 180 days, 360 days, etc.).
3. What agencies can receive student information (all agencies, specific agencies).
4. How information is protected by all agencies covered by the blanket release.
5. How the student or family can revoke the release of information at any time.
6. Assurances that refusal to sign the blanket release will not affect services (Baer, 1996).

In addition to the blanket release of information form, each participating agency will need to sign a member agreement for information sharing. This member agreement needs to specify: (a) how information will be used, (b) information will not be used in criminal manners, except as required by judicial order, and (c) members will maintain information in a secure manner. Both the blanket release of information and the member agreement should be shared with legal experts at each of the agencies to assure that they comply with the law and agency regulations.

(See Appendix B for a sample blanket release of information and member agreement.)

Monitoring Fulfillment of Transition Team Member Responsibilities

The transition coordinator needs to develop mechanisms for monitoring services in IEP/transition plans. This is an area of particular concern since research has indicated that less than 25% of IEP/transition teams were reconvened when adult services could not be provided as planned (Baer et al., 1996). The transition coordinator monitors service provisions by establishing benchmarks and contacting service and support providers periodically to assure that they are on schedule. It is important that the transition coordinator make contacts with key service providers well in advance of transition services deadlines to allow time to correct problems or to revise time lines before deadlines are missed. Additionally, periodic contact with members of a student's IEP/transition team allows the coordinator to gather information and to cement relationships. This investment in relationships with team members is a valuable resource when things go wrong or mistakes are made. If services cannot be provided as planned, the coordinator should reconvene the student's transition team. Reconvening the team offers the student and the family the opportunity to discuss alternative ways of addressing transition objectives.

> **Critical Point**
> The transition coordinator needs to assure that transition planning drives provision of student services and to reconvene the student's transition team if services cannot be provided as planned.

Development of Program Attributes and Structures

Often the transition system at a given school lacks the program structures to promote student-focused planning, student development, family involvement, or interagency collaboration (Kohler, 1998). Relative to the transition planning, this may be manifested in limited time for youth and family input in the development of the IEP/transition plan, use of technical language, inviting only preferred service providers to transition meetings, inconvenient meeting times and places, and excessive bureaucracy. There also may be lack of critical transition programs, such as life skills instruction, career and career/technical and vocational education support services, and structured work experiences (Kohler, 1998).

To deal with these program issues, the transition coordinator must be able to mobilize transition stakeholders in adopting exemplary transition practices (Everson & Guillory, 1998). The transition coordinator may address these issues by forming a school-wide interagency transition team. The membership of the school-level interagency transition team should include all transition stakeholders, including families, adult service providers, administrators, educators, employers, and transition specialists. The makeup of the team may vary from meeting to meeting, depending on the students or issues to be discussed, but it should generally address issues such as:

- Community supports
- Better access to vocational services
- Curriculum enhancement and life skills instruction
- Cross-training for students, parents, and professionals
- Development of work experiences
- Strategies to empower youth with disabilities and their families
- Strategies to empower minority youth with disabilities and their families

A number of surveys have been developed to self-assess transition policy compliance and the best practice (Baer, McMahan, & Flexer, 1999; Johnson, Sharpe, & Sinclair, 1997; McMahan & Baer, 2001; Morgan, Moore, McSweyn, & Salzberg, 1992).

The school-level interagency transition team also can be an effective mechanism for maintaining current information on transition services by bringing school and adult service providers together to discuss the ever-changing system of services available to transition-age youth. Key representatives from major

> **Critical Point**
> The transition coordinator should support or develop a school-wide interagency transition team to address systems issues, planning, and program development.

programs such as rehabilitation services, developmental disabilities programs, WIA (Work Incentive Act), Social Security, mental health, and the Department of Job and Family Services (formerly the Department of Human Services) may be able to provide information pertaining to many other programs in the community.

Generally, the transition coordinator needs to be familiar with group process skills to manage effectively the school-level transition team. Tuckman and Jensen (1977) suggest that groups go through five rather predictable stages of development: forming, storming, norming, performing, and adjourning. In the forming phase, the coordinator needs to recruit representatives of critical transition stakeholder groups and to convince them of the importance of addressing transition issues for youth with disabilities. In the storming phase, the coordinator needs to lead the group in a noncritical generation of ideas about desired transition outcomes and the best practices to achieve those outcomes. In the norming phase, the transition coordinator needs to develop an action plan that outlines who is to do what by when. In the performing stage, the transition coordinator as the leader needs to monitor performance, reward success, and problem-solve failures. At the adjourning phase, the team members are given an option of leaving the team or renewing commitment. Often this is determined by the terms of membership.

Developing Methods to Identify Future Service Needs of Families and Students

The transition coordinator needs to develop a method of determining how many students and families need specific types of transition services prior to and after leaving high school. This information can be shared with programs and agencies that provide these services so that they can plan accordingly. The coordinator can use a number of approaches to identify these needs. These approaches include (a) a review of IEP/transition plans; (b) a survey of students, families, and professionals; or (c) focus groups.

Once the coordinator has obtained the information, it should be shared with all concerned providers and agencies. The school-based interagency transition team can assist the coordinator in this regard by providing a forum where the information can be discussed. The interagency transition team should address questions about whether: (a) services are being utilized effectively, (b) current service capacity meets the future needs of students, and (c) services are of high quality.

Coordinating Student Follow-Up and Follow-Along Studies

Follow-up and longitudinal (or follow-along) studies of students who have exited school provide information on the problems that students encounter after graduation and on the effectiveness of the transition services they received before graduation (Baer et al., 2003). Follow-along studies follow a cohort of students over time; whole follow-up studies collect information on outcomes at a single point in time (Halpern, 1990). These studies may be conducted for all students or for a random sample of students. Typically, follow-up and follow-along studies look at student outcomes one, three, and five years after leaving school. Questions commonly addressed by these studies include:

1. The person's age and date of leaving school (typically from school records)
2. The type of disability (typically from school records)
3. Ethnicity (typically from school records)
4. Employment information (e.g., duration, type, wages, benefits, hours, etc.)
5. Support information (e.g., adult services, financial supports, natural supports, etc.)
6. Community activities (e.g., civic, volunteer, recreation, etc.)
7. Transportation (e.g., car, bus, walking, family, etc.)
8. Living arrangements (e.g., family, independent, supported living, etc.)
9. Postsecondary education enrolled (two-year, four-year, other); postsecondary education completed
10. Transition and school programs that were especially helpful
11. Transition and school programs that were unavailable or unhelpful

Transition Services Coordination

As a transition specialist at an urban school, Ellen and her mother came to me this June to discuss her educational program as she entered high school. Ellen's eighth-grade teacher, Ms. Middleton, had informed them that, since Ellen was 14 years old, her IEP meeting would include a discussion of what she would be doing after graduation and how she would get there. The teacher also told them that we would be talking about other agencies and programs that might help Ellen to reach her goals. Ms. Middleton noted that they were very confused about what "transition" was and what this had to do with Ellen.

Ms. Middleton and I met Ellen and her mother outside the school and had coffee, soft drinks, and donuts while we discussed Ellen's transition to high school and what she would like to do after graduation. Ellen responded "yes" when her mother said "You want to go to school to be a nurse's aide, don't you?" but it was clear that Ellen had no concept of what a nurse's aide did. Ellen clearly was looking for emotional support and guidance, so I surveyed both Ellen and her mother regarding what they saw Ellen doing both before and after graduation. Through this survey, it was clear that Ellen would need a lot more information and that her mother would need to give her more freedom in regard to her choices. We discussed the importance of self-determination and how it could be developed through functional and vocational evaluations, community experiences, informational interviews, and job shadowing. Ellen seemed to be interested, but her mother was concerned that she would miss out on class work. After some discussion, we suggested that Ellen and her mother meet with the guidance counselor and the work-study coordinator to explore this issue further.

> **Critical Point**
> Keep student-focused planning by scheduling meetings at alternative sites and by assuring the student is giving informed consent.

After meeting with the guidance counselor and the work-study coordinator, Ellen and her mother agreed to do the functional-vocational assessment, which identified an interest in library work and a number of areas in which Ellen would need services and supports to pursue this course of study. Ellen had poor spelling skills and no typing skills. It also was clear that while Ellen expressed an interest in library work, she based this decision on the fact that she had no other work experiences. However, it was clear that Ellen liked that type of work environment and enjoyed books. The guidance counselor provided Ellen with a tentative list of classes that would be rigorous enough for entry into two-year college, but that would leave room for community work experiences and job shadowing.

The guidance counselor, the vocational evaluator, and the work-study coordinator were invited to the meeting and Ellen and her mother asked that I describe their plan in the first transition meeting. In the meeting, we focused on transition services and supports that would support Ellen's course of study leading to a two-year college. The guidance counselor agreed to enroll Ellen in business-related English, typing, and math classes. The vocational evaluator suggested a hand speller to help Ellen with her spelling problems. The work-study coordinator agreed to arrange some job-shadowing experiences around office work and related occupations. We discussed time lines and responsibilities for each service and I said that I would be calling monthly to check on Ellen's progress.

> **Critical Point**
> Promote student development by integrating academics and transition activities.

During the ensuing year, everyone involved with Ellen was encouraged to help her identify interests and needs, not only in regard to employment, but also in her home and the community. After a series of job-shadowing experiences and a very positive experience with her typing teacher, Ellen decided that she really wanted to do office work. However, Ellen was having extreme difficulty in English and math courses and it was feared that she would not be able to do the academic work to get into a two-year business school. Ellen and her mother were becoming excited about her new goals, however, and agreed to present their vision at the second IEP/transition meeting. We went over postsecondary goals and needed transition services point by point and rehearsed how their plan would be presented at the meeting. After the discussion, it was decided that Ellen and her mother would like to see her get a chance to try out a community work experience when she turned 16.

(*Continued*)

Critical Point
Promote collaboration and resolve conflict outside the IEP/ transition meeting whenever possible.

It now became clear that Ellen would need a transition plan that addressed instruction, community experiences, and development of her employment objectives in the following year. She also would need linkages with adult service providers to provide the supports she needed to pursue a two-year college degree. Also, the issue of Ellen's low English and math scores would need to be addressed in light of her postsecondary goals. Therefore, I contacted and discussed Ellen's upcoming IEP/transition meeting with the rehabilitation services counselor, the work-study coordinator, local business schools, and Ellen's math and English teachers.

All involved transition stakeholders were invited to Ellen's IEP/transition meeting. Due to a conflict, the counselor from the rehabilitation services could not make the meeting, but she provided written input and committed the agency to developing an Individual Plan for Employment (IPE) so that Ellen could receive support toward a two-year college. Other members attending the meeting included the special education supervisor, the typing teacher, the work-study coordinator, the guidance counselor, Ellen, her mother, a reading resource teacher from a local business college, and the English teacher. At the start of the meeting, an agenda was distributed, as well as a copy of the PowerPoint that Ellen and her mother were going to present to the team. I explained to the team that each member should work toward Ellen's goals and share information and outcomes.

In her transition meeting, Ellen and her mother enthusiastically presented a vision of Ellen working in an office setting and living in an apartment after attending a two-year school. It was noted that Ellen had done very well in typing classes with the help of her speller and enjoyed her job-shadowing experiences in office settings. The reading resource teacher said that they could provide note takers and tutors to assist her in doing the academic work. The work-study coordinator volunteered to provide work experience.

The transition plan reiterated the need for Ellen to have classroom accommodations in regard to spelling and note-taking. Needed transition services were also identified in regard to instruction (applied math and English), community experiences (work study), development of postschool objectives (meeting with the business college), and linkages to adult services (referral to VR). One concern was raised that it was school policy that Ellen would have to pass the state and regional proficiency tests without the use of her spell checker in order to graduate. This issue could not be addressed by Ellen's transition team and was referred to the school-level interagency transition team.

Critical Point
Promote development of transition programs and structures through linkages with administration and other transition stakeholders.

The school-level interagency transition team consisted of parents, students, professionals, administrators, and adult service providers. When Ellen's issue regarding proficiency testing was brought to the team, several other parents agreed that lack of accommodations on this test was a major concern of students with disabilities. One administrator stated that it was a requirement of testing policy that could not be changed. Using conflict management approaches, it became clear that school policy was based on a misperception of state policy on proficiency testing and that the school was not complying with the accommodation requirements outlined in the IDEA and Section 504 of the Rehabilitation Act of 1973. The administrators and parents worked together to generate options regarding accommodations for testing that would match accommodations being provided to Ellen in classes and meet requirements for testing validity. The team also recommended the development of a career portfolio assessment as part of Ellen's final Summary of Performance. This portfolio assessment eventually helped Ellen get a job related to her business school training.

The following year, Ellen was assigned a new transition coordinator. Ellen, her mother, the new coordinator, and I met over coffee, soft drinks, and donuts to discuss where to go from here. Ellen expressed concerns about

Critical Point
Develop ways of following up with students after graduation.

the required credits to graduate. Her expectations for her new transition coordinator would be that he would collaborate with her to address her credit requirements through work study. I bid farewell to Ellen and her mother and offered to keep in touch. I gave Ellen a self-addressed envelope and my phone number for her to contact me and let me know how she was doing. I was confident that Ellen was on the road to a meaningful future, regardless of the barriers that she would encounter along the way.

CONCLUSION

This chapter viewed the role of the transition coordinator from both an individual and systems perspective. It provided a discussion of the four models of service coordination—brokerage, personal strengths, rehabilitation, and full support. The full support model of service coordination was defined as an ecological model of planning that involved an array of professional and natural supports from the student's current and future environments. The personal strengths model was described as aligning well with independent living models of service delivery by minimizing dependence on professionals. The rehabilitation services and broker models of service coordination were described as falling between these two extremes. This chapter also emphasized how the transition coordinator needs to consider individual and family preferences, cultural concerns, and support options in determining which of the service coordination models to emphasize.

This chapter organized the coordination of transition services according to Kohler's taxonomy of transition services: (a) student-focused planning, (b) student development, (c) family involvement, (d) collaboration, and (e) the development of transition programs and structures. These five major categories of transition services were further broken down into eleven specific duties and activities of transition coordination that have been identified by persons in this field. It was noted that these services may be provided by one or more persons at a school under a variety of job titles.

STUDY QUESTIONS

1. Discuss four models of service provision that are considered state of the art for individuals with disabilities.
2. Discuss how student needs, preferences, and cultural background impact upon how services should be provided.
3. List and define the five major categories of transition services under Kohler's (1998) model.
4. Describe why student self-determination is an important objective of transition services coordination.
5. Describe two strategies for developing ongoing linkages and sharing information with adult service providers.
6. Describe how to prepare a student and the family for the IEP/transition meeting.
7. Describe how you would set up a school-wide interagency transition team. Whom would you invite? What would you discuss? How would you involve families and students?

WEBSITES

Transition Research Institute:
   http://www.ed.uiuc.edu/sped/tri/institute.html
Center for Innovation in Transition and Employment:
   http://cite.educ.kent.edu/archives.html
National Center for Learning Disabilities Inc.:
   http://www.ncld.org/
National Center for Research in Vocational Education:
   http://www.ncld.org/
Independent Living Movement:
   http://www.acils.com/acil/ilhistory.html
Ecological Curriculum:
   http://www.ttac.odu.edu/articles/ecolog.html
The Office of Vocational and Adult Education:
   http://www.ed.gov/about/offices/list/ovae/index.html?src=mr
The National Center for Children and Youth with Disabilities (NICHCY):
   http://www.nichcy.org/
The National Longitudinal Transition Study:
   http://www.sri.com/policy/cehs/nlts/nltssum.html
National Institute on Disability and Rehabilitation Research (NIDRR):
   http://www.ncddr.org/
Administration on Developmental Disabilities:
   http://www.acf.dhhs.gov/programs/add/
IDEA Practices:
   http://www.ideapractices.org/
Office of Special Education Programs (OSEP):
   http://www.ed.gov/about/offices/list/osers/osep/index.html?src=mr
Model Transition Projects—The Transition Institute:
   http://www.ed.uiuc.edu/sped/tri/projwebsites.html
Federal Resource Center for Special Education:
   http://dssc.org/frc/
DCDT Transition Specialist Competencies:
   http://www.dcdt.org/pdf/trans_educators.pdf

Accommodation Refers to any alteration of existing facilities or procedures to make them readily accessible to persons with disabilities.

Adult Services Refers to the many agencies and programs that are provided to adults with specific needs such as disability, health, and income.

Advocacy Speaking on behalf of another person or group of persons.

Age of Majority The age that the state has determined persons able to make decisions on their own (usually age 18) unless determined incompetent to do so by a court of law.

Agency Fairs A panel and/or exhibits designed to acquaint participants with the services, eligibility requirements, and referral procedures of adult service agencies.

Apprenticeships Periods of part-time work experience that may extend to a year or more, usually associated with a specific occupation.

Aptitudes The particular strengths, knowledge, or skills that a person has, generally related to an occupation or career.

Audiologist A person who is qualified to assess a person's hearing and provide interventions to improve it.

Backward Planning A step-wise planning process that starts with desired goals and plans backward to the current level of functioning and support.

Bureau of Employment Services A program that helps individuals find jobs through job listings, computer services, and counseling.

Career and Technical Education The educational system that used to be known as vocational education, which includes high school vocational programs, 2+2 programs, and some postsecondary career education programs.

Career Development Index See Career Maturity Index.

Career Fairs Panels and/or exhibits designed to provide information on a range of careers.

Career Maturity Index This assessment, along with the Career Development Inventory (1990), can direct counseling (or the use of a computerized DISCOVER program) to address competencies in the areas of student, leisurite, citizen, worker, and homemaker.

Career Planning Refers to the general planning process related to helping the individual develop and achieve meaningful adult roles. Transition planning is a specific form of career planning.

Career Portfolio Assessment A standardized method of assessing the student's career portfolio activities by measuring mastery (e.g., novice, apprentice, expert) or level of independence.

Career Portfolios Organized samples (often a notebook) of student work and classroom activities that include writing samples, photographs, videos, and other demonstrations of student performance.

Case manager A person from an agency who is responsible for seeing that services are obtained and coordinated for an individual. A transition coordinator is a form of case manager.

ChoiceMaker A self-determination approach that focuses on: (a) choosing goals, (b) expressing goals, and (c) taking action.

COACH A form of person-centered planning that stands for Choosing Options and Accommodations for Children. Includes the family's values and dreams in IEP planning.

Community College A postsecondary education program (generally two-year) that leads to an occupation or entrance into a university.

Course of Study Refers to the type of educational program that a student is enrolled in, including vocational education, college preparation, and apprenticeships.

DD See Developmental Disability.

Developmental Disability A disability that is acquired during the period the person is developing, generally before age 21 or at birth, and that significantly impacts several life activity areas such as self-care, self-direction, learning, mobility, speech, and independent living.

Ecological Approaches A model that focuses on individuals and stresses working with all of the environments that affect their lives.

Education of All Handicapped Children Act Landmark 1975 legislation that required education for all students with disabilities and introduced the terms IEP, Least Restrictive Environment, Free Appropriate Public Education, and the Multifactored Evaluation to Education.

Eligibility A set of rules that determine whether students or families are qualified to receive services based on the nature and severity of the disability, income, or other characteristics.

Employability Life Skills Assessment This criterion-referenced checklist may be used yearly to assess a student's level of performance in 24 critical employability skills areas in the domains of personal, social, and daily living habits.

Employment Specialist In supported employment, a person who provides job placement, training, and sometimes follow-along services to a worker with a disability. Sometimes used interchangeably with job coach.

Empowerment Education and practices aimed at transferring power to or strengthening individuals and groups.

Enclave A form of supported employment where a group of no more than eight persons with disabilities work in an integrated employment setting, often with professional supervision.

Entitlement Programs that must be provided to all eligible persons upon demand. Special education and Social Security are entitlements, many adult services are not.

FAPE See Free Appropriate Public Education.

Follow-Along Services In supported employment this term refers to services and supports provided to a worker with a disability after job training is completed.

Free Appropriate Public Education The requirement, introduced by the EHA of 1975, that requires schools to provide an education relevant to the needs of students with disabilities. The courts have generally stated that appropriateness does not mean optimal, only that the student is progressing at a reasonable rate.

Functional Vocational Evaluation Evaluation that focuses on identifying skills demonstrated by the student in actual vocational and life activities. Situational and work assessments are functional. IQ tests and tests of standardized reading levels are not.

Goals 2000: Educate America Act of 1993 Legislation that established eight educational goals that state and local education agencies were to achieve by the year 2000.

Group Action Planning A self-determination approach that helps students take charge of personal futures planning.

Guardian A person or agency that assumes limited or unlimited authority to make decisions for a minor or an adult who has been determined to be incompetent in a court of law. Includes medical guardianships, guardianship of the person, and guardian of the estate.

Guidance Counselor A person who is qualified to assess an individual's career interests and provide counseling and support in making career decisions.

Housing and Urban Development A federal program that provides or funds subsidized housing for low-income persons.

HUD See Housing and Urban Development.

IDEA See Individuals with Disabilities Education Act.

ILC See Independent Living Center.

Impairment Related Work Expense Certain expenses for things a person with a disability needs because of his/her impairment in order to work may be deducted when determining eligibility for SSDI or SSI.

Inclusion The process of including students with disabilities in the environments, activities, and curriculum of typical students and persons. Inclusion may mean different things to different people. Sometimes used interchangeably with the term "integration."

Independent Living Centers Established by the Rehabilitation Act in response to consumer and People First Movements. ILCs are run predominately by consumers and can fund or support accommodations in vehicles and housing to make persons with disabilities more independent.

Individual with Disabilities Education Act An updated version of the Education of All Handicapped Children's Act (EHA) that required the statement of needed transition services as part of the IEP in 1990.

Individualized Education Program A statement of the programs and services that will be provided to a student with a disability that is eligible under the IDEA.

Individualized Service Plans Plans developed for specific individuals that describe services provided by an agency to help an individual achieve desired goals. These include Individual Habilitation Plans (MR/DD), Individual Work Related Plans (VR), Individual Plans for Employment (VR).

Informational Interviews Interviews with employers to find out about their organization, jobs, and the types of people they employ.

Integration In the disability context, the process of including persons with disabilities in the environments, activities, and social networks of typical persons. Sometimes used interchangeably with the term "inclusion."

Internship See apprenticeships.

IPLAN A form of person-centered planning that stands for Inventory, Plan, Listen, Ask, and Name your goals.

IRWE See Impairment Related Work Expense.

Job Analysis The process of analyzing a job in terms of essential elements, skills needed, and characteristics to aid in job matching and training.

Job Carving A technique used in advanced supported employment programs where a job is divided into components that can be done by a person with a severe disability.

Job Coach See job trainer.

Job Placement The process of helping an individual find a job.

Job Trainer In supported employment, generally a paraprofessional who provides on-site job training and supports to a worker with a disability. Sometimes used interchangeably with employment specialist or job coach.

Job Shadowing The practice of allowing students to observe a real work setting to determine their interest and to acquaint them with the requirements of the job.

Job Sharing The practice of having two or more persons share a job to provide accommodations in work scheduling or job duties.

Language Specialist See speech pathologist.

Least Restrictive Environment A concept introduced to education by the EHA in 1975 that required a continuum of services for students with disabilities so that they could be educated in as integrated an environment as possible while still providing FAPE.

Life-Centered Career Education This career development approach delineates 22 major competencies that can be infused into primary, middle, and secondary curricula to address the major life domains of work, home, and academics.

Lifestyle Planning A form of person-centered planning that describes future goals and defines the steps needed to reach them.

LRE See least restrictive environment.

Mainstreaming A term that was used widely in the 1970s to refer to the practice of placing students with disabilities in the regular education curriculum. This term lost favor when it was found that many students were being placed in regular classes without needed supports.

Making Action Plans (formerly McGill Action Planning System—MAPS) A person-centered planning approach that focuses on seven areas: (a) nonnegotiables, (b) strong preferences, (c) highly desirables, (d) personal characteristics, (e) personal concerns, (f) needed supports, and (g) action steps.

Medicaid A health care program serving eligible low-income persons with disabilities whose income and assets are below specific levels. Generally available to persons receiving SSI or SSI work incentives.

Medicare An insurance program serving persons 65 and older and individuals with disabilities regardless of income if they are eligible for SSDI.

Mental Health Services Services provided to persons with significant behavioral or mood disorders that are not related to mental retardation or developmental disabilities.

Mental Retardation and Development Disability Services Services that are provided to persons with disabilities that were identified at birth or before age 21. In some states referred to as Developmental Disability Services.

Meyers-Briggs This assessment identifies four personality temperaments that can be used to develop self and career awareness (e.g., extroverted, intuitive, feeling, perceptive or ENFP).

MFE See multifactored evaluation.

MH See Mental Health Services

MH/MR In some states mental health and mental retardation and developmental disability services are combined and referred to as MH/MR.

Mobile Work Crew A supported employment placement where a group of no more than eight persons provide contract services to businesses (e.g., janitorial, landscaping) usually under the supervision of a professional.

MR/DD See Mental Retardation and Development Disability Services

Multifactored Evaluation (MFE) Introduced by the EHA of 1975. An evaluation by a variety of professionals to determine whether a student is in need of special education services. Originally, required before entering special education and every three years thereafter. With the IDEA of 1997, the MFE was changed to include assessment by nonprofessionals and parents.

Natural Supports Refers to the use of persons, practices, and things that naturally occur in the environment to meet the support needs of an individual.

Next S.T.E.P. A field-tested student-directed transition approach that consists of 16 lessons that address:

(a) getting started, (b) self-exploration and evaluation, (c) developing goals and activities, and (d) putting a plan into place.

Occupational Therapist A person qualified to develop and implement programs develop fine motor skills and skills and accommodations related to work and daily living.

Occupational Work Adjustment A program that places a person in jobs or environments in order to develop appropriate work and social behaviors.

Occupational Work Experience Refers to programs that allow a person to try one or more jobs for periods of a year or less in order to explore interests and develop job skills.

PASS See Plan for Achieving Self-Support.

People First A movement of persons with disabilities that started in the late 1970s to take greater control of programs affecting them. Originated the concept of person-first language.

Person-Centered Planning Refers to a number of planning approaches that tailor services and supports to meet the needs of the individual, as opposed to programs that try to fit individuals into available services.

Person-First Language The practice of referring to persons with disabilities with the term denoting disability following and not supplanting terms referring to them as an individual (e.g., a person with a visual impairment, a person who uses a wheelchair). Person-first avoids impersonal, negative, and medical terminology (e.g., the disabled, cripples, retardates).

Personal Futures Planning A type of person-centered planning that involves dreaming, describing, and doing with the family and their support system.

Physical Therapist A person qualified to develop and implement programs to develop fine and gross motor skills and rehabilitation services to persons with physical disabilities.

Plan for Achieving Self-Support (PASS) A savings account that can be excluded from income and assets of persons with disabilities to allow them to save up for something that would make them self-sufficient (e.g., college fund).

Postsecondary Education Educational programs that follow high school including colleges, universities, technical and vocational schools, and community colleges.

Postsecondary Programs Programs that occur after high school (secondary education).

Proficiency Tests Tests that are designed to determine if students are measuring up to educational standards set by the state and/or district.

Psychiatrist A medical doctor who can assess an individual's emotional, intellectual, and coping skills and typically provides medical interventions or medications to improve them.

Psychologist A person who is qualified to assess an individual's emotional, intellectual, and coping skills and provide counseling or interventions to improve them.

Referral The process of notifying an agency to request services. A referral is often followed by an eligibility determination.

Rehabilitation Services Commission A name for the agency that oversees the provision of vocational rehabilitation services.

Rehabilitation Technologist A person qualified to apply technology to meet the needs of persons with disabilities.

Related Services Services that are not necessarily educational in nature, but that are provided as part of an educational program. Speech, language, hearing, social work, and psychology services are examples of related services.

SCANS Report See Secretary's Commission on Achieving Necessary Skills Report.

School-to-Work Programs Refers to general education secondary programs developed under the School-to-Work Opportunity Act that include career education, work-based instruction experiences, and efforts to connect students with vocational and postschool programs.

Secretary's Commission on Achieving Necessary Skills Report Competencies identified by employers that will be needed by workers of the future.

Section 8 Housing Refers to housing subsidized by Housing and Urban Development (HUD).

Self-Advocacy The ability and opportunity to speak on behalf of one's self.

Self-Determination Refers to the ability and the opportunity for students to make decisions for themselves.

Self-Directed Search This instrument identifies six personality types and matches them with six matching categories of jobs to help students make a career choice related to their needs and preferences.

SGA See Substantial Gainful Employment.

Social Security Administration The agency that oversees the provision of Social Security Disability and Supplemental Security income and related work incentives.

Social Security Disability Insurance In this context, a monthly check provided to children of parents who have retired or become disabled and have paid into Social Security. Only paid to individuals whose income falls below SGA after accounting for work incentives.

Social Worker A person employed by a school or agency to help individuals, families, or groups in coping with their environments and obtaining needed services.

Speech Pathologist A person who is qualified to assess a person's speech and provide interventions to improve it. Sometimes referred to as a language specialist.

SSA See Social Security Administration. Sometimes used to refer to SSDI payments.

SSI See Supplemental Security Income.

SSDI See Social Security Disability Insurance.

Standards-Based Reform Refers to school accountability efforts to assure that all students attain a common standards and a level of proficiency defined by the state or district.

Statement of Needed Transition Services See Transition Plan.

Student Earned Income Exclusion Income that can be excluded for a student under age 22 in calculating SSI benefits.

STW See School-to-Work.

Subsidized Housing Generally HUD housing where a person pays rent based on income (e.g., 33% of income).

Substantial Gainful Employment The amount of income a person can make after a trial work period and still receive SSDI payments.

Summer Youth Employment Programs Subsidized summer employment for low-income youth, and sometimes youth with disabilities, through the Work Incentive Act.

Supplemental Security Income An income support payment administered by the Social Security Administration that is provided to children with disabilities and adults who are disabled and whose income and assets fall below a prescribed level after accounting for Social Security work incentives.

Supported Employment A form of employment where training is done at the job site and ongoing supports are provided to maintain employment. Supported employment is meant for persons with the most severe disabilities. Supported employment jobs are in integrated settings and may consist of individual placements, mobile work crews, or enclaves.

Supports Refers to accommodations, persons in the environment, or practices that help an individual in conducting life activities, including employment.

Take Charge A student-directed collaborative approach that pairs youth with adults of the same gender with similar challenges, and uses four primary strategies: (a) skill facilitation, (b) mentoring, (c) peer support, and (d) parent support to develop student skills in achievement, partnership, and coping.

Tech-Prep A coordinated curriculum in the final two years of high school with a planned transition to a postsecondary institution, usually for an additional two years in a technical or health field.

Technical Schools Refers to educational programs that lead to certification in a highly specialized vocation such as electrical engineer.

Technology Refers to machines, services, and adaptations that allow the individual to better control his or her environment.

Transition The process of moving from adolescence to adult roles where the child reconciles his or her needs, interests, and preferences with adult norms and roles.

Transition Coordinator A person or agency responsible for assuring that planned services are provided in a timely manner and in a way that complements other services provided to a student. See Coordinator.

Transition Meeting The meeting in which transition is discussed. This meeting should occur *no later than age 14* to discuss the student's course of study, and *no later than age 16* to discuss services and supports needed to achieve the student's desired postschool outcomes.

Transition Plan Also known as the "Statement of Needed Transition Services" or Individual Transition Plan (ITP). The IEP/transition plan states in the IEP what services, supports, and activities will be provided to students to help them reach their career goals.

Transition Planning The process of helping students and their families plan services to help them reach career goals and adult living objectives related to their needs, interests, and preferences. The IDEA requires transition-planning activities documented in the IEP for students aged 14 and older.

Transition Planning Inventory An inventory approach that focuses on student skill and support needs in the areas of: (a) employment, (b) further education, (c) daily living, (d) leisure activities, (e) community participation, (f) health, (g) self-determination, (h) communication, and (i) interpersonal relationships.

Trial Work Period The amount of time that an individual receiving SSDI can exceed SGA without losing benefits (currently up to nine nonconsecutive months in a 60-month period).

Vocational Education Refers to secondary and post-secondary programs that teach skills related to specific occupations. Also referred to as Career and Technical Education.

Vocational Rehabilitation Services A federal and state program that provides a range of services to persons with disabilities, typically to achieve a particular career goal.

VR See Vocational Rehabilitation Services.

Waiting List A list of persons who have been determined eligible for services that are in short supply and cannot be provided until openings arise or services are expanded.

What Color Is Your Parachute? This publication provides an overview of career development and some useful exercises and examples related to identifying interests, researching jobs, developing resumes and conducting interviews.

Whose Future Is It Anyway? A self-determination curriculum designed for persons with cognitive disabilities that consists of thirty-six lessons that address: (a) self-awareness, (b) making decisions, (c) obtaining supports and transition services, (d) writing and evaluating transition objectives, and (e) leadership skills.

Work Adjustment See Occupational Work Adjustment.

Work Experience See Occupational Work Experience.

Work Incentives A number of Social Security Work Incentives that allow a person to exclude part of their income to maintain eligibility for SSI or SSDI. Includes PASS, IRWEs, Student Earned Income Exclusion, and extended eligibility for Medicaid.

Work Study Jobs developed by the high school where the student receives credit toward graduation.

Workforce Investment Act A 1998 Act of Congress that brought a number of job service programs together as part of "one-stop shops." Covers the old Job Training Partnership, Rehabilitation Services (that still maintains separate offices), and the Bureau of Employment Services.

CONSENT FOR RELEASE OF INFORMATION

I understand that my signing or refusing to sign this consent will not affect public benefits or services that I am otherwise entitled to.

CASE INFORMATION:

If the release authorized the disclosure of **Case Information**, consent to such disclosure may include the following types of information, if they are in the files of the agency releasing the information.

1. **Educational records**, including but not limited to the results of diagnostic evaluations, teacher observations, vocational assessments, grades, attendance, individualized education programs (IEPs) and transition plans.

2. **Medical records**, including but not limited to the results of physical and mental examinations, diagnoses of physical and mental disorders, medication history, physical and mental health status and history, summary of treatment or services received, and summary of treatment plans and treatment needs.

3. **Psychological and medical testing**, including but not limited to any IQ tests or other tests, of cognitive or emotional or mental status, and any reports of physical tests such as x-rays, CT scans, diagnostic blood testing, or other results.

4. **HIV, AIDS, and AIDS related diagnoses and test results**, including information about treatment planned and received. (This information will be disclosed only if page 1 is initialed to permit it.)

5. **Drug and alcohol abuse diagnoses and treatment**, including but not limited to results of evaluations, diagnoses, treatment and services received, treatment plans and treatment needs. (This information will be disclosed only if page 1 is initialed to permit it.)

6. All records of services provided by Summit County Children Services except child abuse investigation reports.

7. **Second-hand information** may require an additional release of information from the original source.

TO ALL AGENCIES RECEIVING INFORMATION DISCLOSED AS A RESULT OF THIS SIGNED CONSENT:

1.   If the records released include information of any diagnosis or treatment of drug or alcohol abuse, the following statement applies:

      Information disclosed pursuant to this consent has been disclosed to you from records whose confidentiality is protected by Federal law.

      Federal regulations (42 CFR Part 2) prohibit you from making any further disclosure of it without the specific written consent of the person to whom it pertains, or as otherwise permitted by such regulations. A general authorization for the release of medical or other information is NOT sufficient for this purpose.

2.   If the records released include information of an HIV-related diagnosis or test result, the following Statement applies:

          This information has been disclosed to you from confidential records protected from disclosure by state law. You shall make no further disclosure of this information without the specific, written, and informed release of the individual to whom it pertains, or as otherwise permitted by state law. A general authorization for the release of medical or other information is NOT sufficient for the purpose of the release of HIV test results or diagnoses.

Agencies and/or individuals added to the release will be apprised of the Summit County LITT "Member Agreement for Information Sharing"

SUMMIT COUNTY INTERAGENCY TRANSITION TEAM
Member Agreement for Information Sharing

Member Agencies:

    Alcohol, Drug Addiction, Mental Health Service Board (ADAMH)
    Summit County Health Department
    Akron Public Schools
    Stow City Schools
    Hudson Local Schools
    Nordonia Local Schools
    County of Summit Board of Mental Retardation and Developmental Disabilities
    Summit County of Children Services
    Department of Youth Services
    Department of Human Services
    Private Industry Council
    Rehabilitation Services Commission

This agreement is by and among the member agencies comprising the Summit Local Interagency Transition Team.

This agreement is entered into for the benefit of those who seek to share information without risk of liability from unauthorized release, and for the benefit of students and their families who wish to receive, without unreasonable diminution of their rights of privacy and avoidance of self-incrimination, the improved services which information sharing may produce. The Summit LITT agencies agree to:

1. Share information regarding students in compliance with the "Summit County Local Interagency Transition Team Consent for Release of Information" (here in after "Consent") signed by each student and by his/her parent or guardian if under the age of 18, **unless greater release of information is otherwise required or authorized by law.**

2. Use information only for the purpose of improving the quality, efficiency or coordination of the delivery of transition services to the youth and his/her family. **No information first obtained from the consent may be used or transmitted by a member agency for the purpose of criminal investigation, prosecution, or sentencing, except as required by law or judicial order.**

3. Establish internal management systems to help assure that information-sharing activities will be limited to the terms of this agreement and of the student's Consent and will promptly cease upon expiration or revocation of the Consent.

4. Forward a copy of the signed Consent to all member agencies identified on the Consent.

5. Forward immediately to all member agencies any written notice of revocation of a student's Consent which it may receive.

6. Execute this agreement with all above-named member agencies. Member's information-sharing privileges under this agreement shall extend only to sharing agencies identified in the Consent.

This Agreement shall continue in force and effect for a period of one year, automatically renewed unless earlier terminated. This agreement may be terminated by any member agency, upon written notice. Any amendment to this agreement shall be executed in writing by all member agencies.

AGREED:

_____
_____
_____
_____
_____
_____
_____
_____

          Member Agency   Date

SUMMIT COUNTY LOCAL INTERAGENCY TRANSITION TEAM
CONSENT FOR RELEASE OF INFORMATION

_____ Youth - Full Name	_____ Date of Birth
_____ Social Security Number (Optional)	_____ Student/Case Number

The following agencies have my permission to share information for the purpose of helping the student/youth move from school to adult services and to reduce paperwork:
*(Please check or cross out any agencies you do **not** want to share information)*

- ☐ Akron Child Guidance Center
- ☐ The Summit County Health Department
- ☐ The Summit County Health Department
- ☐ County of Summit Board of Mental Retardation and Developmental Disabilities
- ☐ Summit County Children Services
- ☐ The Summit County Department of Human Services
- ☐ The Private Industry Council
- ☐ Rehabilitation Services Commission
- ☐ The Department of Youth Services
- ☐ Public School Systems (specify): _____

_____

I authorize sharing of the following information: (circle yes or no and initial)

yes	no	_____	Identifying Information: name, birth date, sex, race, address, telephone number, social security number, disability, type of services being received and name of agency providing services to me or the individual named above.
yes	no	_____	Case Information: the above Identifying Information, plus medical and social history, treatment/service history, psychological evaluations, Individualized Education Plans (IEPs), transition plans, vocational assessments, grades and attendance, and other personal information regarding me or the individual named above. Information regarding the following shall not be released unless initialed below: _____ HIV and AIDS related diagnosis and treatment _____ Substance abuse diagnosis and treatment

I understand that the Consent for Release of Information expires 180 days from the date it is signed (*). I also understand that I may cancel this Consent for Release of Information at any time by stating so in writing with the date and my signature. This does not include any information which has been shared between the time that I gave permission to share information and the time that it was canceled.

This consent expires on,_____ 20 ___

_____ Signature of person authorized to consent	_____ Relationship to Youth
_____ Signature of Individual	_____ Date
_____ Witness/Agency Representative	_____ Date

* This release of information will expire in 90 days for information concerning substance and alcohol abuse diagnosis and treatment.

REFERENCES

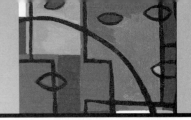

ADAPT (Americans Disabled for Attendant Programs Today). (1999a). *Senators Harkin and Specter introduce landmark legislation, S-1935 supports real choice in the new millennium.* Denver, CO: Author.

ADAPT (Americans Disabled for Attendant Programs Today). (1999b). *Summary of Olmstead Decision.* Denver, CO: Author.

Agran, M., Snow, K., & Swaner, I. (1999). Teacher perceptions of self-determination: Benefits, characteristics, strategies. *Education and Training in Mental Retardation and Developmental Disabilities, 34,* 293-301.

Airasian, P. W. (1994). *Classroom assessment.* New York: McGraw-Hill.

Al-Darmarki, F., & Kivlighan, D. M. (1993). Congruence in client-counselor expectations and the working alliance, *Journal of Counseling Psychology, 40*(4), 379-384.

Algozzine, B., Browder, D., Karvonen, M., Test, D., & Wood, W. (2001). Effects of interventions to promote self-determination for individuals with disabilities. *Review of Educational Research, 71,* 219-277.

Allen, S. K., Smith, A. C., Test, D. W., Flowers, C., & Wood, W. M. (2001). The Effects of *self-directed* IEP on Student Participation in IEP meetings. *Career Development for Exceptional Individuals, 24*(2), 107-120.

Althen, G. (1988). *American ways: A guide for foreigners in the United States.* Yarmouth, MD: Intercultural Press.

American Council on Education. (1996). *Higher education and national affairs.* April 8, pp. 4, 6.

American Vocational Association. (1990). *The AVA guide to the Carl D. Perkins Vocational and Applied Technology Education Act of 1990.* Alexandria, VA: Author.

American Youth Policy Forum/Center on Education Policy. (2002). *Twenty-five years of educating children with disabilities: The good news and the work ahead.* Washington, DC: Author.

Americans with Disabilities Act of 1990, 42 U.S.C.A. § 12101 *et seq.*

Arbona, C. (1996). Career theory and practice in a multicultural context. In M. L. Savickas & W. B. Walsh (Eds.), *Handbook of career counseling theory and practice* (pp. 45-54). Palo Alto, CA: Davies-Black.

Armstrong, D. G. (1990). *Developing and documenting the curriculum.* Boston: Allyn & Bacon.

Arndt, S. A., Konrad, M., & Test, D. W. (2006). Effects of the *Self-Directed IEP* on student participation in planning meetings. *Remedial and Special Education, 27,* 194-207.

Asselin, S. B., Hanley-Maxwell, C., & Syzmanski, E. (1992). Transdisciplinary personnel preparation. In F. R. Rusch, L. DeStefano, J. Chadsey-Rusch, L. A. Phelps, & E. Syzmanski (Eds.). *Transition from school to adult life* (pp. 265-284). Sycamore, IL: Sycamore Publishing.

Asselin, S. B., Todd-Allan, M, & deFur, S. (1998). Transition coordinators: Define yourselves. *Teaching Exceptional Children, 30,* 11-15.

Association on Higher Education and Disability (AHEAD). (1987). *Unlocking the doors: Making the transition from secondary to postsecondary education.* Columbus, OH: Author.

Association on Higher Education and Disability (AHEAD). (1998). *Expanding postsecondary options for minority students with disabilities.* Columbus, OH: Author.

Astin, A. (1993). *What matters in college: Four critical years revisited.* San Francisco: Jossey-Bass.

Aune, E. (1991). A transition model for postsecondary-bound students with learning disabilities. *Learning Disabilities Research & Practice, 6,* 177-187.

Azrin, N. H., & Besalel, V. B. (1979). *A behavioral approach to vocational counseling.* Baltimore: University Park Press.

Azrin, N. H., & Phillips, R. A. (1979). The job club method for handicapped: A comprehensive outcome model. *Rehabilitation Counseling Bulletin, 23,* 144-155.

Baer, R. (1996). *The Summit County L.I.F.E. Project: Linkages for individual and family empowerment* (Report) Kent, OH: Kent State University, Center for Innovation in Transition and Employment.

Baer, R., Flexer, R., Beck, S., Amstutz, N., Hoffman, L., Brothers, J., Steltzer, D., & Zechman, D. (2003). A collaborative followup study on transition. *Career Development for Exceptional Individuals, 26*(1), 7-25.

Baer, R., Flexer, R., & Dennis, L. (in press). Examining the career paths and transition services of students with disabilities exiting high school. *Education and Training of Developmental Disabilities.*

Baer, R., Goebel, G., & Flexer, R. W. (1993). An interdisciplinary team approach to rehabilitation. In R. W. Flexer & P. L. Solomon (Eds.), *Psychiatric rehabilitation in practice.* Boston: Andover Publishers.

Baer, R., Martonyi, E., Simmons, T., Flexer, R., & Goebel, G. (1994). Employer collaboration: A tri-lateral group process model. *Journal of Rehabilitation Administration, 18*(3), 151-163.

Baer, R., McMahan, R., & Flexer, R. (1999). *Effective transition planning: A guide for parents a guide for parents and professionals.* Manual published by Kent State University.

Baer, R., McMahan, R., & Flexer, R. (2004). *Standards-based transition planning: A guide for parents and professionals.* Manual published by Kent State University.

Baer, R., Simmons, T., & Flexer, R. (1996). Transition practice and policy compliance in Ohio: A survey of secondary special educators. *Career Development for Exceptional Individuals, 19*(1), 61-72.

Baer R., Simmons, T., Flexer, R., & Smith, C. (1994). A study of the costs and benefits of supported employment for persons with severe physical and multiple disabilities. *Journal of Rehabilitation Administration, 17*(2), 122-131.

Banks, J. A. (2001). Multicultural education: Characteristics and goals. In J. A. Banks & C. A. McGee Banks (Eds.), *Multicultural education: Issues & perspectives* (4th ed., pp. 3-30). New York: Wiley.

Barrera, I., & Kramer, L. (1997). From monologues to skilled dialogues—Teaching the process of crafting culturally competent early childhood environments. In P. J. Winton, J. A. McCullum, & C. Catlett (Eds.), *Reforming personnel preparation in early intervention* (pp. 217-251). Baltimore: Paul H. Brookes.

Barton, P. E. (2006). The dropout problem: Losing ground. *Educational Leadership, 63*(5), 14-18.

Bates, P. (1990). *Best practices in transition planning: Quality indicators.* Carbondale, IL: Illinois Transition Project.

Bates, P. E. (2002). Instructional assessment. In K. Storey, P. Bates, & D. Hunter (Eds.), *The road ahead: Transition to adult life for persons with disabilities* (pp. 25-45). St. Augustine, FL: Training Resource Network.

Bauder, D., & Lewis, P. (2001). The role of technology in transition planning. In R. W. Flexer, T. J. Simmons, P. Luft, & R. M. Baer (Eds.), *Transition planning for secondary students with disabilities* (pp. 272-301). Upper Saddle River, NJ: Merrill/Prentice Hall.

Bauder, D. K., Lewis, P., Gobert, C., & Bearden, C. (1997). *Assistive technology guidelines for Kentucky schools.* Frankfort, KY: Kentucky Department of Education.

Becker, C. W., & Carnine, D. W. (1982). Direct instruction: A behavior theory model for comprehensive educational intervention with the disadvantaged. In S. W. Bijou & R. Ruiz (Eds.), *Behavior modification: Contributions to education* (pp. 145-210). Hillsdale, NJ: Erlbaum.

Behrmann, M. (1995). Assistive technology training. In K. F. Flippo, K. J. Inge, & J. M. Barcus (Eds.), *Assistive technology: A resource for school, work, and community* (pp. 211-222). Baltimore: Paul H. Brookes.

Behrmann, M. M. (1994). Assistive technology for students with mild disabilities. *Intervention in School and Clinic, 30*(2), 70-83.

Beirne-Smith, M., Ittenbach, R. F., & Patton, J. R. (1998). *Mental retardation.* Upper Saddle River, NJ: Merrill/Prentice Hall.

Bellamy, G. T., Rhodes, L. E., Bourbeau, P. E., & Mank, D. M. (1986). Mental retardation services in sheltered workshops and day activity programs. In F. R. Rusch (Ed.), *Competitive employment: Issues and strategies* (pp. 257-271). Baltimore: Paul H. Brookes.

Bellini, J. (2002). Correlates of multicultural counseling competencies of vocational rehabilitation counselors. *Rehabilitation Counseling Bulletin, 45,* 66-75.

Bender, M., Richmond, L., & Pinson-Millburn, N. (1985). *Careers, computers, and the handicapped.* Austin, TX: PRO-ED.

Benitez, D. T., Lattimore, J., & Wehmeyer, M. L. (2005). Promoting the involvement of students with emotional and behavioral disorders in career and vocational planning and decision-making: the self-determined career development model. *Behavioral Disorders, 30,* 431-447.

Benz, M. R., & Halpern, A. S. (1986). Vocational preparation for high school students with mild disabilities: A statewide study of administrator, teacher, and parent perceptions. *Career Development for Exceptional Individuals, 9*(1), 3-33.

Benz, M. R., & Halpern, A. S. (1987). Transition services for secondary students with mild disabilities: A statewide perspective. *Exceptional Children, 53*(6), 507-514.

Benz, M. R., & Halpern, A. S. (1993). Vocational and transitional services needed and received by students with disabilities during their last year of high school. *Career Development for Exceptional Individuals, 16*(2), 197-212.

Benz, M. R., Johnson, D. K., Mikkelsen, K. S., & Lindstrom, L. E. (1995). Improving collaboration between school and vocational rehabilitation: Stakeholder-identified barriers and strategies. *Career Development for Exceptional Individuals, 18,* 133-144.

Benz, M. R., & Kochhar, C. A. (1996). School-to-work opportunities for all students: A position statement of the division on career development and transition. *Career Development for Exceptional Individuals, 19*(1), 31-48.

Benz, M. R., Lindstrom, L., & Yovanoff, P. (2000). Improving graduation and employment outcomes of students with disabilities: Predictive factors and student perspectives. *Exceptional Children, 66,* 509-529.

Benz, M. R., Yavonoff, P., & Doren, B. (1997). School-to-work components that predict postschool success for students with and without disabilities. *Exceptional Children, 63*(2), 151-166.

Berman, L. M., & Roderick, J. A. (1977). *Curriculum: Teaching what, how, and why of living.* Columbus, OH: Merrill.

Beveridge, S., Craddock, S. H., Liesener, J., Stapleton, M., & Hershenson, D. (2002). INCOME: A framework for conceptualizing the career development of persons with disabilities. *Rehabilitation Counseling Bulletin, 45,* 195-206.

Biklen, D., & Knoll, J. (1987a). The disabled minority. In S. J. Taylor, D. Biklen, & J. A. Knoll (Eds.), *Community integration for people with severe disabilities* (pp. 3-24). New York: Teachers' College Press.

Biklen, D., & Knoll, J. (1987b). The community imperative revisited. In J. A. Mulick & R. F. Antonak (Eds.), *Transitions in mental retardation* (Vol. 3, pp. 1-27), Norwood, NJ: Ablex.

Blackhurst, A. E. (1997). Perspectives on technology in special education. *Teaching Exceptional Children, 29*(5), 41-48.

Blackhurst, A. E., Bausch, M. E., Bell, J. K., Burleson, R. B., Cooper, J. T., Cassaway, L. J., McCrary, N. E., & Zabala, J. S. (1999). *Assistive technology consideration form: The university of Kentucky assistive technology toolkit.* Lexington, KY: Department of Special Education and Rehabilitation Counseling, University of Kentucky.

Blackhurst, A. E., & Cross, D. P. (1993). Technology in special education. In A. E. Blackhurst & W. H. Berdine (Eds.), *An introduction to special education* (3rd ed., pp. 77–103). New York: HarperCollins.

Blackhurst, A. E., & Shuping, M. B. (1990). A philosophy for the use of technology in special education. *Technology and media back-to-school guide.* Reston, VA: Council for Exceptional Children.

Blackorby, J., & Wagner, M. (1996). Longitudinal postschool outcomes of youth with disabilities: Findings from the National Longitudinal Transition Study. *Exceptional Children, 62*(5), 399–414.

Blanck, P. D. (2000). *Employment, disability, and the Americans with Disabilities Act: Issues in law, public policy and research.* Evanston, IL: Northwestern University Press.

Boesel, D., & McFarland, L. (1994). *National assessment of vocational education final report to Congress. Volume 1: Summary and recommendations.* Washington, DC: U.S. Department of Education, Office of Educational Research and Improvement.

Bolles, R. N. (1995). *What color is my parachute? A practical manual for job hunters and career changers.* Berkeley, CA: Ten Speed Press.

Bolles, R. N. (1999). *What color is your parachute?* Berkeley, CA: Ten Speed Press.

Bolles, R. N., & Bolles, M. E. (2006). *What color is your parachute? A practical manual for job hunters and career changers.* Berkeley, CA: Ten Speed Press.

Bond, G. R. (1991). Vocational rehabilitation for persons with severe mental illness: Past, present, and future. In R. Lieberman (Ed.), *Rehabilitation of the psychiatrically disabled.* New York: Pergamon.

Bond, G. R., & Boyer, S. L. (1988). Rehabilitation programs and outcomes. In J. A. Ciardiello & M. D. Bell (Eds.), *Vocational rehabilitation of persons with prolonged mental illness.* (pp. 231–263). Baltimore: Johns Hopkins University Press.

Bond, G. R., Dietzen, L. L., McGrew, J. H., & Miller, L. D. (1995). Accelerating entry into supported employment for persons with severe psychiatric disabilities. *Rehabilitation Psychology, 40*(2), 91–111.

Bose, J. (1996). *Characteristics of the 100 largest public elementary and secondary school districts in the United States: 1993–94: Statistical analysis report.* Washington, DC: National Center for Educational Statistics.

Boyer, E. (1987). *College: The undergraduate experience in America.* New York: Harper & Row.

Braddock, D. (1987). *Federal policy toward mental retardation and developmental disabilities.* Baltimore: Paul H. Brookes.

Braddock, D. (2005). *Disability at the dawn of the 21st century and the state of the states.* AAMR: Washington DC.

Brady, M. P., & Rosenberg, H. (2002). Job observation and behavior scale: A supported employment assessment instrument. *Education and Training in Mental Retardation and Developmental Disabilities, 37*(4), 427–433.

Brame, K. (1995). Strategies for recruiting family members from diverse backgrounds for roles in policy and program development. *Early Childhood Bulletin, 5,* 1–5. (ERIC Document Reproduction Service No. ED 398 721)

Brinckerhoff, L. C., McGuire, J. M., & Shaw. S. F. (2002). *Postsecondary education and transition for students with learning disabilties.* Austin, TX: PRO-ED.

Brinckerhoff, L. C., Shaw, S. F., & McGuire, J. M. (1992). Promoting access, accommodations, and independence for college students with learning disabilities. *Journal of Learning Disabilities, 25,* 417–429.

Brinckerhoff, L. C., Shaw, S. F., & McGuire, J. M. (1993). *Promoting postsecondary education for students with learning disabilities.* Austin, TX: PRO-ED.

Brislin, R. (1993). *Understanding culture's influence on behavior.* Fort Worth, TX: Harcourt Brace.

Brolin, D. E. (1989). *Life-centered career education: A competency-based approach.* Reston, VA: The Council for Exceptional Children.

Brolin, D. E. (1992a). *Competency assessment knowledge batteries: Life-centered career education,* Reston, VA: The Council for Exceptional Children.

Brolin, D. E. (1992b). *Competency assessment performance batteries: Life-centered career education,* Reston, VA: The Council for Exceptional Children.

Brolin, D. E. (1992c). *Life-centered career education: Competency units for occupational guidance and preparation.* Reston, VA: The Council for Exceptional Children.

Brolin, D. E. (1992d). *Life-centered career education: Competency units for personal-social skills.* Reston, VA: The Council for Exceptional Children.

Brolin, D. E. (1993). *Life-centered career education* [videorecording]. Reston, VA: The Council for Exceptional Children.

Brolin, D. E. (Ed.). (1995). *Career education: A functional life skills approach* (3rd. ed.). Upper Saddle River, NJ: Prentice Hall.

Brolin, D. E. (1996). Reflections on the beginning . . . and the future directions! *Career Development for Exceptional Individuals, 19*(2), 93–100. Upper Saddle River, NJ: Merrill/Prentice Hall.

Brolin, D. E. (1997). *Life-centered career education: A competency-based approach.* Reston, VA: The Council for Exceptional Children.

Brolin, D. E., & Gysbers, N. C. (1979). Career education for persons with handicaps. *The Personnel and Guidance Journal, 58,* 258–262.

Brolin, D. E., & Lloyd, R. J. (2004). *Career development and transition services: A functional life skills approach* (4th ed.). Upper Saddle River, NJ: Merrill/Prentice Hall.

Brolin, D. E., & Schatzman, B. (1989). Lifelong career development. In D. E. Berkell & J. M. Brown (Eds.), *Transition from school to work for persons with disabilities.* New York: Longman.

Brookhiser, R. (1991). *The way of the wasp.* New York: Free Press.

Browder, D. M., Courtade-Little, G., Davis, S., Fallin, K., & Karvonen, M. (2005). The impact of teacher training on state alternate assessment scores. *Exceptional Children, 71*(3), 267–282.

Brown, C. (1992). Assistive technology, computers, and persons with disabilities. *Communications of the ACM, 35*(5), 36–45.

Brown, C., McDaniel, R., Couch, R., & McClanahan, M. (1994). *Vocational evaluation and software: A consumer's guide.* (Available from Materials Development Center, Stout Vocational Rehabilitation Institute, University of Wisconsin—Stout, Menomonie, WI 54751.)

Brown, D. (1990). Trait and factor theory. In D. Brown, L. Brooks, & Associates (Eds.), *Career choice and development: Applying contemporary theories to practice* (2nd ed., pp. 13–36). San Francisco: Jossey-Bass.

Brown, D. (1996). Status of career development theories. In D. Brown, L. Brooks, & Associates (Eds.), *Career choice and development: Applying contemporary theories to practice* (3rd ed., pp. 513–526). San Francisco: Jossey-Bass.

Brown, D. (2002). Status of theories of career choice and development. In D. Brown and Associates (Eds.), *Career choice and development* (4th ed., pp. 510–515). San Francisco: Jossey-Bass.

Brown, D., & Brooks, L. (1984). Preface. In D. Brown, L. Brooks, & Associates (Eds.), *Career choice and development: Applying contemporary theories to practice* (pp. ix–xii). San Francisco: Jossey-Bass.

Brown, D., & Brooks, L. (1990). Introduction to theories of career development: Origins, evolution, and current efforts. In D. Brown, L. Brooks, & Associates (Eds.), *Career choice and development: Applying contemporary theories to practice* (2nd ed., pp. 1–12). San Francisco: Jossey-Bass.

Brown, D., & Brooks, L. (1996). Introduction to theories of career development and choice: Origins, evolution, and current efforts. In D. Brown, L. Brooks, & Associates (Eds.), *Career choice and development* (3rd ed., pp. 1–30). San Francisco: Jossey-Bass.

Brown, L., Branston, M. B., Hamre-Nietupski, S., Pumpian, I., Certo, N., & Gruenewald, L. (1979). A strategy for developing chronological age appropriate and functional curricular content for severely handicapped adolescents and young adults. *Journal of Special Education, 13,* 81–90.

Brown, L., Long, E., Udvari-Solner, A., Davis, L., VanDeventer, P., Ahlgren, C., Johnson, F., Gruenewald, L., & Jorgesen, J. (1989). The home school: Why students with severe intellectual disabilities must attend the schools of their brothers, sisters, friends, and neighbors. *Journal of the Association for Persons with Severe Handicaps, 16,* 39–47.

Brown, L., Nietupski, J,. & Hamre-Nietupski, S. (1976). The criterion of ultimate functioning and public school service for severely handicapped students. In M. A. Thomas (Ed.), *Please don't forget about me! Education's investment in the severely, profoundly, and multiple handicapped child.* (pp. 2–15). Reston, VA: The Council for Exceptional Children.

Browning, P. L. (1997). *Transition in action for youth and young adults with disabilities.* Montgomery, AL: Auburn University, Wells Printing.

Bucher, D. E., & Brolin, D. E. (1987). The life-centered career education (LCCE) inventory: A curriculum-based, criterion-related assessment instrument. *Diagnostique, 12,* 131–141.

Bulgren, J. A., Schumaker, J. B., & Deshler, D. D. (1994). *Use and effectiveness of a concept anchoring routine in secondary-level mainstreamed classes.* University of Kansas Center for Research on Learning, Lawrence, KS.

Bull, B. L., Fruehling, R. T., & Chattergy, V. (1992). *The ethics of multicultural and bilingual education.* New York: Teachers College Press.

Bullis, M., & Davis, C. (1996). Further examination of job-related social skills measures for adolescents and young adults with emotional and behavioral disorders. *Behavioral Disorders, 21*(2), 160–171.

Bullis, M. D., Kosko, K., Waintrup, M., Kelley, P., & Issacson, A. (1994). Functional assessment services for transition, education, and rehabilitation: Project FASTER. *American Rehabilitation, 20*(2), 9.

Bureau of Labor Statistics, U.S. Department of Labor. (2001). Monthly Labor Review, Winter 2001–02. *Occupational Outlook Quarterly.*

Bureau of Labor Statistics. (2004, August 25). *Number of jobs held, labor market activity, and earnings growth among younger baby boomers: recent results from a longitudinal survey.* Buearu of Labor Statistics NEWS, USDL 01-1678. Washington, DC: Author. Retrieved June 11, 2006, from *http://www.bls.gov/nls/home.htm.*

Bureau of Labor Statistics. (2005, December 7). *BLS releases 2004-14 employment projections.* USDL 05-2276. Washington, DC: Author. Retrieved May 15, 2006 from *www.bls.gov/emp.*

Burhauser, R. V., & Stapleton, D. C. (2003). *Introduction. The decline in employment of people with disabilities: A policy puzzle.* Retrieved June 4, 2006, from *http://www.ilr.cornell.edu/ped/dep/files/2001PolicyInstitute_Sample Chapter.pdf.*

Burnette, J. (1998). *Reducing the disproportionate representation of minority students in special education.* Reston, VA: ERIC Clearinghouse on Disabilities and Gifted Education, ERIC/OSEP Digest #E566.

Callicott, K. J. (2003). Culturally sensitive collaboration within person-centered planning. *Focus on Autism and Other Developmental Disabilities, 18,* 60–68.

Carl D. Perkins Vocational and Applied Technology Education Act. (1990). Pub. L. No. 101-392, 104, Stat. 756.

Carl D. Perkins Vocational Education Act. (1984). Pub. L. No. 98-524, 98, Stat. 2435.

Carney, I. H., & Orelove, F. P. (1988). Implementing transition programs for community participation. In B. L. Ludlow,

A. P. Turnbull, & R. Luckasson (Eds.), *Transitions to adult life for persons with mental retardation: Principles and practices.* Baltimore: Paul H. Brookes.

Cavalier, A. R., & Brown, C. C. (1998). From passivity to participation: The transformational possibilities of speech-recognition technology. *Teaching Exceptional Children, 30*(6), 60-65.

Center for Applied Special Technology. (1998-1999). *The National Center on Accessing the General Curriculum* [On-line]. Available: *http://www.cast.org/initiatives/nationalcenter.html.*

Chadsey, J., & Sheldon, D. (1998). Moving toward social inclusion in employment and postsecondary school settings. In F. R. Rusch & J. G. Chadsey (Eds.), *Beyond high school: Transition from school to work* (pp. 383-405). Belmont, CA: Wadsworth.

Chadsey-Rusch, J., & Heal, L. (1995). Building consensus from transition experts on social integration outcomes and interventions. *Exceptional Children,* 165-187.

Chadsey-Rusch, J., Rusch, F. R., & O'Reilly, M. F. (1991). Transition from school to integrated communities. *Remedial and Special Education, 12*(6), 23-33.

Chambers, A. C. (1997). *Has technology been considered? A guide for IEP teams.* Albuquerque, NM: Council of Administrators in Special Education.

Chan, F., Reid, C., Kaskel, L., Roldan, G., Rahami, M., & Mpofu, E. (1997). Vocational assessment and evaluation of people with disabilities. *Physical Medicine and Rehabilitation Clinics of North America, 8,* 311-325.

Chan, S. (1998a). Families with Asian roots. In E. W. Lynch & M. H. Hanson (Eds.), *Developing cross-cultural competence: A guide for working with children and their families* (2nd ed., pp. 251-354). Baltimore: Paul H. Brookes.

Chan, S. (1998b). Families with Filipino roots. In E. W. Lynch & M. H. Hanson (Eds.), *Developing cross-cultural competence: A guide for working with children and their families* (2nd ed., pp. 355-408). Baltimore: Paul H. Brookes.

Chen, C. P. (2003). Integrating perspectives in career development theory and practice. *Career Development Quarterly, 51,* 203-216.

Clark, G. M. (1979). *Career education for the handicapped child in the elementary school.* Denver, CO: Love.

Clark, G. M. (1992, April). Providing transition services through a functional curriculum and functional instruction. Paper presented at The Council for Exceptional Children annual conference, Baltimore.

Clark, G. M. (1994). Is a functional curriculum approach compatible with an inclusive education model? *Teaching Exception Children, 26*(2), 36-39.

Clark, G. M. (1996). Transition planning assessment for secondary-level students with learning disabilities. *Journal of Learning Disabilities, 29*(1), 79-92.

Clark, G. M., & Kolstoe, O. P. (1995). *Career development and transition education for adolescents with disabilities* (2nd ed.). Needham, MA: Allyn & Bacon.

Clark, G. M., Carlson, B. C., Fisher, S., Cook, I. D., & D'Alonzo, B. J. (1991). Career development for students with disabilities in elementary schools: A position statement of the Division on Career Development. *Career Development for Exceptional Individuals, 14*(2), 109-120.

Clark, G. M., & Patton, J. R. (1997). *Transition planning inventory: Administration and resource guide.* Austin, TX: PRO-ED.

Clary, G. K. (2001). *Barriers to postsecondary education for rural students with disabilities: A delphi investigation.* Unpublished doctoral dissertation, Kent State University.

Cobb, H. C. (1972). *The forecast of fulfillment.* New York: Teachers College Press.

Cobb, R. B., & Neubert, D. A. (1992). Vocational education models. In F. R. Rusch, L. Destefano, J. Chadsey-Rusch, L. A. Phelps, & E. Syzmanski (Eds.) *Transition from school to adult life:* Models, linkages, and policies. (pp. 93-113) Sycamore IL: Sycamore.

Cobb, R. B., & Neubert, D. A. (1998). Vocational education: Emerging vocationalism. In F. R. Rusch & J. G. Chadsey (Eds.), *Beyond high school: Transition from school to work* (pp. 101-126). Belmont, CA: Wadsworth Publishing.

Cohen, M., & Besharov, D. J. *The role of career and technical education: Implications for the federal government.* Prepared for the Office of Vocational and Adult Education, U.S. Department of Education, March 21, 2002.

Cole, M., & Cole, S. (1993). *The development of children* (2nd ed.). New York: Scientific American Books.

Collignon, F. C., Noble, J. H., & Toms-Barker, L. (1987). Early lessons form the Marin County demonstration integrating vocational and mental health services. *Psychosocial Rehabilitation Journal, 11*(2), 76-85.

Colorado Department of Education. (1998). *Teach access skills.* Denver, CO: Author.

Condeluci, A. (1995). *Interdependence: The route to community.* Winter Park, FL: GR Press.

Cone, J. D., Delawyer, D. D., & Wolfe, V. V. (1985). Assessing parent participation: The parent/family involvement index. *Exceptional Children, 51*(5), 417-424.

Conley, D. T. (2002, April). Preparing students for life after high school. *Educational Leadership,* 60-66.

Conte, L. E. (1983). Vocational development theories and the disabled person: Oversight or deliberate omission? *Rehabilitation Counseling Bulletin, 27,* 316-328.

Conyers, L., Koch, L., & Szymanski, E. (1998). Lifespan perspectives on disability and work: A qualitative study. *Rehabilitation Counseling Bulletin, 42,* 51-75.

Cook, J. A., & Hoffschmidt, S. J. (1995). Comprehensive models of psychosocial rehabilitation. In R. W. Flexer and P. L. Solomon (Eds.), *Psychiatric rehabilitation in practice.* (pp. 81-98) Boston: Andover Publishers.

Cooter, R. B., Jr., & Flynt, E. S. (1996). *Teaching reading in the content areas: Developing content literacy for all students.* Upper Saddle River, NJ: Merrill/Prentice Hall.

Cordeiro, P. A., Reagan, T. G., & Martinez, L. P. (1994). *Multic-ulturalism and* TQE: *Addressing cultural diversity in schools.* Thousand Oaks, CA: Corwin.

Correa, V. I. (1989). Involving culturally diverse families in the educational process. In S. H. Fradd & M. H. Weismantel (Eds.), *Meeting the needs of culturally and linguisti-cally different students: A handbook for educators* (pp. 130–144). Austin, TX: PRO-ED.

Cowen, S. (1993). Transition planning for LD college-bound students. In S. Vogel & P. Adelman (Eds.), *Success for college students with learning disabilities* (pp. 39–56). New York: Springer.

Craddock, G., & Scherer, M. J. (2002). Assessing individual needs for assistive technology. In C. L. Sax & C. A. Thoma (Eds.). *Transition assessment: Wise practices for quality lives* (pp. 87–101). Baltimore: Paul H. Brookes.

Crites, J. (1978). *The career maturity inventory.* Monterey, CA: CTB/McGraw-Hill.

Crites, J. O. (1981). Integrative test interpretation. In D. H. Montross & D. J. Shinkman (Eds.), *Career development in the* 1980s: *Theory and practice* (pp. 161–168). Spring-field, IL: Charles C. Thomas.

Cross, T., Cooke, N. L., Wood, W. M., & Test, D. W. (1999). Comparison of the Effects of MAPS and ChoiceMaker on Student Self-Determination Skills. *Education and Train-ing in Mental Retardation and Developmental Disabli-lities, 34*(4), 499–510.

Cuban, L. (1993). The lure of curricular reform and its pitiful history. *Phi Delta Kappan, 75*(2), 182–186.

Cummins, J. (1986). Psychological assessment of minority students: Out of context, out of focus, out of control? In A. C. Willing & H. F. Greenberg (Eds.), *Bilingualism and learning disabilities: Policy and practice for teachers and administrators* (pp. 3–11). New York: American Library Publishing.

Curnow, T. C. (1989). Vocational development of persons with disabilities. *Career Development Quarterly, 37,* 269–278.

Dattilo, J. (1987). Recreation and leisure literature for individ-uals with mental retardation: Implications for outdoor recreation. *Therapeutic Recreation Journal, 21*(1), 9–17.

Davis, P., & Faw, G. (2002). Residential preferences in person-centered planning: Empowerment through the self-identification of preferences and their availability. In Holburn, S., & Vietze, P. M. (Eds.), *Person-centered planning: Research, practice, and future directions.* (pp. 203–222). Baltimore: Paul H. Brookes.

Daviso, A., Ackerman, G., & Flexer, R. (2003). *A comparison of video based and static line drawing choice-making assessments to determine job preference for students with severe disabilities.* Presentation at The Division of Career Development and Transition, Roanoke, VA.

Dawis, R. (2002). Person-environment-correspondence the-ory. In D. Brown and Associates (Eds.), *Career choice and development* (4th ed., pp. 427–464). San Francisco: Jossey-Bass.

Dawis, R. V. (1996). The theory of work adjustment and person-environment-correspondence counseling. In D. Brown, L. Brooks, & Associates (Eds.), *Career choice and de-velopment* (3rd ed., pp. 75–120). San Francisco: Jossey-Bass.

Dawis, R. V., & Lofquist, L. H. (1984). *A psychological theory of work adjustment: An individual-differences model and its applications.* Minneapolis, MN: University of Min-nesota Press.

Deci, E. L., & Chandler, C. L. (1986). The importance of moti-vation for the future of the LD field. *Journal of Learning Disabilities, 19,* 587–594.

Deci, E. L., & Ryan, R. M. (1985). *Intrinsic motivation and self-determination in human behavior.* New York: Plenum.

Deci, E. L., & Ryan, R. M. (1994). Promoting self-determined ed-ucation. *Scandinavian Journal of Educational Research (38),* 3–14.

deFur, S. H. (2002). Education reform, high-stakes assessment, and students with disabilities: One state's approach. *Remedial and Special Education, 23*(4), 203–211.

deFur, S. H., & Patton, J. R. (1999). *Transition and school-based services: Interdisciplinary perspectives for en-hancing the transition process.* Austin: PRO-ED.

deFur, S. H., & Taymans, J. M. (1995). Competencies needed for transition specialists in vocational rehabilitation, voca-tional education, and special education. *Career Develop-ment for Exceptional Individuals, 62*(1), 38–51.

deFur, S. H., Getzel, E. E., & Kregel, J. (1994). Individual transi-tion plans: A work in progress. *Journal of Vocational Re-habilitation, 4*(2), 139–145.

deFur, S. H., Getzel, E. E., & Trossi, K. (1996). Making the post-secondary education match: A role for transition planning. *Journal of Vocational Rehabilitation, 6,* 231–240.

DeJong, G. (1979) Independent living: From social movement to analytic paradigm. *Archives of Physical Medicine and Rehabilitation, 60, 435–446.*

DeJong, G. (1984). Independent living: From social movement to analytic paradigm. In P. Marinelli & A. Dell Orto (Eds.), *The psychological and social impact of physical disabil-ity* (pp. 39–64). New York: Springer.

Dennis, L. (2006). What's a SOP for special education gradu-ates? *Focus,* newsletter published by the Cuyahoga Special Education Service Center. April-May.

Dennis, R. E., & Giangreco, M. F. (1996). Creating conversation: Reflections on cultural sensitivity in family interviewing. *Exceptional Children, 63,* 103–116.

Dentzer, S. (1992). How to train workers for the 21st century. *U.S. News & World Report,* 21 September, pp. 72–78.

Deshler, D., Ellis, E. S., & Lenz, R. K. (1996). *Teaching adoles-cents with learning disabilities* (2nd ed.). Denver: Love Publishing.

DeStefano, L. (1989). Facilitating the transition from school to adult life for youth with disabilities. In W. E. Kiernan & R. L. Schalock (Eds.), *Economics, industry, and disability: A look ahead* (pp. 169–177). Baltimore: Paul H. Brookes.

DeStefano, L., & Snauwaert, D. (1989). *A value-critical approach to transition policy analysis* [Monograph]. Special Education Programs: Washington, DC.

DeStefano, L., & Wagner, M., (1992). Outcome assessment in special education: Implication for decision-making and long-term planning in vocational rehabilitation. *Career Development for Exceptional Individuals, 16*(2), 147-158.

DeStefano, L., & Wermuth, T. R. (1993). IDEA (P.L. 101-476): Defining a second generation of transition services. In F. R. Rusch, L. DeStefano, J. Chadsey-Rusch, L. A. Phelps, & E. Szymanski (Eds.), *Transition from school to adult life: Models, linkages, and policy* (pp. 537-549). Sycamore, IL: Sycamore.

DeVillar, R. A. (1994). The rhetoric and practice of cultural diversity in U.S. schools: Socialization, resocialization, and quality schooling. In R. A. DeVillar, D. J. Faltis, & J. P. Cummins (Eds.), *Cultural diversity in schools: From rhetoric to practice* (pp. 25-56). Albany, NY: State University of New York.

Dinerstein, R. D., Herr, S. S., & O'Sullivan, J. L. (1999). *A guide to consent.* Washington, DC: American Association on Mental Retardation.

Dinnebell, L. A., & Rule, S. (1994). Congruence between parents' and professionals' judgment about the development of young children with disabilities: A review of the literature. *Topics in Early Childhood Education, 14,* 1-26.

Division of Career Development and Transition. (2000). *Transition specialist competencies.* Reston, VA: Council for Exceptional Children.

Dohm, A., & Wyatt, I. (2002). College at work: Outlook and earnings for college graduates, 2000-10. *Occupational Outlook Quarterly,* fall 2002. Retrieved Feb 20, 2003, from Proquest, *http://proquest.umi.com/pdqweb?*Did = 000000217986161

Donovan, M. S., Bransford, J. D., & Pellegrino, J. W. (1999). *How people learn: Bridging research and practice.* Washington, DC: National Academies Press. [On-line]. Available: *http://books,nap.edu/html/howpeople2/ch2.html.*

Donovan, M. S., & Cross, C. T. (eds.) (2002). *Minority students in special and gifted education.* Washington, DC: National Academy Press, National Research Council Committee on Minority Representation in Special Education.

Downing, J. E. (1996). Working cooperatively: The role of adults. In J. E. Downing (Ed.), *Including students with severe and multiple disabilities in regular classrooms* (pp. 147-162). Baltimore: Paul H. Brookes.

Doyel, A. W. (2000). Entrepreneurs with disabilities can succeed in their own businesses. *Supported Employment InfoLines, 11*(8), 1, 3, 6.

Doyel, A. W. (2001). *No More Job Interviews: Self-employment Strategies for People with Disabilities.* St. Augustine, FL: Training Resource Network.

Doyle, W. (1986). Classroom organization and management. In M. C. Wittrock (Ed.), *Handbook of research on teaching* (3rd ed., pp. 392-431). New York: Macmillan.

Droege, R. C. (1987). The USES testing program. In B. Bolton (Ed.), *Handbook of measurement and evaluation in rehabilitation.* (pp. 169-182). Baltimore: Paul H. Brookes.

Dunham, M., Koller, J. R., & McIntosh, D. (1996). A preliminary comparison of successful and non-successful closure types among adults with specific learning disabilities in the vocational rehabilitation system. *The Journal of Rehabilitation, 62*(1), 42-47.

Dunn, R., & Griggs, S. A. (1995). *Multiculturalism and learning style: Teaching and counseling adolescents.* Westport, CN: Praeger.

Dunst, C., Trivette, C., & Deal, A. (1988). *Enabling and empowering families: Principles and guidelines for practice.* Cambridge, MA: Brookline Books.

Dunst, D. J. (2002). Family-centered practices: Birth through high school. *The Journal of Special Education, 36,* 139-147.

Durlak, C. M., Rose, E., & Bursuck, W. D. (1994). Preparing high school students with learning disabilities for the transition to postsecondary education: Teaching the skills of self-determination. *Journal of Learning Disabilities, 27*(1), 51-59.

Dybwad, G. (1989). Self-determination: Influencing public policy. In R. Perske (Ed.), *National conference on self-determination.* Washington, DC: U.S. Department of Education, Office of Special Education and Rehabilitative Services.

Eber, L., Nelson, C. M., & Miles, P. (1997). School-based wraparound for students with emotional and behavior challenges. *Exceptional Children, 63*(4), 539-556.

Edgar, E. (1987). Secondary programs in special education: Are many of them justifiable? *Exceptional Parent, 53*(6), 555-561.

Edgar, E., & Levine, P. (1986). *Washington state follow-up studies of postsecondary special education students in transition.* Seattle, WA: University of Washington, Networking and Evaluation Team.

Edgar, E., & Polloway, E. A. (1994). Education for adolescents with disabilities: Curriculum and placement issues. *The Journal of Special Education, 27*(4), 438-452.

Education Amendments of 1972, 20 U.S.C. § 1681 *et seq.*

Education Amendments of 1974, Pub. L. No. 93-380, 88 Stat. 580.

Education for All Handicapped Children Act of 1975, 20 U.S.C. § 1401 *et seq.*

Education for All Handicapped Children Act, Pub. L. No. 94-142, 20 U.S.C. 1412 (1975).

Education of the Handicapped Act of 1970, Pub. L. No. 91-230, § 601-662, 84 Stat. 175.

Education of the Handicapped Amendments of 1986, 20 U.S.C. § 1401 *et seq.*

Elementary and Secondary Education Act of 1965, Pub. L. No. 89-10, 79 Stat. 27.

Elementary and Secondary Education Act of 1965 (20 U.S.C. 6301 *et seq.*).

Elementary and Secondary Education Act, amended by Pub. L. No. 89-750. § 161 [Title VI], 80 Stat. 1204 (1966).

Erikson, E. (1963). *Childhood and society* (2nd ed.). New York: W. W. Norton.

Erikson, E. (1968). *Identity, youth, and crisis.* Toronto: W. W. Norton.

Esposito, L., & Campbell, P. H. (1993). Computers and severely and physically handicapped individuals. In J. D. Lindsey (Ed.), *Computers and exceptional individuals* (2nd ed., pp. 159–171). Austin, TX: PRO-ED.

Eubanks, S. C. (1996). *The urban teacher challenge: A report on teacher recruitment and demand in selected great city schools.* Belmont, MA: Recruiting New Teachers.

Evers, R. B., & Elksnin, N. (1998). *Working with students with disabilities in vocational-technical settings.* Austin, TX: Pro-Ed.

Everson, J. M. (1990). A local team approach. *Teaching Exceptional Children, 23*(1), 44–46.

Everson, J. M., & Guillory, J. D. (1998). Building statewide transition services through collaborative interagency teamwork. In F. Rusch & J. Chadsey (Eds.), *Beyond high school: Transition from school to work* (pp. 299–317). Belmont, CA: Wadsworth.

Everson, J. M., & McNulty, K. (1992). Interagency teams: Building local transition programs through parental and professional partnerships. In F. R. Rusch, L. DeStefano, J. Chadsey-Rusch, L. A. Phelps, & E. Szymanski (Eds.), *Transition from school to adult life: Models, linkages, and policy* (pp. 341–352). Sycamore, IL: Sycamore.

Everson, J. M., & Moon, M. S. (1987). Transition services for young adults with severe disabilities: Defining professional and parental roles and responsibilities. *Journal of the Association for Persons with Severe Handicaps, 12*(2), 87–95.

Everson, J. M., Barcus, M., Moon, M. S., & Morton, M. V. (1987). *Achieving outcomes: A guide to interagency training in transition and supported employment.* Richmond, VA: Virginia Commonwealth University, Project Transition into Employment.

Everson, J. M., & Rachal, P. (1996). *What are we learning about state and local interagency partnerships? An analysis of state and interagency activities for students who are deaf-blind in seventeen states.* Sands Point, NY: Helen Keller National Center—Technical Assistance Center.

Fabian, E., Lent, R., & Willis, S. (1998). Predicting work transition outcomes for students with disabilities: Implications for counselors. *Journal of Counseling and Development, 76,* 311–316.

Fairweather, J. S., & Shaver, D. M. (1991). Making the transition to postsecondary education and training. *Exceptional Children, 57*(3), 264–270.

Federal Register. (1981, January 19). Washington, DC: U.S. Government Printing Office.

Ferguson, D., Droege, C., Lester, J., Meyer, G., Ralph, G, Sampson, N., & Williams, J. (2001). *Designing personalized learning for every student.* The Association for Supervision and Curriculum Development (ASCD).

Ferguson, G. (2001, Summer). The use of ritual in rites of passage. *The Voice for Adventure Edcuation, 43,* 14–19.

Ferguson, P. M., & Ferguson, D. L. (2000). The promise of adulthood. In M. E. Snell & F. Brown, *Instruction of students with severe disabilities* (5th ed., pp. 629–656). Upper Saddle River, NJ: Merrill/Prentice Hall.

Ferguson, P. M., & Olsen, D. (Eds.). (1989). *Supported community life: Connecting policy to practice in disability research.* Eugene, OR: Specialized Training Program.

Fichten, C. S., & Ansel, R. (1988). Thoughts concerning interactions between college students who have a physical disability and their nondisabled peers. *Rehabilitation Counseling Bulletin, 32,* 23–40.

Field, S., & Hoffman, A. (1994). Development of a model for self-determination. *Career Development for Exceptional Individuals, 17*(2), 159–169.

Field, S., & Hoffman, A. (1995). *Steps to self-determination.* Austin, TX: PRO-ED.

Field, S., Hoffman, A., & Spezia, S. (1998). *Self-determination strategies for adolescents in transition.* Austin, TX: Pro-Ed.

Field, S., Martin, J, Miller, R., Ward, M., & Wehmeyer, M. (1998). *A practical guide for teaching self-determination.* Reston, VA: The Council for Exceptional Children.

Field, S., Martin, J. E., Miller, R., Ward, M., & Wehmeyer, M. (1998). Self-determination for persons with disabilities: A position paper of the Division on Career Development and Transition. *Career Development for Exceptional Individuals, 21*(2), 113–128.

Fisher, S. K., & Gardner, J. E. (1999). Introduction to technology in transition. *Career Development for Exceptional Individuals, 22*(2), 131–152.

Fitcher, J. M. (1991). *Endangered spaces, enduring places: Change, identity, and survival in rural America.* Boulder, CO: Westview.

Flexer, R. (1996). Federal laws and program accessibility. In C. Flexer, D. Wray, R. Leavitt, & R. Flexer (Eds.), *How the student with hearing loss can succeed in college: A handbook for students, families, and professional* (2nd ed., pp. 13–27). Washington, DC: Alexander Graham Bell Association for the Deaf.

Flexer, R., Simmons, T., & Tankersley, M. (1997). Graduate interdisciplinary training at Kent State University. *Journal of Vocational Rehabilitation, 8,* 183–195.

Flexer, R. W. (2005). History and transition legislation. In Flexer, R.W., Simmons, T.J., Luft, P., & Baer, R. M. (Eds.). *Transition planning for secondary students with disabilities* (2nd ed., pp. 20–52). Upper Saddle River, NJ: Merrill/Prentice Hall.

Flexer, R. W. & Baer, R.M. Description and evaluation of a university-based transition endorsement program. *Career Development for Exceptional Individuals, 28,* 80–91.

Flexer, R. W., Goebel, G. W., Simmons, T. J., Baer, R., Shell, D., Steele, R., & Sabousky, R. (1994). Participant, employer, and rehabilitation resources in supported employment: A collaborative approach. *Journal of Applied Rehabilitation Counseling, 25*(4), 9-15.

Foley, R. M., & Munschenck, N. A. (1997). Collaboration activities and competencies of secondary school special educators: A national survey. *Teacher Education and Special Education, 20,* 47-60.

Ford, A., Schnorr, R., Meyer, L., Davern, L., Black, J., & Dempsey, P. (1989). *The Syracuse community-referenced curriculum guide for students with moderate and severe disabilities.* Baltimore: Paul H. Brookes.

Forest, M., & Lusthaus, E. (1989). Promoting educational equality for all students: Circles and MAPS. In S. Stainback, W. Stainback, & M. Forest (Eds.), *Educating all students in the mainstream of regular education* (pp. 43-57). Baltimore: Paul H. Brookes.

Forest, M., Pearpoint, J., & Snow, J. (1993). Natural support systems: Families, friends, and circles. In J. Pearpoint, M. Forest, & J. Snow (Eds.), *The inclusion papers: Strategies to make inclusion work* (pp. 116-132). Toronto: Inclusion Press.

Foss, G., Bullis, M. D., & Vilhauer, D. A. (1984). Assessment and training of job-related social competence for mentally retarded adolescents and adults. In A. S. Halpern & M. J. Fuhrer (Eds.), *Functional assessment in rehabilitation* (pp. 145-157). Baltimore: Paul H. Brookes.

Foss, G., Cheney, D., & Bullis, M. D. (1986). *TICE: Test of interpersonal competence for employment.* Santa Monica, CA: James Stanfield.

Foss, G., & Vilhauer, D. A. (1986). *Working II: Interpersonal skills assessment and training for employment: Teachers guide.* Santa Monica, CA: James Stanfield.

Fox, L., Zakely, J., Morris, R., & Jundt, M. (1993). Orientation as a catalyst: Effective retention through academic and social integration. In M. L. Upcraft, R. H. Mullendore, B. O. Barefoot, & D. S. Fidler (Eds.), *Designing successful transitions: A guide for orienting students to college* [Monograph Series No. 13] 49-59. Columbia, SC: University of South Carolina.

Fradd, S. H., & Weismantel, M. J. (1989). Developing and evaluating goals. In S. H. Fradd & M. H. Weismantel (Eds.), *Meeting the needs of culturally and linguistically different students: A handbook for educators* (pp. 34-62). Austin, TX: PRO-ED.

Francese, P. (2002). The college-cash connection. *American Demographics, 24*(3), 42-43.

Frank, K., & Wade, P. (1993). Disabled student services in post-secondary education: Who's responsible for what? *Journal of College Student Development, 34,* 26-30.

French, M. M. (1999). *Starting with assessment: A developmental approach to deaf children's literacy.* Washington, DC: Pre-College National Mission Programs, Gallaudet University.

Frey, R. M., & Kolstoe, O. P. (1965). *A high school work-study program for mentally subnormal students.* Carbondale, IL: Southern Illinois University Press.

Friend, M., & Bursuck, W. D. (2002). *Including students with special needs: A practical guide for classroom teachers* (3rd ed.). Boston: Allyn & Bacon.

Friend, M., & Bursuck, W. D. (2006). *Including students with special needs: A practical guide for classroom teachers* (4th ed.). Boston: Allyn & Bacon.

Friend, M., & Cook, L. (1990). Collaboration as a predictor for success in school reform. *Journal of Educational and Psychological Consultation, 1,* 69-86.

Fujiura, G. T., & Yamaki, K. (1997). Analysis of ethnic variations in developmental disability prevalence and household economic status. *Mental Retardation, 35,* 286-294.

Gajar, A. (1998). Post-secondary education. In F. R. Rusch & J. G. Chadsey (Eds.), *Beyond high school: Transition from school to work* (pp. 383-405). Belmont, CA: Wadsworth.

Gajar, A., Goodman, L., & McAfee, J. (1993). *Secondary schools and beyond: Transition of individuals with mild disabilities.* Upper Saddle River, NJ: Merrill/Prentice Hall.

Gallivan-Fenlon, A. (1994). "Their senior year": Family and service provider perspectives on the transition from school to adult life for young adults with disabilities. *Journal of the Association for Persons with Severe Handicaps, 19*(1), 11-23.

Garcia, E. (2002). *Student cultural diversity: Understanding and meeting the challenge* (3rd ed.). Boston: Houghton Mifflin.

Garcia, S. B., & Yates, J. R. (1986). Policy issues associated with serving bilingual exceptional children. In A. C. Willing & H. F. Greenberg (Eds.), *Bilingualism and learning disabilities: Policy and practice for teachers and administrators* (pp. 113-134). New York: American Library Publishing.

Gartin, B. C., Rumrill, P., & Serebreni, R. (1996). The higher education transition model: Guidelines for facilitating college transition among college-bound students with disabilities. *Teaching Exceptional Children, 29*(1), 30-33.

Gartner, A., & Lipsky, D. K. (1987). Beyond special education: Toward a quality system for all students. *Harvard Educational Review, 57,* 367-395.

Gaylord-Ross, R., & Browder, D. (1991). Functional assessment: Dynamic and domain properties. In L. Meyer, C. Peck, & L. Brown (Eds.), *Critical issues in the lives of people with severe disabilities* (pp. 45-66). Baltimore: Paul H. Brookes.

Gerber, P. J., Ginsberg, R., & Reiff, H. B. (1992). Identifying alterable patterns in employment success for highly successful adults with learning disabilities. *Journal of Learning Disabilities, 25,* 475-487.

Gerber, P. J., Reiff, H. B., & Ginsberg, R. (1994). Critical incidents of highly successful adults with learning disabilities. *The Journal of Vocational Rehabilitation, 4*(2), 105-112.

German, S., Martin, J. E., Huber Marshall, L., & Sale, R. P. (2000). Promoting self-determination: Teaching goal attainment with the *Take Action* process. *Career Development for Exceptional Individuals, 23,* 27-38.

Getzel, E., Emanuel, E. J., Fesko, S., & Parent, W. (2000). *Factors that inhibit and facilitate transition-age youth in ac-*

cessing and using SSI work incentives: Implications for policy, research, and practice. Paper presented at Annual Project Directors' Meeting, National Transition Alliance for Youth with Disabilities, Washington, DC.

Getzel, E., Stodden, R., & Briel, L. (2000). Pursuing postsecondary educational opportunities for individuals with disabilities. In Wehman, P. (Ed.), *Life beyond the classroom: Transition strategies for young people with disabilities* (3rd ed., pp. 247–259). Baltimore: Paul H. Brookes.

Getzel, E. E., & Kregel, J. (1996). Transitioning from the academic to the employment setting: The employment connection program. *Journal of Vocational Rehabilitation, 6,* 273–287.

Ghilani, M. E. (2005). *Web-based career counseling: A guide to Internet resources for researching a career and choosing a major.* Scranton, PA: University of Scranton.

Gill, D., & Edgar, E. (1990). Outcomes of vocational programs designed for students with mild disabilities: The Pierce County Vocational Special Education Cooperative. *Journal for Vocational Special Needs Education, 12*(3), 17–22.

Gillingham, M. G., & Topper, A. (1999). Technology in teacher preparation: Preparing teachers for the future. *Journal of Technology and Teacher Education, 7,* 303–321.

Gilmore, D., & Butterworth, J. (1996). *Work status trends for people with mental retardation.* Boston: Institute for Community Inclusion.

Gliedman, J., & Roth, W. (1980). *The unexpected minority: Handicapped children in America.* New York: Carnegie Council on Children.

Goals 2000: Educate America Act of 1994, 20 U.S.C.S. § 5801 *et seq.*

Goldberg, R. J., Higgins, E. L., Raskind, M. H., & Herman, K. L. (2003). Predictors of success in individuals with learning disabilities: A qualitative analysis of a 20-year longitudinal study. *Learning Disabilities Research & Practice, 18,* 222–236.

Goldman, H. H., & Mandershied, R. W. (1987). The epidemiology of psychiatric disabilities. In A. T. Meyerson & T. Fine (Eds.), *Psychiatric disability: Clinical, legal, and administrative dimensions* (pp. 13–21). Washington, DC: American Psychiatric Association Press.

Goode, D. (1990). Thinking about and discussing quality of life. In R. Schalock & M. Begab (Eds.), *Quality of life: Perspectives and issues* (pp. 41–58). Washington, DC: American Association on Mental Retardation.

Granger, M. (1996, March 22). Accommodating employees with disabilities: A matter of attitude. *Journal of Managerial Issues, 8*(14), 78.

Gray, A. (1997). Modeling transcultural leadership for transformational change. *The Journal for Vocational Special Needs Education, 19,* 78–84.

Gray, K. (1996). The baccalaureate game: Is it right for all teens? *Phi Delta Kappan, 77*(8), 528–534.

Gray, K. (2002). *The role of career and technical education in the American high school: A student centered analysis.* Washington, DC: U.S. Department of Education.

Grayson T. E. (1998). *Dropout prevention and special services.* In F. R. Rusch & J. G. Chadsey (Eds.), *Beyond high school: Transition from school to work* (pp. 77–98). New York: Wadsworth.

Green, J. W. (1999). *Cultural awareness in the human services: A multi-ethnic approach.* Boston: Allyn & Bacon.

Greenberg, H. F. (1986). Preface. In A. C. Willing & H. F. Greenberg (Eds.), *Bilingualism and learning disabilities: Policy and practice for teachers and administrators* (pp. xv–xvi). New York: American Library.

Greenberger, E. & Steinberg, L. (1986). *When teenagers work: The psychological and social costs of adolescent employment.* New York: Basic Books.

Greene, G. (1996). Empowering culturally and linguistically diverse families in the transition planning process. *The Journal for Vocational Special Needs Education, 19,* 26–30.

Greene, G. (2003). Best practices in transition. In G. Greene & C. A. Kochar-Bryant (Eds.), *Pathways to successful transition for youth with disabilities* (pp. 154–196). Upper Saddle River, NJ: Merrill/Prentice Hall.

Greene, G. (2003). Transition pathways. In G. Greene & C. A. Kochhar-Bryant (Eds.) *Pathways to successful transition for youth with disabilities.* (pp. 199–229). Columbus, Ohio: Merrill/Prentice-Hall.

Greene, G., & Kochhar-Bryant, C. A. (2003). *Pathways to successful transition for youth with disabilities.* Columbus, OH: Merrill.

Greenfield, P. M. (1994). Independence and interdependence as developmental scripts: Implications for theory, research, and practice. In P. M. Greenfield & R. R. Cocking (Eds.), *Cross-cultural roots of minority child development* (pp. 1–37). Hillsdale, NJ: Erlbaum.

Griffin, C., & Hammis, D. (2001). Self-employment as the logical descendant of supported employment. In P. Wehman (Ed.), *Supported employment in business: Expanding the capacity of workers with disabilities* (pp. 251–268). St. Augustine, Fl: Training Resource Network.

Griffin, C., & Targett, P. (2001). Finding jobs for young people with disabilities. In P. Wehman (Ed.), *Life beyond the classroom: Transition strategies for young people with disabilities* (pp. 247–260). Baltimore: Paul H. Brookes.

Grigal, M., Test, D. W., Beattie, J., & Wood, W. M. (1997). An evaluation of transition components of individualized education programs. *Exceptional Children, 63*(3), 357–372.

Gunning, T. G. (2003). *Creating literacy instruction for all children* (4th ed.). Boston: Allyn & Bacon.

Hagen, J. L. (1998). Jobs and case management development in 10 states. *Social Work, 39,* 197–204.

Hagner, D., & Dileo, D. (1993). *Working together: Workplace culture, supported employment, and persons with disabilities.* Cambridge, MA: Brookline Books.

Hagner, D., & Vander-Sande, J. (1998). School sponsored work experience and vocational instruction. In F. R. Rusch & J. G. Chadsey (Eds.), *Beyond high school: Transition from school to work* (pp. 340–366). Belmont, CA: Wadsworth.

Hagner, D., Fesko, S., Cadigan, M., Kiernan, W., & Butterworth, J. (1996). Securing employment: Job search and employer negotiation strategies in rehabilitation. In E. M. Szymanski & R. M. Parker (Eds.), *Work and disability: Issues and strategies in career development and job placement* (pp. 309–340). Austin, TX: PRO-ED.

Hagner, D., Helm, D., & Butterworth, J. (1996). "This is your meeting": A qualitative study of person-centered planning. *Mental Retardation, 34,* 159–171.

Hagner, D., Rogan, P., & Murphy, S. (1992). Facilitating natural supports in the workplace: Strategies for support consultants. *Journal of Rehabilitation, 58,* 29–34.

Hall, M., Kleinert, H., & Kearns, J. F. (2000). Going to college: Post-secondary programs for students with moderate and severe disabilities. *Teaching Exceptional Children, 32*(3), 58–65.

Halloran, W. D. (1993). Transition services requirement: Issues, implications, challenge. In R. C. Eaves & P. J. McLaughlin (Eds.), *Recent advances in special education and rehabilitation* (pp. 210–224). Boston: Andover Medical Publishers.

Halpern, A. S. (1985). Transition: A look at the foundations. *Exceptional Children, 51,* 479–502.

Halpern, A. S. (1990). A methodological review of follow-up and follow-along studies tracking post-school leavers of special education. *Career Development for Exceptional Individuals, 13,* 13–27.

Halpern, A. S. (1992). Transition: Old wine in new bottles. *Exceptional Children, 58*(3), 202–211.

Halpern, A. S. (1993). Quality of Life as a framework for evaluating transition outcomes. *Exceptional Children, 59.*

Halpern, A. S. (1994). The transition of youth with disabilities to adult life: A position statement of the Division on Career Development and Transition, The Council for Exceptional Children. *Career Development of Exceptional Individuals, 17*(2), 115–124.

Halpern, A. S. (1996). *Transition skills inventory.* Eugene, OR: Secondary Transition Program College of Education, University of Oregon.

Halpern, A. S., & Benz, M. R. (1987). A statewide examination of secondary special education for students with mild disabilities: Implications for the high school curriculum. *Exceptional Children, 54*(2), 122–129.

Halpern, A. S., Benz, M. R., & Lindstrom, L. E. (1992). A systems change approach to improving secondary special education and transition programs at the community level. *Career Development for Exceptional Individuals, 15*(1), 109–120.

Halpern, A. S., Doren, B., & Benz, M. R. (1993). Job experiences of students with disabilities during their last two years in school. *Career Development for Exceptional Individuals, 16*(1), 63–73.

Halpern, A. S., & Fuhrer, M. J. (Eds.). (1984). *Functional assessment in rehabilitation.* Baltimore: Paul H. Brookes.

Halpern, A. S., Herr, C. M., Wolf, N. K., Lawson, J. D., Doren, B., & Johnson, M. D. (1997). *Next S.T.E.P.: Student transition and education.* Austin, TX: PRO-ED.

Halpern, A. S., & Irvin, L. (1986). *Social and prevocational information battery-revised.* Monterey, CA: CTB McGraw-Hill.

Halpern, A. S., Irvin, L., & Landman, J. (n.d.). *Tests for everyday living.* Monterey, CA: CTB/McGraw-Hill.

Halpern, A. S., Lehmann, J., Irvin, L., & Heiry, T. (1982). *Contemporary assessment for mentally retarded adolescents and adults.* Baltimore: University Park.

Halpern, A. S., Yavonoff, P., Doren, B., & Benz, M. R. (1995). Predicting participation in postsecondary education for school leavers with disabilities. *Career Development for Exceptional Individuals, 62*(2), 151–164.

Hamburg, D. (1993). The opportunities of early adolescence. *Teachers College Record, 94,* 468.

Hammond, J., & Morrison, J. (1996). *The stuff Americans are made of.* New York: Macmillan.

Hamre-Nietupski, S., Krajewski, L., Nietupski, J., Ostercamp, D., Sensor, K., & Opheim, B. (1988). Parent/professional partnerships in advocacy: Developing integrated options within resistive systems. *Journal of the Association for Persons with Severe Handicaps, 13*(4), 251–259.

Hanley-Maxwell, C., & Collet-Klingenberg, L. (1994). *Synthesis in design of effective curricular practices in transition from school to the community.* Available: *http://darkwing. uoregan.edu/_ncite/otherRsc/research.html*

Hanley-Maxwell, C., & Szymanski, E. M. (1992). School-to-work transition and supported employment. In R. M. Parker & E. M. Szymanski (Eds.), *Rehabilitation counseling: Basics and beyond* (pp. 135–164). Austin, TX: PRO-ED.

Hanley-Maxwell, C. Pogoloff, S. M. & Whitney-Thomas J. (1998). Families: The heart of transition. In F. R. Rusch & J. G. Chadsey (Eds.), *Beyond high school: Transition from school to work* (pp. 234–264). New York: Wadsworth.

Hanley-Maxwell, C., Szymanski, E., & Owens-Johnson, L. (1998). School-to-adult life transition and supported employment. In E. M. Szymanski & R. M. Parker (Eds.), *Rehabilitation counseling: Basics and beyond* (3rd ed., pp. 143–179). Austin, TX: PRO-ED.

Hanson, M. J. (1998a). Ethnic, cultural, and language diversity in intervention settings. In E. W. Lynch & M. H. Hanson (Eds.), *Developing cross-cultural competence: A guide for working with children and their families* (2nd ed., pp. 3–22). Baltimore: Paul H. Brookes.

Hanson, M. J. (1998b). Families with Native American roots. In E. W. Lynch & M. H. Hanson (Eds.), *Developing cross-cultural competence: A guide for working with children and their families* (2nd ed., pp. 93–126). Baltimore: Paul H. Brookes.

Hanson, M. J., & Carta, J. J. (1996). Addressing the challenges of families with multiple risks. *Exceptional Children, 62,* 201–212.

Haring, K. A., Lovett, D. L., & Smith, D. D. (1990). A follow-up study of recent special education graduates of learning disabilities programs. *Journal of Learning Disabilities, 23*(2), 108–113.

Harmon, L. W. (1996). A moving target: The widening gap between theory and practice. In M. L. Savickas & W. B. Walsh (Eds.), *Handbook of career counseling theory and practice* (pp. 37–44). Palo Alto, CA: Davies-Black.

Harmon, L. W., Hansen, J. C., Borgen, F. H., & Hammer, A. L. (1994). *Applications and technical guide for the Strong Interest Inventory.* Palo Alto, CA: Consulting Psychologists Press.

Harrington, T. F. (2003). Career development theory. In T. F. Harringon (Ed.), *Handbook of career planning for students with special needs* (3rd ed., pp. 3–44). Austin, TX: Pro-Ed.

Harris, L., & Associates, Inc. (1986). *The ICD survey of disabled Americans: Bringing disabled Americans into the mainstream.* New York: Author.

Harris, L. & Associates, Inc. (1994). N.O.D./Harris survey of Americans with disabilities (Study No. 942003). New York: Author.

Harris, L., & Associates, Inc. (2001). *N.O.D./Harris survey of Americans with disabilities.* New York: Author.

Harry, B. (1992a). *Cultural diversity, families, and the special education system: Communication and empowerment.* New York: Teachers College Press.

Harry, B. (1992b). Making sense of disability: Low-income, Puerto Rican parents' theories of the problem. *Exceptional Children, 59,* 27–40.

Harry, B. (1992c). Restructuring the participation of African-American parents in special education. *Exceptional Children, 59,* 123–131.

Harry, B. (2002). Trends and issues in serving culturally diverse families of children with disabilities. *The Journal of Special Education, 36,* 131–138, 147.

Harry, B., Grenot-Scheyer, M., Smith-Lewis, M., Park, H., Xin, F. & Schwartz, I. (1995). Developing culturally inclusive services for individuals with severe disabilities. *The Journal of the Association for Persons with Severe Handicaps, 20,* 99–109.

Harry, B., & Klingner, J. (2006). *Why are so many minority students in special education? Understanding race and disability in schools.* New York: Teachers College, Columbia University.

Hart, D., Mele-McCarthy, J., Pasternak, R. H., Zimbrich, K., & Parker, D. R. (2004). Community college: A pathway to success for youth with learning, cognitive, and intellectual disabilities in secondary settings. *Education and Training in Developmental Disabilities, 39,* 54–67.

Hasazi, S. B., Furney, K. S., & DeStefano, L. (1999). Implementing the IDEA transition mandates. *Exceptional Children, 65*(4), 555–566.

Hasazi, S. B., Gordon, L. R., & Roe, C. A. (1985). Factors associated with the employment status of handicapped youth exiting high school from 1979 to 1983. *Exceptional Children, 51,* 455–469.

Hayden, M. F., & Goldman, J. (1996). Families of adults with mental retardation: Stress levels and need for services. *Social Work, 41*(6), 657–667.

Heal, L. W., Copher, J. I., Destefano, L. D., & Rusch, F. R. (1989). A comparison of successful and unsuccessful placements of secondary students with mental handicaps into competitive employment, *Career Development for Exceptional Individuals, 12*(2), 167–177.

Heal, L. W., Copher, J. I., & Rusch, F. R. (1990). Interagency agreements (IAA's) among agencies responsible for the transition education of students with handicaps from secondary schools to post-school setting. *Career Development for Exceptional Children, 13*(2), 121–127.

Heal, L. W., Gonzalez, P., Rusch, F. R., Copher, J. I., & DeStefano, L. (1990). A comparison of successful and unsuccessful placements of youths with mental handicaps into competitive employment. *Exceptionality, 1*(3), 181–196.

HEATH Resource Center. (1995). *Getting ready for college: Advising high school students with learning disabilities.* Washington, DC: American Council on Education, U.S. Department of Education.

HEATH Resource Center. (1996). Vast spaces and stone walls: Overcoming barriers to postsecondary education for rural students with disabilities. *Information from HEATH, 15*(2-3), 1–4.

HEATH Resource Center. (1997). *How to choose a college: Guide for the student with a disability.* Washington, DC: American Council on Education, U.S. Department of Education.

HEATH Resource Center. (2003, May). *Summer pre-college programs for students with disabilities* 2003. Retrieved May 22, 2003, from *http://www.heath.gwu.edu/SummerPreCollege.htm*

Heaven, P. C. L. (2001). *The social psychology of adolescence.* (2nd ed.). New York: Palgrave.

Helge, D. I. (1984a). The state of the art of rural special education. *Exceptional Children, 50,* 294–305.

Helge, D. I. (1984b). Models for serving rural students with low-incidence handicapping conditions. *Exceptional Children, 50,* 313–324.

Henderson, C. (1995). *College freshman with disabilities: A statistical profile.* Washington, DC: HEATH Resource Center, American Council on Education, U. S. Department of Education.

Henn, J., & Henn, M. (2005). Defying the odds: You can't put a square peg in a round hole no matter how hard you try. *Journal of Vocational Rehabilitation, 22,* 129–130.

Herr, E. L. (1996). Toward the convergence of career theory and practice: Mythology, issues, and possibilities. In M. L. Savickas & W. B. Walsh (Eds.), *Handbook of career counseling theory and practice* (pp. 13–35). Palo Alto, CA: Davies-Black.

Herr, E. L., & Cramer, S. H. (1992). *Career guidance and counseling through the lifespan: Systematic approaches* (4th ed.). New York: HarperCollins.

Herr, E. L., Rayman, J. R., & Garis, J. W. (1993). *Handbook for the college and university career center.* Westport, CT: Greenwood Press.

Hershenson, D. B., & Szymanski, E. M. (1992). Career development of people with disabilities. In R. M. Parker & E. M. Szymanski (Eds.), *Rehabilitation counseling: Basics and beyond* (2nd ed., pp. 273–303). Austin, TX: PRO-ED.

Heyward, S. M. (1996). *Frequently asked questions: Postsecondary education and disability.* Cambridge, MA: Heyward, Lawton & Associates.

Hitchcock, C. (2001). *Balanced instructional support and challenge in universally designed learning environments.* OSEP Futures Paper, Project Director's Meeting, Washington, D.C.

Hitchcock, C., Meyer, A., Rose, D., & Jackson, R. (2002). Providing new access to the general curriculum: Universal design for learning. *Teaching Exceptional Children, 35*(2) 8–17.

Hobbs, N. (1975). *The futures of children: Categories, labels, and their consequences: Report of the project on classification of exceptional children.* San Francisco: Jossey-Bass.

Hobbs, T., & Westling, D. L. (1998). Promoting successful inclusion through collaborative problem-solving. *Teaching Exceptional Children, 31,* 12–19.

Hodge, M. & Draine, J. (1993). Case management. In R. W. Flexer and P. Soloman, (Eds.) *Psychiatric rehabilitation in practice.* Boston: Andover medical.

Hoffman, A., Field, S., & Sawilowsky, S. (1996). *Self-determination knowledge scale.* Austin, TX: PRO-ED.

Holburn, S., & Vietze, P. (1998). Has person-centered planning become the alchemy of developmental disabilities? *Mental Retardation, 36*(6), 485–488.

Holburn, S., & Vietze, P. M. (2002). *Person-centered planning: Research, practice, and future directions.* Baltimore: Paul H. Brookes.

Holder-Brown, L., & Parette, H. P. (1992). Children with disabilities who use assistive technology: Ethical considerations. *Young Children 47*(6), 73–77.

Holland, J. L. (1985a). *Making vocational choices: A theory of vocational personalities and work environments.* Upper Saddle River, NJ: Prentice Hall.

Holland, J. L. (1985b). *Manual for vocational preference inventory.* Odessa, FL: Psychological Assessment Resources.

Holland, J. L. (1992). *Making vocational choices: A theory of vocational personalities and work environments* (3rd ed.). Odessa, FL: Psychological Assessment Resources.

Holland, J. L. (1996). Integrating career theory and practice: The current situation and some potential remedies. In M. L. Savickas & W. B. Walsh (Eds.), *Handbook of career counseling theory and practice* (pp. 1–11). Palo Alto, CA: Davies-Black.

Holland, J. L., Fritzche, B. A., & Powell, A. B. (1994). *Self-directed search technical manual.* Odessa, FL: Psychological Assessment Resources.

Home of Your Own Project. (1995). *Extending the American dream: Home ownership through creative financing.* Durham, NH: University of New Hampshire, Institute on Disability.

Homstem, B. (1997). How the religious community can support the transition to adulthood: A parent's perspective. *Mental Retardation, 35,* 485–487.

Hoye, J. D. (1998, July). *Integrating school-to-work into preservice teacher education.* Paper presented at Conference for Professors of Education in Ohio, Kent, OH.

Hoyt, K. B. (1975). *Career education: Contributions to an evolving concept.* Salt Lake City, UT: Olympus.

Hoyt, K. B. (1977). *A primer for career education.* Washington, DC: U.S. Government Printing Office.

HSRI (Human Services Research Institute). (1991). *New models for the provision of personal assistance services: Final report.* Bethesda, MD: Human Services Research Institute.

Huber Marshall, L. H., Martin, J. E., Hughes, C., Jerman, P., & Maxson, L. (1997). *Choosing personal goals.* Longmont, CO: Sopris West.

Huber Marshall, L. H., Martin, J. E., Maxson, L., Hughes, W., Miller, T. L., McGill, T., & Jerman, P. (1996). *Take action: Making goals happen.* Longmont, CO: Sopris West.

Huber Marshall, L. H., Martin, J. E., Maxson, L., & Jerman, P. (1997). *Choosing employment goals.* Longmont, CO: Sopris West.

Hudson, P. J., Schwartz, S. E., Sealander, K. A., Campbell, P., & Hensel, J. W. (1988). Successfully employed adults with handicaps: Characteristics and transition strategies. *Career Development for Exceptional Individuals, 11*(1), 7–14.

Hughes, C., & Carter, E. W. (2002). Informal assessment procedures. In C. L. Sax & C. A. Thoma (Eds.), *Transition assessment: Wise practices for quality lives* (pp. 51–69). Baltimore: Paul H. Brookes.

Hughes, C., & Kim, J. (1998). Supporting the transition from school to adult life. In F. Rusch & J. Chadsey, *Beyond high school: Transition from school to work* (pp. 367–380). Belmont, CA: Wadsworth.

Hughes, Catherine, Bailey Thomas, & Mechur Melinda (2001). *School to work: Making a difference in education.* New York: Institute on Education and the Economy, Teachers College, Columbia University.

Individuals with Disabilities Education Act Amendments of 1997, 20 U.S.C. §1400 *et seq.*

Individuals with Disabilities Education Act Amendments of 1997, Pub. L. No. 105-17, 105th Cong., 1st sess.

Individuals with Disabilities Education Act of 1990, 20 U.S.C. §1400 et seq.

Individuals with Disabilities Education Act Regulations, 34 C.F.R. § 300.533 *et seq.* (1997).

Individuals with Disabilities Education Improvement Act of 2004, 20 U.S.C. § 1400 *et esq.* (2004) (reauthorization of Individuals with Disabilities Act of 1990).

Inge, K. J., & Shepherd, J. (1995). Assistive technology applications and strategies for school system personnel. In K. F. Flippo, K. J. Inge, & J. M. Barcus (Eds.), *Assistive technology: A resource for school, work, and community* (pp. 133–166). Baltimore, MD: Paul H. Brookes.

Intagliata, J. & Baker, F. (1983). Factors affecting case management for the chronically mentally ill. *Administration in Mental Health, 11,* 73–91.

International Survey of Faculty Attitudes. (1994, June 9). *The Chronicle of Higher Education,* pp. A35–A38.

Iowa Department of Education. (1998). *School to adult life: Working together towards successful transition.* Des Moines, IA: Author.

Iowa Department of Education, Division of Early Childhood, Elementary, and Secondary Education. (1998). *Working together towards successful transition: School to adult life.* Des Moines, IA: Author.

Ippoliti, C., Peppey, B., & Depoy, E. (1994). Promoting self-determination for persons with developmental disabilities. *Disability & Society* (9), 453–460.

Izzo, M. V., Cartledge, G., Miller, L., Growick, B., & Rutkowski, S. (2000). Increasing employment earnings: Extended transition services that make a difference. *Career Development for Exceptional Children, 23*(2), 139–156.

Janesick, V. J. (1995). Our multicultural society. In E. L. Meyen & T. M. Skrtic (Eds.), *Special education and student disability, an introduction: Traditional, emerging, and alternative perspectives* (4th ed., pp. 713–728). Denver, CO: Love.

Jansma, P. & French, R. (1994). *Special physical education: Physical activity sports & recreation.* Englewood Cliffs, NJ: Prentice-Hall.

Jarrow, J. (1992). *Title by title: The ADA's impact on postsecondary education.* Columbus, OH: Association on Higher Education and Disability (AHEAD).

Jayanthi, M., & Friend, M. (1992). Interpersonal problem-solving: A selected literature review to guide practice. *Journal of Educational and Psychological Consultation, 3,* 147–152.

Job Accommodation Network. (1995). *Accommodation benefit/cost data summary.* West Virginia University, Morgantown, WV: Author.

Joe, J. R., & Malach, R. S. (1998). Families with Native American roots. In E. W. Lynch & M. H. Hanson (Eds.), *Developing cross-cultural competence: A guide for working with children and their families* (2nd ed., pp. 127–164). Baltimore: Paul H. Brookes.

Johnson, D., Bruininks, R., & Thurlow, M. (1987). Meeting the challenge of transition service planning through improved interagency cooperation. *Exceptional Children, 53*(6), 522–530.

Johnson, D., & Guy, B. (1997). Implications of lessons learned from a state systems change initiative on transition for youth with disabilities. *Career Development for Exceptional Individuals, 20*(2), 191–200.

Johnson, D. R. (2005). Key provisions on transition: A comparison of IDEA 1997 and IDEA 2004. *Career Development for Exceptional Individuals, 28,* 60–63.

Johnson, D. R., McGrew, K. S., Bloomberg, L., Bruininks, R. H., & Lin, H. C. (1997). Results of a national follow-up study of young adults with severe disabilities. *Journal of Vocational Rehabilitation, 8,* 119–133.

Johnson, D. R., Sharpe, M., & Sinclair, M. F. (1998). *Report on the national survey of the implementation of the IDEA transition requirements.* Minneapolis: National Transition Network, Institute on Community Integration, University of Minnesota.

Johnson, D. R., Stodden, R. A., Emanuel, E. J., Luecking, R., & Mack, M. (2002). Current challenges facing secondary education and transition services: What research tells us. *Exceptional Children, 68*(4), 519–531.

Johnson, J. & Rusch, F. (1993). Secondary special education and transition services: Identification and recommendations for future research and demonstration. *Career Development for Exceptional Individuals, 16*(1), 1–18.

Judge, S. (2002). Family-centered assistive technology assessment and intervention practices for early intervention. *Infants and Young Children, 15*(1), 60–68.

Karvonen, M., Test, D. W., Wood, W. M., Browder, D., & Algozzine, B. (2004). Putting self-determination into practice. *Exceptional Children, 71*(1), 23–41.

Kauffman, J. M. (1998). Are we all postmodernists now? *Behavioral Disorders, 23,* 149–152.

Kauffman, J. M. (1999). The role of science in behavioral disorders. *Behavioral Disorders, 24,* 265–272.

Kazdin, A. E. (1989). *Behavior modification in applied settings* (4th ed.). Pacific Grove, CA: Brooks/Cole.

Kazis, R., & Liebowitz, M. (2003). *Instructional innovations that help low-income students succeed in community college,* Manpower Demonstration Research Corporation (MDRC). Retrieved August 4, 2006, from www.mdrc.org

Keitel, M. A., Kopala, M., & Adamson, W. S. (1996). Ethical issues in multicultural assessment. In L. A. Suzuki, P. J. Meller, & J. G. Ponterotto (Eds.), *Handbook of multicultural assessment* (pp. 29–48). San Francisco: Jossey-Bass.

Kezar, A. (1997a). At the fork in the path: Some guidance from the research. *The ERIC review: The path to college, 5*(3), 26–29.

Kezar, A. (1997b). How colleges are changing. *The ERIC review: The path to college, 5*(3), 29–32.

Khattri, N., Riley, K., & Kane, M. (1997). Students at risk in poor, rural areas: A review of the research. *Journal of Research in Rural Education, 13*(2), 79–100.

Kim, V., & Choi, S. H. (1994). Individualism, collectivism, and child development. In P. M. Greenfield & R. R. Cocking (Eds.), *Cross-cultural roots of minority child development* (pp. 226–257). Hillsdale, NJ: Erlbaum.

Kleinert, H. L., Kearns, F. K., & Kennedy, S. (1997). Accountability for all students: Kentucky's alternate portfolio assessment for students with moderate and severe cognitive disabilities. *Journal of Association for Persons with Severe Disabilities, 22*(2), 88–101.

Knoll, J. & Ford, A. (1987). Beyond caregiving: A reconceptualization of the role of the residential service provider. In S. J. Taylor, D. Biklen, & J. A. Knoll (Eds.), *Community integration for people with severe disabilities* (pp. 129–146). New York: Teachers' College Press.

Knoll, J. A., & Wheeler, C. B. (2005). My home and community: Developing supports for adult living. In Flexer, R. W., Simmons, T. J., Luft, P., & Baer, R. M. (Eds.), *Transition planning for seconding students with disabilities* (pp. 424–459). Upper Saddle River, NJ: Merrill/Prentice Hall.

Knopp, L., & Otuya, E. (1995). Who is teaching America's school children? *Research Briefs, 6,* 1-13.

Knowlton, H., Turnbull, D. R., Backus, L., & Turnbull, H. R. (1988). Letting go: Consent and the yes but … "problem in transition." In B. L. Ludlow, A. P. Turnbull, & R. Luckasson (Eds.), *Transitions to adult life for people with mental retardation* (pp. 45-66). Baltimore: Paul H. Brookes.

Koch, L., & Johnston-Rodriguez, S. (1997). The career portfolio: A vocational rehabilitation tool for assessment, planning, and placement. *Journal of Job Placement, 13*(1), 19-22.

Koch, L. C., & Rumrill, P. D. (1998a). Interpersonal communication skills for case managers. *Healthcare and rehabilitation managers' desk reference.* Lake Zurich, IL: Vocational Consultants Press.

Koch, L. C., & Rumrill, P. D. (1998b). The working alliance: An interdisciplinary case management strategy for health professionals. *Work, 10,* 55-62.

Kochany, L., & Keller, J. (1981). An analysis and evaluation of the failures of severely disabled individuals in competitive employment. In P. Wehman (Ed.), *Competitive employment: New horizons for severely disabled individuals* (pp. 181-198). Baltimore: Paul H. Brookes.

Kochar-Bryant, C. A. (2003). Coordinating systems and agencies for successful transition. In Greene, G. & Kochar-Bryant, C.A. (Eds.), *Pathways to successful transition for youth with disabilities* (pp. 109-152). Upper Saddle River, NJ: Merrill/Prentice Hall.

Kochhar-Bryant, C. A., & Deschamps, A. B. (1992). Policy crossroads in preserving the right of passage to independence for learners with special needs: Implications of current change in national vocational and special education policies. *Journal for Vocational Special Needs Education, 14*(2-3), 9-19.

Kochhar-Bryant, C. A., & West, L. L. (1995). Future directions for federal legislation affecting transition services for individuals with special needs. *Journal for Vocational Special Needs Education, 17*(3), 85-93.

Kohler, P. D. (1993). Best practices in transition: Substantiated or implied? *Career Development for Exceptional Individuals, 16,* 107-121.

Kohler, P. D. (1996). Preparing youths with disabilities for future challenges: A taxonomy for transition planning. In P. D. Kohler (Ed.), *Taxonomy for transition planning: Linking research and practice* (pp. 1-62). Champaign, IL: Transition Research Institute at Illinois, University of Illinois at Urbana-Champaign [Monograph].

Kohler, P. D. (1998). Implementing a transition perspective of education: A comprehensive approach to planning and delivering secondary education and transition services. In F. R. Rusch & J. G. Chadsey (Eds.), *Beyond high school: Transition from school to work* (pp. 179-205). New York: Wadsworth.

Kohler, P. D., DeStefano, L., Wermuth, T., Grayson, T., & McGinty, S. (1994). An analysis of exemplary transition programs: How and why are they selected? *Career Development for Exceptional Individuals, 17*(2), 187-202.

Kokaska, C., & Brolin, D. E. (1985). *Career education for handicapped individuals* (2nd ed.). Columbus, OH: Merrill.

Kolstoe, O. P., & Frey, R. M. (1965). *A high school work study program for mentally subnormal students.* Carbondale, IL: Southern Illinois University Press.

Konrad, M., Fowler, C. H., Walker, A. R., Test, D. W., & Wood, W. M. (2005). *Effects of self-determination interventions on the academic skills of students with learning disabilities.* Manuscript submitted for publication.

Kortering, L. J., & Edgar, E. B. (1988). Vocational rehabilitation and special education: A need for cooperation. *Rehabilitation Counseling Bulletin, 3*(3), 178-184.

Kozol, J. (1996). Amazing grace: The lives of children and the conscience of a nation. New York: Harper Perennial.

Kregel, J., & Unger, D. (1993). Employer perceptions of the work potential of individuals with disabilities: An illustration from supported employment. *Journal of Vocational Rehabilitation. 3*(4). 17-25.

Kregel, J., Wehman, P., & Banks, P. D. (1989). The effects of consumer characteristics and type of employment model on individual outcomes in supported employment. *Journal of Applied Behavior Analysis, 22,* 407-415.

Kregel, J., Wehman, P., Seyfarth, J., & Marshall, K. (1986). Community integration of young adults with mental retardation: Transition from school to adulthood. *Education and Training of the Mentally Retarded, 21,* 35-42.

Kreiner, J.L. (2005) Development of a vocabulary-free leisure assessment instrument for individuals with severe developmental disabilities and communication difficulties. Unpublished doctoral dissertation, Kent State University, Kent Ohio.

Krom, D. M. & Prater, M. A. (1993). IEP goals for intermediate aged students with mild mental retardation. *Career Development for Exceptional Individuals, 16*(1), 87-95.

Krouse, J. & Sabousky, R. (2001). Curriculum development and transition. In Robert W. Flexer, Thomas J. Simmons, Pamela Luft, & Robert M. Baer, *Transition planning for secondary students with disabilities* (pp. 227-246). Columbus, OH: Merrill.

Krumboltz, J. D. (1996). A learning theory of career counseling. In M. L. Savickas & W. B. Walsh (Eds.), *Handbook of career counseling theory and practice* (pp. 55-80). Palo Alto, CA: Davies-Black.

Lahm, E. A, & Sizemore, L. (2002). Factors that influence assistive technology decision making. *Journal of Special Education Technology, 17*(1), 15-25.

Lai, Y., & Ishiyama, F. I. (2004). Involvement of immigrant chinese canadian mothers of children with disabilities. *Exceptional Children, 71,* 97-108.

Lakin, K., Hill, B., White, C., & Write, E. (1988). *Longitudinal change and interstate variability in the size of residential facilities for persons with mental retarda-*

tion. Minneapolis, MN: Center on Residential and Community Services, University of Minnesota.

LaPlante, M. P., Kennedy, J., Kaye, S. H., & Wenger, B. L. (1997). Disability and employment. *Disability statistics abstract, 11,* San Francisco: Disability Statistics Rehabilitation Research and Training Center, University of California.

Lareau, A. (1989). *Home advantage: Social class and parental intervention in elementary education.* London: Falmer Press.

Lawn, B., & Meyerson, A. T. (1995). A modern perspective on psychiatry in rehabilitation. In R. W. Flexer & P. L. Solomon (Eds.), *Psychiatric rehabilitation in practice.* (pp. 31–44). Boston, MA: Andover Publishers.

Leake, D. W., & Black, R. S. (2005, November/December). Implications of individualism and collectivism for the transition of youth with significant disabilities. *TASH Connections,* 12–16.

Leake, D., & Stodden, B. (1994). Getting to the core of transition: A re-assessment of old wine in new bottles. *Career Development for Exceptional Individuals, 17*(1), 65–76.

LeConte, P. (1986). Vocational assessment of special needs learners: A vocational education perspective. Paper presented at Annual meeting of American Vocational Association in Atlanta, GA.

Lehmann, J. P., Bassett, D. S., & Sands, D. J. (1999). Students' participation in transition-related actions: A qualitative study. *Remedial and Special Education, 20,* 160–169.

Lent, R. W., Brown, S. D., & Hackett, G. (2002). Social cognitive career theory. In D. Brown and Associates (Eds.,) *Career choice and development* (4th ed., pp. 255–311). San Francisco: Jossey-Bass.

Leong, F. T. L., & Serafica, F. C. (2001). Cross-cultural perspective on Super's career development theory: Career maturity and cultural accommodation. In F. T. L. Leong & A. Barak (Eds.), *Contemporary models in vocational psychology* (pp. 167–205), Mahwah, NJ: Lawrence Erlbaum.

Levesque, K., Lauen, D., Teitelbaum, P., Martha, A., & Librera, S. (2000). Vocational Education in the United States: Toward the Year 2000, National Center for Education Statistics. U.S. Department of Education, Office of Educational Research and Improvement NCES 2000-02.

Lewis, R. D. (1997). *When cultures collide: Managing successfully across cultures.* London: Nicholas Brealey.

Lichstenstein, S. (1998). Characteristics of youth and young adults. In F. R. Rusch & J. G. Chadsey (Eds), *Beyond high school: Transition from school to work* (pp. 3–35). New York: Wadsworth.

Lindstrom, L., Benz, M., & Johnson, M. (1996). Developing job clubs for students in transition. *Teaching Exceptional Children, 29*(2), 18–21.

Lindstrom, L. E., & Benz, M. R. (2002). Phases of career development: Case studies of young women with learning disabilities. *Exceptional Children, 69*(1). 67–83.

Linn, R., & DeStefano, L. (1986). *Review of student assessment instruments and practices in use in the second-*

ary/transition project. Champaign, IL: Secondary Transition Intervention Effectiveness Institute, University of Illinois at Urbana-Champaign. (ERIC Document Reproduction Service No. ED 279 123)

Loewen, G., & Iaquinto, M. (1990). Rebuilding a career plan: Issues for head injured students. In J. J. Vander Putten (Ed.), *Reaching new heights: Proceedings of the 1989 AHSSPPE Conference.* Columbus, OH: Association on Handicapped Student Service Programs in Postsecondary Education.

Lofquist, L. H., & Dawis, R. V. (1969). *Adjustment to work: A psychological view of man's problems in a work-oriented society.* New York: Appleton-Century-Crofts, Education Division, Meredith Corporation.

Lombard, R. C., Hazelkorn, M. N., & Miller, R. J. (1995). Special populations and tech prep. A national study of state policy and practice. *Career Development for Exceptional Individuals, 18*(2), 145–156.

Lombard, R. C., Hazelkorn, M. N., & Neubert, D. A. (1992). A survey of accessibility to secondary vocational education programs and transition services for students with disabilities in Wisconsin. *Career Development for Exceptional Individuals, 15*(2), 179–188.

Lovitt, T. C., Cushing, S. S., & Stump, C. S. (1994). High school students rate their IEPs: Low opinions and lack of ownership. *Intervention in School and Clinic, 30,* 34–37.

Loyd, R. J., & Wehmeyer, M. (2004). Self-determination. In D. E. Brolin & R. J. Loyd (Eds.), *Career development and transition services: A functional life skills approach* (4th ed., pp. 250–281). Upper Saddle River, NJ: Merrill/ Prentice Hall.

Luft, P. (1995, April). *Addressing minority overrepresentation in special education: Cultural barriers to effective collaboration.* Presentation at the annual convention of the Council for Exceptional Children, Indianapolis, IN.

Luft, P. (1999). Assessment and collaboration: Key elements in comprehensive and cohesive transition planning. *Work, 13,* 31–41.

Luft, P. (2005). Instructional strategies and transition settings. In Flexer, R. W., Simmons, T. J., Luft, P. & Baer, R. M. (Eds.). *Transition planning for secondary students with disabilities* (2nd ed., pp. 178–210). Upper Saddle River, NJ: Merrill/Prentice Hall.

Luft, P., & Koch, L. (1998). Transition of adolescents with chronic illness: Overlooked needs and rehabilitation considerations. *Journal of Vocational Rehabilitation, 10,* 205–217.

Luft, P., & Koch, L. C. (2001). Career development: Theories for transition planning. In Robert W. Flexer, Thomas J. Simmons, Pamela Luft, and Robert M. Baer. *Transition planning for secondary students with disabilities* (pp. 69–94). Columbus, OH: Merrill.

Luft, P., Koch, L. C., Headmen, D., & O'Connor, P. (2001). Career and vocational education. In Robert W. Flexer, Thomas J. Simmons, Pamela Luft, & Robert M. Baer, *Transition planning for secondary students with disabilities* (pp. 162-196). Columbus, OH: Merrill.

Luft, P., Rumrill, P., Snyder, J., & Hennessey, M. (2001). Transition strategies for youths with sensory impairments. *Work: A Journal of Prevention, Assessment, and Rehabilitation, 17.*

Lusthaus, C. S., Lusthaus, E. W., & Gibbs, H. (1981). Parents' role in the decision process. *Exceptional Children, 48*(3), 256-257.

Lynch, E. C., & Beare, P. L. (1990). The quality of IEP objectives and their relevance to instruction for students with mental retardation and behavioral disorders. *Remedial and Special Education, 11*(2), 48-55.

Lynch, E. W. (1998a). Conceptual framework: From culture shock to cultural learning. In E. W. Lynch & M. H. Hanson (Eds.), *Developing cross-cultural competence: A guide for working with children and their families* (2nd ed., pp. 23-46). Baltimore: Paul H. Brookes.

Lynch, E. W. (1998b). Developing cross-cultural competence. In E. W. Lynch & M. H. Hanson (Eds.), *Developing cross-cultural competence: A guide for working with children and their families* (2nd ed., pp. 47-90). Baltimore: Paul H. Brookes.

Lynch, E. W., & Stein, R. C. (1982). Perspectives on parent participation in special education. *Exceptional Education Quarterly, 3,* 56-63.

Lynch, E. W., & Stein, R. C. (1987). Parent participation by ethnicity: A comparison of Hispanic, Black, and Anglo families. *Exceptional Children, 54,* 105-111.

MacDonald-Wilson, K. L., Revell, Jr., W. G., Nguyen, N. H., & Peterson, M. (1991). Supported employment outcomes for people with psychiatric disability: A comparative analysis. *Journal of Vocational Rehabilitation, 1*(3), 30-44.

Mackelsprang, R. W., & Salsgiver, R. O. (1996). People with disabilities and social work: Historical and contemporary issues. *Social Work, 41*(1), 7-14.

Maddy-Bernstein, C. (1997). Vocational preparation for students with disabilities. In H. M. Wallace, R. F. Bieh, J. C. MacQueen, & J. A. Blackman (Eds.), *Mosby's resource guide to children with disabilities and chronic illness* (pp. 381-392). St. Louis, MO: Mosby-Year Book.

Mager, R. F. (1962). *Preparing instructional objectives.* Belmont, CA: Fearon.

Mahoney, J. & Cairns, R. (1997). Do extracurricular activities protect against early school dropout? *Developmental Psychology, 33*(2), 241-253.

Malian, I. M., & Love, L. L. (1998). Leaving high school: An ongoing transition study. *Teaching Exceptional Children, 30* (1), 4-10.

Malone, B. L. (1995). Job clubs: Providing an empathetic ear, moral support, and a built-in EEO procedure. *Equal Employment Opportunity Career Journal, 31* October, Vol. 30 (pp. 20-32).

Mangrum, C. T., & Strichart, S. S. (Eds.). (1997). *Peterson's colleges with programs for students with learning disabilities or attention deficit disorders* (5th ed.). Princeton, NJ: Peterson's Guides.

Mank, D., Cioffi, A. & Yovanoff, P. (1997). An analysis of the typicalness of supported employment jobs, natural supports, and wage and integration outcomes. *Mental Retardation, 35*(3), 185-197.

Mank, D., Oorthuys, J., Rhodes, L., Sandow, D., & Weyer, T. (1992). Accommodating workers with mental disabilities. *Training and Development Journal, 46,* 49-52.

Marder, C. (1992). *How well are youth with disabilities really doing? A comparison of youth with disabilities and youth in general.* Menlo Park, CA: SRI International.

Markowitz, J. (1996, May). *Strategies that address the disproportionate number of students from racial/ethnic minority groups receiving special education services: Case studies of selected states and school districts, final report.* Paper presented at the National Association of State Directors of Special Education, Alexandria, VA.

Martin, J. E., Greene, B. A., & Borland, B. J. (2004). Secondary students' involvement in their IEP meetings: Administrators' perceptions. *Career Development for Exceptional Individuals, 27,* 177-188.

Martin, J. E., & Huber Marshall, L. H. (1995). ChoiceMaker: A comprehensive self-determination transition program. *Intervention in School and Clinic, 30*(3), 147-156.

Martin, J. E., & Huber Marshall, L. H. (1996a). ChoiceMaker: Infusing self-determination instruction into the IEP and transition process. In D. J. Sands & M. L. Wehmeyer (Eds.), *Self-determination across the life span* (pp. 215-236). Baltimore: Paul H. Brookes.

Martin, J. E., & Huber Marshall, L. H. (1996b). *ChoiceMaker self-determination transition assessment.* Longmont, CO: Sopris West, Inc.

Martin, J. E., Huber-Marshall, L., Maxson, L. L., & Jerman, P. (1996). *Self-directed. IEP.* Longmont, CO: Sopris West.

Martin, J. E., Huber Marshall, L., & Sale, R. P. (1999). *IEP Team Tells All!* Manuscript submitted for publication.

Martin, J. E., Huber Marshall, L., & Sale, R. P. (in press). Student participation in their own IEP meetings: A three-year study. *Exceptional Children.*

Martin, J. E., Huber Marshall, L., Wray, D., O'Brien, J., & Snyder, L. (1999). *Choose and take action.* Software and lesson package submitted for publication.

Martin, J. E., Huber Marshall, L., Wray, D., Wells, L., O'Brien, J., Olvey, G., & Johnson, Z. (2004). *Choose and take action: Finding the right job for you.* Longmont, CO: Sopris West.

Martin, J. E., Hughes, W., Huber Marshall, L. H., Jerman, P., & Maxson, L. (1999). *Choosing education goals.* Longmont, CO: Sopris West.

Martin, J. E., Marshall, L. H., & Maxson, L. L. (1993). Transition policy: Infusing self-determination and self-advocacy into transition programs. *Career Development for Exceptional Individuals, 16*(1), 53-61.

Martin, J. E., Marshall, L. H., & Sale, P. (2004). A 3-year study of middle, junior high, and high school IEP meetings. *Exceptional Children, 70,* 285-297.

Martin, J. E., Marshall, L. H., Wray, D., Wells, L., O'Brien, J., Olvey, G. H., & Johnson, Z. (2004). *Choose and Take Action: Finding the right job for you.* Longmont, CO: Sopris West.

Martin, J. E., Mithaug, D. E., Cox, P., Peterson, L. Y., Van Dycke, J. L., & Cash, M. E. (2003). Increasing self-determination: Teaching students to plan, work, evaluate, and adjust. *Exceptional Children, 69*(4), 431–447.

Martin, J. E., Mithaug, D. E., Oliphint, J., & Husch, J. V. (2002). *ChoiceMaker employment: A self-determination transition and supported employment handbook.* Baltimore: Paul H. Brookes.

Martin, J. E., Mithaug, D. E., Oliphint, J. H., Husch, J. V., & Frazier, E. S. (2002). *Self-directed employment: A handbook for transition teachers and employment specialists.* Baltimore: Paul H. Brookes.

Martin, J. E., Peterson, L. Y. & Goff, C. D. (in press). How to increase self-determination at school and work. In D. E. Mithaug, D. K., Mithaug, M. Agran, J. E. Martin, & M. L. Wehmeyer (Eds.), *Self-instruction pedagogy: How to teach self-determined learning.* Springfield, IL: Charles Thomas.

Martin, J. E., Van Dycke, J., D'Ottavio, M., & Nickerson, K. (in press). *The student-directed summary of performance: Increasing student and family involvement in the transition planning process.* Career Development for Exceptional Individuals.

Martin, J. E., Van Dycke, J. L., Christensen, W. R., Greene, B. A., Gardner, J. E., & Lovett, D. L. (2006) Increasing student participation in IEP meetings: Establishing the *Self-Directed IEP* as an evidenced-based practice. *Exceptional Children, 72,* 299–316.

Martin, J. E., Van Dycke, J. L., Greene, B. A., Gardner, J. E., Christensen, W. R., Woods, L. L., & Lovett, D. L. (2006). Direct observation of teacher-directed IEP meetings: Establishing the need for student IEP meeting instruction. *Exceptional Children, 72,* 187–200.

Martin, J. E., Woods, L. E., Sylvester, L., & Gardner, J. E. (2005). A challenge to self-determination: Disagreement between the vocational choices made by individuals with severe disabilities and their caregivers. *Research and Practice for Persons with Severe Disabilities, 30,* 147–153.

Marzono, R. (2001). Classroom instruction that works: Research-based strategies for increasing student achievement. Alexandria, VA: ASCD.

Mason, C., Field, S., & Sawilowsky, S. (2004). Implementation of self-determination activities and student participation in IEPs. *Exceptional Children, 70,* 441–451.

Massenzio, S. (1983). Legal resource networks for parents of individuals with special needs. *Exceptional Children, 50*(3), 273–275.

Mastropieri, M. A., & Scruggs, T. E. (2000). *The inclusive classroom: Strategies for effective instruction.* Upper Saddle River, NJ: Merrill/Prentice Hall.

Mastropieri, M. A., & Scruggs, T. E. (2002). *Effective instruction for special education* (3rd ed.). Upper Saddle River, NJ: Merrill/Prentice Hall.

Mastropieri, M. A., & Scruggs, T. E. (2007). *The inclusive classroom: Strategies for effective instruction* (3rd ed.). Upper Saddle River, NJ: Merrill/Prentice Hall.

Mattie, H. D. (2000). The Suitability of Holland's Self-Directed Search for Non-Readers with Learning Disabilities or Mild Verbal Retardation: CDEI, 23, 57–72.

McCarthy, D., Thompson, T., & Olson, S. (1998). Planning a statewide project to convert day treatment to supported employment. *Psychiatric Rehabilitation Journal, 22*(1), 30–33.

McCaughrin, W., Ellis, W., Rusch, F., & Heal, L. (1993). Cost-effectiveness of supported employment. *Mental Retardation, 31*(1), 41–48.

McDonnell, J., Ferguson, B., & Mathot-Buckner, C. (1992). Transition from school to work for students with severe disabilities: The Utah community employment placement project. In F. R. Rusch, L. DeStefano, J. Chadsey-Rusch, L. A. Phelps, & E. Szymanski (Eds.), *Transition from school to adult life: Models, linkages, and policy* (pp. 33–50). Sycamore, IL: Sycamore.

McDonnell, J., Hardman, M. L., & Hightower, J. (1989). Employment preparation for high school students with severe handicaps. *Mental Retardation, 27*(6), 396–405.

McDonnell, J., Wilcox, B., & Boles, S. M. (1986). Do we know enough to plan for transition? A national survey of state agencies responsible for services to persons with severe handicaps. *Journal of The Association for Persons with Severe Handicaps, 11*(1), 53–60.

McDonnell, J. J., Wilcox, B., Boles, S. M., & Bellamy, G. T. (1985). Issues in transition from school to adult services: A survey of parents of secondary students with severe handicaps. *The Journal of the Association for Persons with Severe Handicaps, 10*(1), 61–65.

McGahee-Kovac, M. (1995). *A student's guide to the IEP.* Washington, DC: National Information Center for Children and Youth with Disabilities.

McKnight, J. (1987). Regenerating community. *Social Policy,* Winter, 54–58.

McMahan, R. (2005). *Transition policy compliance and best practice in Ohio.* Unpublished doctoral dissertation, Kent State University, Kent, Ohio.

McMahan, R. K., & Baer, R. (2001). *Survey on transition policy compliance and best practices: Final report.* Kent, OH: Transition Center, Kent State University.

McNair, J., & Rusch, F. R. (1987). Parent survey: Identification and validation of transition issues. *Interchange, 7*(4), Urbana-Champaign, IL: University of Illinois, Transition Institute.

McNair, J., & Rusch, F. R. (1991). Parent involvement in transition programs. *Mental Retardation, 29*(2), 93–101.

Menchetti, B. M., & Piland, V. C. (1998). A person-centered approach to vocational evaluation and career planning. In

F. R. Rusch & J. Chadsey (Eds.), *Beyond high school: Transition from school to work.* New York: Wadsworth.

Menchetti, B. M., Rusch, F. R., & Owens, D. M. (1983). Vocational training. In J. Matson & S. Breuing (Eds.), *Assessing the mentally retarded* (pp. 247–285). New York: Grune & Stratton.

Mercer, C. D., & Mercer, A. R. (2000). *Teaching students with learning problems* (6th ed.). Upper Saddle River, NJ: Merrill/Prentice Hall.

Mertz, M. K. (1997). After inclusion: Next S.T.E.P.s for high-school graduates. *Exceptional Parent, 27*(9), 44–49.

Middleton, R. A., Rollins, C. W., Sanderson, P. L., Leung, P., Harley, D. A., Ebener, D., & Leal-Idrogo, A. (2000). Endorsement of professional multicultural rehabilitation competencies and standards: A call to action. *Rehabilitation Counseling Bulletin, 43,* 219–240.

Miller, R. J., Lombard, R. C., & Corbey, S. A. (2007). *Transition assessment: Planning transition and IEP development for youth with mild to moderate disabilities.* Boston: Pearson Education.

Miller, S. M., & Roby, P. (1970). Poverty: Changing social stratification. In P. Townsend (Ed.), *The concept of poverty: Working papers on methods of investigation and lifestyles of the poor in different countries* (pp. 124–145). New York: American Elsevier Publishing.

Miner, C. A., & Bates, P. E. (1997). The effect of person-centered planning activities on the IEP/transition planning process. *Education and Training in Mental Retardation and Developmental Disabilities, 32*(2), 105–112.

Minnesota Governor's Planning Council on Developmental Disabilities. (1987). *A new way of thinking.* St. Paul, MN: Author.

Mitchell, K. (1997). Making the grade: Help and hope for the first-generation college student. *The ERIC Review: The Path to College, 5*(3), 13–15.

Mitchell, L. K., & Krumboltz, J. D. (1996). Krumboltz's learning theory of career choice and counseling. In D. Brown, L. Brooks, & Associates (Eds.), *Career choice and development* (3rd ed., pp. 233–280). San Francisco: Jossey-Bass.

Mithaug, D. E. (1993). *Self-regulation theory: How optimal adjustment maximizes gain.* Westport, CT: Praeger.

Mithaug, D. E. (2005). On persistent pursuits of self-interest. *Research and Practice for Persons with Severe Disabilities, 30,* 163–167.

Mithaug, D. E., Horiuchi, C. N., & Fanning, P. N. (1985). A report on the Colorado statewide follow-up survey of special education students. *Exceptional Children, 51,* 397–404.

Mithaug, D. E., & Mar, D. K. (1980). The relation between choosing and working prevocational tasks in two severely retarded young adults. *Journal of Applied Behavior Analysis* (13), 177–182.

Mithaug, D. E., Mithaug, D., Agran, M., Martin, J. E., & Wehmeyer, M. (in press). *Self-instruction pedagogy: How to teach self-determined learning.* Springfield, Il: Charles Thomas.

Mithaug, D. E., Mithaug, D. K., Agran, M., Martin, J. E., & Wehmeyer, M. L. (2003). *Self-determined learning theory.* Mahwah, NJ: Lawrence Erlbaum.

Mithaug, D. E., Wehmeyer, M. L., Agran, M., Martin, J. E., & Palmer, S. (1998). The self-determined learning model of instruction. In M. L. Wehmeyer & D. J. Sands (Eds.), *Making it happen: Student involvement in education planning, decision making, and instruction* (pp. 299–328). Baltimore: Paul H. Brookes.

Mokuau, N., & Tauili'ili, P. (1998). Families with native Hawaiian and Samoan roots. In E. W. Lynch & M. H. Hanson (Eds.), *Developing cross-cultural competence: A guide for working with children and their families* (2nd ed., pp. 409–440). Baltimore: Paul H. Brookes.

Monette, G. C. (1997). Tribal colleges: Tradition, heritage, and community. *The ERIC Review: The Path to College, 5*(3), 24–25.

Moon, M. S., Hart, D., Komissar, C., & Friedlander, R. (1995). Making sports and recreation activities accessible. In K. F. Flippo, K. J. Inge, & J. M. Barcus (Eds.), *Assistive technology: A resource for school, work, and community* (pp. 187–197). Baltimore, MD: Paul H. Brookes.

Moores, D. (1996). *Educating the deaf: Psychology, principles, and practices* (4th ed.). Boston: Houghton Mifflin.

Morgan, R. L., Moore, S. C., McSweyn, C. A., & Salzberg, C. L. (1992). Transition from school to work: Views of secondary special educators. *Education and Training in Mental Retardation, 27*(4), 315–323.

Morningstar, M. (1997). Critical issues in career development and employment preparation for adolescents with disabilities. *Remedial and Special Education, 18,* 307–320.

Morningstar, M. E., Turnbull, A. P., & Turnbull, H. R. (1996). What do students with disabilities tell us about the importance of family involvement in the transition from school to adult life? *Exceptional Children, 62,* 249–260.

Morse, T. E. (2001). Designing appropriate curriculum for special education students in urban schools. *Education and Urban Society, 34*(1), 4–17.

Mosston, M. (1972). *Teaching: From command to discovery.* Belmont, CA: Wadsworth.

Mosston, M., & Ashworth, S. (1990). *The spectrum of teaching styles: From command to discovery.* New York: Longman.

Mount, B. (1989). *Making futures happen: A manual for facilitators of personal futures planning.* St. Paul, MN: Governor's Council on Developmental Disabilities.

Mount, B. (1992). *Personal futures planning: Promises and precautions.* New York, NY: Graphic Futures.

Mount, B. (1994). Benefits and limitations of personal futures planning. In J. Bradlley, J. W. Ashbaugh, & B. C. Blaney (Eds.), *Creating individual supports for people with developmental disabilities* (pp. 97–98). Baltimore: Paul H. Brookes.

Mount, B., Beeman, P., & Ducharme, G. (1988). What are we learning about circles of support? Manchester, CT: Communitas.

Mount, B., & Zwernick. (1988). *It's never too early, it's never too late: A booklet about personal futures planning.* St. Paul, MN: Governor's Planning Council on Developmental Disabilities. Publication No. 421, 88–109.

Munk, D. D., & Repp, A. C. (1994). The relationship between instructional variables and problem behavior: A review. *Exceptional Children, 60,* 390–401.

Murray, C., Goldstein, D. E., Nourse, S., & Edgar, E. (2000). The postsecondary school attendance and completion rates of high school graduates with learning disabilities. *Learning Disabilities Research, 15,* 119–127.

Myers, L. B., & McCauley M. H. (1985). *Manual: A guide to the development and use of the Myers-Briggs type indicator.* Palo Alto, CA: Consulting Psychologists Press.

National Association of Private Residential Resources (NAPRR). (1991). *Supported living.* Annandale, VA: Author.

National Association of Private Residential Resources (NAPRR), (1992) *Supported living,* Vol. II. Annandale, VA: Author.

National Association of Protection and Advocacy Systems. (1999, October). *Questions and answers about the Olmstead v. L. C. and E. W. decision.* Washington, DC: Author.

National Center for Educational Statistics (NCES). (1993). *Baccalaureate and beyond: Longitudinal study. 1st and 2nd follow-up.* Washington, DC: U.S. Government Printing Office.

National Center for Education Statistics. (1993). *Education of the Handicapped Act Amendment of 1990 (PL 101-476): Summary of major changes in parts A through H of the Act.* Washington, DC: U.S. Department of Education.

National Center for Education Statistics. (1999a). *Students with disabilities in postsecondary education: A profile of preparation, participation, and outcomes.* NCES 1999-187. Washington, DC: U.S. Department of Education.

National Center for Education Statistics. (1999b). *An institutional perspective on students with disabilities in postsecondary education.* NCES 1999-046. Washington, DC: U.S. Department of Education.

National Center for Education Statistics (2004). Retrieved August 4, 2006, from http://nces.ed.gov/programs/digest/d04/tables/d04_211.asp

National Council on Disability. (2000). *Back to school on civil rights.* Washington, DC: Author.

National Information Center for Children and Youth with Disabilities. (1993). *Transition services in the IEP: Transition summary, 3*(1), Washington, DC: Office of Special Education Programs of the U.S. Department of Education.

National Institute of Disability and Rehabilitation Research/Social Security Administration (1999). *The summary of data on young people with disabilities.* Washington DC: Author.

Neel, R. S., & Billingsley, F. F. (1989). *Impact: A functional curriculum handbook for students with moderate to severe disabilities.* Baltimore: Paul H. Brookes.

Neubert, D. (1985). Use of vocational evaluation recommendations in selected public school settings. *Career Development for Exceptional Individuals, 9,* 98–105.

Neubert, D. A. (1997). Time to grow: The history and future of preparing youth for adult roles in society. *Teaching Exceptional Children, 29*(5), 5–17.

Neubert, D. A., & Moon, M. S. (2000, Nov/Dec). How a transition profile helps students prepare for life in the community. *Teaching Exceptional Children, 33*(2), 20–25.

Neubert, D. A., Moon, S., & Grigal, M. (2004). Activities of students with significant disabilities receiving services in postsecondary settings. *Education and Training in Developmental Disabilities, 39*(1), 16–25.

Neubert, D. A., & Repetto, J. B. (1992). Serving individuals with special needs through professional development: Meeting the intent of the Act. *Journal for Vocational Special Needs Education, 2-3*(14), 37–41.

Nevill, D., & Super, D. E. (1986). *The values scale: Theory, application, and research manual* (Research Edition). Palo Alto, CA: Consulting Psychologists Press.

Newman, L. (1991). Social activities. In M. Wagner, L. Newman, R. D'Amico, E. Jay, P. Butler-Nalin, C. Marder, & R. Cox (Eds.), *Youth with disabilities: How are they doing? The first comprehensive report from the National Longitudinal Transition Study of Special Education Students* (pp. 6-1 to 6-50). Menlo Park, CA: SRI International.

Newman, L. (2005). Changes in postsecondary education participation of youth with disabilities. In M. Wagner, L. Newman, R. Cameto, & P. Levine (Eds.), (2005). *Changes over time in the early postschool outcomes of youth with disabilities.* A report from the National Longitudinal Transition Study-2 (NLTS2). Menlo Park, CA: SRI International. Retrieved from www.nlts2.org/pdfs/str6/completereport.pdf

Newman, L., & Cameto, R. (1993). *What makes a difference? Factors related to postsecondary school attendance for young people with disabilities.* Paper presented at the Division J: Postsecondary Education of the American Educational Research Association annual meeting, Atlanta, GA.

Nezu, A., & D'Zurilla, T. (1981). Effects of problem definition and formulation on the generation of alternatives in the social problem-solving process. *Cognitive Therapy and Research, 5,* 265–271.

NICHCY *News Digest.* (1993). *2*(2) , 1–7. Washington, DC: The National Information Center for Children and Youth with Disabilities: Author.

NICHCY *Transition Summary.* (1990, December). *Vocational assessment: A guide for parents and professionals.* Washington DC: The National Information Center for Children and Youth with Disabilities: Author.

NICHCY. (1988). *Individualized education programs.* (2–17), Washington DC: The National Information Center for Children and Youth with Disabilities: Author.

NICHCY. (1993, March). *Transition services defined by IDEA. 3*(1), 2–19. Washington DC: The National Information Center for Children and Youth with Disabilities: Author.

Nieto, S. (2000). *Affirming diversity: The sociopolitical context of multicultural education* (3rd ed.). New York: Longman.

Nieto, S. (2001). School reform and student learning: A multicultural perspective. In J. A. Banks & C. A. McGee Banks (Eds.), *Multicultural education: Issues & perspectives* (4th ed., pp. 381-401). New York: Wiley.

Nietupski, J., Verstegen, D., Reilly, J., Hutson, J., & Hamre-Nietupski, S. (1997). A pilot investigation into the effectiveness of cold call and referral job development models in supported employment. *Journal of Vocational Rehabilitation, 8*(2), 89-98.

Nirje, B. (1972). The right to self-determination. In W. Wolfensberger (Ed.). *The principle of normalization in human services* (pp. 176-193). Toronto: National Institute on Mental Retardation.

Nisbet, J., & Hagner, D. (1988). Natural supports in the workplace: A reexamination of supported employment. *Journal of the Association for Persons with Severe Handicaps, 13,* 260-267.

Nolet, V., & McLaughlin, M. J. (2005). *Accessing the general curriculum.* (2nd ed.). Thousand Oaks, CA: Corwin.

Noll, S., & Trent, W. J. (2004). *Mental Retardation in America: A Historical Reader (The History of Disability).* New York: New York University Press.

Norman, M. E., & Bourexis, P. S. (1995). *Including students with disabilities in school-to-work opportunities.* Washington, DC: Council of Chief State School Officers.

Obiakor, F. E., & Utley, C. A. (1996). *Rethinking preservice and inservice training programs for teachers in the learning disabilities field: Workable multicultural models.* (ERIC Document Reproduction Service No. ED 397 594).

O'Brien, C., & O'Brien, J. (1992a). *Checklist for evaluating personal assistance services (PAS) policies and programs.* Livonia, GA: Responsive Systems Associates.

O'Brien, J. (1987). A guide to life-style planning: Using the activities catalogue to integrate services and natural support system. In G. T. Bellamy & B. Wilcox (Eds.), *A comprehensive guide to the activities catalogue: An alternative curriculum for youth and adults with severe disabilities* (pp. 175-190). Baltimore: Paul H. Brookes.

O'Brien, J. (1993). *Supported living: What's the difference?* Livonia, GA: Responsive Systems Associates.

O'Brien, J., & Lovett, H. (1992) *Finding a way toward everyday lives: The contribution of person-centered planning.* Harrisburg, PA: Pennsylvania Office of Mental Retardation.

O'Brien, J., & O'Brien, C. (1991). *More than just a new address: Images of organizations for supported living agencies* Syracuse, NY: Center on Human Policy, Syracuse University.

O'Brien, J., & O'Brien, C. (1992b). *Remembering the soul of our work: Stories by staff of Options in Community Living, Madison, Wisconsin.* Madison, WI: Options in Community Living.

O'Brien, J., O'Brien, L., & Mount, B. (1997). Person-centered planning has arrived . . . or has it? *Mental Retardation, 35*(6), 480-484.

Ochs, L. A., & Roessler, R. T. (2001). Students with disabilities: How ready are they for the 21st century? *Rehabilitation Counseling Bulletin, 44,* 170-176.

Office of Special Education Programs, (1997). *The Individuals with Disabilities Education Act Amendments of 1997: Curriculum.* Washington, DC. U. S. Department of Education.

Ohio Department of Education, Division of Special Education. (1999). *District self-study for the* 1999-2000 *school improvement review.* Worthington, OH: Author.

Ohio Department of Education. (1990). *Ohio speaks.* Columbus, OH: Author.

Ohio Rehabilitation Services Commission (1997). *Transition guidelines and best practices.* Columbus, OH: RSC Office of Public Information.

Olson, W. (1999). Under the ADA, we may all be disabled. *The Wall Street Journal,* May 17, A27.

O'Neill, R. E., Horner, R. H., Albin, R. W., Sprague, J. R., Storey, K., & Newton, J. S. (1997). *Functional assessment and program development for problem behavior: A practical handbook* (2nd ed.). Pacific Grove, CA: Brooks/Cole Publishing.

Osborne, A. G. (1996). Legal issues in special education, Boston: Allyn and Bacon.

PACER Center. (2002). *Technology. http://www.pacer.org/*

Page, B., & Chadsey-Rusch, J. (1995). The community college experience for students with and without disabilities: A viable transition outcome? *Career Development for Exceptional Individuals, 18*(2), 85-96.

Pallas, A. (1993, Winter). Schooling in the course of human lives: The social context of education and the transition to adulthood in industrial society. *Review of Education Research, 63,* 409-447.

Palmer, S. B., & Wehmeyer, M. L. (2003). Promoting self-determination in early elementary school. *Remedial and Special Education, 24,* 115-127.

Pancsofar, E. L. (1986). Assessing work behavior. In F. R. Rusch (Ed.), *Competitive employment issues and strategies* (pp. 93-102). Baltimore: Paul H. Brookes.

Pancsofar, E. L., & Steere, D. E. (1997). The C.A.P.A.B.L.E. process: Critical dimensions of community-based assessment. *Journal of Vocational Rehabilitation, 8,* 99-108.

Parent, W. (1996). Consumer choice and satisfaction in supported employment. Paper presented at International Symposium on Supported Employment, Norfolk Virginia, *The Journal of Vocational Rehabilitation, 6*(1), 15-22.

Parent, W. Sherron, P., Stallard, D., & Booth, M. (1993). Job development and placement: Strategies for success. *Journal of Vocational Rehabilitation, 3*(3), 17-26.

Parent, W., Unger, D., Gibson, K., & Clements, C. (1994). The role of the job coach: Orchestrating community and natural supports. *American Rehabilitation, 20*(3), 2-11.

Parette, H. P., Huer, M. B., & Scherer, M. (2004). Effects of acculturation on assistive technology service delivery. *Journal of Special Education Technology, 19,* 31-41.

Pascarella, E., & Terenzini, P. (1991). *How college affects students: Findings and insights from twenty years of research.* San Francisco: Jossey-Bass.

PA-TASH. (1994). PA-TASH supports the right to communicate. *PA-TASH Newsletter, 4*(2), 1-4.

Patton, J. R., Cronin, M. E., Bassett, D. S., & Koppel, A. E. (1997). A life skills approach to mathematics instruction: Preparing students with learning disabilities for the real-life math demands of adulthood. *Journal of Learning Disabilities, 30*(2), 178-187.

Patton, J. R., & Polloway, E. A. (1990). Mild mental retardation. In N. G. Haring, L. McCormick, & T. G. Haring (Eds.), *Exceptional children and youth* (6th ed., pp. 212-256). Upper Saddle River, NJ: Merrill/Prentice Hall.

Patton, J. R., Smith, T. E. C., Clark, G. M., Polloway, E. A., Edgar, E., & Lee, S. (1996). Individuals with mild mental retardation: Postsecondary outcomes and implications for educational policy. *Education and Training in Mental Retardation and Developmental Disabilities, 31*(2), 75-85.

Patton, W., & McMahon, M. (1999). *Career development and systems theory: A new relationship.* Pacific Grove, CA: Brooks/Cole.

Patton, W., & Polloway, E. A. (1990). Mild mental retardation. In N. G. Haring, L. McCormick, & T. G. Haring (Eds.), *Exceptional children and youth* (6th ed., pp. 212-256). Upper Saddle River, NJ: Merrill/Prentice Hall.

Paulson, R. I. (1993). Interagency collaboration among rehabilitation, mental health, and other systems. In R. W. Flexer and P. Solomon (Eds.) *Psychiatric rehabilitation in practice.* Boston: Andover Medical.

Payne, J. (2001). *Patterns of participation in full time education after 16: An analysis of the England and Wales youth cohort study.* (Department for Education and Skills Rep. No. RR307).

Pearlman, B. (2002, April). Reinventing the high school experience. *Educational Leadership,* 72-79.

Pennsylvania Association of Retarded Citizens v. Commonwealth of Pennsylvania, 343 F. Suppl. 279 (E.D. Pa. 1972).

Perske, R. (1973). *New hope for the families.* Nashville, TN: Abingdon.

Perske, R. (1988). Circles of friends: People with disabilities and their friends enrich the lives of one another. Nashville, TN: Abingdon Press.

Petric, J. (2002, May). *Labor laws and their effect on training programs.* Paper presented at 2002 Ohio Topical Conference, Columbus, OH.

Peterson, L. Y., Van Dycke, J. L., Crownover, C. A., Roberson, R. L., Borland, B. J., & Martin, J. E. (2004). Teaching students with high incidence disabilities to complete IEP plans of study. Manuscript submitted for publication.

Phelps, L. A., & Hanley-Maxwell, C. (1997). School-to-work transitions for youth with disabilities: A review of outcomes and practices. *Review of Educational Research, 67*(2), 197-226.

Phelps, L. A., & Maddy-Bernstein, C. (1992). Developing effective partnerships for special populations: The challenge of partnerships and alliances. *The Journal for Vocational Special Needs Education, 14*(2-3), 33-36.

Phillips, S., & Sandstrom, K. (1990). Parental attitudes toward youth work. *Youth and Society, 22,* 160-183.

Piaget, J. (1966). *The child's conception of physical causality.* London: Routledge & K. Paul.

Pinderhughes, E. (1995). Empowering diverse populations: Family practice in the 21st century. *Families in Society, 76,* 131-140.

Pitman, J. A., & Slate, J. R. (1994). Students' familiarity with and attitudes toward the rights of students who are disabled. *Journal of Applied Rehabilitation Counseling, 25*(2), 38-40.

Plank, S. (2001). *Career and technical education in the balance: An analysis of high school persistence, academic achievement, and postsecondary destinations.* Columbus, OH: Ohio State University, National Center for Dissemination.

Post, M., & Storey, K. (2006). Self-determination and informed choice. *TASH Connections, 32,* 30-33.

Powell, T., Pancsofar, E. L., Steere, D., Butterworth, J., Itzkowitz, J., & Rainforth, B. (1991). *Supported employment: Providing integrated employment opportunities for person with disabilities.* New York: Longman.

Power, P. (1991). *A guide to vocational assessment* (2nd ed.). Austin, TX: PRO-ED.

Powers, L. E. (1997). *Self-determination research results.* Colorado Springs, CO: Presentation at University of Colorado Self-Determination Meeting.

Powers, L. E., Sowers, J., Turner, A., Nesbitt, M., Knowles, E., & Ellison, R. (1996). TAKE CHARGE: A model for promoting self-determination among adolescents with challenges. In L. E. Powers, G. H. S. Singer, & J. Sowers (Eds.), *On the road to autonomy: Promoting self-competence for children and youth with disabilities* (pp. 291-322). Baltimore: Paul H. Brookes.

Presidents Panel on Mental Retardation. (1962). *A proposed program for national action to combat mental retardation.* Washington, DC: U.S. Government Printing Office.

Pruitt, P., & Wandry, D. (1998). Listen to us! Parents speak out about their interactions with special educators. *Preventing School Failure, 42,* 161-167.

Pugach, M. C., & Warger, C. L. (2001). Curriculum matters: Raising expectations for students with disabilities. *Remedial and Special Education, 22*(4) 194-196.

Pumpian, I., Campbell, C., & Hesche, S. (1992). Making person-centered dreams come true. *Resources, 4*(4), 1-6.

Pumpian, I., & Fisher, D. (1993). *Job placement: The final frontier?* Washington, DC: National Institute on Disabilities and Rehabilitation Research [NIDRR].

Pumpian, I., Fisher, D., Certo, N. J., & Smalley, K. A. (1997). Changing jobs: An essential part of career development.

Career Development for Exceptional Individuals, 35, 39-48.

Quinn, M. M., Gable, R. A., Rutherford, Jr., R. B., Nelson, C. M., Howell, K. W. (1998) Functional Behavioral Assessment. Center for Effective Collaboration and Practice. Retrieved July 9, 2003, from *http://www.air.org/cecp/fba/default.htm.*

Rainforth, B., York, J., & MacDonald, C. (1992). *Collaborative teams for students with severe disabilities.* Baltimore: Paul H. Brookes.

Raskind, M. H. (1997/1998). A guide to assistive technology. *Their World,* 72-74.

Raskind, M. H., Goldberg, R. J., Higgins, E. L., Herman, K. L. (1999). Patterns of change and predictors of success in individuals with learning disabilities: Result from a twenty-year longitudinal study. *Learning Disabilities Research & Practice, 14*(1), 35-49.

Reed, C., & Rumrill, P. (1997). Supported employment: Principles and practices for interdisciplinary collaboration. *Work: A Journal of Prevention, Assessment, and Rehabilitation, 9,* 237-244.

Reed, P. (1997). *Assessing students' need for assistive technology.* Oshkosh, WI: Wisconsin Assistive Technology Initiative.

Rehabilitation Act Amendments of 1992, 29 U.S C. § 794 *et seq.*

Rehabilitation Act of 1973, Section 504, 29 U.S.C. § 794.

Rehabilitation, Comprehensive Services, and Developmental Disabilities Act of 1978, Pub. L. No. 95-062.

Rehabilitation Research and Training Center on Disability Demographics and Statistics, (2005). *2004 disability status reports.* Ithaca, NY: Cornell University. Retrieved June 4, 2006, from *http://www.disabilitystatistics.org/.*

Rehabilitation Services Administration, Office of Special Education and Rehabilitation Services, U.S. Department of Education. (1999). Rehabilitation Services Administration (RSA) Programs: Centers for Independent Living. Retrieved January 15, 2000 from the World Wide Web: *http://www.ed.gov/offices/OSERS/RSA/rsa.html*

Repetto, J. B., & Correa, V. I. (1996). Expanding views on transition. *Exceptional Children 62*(6), 551-563.

Repetto, J. B., White, W. J., & Snauwaert, D. T. (1990). Individualized transition plans (ITP): A national perspective. *Career Development for Exceptional Individuals, 13*(2), 109-119.

Reschly, D. J. (1997). *Disproportionate minority representation in general and special education: Patterns, issues, and alternatives.* Washington, DC: Office of Special Education and Rehabilitative Services, and Mountain Plains Regional Resource Center.

Research and Training Center on Residential Services and Community Living. (1994). *Housing policy and persons with mental retardation.* Minneapolis, MN: Institute on Community Integration.

Reutzel, D. R., & Cooter, R. B. Jr. (1999). *Balanced reading strategies and practices: Assessing and assisting readers with special needs.* Upper Saddle River, NJ: Merrill/Prentice Hall.

Rhodes, L., Sandow, D., Mank, D., Buckley, J., & Albin, J. (1991). Expanding the role of employers in supported employment. *The Journal of the Association for Persons with Severe Handicaps, 16*(4), 213-217.

Richmond, W. V. (1934). *An introduction to sex education.* New York: New Home Library.

Robertson, N. (2006). Preparing students for community living opportunities. In D. W. Test, N. P. Aspel, & J. M. Everson (Eds.), *Transition methods for youth with disabilities.* (pp. 303-333). Upper Saddle River, NJ: Merrill/Prenlic Hall.

Robinson, G. K. (1991). Choices in case management. *Community Support Network News, 7,* 11-12.

Rodriquez, R. F. (1994). Administrators' perceptions of teaching competencies for rural minority group children with exceptionalities. *Rural Special Education Quarterly, 13,* 40-44.

Roessler, R., & Bolton, B. (1985). Employment patterns of former vocational rehabilitation clients and implications for rehabilitation practice. *Rehabilitation Counseling Bulletin, 28*(3), 179-187.

Roessler, R., & Rumrill, P. (1995). Promoting reasonable accommodations: An essential postemployment service. *Journal of Applied Rehabilitation Counseling, 26*(4), 3-7.

Roessler, R. T., Brown, P. L., & Rumrill, P. D. (1998). Self-advocacy training: Preparing students with disabilities to request classroom accommodations. *The Journal on Postsecondary Education and Disability, 13*(3). Retrieved August 4, 2006, from: http://www.ahead.org/members/jped/articles/Volume13/13_3/jped133 roesslerselfadvocacy.doc

Rogan, P., Grossi, T., Mank, D., Haynes, D., Thomas, F., & Majad, C. (2002). What happens when people leave the workshop? Outcomes of workshop participants now in SE. *Supported Employment Infolines, 13*(4), 1,3.

Rogan, P., Grossi, T. A., & Gajewski, R. (2002). Vocational career assessment. In C. L. Sax & C. A. Thoma (Eds.), *Transition assessment: Wise practices for quality lives* (pp. 103-118). Baltimore: Paul H. Brookes.

Rogers-Adkinson, D. L., Ochoa, T. A., & Delgado, B. (2003). Developing cross-cultural competence: Serving families of children with significant developmental needs. *Focus on Autism and Other Developmental Disabilities, 18,* 4-8.

Rojewski, J. W. (1993). Theoretical structure of career maturity for rural adolescents with learning disabilities. *Career Development for Exceptional Individuals, 16*(1), 39-52.

Rojewski, J. W. (1996). Educational and occupational aspirations of high school seniors with learning difficulties. *Exceptional Children, 62*(5), 463-476.

Rojewski, J. W. (1999). Career-related predictors of work-bound and college-bound status of adolescents in rural and non-rural areas. *Journal of Research in Rural Education, 15*(3), 141-156.

Rojewski, J. W. (2002). Career assessment for adolescents with mild disabilities: Critical concerns for transition planning. *Career Development for Exceptional Individuals, 25*(1), 73-95.

Rose, S. M. (1972). *The betrayal of the poor: The transformation of community action.* Cambridge, MA: Schenkman Publishing.

Ruben, B. D. (1976). Assessing communication competency for intercultural adaptation. *Group and Organizational Studies, 1,* 334-354.

Rueda, R., Monzo, L., Shapiro, J., Gomez, J., & Blacher, J. (2005). Cultural models of transition: Latina mothers of young adults with developmental disabilities. *Exceptional Children, 71,* 401-414.

Rumrill, P., & Koch, L. (1998). The career maintenance specialist: Broadening the scope of successful rehabilitation. *Journal of Rehabilitation Administration, 22*(2), 111-121.

Rumrill, P. D. (1994). The "win-win" approach to Title I of the Americans with Disabilities Act: Preparing college students with disabilities for career-entry placements after graduation. *Journal of Postsecondary Education and Disability, 11*(1), 15-19.

Rusch, F. R. (1979). Toward the validation of social/vocational survival skills. *Mental Retardation, 17,* 143-145.

Rusch, F. R. (1986). *Competitive employment: Issues, theories, and models.* Baltimore: Paul H. Brookes.

Rusch, F. R., & Chadsey, J. G. (1998). *Beyond high school: Transition from school to work.* The Wadsworth Special Education Series. Belmont, CA: Wadsworth.

Rusch, F. R., & DeStefano, L. (1989). Transition from school to work: Strategies for young adults with disabilities. *Interchange, 9*(3), 1-2. Urbana-Champaign, IL: University of Illinois, Secondary Transition Intervention Effectiveness Institute.

Rusch, F. R., DeStefano, L., Chadsey-Rusch, J., Phelps, L. A., & Szymanski, E. (1992). *Transition from school to adult life: Models, linkages, and policy.* Sycamore, IL: Sycamore.

Rusch, F. R., & Millar, D. M. (1998). Emerging transition best practices. In F. R. Rusch & J. G. Chadsey (Eds.), *Beyond high school: Transition from school to work* (pp. 36-60). New York: Wadsworth.

Russo, C. J., & Talbert-Johnson, C. (1997). The overrepresentation of African American children in special education: The resegregation of educational programming? *Education and Urban Society, 29,* 136-148.

Rylance, B. J. (1997). Predictors of high school graduation or dropping out for youth with severe emotional disturbances. *Behavior Disorders, 23*(1), 5-17.

Sale, P., & Martin, J. E. (1997). Self-determination. In P. Wehman & J. Kregel (Eds.), *Functional curriculum for elementary, middle, and secondary age students with special needs* (pp. 43-67). Austin, TX: PRO-ED.

Sale, R. P., & Martin, J. E. (2004). Self-determination instruction. In P. Wehman & J. Kregel (Eds.), *Community-based instruction* (2nd edition, pp. 67-94). Austin, TX: Pro-Ed.

Salembier, G., & Furney, K. S. (1997). Facilitating participation: Parents' perceptions of their involvement in the IEP/transition planning process. *Career Development for Exceptional Children, 20,* 29-42.

Salend, S. J. (2005). *Creating inclusive classrooms: Effective and reflective practices* (5th ed.). Upper Saddle River, NJ: Merrill.

Salisbury, D. L., Evans, I. M., & Palombaro, M. M. (1997). Collaborative problem-solving to promote inclusion of young children with significant disabilities in the primary grades. *Exceptional Children, 63,* 195-209.

Sanoff, A. P. (2006). A perception gap over students' preparation. The Chronicle of Higher Education, *52*(27), B9.

Sarason, S. B., & Doris, J. (1979). *Educational handicap, public policy, and social history: A broadened perspective on mental retardation.* New York: Free Press.

Sarkees, M. D., & Scott, J. L. (1985). *Vocational special needs* (2nd ed.). Home wood, IL: American Technical Publishers.

Sarkees-Wincenski, M., & Scott, J. L. (1995). *Vocational special needs* (3rd ed.). Homewood, IL: American Technical Publishers.

Sarkees-Wircenski, M., & Wircenski, J. (1994). Transition planning: Developing a career portfolio for students with disabilities. *Career Development for Exceptional Individuals, 17,* 203-214.

Savickas, M. L. (1989). Career-style assessment and counseling. In T. Sweeney (Ed.), *Adlerian counseling: A practical approach for a new decade* (3rd ed., pp. 289-320). Muncie, IN: Accelerated Development Press.

Savickas, M. L. (1996). A framework for linking career theory and practice. In M. L. Savickas & W. B. Walsh (Eds.), *Handbook of career counseling theory and practice* (pp. 191-208). Palo Alto, CA: Davies-Black.

Savickas, M. L. (2001). Toward a comprehensive theory of career development: Dispositions, concerns, and narratives. In F. T. L. Leong & A. Barak (Eds.), *Contemporary models in vocational psychology* (pp. 295-320). Mahwah, NJ: Lawrence Erlbaum.

Savickas, M. L. (2002). Career construction: A developmental theory of vocational behavior. In D. Brown and Associates (Eds.), *Career choice and development* (4th ed., pp. 149-205). San Francisco: Jossey-Bass.

Sax, C., Pumpian, I., & Fisher, D. (March, 1997). Assistive technology and inclusion. *CISP Issue Briefs,* 1-5.

Sax, C. L., & Thoma, C. A. (2002). *Transition assessment: Wise practices for quality lives.* Baltimore: Paul H. Brookes.

SCANS (Secretary's Commission on Acheiveing Necessary Skills). (1991). *What work requires of schools: A SCANS report for America 2000.* Washington DC: U.S. Department of Labor.

SCANS: Secretary's Commission on Achieving Necessary Skills (1992, June). *SCANS in the schools.* Washington, DC: SCANS, U.S. Dept. of Labor, Pelavin Assoc.

Schalock, R. L., Verdugo, M. A., Jenaro, C., Wang, M, Wehmeyer, M, Jiancheng, X., et al. (2005). A cross-cultural study of core quality of life domains and indicators: An exploratory analysis. *American Journal on Mental Retardation, 110*(4) 298–311.

Schalock, R. L., Wolzen, B., Ross, I., Elliott, B., Werbel, G., & Peterson, K. (1986). Post-secondary community placement of handicapped students: A five-year follow-up. *Learning Disability Quarterly, 9*(4), 295–303.

Scheerenberger, R. C. (1983). *A history of mental retardation.* Baltimore, Paul H. Brookes.

Scherer, M. J. (1997). Assessing individuals' predispositions to the use, avoidance, or abandonment of assistive technologies. *Journal of Rehabilitation Research & Development, 31,* 135–136.

Schirmer, B. R. (2000). *Language and literacy development in children who are deaf* (2nd ed.). New York: Macmillan.

Schloss, P. J., & Smith, M. A. (1998). *Applied behavior analysis in the classroom* (2nd ed.). Boston: Allyn & Bacon.

Schloss, P. J., Smith, M. A., & Schloss, C. N. (1995). *Instructional methods for adolescents with learning and behavior problems* (2nd ed.). Boston: Allyn & Bacon.

School to Work Opportunity Act of 1994, Pub. L. No. 103–239, 20 U.S.C. § 6101 et seq.

Scott, S. S. (1996). Understanding colleges: An overview of college support services and programs available to clients from transition planning through graduation. *Journal of Vocational Rehabilitation, 6,* 217–230.

Scuccimarra, D., & Speece, D. (1990). Employment outcomes and social integration of students with mild handicaps: The quality of life two years after high school. *Journal of Learning Disabilities, 23*(4), 213–219.

Secretary's Commission on Achieving Necessary Skills. (1991). *What work requires of schools: A SCANs report for America 2000.* Washington D.C.: U.S. Department of Labor.

Section 504 of the Rehabilitation Act of 1973, 29 U.S.C. § 794 et seq.

Serebreni, R., Rumrill, P. D., Mullins, J. A., & Gordon, S. E., (1993). Project Excel: A demonstration of the higher education transition model for high-achieving students with disabilities. *Journal of Postsecondary Education and Disability, 10,* 15–23.

Sexton, D., Lobman, M., Constans, T., Snyder, P., & Ernest, J. (1997). Early interventionists' perspectives of multicultural practices with African-American families. *Exceptional Children, 63,* 313–328.

Shapiro, J. P. (1993). *No Pity.* New York: Times Books.

Sharifzadeh, V. S. (1998). Families with Middle Eastern roots. In E. W. Lynch & M. H. Hanson (Eds.), *Developing cross-cultural competence: A guide for working with children and their families* (2nd ed., pp. 441–482). Baltimore: Paul H. Brookes.

Shaw, S., Brinckerhoff, L. C., Kistler, J. K., & McGuire, J. M. (1991). Preparing students with learning disabilities for postsecondary education: Issues and future needs. *Learning Disabilities: A Multidisciplinary Journal, 2*(1), 21–26.

Siegel, S. (1998). Foundations for a school-to-work system that serves all students. In F. R. Rusch & J. G. Chadsey (Eds.), *Beyond high school: Transition from school to work* (pp. 146–178). New York: Wadsworth.

Siegel, S., Robert, M., Greener, K., Meyer, G., Halloran, W., & Gaylord-Ross, R. (1993). *Career ladders for challenged youths in transition from school to adult life.* Austin, TX: PRO-ED.

Siegel, S., & Sleeter, C. S. (1991). Transforming transition: Next stages for the school-to-work transition movement. *Career Development for Exceptional Individuals, 14*(2), 27–41.

Simich-Dudgeon, C. (1986). A multidisciplinary model to educate minority language students with handicapping conditions. In A. C. Willing & H. F. Greenberg (Eds.), *Bilingualism and learning disabilities: Policy and practice for teachers and administrators* (pp. 95–110). New York: American Library Publishing.

Simmons, T., & Baer, R. (1996). What I want to be when I grow up: Career planning. In C. Flexer, D. Wray, R. Leavitt & R. Flexer (Eds.), *How the student with hearing loss can succeed in college: A handbook for students, families, and professionals* (2nd ed., pp. 117–130). Washington, DC: Alexander Graham Bell Association for the Deaf.

Simmons, T. J. (1996). *Postsecondary higher educational settings: Model environment for the delivery of secondary special education services.* Model demonstration Grant funded by the Office of Special Education. Washington, DC: S. Department of Education.

Simmons, T. J., & Flexer, R. W. (1992). Community based job training for persons with mental retardation: An acquisition and performance replication. *Education and Training in Mental Retardation, 15,* 261–272.

Simmons, T. J., Selleck, V., Steele, R. B., & Sepetauc, F. (1993). Supports and rehabilitation for employment. In R. W. Flexer and P. L. Solomon (Eds.), *Psychiatric rehabilitation in practice,* (pp. 119–136), Boston: Andover Medical Publishers.

Simmons, T. J., & Whaley B. (2001). Transition to employment. In R. W. Flexer, Simmons, T. J. Luft, P. & Bion, R. (Eds.) *Transition planning for students with disabilities.* Columbus, OH: Merrill.

Simon, M., Cobb, B., Halloran, W., Norman, M., & Bourexis. (1994). *Meeting the needs of youth with disabilities: Handbook for implementing community-based vocational education programs according to the Fair Labor Standards Act.* Minneapolis: National Transition Network.

Simpson, G. W. (1997). To grow a teacher. *American School Board Journal, 184,* 42–43.

Sitlington, P. L. (1996a). Transition assessment: Where have we been and where should we be going? *Career Development for Exceptional Individuals, 19,* 159–168.

Sitlington, P. L. (1996b). Transition assessment—Where have we been and where should we be going? *Career Development for Exceptional Children, 19,* 159–168.

Sitlington, P. L. (1996c). Transition to living: The neglected component of transition programming for individuals with learning disabilities. *Journal of Learning Disabilities, 29*(1), 31–41.

Sitlington, P. L., & Clark, G. M. (2006). *Transition education and services for students with disabilities.* (4th ed.). Boston: Allyn & Bacon.

Sitlington, P. L., Clark, G. M., Kolstoe, O. P. (Eds.). (2000) *Transition education and services for adolescents with disabilities* (3rd ed.). Boston: Allyn & Bacon.

Sitlington, P. L., & Frank, A. R. (1990). Are adolescents with learning disabilities successfully crossing the bridge into adult life? *Learning Disabilities Quarterly, 13*(2), 97–111.

Sitlington, P. L., Neubert, D., Begun, W., Le Conte, W., & Lombard, R. (1996). *Assess for success: Handbook for transition assessment.* Reston, VA: The Council for Exceptional Children.

Sitlington, P. L., Neubert, D. A., & LeConte, P. J. (1997). Transition assessment: The position of the Division on Career Development and Transition. *Career Development for Exceptional Individuals, 20*(1), 69–79.

Siu-Runyan, Y., & Faircloth, C. V. (1995). *Beyond separate subjects: Integrative learning at the middle level.* Norwood, MA: Christopher Gordon.

Skinner, D., Bailey, D. B., Jr., Correa, V., & Rodriguez, P. (1999). Narrating self and disability: Latino mothers' construction of identities vis-à-vis their child with special needs. *Exceptional Children, 65,* 481–495.

Smith, C., & Rojewski, J. (1993). School-to-work transition: Alternatives for educational reform. *Youth & Society, 25,* 222–250.

Smith, F., Lombard, R., Neubert, D., Le Conte, P., Rothenbacher, C., & Sitlington, P. (1996). The position statement of the interdisciplinary council on vocational evaluation and assessment. *Career Development for Exceptional Individuals, 19,* 73–76.

Smith, T. E. C., Polloway, E. A., Patton, J. R., & Dowdy, C. A. (2001). *Teaching students with special needs in inclusive settings* (3rd ed.). Boston: Allyn & Bacon.

Smull, M., & Burke-Harrison, S. (1992). Supporting people with severe reputations in the community. Alexandria, VA: National Association of State Mental Retardation Program Directors.

Snell, M. E. (1981). Daily living skills. In J. M. Kauffman & D. P. Hallahan (Eds.), *Handbook of special education* (pp. 530–551). Upper Saddle River, NJ: Prentice Hall.

Snell, M. E. (1987). *Systematic instruction of the moderately to severely handicapped* (3rd ed.). Columbus, OH: Merrill.

Snyder, E. P. (2002). Teaching students with combined behavioral disorders and mental retardation to lead their own IEP meetings. *Behavioral Disorders, 27*(4), 340–357.

Snyder, E. P., & Shapiro, E. D. (1997). Teaching students with emotional/behavioral disorders the skills to participate in the development of their own IEPs. *Behavioral Disorders, 22,* 246B–259.

Social Security Administration. (2003). *Fast Facts and Figures about Social Security,* 2003 [data file]. Available from Social Security online website, *http://www.ssa.gov*

Sowers, J. & Powers, L. (1991). *Vocational preparation and employment of students with physical and multiple disabilities.* Baltimore: Paul H. Brookes.

Sowers, J., & Powers, L. (1995). Enhancing the participation and independence of students with severe physical and multiple disabilities in performing community activities. *Mental Retardation, 33*(4), 209–220.

Staab, M. J. (1996). *The role of the school psychologist in transition planning* (Doctoral dissertation, University of Kansas, Lawrence, 1996). Dissertation Abstracts International, 58, 281.

Stageberg, D., Fischer, J., & Barbut, A. (1996). University students' knowledge of civil rights laws pertaining to people with disabilities. *Journal of Applied Rehabilitation Counseling, 27*(4), 25–29.

Stanford Research Institute (SRI) International. (1990). *National longitudinal transition study of special education students.* Washington, DC: The Office of Special Education Programs.

Stanford Research Institute (SRI) International. (1992). *What happens next? Trends in postschool outcomes of youth with disabilities.* Washington, DC: The Office of Special Education Programs.

State Agency Exchange. (1969). *The rehabilitation agency focus.* Washington, DC: U.S. Government Printing Office.

Steele, L. (1991). Early work experience among white and non-white youths: Implications for subsequent enrollment and employment. *Youth and Society, 22,* 419–447.

Steere, D. E., & Cavaiuolo, D. (2002). Connecting outcomes, goals, and objectives in transition planning. *Teaching Exceptional Children, 34*(6), 54–59.

Steere, D. E., Panscofar, E., Wood, R., & Hecimovic, A. (1990). Principals of shared responsibility. *Career Development for Exceptional Individuals, 13*(2), 143–153.

Steere, D. E., Wood, R., Panscofar, E. L., & Butterworth, J. (1990). Outcome-based school-to-work transition planning for students with severe disabilities. *Career Development for Exceptional Individuals, 13*(1), 57–70.

Stern, D., McMillion, M., Hopkins, C., & Stone, J. (1990). Work experience for students in high school and college. *Youth and Society, 21,* 355–389.

Stevens, R. J., & Slavin, R. (1995). The cooperative elementary school: Effects on students' achievement, attitudes, and social relations. *American Educational Research Journal, 32,* 321–351.

Stewart, E. D., Danielian, J., & Festes, R. J. (1969). *Simulating intercultural communication through role playing.* Alexandria, VA: Human Resources Research Organization.

Stodden, R. A. (1998). School-to-work transition: Overview of disability legislation. In F. R. Rusch & J. G. Chadsey (Eds.), *Beyond high school: Transition from school to work* (pp. 60–76). Belmont, CA: Wadsworth.

Stodden, R. A. (2001). Postsecondary education supports for students with disabilities: A review and response. *The Journal for Vocational Special Needs Education, 23*(2), 4–11.

Stodden, R. A. (2005). The status of persons with disabilities in postsecondary education. *TASH Connections, 31*(11/12), 4–7.

Stodden, R. A., & Leake, D. W. (1994). Getting to the core of transition: A re-assessment of old wine in new bottles. *Career Development for Exceptional Individuals, 17*(1), 65–76.

Stodden, R. A., & Whelley, T. (2004). Postsecondary education and persons with intellectual disabilities: An introduction. *Education and Training in Developmental Disabilities, 39*(1), 6–15.

Storey, K. (2002). Introduction: Curriculum design and programmatic issues involving youth in transition. In K. Storey, P. Bates, & D. Hunter (Eds.), *The road ahead: Transition to adult life for persons with disabilities* (pp. 1–5). St. Augustine, FL: Training Resource Network.

Storey, K., Bates, P., & Hunter, D. (Eds.). (2002). *The road ahead: Transition to adult life for persons with disabilities.* St. Augustine, FL: Training Resource Network.

Storey, K., & Mank, D. (1989). Vocational education of students with moderate and severe disabilities: Implications for service delivery and teacher preparation. *Career Development for Exceptional Individuals, 12*(1), 11–24.

Storms, J., O'Leary, E., & Williams, J. (2000). *IDEA 1997 transition requirements: A guide for states, districts, schools, universities, and families.* (Available from Publications Office, Institute on Community Integration, University of Minnesota, 109 Pattee Hall, 150 Pillsbury Drive, SE, Minneapolis, MN 55455).

Stowitschek, J. J., & Kelso, C. A. (1989). Are we in danger of making the same mistakes with ITPs as were made with IEPs? *Career Development for Exceptional Individuals, 12*(2), 139–151.

Stroul, B. A. (1989). Rehabilitation in community support systems. In R. W. Flexer and P. L. Solomon (Eds.), *Psychiatric rehabilitation in practice.* (pp. 45–61). Boston: Andover Publishers.

Sue, D. W. (1996, Fall). ACES endorsement of multicultural counseling competencies: Do we have the courage? *ACES Spectrum Newsletter,* 9–10.

Super, D. (1957). *The psychology of careers: An introduction to vocational development.* New York: Harper & Brothers.

Super, D. E. (1954). Career patterns as a basis for vocational counseling. *Journal of Counseling Psychology, 1,* 12–20.

Super, D. E. (Ed.). (1974). *Measuring vocational maturity for counseling and evaluation.* Washington, DC: National Career Development Association.

Super, D. E. (1975). *The psychology of careers.* New York: Harper & Row.

Super, D. E. (1984). Career and life development. In D. Brown, L. Brooks, & Associates (Eds.), *Career choice and devel-*

opment: Applying contemporary theories to practice (pp. 192–234). San Francisco: Jossey-Bass.

Super, D. E. (1990). A life-span, life-space approach to career development. In D. Brown, L. Brooks, & Associates (Eds.), *Career choice and development: Applying contemporary theories to practice* (2nd ed., pp. 197–261). San Francisco: Jossey-Bass.

Super, D. E., Osborne, W. L., Walsh, D. J., Brown, S. D., & Niles, S. G. (1992). Developmental career assessment and counseling: The C-DAC model. *Journal of Counseling and Development, 71,* 74–79.

Super, D. E., Savickas, M. L., & Super, C. M. (1996). The life-span, life-space approach to careers. In D. Brown, L. Brooks, & Associates (Eds.), *Career choice and development* (3rd ed., pp. 121–178). San Francisco: Jossey-Bass.

Super, D. E., Thompson, A. S., Lindeman, R. H., Jordaan, J. P., & Myers, R. A. (1981). *Career development inventory.* Palo Alto, CA: Consulting Psychologists Press.

Sweeney, M. (1996). *The effects of self-determination training on student involvement in the IEP process.* Unpublished doctoral dissertation., Tallahassee, FL: Florida State University.

Szymanski, E., Fernandez, D., Koch, L., & Merz, M. (1996). *Career development: Planning for placement.* Madison, WI: University of Wisconsin, Rehabilitation Research and Training Center on Career Development and Advancement.

Szymanski, E. M. (1994). Transition: life-span, life-space considerations for empowerment. *Exceptional Children, 60,* 402–410.

Szymanski, E. M. (1998). Career development, school to work transition, and diversity: An ecological approach. In F. R. Rusch & J. G. Chadsey (Eds.), *Beyond high school: Transition from school to work* (pp. 127–145). New York: Wadsworth.

Szymanski, E. M., & Hanley-Maxwell, C. (1997). Career development of people with developmental disabilities: An ecological model. *The Journal of Rehabilitation, 62*(1), 48–55.

Szymanski, E. M., Hanley-Maxwell, C., & Asselin, S. (1990). Rehabilitation counseling, special education, and vocational special needs education: Three transitional disciplines. *Career Development for Exceptional Individuals, 13*(1), 29–38.

Szymanski, E. M., Hanley-Maxwell, C., & Asselin, S. B. (1992). Systems interface: Vocational rehabilitation, special education, and vocational education. In F. R. Rusch, L. Destefano, J. Chadsey-Rusch, L. A. Phelps, & E. Szymanski (Eds.), *Transition from school to adult life: Models, linkages, and policy.* (pp. 153–172). Sycamore, IL: Sycamore.

Szymanski, E., & Hershenson, D. (1998). Career development of people with disabilities: An ecological model. In E. M. Szymanski & R. M. Parker (Eds.), *Rehabilitation counseling: Basics and beyond* (3rd ed., pp. 327–378). Austin, TX: PRO-ED.

Szymanski, E. M., & Hershenson, D. B. (2005). An ecological approach to vocational behavior and career development of people with disabilities. In R. M. Parker, E. M. Szymanski, & J. B. Patterson (Eds.), *Rehabilitation counseling: Basics and beyond* (pp. 225–280). Austin, TX: Pro-Ed.

Szymanski, E. M., Hershenson, D. B., Enright, M. S., & Ettinger, J. M. (1996). Career development theories, constructs, and research: Implications for people with disabilities. In E. M. Szymanski & R. M. Parker (Eds.), *Work and disability: Issues and strategies in career development and job development* (pp. 79–126). Austin, TX: PRO-ED.

Szymanski, E. M. & Parker, R. M. (1996). Work and disability: Introduction. In E. M. Szymanski & R. M. Parker (Eds.). *Work and disability: Issues and strategies in carrer development and job placement* (pp. 1–7). Austin. TX: PRO-ED.

Szymanski, E. M., Turner, K. D., & Herschenson, D. B. (1992). Career development and work adjustment of persons with disabilities: Theoretical perspectives and implications for transition. In F. R. Rusch, L. Destefano, J. Chadsey-Rusch, L. A. Phelps, & E. Szymanski (Eds.), *Transition from school to adult life: Models, linkages, and policy* (pp. 391–406). Sycamore, IL: Sycamore.

Talbert-Johnson, C. (1998). Why [are] so many African-American children in special ed? *School Business Affairs, 64,* 30–35.

Taylor, R. (1997). *Assessment of exceptional students: Educational and psychological procedures* (4th ed.). Boston: Allyn & Bacon.

Taylor, S. J. (1988). Caught in the continuum: A critical analysis of the principle of the least restrictive environment. *Journal of the Association for Persons with Severe Handicaps, 13,* 41–53.

Taylor, S. J., Racino, J., Knoll, J., & Lutfiyya, Z. (1987). *The nonrestrictive environment: A resource manual on community integration for people with the most severe disabilities.* Syracuse, NY: Human Policy Press.

Technology-Related Assistance for Individuals with Disabilities Act of 1988, 29 U.S.C § 2201 *et seq.*

Test, D., Hinson, K., Solow, J., & Kuel, P. (1993). Job satisfaction of persons in supported employment. *Education and Training in Mental Retardation, 28*(1), 38–46.

Test, D. W., Aspel, N. P., & Everson, J. M. (2006). *Transition methods for youth with disabilities.* Upper Saddle River, NJ: Pearson/Merrill/Prentice Hall.

Test, D. W., Fowler, C. H., Brewer, D. M., & Wood, W. M. (2005). A content and methodological review of self-advocacy intervention studies. *Exceptional Children, 72*(1), 101–125.

Test, D. W., Fowler, C. H., Wood, W. W., Brewer, D. M., & Eddy, S. (2005). A conceptual framework of self-advocacy for students with disabilities. *Remedial and Special Education, 26,* 43–54.

Test, D. W., Spooner, F., Keul, P. K., & Grossi T. (1995). Teaching adolescents with severe disabilities to use the public telephone. *Behavior Modification, 14*(2), 157–171.

Thomas, A. & Grimes, J. (1995). Best practices in school psychology III. Washington, DC: NASP.

Thompson, S.J., & Thurlow, M.L. (2000). State alternate assessments: *Status as IDEA alternate assessment requirements take effect* (Synthesis Report 35). Minneapolis, MN: National Center on Educational Outcomes, University of Minnesota. (Eric Document Reproduction Service No. ED447613)

Thorkildsen, R. (1994). *Research synthesis on quality and availability of assistive technology devices. Executive summary.* Technical report No. 8. (ERIC Document Reproduction Service No. ED 386 856)

Thurlow, M. (2002). Positive educational results for all students. The promise of standards-based reform. *Remedial and Special Education, 23*(4) 195–202.

Thurlow, M., & Elliott, J. (1998). Student assessment and evaluation. In J. R. Rusch & J. G. Chadsey (Eds.), *Beyond high school: Transition from school to work* (pp. 265–296). New York: Wadsworth Publishing Company.

Tileston, D. W. (2000). *Ten best teaching practices: How brain research, learning styles, and standards define teaching competencies.* Thousand Oaks, CA: Corwin.

Tilson, G. P., Lueking, R. G., & Donavan, M. R. (1994). Involving employers in transition: The BRIDGES from school to work model. *Career Development for Exceptional Individuals, 17*(1), 77–89.

Tilson, G. P., Jr., & Neubert, D. A. (1988). School-to-work transition of mildly disabled young adults: Parental perceptions of vocational needs. *The Journal for Vocational Special Needs Education, 11*(1), 33–37.

Tinto, V. (1993). *Leaving college: Rethinking the causes and cures of student attrition* (2nd ed.). Chicago: University of Chicago Press.

Todis, B., & Walker, H. (1993). User perspective on assistive technology in educational settings. *Focus on Exceptional Children, 26,* 1–16.

Tomlinson, C. A. & McTighe, J. (2006). *Integrating differentiated instruction & understanding by design.* Alexandria, VA: Association for Supervision and Curriculum Development.

Tower, K. D. (1994). Consumer-centered social work practice: Restoring client self-determination. *Social Work, 39*(2), 191–196.

Trace Center. (1996). CO-Net, HyperAbleDATA [CD-Rom program]. Madison: University of Wisconsin, Author.

Trainor, A. A., Patton, J. R., & Clark, G. M. (2005). *Case studies in assessment for transition planning.* Austin, TX: Pro-Ed.

Trivette, C. M., Dunst, C. J., Boyd, K., & Hamby, D. W. (1996). Family-orientated program models, helping practices and parental control appraisals. *Exceptional Children, 62*(3), 237–248.

Tuckman, B. W., & Jensen, M. A. C. (1977). States in small group development revisited. *Group and Organizational Studies, 2,* 419–442.

Turnbull, A. P., Barber, P., Kerns, G. M., & Behr, S. K. (1995). The family of children and youth with exceptionalities. In E. L. Meyen & T. M. Skrtic (Eds.), *Special education and student disability, an introduction: Traditional, emerging, and alternative perspectives* (4th ed., pp. 141-170). Denver, CO: Love.

Turnbull, A. P., & Morningstar, M. E. (1993). Family and professional interaction. In M. E. Snell (Ed.), *Instruction of students with severe disabilities* (4th ed., pp. 31-60). Upper Saddle River, NJ: Merrill/Prentice Hall.

Turnbull, A. P., & Turnbull, H. R. (1990). *Families, professionals, and exceptionality: A special partnership* (2nd ed.). Upper Saddle River, NJ: Merrill/Prentice Hall.

Turnbull, A. P., & Turnbull, H. R. (1993). Empowerment and decision-making through Group Action Planning. In *Life-long transitions: Proceedings of the third annual parent/family conference.* Washington, DC: U.S. Department of Education.

Turnbull, H. Rutherford, III. (1993). *Free appropriate public education: The law and children with disabilities* (4th ed.). Denver, CO: Love.

Turnbull, H. R., Turnbull, A. P., Wehmeyer, M. L., & Park, J. (2003). A quality of life framework for special education outcomes. *Remedial and Special Education, 24*(2), 67-74.

Turnbull, A., Turnbull, R., Erwin, E. J., & Soodak, L. C. (2006). *Families, professionals, and exceptionality: Positive outcomes through partnerships and trust* (5th ed.). Columbus, OH: Pearson/Merrill/Prentice Hall.

Turner, L. (1996). Selecting a college option: Determining the best fit. In C. Flexer, D. Wray, R. Leavitt, & R. Flexer (Eds.), *How the student with hearing loss can succeed in college: A handbook for students, families, and professionals* (pp. 142-164). Washington, DC: Alexander Graham Bell Association for the Deaf.

Turner, L. P. (1996). *Parent involvement in transition planning.* Unpublished doctoral dissertation, Kent State University, Kent, OH.

Turner, L. P., & Simmons, T. J. (1996). Getting ready for transition to college. In C. Flexer, D. Wray, R. Leavitt, & R. Flexer (Eds.), *How the student with hearing loss can succeed in college: A handbook for students, families, and professionals* (2nd ed., pp. 131-145). Washington, DC: Alexander Graham Bell Association for the Deaf.

U. S. Census Bureau. (2001, March). *Overview of race and Hispanic origin: Census 2000 brief.* Washington, DC: U.S. Department of Commerce, U.S. Census Bureau. Available online: *www.census.gov/prod/2002pubs/censr.4.pdf*

U.S. Census Bureau. (2002, November). *Demographic trends in the 20th century: Census 2000 special reports.* Washington, DC: U.S. Department of Commerce, U.S. Census Bureau. Available online: *www.census.gov/prod/2002pubs/censr.4.pdf*

U.S. Census Bureau. (2003, August). *School enrollment 2000: Census 2000 brief.* Washington, DC: U.S. Department of Commerce, U.S. Census Bureau. Available online: *www.census.gov/prod/2002pubs/censr.4.pdf*

U.S. Census Bureau. (2003, May). *Poverty: 1999: Census 2000 brief.* Washington, DC: U.S. Department of Commerce, U.S.

Census Bureau. Available online: *www.census.gov/prod/2002pubs/censr.4.pdf*

U.S. Census Bureau (2004). *2004 American community survey—race.* Washington, DC: U.S. Department of Commerce, U.S. Census Bureau. Available online: http://factfinder.census.gov/home/saff/main.html?_lang=en

U.S. Department of Education. (1995). *Seventeenth annual report to Congress on the implementation of the Individuals with Disabilities Education Act.* Washington, DC: Author.

U.S. Department of Education. (1996). *Eighteenth annual report to Congress on the implementation of the Individuals with Disabilities Education Act.* Washington, DC: Author.

U.S. Department of Education. (1997). *Nineteenth annual report to Congress on the implementation of the Individuals with Disabilities Education Act.* Washington DC: Author.

U.S. Department of Education. (2004). *Twenty-sixth annual report to congress on the implementation of the Individuals with Disabilities Act.* Washington, DC: Author.

U.S. Department of Education, Office for Civil Rights. (1987). *1986 elementary and secondary school civil rights survey: National summaries.* Arlington, VA: DBS Corporation, subcontract from Opportunity Systems, Inc.

U.S. Department of Education, Office for Civil Rights. (1994). *1992 elementary and secondary school civil rights compliance report (draft).* Washington, DC: Author.

U.S. Department of Education, Office of Special Education Programs. (2001). Students with disabilities' secondary education, transition, and employment (Expert Strategy Panel Report). Available: *http://www.ed.gov/offices/osers/osep.* Washington, DC: Author.

U.S. Department of Labor. (1991). *The revised handbook for analyzing jobs.* Washington, DC: Employment and Training Administration.

U.S. Department of Labor. (1993). Learning a living: A blueprint for high performance (SCANS report). Washington, DC: U.S. Government Printing Office.

van Keulen, J. E., Weddington, G. T., & DeBose, C. E. (1998). *Speech, language, learning, and the African American child.* Boston: Allyn & Bacon.

Van Reusen, A. K., & Bos, C. S. (1990). I Plan: Helping students communicate in planning conferences. *Teaching Exceptional Children 22*(4), 30-32.

Van Reusen, A. K., & Bos, C. (1994). Facilitating student participation in individual educational programs through motivation strategy instruction. *Exceptional Children, 60*(5), 466-475.

Van Reusen, A. K., Bos, C. S., Schumaker, J. B., & Deshler, D. D. (1994). *Self-advocacy strategy for education and transition planning.* Lawrence, KS: Edge Enterprises.

Vandercook, T., York, J., & Forest, M. (1989). The McGill action planning system (MAPS): A strategy for building the vision. *Journal of the Association for Persons with Severe Handicaps, 14*(3), 205-215.

Vaughn, S., Bos, C. S., & Schumm, J. S (2000). *Teaching exceptional, diverse, and at-risk students in the general education curriculum* (2nd ed.). Boston: Allyn & Bacon.

VEWAA glossary. (1988). (Available from Materials Development Center, Stout Vocational Rehabilitation Institute, University of Wisconsin–Stout, Menomonie, WI 54751). Author.

Vogel, S. A., & Adelman, P. B. (1992). The success of college students with learning disabilities: Factors related to educational attainment. *Journal of Learning Disabilities, 25*(7), 430–441.

Vondracek, F. W., & Porfeli, E. (2002). Integrating person- and function-centered approaches in career development theory and research. *Journal of Vocational Behavior, 61,* 386–397.

Wagner, M. (1989). *Youth with disabilities during transition: An overview of descriptive findings from the national longitudinal transition study.* Menlo Park, CA: SRI International.

Wagner, M. (1991). *Dropouts with disabilities: What do we know? What can we do?* (A report from the National Longitudinal Transition Study of Special Education Students). Menlo Park, CA: SRI International.

Wagner, M., & Blackorby, J. (1996). Transition from high school to work or college: How special education students fare. *The Future of Children: Special Education for Students with Disabilities, 6*(1), 103–110.

Wagner, M., Blackorby, J., Cameto, R., & Newman, L. (1993). *What makes a difference? Influence on post-school outcomes of youth with disabilities: The third comprehensive report from the National Longitudinal Transition Study of Special Education Students.* Menlo Park, CA: SRI International.

Wagner, M., Cameto, R., & Newman, L. (2003). *Youth with disabilities: A changing population. A report of findings from the National Longitudinal Transition Study* (NLTS) *and the National Longitudinal Transition Study-2* (NLTS2). [Executive Summary]. Menlo Park, CA: SRI International.

Wagner, M., D'Amico, R., Marder, C., Newman, l., & Blackorby, J. (1992). *What happens next? Trends in postschool outcomes of youth with disabilities.* Menlo Park, CA: SRI International.

Wagner, M., Newman, L., Cameto, R., Garga, N., & Levine, P. (2005). *After high school: A first look at the postschool experience of youth with disabilities.* Menlo Park, CA: SRI International.

Wagner, M., Newman, L., Cameto, R., & Levine, P. (2005). *Changes over time in the early postschool outcomes of youth with disabilities. A report of findings from the National Longitudinal Study (NLTS) and the National Longitudinal Transition Study-2 (NLTS2).* Menlo Park, CA: SRI International.

Wagner, M., Newman, L., & Shaver, D. M. (1989). The *National Longitudinal Transition Study of Special Education Students: Report on procedures for the first wave of data collection (1987).* Menlo Park, CA: SRI International.

Wald, J. L. (1996). *Culturally and linguistically diverse professionals in special education: A demographic analysis.* Reston, VA: National Clearinghouse for Professions in Special Education and OSERS.

Walden, R. J. (2002). *Teaching a goal attainment process to university students with learning disabilities.* Unpublished doctoral dissertation University of Oklahoma, Norman.

Ward, M. J. (1988). The many facets of self-determination. *National Information Center for Children and Youth with Handicaps: Transition Summary, 5,* 2–3. Washington, DC: Office of Special Education Programs of the U.S. Department of Education.

Ward, M. J. (1994, Winter). Self-determination: A means to an end. *Impact, 6,* 8.

Ward, M. J. (1996). Coming of age in the age of self-determination: An historical and personal perspective. In D. J. Sands & M. L. Wehmeyer (Eds.), *Self-determination across the life span* (pp. 1–14). Baltimore: Paul H. Brookes.

Ward, M. J., & Halloran, W. J. (1989). Transition to uncertainty: Status of many school leavers with severe disabilities. *Career Development for Exceptional Individuals, 12*(2), 71–78.

Ward, M. J., & Halloran, W. (1993, Fall). Transition issues for the 1990s. *OSERS News in Print, 6*(1) 4–5. (ERIC Document Reproduction Service No. ED 364035)

Weaver, R., & DeLuca, J. R. (1987). *Employability life skills assessment: Ages 14–21.* Dayton, OH: Miami Valley Special Education Center.

Webster, D. D. (1999, July). *Developing the leadership potential of postsecondary students with disabilities.* Paper presented at AHEAD Conference, Atlanta, GA.

Webster, D. D. (2001). *Giving voice to students with disabilities who have transitioned to college: Or how LL Slim became "the best darn gimp on the planet"* (Doctoral dissertation, Kent State University, 2001). Dissertation Abstracts International, 62/05, 1796.

Webster, D. D. (2004). Giving voice to students with disabilities who have successfully transitioned to college. *Career Development for Exceptional Individuals, 27*(2), 151–175.

Wehman, P. (1990). School-to-work: Elements of successful programs. *Teaching Exceptional Children, 23*(1), 40–43.

Wehman, P. (1992). Transition for young people with disabilities: Challenges for the 1990's. *Education and Training in Mental Retardation; 27,* 112–118.

Wehman, P. (1997b). *Exceptional individuals in school, community, and work.* Austin Texas: PRO-ED.

Wehman, P. (Ed.). (2001). *Life beyond the classroom: Transition strategies for young people with disabilities* (3rd ed.). Baltimore: Paul H. Brookes.

Wehman, P. (2006). *Life beyond the classroom: Transition strategies for young people with disabilities.* (4th ed.). Baltimore: Paul H. Brookes.

Wehman, P., & Bricout, J. (2001). Supported Employment: New directions for a new millenium. In P. Wehman (Ed.)

Supported employment in business: Expanding the capacity of workers with disabilities. (pp. 3–22). St. Augustine, Fl: Training Resource Network.

Wehman, P., Everson, J., & Reid, D. (2001). Beyond programs and placements: using person-centered practices to individualize the transition process and outcomes. In P. Wehman (Ed.), (2001). *Life beyond the classroom: Transition strategies for young people with disabilities* (pp. 91–124). Baltimore, MD: Paul H. Brookes.

Wehman, P., & Kregel, J. (1985). A supported work approach to competitive employment of individuals with moderate and severe handicaps. *Journal of the Association for Persons with Severe Handicaps, 10,* 3–11.

Wehman, P., Kregel, J., & Barcus, J. M. (1985). From school to work: A vocational transition model for handicapped students. *Exceptional Children, 52*(1), 25–37.

Wehman, P., Moon, M. S., Everson, J. M., Wood, W., & Barcus, J. M. (1988). *Transition from school to work: New challenges for youth with severe disabilities.* Baltimore: Paul H. Brookes.

Wehman, P., Revell, W. G., & Kregel, J. (1998a). Expanding supported employment opportunities for persons with severe disabilities. *TASH Newsletter, 22*(6), 24–25.

Wehman, P., Revell, W. G., & Kregel, J. (1998b). Supported employment: A decade of rapid growth and impact. *American Rehabiliation, 24*(1), 31–43.

Wehmeyer, M. (2002). Transition principles and access to the general education curriculum. In C. A. Kochar-Bryant & D. Bassett (Eds.). *Aligning transition and standards-based education: Issues and strategies.* Arlington, VA: Council for Exceptional Children.

Wehmeyer, M., Agran, M., & Hughes, C. (2000). A national survey of teachers' promotion of self-determination and student-directed learning. *Journal of Special Education, 34*(2), 58–68.

Wehmeyer, M., & Lawrence, M. (1996). Whose future is it anyway? Promoting student involvement in transition planning. *Career Development for Exceptional Individuals, 18*(2), 69–84.

Wehmeyer, M., & Schwartz, M. (1997). Self-determination and positive adult outcomes: A follow-up of youth with mental retardation or learning disabilities. *Exceptional Children, 63*(2), 245–255.

Wehmeyer, M., & Schwartz, M. (1998). The self-determination focus of transition goals for students with mental retardation. *Career Development for Exceptional Children, 21,* 75–86.

Wehmeyer, M. L. (1992). Self-determination: Critical skills for outcome-oriented transition services. *The Journal for Vocational Special Needs Education, 15,* 3–9.

Wehmeyer, M. L. (1993). Perceptual and psychological factors in career decision-making of adolescents with and without cognitive disabilities. *Career Development for Exceptional Individuals, 16*(2), 135–146.

Wehmeyer, M. L. (1994). Perceptions of self-determination and psychological empowerment of adolescents with mental retardation. *Education and Training in Mental Retardation and Developmental Disabilities, 29,* 9–21.

Wehmeyer, M. L. (1995). *The ARC's self-determination scale: Procedural guidelines.* (Available from The ARC of the United States, 500 E. Border Street, Suite 300, Arlington, TX 76010.)

Wehmeyer, M. L. (1996). Self determination as an educational outcome. In D. J. Sands & M. L. Wehmeyer (Eds.), *Self-determination across the life span: Independence and choice for people with disabilities* (pp. 17–36). Baltimore: Paul H. Brookes.

Wehmeyer, M. L. (1997). Student-directed learning and self-determination. In M. Agran (Ed.), *Student directed learning: Teaching self-determination skills* (pp. 28–59). Pacific Grove, CA: Brooks/Cole Publishers.

Wehmeyer, M. L. (1998). National survey of the use of assistive technology by adults with mental retardation. *Mental Retardation, 36,* 44–51.

Wehmeyer, M. L. (1998). Student involvement in transition-planning and transition-program implementation. In F. R. Rusch & J. G. Chadsey (Eds.), *Beyond high school: Transition from school to work.* (pp. 206–233). Belmont CA: Wadsworth.

Wehmeyer, M. L. (1999). Assistive technology and students with mental retardation: Utilization and barriers. *Journal of Special Education Technology, 14,* 48–58.

Wehmeyer, M. L., Agran, M., & Hughes, C. (1998). *Teaching self-determination to students with disabilities: Basic skills for successful transition.* Baltimore: Paul H. Brookes.

Wehmeyer, M. L., & Kelchner, K. (1995a). *The ARC's self-determination scale.* Arlington, TX: ARC.

Wehmeyer, M. L., & Kelchner, K. (1995b). *Whose future is it anyway?* Arlington, TX: ARC.

Wehmeyer, M. L., & Palmer, S. B. (2003). Adult outcomes for students with cognitive disabilities three-years after high school: The impact of self-determination. *Education and Training in Developmental Disabilities, 38*(2), 131–144.

Wehmeyer, M. L., Palmer, S. B., Agran, M., Mithaug, D. E., & Martin, J. E. (2000). Promoting casual agency: The self-determined learning model of instruction. *Exceptional Children, 66*(4), 439–453.

Wehmeyer, M. L., Lattin, D., & Agran, M. (2001). Achieving access to the general curriculum for students with mental retardation: A curriculum decision-making model. *Education and Training in Mental Retardation and Development Disabilities, 36,* 327–342.

Wehmeyer, M. L., & Ward, M. J. (1995). The spirit of IDEA mandate: Student involvement in transition planning. *Journal of the Association for Vocational Special Needs Education, 17,* 108–111.

Welsh Office, Department of Education. (1994). *Code of practice on the identification and assessment of special education needs.* Cardiff, Wales, UK: Author.

Wermuth, T. (1991). Impact of educational legislation on transition and supported employment programs. *The Advance, 3,* 3–4. Richmond, VA: Association for Persons in Supported Employment [APSE].

West, J. (1991). *The Americans with Disabilities Act: From policy to practice.* New York: Milbank Fund.

West, M., Wehman, P., & Revell, G. (1996). Use of Social Security Work Incentives by supported employment agencies and consumers: Findings from a national survey. *Journal of Vocational Rehabilitation, 7,* 117-123.

Westling, D. L., & Fox, L. (2000). *Teaching students with severe disabilities* (2nd ed.). Upper Saddle River, NJ: Merrill/Prentice Hall.

Whitehead, C. W. (1977). *Sheltered workshop study: A nationwide report on sheltered workshops and their employment of handicapped individuals* (Workshop Survey, Vol. I, U.S. Department of Labor Services Publications). Washington, DC: U.S. Government Printing Office.

Whitney-Thomas, J., & Hanley-Maxwell, C. (1996). Packing the parachute: Parents experiences as their children prepare to leave high school. *Exceptional Children, 63*(1), 75-88.

Whitney-Thomas, J., Shaw, D., Honey, K., & Butterworth, J. (1998). Building a future: A study of student participation in person-centered planning, *The Journal of the Association for Persons with Severe Handicaps, 23*(2), 119-133.

Wiggins, G., & McTighe, J. (1998). *Understanding by design.* Alexandria, VA: Association for Supervision and Curriculum Development.

Wilcox, B., & Bellamy, G. T. (1987). *The activities catalog: An alternative curriculum for youth and adults with severe disabilities.* Baltimore: Paul H. Brookes.

Will, M. (1983). *OSERS programming for the transition of youth with disabilities: Bridges from school to working life.* Washington, DC: U.S. Department of Education, Office of Special Education and Rehabilitative Services. (ERIC Document Repro-duction Service No. ED 256 132)

Will, M. (1984). Supported employment for adults with severe disabilities: An OSERS program initiative. Washington, DC.

Williams, J. M., & O'Leary, E. (2001). What we've learned and where we go from here. *Career Development for Exceptional Individuals, 24*(1), 51-71.

Willig, A. C. (1986). Special education and the culturally and linguistically different child: An overview of issues and challenges. In A. C. Willing & H. F. Greenberg (Eds.), *Bilingualism and learning disabilities: Policy and practice for teachers and administrators* (pp. 191-209). New York: American Library Publishing.

Willis, W. (1998). Families with African American roots. In E. W. Lynch & M. H. Hanson (Eds.), *Developing cross-cultural competence: A guide for working with children and their families* (2nd ed., pp. 165-208). Baltimore: Paul H. Brookes.

Wilson, K., & Getzel, E. (2001). Creating a supportive campus: The VCU professional development academy. *The Journal for Vocational Special Needs Education, 23*(2), 12-18.

Winterbottom, C., Liska, D. W., & Obermaier, K. M. (1995). *State-level databook on health care access and financing.* Washington, DC: The Urban Institute.

Winup, K. (1994). The role of a student committee in promotion of independence among school leavers. In J. Coupe-O'Kane & B. Smith (Eds.), *Taking control* (pp. 103-116). London: David Fulton Publishers.

Winzer, M. A., & Mazurek, K. (1998). *Special education in multicultural contexts.* Upper Saddle River, NJ: Merrill/Prentice Hall.

Wolfe, P. S., Boone, R. S., and Barrera, M. (1997). Developing culturally sensitive transition plans: A reflective process. *The Journal for Vocational Special Needs Education, 20,* 30-33.

Wolfensberger, W. (1972). *The principal normalization in human services.* Toronto: National Institute on Mental Retardation.

Wolfensberger, W. (1991). *A brief introduction to SRV as a high-order concept for structuring human services.* Syracuse, NY: Training Institute for Human Service Planning, Leadership and Change Agency.

Wolffe, K. (1997). *Career counseling for people with disabilities: A practical guide to finding employment.* Austin, TX: PRO-ED.

Wolman, J. M., Campeau, P. L., DuBois, P. A., Mithaug, D. E., & Stolarski, V. S. (1994). *AIR Self-Determination Scale and user guide.* New York: Teachers College at Columbia University.

Wood, J. W. (2002). *Adapting instruction to accommodate students in inclusive settings* (4th ed.). Upper Saddle River, NJ: Prentice Hall.

Wood, W. M., Fowler, C. H., Uphold, N., & Test, D. W. (2005). A review of self-determination interventions with individuals with severe disabilities. *Research and Practice for Persons with Severe Disabilities, 30,* 121-146.

Woolcock, W. W., Stodden, R. A., & Bisconer, S. W. (1992). Process and outcome-focused decision making. In F. R. Rusch, L. DeStefano, J. Chadsey-Rusch, L. A. Phelps & E. Szymanski (Eds.), *Transition from school to adult life: Models, linkages, and policy* (pp. 219-244). Sycamore, IL: Sycamore.

World Institute on Disability. (1991). *Personal assistance services: A new millennium. Resolution on personal assistance services passed by participants of the international personal assistance services symposium.* Oakland, CA: World Institute on Disability.

Ysseldyke, J. E., Algozzine, B., & Thurlow, M. L. (1992). *Critical issues in special education* (2nd ed.). Boston: Houghton Mifflin.

Zabala, J. (1994). *The SETT framework: Critical questions to ask when making informed assistive technology decisions.* Paper presented at Closing the Gap Conference, Oct, 1994, Minneapolis, MN.

Zuniga, M. E. (1998). Families with Latino roots. In E. W. Lynch & M. H. Hanson (Eds.), *Developing cross-cultural competence: A guide for working with children and their families* (2nd ed., pp. 209-250). Baltimore: Paul H. Brookes.

NAME INDEX

Residential programs (*Cont.*)
    transportation, role of, 302–303
    U.S. Department of Housing and Urban Development
      (HUD), 305–306
Residential transition planning, 297–307
Responsibilities of transition coordinators, 369–370
Risk taking, 7
Role release, 207
Rural college students, 285–286

Same-skill groupings, 171
Satisfaction, 91
Satisfactoriness, 91
Scale of Job-Related Social Skill Knowledge (SSSK), 112
Scale of Job-Related Social Skill Performance (SSSP), 112
SCANS foundational skills, 141
Scheduling and facilitating transition meetings, 371–373
Scheerenberger, 1983, 5
School to work program, 237–238
School-Based Career Development and Transition
    Education Model, 39
School-based enterprise, 239
School-to-Work Opportunities Act of 1994, 45–46
Schoolwide professional and in-service training, 70–72
Science of teaching, 165
Section 504 of the Rehabilitation Act of 1973, 22, 271–272
Section 8 Housing, 306
Segregated day programs, 4
Self-advocacy strategies, 227
Self-awareness and advocacy, 268–273
Self-care, role of, 301–302
Self-determination, 15–17, 148–149
    approaches, 322
    Choice Maker, 351–353
    choice strand, 343–344
    Choose and Take Action, 361–364
    choosing goals process, 353
    components of, 344–345
    education goals, choosing, 354–356
    employment goals, choosing, 353–354
    federal laws, regulations, and state practice, 341
    functional behavioral
      assessment, 365
    goal-setting and attainment strand, 344
    IEP, and the, 347–351
    importance of, 345–347
    opportunities to practice self-determination, 364–365
    personal goals, choosing, 356–357
    self-directed IEP, 357–359
    severe cognitive needs, in students with, 360–364
    student-directed summary of performance, 365
    Take Action, 359–360
Self-Determination Knowledge
    Scale, 347
Self-Determination Scale, 113, 347
Self-directed IEP, 357–359
Self-Directed Search, 90, *111, 322*
Self-perceptions, ideal and actual, 5
Service coordination
    broker models, 368
    collaboration, 379–381

communication strategies, developing, 380–381
criteria of the next environment, 368
criterion of ultimate function, 368
family involvement, 378–379
full support models, 368
interdisciplinary models, 379
multidisciplinary models, 379
program attributes and structures, development of,
    381–382
range of, 368–369
referrals, coordinating, 373
responsibilities of transition coordinators, 369–370
scheduling and facilitating transition meetings, 371–373
student development, 373–378
student-focused planning, 370–373
transdisciplinary models, 379
Service delivery system, 206
Service model comparison, 208
Services and agency delivery matrix, 227, 229
Singer Vocational Evaluation System, 112
Situational assessments, 119, 126, 215
Skills Confidence Inventory, 94
Small group instruction, 171
Small-business incentives, 246
Smith-Fess Act, 31, 34
Smith-Hughes Act, 31, 34
Smith-Sears Act, 34
Social and Prevocational Information Battery (SPIB), 114
Social cognitive career theory (SCCT), 93–94
Social entitlements, 245
Social role valorization, 295
Social Security Administration, 41
Social Security Disability Income (SSDI), 4, 245
Social welfare, 245
Sociohistorical deviancy role perceptions, 31
Special education, scope of, 207
Special needs career and technical education, 239–240
Special needs vocational education, 42
Specialized programs, 283–285
Speech and language therapy (SLP), 217
Standards-based curriculum model, 150
Standards-based education
    application, 142
    benchmarks, 143–144
    content standards, 142–143
    performance standards, 144–145
Standards-based reform, 136
State Bureau of Employment Services, 250
Street Survival Skills Questionnaire, 113
Strong Interest Inventory, 94
Student and family-led transition meetings, 327–328
Student development, 373–378
Student Earned Income Exclusion, 338
Student internships, 239
Student participation, supporting, 76
Student-directed learning, 192–193
Student-directed summary of performance, 365
Student-focused planning, 370–373
Student-guided or project-based learning, 190–192
Substantial Gainful Activity, 245
Summary of performance (SOP), 157–158